Praise for Best Plac

"Best Places *covers must-see portions of the* \
In-the-know locals offer thorough info on res
—NATIONAL GEOGRAPH

"Best Places *are the best regional restaurant and guide books in America.*"
—THE SEATTLE TIMES

". . . *travelers swear by the recommendations in the Best Places guidebooks . . .*"
—SUNSET MAGAZINE

"*Known for their frank yet chatty tone . . .*"
—PUBLISHERS WEEKLY

"Best Places Northern California *is great fun to read even if you're not
going anywhere.*"
—SAN FRANCISCO CHRONICLE

"Best Places Southern California *is just about all the inspiration you need
to start planning your next road trip or summer vacation with the kids.*"
—THE FRESNO BEE

"Best Places Southern California *and* Best Places San Diego *are quite good, and
any traveler to the area would do well to pick one up.*"
—LIBRARY JOURNAL

"*Eat, surf, and shop like a local with this insider's guide,* Best Places San Diego."
—AMERICAN WAY

"Best Places San Francisco *has frank assessments of restaurants
and accommodations . . .*"
—THE SEATTLE TIMES

"*For travel collections covering the Northwest, the* Best Places *series takes
precedence over all similar guides.*"
—BOOKLIST

"*The best guide to Seattle is the locally published* Best Places Seattle . . ."
—JONATHAN RABAN, MONEY MAGAZINE

TRUST THE LOCALS

The original insider's guides, written by local experts

COMPLETELY INDEPENDENT

- No advertisers
- No sponsors
- No favors

EVERY PLACE STAR-RATED & RECOMMENDED

★★★★ The very best in the region

★★★ Distinguished; many outstanding features

★★ Excellent; some wonderful qualities

★ A good place

NO STARS Worth knowing about, if nearby

MONEY-BACK GUARANTEE

We're so sure you'll be satisfied, we guarantee it!

HELPFUL ICONS

Watch for these quick-reference symbols throughout the book:

 FAMILY FUN

 GOOD VALUE

 ROMANTIC

 UNIQUELY NORTHERN CALIFORNIA

BEST PLACES®
NORTHERN
CALIFORNIA

Edited by
LINDA WATANABE MCFERRIN

EDITION

SASQUATCH BOOKS
SEATTLE

Printed in the United States of America
Distributed in Canada by Raincoast Books, Ltd.

Fourth edition
07 06 05 04 03 02 01   5 4 3 2 1

ISBN: 1-57061-270-6
ISSN: 1533-3981

Series editor: Kate Rogers
Cover and interior design: Nancy Gellos
Maps: GreenEye Design
Composition: Patrick David Barber and Holly McGuire

SPECIAL SALES

BEST PLACES® guidebooks are available at special discounts on bulk purchases for corporate, club, or organization sales promotions, premiums, and gifts. Special editions,
including personalized covers, excerpts of existing guides, and corporate imprints,
can be created in large quantities for specific needs. For more information, contact
your local bookseller or Special Sales, Best Places Guidebooks, 615 Second Avenue,
Suite 260, Seattle, Washington 98104, 800/775-0817.

SASQUATCH BOOKS
615 Second Avenue
Seattle, Washington 98104
206/467-4300
books@SasquatchBooks.com
www.SasquatchBooks.com

CONTENTS

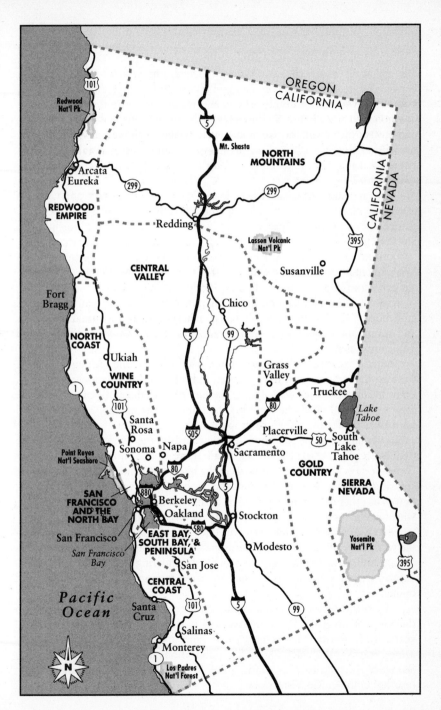

Contributors

One night in a superb San Francisco neighborhood restaurant, sometime between a bite of monkfish on pumpkin risotto and a sip of good French wine, **DANIELLE MACHOTKA** decided she would rather eat out in the city than save her money to buy a house. So she explores the restaurant scene with dedication, and always with room for one more bite. A freelance writer and world traveler who grew up in Santa Cruz, Danielle's work has appeared in newsletters, newspapers and magazines including the *San Francisco Examiner* and *Landscape Architecture.*

Born and raised in the sand hills of South Carolina, **MARY BRENT CANTARUTTI** is a happy Northern California transplant. She is the author of a Marin County guidebook and is currently at work on two new books about the North Coast. She lives in San Rafael with her husband, Lido, and her enormous cat, Fellini.

CHRISTI PHILLIPS knew she was a writer at the age of ten, when she found herself mentally adding "she said" to friends' sentences. When she isn't off traveling in some exotic location, she's exploring her own back yard—in this case, Northern California's Central Coast. A past contributor to many California guidebooks, she has also contributed to newspapers and national magazines and travel anthologies including the *San Francisco Examiner, Esquire,* and *Travelers' Tales.*

BRIAN TACANG is a freelance writer, graphic artist, and lifelong resident of the East Bay whose work has appeared in both print publications and online. Brian has munched his way all over the Bay Area in the name of research. He lives in Oakland where he can often be found in the garage, crouched on all fours, waiting for the SASE's to drop through the mail slot.

After haunting the backroads and vineyards of the Wine Country for more than a decade, **CATHLEEN MILLER** finally gave in and moved to the town of Napa. Today she lives in a Victorian in the historic downtown area. A frequent contributor to the *Washington Post,* she has previously written for guidebooks, as well as other newspapers and travel anthologies. Her hobby is—what else?— wine tasting, a passion she pursues with her eternally thirsty husband, Kerby.

SUSAN LYN MCCOMBS has traveled the world, but her favorite spots are in the wilds of her home state of California. She's recently decided to settle into a cottage and garden of her very own, but her wandering feet are already itching. Susan's writing on world travel has appeared in magazines, anthologies, and online.

A Central Valley resident and part-time teacher, **LORI MAKABE** has lived in the Sacramento River Delta and worked in the Central Valley for nearly 20 years. She has written about sports, adventure, and travel for newspapers, magazines, travel anthologies, and online publications including *Salon.com* and *In Search of Adventure.* If it's windy, you'll find her kiteboarding or windsurfing near her home in Rio Vista.

MARY ANNE MOORE and **MAURICE READ** are freelance writers and editors, and contributors to several other travel guides including *Northern California Cheap Sleeps*. They are authors of a recently published book on bed-and-breakfasts in California. Moore is also a legislative consultant at the California State Capitol and loves to travel. Read is a Sacramento-based lobbyist and gourmet chef always on the lookout for dog-friendly lodgings, great fly-fishing, and memorable meals. Mary Anne and Maurice have contributed to previous editions of *Best Places Northern California*.

LINDA WATANABE MCFERRIN started traveling at the age of two and writing about it at age six. Decades later she's still traveling, although these days her destinations span the globe. An award-winning poet, travel writer, novelist, and contributor to numerous journals, newspapers, magazines, anthologies and online publications including the *San Francisco Examiner,* the *Washington Post, Modern Bride, Travelers' Tales, Salon.com,* and *Women.com,* she divides her time between the open road and a seat in front of her computer. She lives in Oakland.

About Best Places® Guidebooks

People trust us. Best Places® guidebooks, which have been published continuously since 1975, represent one of the most respected regional travel series in the country. Each guide is written completely independently: no advertisers, no sponsors, no favors. Our reviewers know their territory, work incognito, and seek out the very best a city or region has to offer. Because we accept no free meals, accommodations, or other complimentary services, we are able to provide tough, candid reports about places that have rested too long on their laurels, and to delight in new places that deserve recognition. We describe the true strengths, foibles, and unique characteristics of each establishment listed.

Best Places Northern California is written by and for locals, and is therefore coveted by travelers. It's written for people who live here and who enjoy exploring the region's bounty and its out-of-the-way places of high character and individualism. It is these very characteristics that make *Best Places Northern California* ideal for tourists, too. The best places in and around the region are the ones that denizens favor: independently owned establishments of good value, touched with local history, run by lively individuals, and graced with natural beauty. With this fourth edition of *Best Places Northern California*, travelers will find the information they need: where to go and when, what to order, which rooms to request (and which to avoid), where the best music, art, nightlife, shopping, and other attractions are, and how to find the region's hidden secrets.

We're so sure you'll be satisfied with our guide, we guarantee it.

NOTE: *The reviews in this edition are based on information available at press time and are subject to change. Readers are advised that places listed in previous editions may have closed or changed management, or may no longer be recommended by this series. The editors welcome information conveyed by users of this book. A report form is provided at the end of the book, and feedback is also welcome via email: books@SasquatchBooks.com.*

How to Use This Book

This book is divided into ten major regions, encompassing the Sierra Nevada, the San Francisco Bay Area, the Central Valley, and all destinations north to the Oregon border. All evaluations are based on numerous reports from local and traveling inspectors. Best Places® reporters do not identify themselves when they review an establishment, and they accept no free meals, accommodations, or any other services. Final judgments are made by the editors. **EVERY PLACE FEATURED IN THIS BOOK IS RECOMMENDED.**

STAR RATINGS Restaurants and lodgings are rated on a scale of zero to four stars (with half stars in between), based on uniqueness, loyalty of local clientele, performance measured against the establishment's goals, excellence of cooking, cleanliness, value, and professionalism of service. Reviews are listed alphabetically.

★★★★   The very best in the region

★★★   Distinguished; many outstanding features

★★   Excellent; some wonderful qualities

★   A good place

NO STARS   Worth knowing about, if nearby

(For more on how we rate places, see the Best Places® Star Ratings box below.)

PRICE RANGE Prices for restaurants are based primarily on dinner for two, including dessert, tax, and tip (no alcohol). Prices for lodgings are based on peak season rates for one night's lodging for two people (i.e., double occupancy). Peak season is typically Memorial Day to Labor Day; off-season rates vary but can sometimes be significantly less. Call ahead to verify, as all prices are subject to change.

$$$$ Very expensive (more than $100 for dinner for two; more than $200 for one night's lodging for two)

$$$ Expensive (between $65 and $100 for dinner for two; between $120 and $200 for one night's lodging for two)

$$ Moderate (between $35 and $65 for dinner for two; between $75 and $120 for one night's lodging for two)

$ Inexpensive (less than $35 for dinner for two; less than $75 for one night's lodging for two)

RESERVATIONS (FOR RESTAURANTS ONLY) We used one of the following terms for our reservations policy: reservations required, reservations recommended, no reservations. "No reservations" means either reservations are not necessary or are not accepted.

ACCESS AND INFORMATION At the beginning of each chapter, you'll find general guidelines about how to get to a particular region and what types of transportation are available, as well as basic sources for any additional tourist information you might need. Also check individual town listings for specifics about visiting those places.

THREE-DAY TOURS In every chapter, we've included a quick-reference, three-day itinerary designed for travelers with a short amount of time. Perfect for weekend getaways, these tours outline the highlights of a region or town; each of the establishments or attractions that appear in boldface within the tour are discussed in greater detail elsewhere in the chapter.

ADDRESSES AND PHONE NUMBERS Every attempt has been made to provide accurate information on an establishment's location and phone number, but it's always a good idea to call ahead and confirm. If an establishment has two area locations, we list both at the top of the review. If there are three or more locations, we list only the main address and indicate "other branches."

CHECKS AND CREDIT CARDS Many establishments that accept checks also require a major credit card for identification. Note that some places accept only local checks. Credit cards are abbreviated in this book as follows: American Express (AE); Carte Blanche (CB); Diners Club (DC); Discover (DIS); Japanese credit card (JCB); MasterCard (MC); Visa (V).

EMAIL AND WEB SITE ADDRESSES Email and web site addresses for establishments have been included where available. Please note that the web is a fluid and evolving medium, and that web pages are often "under construction" or, as with all time-sensitive information, may no longer be valid.

MAPS AND DIRECTIONS Each chapter in the book begins with a regional map that shows the general area being covered. Throughout the book, basic directions are provided with each entry. Whenever possible, call ahead to confirm hours and location.

HELPFUL ICONS Watch for these quick-reference symbols throughout the book:

 FAMILY FUN Family-oriented places that are great for kids—fun, easy, not too expensive, and accustomed to dealing with young ones.

 GOOD VALUE While not necessarily cheap, these places offer you the best value for your dollars—a good deal within the context of the region.

 ROMANTIC These spots offer candlelight, atmosphere, intimacy, or other romantic qualities—kisses and proposals are encouraged!

 UNIQUELY NORTHERN CALIFORNIA These are places that are unique and special to Northern California and beyond, such as a restaurant owned by a beloved local chef or a tourist attraction recognized around the globe.

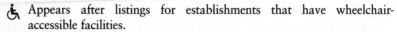 Appears after listings for establishments that have wheelchair-accessible facilities.

INDEXES All restaurants, lodgings, town names, and major tourist attractions are listed alphabetically in the back of the book.

MONEY-BACK GUARANTEE Please see "We Stand by Our Reviews" at the end of this book.

READER REPORTS At the end of the book is a report form. We receive hundreds of reports from readers suggesting new places or agreeing or disagreeing with our assessments. They greatly help in our evaluations, and we encourage you to respond.

BEST PLACES® STAR RATINGS

Any travel guide that rates establishments is inherently subjective—and Best Places®️ is no exception. We rely on our professional experience, yes, but also on a gut feeling. And, occasionally, we even give in to a soft spot for a favorite neighborhood hangout. Our star-rating system is not simply a checklist; it's judgmental, critical, sometimes fickle, and highly personal. And unlike most other travel guides, we pay our own way and accept no freebies: no free meals or accommodations, no advertisers, no sponsors, no favors.

For each new edition, we send local food and travel experts out to review restaurants and lodgings anonymously, and then to rate them on a scale of one to four, based on uniqueness, loyalty of local clientele, performance measured against the establishment's goals, excellence of cooking, cleanliness, value, and professionalism of service. That doesn't mean a one-star establishment isn't worth dining or sleeping at—far from it. When we say that all the places listed in our books are recommended, we mean it. That one-star pizza joint may be just the ticket for the end of a whirlwind day of shopping with the kids. But if you're planning something more special, the star ratings can help you choose an eatery or hotel that will wow your new clients or be a stunning, romantic place to celebrate an anniversary or impress a first date.

We award four-star ratings sparingly, reserving them for what we consider truly the best. And once an establishment has earned our highest rating, everyone's expectations seem to rise. Readers often write us letters specifically to point out the faults in four-star establishments. With changes in chefs, management, styles, and trends, it's always easier to get knocked off the pedestal than to ascend it. Three-star establishments, on the other hand, seem to generate healthy praise. They exhibit outstanding qualities, and we get lots of love letters about them. The difference between two and three stars can sometimes be a very fine line. Two-star establishments are doing a good, solid job and gaining attention, while one-star places are often dependable spots that have been around forever.

The restaurants and lodgings described in *Best Places Northern California* have earned their stars from hard work and good service (and good food). They're proud to be included in this book—look for our Best Places®️ sticker in their windows. And we're proud to honor them in this, the fourth edition of *Best Places Northern California*.

SAN FRANCISCO AND THE NORTH BAY

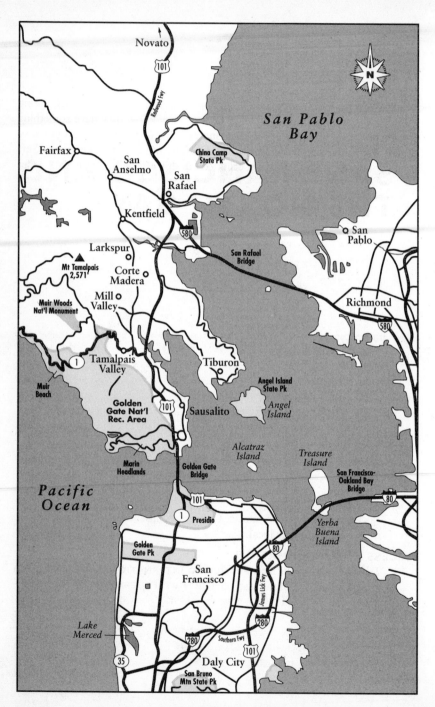

Novato

San Pablo Bay

Fairfax

San Anselmo

China Camp State Pk

San Rafael

Kentfield

Larkspur

San Rafael Bridge

San Pablo

Mt Tamalpais 2,571'

Corte Madera

Richmond

Muir Woods Nat'l Monument

Mill Valley

Tamalpais Valley

Tiburon

Angel Island State Pk

Muir Beach

Golden Gate Nat'l Rec. Area

Angel Island

Sausalito

Alcatraz Island

Treasure Island

San Francisco-Oakland Bay Bridge

Marin Headlands

Pacific Ocean

Golden Gate Bridge

Golden Gate Pk

Presidio

Yerba Buena Island

San Francisco

Lake Merced

Daly City

San Bruno Mtn State Pk

SAN FRANCISCO AND THE NORTH BAY

San Francisco

Please don't call it Frisco. It's San Francisco. Locals call it "the city," using the shorthand with confidence because they know they have something special. In no other urb in the country is the meeting of land and sea so spectacular or the combination of nature and culture so enticing. Surrounded by ocean and bay, crinkled into hill after hill, the city sits under a downy layer of fog one moment and sparkles in the clear Northern California sunlight the next.

But the attraction isn't just the setting; San Francisco's neighborhoods exude a personality that makes this place much more than a pretty collection of natural gifts. A walk around the city feels like a walk among many cities, with tolerance crossing the borders and creating a structure that holds the disparate quarters together. A trendy energy radiates from the Marina on summer days, with residents and visitors jogging, cycling, and inline skating along the Marina Green. Tie-dye and the Grateful Dead are alive and well in the Haight. The Mission District moves to a multiethnic beat, stirring the cultural pot in its eateries and its public artwork. The city's neighborhoods are as varied as its topography. And while it's true that on some days the fog never clears, that prices can strain even the fattest wallets, and that freeways clog like arteries on the verge of emergency bypass surgery, it's still easy to adore the town that columnist Herb Caen affectionately dubbed Baghdad by the Bay.

Lovers of all persuasions kiss on street corners. Poets scribble in coffee shops. Culture fiends are on a perpetual high. Stunning views can be had at the cost of a brisk walk to the top of a staircase. There's as much to do outdoors as indoors, and the climate is downright pleasant.

It's not an exaggeration. Climb a hill. Take a cable car. Peek into doorways, seek a variety of views, and sample everything your stomach can hold. Listen to live music. Cruise the museums. You'll leave calling it "the city" like any local.

ACCESS AND INFORMATION

Trips to or from the SAN FRANCISCO INTERNATIONAL AIRPORT (SFO) are easy with one of the fast, reliable SHUTTLE SERVICES, such as Super-Shuttle (415/558-8500; www.supershuttle.com) or Quake City (415/255-4899). TAXIS wait at each terminal's arrival area and will relieve you of $30 to $35 for the half-hour trip downtown. Note: A $1.2 billion BAY AREA RAPID TRANSIT (BART) train line extension to the airport is currently under construction but won't be in service until late 2001.

PARKING in San Francisco can be an ordeal; many neighborhoods limit nonresidents to only two hours, and most downtown meters have a maddening maximum time limit of 30 minutes. To make things even more frustrating, traffic cops are quick, ruthless, and in abundance. If you see a tow-away warning, take it seriously. Public parking garages abound, and if you look hard enough, you can find some garages or park-and-pay lots that don't charge Manhattan rates.

Major hotels have taxi stands; otherwise, telephone for a cab, since taxis usually only cruise along the most populated streets.

Public transportation reaches every neighborhood but grows sparse after midnight. **MUNI**, the **SAN FRANCISCO MUNICIPAL RAILWAY** (415/673-6864), includes buses, above-ground/underground streetcars, and cable cars. Exact change is required ($1 bills are OK), and free transfers (except for cable cars) grant two more rides within the next 1½ hours (be sure to ask for a transfer as soon as you board the bus). Short-term (one-, three-, and seven-day) and monthly Muni passes allowing unlimited rides are available at the Visitor Information Center (see below) and at City Hall during weekday business hours. (For information on cable cars, see Major Attractions, below.)

BART (650/992-2278) is a clean, reliable, high-speed underground commuter train system that runs through the southeastern side of the city, with routes to Daly City and the East Bay, including Berkeley and Oakland.

San Franciscans have become masters at dressing in layers, never sure exactly what the day's **WEATHER** holds. Sunny afternoons can be warm and spectacular, but are often preceded by foggy mornings or followed by cool evenings. The climate is mild, rarely rising above 70°F or falling below 40°F, but bring a sweater or coat—chances are you'll need it. Spring and fall months are warmest, as the fog makes its most frequent appearances in summer.

For more details on San Francisco sites and attractions, visit the helpful staff at the Convention and Visitors Bureau's **VISITOR INFORMATION CENTER** (lower level of Hallidie Plaza at Market and Powell Sts; 415/391-2000; www.sfvisitor.org), open seven days a week, Monday through Friday 9am to 5pm, Saturday and Sunday 9am to 3pm. Free info is available by fax 24 hours a day (800/220-5747). The bureau has a hotel reservation service (888/782-9673; www.sfvisitor.org) with photos, descriptions, and features of more than 200 Bay Area hotels. The Visitor Information Center also sells a terrific pass called the **CITYPASS**, which includes a Blue & Gold Fleet Bay Cruise, a seven-day unlimited cable car and Muni pass, and entry to the Exploratorium, the California Academy of Sciences and Steinhart Aquarium, the Museum of Modern Art, and the Palace of the Legion of Honor. CityPasses are also sold at the entrance to any of those venues.

MAJOR ATTRACTIONS

San Francisco, like Paris, is a great walking town, and one of the city's most spectacular scenic walks is along the **GOLDEN GATE PROMENADE**, a 4-mile stretch from **AQUATIC PARK** in front of the Cannery through the beautiful **MARINA GREEN** and **CRISSY FIELD** to historic **FORT POINT**, a fortification built in 1861 that's nestled under the south end of the Golden Gate Bridge. If you have the energy, continue your tour with a walk across the bridge for a breathtaking view of the Bay Area and the Pacific. Another gorgeous waterfront stroll follows the Embarcadero north from Market Street, past the landmark **FERRY BUILDING** to handsome Pier 7, where you'll get a good look at **TREASURE ISLAND** and the yachts and freighters sailing beneath the San Francisco–Oakland Bay Bridge. A hop on the **F LINE**, which runs vintage trolleys up the palm-filled center of the Embarcadero, takes you to touristy Pier 39. There you can watch the hundreds of silly **SEA LIONS** playing and basking in the sun on the west side of the pier.

The third-most-visited amusement attraction in the nation, **PIER 39** is packed with kitschy shops and overpriced, touristy restaurants, but it boasts beautiful views of Angel Island, Alcatraz, and the bay. It has great entertainment for kids with its **VENETIAN CAROUSEL**, jugglers, mimes, the "motion theater" **TURBO RIDE**, the fun (but slightly overrated and expensive) **UNDERWATER WORLD** aquarium, and an arcade stocked with every gizmo and quarter-sucking machine the young-at-heart could dream of. Once you've had your fill of the tourist-packed pier, jump aboard the ferry for the **ISLAND HOP TOUR** and make your way around both Angel Island and Alcatraz (make advance reservations), or take a **SAN FRANCISCO BAY CRUISE** or a scenic trip to the pretty towns across the bay, **SAUSALITO** and **TIBURON**. For tour information and ferry schedules, call the Blue & Gold Fleet (Piers 39–41; 415/705-5444 or 415/773-1188, recordings; or 415/705-5555, reservations; www.blueand goldfleet.com).

Just a short jaunt west of Pier 39 are world-famous **FISHERMAN'S WHARF**, **THE CANNERY**, and **GHIRARDELLI SQUARE** (www.citysearch.com/ sfo/fishermanswharf). They're always mobbed with tourists, but they offer some interesting shops. It's also still a working waterfront—stroll along the north side of Jefferson Street, between Taylor and Jones Streets, to see the colorful fishing boat fleet. And from mid-November through June, this is where you'll see the city's highly touted (and delicious) **DUNGENESS CRABS** boiling in large metal pots on the sidewalks lining the wharf.

While tourists flock to Fisherman's Wharf and Pier 39, locals often head in the other direction to the extraordinary **CALIFORNIA ACADEMY OF SCIENCES** (in Golden Gate Park, on the Music Concourse; 415/750-7145; www.calacademy.org). There, under one roof, you'll find the **NATURAL**

SAN FRANCISCO THREE-DAY TOUR

DAY ONE: Northern lights. Watch most of **North Beach** rub sleepy eyes while you're sipping a cappuccino and nibbling on an Italian pastry or the house specialty, *sacripantina*, at Stella Pastry (446 Columbus Ave; 415/986-2914). Spend the morning wandering the streets of North Beach and **Chinatown**; buy some rice candy to munch on while you walk and browse. Lunch outdoors on **Belden Lane** (between Bush and Pine Sts, and Kearny and Montgomery Sts), at one of the terrific restaurants lining the little alley, such as Plouf or Café Bastille. Walk to Powell Street and ride the Powell-Hyde **cable car** line to the end at Victorian Park. Explore **Fisherman's Wharf** and **Ghirardelli Square** (test your faith at Ripley's Believe It Or Not! Museum). Snack on cooked and cracked Dungeness crab and take the historic F line trolley back to Market Street. Walk up to Jackson Square and window-shop before dining at **Restaurant Elisabeth Daniel**. Enjoy an aerial view of your day over a nightcap and dancing at the **Top of the Mark** before you check in to your room at **Hotel Behème**.

DAY TWO: Urban edge. Fuel up early at the **Universal Cafe** for a morning at **Yerba Buena Gardens** and the **Museum of Modern Art**. Cruise the building and peruse the art at **SFMOMA**, and take a rest on the lush lawn in the middle of the main garden. Hop the California cable car line at Market and California Streets and enjoy the

HISTORY MUSEUM, MORRISON PLANETARIUM, the **LASERIUM**, and the superb **STEINHART AQUARIUM**, offering one of the most varied collections of aquatic life in the world—more than 6,000 creatures, including dolphins and alligators, from diverse underwater habitats. Another San Francisco favorite is the **EXPLORATORIUM** (415/561-0360), a unique interactive museum that brings scientific concepts to vivid life—it's a blast at any age. The Exploratorium's marvelous **TACTILE DOME** (415/561-0362), where visitors must feel their way through a maze of hurdles in total darkness, requires reservations and a certain amount of nerve. The Exploratorium is housed within the magnificent **PALACE OF FINE ARTS** (3601 Lyon St, between Jefferson and Bay Sts), designed by renowned architect Bernard Maybeck for the 1915 Panama-Pacific International Exposition. Surrounded by a natural lagoon, the Palace is an ideal spot for a picnic and for tossing your leftovers to grateful swans, seagulls, and pigeons.

In the southwest corner of the city, near the ocean and Lake Merced, is the popular **SAN FRANCISCO ZOO** (45th Ave and Sloat Blvd; 415/753-7061). Don't miss the famed Primate Discovery Center, where several species of apes and monkeys live in glass-walled condos. The zoo also has rare Sumatran and Siberian tigers, African lions (visit during their mealtimes), a children's petting zoo, and even an insect zoo. On the other side of the Golden Gate Bridge, in Sausalito, is the **BAY AREA DISCOVERY**

hilly ride to the end of the line. For lunch, savor fresh-from-the-ocean seafood at **Swan Oyster Depot** (check out those shuckers!) and walk off the calories along the **Golden Gate Promenade**, between the Marina Green and the Golden Gate Bridge. Hop on a **Blue & Gold Fleet** ferry for the Evening on Alcatraz tour ("the Rock" is most atmospheric at night). Show up for a late Spanish tapas dinner at **Zarzuela**, then sample the midnight blues scene at **Biscuits & Blues**.

DAY THREE: Elegant and outdoors. Flip through French fashion magazines and spread some jam on a croissant (or dip it in your cafe au lait) while sitting at the sidewalk table at Cafe de la Presse (352 Grant Ave at Bush St). Pass a bucolic morning in **Golden Gate Park**, floating on **Stow Lake** in a rented boat and strolling through the **Japanese Tea Garden** and **Strybing Arboretum**. Grab a quick tapas lunch on the way at **Cha Cha Cha** if you're famished, then follow a leisurely, harp-accompanied afternoon tea at the **Ritz-Carlton** with a relaxing jaunt in Pacific Heights, marveling at the homes along Pacific Avenue and Broadway, between Steiner and Baker Streets, and taking in the views from all four corners of the intersection at Broadway and Divisadero. Head toward the water again for dinner at **Boulevard**. Cap off the outdoor elegance with a short walk up the Embarcadero through the new Harry Bridges Plaza at the Ferry Building and out to Pier 7 to see the city and the bay sparkling at night.

MUSEUM (East Fort Baker; 415/289-7268), a wonderland of hands-on science, art, and multimedia exhibits designed for kids. Go north across the bridge, exit at Alexander Avenue, and follow the signs.

For a sweeping view of the Pacific Ocean, visit the historic **CLIFF HOUSE** (415/386-3330) and sip a cocktail at a windowside table, then climb around the neighboring ruins of the once-spectacular **SUTRO BATHS** (1090 Point Lobos Ave).

To explore some of the city's multiethnic neighborhoods and architectural masterpieces, strap on your heavy-duty walking shoes and hike around the **RUSSIAN HILL** neighborhood, starting at the top of the crookedest street in the world, **LOMBARD STREET** (at Hyde St). Wind your way down Lombard's multiple, flower-lined curves and continue east until Lombard intersects with Columbus Avenue, then turn right and stay on Columbus for a tour of charming **NORTH BEACH**—a predominantly Italian and Chinese neighborhood where residents practice tai chi in **WASHINGTON SQUARE** on weekend mornings or sip espresso as they peruse Proust or the *Bay Guardian*'s really racy personal ads (guaranteed to make you blush—or send you running for the nearest pay phone). You can extend this tour by turning right off Columbus onto Grant Avenue, which will take you through the heart of the ever-bustling and fascinating **CHINATOWN**—the only part of the city where vendors sell live, 3-foot-long slippery eels next to X-rated fortune cookies and herbs meant to cure whatever ails you.

If you're in need of an aerobic workout, take a different tour: instead of turning off Lombard onto Columbus, keep following Lombard Street east all the way up to COIT TOWER (415/362-0808) on the top of TELE-GRAPH HILL, then reward yourself for making the steep ascent (*gasp, gasp*) with an elevator trip to the top of the tower for a panoramic view of the Bay Area. For views without the exercise, go to the VIRTUAL OBSERVATION DECK in the lobby of the Transamerica Pyramid (600 Montgomery St at Washington St). There, on four monitors connected to cameras on the tip of the spire (853 feet up!), you can pan and zoom the entire city. And it's not even windy.

If you'd rather ride than walk the hills of San Francisco, an outside perch on one of the city's famed CABLE CARS is always a kick. The three cable car routes are named after the streets on which they run (you can take them in either direction) and operate daily from 6:30am to 12:30am, rain or shine. The Powell-Mason line starts at Powell and Market Streets and terminates at Bay Street near Fisherman's Wharf; the Powell-Hyde line also begins at Powell and Market Streets but ends at Victorian Park near Aquatic Park and the bay, making it the most scenic route; and the California line runs from California and Market Streets through China-town to Van Ness Avenue. Expect very long lines during peak travel times, especially when the weather is warm. For more information on the cable cars, call the Visitor Information Center (415/391-2000) or Muni (415/673-6864).

MUSEUMS

The SAN FRANCISCO MUSEUM OF MODERN ART (151 3rd St, between Mission and Howard Sts; 415/357-4000), housed in a dramatic new modernist building designed by Swiss architect Mario Botta, offers works by Picasso, Matisse, O'Keeffe, Rivera, Pollock, Warhol, Klee, De Forest, and Lichtenstein. The M. H. DE YOUNG MEMORIAL MUSEUM (in Golden Gate Park, on the Music Concourse; 415/863-3330) will be closed until 2005 while a flashy new building is constructed on the site of the old one. Some of the collection will travel, some will be loaned to the San Francisco Airport and the Oakland Museum, and the rest will be put in storage. On the west side of the de Young is the ASIAN ART MUSEUM (415/668-8921), the largest museum in the Western world devoted exclusively to Asian art, with many masterpieces from the Avery Brundage collection. (The museum will move to the former San Francisco Main Library building in the Civic Center late in 2002.)

The CALIFORNIA PALACE OF THE LEGION OF HONOR (in Lincoln Park near 34th Ave and Clement St; 415/863-3330 or 415/750-3600), a three-quarter-scale replica of Paris's grand Palais de la Légion d'Honneur,

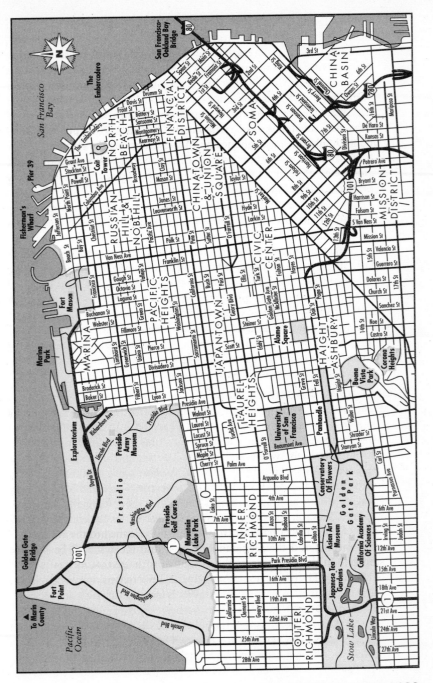

DOWNTOWN SAN FRANCISCO

features European paintings (including works by Monet, Cézanne, and Rembrandt), sculptures (a large collection of Rodin), and decorative art. It also has a small collection of ancient art and hosts a constant stream of interesting international exhibits. The city has several terrific folk-art museums, most notably the **MEXICAN MUSEUM** (Fort Mason Center, Building D, off Marina Blvd at Buchanan St; 415/441-0404), the first in the United States to feature Mexican and Chicano art. (The museum will move to a new building in Yerba Buena Gardens in 2002.) Photography buffs should not miss the **ANSEL ADAMS CENTER FOR PHOTOGRAPHY** (655 Mission St; 415/495-7000), where the work of the master himself, along with that of Imogen Cunningham, Dorothea Lange, and many other notables, is showcased.

Galleries for established San Francisco artists are located primarily on lower Grant Avenue and near Union Square; up-and-coming artists tend to exhibit in SoMa (the South of Market Street area).

Fantastic **MURALS** decorate many public spaces in the city, particularly in the **MISSION DISTRICT**, the city's vibrant, primarily Hispanic neighborhood; for maps outlining self-guided walks or for very good two-hour guided tours, contact the **PRECITA EYES MURAL ARTS CENTER** (2981 24th St at Harrison St; 415/285-2287; www.precitaeyes.org). If you don't have time for a tour, at least stroll down narrow **BALMY ALLEY** (near Harrison and 25th Sts), which is lined with about 30 incredibly colorful murals on the garages and fences of the homes and is the birthplace of mural painting in San Francisco.

SHOPPING AND BOOKSTORES

The famous and oh-so-trendy **UNION SQUARE** area and the nearby **SAN FRANCISCO SHOPPING CENTRE** (Market and 5th Sts; 415/495-5656) together boast many major department stores (including Macy's, Nordstrom, Saks Fifth Avenue, and Neiman Marcus) and more specialty shops than you can shake a credit card at. A short walk away is the chichi **CROCKER GALLERIA** (bounded by Post, Kearny, Sutter, and Montgomery Sts), a 70-foot-high, glass-domed, three-level shopping mall with Ralph Lauren, Versace, and similar boutiques, which was modeled after Milan's 1867 Galleria Vittoria Emmanuelle II. The vast **EMBARCADERO CENTER** (between Clay, Sacramento, Battery, and Drumm Sts) is a sophisticated three-level, open-air neo-mall also well worth a spree.

Many famed fashion firms have factory outlets south of Market Street. Among them are **ESPRIT** (499 Illinois St off 16th St; 415/957-2500) and **GEORGIOU** (925 Bryant St, between 7th and 8th Sts; 415/554-0150). Outdoor enthusiasts should check out **THE NORTH FACE** outlet (1325 Howard St, between 9th and 10th Sts; 415/626-6444) for skiwear, sweaters, sleeping bags, and other high-quality outdoor gear.

Stroll down **SACRAMENTO STREET** (between Lyon and Spruce Sts) for elegant clothing and furnishings. For vintage, cutting-edge, and folksy fashions and crafts, shop on **24TH STREET** (between Castro and Church Sts) and **HAIGHT STREET** (between Masonic Ave and Shrader St). Hip, eclectic, and classic items abound on **CASTRO STREET** (between Market and 19th Sts), **FILLMORE STREET** (between Jackson and Sutter Sts), and **UNION STREET** (between Gough and Steiner Sts). The 5-acre **JAPAN CENTER** (Post St, between Laguna and Fillmore Sts; 415/922-6776) houses several shops selling Japanese crafts, housewares, and books, with numerous sushi bars and other Japanese-style eateries sandwiched in between.

Cosmopolitan cooks can stock up on Asian foodstuffs in **CHINATOWN** along Stockton Street (between California St and Broadway) or in **NEW CHINATOWN** on Clement Street (between Arguello Blvd and 10th Ave, and 18th and 25th Aves). Shops along **COLUMBUS AVENUE** (between Broadway and Bay Sts) in North Beach sell Italian treats, while the **MISSION DISTRICT'S** stores offer Latin specialties on 24th Street (between Guerrero St and Potrero Ave).

Good bookstores include **CITY LIGHTS** (261 Columbus Ave at Broadway; 415/362-8193), still Beat after all these years; **A CLEAN WELL-LIGHTED PLACE FOR BOOKS** (601 Van Ness Ave, in Opera Plaza between Golden Gate Ave and Turk St; 415/441-6670); **STACEY'S BOOKSTORE** (581 Market St at 2nd St; 415/421-4687). **GET LOST TRAVEL BOOKS** (1825 Market St at Gough St; 415/437-0529); **RAND MCNALLY MAP & TRAVEL STORE** (595 Market St at 2nd St; 415/777-3131); and **THOMAS BROS. MAPS AND BOOKS** (550 Jackson St at Columbus Ave; 415/981-7520 or 800/969-3072) are great stops for any traveler.

PERFORMING ARTS

San Franciscans' love of the arts is evident not only in the number of artsy goings-on but also in the number of ways to discover them. For up-to-the-moment information, surf to the **SAN FRANCISCO ARTS MONTHLY** web site (artsmonthlysf.org) or check the *San Francisco Chronicle*'s Datebook (more commonly known as "the pink section") in the Sunday paper.

TIX BAY AREA (251 Stockton St, on the east side of Union Square; 415/433-7827; www.theatrebayarea.org) sells half-price tickets to many of San Francisco's dance, music, and theater events on the day of the performance only (tickets for Sunday and Monday events are sold on Saturday). You must purchase the tickets in person and pay in cash or with traveler's checks. Advance full-price tickets are sold here, too, and may be purchased with Visa, MasterCard, traveler's checks, or cash. Tickets to most dance and theater events are also sold by phone through the **CITY BOX OFFICE** (415/392-4400) and **BASS TICKETMASTER** (510/762-2277).

MUSIC: San Francisco's bountiful music scene has a 24-hour-a-day tempo. The accordion is the city's official musical instrument, but don't look for the squeeze box in the venues below. It makes most of its appearances in street performances.

The world-class **SAN FRANCISCO OPERA** (415/864-3330, box office; or 415/861-4008, general information), led by Lotfi Mansouri, alternates warhorses with rarities from September through January at the beautiful War Memorial Opera House. This beloved Beaux Arts beauty was modeled on Garnier's Paris Opéra and first opened on October 15, 1932, with a production of Puccini's *Tosca*. Sixty-five years later, on September 5, 1997, the same Puccini production launched the reopening after an 18-month, $86.5 million renovation that included seismic retrofitting, regilding of the 530 rosettes on the lobby's barrel-vaulted ceiling, and replacing of the old stage curtain with an elaborate 3,000-pound, gold silk organza number. Subscribers grab up most of the red velvet seats, but fans with smaller bankrolls can stand in line early on performance mornings to buy one of the 200 standing-room tickets, which go on sale at 10am (50 of these inexpensive tickets are held until two hours before the performance). The **SAN FRANCISCO SYMPHONY** (415/864-6000), under the heralded baton of music director Michael Tilson-Thomas, performs from September through July at the modern Louise M. Davies Symphony Hall (201 Van Ness Ave at Grove St), a gorgeous $38 million construction with a wraparound glass facade. Other classical groups include the **WOMEN'S PHILHARMONIC** (415/437-0123) and the **SAN FRANCISCO EARLY MUSIC SOCIETY** (510/528-1725).

On summer Sundays, families and couples tote blankets and picnic baskets to free outdoor performances (everything from jazz to opera to symphony) at the pretty **STERN GROVE** (Sloat Blvd and 19th Ave; 415/252-6252). The **SAN FRANCISCO JAZZ FESTIVAL** (415/788-7353; www.sfjazzfest.org), one of the largest in the country, toots its horn every fall with concerts, dances, films, and lectures. (For the scoop on the city's best nightclub performances, see Nightlife, below.)

THEATER AND COMEDY: AMERICAN CONSERVATORY THEATER (415/749-2ACT; www.act-sfbay.org), the city's best-known theater company, presents solid productions of new works and classics under the artistic direction of Carey Perloff from September through July in the Geary Theater (415 Geary St). Broadway shows on tour are performed at the **GOLDEN GATE, CURRAN,** and **ORPHEUM THEATERS** (415/551-2000). **THEATRE ON THE SQUARE** (450 Post St, between Powell and Mason Sts; 415/433-9500) and **MARINES MEMORIAL THEATRE** (609 Sutter St at Mason St; 415/771-6900) showcase off-Broadway acts.

Among the small local theater companies offering wonderful performances are the **LORRAINE HANSBERRY THEATRE** (620 Sutter St at Mason St; 415/474-8800 or 415/288-0336); the **LAMPLIGHTERS MUSIC THEATER** (415/978-2787), which performs primarily Gilbert and Sullivan comic operas at Yerba Buena Gardens' Center for the Arts (701 Mission St at 3rd St) and the Ira & Leonore S. Gershwin Theater (2350 Turk St at Masonic St); and the **MAGIC THEATRE** (Fort Mason Center, Building D, off Marina Blvd at Buchanan St; 415/441-8822). **THEATRE RHINOCEROS** (2926 16th St at South Van Ness Ave; 415/861-5079) specializes in gay and lesbian drama. Summer and early autumn bring free outdoor performances at various venues by America's oldest political musical-comedy theater group, the Tony award–winning **SAN FRANCISCO MIME TROUPE** (415/285-1717). The more serious **SHAKESPEARE IN THE PARK** (415/422-2221; www.sfshakes.org) theater group also performs for free in the summer in Golden Gate Park. **BEACH BLANKET BABYLON,** the longest-running musical revue in the world, is a cabaret-style show full of silly jokes that's famous for its wild costumes and humongous hats. It remains a favorite of residents and visitors alike, so be sure to reserve seats in advance at Club Fugazi (678 Green St near Powell St; 415/421-4222).

San Francisco has launched many comedians' careers, including Robin Williams and Whoopi Goldberg. See the latest talents at the **PUNCHLINE** (444 Battery St, 2nd Fl, between Clay and Washington Sts; 415/397-7573), and **COBB'S COMEDY CLUB,** in the Cannery (2801 Leavenworth St, Building S, courtyard entrance at Beach St; 415/928-4320).

DANCE: The internationally renowned **SAN FRANCISCO BALLET** (415/865-2000), led by artistic director Helgi Tomasson, leaps into its season in December with the classic *Nutcracker* and begins its repertory season in February; performances are held at the War Memorial Opera House (301 Van Ness Ave at Grove St). Ethnic dance troupes abound in the Bay Area, and they come together in June for the **SAN FRANCISCO ETHNIC DANCE FESTIVAL** (415/474-3914). For modern and contemporary performances, see the **ODC/SAN FRANCISCO** dance troupe (415/ 863-6606); for contemporary ballet, **LINES** (415/863-3360; www.lines-ballet.org) is a local favorite and often performs at Yerba Buena Gardens' Center for the Arts (701 Mission St at 3rd St). Modern dance recitals also are frequently held at **THEATER ARTAUD** (450 Florida St at 17th St; 415/621-7797).

FILM: The **SAN FRANCISCO INTERNATIONAL FILM FESTIVAL** (415/931-3456) attracts film fanatics for a fortnight every spring; screenings are held at various venues in San Francisco, Berkeley, and Marin County. Another popular event is the **SAN FRANCISCO INTERNATIONAL LESBIAN AND GAY FILM FESTIVAL** (415/703-8650), which takes place in June. For rare revivals and premieres, check out the palatial **CASTRO THEATRE** (429 Castro St off Market St; 415/621-6120), a flamboyant Spanish baroque-style movie palace designed by Timothy Pflueger in 1923; the funky (but finely programmed) **ROXIE CINEMA** (3117 16th St at Valencia St; 415/863-1087); and the homey **RED VIC MOVIE HOUSE** (1727 Haight St, between Cole and Shrader Sts; 415/668-3994).

PARKS, GARDENS, AND BEACHES

GOLDEN GATE PARK, encompassing 1,017 acres of lush grounds dotted with magnificent museums, lakes, and gardens, is a masterpiece of park design. For a good introduction to its attractions, join one of the **FREE GUIDED WALKING TOURS** offered by Friends of Recreation and Parks (415/263-0991 or 415/750-5105) every weekend from May through October. Plant enthusiasts mustn't miss the **STRYBING ARBORETUM AND BOTANICAL GARDENS** (near 9th Ave and Lincoln Wy; 415/661-1316), home to more than 7,000 plant and tree varieties. A somewhat more Zen-like experience is offered by the lovely **JAPANESE TEA GARDEN**, the oldest Japanese-style park in the United States, which always attracts crowds but particularly when the cherry blossoms and azaleas bloom in March and April (*pssst . . . to avoid the hordes, visit when it's raining*). In the northeast corner of the park is the spectacular **CONSERVATORY OF FLOWERS** (John F. Kennedy Dr, near Conservatory Dr; 415/831-2700), an 1879 Victorian fairyland hothouse that was full of tropical flora until massive storms destroyed much of the glass-paneled landmark in 1995. It's still an architectural beauty worth admiring from the outside but is closed until spring of 2003. In the middle of the park, serene **STOW LAKE** compels you to rent a rowboat, paddleboat, or electric boat (415/752-0347) and circle the 430-foot-high artificial island known as **STRAW-BERRY HILL**, the highest peak in the park. Look for the hill's waterfall and Chinese moon-watching pavilion as well as the numerous turtles and ducks that live on the lake. If you have youngsters in tow, don't skip the **CHILDREN'S PLAYGROUND** (off Kezar Dr), which has a dazzling Golden Age 1912 carousel (the oldest one in a public park) that's guaranteed to make every child's heart go pitter-patter. Every Sunday, Golden Gate Park's main drag is closed to auto traffic so skaters and joggers can let loose on the tree-lined street. **SKATE RENTALS** are readily available on Fulton and Haight Streets.

The city's entire northwest corner is part of the **GOLDEN GATE NATIONAL RECREATION AREA (GGNRA)**, the largest urban park in the world. Take a hike along its gorgeous wildflower-laced **COASTAL TRAIL**, which hugs the headlands for more than 10 miles and offers fantastic views of the Pacific Ocean; start at Point Lobos (at the end of Point Lobos Ave, near the Sutro Baths) and wind your way to the Golden Gate Bridge. **THE PRESIDIO**, a lush 1,480-acre former military base, has become part of the GGNRA and offers superb views to hikers (and drivers) as well as historic buildings, a scenic golf course, walking and biking tours, and a national cemetery. Also part of the GGNRA are **CRISSY FIELD**, a fabulous windsurfing spot, and the **MARINA GREEN**, prime kite-flying and jogging territory; both are located off Marina Boulevard, near the on-ramp to the Golden Gate Bridge. For maps and more details on the GGNRA, call the National Park Information Center (415/556-0560).

In the heart of the city, across from the Museum of Modern Art, is **YERBA BUENA GARDENS** (Mission St between 3rd and 4th Sts), San Francisco's 5-acre urban park featuring a walk-through waterfall enclosing a beautiful memorial for Martin Luther King Jr., a sculpture garden, and terrace cafes. The Yerba Buena **CHILDREN'S CENTER**, cleverly situated on the roof of the Moscone Convention Center, has plenty of diversions for little tykes, including a carousel, ice-skating rink, bowling alley, arts and technology center, and children's garden. For consumers of all ages, **SONY'S METREON ENTERTAINMENT COMPLEX** has shops, restaurants, a 15-screen cinema, an IMAX theater, and a children's play center designed by author-illustrator Maurice Sendak. Tours of Yerba Buena Gardens are available by appointment for a nominal fee (415/541-0312; YBAlliance@yerbabuena.org).

Riptide-ridden and blustery **OCEAN BEACH** is a haven for seasoned surfers as well as families, dog-walkers, joggers, and lovers who enjoy the long, sandy beach located off the Great Highway. On warm days, sun worshippers prefer to bask at **BAKER BEACH** (at the south end of Lincoln Blvd) while gazing at the stupendous view of the Golden Gate (as at most of the city's beaches, however, swimming is unsafe here). The east side of the beach is a popular gay hangout, where sunbathers wear nothing but sunscreen. Other scenic spots include **GLEN CANYON PARK** (Bosworth St and O'Shaughnessy Blvd), which has a playground; the lush **STERN GROVE** (Sloat Blvd at 19th Ave); and **LAKE MERCED** (off Harding Dr between Hwy 35 and Sloat Blvd, near the zoo), where you can rent a rowboat, canoe, or paddleboat (415/681-3310) and fish for trout.

NIGHTLIFE

BARS: San Franciscans need something to cut the chill of those long, foggy nights, so many head to North Beach, which has more than its fair share of popular watering holes, including **LITTLE CITY** (673 Union St at Powell St, near Washington Sq; 415/434-2900), a great spot for flirting over drinks and plates of antipasto. There's also the pleasant (and semisecret) **SPECS** (Saroyan Alley off Columbus Ave; 415/421-411), an old Beat generation hangout; the charming but rough-around-the-edges **SAVOY TIVOLI** (1434 Grant Ave, between Union and Green Sts; 415/362-7023); and **TOSCA CAFE** (242 Columbus Ave, between Pacific Ave and Broadway; 415/391-1244), where locals hang out (and celebs hide in the back room) sipping the house specialty: coffeeless cappuccinos made with brandy, milk, and chocolate.

When the fog burns off and the weather heats up, grab a chair on the patio of **CAFE FLORE** (2298 Market St at Noe St; 415/621-8579) in the Castro District and order a glass of white wine or a latte. Or get the full array of spirits on the outdoor decks of such funky local favorites as the **RAMP** (855 China Basin St off 3rd St; 415/621-2378) and **PIER 23** (the Embarcadero between Broadway and Bay Sts; 415/362-5125).

For a more romantic retreat, make your toasts at the lounge of the **CARNELIAN ROOM** restaurant at the top of the 52-story Bank of America building (555 California St, between Kearny and Montgomery Sts; 415/433-7500), which offers a dizzying view of the city when the sky is clear; the plush **CROWN ROOM** in the Fairmont Hotel (950 Mason St at California St, 24th Fl; 415/772-5131); the scenic, glass-walled **TOP OF THE MARK** lounge in the Mark Hopkins Hotel (999 California St at Mason St; 415/392-3434), with dancing to live music after 8:30pm; or **EQUINOX**, the unique revolving rooftop lounge and restaurant at the Hyatt Regency (5 Embarcadero Center; 415/788-1234) that slowly spins in a circle, giving patrons a varying 360-degree panorama.

If you haven't tired of the cigar craze, puff on a stogie at **850** (850 Montgomery St; 415/291-0850), a cigar bar with more than 20 varieties in its humidor and an outside patio and pool tables to boot. Just down the street, catch the scene at the **BUBBLE LOUNGE** (714 Montgomery St; 415/434-4204). With over 300 champagnes, 30 by the glass, you're sure to find something that tickles your palate while lounging in the oversize, hip chairs and sofas that make up the "salons" in the main upstairs room.

Union Square's best bustling bars are at **KULETO'S** restaurant (221 Powell St, between Geary and O'Farrell Sts; 415/397-7720) and the **COMPASS ROSE** in the Westin St. Francis Hotel (335 Powell St, between Post and Geary Sts; 415/397-7000), which boasts the largest martini in the city—10 ounces! For the best Irish coffee in town, the **BUENA VISTA** (2765 Hyde St at the corner of Beach St; 415/474-5044) takes top honors.

CLUBS: Great clubs abound in San Francisco, the city that never seems to sleep. Most of San Francisco's clubs present an ever-changing lineup of bands or recorded music, so call ahead for up-to-date recorded listings at each venue. The **BE-AT LINE** (415/626-4087) recorded hotline will also tell you where you can find the night's hot musical acts. Locals tend to pick up a copy of the free *San Francisco Bay Guardian* weekly newspaper (available at cafes and most major street corners) for the straight scoop on the city's wild and ever-changing club scene.

For live blues, jazz, and rock, **SLIM'S** (333 11th St, between Folsom and Harrison Sts; 415/522-0333) can't be beat. The famous **FILLMORE** (1805 Geary Blvd at Fillmore St; 415/346-6000) always books top talents, and **BRUNO'S** (2389 Mission St at 20th St; 415/648-7701) is boffo. For hip-hop, rock, purple hair, and nipple rings, venture into the **DNA LOUNGE** (375 11th St at Harrison St; 415/626-1409). If dancin' among the masses is your thing, go to **CLUB 1015** (1015 Folsom St at 6th St;

415/431-1200). For a mix of live music, the trendy set kicks up its heels at **CAFE DU NORD** (2170 Market St, between Church and Sanchez Sts; 415/861-5016) and the rowdy **LAST DAY SALOON** (406 Clement St, between 5th and 6th Aves; 415/387-6343). If you want to shake, rattle, and roll with the high-fashion crowd, put on your best dancing shoes and go to **HARRY DENTON'S STARLIGHT ROOM** at the top of the Sir Francis Drake Hotel (450 Powell St, between Sutter and Post Sts; 415/395-8595).

To hear the sounds of the city's new bands, stroll Haight Street. Numerous venues line both sides of this famous strip, still populated by dazed youth, the homeless, and various eccentrics. Great cocktails and live swing bands will get you out of your seat and onto the dance floor at **CLUB DELUXE** (1511 Haight St at Ashbury St; 415/552-6949). Elsewhere, the ornate **GREAT AMERICAN MUSIC HALL** (859 O'Farrell St, between Polk and Larkin Sts; 415/885-0750) hosts hundreds of concerts a year, ranging from Motown, rock, and jazz to bluegrass, folk, and zydeco. **PARADISE LOUNGE** (11th and Folsom Sts; 415/861-6906) offers a stellar lineup of all kinds of music. For a blast of the blues, go to the candlelit **BISCUITS & BLUES** (401 Mason St at Geary St; 415/292-2583). Jumpin' jazz joints include **JAZZ AT PEARL'S** (256 Columbus Ave just north of Broadway; 415/291-8255) and **RASSELAS** (2801 California St at Divisadero St; 415/567-5010).

SPORTS AND RECREATION

Bay Area sports buffs are proud of their **SAN FRANCISCO 49ERS** football team (415/468-2249), which plays home games at **3COM PARK** (previously named Candlestick Park, and still called "the Stick" by Bay Area residents). The **SAN FRANCISCO GIANTS** (415/972-2000; www.sfgiants. com) play at the new, home-run-friendly **PACIFIC BELL PARK** in China Basin (3rd and King Sts). PacBell Park, as it's known, is of the "new" intimate ballpark genre, so there are good views of the field even from on high. Perhaps even more enticing, depending on the game, are views of the bay and downtown San Francisco. True to the foodie spirit of the city, regular ballpark fare is enhanced by concession stands and bistros serving pan-Latin and Asian cuisine as well as *bazurros*, salads rolled into fresh flat bread. If none of that appeals, restaurants are springing up all around the park. (Fans of the **OAKLAND A'S** and the **GOLDEN STATE WARRIORS** should turn to the Oakland section in the following pages.)

The **SAN FRANCISCO MARATHON** is usually run in July, but if you'd rather race against two-legged Brillo boxes, centipedes, Snow White and the Seven Dwarfs, and a Whitney Houston clone in drag, sign up for the wild-and-wacky, 7.5-mile **BAY TO BREAKERS** race and walk (415/777-7770, ext. 4) held in mid-May.

FESTIVALS

Every winter, the two-week-long **CHINESE NEW YEAR** (415/982-3071 or 415/982-3000) celebration culminates explosively with an electrifying parade that winds through downtown, Union Square, and Chinatown. In summer and spring, **STREET FAIRS** that typify their neighborhoods pop up (from upscale Union Street to the still-hairy Haight). Japantown launches its **CHERRY BLOSSOM FESTIVAL** with a parade in April; the Mission District draws crowds with its **CINCO DE MAYO PARADE**; and the **SAN FRANCISCO LESBIAN, GAY, BISEXUAL, TRANSGENDER PRIDE CELEBRATION PARADE** (415/864-3733) attracts thousands of revelers on the last weekend of June.

All heads turn skyward when the U.S. Navy flaunts its amazing acrobatic flight team—the **BLUE ANGELS**—during **FLEET WEEK CELEBRATION** (near Fisherman's Wharf and Pier 39; 415/705-5500) in early October. Bands, boat rides, and a parade of ships and submarines on the bay round out the festivities.

Restaurants and Lodgings by Neighborhood

This restaurant scene keeps reviewers busy inventing new adjectives and diners tottering on the verge of gluttony.

North Beach

Your eyes will say you're in the United States. Your other senses, though, will shout, "Italy, Italy, Italy!" Shopkeepers stand on their stoops firing Italian at friends on the sidewalks. Cafes and restaurants send up aromatic espresso, focaccia, and saucy pasta greetings. North Beach is most definitely an Italian enclave. These days, Chinatown—just to the west—also exerts an influence on the community. Saints Peter and Paul Roman Catholic Church, the neighborhood's spiritual anchor, now offers services in English, Italian, and Chinese. Tai chi is as ubiquitous in Washington Square Park as sunbathing. Always a haven for bohemian society, North Beach also treasures a literary history that embraces Beat writers like Allen Ginsberg, Lawrence Ferlinghetti, and Jack Kerouac, and local bars and bookstores still celebrate their presence.

RESTAURANTS

Helmand / ★★

430 BROADWAY, SAN FRANCISCO; 415/362-0641

An oasis of good taste on Broadway's less-than-tasteful topless strip, Helmand serves delicious renditions of Afghan cuisine in a pretty room lit by brass chandeliers and small table lanterns. The restaurant's light and variously spiced house-made yogurts, a staple of Afghani cooking, dress several favorite appetizers, including *mantwo* (a house-made dumpling filled with sautéed onions and beef, topped with a carrot, yellow split pea, and beef sauce, and served on yogurt) and *kaddo borawni* (sweet baby pumpkin that's pan-fried, then baked, and tempered by a piquant yogurt-garlic sauce). For a main course, try the *chowpan*—a tender, juicy half rack of lamb marinated, then grilled and served with sautéed eggplant and rice pilau. Other fine choices include *sabzi challow* (a wonderfully seasoned mixture of spinach with lamb), *mourgh challow* (chicken sautéed with split peas and curry), and *koufta challow* (light, moderately spicy meatballs with sun-dried tomatoes, peppers, and peas), each served with a ramekin of flavorful fresh cilantro sauce and aromatic white or brown rice. Servers are personable, if sometimes slightly scattered, and the wine list is well chosen and well priced. Parking is scarce in this neighborhood, so take advantage of the time-limited validated parking at the lot down the block. *$$; AE, MC, V; no checks; dinner Tues–Sun; full bar; reservations required; between Montgomery and Kearny Sts.* &

MC² / ★★★

470 PACIFIC AVE, SAN FRANCISCO; 415/956-0666

One of the best-looking restaurants in the city, this sleek, modern establishment has earned awards and acclaim as much for its architecture as for its food. Built into a historic brick warehouse from the Barbary Coast era, the room features wood ceilings, brick walls, and exposed beams, a stylish aesthetic that threatens to make the meals here a second act. Luckily, chef Yoshi Kojima is behind the stoves in the exhibition kitchen, and his light, flavorful, contemporary California-French cuisine is among the best in town. Kojima's Japanese heritage is evident in some of the better dishes, such as the appetizer of seared tuna and tuna tartare with shiitake mushrooms or the dinner entrees of roasted day-boat scallops and shiitake-crusted fillet of beef with root vegetables. The Sonoma duck breast with caramelized turnip tart and foie gras sauce is also outstanding. The massive wine list can be a bit daunting, but the sommelier is friendly and quick with a perfect recommendation. Service is generally flawless but can be distant. *$$$; AE, DC, MC, V; no checks; lunch Mon–Fri, dinner Mon–Sat; full bar; reservations recommended; between Montgomery and Sansome Sts.* &

Moose's / ★★

1652 STOCKTON ST, SAN FRANCISCO; 415/989-7800

Every major city has a place where the prime movers-and-shakers hang out, and in this city it's Moose's. Run by well-respected San Francisco restaurateur Ed Moose, the lively, ever-so-friendly establishment facing Washington Square is abuzz every night with lawyers, politicians, and local celebrities who come to sup and schmooze within the spacious,

WALKABOUT

Think your dry cleaner is slow? In the 19th century, San Francisco's elite sent their laundry to China, waiting five months for their shirts to return, cleaned and pressed. These well-traveled garments spent more time on boats than on backs. Enterprising Chinese in San Francisco, unemployed after work on the Transcontinental Railroad ended, offered to pick up, clean, and deliver the clothing locally, launching the laundry business in America—on tiny Waverly Place in Chinatown.

Snippets like that are the special surprises that await you when you take a San Francisco walking tour. Want to visit Mark Twain's favorite haunts? Sample Chinatown's best eats? Find the treats hidden in various neighborhoods all over town? There's a tour for nearly every taste (bud), and you're guaranteed to learn things even locals don't know.

Wok Wiz (415/981-8989; www.wokwiz.com) offers food and culture tours, ranging from the extravagant "I Can't Believe I Ate My Way Through Chinatown" to "Walk 'n Wok," in which you shop for the ingredients, then cook and consume a meal. The "Ciao, Chow!" tour meanders through North Beach and Chinatown, providing a truly multicultural introduction to the adjoining neighborhoods. Food writer **GraceAnn Walden** (415/397-8530) offers her own "Mangia North Beach!" tour, which includes behind-the-scenes looks at bakeries, pubs, truffle makers, and restaurants, as well as visits to Italian book and ceramics stores. Feeling low on energy? Get a buzz with the brisk **Javawalk** (415/673-9255), two hours of tracing the vein of caffeine in San Francisco history. Coffee lover Elaine Sosa shares colorful stories of North Beach and Jackson Square while exploring cafes, a coffee roastery, and a shop that sells—what else?—

high-energy dining room. Chef Jason Miller runs the exhibition kitchen, offering a monthly changing menu of upscale American dishes that have garnered many a favorable review. The most recommended dishes are anything that's cooked in the wood-burning oven. When in doubt, stick with the legendary Caesar salad and juicy Mooseburger, washed down with a glass of spicy zinfandel. A jazz combo plays nightly, and the adjacent bar—separated from the main dining room by a frosted-glass partition—stays busy long after the kitchen closes. Moose's hosts a popular weekend brunch as well. *$$–$$$; AE, DC, MC, V; no checks; lunch Thurs–Sun, dinner every day, brunch Sun; full bar; reservations recommended; www.mooses.com; between Union and Filbert Sts.* &

Peña PachaMama / ★★☆

1630 POWELL ST, SAN FRANCISCO; 415/646-0018

 The moment you walk past the neon-orange-clad figure of Kusillo at the door, you are folded into the musical family of Sukay. This Andean

espresso machines.

Lest you get the impression that San Franciscans only think about food, **tactileHeart** (415/721-1763; www.tactileheart.com) offers the "FootNotes Street Theater Living Literature Tour," a performance walk through North Beach, following in the footsteps of writers like Jack Kerouac and Maya Angelou. **Artline's** (650/494-1368; www.e-artline. com) fine art walking tours are customized to group preferences. Organized by either theme or location, the tours explore art galleries, artists' studios, printmaking ateliers, and photography galleries.

Celebrating San Francisco's folklore, history, and diversity is the goal of **City Guides'** (415/557-4266; www.wenet.net/~jhum/cgtours.html) 200 volunteers. They lead free walking tours covering every imaginable corner of the city. Architecture buffs might take the "Art Deco Marina" or "Pacific Heights Mansions" tours. Fans of the Barbary Coast period of San Francisco's history can enjoy "Brothels, Boardinghouses, & Bawds." The alphabet soup of tours will move you from "Alamo Square" to the "Zakheim Mural."

If you'd rather walk at your own pace, follow the bronze medallions in the sidewalk on the "Barbary Coast Trail," a 3.8-mile tour of the city's history that runs from the Old Mint at Fifth and Mission Streets to Aquatic Park near the Wharf. Or pick up a copy of the **Convention and Visitors Bureau's** (415/391-2000; www.sfvisitor.org) pamphlet of self-guided walking tours. The pamphlet even offers helpful tips, like what to look for when choosing a walking shoe. It's a good idea to check your hoofers against this list before starting out on any of these excursions. —Danielle Machotka

ensemble, which has been performing together for more than 20 years, opened Peña PachaMama (Mother Earth, in the ancient Quechua language) to create a center for Bolivian food and music in San Francisco. The Nuevo Latino cuisine—a fusion of traditional Bolivian dishes with the lighter, organic California sensibility—is the perfect opening act for the show; Friday and Saturday nights, the cozy restaurant gets even cozier, as the group plays an invigorating, nonamplified collection of traditional and new Bolivian music on a stage next to the dining room. Pan pipes, flutes, guitarlike instruments, drums, masks, festival costumes, and one very large inverted-cone hat made of long feathers and ribbon—all spring around the room under the power of the lively band members. Peña PachaMama's engaging warmth gives it the feel of a neighbor's house, but chef James Canter (formerly of the local restaurants Fringale and Foreign Cinema) spins the organic produce and hormone-free meat into savory concoctions that your next-door neighbor might never imagine. Appetizers include Bolivian Rock Soup—a purée of corn tortillas, roasted peppers, tomatoes, and spices—and a wonderful green salad with a dab of ground nut and drizzle of mango-lime sauces. For the main course, Pacha Pollo is a succulent pan-seared chicken with Andean spices, a purée of Peruvian potatoes (they're purple!), and organic greens. Vegetarians can happily put themselves in Canter's hands with the Chef's Vegetarian Selection. An evening here is a full night out on the town— food, culture, and entertainment—all for the very reasonable price of dinner. *$$; AE, MC, V; checks OK; dinner Tues–Sat; beer and wine; reservations recommended; sukay@sirius.com; www.penapachamama. com; between Union and Green Sts.* &

Rose Pistola / ★★★

532 COLUMBUS AVE, SAN FRANCISCO; 415/399-0499

A star has been born in North Beach, and her name is Rose Pistola. The brainchild of Midas-like chef-restaurateur Reed Hearon (who launched the reputations of LuLu and Cafe Marimba), this sleek and sexy addition to the Columbus Avenue promenade is as pleasing to behold as it is to dine in (it's actually named after a popular octogenarian North Beach restaurateur). If you prefer to oversee the preparation of your meal, sit at the counter overlooking the grill; however, the family-style meals are best enjoyed in the large dining room's comfy booths. Tables on the sidewalk offer an alfresco option. The food is rustic Italian with a California flair (less fats, more flavors) inspired by the cuisine of Liguria: roast rabbit with fresh shell-bean ragout and polenta; pumpkin-filled ravioli; or roast pork chop with panzanella, an Italian bread salad infused with onions, basil, and tomatoes. The pastas, wood-fired pizzas, and antipasto are also very well prepared, but the fish dishes (particularly the whole roasted fish) are Hearon's specialty. A late-night menu is served until 1am on weekends. *$$$; AE, DC, MC, V; no checks; lunch, dinner every day; full bar; reservations recommended; between Union and Green Sts.* &

LODGINGS

Hotel Bohème / ★★

444 COLUMBUS AVE, SAN FRANCISCO; 415/433-9111

Hopelessly chic is perhaps the best way to describe the Hotel Bohème, one of the sexiest small hotels in the city and a favorite retreat of visiting writers and poets. Hovering two stories above Columbus Avenue—the Boulevard Saint-Michel of San Francisco streets—the Bohème artfully reflects North Beach's bohemian flair dating from the late 1950s and early 1960s. The time trip starts with a gallery of moody black-and-white photographs lining the hallways and segues into the 15 guest rooms decorated in soothing shades of sage green, cantaloupe, lavender, and black. The rooms feature handmade light fixtures crafted from glazed collages of jazz sheet music, Ginsberg poetry, and old menus and headlines, as well as black iron beds with sheer canopies, European armoires, bistro tables, wicker chairs, and Picasso and Matisse prints. Modern amenities abound, including private baths, remote-control cable TV, and telephones with modem jacks. A couple of minor caveats: Most rooms are quite small, and those facing Columbus Avenue aren't kind to light sleepers (though views of the ever-bustling cafes and shops are entrancing). Otherwise, Hotel Bohème's engaging amalgamation of art, poetry, and hospitality will forever turn you away from America's cookie-cutter corporate hotels. *$$$; AE, DC, DIS, MC, V; no checks; mail@hotelboheme.com; www.hotelboheme.com; between Green and Vallejo Sts.*

Chinatown

Mysterious aromas, jostling crowds, energetic bartering, unfamiliar writing on buildings and merchandise—Chinatown envelops you. The narrow streets sport Western architecture embellished with Chinese flourishes, like cinnabar- and jade-colored columns. Curled corners of roofs and overhangs send evil spirits back into the air, while lions, dragons, and serpents stand sentry at building entrances or wrap themselves around lampposts. San Francisco has the largest Asian population outside Asia, and Chinatown's 20,000 inhabitants live in the second most densely packed community in the country—160 people per acre. Only New York's Chinatown fits more people into a city block. If you couldn't see the skyscrapers, you might not know you were in an American city. Pedestrians rule the roadway. Everyone has a shopping bag or a school backpack. Daily life is lived in the streets, and no matter where you're from, you're an onlooker.

RESTAURANTS

Great Eastern / ★★

649 JACKSON ST, SAN FRANCISCO; 415/986-2500

If you love seafood and Chinese food and have an adventurous palate, this is the restaurant for you. The venerable Great Eastern restaurant in Chinatown is renowned for its hard-to-find seafood, yanked fresh from the myriad huge fish tanks that line the back wall. If it swims, hops, slithers, or crawls, it's probably on the menu. Frogs, sea bass, soft-shell turtles, abalone, sea conch, steelhead, and lord only knows what else are served sizzling on large, round, family-style tables. Check the neon board in back to peruse the day's catch, which is sold by the pound. Some advice: Unless you're savvy at translating an authentic Hong Kong menu, order one of the set dinners (the crab version is fantastic) or point to another table and say, "I want that." (Don't expect much help from the harried servers.) The crystal chandeliers and glimmering emerald-and-black furnishings make an attempt at elegance, but it's the gaudy fish tanks filled with edible creatures that capture everyone's eye. *$$; AE, MC, V; no checks; lunch, dinner every day; beer and wine; reservations recommended; between Grant Ave and Kearny St.* &

Financial District

The Financial District is the shadiest neighborhood in the city. Not because of the deals that are made here—although some might argue that—but because it lies at the base of the tallest buildings. This fiscal quarter vibrates with activity during the day, only to fall silent at night. Except for the restaurants. A number of fabulous eateries keep bankers in the neighborhood after hours and bring aficionados from all corners of town. Wandering the crowded chiaroscuro streets in the daytime, you can bask in the leisure of your vacation while the bankers scurry past. Fans of the stock market already know that the Pacific Exchange (301 Pine St at Sansome St) is the third most active in the country. Its hallowed floors are not open to the public, but its columned facade is worth a pass-by. If you're drawn to currency, descend into the Museum of Money in the basement of the Union Bank of California (California St at Sansome St). The Financial District sports the greatest concentration of grand institutional architecture in San Francisco, from neoclassical 19th-century money houses to slick, glass-skinned, late-stock-market-boom structures—and don't forget the pyramid. Big buildings and big business—it's clear that the greenback is the commodity bartered here.

RESTAURANTS

Boulevard / ★★★☆

I MISSION ST, SAN FRANCISCO; 415/543-6084

Nancy Oakes, a self-taught chef whose cooking career began in 1977 at a scruffy San Francisco saloon, teamed up with nationally renowned restaurant designer Pat Kuleto in 1993 and created this glittering jewel that sits squarely in the center of the city's culinary crown. Hailed as one of the nation's 10 best chefs by *Food & Wine* magazine, Oakes has come a long way from her days of dishing out saloon-style grub to an audience of longshoremen. These days her patrons tend to be well-heeled gastronomes who have been fans ever since she opened her first restaurant, L'Avenue, in 1988. At big, bustling Boulevard, she now serves hearty American-style cuisine with French and Italian influences. Before you indulge in her fabulous fare, feast your eyes on Kuleto's fantastic Parisian-inspired interior design, which he has dubbed "industrial art nouveau." On the seasonal menu you'll find a well-chosen mix of dishes. Oysters, giant beluga caviar, and fresh sautéed Sonoma foie gras served on an apple and fig strudel top the extensive appetizer list. Main courses might include a boneless rabbit stuffed with fresh chicken-and-sun-dried-tomato sausages, roasted to perfection in the wood-fired oven; asparagus risotto accompanied by roasted prawns and shiitake mushrooms filled with herbed goat cheese; and oven-roasted northern halibut resting on a large bed of wilted baby spinach sprinkled with chanterelle mushrooms and a side of buttery potato-chive fritters. For dessert, the ganache-mousse tart with fresh raspberries or pecan pie topped with vanilla ice cream and chocolate sauce push the sated diner over a blissful edge. *$$$$; AE, DC, DIS, MC, V; no checks; lunch Mon–Fri, dinner every day; full bar; reservations recommended; blvd@sirius.com; www.boulevard restaurant.com; at the Embarcadero.* &

Oritalia / ★★★

586 BUSH ST, SAN FRANCISCO; 415/782-8122

Oritalia is an amalgamation of "Oriental" and "Italian," which is precisely what the menu delivers at this plush and popular downtown restaurant. Actually, the flavors of Italy, China, Korea, France, and Southeast Asia are all represented in various combinations on the sophisticated menu, often with outstanding results. The restaurant's decor—silk chandeliers, Oriental rugs, curtained booths—offers both artistry and intimacy, but the most attractive items are on the dinner plate, such as the heavenly satsuma potato gnocchi made with sautéed Maine lobster, asparagus, and lime beurre blanc. Other dishes that are simply incredible are the sake-steamed sea bass with Chinese black-bean sauce and the five-spice duck confit and frisée salad. End the world tour with a slice of dreamy passion fruit cheesecake. Even restaurant-jaded San Franciscans are consistently surprised and impressed with what Oritalia has to offer. *$$$; AE, DC, MC, V; no checks; dinner every day; full bar; reservations recommended; at Stockton St.* &

Pastis / ★★

1015 BATTERY ST, SAN FRANCISCO; 415/391-2555

Named after the anise-flavored apéritif, Pastis continues co-owner Gerald Hirigoyen's tradition of hearty brasserie fare at reasonable prices. Like Fringale (see review under the SoMa section, below), his other top-flight San Francisco restaurant, this is a classy little bistro. Inside, there's an industrial feel, with tile floors, hardwood banquettes, brick walls, a beamed ceiling, and a curved concrete bar. The French-American fusion fare comes across as sophisticated and European. For starters, try the tender spinach salad with crisp pieces of bacon and hard-cooked eggs; generous slices of crisp foie gras with grapes and verjus (a tart grape juice); or prawns marinated in pastis, garlic, and thyme. Entrees might include a tender rack of lamb served in a soup plate over a bed of meaty beans mixed with a tomato broth, a steak with Roquefort and basil butter, and baked halibut with quinoa risotto and papaya. End your meal with the sophisticated warm chocolate tart topped with purple-basil ice cream. Portions are moderate, as they are in Paris, but you'll get value for your dollar and you'll dine in style. *$$$; AE, MC, V; no checks; lunch Mon–Fri, dinner Mon–Sat; full bar; reservations recommended; between Union and Green Sts.* &

Restaurant Elisabeth Daniel / ★★★⯨

550 WASHINGTON ST, SAN FRANCISCO; 415/397-6129

The first thing you notice about this refined restaurant is the quiet. While the streets outside remind you that you're in the heart of a city, Restaurant Elisabeth Daniel pampers you with the illusion that the world begins and ends within a few feet of your brocade-draped table. The intimate room holds only 16 of them, spaced so that your neighbors' conversation is almost inaudible. Meals are a leisurely affair; for lunch, a three-course meal and a five-course tasting menu compete for your favor. Dinner comprises six tantalizing courses, with three options for each. With alternatives like peppercorn-encrusted venison with spinach and a crisp potato galette, herb-scented black bass on a bed of lobster risotto, and a ragout of mushrooms, herbed gnocchi and peas, the only disappointment is that you can't try it all. Portions are sized appropriately for the number of courses, and you will have room for dessert. Chilled tropical fruit soup with passion fruit sorbet, perhaps? Refreshingly, the service is attentive and prompt, without fawning. *$$$$; AE, DIS, MC, V; no checks; lunch Mon–Fri, dinner Mon–Sat; wine only; reservations recommended; between Sansome and Montgomery Streets.* &

Rubicon / ★★★

558 SACRAMENTO ST, SAN FRANCISCO; 415/434-4100

Thanks to Rubicon's star-studded cast of financial backers—Robert De Niro, Robin Williams, and Francis Ford Coppola—this Financial District restaurant received so much advance publicity that San Franciscans were setting dates to eat here long before the seismic reinforcements were bolted to the floorboards. Chances are slim that you'll see any Tinseltown talent at the table next to you, but if you want to catch a rising star, keep an eye out for Rubicon's young chef, Scott Newman. A native New Yorker who once studied acting, Newman swapped Broadway aspirations for the culinary stage. After graduating from the California Culinary Academy, he worked with famed chef Julian Serrano and Rubicon's founding chef, Traci Des Jardins, who left to launch her own restaurant, Jardinière (see review under the Hayes Valley section, below). Newman's superb starters have included pan-seared rouget (a mild, pink-fleshed French fish) with ratatouille vegetables in a lobster broth, and a luscious lobster ravioli with spinach and chervil butter. Main courses on the French-inspired menu may include a crispy polenta cake with wild mushrooms, roasted pork loin with black-eyed peas, and halibut with chanterelles and cranberry beans. There's also a pair of prix-fixe menus and a tasting menu. The excellent, extensive, and expensive wine list is presented by Larry Stone, one of the nation's premier sommeliers. *$$$; AE, DC, MC, V; no checks; lunch Mon–Fri, dinner Mon–Sat; full bar; reservations recommended; www.myriadrestaurantgroup.com; between Montgomery and Sansome Sts.* &

LODGINGS

Mandarin Oriental / ★★★

222 SANSOME ST, SAN FRANCISCO; 415/276-9888 OR 800/622-0404

The rooms at the award-winning Mandarin Oriental offer some of the most remarkable views in the city. Because it's perched high in the sky (on the top 11 floors of the 48-story First Interstate Building, San Francisco's third-tallest skyscraper), you're not only guaranteed a bird's-eye view of the city, you'll be gazing at the entire Bay Area. The 158 rooms are comfortable and deceptively austere. Well hidden among the simple blond-wood furniture and fine Asian artwork are all the latest deluxe amenities: three two-line speakerphones with fax hookups, remote-control televisions with access to videos, and fully stocked minibars and refrigerators, as well as jumbo marble bathrooms with stall showers and extra-deep soaking tubs (you can even admire the city's skyline from some of the bathtubs). Once settled in your room, you'll be treated to jasmine tea and Thai silk slippers. Contrary to the policy of many other hotels, the room rates at the Mandarin don't vary according to scenery, so request one of the corner rooms (numbers ending with 6 or 11) for the best views. Additional perks include access to numerous business services, valet parking, a continental breakfast served in the lounge, shoe shines, 24-hour room service, and a state-of-the-art fitness center. The hotel's award-winning restaurant, Silks, recently underwent a complete renovation. The Silk Road theme is reflected in soft, spicy earth tones—think cardamom and turmeric—and the elegantly spaced tables allow for almost-private conversation. It's an evocative setting for the innovative California–Pacific Rim cuisine. *$$$$; AE, DC, DIS, MC, V; checks OK; sfo-reservations@mohg.com; www.mandarinoriental.com; between California and Pine Sts.* &

Palace Hotel / ★★★

2 NEW MONTGOMERY ST, SAN FRANCISCO; 415/512-1111 OR 800/325-3535

Reminiscent of more romantic times, this opulent hotel built in 1875 has housed such luminaries as Thomas Edison, D. H. Lawrence, Amelia Earhart, and Winston Churchill, as well as 10 American presidents and numerous aristocrats and royalty from around the world. Hoping to attract a similarly high-class clientele in the future, the management closed the Palace in 1989 for 27 months and poured $170 million into restoring it to its original splendor. And splendid it is. The downstairs decor is truly breathtaking, from the multiple sparkling Austrian-crystal chandeliers, the double row of white Italian marble Ionic columns, and the 80,000-pane stained-glass dome of the Garden Court to the three grand ballrooms and early 19th-century French tapestry gracing the walls. Unfortunately, all this impressive glitz comes to a screeching halt when you open the door to one of the 550 guest rooms. Although comfortable and attractive, the rooms are more akin to dolled-up generic hotel rooms than to any palace chamber. However, this place does offer all the perks you'd look for in a luxury hotel, including a concierge, 24-hour room service, valet parking, and an elaborate business center, plus a new, palm-embellished health club with an exercise room, co-ed sauna, whirlpool, and stunning white-tiled lap pool capped by a dome of clear glass. Restaurants include the Garden Court, famous for its elaborate breakfast buffet and elegant afternoon tea; Kyo-ya, a rather austere Japanese dining room serving the best (and most expensive) sushi and sashimi in town; and Maxfield's Pied Piper Bar, which is dominated by a stunning, $2.5 million, 1909 Maxfield Parrish painting of the Pied Piper of Hamelin leading a band of 27 children. Even if you don't have the resources to recline or dine here, this place, like most palaces, is worth a self-guided tour. *$$$$; AE, DC, DIS, MC, V; checks OK; www.luxury collection.com; at Market St.* &

Union Square

For shopping fanatics, this is the heart of it all, ground zero for credit card aerobics. But don't despair if Saks Fifth Avenue, Neiman Marcus, Macys, Gump's, and Tiffany & Co. are not on your top-ten list of vacation destinations. The theater district is right around the corner, and a "French Quarter" hides on Bush Street, between Grant and Montgomery Streets, and down tiny Claude and Belden Lanes. Dining options range from the relaxed bistros to some of the most elegant restaurants in town. The square is named for the fiery pro-Union rallies that took place there during the Civil War; today it is on the verge of a massive redesign and renovation that will make it a more inviting civic space, with outdoor cafes and room for entertainment. The number and quality of the hotels in this area make it the ideal launch for excursions into other neighborhoods.

RESTAURANTS

Campton Place / ★★★

340 STOCKTON ST (CAMPTON PLACE HOTEL), SAN FRANCISCO; 415/955-5555

Just off the lobby of the Campton Place Hotel, Campton Place pairs an ambience steeped in serene, old-money traditionalism with a kitchen that delights in inventive, newfangled ideas. Since its unveiling in 1983, the pricey restaurant has been the proving ground for such noteworthy chefs as Bradley Ogden (who went on to Lark Creek Inn fame), Jan Birnbaum, and, most recently, Todd Humphries. Humphries's replacement, Frenchman Laurent Manrique, is now at the helm and has been wowing hard-to-please San Franciscans with his simple yet sophisticated Gascony cooking. Try the Serrano ham, the asparagus and wild mushroom appetizer, the halibut in squid ink jus with artichoke and calamari, the rack of lamb crusted with mustard seed, or his signature poached chicken Aurélie. Desserts are as decadent as one would expect from this lush brand of cuisine. The service is quietly attentive, and the decor is a study in understated elegance. Campton Place also serves a superb breakfast. *$$$$; AE, DC, MC, V; checks OK; breakfast, lunch, dinner every day; full bar; reservations recommended; reserve@camptonplace.com; www.camptonplace.com; between Sutter and Post Sts.* &

Farallon / ★★★

450 POST ST, SAN FRANCISCO; 415/956-6969
Diving into the undersea world of chef Mark Franz (of Stars restaurant fame) and designer Pat Kuleto can leave one breathless. In the fall of 1997, the two co-owners opened a dazzling $4 million, 160-seat restaurant offering seafood dishes that are as innovative as Kuleto's elegant, aquatic-themed decor. Giant handblown jellyfish chandeliers with glowing tentacles seemingly float beneath a sea-blue ceiling in the Jelly Bar cocktail lounge, where sculpted strands of kelp climb up illuminated pillars. Upstairs, the marine motif continues with huge sea-urchin chandeliers dangling from the arched, painted mosaic ceiling—all a dramatic but enchanting stage for Franz's excellent coastal cuisine. For starters, consider delectable asparagus bisque with cardamom cream; truffled mashed potatoes with crab and salmon caviar artfully stuffed into a real sea-urchin shell; Maine lobster and wild-mushroom gnocchi with a leek, tarragon, and champagne lobster sauce; or giant tiger prawns—the best thing on the menu. Entrees change daily and might include ginger-steamed salmon and sea-scallop pillows with a prawn mousse or sautéed gulf prawns with potato risotto, English peas, pearl onions, and truffle portobello coulis. While Franz's forte is fish, he also has a flair for meat dishes such as a juicy grilled fillet of beef served with a portobello mushroom and potato galette, haricots verts, and black truffle aioli, and he offers a vegetarian menu. The 300-item wine list fits in swimmingly with the entire menu (though prices are high), and about two dozen wines are available by the glass. The attentive staff helps make Farallon a deep-sea affair to remember. *$$$$; AE, DC, DIS, MC, V; no checks; lunch Mon–Sat, dinner every day; full bar; reservations recommended; between Powell and Mason Sts.* &

Le Colonial / ★★☆

20 COSMO PL, SAN FRANCISCO; 415/931-3600

The once-popular Trader Vic's restaurant thrived for many years on this tiny, tucked-away side street near the Tenderloin and Union Square. Today this hideaway is the home of Le Colonial, which serves excellent Vietnamese food that is much more expensive than what you'll find at the usual Asian restaurants around town. But this is no typical Asian restaurant. It's a place to be seen, to dress up, and to pose (jackets are required for men). Fashioned after a 1920s Vietnamese plantation, complete with wicker, fans, and rich wood, Le Colonial offers a blend of French and Vietnamese cooking. Upstairs in the lounge, relax with a drink and choose from an extensive list of appetizers. The dinner menu also offers a wide selection, and most dishes are a tantalizing blend of sweet, spicy, sour, and aromatic flavors. Selections can be ordered individually as entrees or served family style. Some good choices include the coconut curry prawns with mango and eggplant, wok-seared beef tenderloin with watercress and onion salad, cold beef salad with tender chunks marinated in lime, ginger roast duck, and steamed sea bass wrapped in a banana leaf. *$$$; AE, DC, MC, V; no checks; dinner every day; full bar; reservations recommended; off Taylor St, between Sutter and Post Sts.* &

Postrio / ★★★

545 POST ST, SAN FRANCISCO; 415/776-7825

Owned by Southern California superstar chef Wolfgang Puck and the Kimpton Hotel & Restaurant Group, Postrio is a splashy slice of Hollywood set in the heart of San Francisco, with superglitzy decor à la restaurant designer Pat Kuleto, delightful culinary combinations, and the perpetual hope of catching sight of some celeb at the next table. One enters through a spiffy street-level bar that serves tapas and little Puckish pizzas to the unreserving; from there a grand sculpted-iron and copper staircase—on which everybody can at least play a star—descends dramatically into a crowded, pink-lighted dining room ringed with paintings and plants. It's a lovely, sophisticated setting for some terrific food, prepared by Mitchell and Steven Rosenthal, who proved themselves capable successors when founding chefs Anne and David Gingrass jumped ship to open Hawthorne Lane in '95. Working closely with Puck, the brothers Rosenthal have crafted an exciting hybrid of California-Asian-Mediterranean cuisine that includes such creations as grilled quail accompanied by spinach and a soft egg ravioli with port wine glaze; sautéed salmon with plum glaze, wasabi mashed potatoes, and miso vinaigrette; Chinese duck with mango sauce; and roasted leg of lamb with garlic potato purée and niçoise olives. Tempting choices indeed, but the dessert menu offers its own array of showstoppers—from the potato-pecan pie to the caramel pear tart with Grand Marnier crème fraîche. The wine list is excellent, the service professional, and reservations are essential—make them several weeks in advance. *$$$$; AE, DC, DIS, MC, V; no checks; breakfast Mon–Fri, lunch Mon–Sat, dinner every day, brunch Sun; full bar; reservations recommended; www.postrio.com; between Taylor and Mason Sts.* &

LODGINGS

Campton Place Hotel / ★★★★

340 STOCKTON ST, SAN FRANCISCO; 415/781-5555 OR 800/235-4300
Almost as soon as Campton Place reopened after an extensive restoration in 1984, its posh surroundings, stunning objets d'art, superlative service, and elegant accommodations began swaying the patrons of the carriage trade away from traditional San Francisco hotels. The lobby, reminiscent of a gallery with its domed ceiling, miles of marble, crystal chandeliers, and striking Asian art, alone is worth the price of admission. The 110 guest rooms are very comfortable, and the Henredon armoires, custom-built chairs, and handsome desks help create a pervasive air of luxury. The travertine-marble bathrooms are equipped with telephones, terry-cloth robes, hair dryers, French-milled soaps, and bath scales. For the best views, ask for one of the larger double deluxe corner rooms on the upper floors. The view from room 1501, which overlooks Union Square, is particularly stunning. For help with your laundry, dry cleaning, a shoe shine, or even baby-sitting, just pick up the phone and you'll be accommodated tout de suite. The concierge will make any and all of your arrangements (a reservation for the hotel's limo, perhaps?), and 24-hour room service will deliver whatever you're craving from the menu at the well-regarded Campton Place restaurant, one of the city's prettiest—and priciest—dining establishments (see review, above). *$$$$; AE, DC, MC, V; checks OK; reserve@camptonplace.com; www.camptonplace.com; between Sutter and Post Sts.* &

Hotel Diva / ★★★

440 GEARY ST, SAN FRANCISCO; 415/885-0200 OR 800/553-1900
Ever since it opened in 1985, Hotel Diva has been the prima donna of San Francisco's modern hotels, winning the Best Hotel Design prize from *Interiors* magazine for its suave, ultramodern design. The hotel's facade is still a veritable work of art, a fashionable fusion of concrete, steel, and glass that is très chic. But the high style doesn't stop here: even the 111 guest rooms are works of art, decorated with handsome Italian modern furnishings. Standard luxury amenities in each room include an individually controlled air conditioner, a television with interactive multimedia and VCR, two telephones with extra-long cords, a data port, voice mail, and a personal safe. Guest services include a complimentary breakfast of

fresh fruit, breads, yogurt, coffee, and orange juice delivered to your room, as well as room service, a concierge, a 24-hour fitness center, and a business center offering free use of computers, software, and a laser printer. Best of all, the Diva is in a prime location, just around the corner from Union Square. Insider tip: Reserve one of the rooms ending in "09," which have extra-large bathrooms with vanity mirrors and makeup tables. *$$$$; AE, DC, DIS, MC, V; checks OK; www.personalityhotels.com; between Mason and Taylor Sts.* &

Hotel Monaco / ★★★★

501 GEARY ST, SAN FRANCISCO; 415/292-0100 OR 800/214-4220

"Wow!" is a common exclamation among first-time guests at Hotel Monaco, one of the hottest new hotels in a city brimming with top-notch accommodations. After a $24 million renovation, Monaco opened in June 1995 and has received nothing but kudos for its sumptuous, stunning decor. Expect a melding of modern European fashion with flourishes of the American Beaux Arts era—the trademark of award-winning designer Cheryl Rowley, who envisioned the 201-room hotel as a "great ship traveling to the farthest reaches of the world, collecting exotic, precious treasures and antiquities." Hence the guest rooms replete with canopy beds, Chinese-inspired armoires, bamboo writing desks, old-fashioned decorative luggage, and a profusion of bold stripes and vibrant colors. The entire hotel is truly a feast for the eyes, particularly the Grand Cafe with its 30-foot ceilings, cascading chandeliers, plethora of stately columns, and many art nouveau frills—all vestiges of its former incarnation as the hotel's grand ballroom. A chic see-and-be-seen crowd typically fills the impressive dining room, noshing on trendy California-French cuisine. And of course, there are the requisite hotel toys (health club, steam room, whirlpool spa, sauna), services (massages, manicures, valet parking, business and room service), and complimentary perks (newspaper delivery, morning coffee, evening wine reception). You'll like the location as well: in the heart of San Francisco's theater district, a mere two blocks from Union Square and the cable cars. *$$$$; AE, DC, DIS, JCB, MC, V; checks OK; sales@hotelmonaco.com; www.hotelmonaco.com; at Taylor St.* &

Hotel Rex / ★★★

562 SUTTER ST, SAN FRANCISCO; 415/433-4434 OR 800/433-4434

The Joie de Vivre hotel company has created another winner with the 94-room Hotel Rex, the latest addition to its cadre of fashionable yet affordable accommodations. The hotel's sophisticated and sensuous lobby lounge is cleverly modeled after a 1920s library, meant to create a stylish sanctuary for San Francisco's arts and literary community (hence the adjoining antiquarian bookstore). To keep costs and rates down, many of the site's former Orchard Hotel's imported furnishings have been retained, which adds a bit of authenticity to the European boutique hotel–style ambience. All of the spacious (for a downtown hotel) and newly renovated rooms feature CD players, two-line telephones with voice mail and data port, and an electronic key-card system. The rooms in the back are not only quieter, they also overlook a tranquil, shaded courtyard. Perks include room service, same-day laundry/dry cleaning, complimentary newspaper, an evening wine hour, concierge service, and morning car service to the Financial District. The hotel is in a key location as well, within walking distance of Union Square and surrounded by first-rate galleries, theaters, and restaurants. *$$$–$$$$; AE, DC, DIS, MC, V; no checks; www.citysearch.com/sfo/hotelrex; between Powell and Mason Sts.* &

Hotel Triton / ★★★
342 GRANT AVE, SAN FRANCISCO; 415/394-0500 OR 800/433-6611

The Hotel Triton has been described as modern, whimsical, sophisticated, chic, vogue, neo-baroque, ultrahip, and retro-futuristic—but words just don't do justice to this unique hostelry-cum-art-gallery that you'll simply have to see to appreciate. The entire hotel, from the bellhop's inverted pyramid-shaped podium to the iridescent throw pillows on the beds and the ashtrays ringed with faux pearls, is the original work of four imaginative San Francisco artisans. For a preview of what's behind the bedroom doors, peek into the lobby, where you'll see curvaceous chairs shimmering in gold silk taffeta, an imposing duo of floor-to-ceiling pillars sheathed in teal, purple, and gold leaf, and a pastel mural portraying mythic images of sea life, triton shells, and human figures. Add to this visual extravaganza all the amenities you'd find in any luxury hotel, including a concierge, valet parking, room service, complimentary wine and coffee, business and limousine services, and even a fitness center. The 147 rooms and designer suites (designed with the help of such celebs as Carlos Santana, Joe Boxer, and the late Jerry Garcia) continue the modern wonderland theme: walls are splashed with giant, hand-painted yellow and blue diamonds; king-size beds feature navy-and-khaki-striped camelback headboards; and armoires that hide TVs are topped with golden crowns. The tree-hugger in all of us can embrace the EcoFloor, the Triton's environmentally conscious seventh floor, where almost everything is made from recycled, biodegradable, or organically grown materials, and the air and water are passed through fancy filtration systems. Heck, the Triton is so utterly hip, even the elevator swings to Thelonious Monk. *$$$$; AE, DC, DIS, JCB, MC, V; checks OK; www.hotel-tritonsf.com; between Bush and Sutter Sts.* &

The Prescott Hotel / ★★★
545 POST ST, SAN FRANCISCO; 415/563-0303 OR 800/283-7322

Opened in 1989 by San Francisco hotel magnate Bill Kimpton, the Prescott has put pressure on Union Square's neighboring luxury hotels by offering first-rate accommodations at a fairly reasonable price. This, combined with dining privileges at one of the city's most popular restaurants (the adjoining Postrio; see review above), superlative service from an intelligent, youthful staff, and a prime location in the heart of San Francisco, places the Prescott at the top of the Union Square hotel list. The rooms, decorated with custom-made cherry-wood furnishings, black-granite-topped nightstands and dressers, and silk wallpaper, have rich color schemes of hunter green, deep purple, cerise, taupe, and gold. The Prescott offers 164 rooms, including numerous suites and a wildly posh penthouse complete with a grand piano, a rooftop Jacuzzi, a formal dining room, and twin fireplaces. For an additional $30 per night, you may gain "Club Concierge Level" status, which grants you access to a plush lounge (complete with a complimentary premium bar), an hors d'oeuvres reception, and a continental breakfast, as well as a host of other privileges—not a bad investment for 30 bones. Standard perks include limo service to the Financial District, overnight shoe shine, valet parking, laundry service, a daily newspaper delivered to your room, and access to the adjacent fitness facility. *$$$$; AE, DC, DIS, MC, V; checks OK; www.prescotthotel.com; between Taylor and Mason Sts.* &

Savoy Hotel / ★★

580 GEARY ST, SAN FRANCISCO; 415/441-2700 OR 800/227-4223
Originally built in 1913 for the Panama-Pacific International Exposition, this seven-story hotel is a posh French country-style inn with a gorgeous facade of richly veined black marble, beveled glass, mahogany, and polished brass. It's ideally located in the center of the theater district, just 2-½ blocks from Union Square. The 83 guest rooms and suites are small but beautifully appointed, with reams of toile de Jouy fabrics, heavy French cotton bedspreads, imported Provençal furnishings, plump featherbeds, goose-down pillows, two-line telephones with modem jacks, and mini-bars. A few of the suites come with Jacuzzi tubs. The most tranquil rooms are on the northeast corner (farthest from the traffic noise) facing a rear courtyard. Guests are nurtured with a continental breakfast and afternoon tea and sherry; a full breakfast is also available. Additional amenities include an overnight shoe shine and room service from the hotel's popular Brasserie Savoy. This restaurant is a replica of an authentic French brasserie, right down to the zinc bar, black-and-white marble floors, comfy banquettes, woven-leather chairs, and a staff clad in long, starched white aprons. Its air of casual sophistication, reasonable prices, and generally very good food—foie gras, filet mignon with truffle sauce, crispy sweetbreads, duck confit—make it a reliable bet, especially for a meal before show time (ask about the well-priced three-course dinner special offered from 5 to 8pm daily). *$$$; AE, DC, DIS, MC, V; no checks; savoysf@usa.com; www.savoyhotel.net; at Jones St.*

Sir Francis Drake Hotel / ★★☆
450 POWELL ST, SAN FRANCISCO; 415/392-7755 OR 800/227-5480
While nowhere near as resplendent as the nearby Westin St. Francis, the 21-story Sir Francis Drake gives us ordinary folks a reasonably priced opportunity to stay in one of San Francisco's grande dames. A recent $5 million renovation has spruced up the 417 rooms a bit, but there's still a little wear around the edges. No matter—it's the experience of listening to the sounds of Union Square wafting through your window that makes staying here an enjoyable experience. Then there are the ever-jovial Beefeater doormen; the top-floor Harry Denton's Starlight Room, one of the most fun and fashionable cocktail/dance lounges in the city; and Scala's Bistro, next door on the lower level, an upscale yet affordable restaurant you are sure to enjoy; and all the requisite big-hotel services such as room service, newspaper delivery, business services, baby-sitting, in-room massage, and laundry. So considering that you can get a standard room here for about half the price of rooms at the St. Francis—and with far better eating, drinking, and dancing—the Drake is definitely worth looking into. *$$$$; AE, DC, DIS, MC, V; checks OK; www.sir franciscdrake.com; between Sutter and Post Sts.* &

Nob Hill
The nob of this hill is indeed the highlight of the neighborhood. Ringing the top o' the hill like mismatched guests at a cocktail party are the imposingly spiritual Grace Cathedral and those bastions of luxury, the Fairmont, Mark Hopkins, and Huntington Hotels. In the midst of that impressive circle, Huntington Park sits quietly next to the Flood Mansion, now the Pacific Union Club, the only remaining manor of several that once graced Nob Hill's summit, a remnant of the days when "nabobs" (Urdu for "very rich men") like the Big Four (Leland Stanford, Collis Huntington, Charles Crocker, and Mark Hopkins) called the shots.

RESTAURANTS

The Dining Room at the Ritz-Carlton / ★★★
600 STOCKTON ST, SAN FRANCISCO; 415/773-6198
For those special occasions or when the other person is buying, few restaurants go the extra distance to spoil you rotten like the Dining Room at the Ritz-Carlton hotel. No less than five tuxedoed wait staff are at your beck and call, surreptitiously attending to your needs as you bask in your evening of opulence. The setting is, as one would expect, sumptuous and regal. The room was redecorated in the fall of '97: cushy high-backed chairs, rich brocade, crystal chandeliers, elegant table settings, and live harp music provide a definite air of formality. Celebrity chef Gary Danko

left the Ritz in the summer of 1996 to open his own restaurant; his replacement, chef Sylvain Portay, a Frenchman from the famed Le Cirque restaurant in New York, continues the Ritz-Carlton tradition of using only the finest, freshest ingredients from around the world. The seasonal menu is strictly prix fixe, offering a choice of three-, four-, or five-course dinners; the latter includes wine pairings per course by master sommelier Emmanuel Kemiji (one of only 31 master sommeliers in the United States) for a hefty additional fee. Notable dishes have included the frothy crayfish bisque, risotto with butternut squash and roasted squab, sweetbreads with scallions and bok choy, a juicy roasted rack of Colorado lamb, and grilled John Dory—a New Zealand fish—spiked with basil and olives. For the finale, indulge in the ultimate French dessert: dark chocolate soufflé with bitter almond ice cream. The Dining Room also features a rolling cheese cart laden with at least two dozen individually ripened cheeses. *$$$$; AE, DC, DIS, MC, V; no checks; dinner Mon–Sat; full bar; reservations required; www.ritzcarlton.com; between California and Pine Sts.* &

Fleur de Lys / ★★★★

777 SUTTER ST, SAN FRANCISCO; 415/673-7779

Fleur de Lys is definitely a Grand Occasion restaurant, with fantastic food, formal service, breathtaking decor, and a superb wine list. Trained by such French superstars as Paul Bocuse and Roger Vergé, wunderkind chef and co-owner Hubert Keller displays a formidable technique—beautifully prepared ingredients accompanied by surprising garnishes and subtle sauces—and many of his contemporary French dishes are near-miracles. Recent standouts include the terrine of Hudson Valley foie gras in a fresh herb and black pepper gelée with brioche, fresh Atlantic salmon baked in a tender corn pancake topped with imperial caviar and a watercress sauce, marinated loin of venison with a mustard seed sabayon, and his five-course vegetarian feast, which prompted a flurry of favorable press when it debuted several years ago. Critics sometimes sniff that particular dishes are too complex, portions seem small, and prices loom large, but these are small dents in Fleur de Lys' mighty armor. The restaurant's decor matches the splendor of its food step for step: the romantic dining area is draped in a luxurious tentlike fashion with 700 yards of rich, red-and-gold hand-painted floral fabrics, and in the center of the room sits a spectacular crown of fresh flowers on a pedestal. Mirrored walls double this visual spectacle while simultaneously allowing you to admire yourself and your glitteringly attired companion. Fleur de Lys isn't always crowded, but reservations are required; this is the sort of establishment that doesn't want to guess who's coming to dinner. *$$$$; AE, DC, MC, V; no checks; dinner Mon–Sat; full bar; reservations recommended; between Jones and Taylor Sts.* &

Swan Oyster Depot / ★★☆

1517 POLK ST, SAN FRANCISCO; 415/673-1101
You won't find white linen tablecloths at this oyster bar—in fact, you won't even find any tables. Since 1912, patrons have balanced themselves on the 19 hard, rickety stools lining the long, narrow marble counter cluttered with bowls of oyster crackers, fresh-cut lemons, napkin holders, Tabasco sauce, and other seasonings. On the opposite side stands a quick-shucking team of some of the most congenial men in town, always ready and eager to serve. Lunch specialties include Boston clam chowder, sizable salads (crab, shrimp, prawn, or a combo), seafood cocktails, cracked Dungeness crab, lobster, and smoked salmon and trout. If you want to take home some fish for supper, take a gander at all the fresh offerings in the display case: salmon, swordfish, delta crawfish, red snapper, trout, shrimp, lingcod, and whatever else the boat brought in that day. *$$; no credit cards; checks OK; lunch Mon–Sat (open 8am–5:30pm); beer and wine; no reservations; between Sacramento and California Sts.* &

LODGINGS

Fairmont Hotel & Tower / ★★★

950 MASON ST, SAN FRANCISCO; 415/772-5000 OR 800/527-4727
The Fairmont is another one of San Francisco's grand old hotels that is part hotel, part tourist attraction. Designed by architect Julia Morgan just after the 1906 earthquake, it recently underwent an extensive renovation that restored several original elements. The lobby's large restaurant and bar is back, full of the tinkling of the piano, soft clinking of dishes, and animated conversation. The fantastic entrance is more dazzling than ever: massive Corinthian columns of solid marble, vaulted ceilings, marble floors, velvet sofas and smoking chairs, enormous gilded mirrors, and a colossal wraparound staircase. A small plaque tells visitors—and you should visit if you're not staying there—that the United Nations charter was drafted at the Fairmont. The rooms have been completely redesigned: marble bathrooms, new color scheme, new carpeting, new fabrics. Yes, they're expensive, but they're luxurious—amenities include the 24-hour concierge and room service, complimentary morning limousine to the Financial District, business center, baby-sitting services, and free shoe shine. Within the hotel there's a beauty salon, barbershop, shopping arcade, and even a pharmacy. There are several restaurants and bars as well, including the famous Polynesian-style Tonga Room bar and restaurant, fine dining at Masons, and the top-floor Crown Room restaurant and bar, which has a spectacular panoramic view of the city. *$$$$; AE, DC, DIS, JCB, MC, V; checks OK; reserve@grc.cphotels.com; www.fairmont.com; between Sacramento and California Sts.* &

Huntington Hotel / ★★★

1075 CALIFORNIA ST, SAN FRANCISCO; 415/474-5400 OR 800/227-4683
The modest lobby of this imposing Nob Hill landmark belies its lavish interiors. The Huntington is graced with a remarkable array of antiques, plush sofas, and museum-quality objets d'art; the doorman is subdued and genteel but always seems delighted to see you; the staff maintains a professional attitude and at the same time treats you like a favored guest. These things, along with superb security, explain why the Huntington has long been a favorite of many of San Francisco's visiting dignitaries and celebrities, from Archbishop Desmond Tutu to Robert Redford. The 12-story hotel's 140 rooms are spacious and lavish, with imported silks, 17th-century paintings, and stunning views of the city and the bay. The rooms are individually decorated, and some are so handsome they have been featured in *Architectural Digest*. Several flaunt gold velvet sofas and fringed, tufted hassocks surrounded by antiques, while others boast modern leather couches, faux-leopard-skin hassocks, and marble bars. Guests are treated to a formal afternoon tea and complimentary sherry, nightly turndown service, and a morning paper. Valet parking and room service are also available, along with a full range of business services and access to the Nob Hill Club, a top-of-the-line fitness center one block away. Yes, Virginia, it's expensive, but offers such as the Romance Package (including free champagne, sherry, and limousine service) make the Huntington worth considering for that special occasion. *$$$$; AE, DC, DIS, MC, V; checks OK; reservations@huntingtonhotel.com; www.huntingtonhotel.com; at Taylor St.* &

The Ritz-Carlton, San Francisco / ★★★★

600 STOCKTON ST, SAN FRANCISCO; 415/296-7465 OR 800/241-3333
In 1991, after a four-year, multimillion-dollar renovation, this 1909 17-columned neoclassical beauty—formerly the Metropolitan Life Insurance Company building—reopened as the Ritz-Carlton hotel. Since then, it's been stacking up heady accolades, including *Condé Nast Traveler*'s Gold List, "best in San Francisco," from 1993 to 2000. The hotel's lobby is breathtaking, with a series of enormous, high-ceilinged lounges, gigantic floral arrangements, an abundance of museum-quality paintings and antiques, and crystal chandeliers at every turn. The spectacular Lobby Lounge is the place to mingle over afternoon tea or sushi, and live piano performances perk up the scene every day. The 336 guest rooms are also luxury personified, though the decor is rather staid, to say the least; people looking for a more artistic ambience might want to try Hotel Monaco or W Hotel. Regardless, the rooms are sinfully plush and loaded with high-society amenities such as spiffy marble bathrooms, fully stocked honor bars, thick terry-cloth robes, in-room safes, phones, and TVs. Some (though not many) have wonderful views of the city and the

bay, but your best bets are the quieter rooms overlooking the landscaped courtyard. The hotel's ritzy fitness center has an indoor lap pool, whirlpool, sauna, fully equipped training room, and massage services. Two restaurants are located in the hotel: the formal Dining Room at the Ritz-Carlton, one of the top restaurants in the city (see review above), and the more casual Terrace, serving excellent Mediterranean fare and sensational desserts in a pleasant dining room adorned with handsome oil paintings. *$$$$; AE, DC, DIS, MC, V; no checks; www.ritz-carlton.com; between California and Pine Sts.* &

Russian Hill

Russian Hill didn't get its name from Russians *living* in the vicinity. It's so named because many Russian explorers and trappers in the early 1800s, in San Francisco to trade with the Spanish and Native Americans, died before making the long journey home and were buried on the empty hill. Their graves, marked by black crosses with Russian inscriptions, were the only defining characteristic of this topographical bump for many years. The graves are long covered over, and today even the literati who once populated the summit of the hill—Mark Twain, Jack London, Ambrose Bierce, and Jack Kerouac among them—couldn't afford an apartment here. Polk and Hyde Streets give Russian Hill plenty of atmosphere and fine dining, but the residential architecture near the top of the hill really steals the show. Polk Street is the neighborhood commercial center, with shops, cafes, and restaurants that keep locals happy and draw those brave enough to try to find parking. Hyde Street has several excellent little restaurants tucked between apartment buildings and grocery stores. Take an hour to wander the area, marveling at the views. If you're in search of the crookedest street in the world (Lombard St, between Hyde and Leavenworth), you'll find it on Russian Hill.

RESTAURANTS

Antica Trattoria / ★★★

2400 POLK ST, SAN FRANCISCO; 415/928-5797
Soon after Antica Trattoria opened its doors in 1996, the surrounding neighborhood was abuzz with talk of chef Ruggero Gadaldi's incredible Italian fare (he previously wore the toque at the now-closed Etrusca). Occupying a moderately busy corner on Polk and Union Streets, this simply decorated restaurant with dark wood floors and cream-colored walls has developed a deserved reputation as one of the city's best Italian trattorias. Appetizers might include a purée of potato and vegetable soup seasoned with bacon, or delicate, divine slices of beef carpaccio enhanced with capers, arugula, mustard, and Parmesan shavings. A recent rendition of the creamy risotto was prepared with pears and Taleggio cheese,

while a memorable chestnut-flavored *fedellini* (angel hair pasta) was dressed with leeks and a smoked-chicken cream sauce. Main dishes might include a savory monkfish wrapped in pancetta, potatoes, and wild mushrooms, or a perfectly grilled pork tenderloin with Gorgonzola, crispy pancetta, and polenta. It's not the most surprising Italian fare in the city, but it's some of the best prepared and most reasonably priced. Top it off with the terrific tiramisu. *$$; DC, MC, V; no checks; dinner Tues–Sun; beer and wine; reservations recommended; at Union St.* ♿

La Folie / ★★★★
2316 POLK ST, SAN FRANCISCO; 415/776-5577

After a stingy San Francisco restaurateur fired him for spending too much on ingredients and serving overly generous portions, French-born chef Roland Passot decided to open his own restaurant where he could spend as much as he liked to make the food perfect. The paradisiacal result is the charming, small, family-run La Folie, now glistening after a much-needed interior refurbishing completed in the summer of '97. The intimate, whimsical, theatrical dining room with white puffy clouds painted on the sky-blue ceiling now has red-patterned carpeting, new chairs, a colorful stained-glass entryway, and even marionettes from Lyon dangling from the wall—an appropriate stage for Passot's creative, exuberant, but disciplined menu. His Roquefort soufflé with grapes, herbs, and walnut bread alone is worthy of four stars. Other memorable starters are the wonderful foie gras dishes; the potato blinis with golden Osetra caviar, salmon, asparagus, and crème fraîche; the rabbit loin stuffed with exquisitely fresh vegetables and roasted garlic; the velvety corn-and-leek soup; the parsley and garlic soup with snails and shiitake mushrooms; and the lobster consommé. For an entree, choose whatever meat or fish suits your fancy, for it surely will be exquisitely prepared. To accommodate vegetarians, Passot has thoughtfully included a separate Vegetable Lovers' menu. And for those who can't make up their minds, there's a discovery menu that allows you to choose five courses à la carte (though it's pricey). For dessert, indulge in clafoutis with chocolate sauce or croquettes of chocolate with orange zest sauce. The wine list is extensive but the prices are steep. *$$$$; AE, DC, DIS, MC, V; no checks; dinner Mon–Sat; full bar; reservations recommended; between Union and Green Sts.* ♿

Zarzuela / ★★★
2000 HYDE ST, SAN FRANCISCO; 415/346-0800

It's almost as good as being there—really. Waiters with Spanish accents bring plate after plate of just-like-the-old-country tapas, and you feel like a member of an extended family. This excellent Spanish restaurant atop Russian Hill has been popular since day one. Drenched in soothing colors, it is an elegant, sophisticated spot for well-priced Spanish cuisine.

Fresh bread and Spanish olives are whisked to your table as soon as you sit down, and sangria and a selection of Spanish wines are offered immediately. The tapas are prepared with fresh ingredients and a liberal use of seasonings that sets them apart from the usual tapas fare. Nibble on the favorite *gambas al ajillo*, shrimp bathed in olive oil and garlic, which arrives in a small iron skillet, or the cool, colorful seafood salad—check inside the beautifully carved tomato for an extra helping. The paella is excellent, arguably the best in town; it's available only for two or more and requires a 30-minute wait—but it's more than worth it. Zarzuela takes its name from one of the menu's dishes, a traditional seafood stew. Fortunately for American diners, this Spanish treasure keeps American dinner hours. *$$; DC, MC, V; no checks; dinner Tues–Sat; full bar; no reservations; at Union St.* &

Marina/Cow Hollow

The Marina is the city's northern waterfront neighborhood, setting for some of San Francisco's priciest real estate. Anchoring the quarter on the north and west, the Marina Green and the Palace of Fine Arts entice joggers, kite flyers, and picnickers. Mediterranean-inspired homes line Marina Boulevard, overlooking the place-to-be-seen Green and the actual marina. This neighborhood, filled with art deco–inspired houses, was formerly a marsh. Built on fill material and notoriously lacking in stability, the Marina sustained a good deal of damage in the 1989 Loma Prieta earthquake. Happily, the damage has largely been repaired, and a walk among the low-rise buildings yields plenty of architectural eye candy. Bouncy Chestnut Street sports numerous restaurants, cafes, shops, and theaters. On the eastern end of the Marina, Fort Mason, formerly a World War II–era shipping port, plays host to a number of small museums such as the Museo Italo Americano, the Mexican Museum, and the Craft and Folk Art Museum.

Cow Hollow sits south of Lombard Street, at the base of Pacific Heights, wrapped around stylish Union Street. A profusion of dairies in the 19th century gave this area its name. In the 1880s, the board of health realized that cows were a health risk to the ever-expanding city, the dairies were banished to the suburbs, and the bovine presence was gradually replaced by a human one. Today the neighborhood is populated with young families and single professionals. Although the houses and avenues don't approach Pacific Heights in grandeur or leafy peacefulness, Union Street makes up for it with chic boutiques, including Armani Exchange and Kenneth Cole, and plenty of good restaurants. At night, bars call the 20- and 30-somethings out to play as the street puts on its party hat.

RESTAURANTS

Betelnut / ★★

2030 UNION ST, SAN FRANCISCO; 415/929-8855

A member of the Real Restaurants company, which includes such successes as Tra Vigne and Bix, this sumptuously decorated Asian "beerhouse" has the ever-so-slightly-tarty feel of an exotic 1930s Shanghai brothel. Named after a popular seed that is chewed throughout Asia for its intoxicating side effects, Betelnut became a huge success in a short time, and it's still on everyone's list of places to try (though, alas, the namesake nut is not offered here). The mixed menu is pan-Asian, with an array of authentic dishes from Vietnam, Singapore, China, Thailand, Indonesia, and Japan. Although the unusual concept entices diners, the reality is not always up to par. With more than a dozen cooks in the kitchen on busy nights, results can vary. Some dishes consistently get raves, including the spicy coconut chicken with eggplant, lemongrass, and basil; the crunchy tea-smoked duck; the succulent short ribs; and the sun-dried anchovies with peanuts, chiles, and garlic. But the green papaya salad gets mixed reviews, and Betelnut's dumplings can be downright disappointing. Expect an attitude from the hostess if you haven't made reservations. *$$$; DC, DIS, MC, V; no checks; lunch, dinner every day; full bar; reservations recommended; www.citysearch7.com; between Buchanan and Webster Sts.* &

Cafe Marimba / ★★★☆

2317 CHESTNUT ST, SAN FRANCISCO; 415/776-1506

This exuberant little restaurant sandwiched between shops in the Marina district is easy to miss, despite its vibrant sunset-purple facade and the seemingly endless stream of people who squeeze through its lime-green doors every evening. Step inside and you'll be bowled over by a profusion of more screaming colors—pink, turquoise, green, orange—not to mention a fiery-red, 10-foot-tall papier-mâché diablo towering above the room. The secret to eating at Marimba is to make a reservation for early in the evening so you won't have to wait long for a table. San Francisco chef Reed Hearon, famous for his Black Cat and Rose Pistola restaurants, pioneered this festive place, and although he has since moved on to other projects, Marimba still thrives under owners Louise Clement and Bill Susky's inspired creations. The quite reasonably priced fare here is real Mexican—not an overpriced upscale version of Taco Bell. Once you're seated, immediately order the wonderful guacamole and chips. The restaurant has a changing repertoire of more than 50 salsas; the nightly selections might include roasted corn, avocado-tomatillo, or tomato with smoked chiles. Have a margarita to douse the flames, or sip a delicious fresh-fruit juice. Then move on to the sublime shrimp *mojo de ajo,* drenched in garlic, chiles, and lime; spicy snapper tacos with pineapple salsa; or grilled chicken spiced with mild, smoky achiote seed. Even the more common fare has a twist: the seafood comes with a choice of five sauces, including garlic, caramelized onions, and fresh jalapeño sauces, or a combination of capers, olives, tomatoes, and jalapeños. Top it all off with the fantastic flan. *$$; AE, MC, V; no checks; lunch Tues–Fri, dinner every day, brunch Sat–Sun; full bar; reservations recommended; between Scott and Divisadero Sts.* &

Greens / ★★☆

FORT MASON CENTER, BUILDING A, SAN FRANCISCO; 415/771-6222

As Le Tour d'Argent in Paris is to the dedicated duck fancier and the Savoy Grill in London is to the roast beef connoisseur, so is Greens at Fort Mason to the vegetarian aesthete. Not only is the food politically correct here, it's often so good that even carnivores find it irresistible. Part of the Greens treat is visual: located in a converted barracks in the historic Fort Mason Center, the enormous, airy dining room is surrounded by huge windows with a spectacular view of the bay and the Golden Gate Bridge, and a gigantic sculpted redwood burl is a Buddhist-inspired centerpiece in the waiting area. Yes, Greens is owned and operated by the Zen Center—but this is a restaurant, not a monastery. The menu changes daily; expect to see such dishes as mesquite-grilled polenta; filo turnovers filled with mushrooms, spinach, and Parmesan; pizza sprinkled with onion confit, goat cheese, and basil; and fettuccine with mushrooms, peas, goat cheese, and crème fraîche. Greens to Go, a takeout counter inside the restaurant, also sells baked goods, savory soups, sandwiches, and black-bean chili. An à la carte dinner menu is offered Monday through Friday; guests may order from the prix-fixe five-course dinner menu only on Saturday. The restaurant is also open for late-night desserts, coffee, and wine from Monday through Saturday, 9:30 to 11pm. *$$$; DIS, MC, V; local checks only; lunch Tues–Sat, dinner Mon–Sat, brunch Sun; beer and wine; reservations recommended; off Marina Blvd at Buchanan St.* &

Pane e Vino / ★★★

3011 STEINER ST, SAN FRANCISCO; 415/346-2111

This dark-wood-trimmed trattoria framed by a cream-colored awning is a local favorite. The two tiny, simply furnished dining rooms with small white-clothed tables fill up fast, and as waiters spouting rapid-fire Italian dart back and forth between the kitchen and their customers, folks waiting for a table are often left frantically searching for a place to stand out of the way. It's all enchantingly reminiscent of the real ristorante scene in Italy, which is perhaps one of the reasons people keep coming back. Do yourself a favor and indulge in the amazing chilled artichoke appetizer, stuffed with bread and tomatoes and served with a vinaigrette—it's divine! Follow that lead with one of the perfectly prepared pastas, ranging from the simple but savory capellini tossed with fresh tomatoes, basil, garlic, and extra-virgin olive oil to the zesty bucatini (hollow straw pasta) smothered with pancetta, hot peppers, and tomato sauce. The excellent entrees vary from rack of lamb marinated in sage and rosemary to the whole roasted fresh fish of the day. Before you raise your napkin to your lips for the last time, dive into the delightful dolci: a luscious crème caramel, assorted gelati, and a terrific tiramisu are the standouts. *$$; AE, MC, V; no checks; lunch Mon–Sat, dinner every day; beer and wine; reservations recommended; between Union and Filbert Sts.* &

LODGINGS

The Bed and Breakfast Inn / ★★

4 CHARLTON CT, SAN FRANCISCO; 415/921-9784

San Francisco's first bed-and-breakfast maintains the convincing illusion that it's a charming old English inn in a picturesque mews somewhere in Cornwall. Instead, this B&B tucked into a cul-de-sac is just steps away from the popular boutiques, bars, and restaurants lining Union Street, one of the city's most popular shopping areas. The three adjoining green Victorian buildings—graced with twining ivy, window boxes bursting with bright red geraniums, and a birdhouse bobbing from a tree out front—offer 13 enchanting guest rooms, each individually decorated with family antiques, floral prints, and appealing personal touches. Ask for a room that opens directly onto the alluring back garden. The least expensive rooms have shared baths. Of the two sunny penthouses, the Mayfair offers a living room, kitchen, latticed balcony, and spiral staircase leading to a bedroom loft with a king-size bed; the Garden Suite, popular with groups of four, has a king-size bed in the master bedroom, a double bed in the loft, a fully stocked kitchen, a living room with a fireplace, two bathrooms (one with a Jacuzzi tub), and French doors leading to a private atrium and garden. You may enjoy your simple continental breakfast in your room, the garden, or the diminutive English tearoom. *$$$; MC, V; checks OK; www.thebandb.com; between Laguna and Buchanan Sts.* &

Marina Inn / ★★★

3110 OCTAVIA ST, SAN FRANCISCO; 415/928-1000 OR 800/274-1420

If you don't have strong feelings about where you want to stay in San Francisco and you want the most for your money, book a room here; of all the inexpensive lodgings in the city, none comes close to offering a better deal. The building, located on busy Lombard Street, is a handsome 1924 four-story Victorian, and the guest rooms are equally impressive: four-poster beds with cozy comforters and mattresses, rustic pine-wood furnishings, attractive wallpaper, and a pleasant color scheme of rose, hunter green, and pale yellow. The location is fine as well—within easy walking distance of the shops and restaurants along Chestnut and Union Streets, and right on the bus route to downtown. *$$; AE, MC, V; no checks; www.marinainn.com; at Lombard St.* &

Pacific Heights

This chic and blatantly prosperous neighborhood stretches languidly over the hills between Van Ness Avenue and the Presidio. Even the fog likes it here, often refusing to leave after pulling away from downtown and the southern neighborhoods. Whether your architectural tastes lean toward Victorians, over-the-top neoclassical manors, or something elegantly in between, there are jaw-dropping buildings for you to admire and many to tour. The views from the higher intersections are stunning—imagine what residents must enjoy over their morning coffee. Two parks, Alta Plaza and Lafayette, offer greenery, which is already in abundance, and open space, which is not. Shopping on Fillmore Street is elegant, comfortable, and varied. You can browse sleek furniture stores, visit charming thrift shops, have lunch in a stylish restaurant, or grab a quick burrito.

RESTAURANTS

Cafe Kati / ★★★

1963 SUTTER ST, SAN FRANCISCO; 415/775-7313

Cafe Kati may not have the elbow room of some of San Francisco's other top restaurants, but there are few chefs on the West Coast who can match Kirk Webber—a California Culinary Academy graduate—when it comes to culinary artistry. Obscurely located on a residential block off Fillmore Street, this tiny, modest, 60-seat cafe has garnered a monsoon of kudos for Webber's weird and wonderful arrangements of numerous cuisines. Even something as mundane as a Caesar salad is transformed into a towering monument of lovely romaine lettuce arranged upright on the plate and held in place by a ribbon of thinly sliced cucumber. Fortunately, it tastes as good as it looks. Although the menu changes monthly, it always spans the globe: miso-marinated Chilean sea bass topped with tempura kabocha squash; pancetta-wrapped pork tenderloin bathed in a ragout of baby artichokes and chanterelle mushrooms; walnut-crusted chicken with Gorgonzola; crispy duck confit with sweet potato polenta and wild mushrooms. Complete the gustatory experience with the to-die-for butterscotch pudding. When making a reservation, request a table in the front room—and don't make any plans after dinner because the kitchen takes its sweet time preparing your objet d'art. *$$$$; MC, V; no checks; dinner Tues–Sun; beer and wine; reservations recommended; katikwok@aol.com; www.cafekati.com; between Fillmore and Webster Sts.*

The Meetinghouse / ★★★

1701 OCTAVIA ST, SAN FRANCISCO; 415/922-6733

Without the forest-green awning jutting from its Victorian facade, the Meetinghouse could easily be mistaken for a residence. Luckily for lovers of good American food, it's not one. In 1996 owner-chefs John Bryant Snell and Joanna Karlinsky converted an old apothecary space into one of the very best restaurants in San Francisco. Custard-yellow walls, dark green trim, wood ceiling fans, and hardwood floors make this warm, intimate space utterly inviting. This dinner-only establishment offers superb seasonal American cuisine served by an exceptionally professional staff. Baskets of warm biscuits and homemade breads arrive at your table immediately. A small seasonal menu typically boasts no more than five enticing entrees. A fall offering included a marvelous rock shrimp and scallion johnnycake appetizer with a sweet-pepper relish, and an exquisite tomato salad drizzled with a lightly sweetened balsamic vinaigrette and toasted pine nuts. Unforgettable entrees have included a grilled pork loin chop with applesauce served with braised baby greens; a pan-seared Chilean sea bass in a sumptuous red-wine jus; and braised short ribs smothered in a sweet barbecue sauce. For dessert, try the utterly delectable strawberry shortcake with sweet berries nestled in a cloud of whipped cream atop a strawberry and wine purée. A carefully selected, reasonably priced list of primarily California wines is perfectly matched with the extraordinary American cuisine. *$$$$; AE, DC, MC, V; no checks; dinner Mon–Sat; beer and wine; reservations recommended; at Bush St.* &

LODGINGS

El Drisco / ★★★

2901 PACIFIC AVE, SAN FRANCISCO; 415/346-2880 OR 800/634-7277

If you're a fan of San Francisco's Ritz-Carlton, you'll adore El Drisco. The six-story structure, perched on one of the most coveted blocks in the city, was built in 1903 as a boardinghouse for neighborhood servants. After surviving the great fire of 1906, it was converted into a hotel in the mid-'20s but eventually fell into major disrepair. Combining the financial might of hotelier Tom Callinan (Meadowood, the Inn at Southbridge) and the interior design skills of Glenn Texeira (Ritz-Carlton, Manila), El Drisco's proprietors transformed years of blood, sweat, and greenbacks into one of the finest small hotels in the city. The 24 rooms and 19 suites are bathed in soothing shades of alabaster, celadon, and buttercup yellow and feature rich fabrics, quality antiques, and superior mattresses. Standard amenities include a two-line phone with modem hookup, a CD player, a discreetly hidden TV with a VCR, and a minibar; suites include a handsome sofa bed, an additional phone and TV, and terrific views. The spacious marble-clad bathrooms are equipped with hair dryers, plush robes, and (in most units) bathtubs. Room 304A—a corner suite with an extraordinary view of Pacific Heights mansions and the surrounding bay—is a favorite. An extended continental breakfast is served in one of the three quiet, comfortable common rooms. *$$$$; AE, DC, DIS, MC, V; no checks; resinfo@eldriscohotel.com; www.eldrisco hotel.com; between Broderick and Baker Sts.* &

Hayes Valley

Hayes Valley gets traffic. Highway 101 scoops up and drops off motorists on Oak and Fell Streets, respectively, making the neighborhood an unwilling stage for the morning and evening commutes. It also sits next to the War Memorial Opera House and Davies Symphony Hall, making it the quarter of choice for pre-performance dining (a plethora of good restaurants doesn't hurt). City residents are also beginning to discover its shopping opportunities (on Hayes St between Laguna and Franklin and on Laguna St). Formerly a poor and working-class African-American neighborhood, the never-ending search for affordable housing is bringing new residents to Hayes Valley. It's now also home to young, white hipsters, and the housing mix illustrates the transition—an interesting combination of tidy Victorians, housing projects from the '60s and '70s, and, of course, new multicolored condominium units.

RESTAURANTS

Absinthe Brasserie and Bar / ★★

398 HAYES ST, SAN FRANCISCO; 415/551-1590

Stylish Absinthe, named for the green herbal liqueur so potent it was banned in turn-of-the-century France, re-creates the romance and mystery of the bygone Belle Epoque. The sumptuous decor begins at the entry with French rattan cafe chairs, copper-topped tables, and a mosaic checkerboard floor. Chef Ross Browne, who relocated here along with the owner and general manager from the now-shuttered Rosmarino, prepares a brasserie-style French and Italian menu with such starters as veal sweetbreads sautéed in a sweet marsala sauce, a delicious version of the classic pissaladière, and fluffy ricotta dumplings. A generous seafood platter loaded with Dungeness crab, shrimp, and mussels is a highlight. Entrees change daily and vary in consistency (much like, alas, the service). You'll find everything from roasted veal chops and seasonal risottos to inventive vegetarian creations. Desserts are more dependable: a Scharffen Berger chocolate pot de crème is sublime, as is the lavender crème brûlée. And while you won't find actual absinthe on the menu, professional bartenders mix a range of amusingly named cocktails, including one named after Hemingway's Death in the Afternoon—an unusual combination of Pernod and champagne. *$$$; AE, DC, DIS, MC, V; no checks; breakfast, lunch Tues–Fri, dinner Tues–Sun, brunch Sat–Sun; full bar; reservations recommended; www.absinthe.com; at Gough St.* &

Jardinière / ★★★⯨

300 GROVE ST, SAN FRANCISCO; 415/861-5555

A native Californian, chef Traci Des Jardins worked in many notable restaurants in France, New York, and Los Angeles before co-opening Rubicon restaurant in San Francisco, which launched her culinary reputation nationwide. She won the prestigious James Beard Rising Star Chef of the Year award in 1995 and was named one of *Food & Wine*'s Best New Chefs in America. With those kudos, it's no wonder that her own restaurant, Jardinière, was a smashing success as soon as the highly stylized glass doors swung open in September 1997. With award-winning designer-restaurateur Pat Kuleto as her business partner, Des Jardins was assured of an impressive setting for her French-California cuisine. Formerly home to a jazz club, the two-story interior is elegantly framed with violet velvet drapes, and the focal point is the central oval mahogany and marble bar, frequently mobbed with local politicos and patrons of the arts. Appetizers are Des Jardins's strong point, especially the flavor-packed lobster, leek, and chanterelle strudel and the delicate kabocha squash ravioli with chestnuts and sage brown butter. Some of her best entrees thus far have included the crisp chicken with chanterelles and applewood-smoked bacon, herbed lamb loin with cranberry beans and tomato confit, and pan-roasted salmon with lentils, celery root salad, and red-wine sauce. After your meal, consider the chef's selection of domestic and imported cheeses, which are visible in the temperature-controlled cheese room on the main floor. The live entertainment makes this restaurant ideal for a special night on the town. *$$$$; AE, DC, DIS, MC, V; no checks; dinner, late-night menu every day; full bar; reservations recommended; jardin1997@aol.com; at Franklin St.* &

Zuni Cafe / ★★★

1658 MARKET ST, SAN FRANCISCO; 415/552-2522

Before it got famous, Zuni was a tiny Southwestern-style lunch spot in a low-class neighborhood. When Chez Panisse alumna Judy Rodgers came on board as chef and co-owner, the cafe became so popular it had to more than double its size. Today, with its roaring copper-topped bar, grand piano, and exposed-brick dining room, it's nearly as quintessential a San Francisco institution as Dungeness crab and sourdough bread, though many loyal patrons miss the days when it was little more than a hole in the wall. It wouldn't be stretching the truth to say that one reason the neighborhood started improving was Zuni's Mediterranean-influenced upscale food, as divinely simple as only the supremely sophisticated can be. Picture a plate of mild, house-cured anchovies sprinkled with olives, celery, and Parmesan cheese; polenta with delicate mascarpone; a terrific Caesar salad; a small, perfectly roasted chicken for two on a delicious bed of Tuscan bread salad; a grilled rib-eye steak accompanied by sweet white corn seasoned with fresh basil. At lunchtime and after 10pm, you can get some of the best burgers in town here, too, served on focaccia with aioli and house pickles—and be sure to order a side of the great shoestring potatoes. Service is first-rate for regulars and those who resemble them. *$$$; AE, MC, V; no checks; lunch, dinner, late dinner Tues–Sun; full bar; reservations recommended; between Franklin and Gough Sts.* &

The Richmond

Former mayor and silver baron Adolph Sutro drew San Franciscans "out west" by building the original Cliff House and Sutro Baths along the coast and bringing visitors in with a steam railroad he constructed along California Street. Over the years, immigrants from Russia, Eastern Europe, Ireland, and China settled in the area, giving it a cosmopolitan flair despite the monotony of the stucco architecture. This huge district is one big grid of crisscrossing streets surrounded by green. To the north, verdant Lake Street borders the Presidio, offering peekaboo views of the ocean and the Marin headlands. Sea Cliff, a community of mansions along the coast, sits between the Presidio and Lincoln Park, which houses the stately Palace of the Legion of Honor art museum. Golden Gate Park occupies the southern border of the Richmond, from the Haight to Ocean Beach. Do your walking and exploring along the coast; Geary Boulevard, the noisy commercial artery that runs through the neighborhood, doesn't invite strolling. Clement Street and Geary Boulevard do, however, provide some excellent Chinese and Southeast Asian cuisine.

RESTAURANTS

Hong Kong Flower Lounge / ★★

5322 GEARY BLVD, SAN FRANCISCO; 415/668-8998

This popular branch in a series of Flower Lounges that serves delicious Chinese dishes prepared by Hong Kong chefs is a long-standing favorite. For a full review, see the Restaurant section under Millbrae in the East Bay, South Bay, and Peninsula chapter. *$$; AE, DC, DIS, MC, V; no checks; lunch, dinner every day; full bar; reservations recommended; between 17th and 18th Aves.*

The Haight

Formerly known as Haight-Ashbury, it's now simply called the Haight by most San Franciscans, and it hasn't lost its '60s aura in the name change, either. Visitors drawn to its atmospheric streets are rewarded with plenty of psychedelia. Two parks—Golden Gate and Buena Vista—give the Haight a peaceful frame. What you can't find in the parks you'll encounter on Haight Street, a diverse retail potpourri now populated by the young and the unkempt. The intersection of Haight and Ashbury

Streets was ground zero for the Summer of Love; 15 months (between 1965 and 1967) of flower children, rock 'n' roll, gurus of all persuasions, and hippies. Parts of Haight Street haven't aged at all; many of the stores will take you back a decade or four. The Gap and tourists have moved in, however, giving The Haight the feeling of a cultural exhibit, even while many still claim it as their hood.

RESTAURANTS

Cha Cha Cha / ★★☆

1801 HAIGHT ST, SAN FRANCISCO; 415/386-5758
2327 MISSION ST, SAN FRANCISCO; 415/648-0504

Cha Cha Cha is fun. It's festive, the Caribbean food is very good, the prices are totally reasonable, and the sangría is addictive. What's not to like? The cafe is wildly decorated with Santeria altars and glittery bric-a-brac, which blend in perfectly with the varied mix of pumped-up patrons quaffing pitchers of sangría while waiting for a table, which often takes up to an hour on weekends, though nobody seems to mind. The tapas-style dishes not to miss: sautéed mushrooms, fried calamari, fried new potatoes with a fab spicy sauce, Cajun shrimp, mussels in saffron, and plantains with black-bean sauce. Check the specials board for outstanding seafood dishes as well, but skip the so-so steak. The second branch, recently opened in the Mission, serves exactly the same food as the Haight location in a much larger space; not only is the wait shorter, but there's also a full bar. Still, the original is best if you want the only-in-SF Cha Cha Cha experience. *$$; MC, V; no checks; lunch, dinner every day; beer and wine; no reservations; Haight St at Shrader St, Mission St between 19th and 20th Sts.* &

Thep Phanom / ★★★

400 WALLER ST, SAN FRANCISCO; 415/431-2526

Thailand's complex, spicy, cosmopolitan cuisine has always been adaptive, incorporating flavors from India, China, Burma, Malaysia, and, more recently, the West. San Francisco boasts dozens of Thai restaurants; virtually all of them are good, and many are excellent. Why, then, does Thep Phanom alone have a permanent line out its front door even though it takes reservations? At this restaurant, a creative touch of California enters the cultural mix, resulting in sophisticated preparations that have a special sparkle. The signature dish, *ped swan*, is a boneless duck in a light honey sauce served on a bed of spinach—and it ranks with the city's greatest entrees. Tart, minty, spicy *yum plamuk* (calamari salad), *larb ped* (minced duck salad), coconut chicken soup, and the velvety basil-spiked seafood curry served on banana leaves—available Wednesday and Thursday only—are superb choices, too. Service is charming and efficient; the tasteful decor, informal atmosphere, eclectic crowd, and discerning wine list are all very San Francisco. *$$; AE, DC, DIS, MC, V;*

no checks; dinner every day; beer and wine; reservations recommended; at Fillmore St. ⅃

LODGINGS

Red Victorian Bed, Breakfast & Art / ★★☆

1665 HAIGHT ST, SAN FRANCISCO; 415/864-1978

The Red Vic, located smack-dab on an exciting stretch of Haight Street, is one of the most eclectic and groovy lodgings in the city. You'll have the quintessential Haight experience staying in any of the 18 colorfully decorated rooms, each with its own Summer of Love theme. For example, the Flower Child room has rainbow-colored walls, a mural of the sun on the ceiling, and a hand-crocheted shawl on the bed's headboard. The Peacock Suite features psychedelic, multicolored patterns, hanging beads, and a canopy bed. Four of the guest rooms have private baths, while the remaining rooms share four bathrooms down the hall. A complimentary continental breakfast is served family style, offering an opportunity to meet the other guests (and what an interesting lot they are). Former flower child Sami Sunchild owns and runs this one-of-a-kind tribute to the '60s, and you couldn't dream up a more perfect, gracious host. So c'mon, inject a little peace, love, and happiness into your vacation—give Sami a call. *$$; AE, DIS, MC, V; checks OK; redvic@linex.com; www.redvic.com; between Cole and Belvedere Sts.*

Cole Valley

Cole Valley survived the 1989 earthquake mostly intact, with the exception of buildings at the corner of Parnassus and Cole Streets. The trouble was the ground underneath the intersection. Formerly a farm pond, it was filled to allow the construction of the road and buildings—and everyone knows that fill soil is the worst soil to be sitting on in an earthquake. This peaceful neighbor to the Haight revels in its isolation from the hubbub of the rest of the city. Residents here seek their creature comforts close to home, along a small segment of Cole Street, between Frederick and Parnassus Streets, where great restaurants, cafes, and grocery and hardware stores cater to their needs. The streets surrounding Cole are intimate and tree-lined, yet vast Golden Gate Park is a few minutes' walk away, and major east-west arteries nearby can whisk (on a good day) residents across town if the mood moves them.

RESTAURANTS

EOS Restaurant & Wine Bar / ★★★

901 COLE ST, SAN FRANCISCO; 415/566-3063

It's not so much the menu—the Euro-Asian fusion theme is hardly original—as it is the portions (generous) and presentations (brilliant) that have brought throngs of visitors and residents to this once-little-known

San Francisco neighborhood. Chef/owner Arnold Wong has taken the art of arrangement to a whole new level: every dish is masterfully crafted to take full advantage of the shape, color, and texture of each ingredient. It's almost a desecration to dig in to such culinary artwork, though one's guilt is soon assuaged after the feasting begins, particularly when it's upon the tender breast of Peking duck, smoked in ginger-peach tea leaves and served with a plum-kumquat chutney. Other notable dishes are the almond-encrusted soft-shell crab appetizer dipped in spicy plum ponzu sauce, shiitake mushroom dumplings, blackened Asian catfish atop a bed of lemongrass risotto, five-pepper calamari, and the red curry-marinated rack of lamb. Desserts are as fetching as the entrees, particularly the Bananamisu (akin to tiramisu) with caramelized bananas, and the warm bittersweet chocolate soufflé cake. Unfortunately, a quiet, romantic dinner is out of the question here, since the stark deco-industrial decor merely amplifies the nightly cacophony. After dinner, adjourn to the restaurant's popular wine bar around the corner, which stocks more than 400 bottles from around the globe. Nearly 50 red and white wines are available by the glass, too. *$$$$; AE, MC, V; no checks; dinner every day; beer and wine; reservations recommended; at Carl St.* &

SoMa (South of Market Street)

This section of the city is almost too big and diverse to call a neighborhood. SoMa is a geographic moniker only, comprising several distinct areas, many in transition. The western end, between Eleventh and Fifth Streets, is full of low-rise, light-industrial buildings, slowly being converted to architects' offices and Internet start-up work space. Nighttime sees these blocks pulsing to the club-scene beat. Between Fourth and Third Streets, the Moscone Convention Center, Yerba Buena Gardens/Center for the Arts, and the San Francisco Museum of Modern Art hold court, surrounded by a coterie of hip new restaurants. The area south of Highway 80 is known as "Multimedia Gulch." Finally, the neighborhood's eastern frontier, between Third Street and the Embarcadero, feels like an extension of downtown, as high-rise buildings go up in every empty square foot of space. Check out SoMa now—it's bound to be different next time you visit.

RESTAURANTS

Azie / ★★★

826 FOLSOM ST, SAN FRANCISCO; 415/538-0918

Chef-restaurateur Jody Denton wants to corner the culinary market on the up-and-coming scene on Folsom Street. With Azie, wedged in next door to his wildly popular LuLu, he's well on his way. This stylish restaurant bears its warehousey South of Market surroundings in mind, with

22-foot ceilings vaulted by four huge columns. The dining room is split-level; in the booths on the main level, you can draw a set of curtains for a truly exclusive feel. The main level is also home to the exhibition kitchen, where chef Donnie Masterton prepares Asian-inspired French cuisine. One recent menu included such dishes as roulade of monkfish, grilled veal medallions with sea urchin–wasabi butter, and aromatic oxtail bundles. Adventurous, to be sure; if you have trouble making a decision, opt for the nightly tasting menu. Dining is also available at the bar, where a DJ plays music nightly. *$$$$; AE, DC, MC, V; no checks; lunch Mon–Fri, dinner every day; full bar; reservations recommended; www.restaurantlulu.com; between 4th and 5th Sts.* &

Bizou / ★★★

598 4TH ST, SAN FRANCISCO; 415/543-2222
Bizou means "a little kiss" in French, but San Francisco foodies seem to have planted a big fat wet one on this lively bistro with the rustic Mediterranean menu. Since April 1993, chef/owner Loretta Keller, formerly of Stars, has seduced even normally conservative diners into eating such exotica as beef cheeks, parsnip chips, cod ravioli, and house-cured anchovies, winning them over with her deceptively simple, flavorful preparations. There are plenty of less-adventurous items, to be sure, including a wonderful salad of pear, Gorgonzola, radicchio, frisée, and toasted walnuts; day-boat scallops with wild mushrooms, endive, and balsamic vinegar; stuffed young chicken with celeriac, grilled apples, and goat cheese; and desserts like French cream with persimmon and fig sauces and a Seville orange and Meyer lemon curd cake. Housed in a 1906 building, the corner storefront restaurant has an updated bistro feel, with window boxes, vintage light fixtures, weathered mustard-colored walls, large windows, and an oak bar. A few caveats, though: the tables are packed tightly together, the place can get very noisy, and the service can range from rare to well-done. *$$$; AE, MC, V; no checks; lunch Mon–Fri, dinner Mon–Sat; full bar; reservations recommended; at Brannan St.* &

Fringale / ★★★★

570 4TH ST, SAN FRANCISCO; 415/543-0573
Chef/co-owner Gerald Hirigoyen, named one of the 10 best chefs in the nation by *Food & Wine* magazine, draws crowds to his tiny, boisterous 50-seat French restaurant. Behind this restaurant's yellow facade, plenty of charm emanates from the casual, blond-wood-trimmed interior, petite curved bar, and friendly, largely French wait staff. Hirigoyen was born and raised in the Basque country of southwestern France, and his origins serve as the abiding inspiration for his gutsy, flavor-packed, and extremely reasonably priced fare. Outstanding dishes include the frisée salad topped with a poached egg and warm bacon dressing, steamed

mussels sprinkled with garlic and parsley, wild mushroom ravioli, rack of lamb, and his signature pork tenderloin confit with onion and apple marmalade. Hirigoyen was originally a pastry chef, and he flaunts his talents with his incredible crème brûlée and rich chocolate Basque cake topped with chocolate mousse. Fringale (French for "raging hunger") is perpetually packed with famished folks at dinnertime, so expect a noisy crowd and a wait for a table, even if you've made a reservation. *$$$; AE, MC, V; no checks; lunch Mon–Fri, dinner Mon–Sat; full bar; reservations recommended; between Bryant and Brannan Sts.* &

Hawthorne Lane / ★★★☆

22 HAWTHORNE ST, SAN FRANCISCO; 415/777-9779

When Hillary Rodham Clinton was in town to promote her book *It Takes a Village*, she ate a late dinner at Hawthorne Lane. Probably learned about it from hubby Bill, who supped here the year before and might have raved about the miso-glazed black cod with sesame spinach rolls, the special lobster tempura, the roasted Sonoma lamb with butternut squash and Parmesan risotto, or the house-made fettuccine with chanterelle mushrooms. Ever since it opened in June 1995, Hawthorne Lane has been one of the city's hottest restaurants, its popularity fueled by its lovely design, its proximity to the happening SoMa scene, and the pedigree of owner-chefs David and Anne Gingrass (formerly of Spago and Postrio fame). The dining room is a refined, beguiling space, with wrought-iron cherry blossoms, a massive skylight, giant urns with dazzling fresh floral displays, and light-colored woods creating an air of perennial spring. Hawthorne Lane also wins raves for its varied selection of wonderful breads and desserts. If you can't get a reservation, snag one of the seats at the long, oval bar, where you can order from the dining room menu, or sign up for one of the many tables set aside for walk-ins. *$$$$; DC, DIS, MC, V; no checks; lunch Mon–Fri, dinner every day; full bar; reservations recommended; www.hawthornelane.com; off Howard St, between 2nd and 3rd Sts.* &

LODGINGS

Harbor Court Hotel / ★★★

165 STEUART ST, SAN FRANCISCO; 415/882-1300 OR 800/346-0555

Not far from the Financial District, this low-key, high-style hotel caters mainly to business travelers but will equally impress the weekend vacationer. It was once a YMCA, which shouldn't dissuade you. The high-quality accommodations, gorgeous views of the bay, and complimentary use of the adjoining fitness club—complete with indoor Olympic-size swimming pool—add up to one sweet deal. Guest rooms are nicely equipped with soundproof windows, half-canopy beds, large armoires, and writing desks. Amenities range from limited room service to secretarial services, laundry and dry cleaning, newspaper delivery, valet service, and car service to the Financial District. When the sun drops, slip on down to the bar at Boulevard (see review under Financial District) and mingle with the swinging yuppie singles. *$$$$; AE, DC, DIS, JCB, MC, V; checks OK; www.kimptongroup.com; between Mission and Howard Sts.* &

W Hotel / ★★★
181 3RD ST, SAN FRANCISCO; 415/777-5300 OR 877/W-HOTELS
Hip hotels are all the rage now, and the Westin hotel corporation has capitalized on the craze with a San Francisco version of its popular W Hotel in New York. Art, technology, service, and sex appeal are all applied in force from the moment you walk into the lobby. In fact, you don't even know you're in a hotel at first, because the first person to greet you is the bartender (brilliant). To your right is a gaggle of hip, young, beautiful people lounging in the ever-so-chic lobby, and to the left is XYZ restaurant. The room decor mimics the overall theme—bold colors, soft fabrics, sensual curves. It's almost enough to make you not notice how small the rooms actually are. No matter: dive onto the thick, luscious goose-down comforter and you won't ever want to leave. High-tech toys include a 27-inch TV, CD player, and modem jacks for your laptop. The location is fantastic as well, literally sharing real estate with the beautiful San Francisco Museum of Modern Art and Yerba Buena Gardens. *$$$$; AE, DC, DIS, JCB, MC, V; checks OK; www.whotels.com; at Howard St.* &

Potrero Hill

Sitting between two freeways and on a rise directly south of downtown, Potrero Hill flutters between industrial chic and leafy residential. Sometimes the lines cross, and the results are brightly hued, high-tech abodes in the middle of sleepy old streets. Once called Goat Hill, this former home to ungulates is now an up-and-coming residential area, shedding its former incarnation as a site for affordable housing "projects." Interior design heaven (furniture and antique shops as well as design studios) lies at its base, in the area between 16th and Division Streets. Climb the hill, and the views of downtown and the bay are expansive. On 18th Street, a little commercial area (between Arkansas and Texas Sts) features several charming restaurants.

RESTAURANTS

42 Degrees / ★★★
235 16TH ST, SAN FRANCISCO; 415/777-5559
Like Caffe Esprit, the former occupant of this bayside site hidden behind a thick line of hedges, 42 Degrees is popular with a discerning crowd of young professionals and boasts a spare, high-tech warehouse look, with a soaring ceiling and lots of concrete, metal, and glass. As night falls,

however, candlelight, table linens, and strains of live jazz soften the effect, transforming the stark 100-seat space into an appealing supper club. The name refers to the latitude of Provence and the Mediterranean Sea, and chef/owner James Moffat's ever-changing menu reflects this sun-splashed influence with starters like watercress salad with duck confit, walnuts, and pomegranates; Medjool dates with Parmesan and celery; and grilled artichokes with Meyer lemons. Entrees might include risotto with shaved truffles and mushrooms, pan-roasted chicken with lemon and black olive sauce, or grilled pancetta-wrapped salmon. Lighter eaters can look to the chalkboard for small plates such as pizzettas, Iberian blood sausage, and herb-roasted potatoes with aioli. Desserts include a sublime chocolate pot de crème, milk chocolate crème brûlée, and a warm apple Napoleon with vanilla ice cream and huckleberry sauce. The service is courteous and professional, the mezzanine-level windows afford a view of the bay, and there's a large, pleasant courtyard patio for dining alfresco on warm days. *$$$$; AE, MC, V; no checks; dinner Wed–Sun; full bar; reservations recommended; at Illinois St, behind the Esprit Outlet.* &

The Mission

One of the most colorful neighborhoods in San Francisco, the Mission District is definitely not the tidiest. On the other hand, it is a diverse community with some of the hippest new restaurants and best ethnic cuisine in the city. The heart and namesake of the neighborhood, Mission Dolores, sits on Dolores Street at 16th Street. The newer basilica's spires tower above the much smaller mission next door, which was dedicated in 1791, and still has original adobe walls and roof tiles. Cruise Valencia and 16th Streets for interesting shopping and good restaurants, 24th Street between Guerrero and South Van Ness for the epicenter of the Mission's Latino culture, and the entire neighborhood for ethnic markets, inexpensive taquerias, and vibrant murals.

RESTAURANTS

Blowfish Sushi to Die For / ★★

2170 BRYANT ST, SAN FRANCISCO; 415/285-3848

Japanese animation films play on two suspended television sets for the young and restless who pack this place, lounging against a backdrop of velvet walls, techno dance music, and acid jazz. Clearly, Blowfish caters to a crowd that wants more than just good sushi. Located in the industrial northeast Mission District, the restaurant offers a combination of traditional and more adventurous sushi by chef Ritsuo Tsuchida. If you're intent on trying blowfish, the Japanese delicacy otherwise known as puffer fish, expect to fork over about $30 if it's in season, and be prepared for a letdown: it's fairly bland. Move on to the mavericks: Maui

Maki (tuna, mango, and macadamia nuts); double crab salad with soft-shell crab; tempura-battered asparagus maki wrapped in rice; and the restaurant's namesake, Blowfish Maki (a roll of yellowtail, scallions, and tobiko, draped with salmon—but, ironically, no blowfish). Non-fish-eaters also have choices: filet mignon with rosemary garlic butter, chicken pot stickers, or asparagus spring rolls with duck. Chef Tsuchida likes to tempt his regular customers with some of his more unusual creations: seared ostrich on portobello-mushroom tempura, anyone? Service is friendly and efficient. *$$$; AE, DC, DIS, MC, V; no checks; lunch Mon–Fri, dinner every day; full bar; reservations recommended; between 19th and 20th Sts.* &

Foreign Cinema / ★★

2534 MISSION ST, SAN FRANCISCO; 415/648-7600

Like a Steven Spielberg movie, the opening of this Mission District restaurant was anticipated at least a year in advance. The hype reached such a fevered pitch, locals were half expecting to see a line of product tie-ins in local stores. When the place finally opened, in the summer of 1999, it was quickly apparent the throngs hadn't waited in vain. The concept behind this contemporary French restaurant is to combine dinner and a movie in a single location. Accessed through an unassuming door along Mission Street, the restaurant has an industrial-chic appearance, with deliberately unfinished walls, exposed mechanics in the ceiling, and hard surfaces throughout. On one wall in a center courtyard, classic foreign films are projected in all their grainy black-and-white glory. Drive-in-movie-type speaker boxes are placed at each table so you can listen along as you dine. But mostly the films are just an imaginative distraction from the main attraction: the food. The lobster and monkfish bouillabaisse is rich and decadent; the roasted Sonoma duck breast is tender and bursting with flavor; the rosemary-marinated lamb melts in your mouth. It's quite a production. *$$$; MC, V; no checks; dinner Tues–Sun; full bar; reservations recommended; between 21st and 22nd Sts.* &

La Taqueria / ★★

2889 MISSION ST, SAN FRANCISCO; 415/285-7117

Among colorful fruit stands, thrift shops, and greasy panhandlers lining bustling Mission Street sits La Taqueria, the Bay Area's best burrito factory. Its lackluster interior is brightened only by a vibrant mural depicting south-of-the-border scenes and a shiny CD jukebox pumping out merry Mexican music, all of which could mean only one thing: people come here for the food. Don't expect a wide variety, for the folks behind the counter just churn out what they do best: burritos, tacos, and quesadillas. It's all fresh, delicious, and guaranteed to fill you up—for little more than pocket change. The moist, meaty fillings include grilled beef, pork, sausage, beef tongue, and chicken—you won't find any rice in these burritos; and the *bebidas* vary from beer and soda to cantaloupe juice and even *horchata* (a sweet rice drink). Stand in line to place your order and pay, then take a seat at one of the shared, long wooden tables and wait for someone to bellow out your number (somehow they just know whether to say it in Spanish or English). *$; cash only; lunch, dinner every day; beer only; no reservations; at 25th St.* &

The Slanted Door / ★★★

584 VALENCIA ST, SAN FRANCISCO; 415/861-8032

Thank goodness chef Charles Phan abandoned his original plan to build a crepe stand in San Francisco, because otherwise we never would have had the opportunity to sink our teeth into his superb green papaya salad or stir-fried caramelized shrimp. When Phan and his large extended family discovered a vacant space on a slightly run-down stretch of Valencia Street, they ditched the crêperie plan in late 1995 and transformed the high-ceilinged room into a small, bi-level restaurant specializing in country Vietnamese food. Phan's design talents—he's a former UC Berkeley architecture student—are evident from the moment you enter the stylish, narrow dining room and take a seat at one of his green-stained wood tables. But even more impressive is Phan's unique fare, which attracts droves of people for lunch and dinner. The dinner menu changes weekly to reflect the market's offerings, but look for the favored spring rolls stuffed with fresh shrimp and pork; crab and asparagus soup; caramelized shrimp; curried chicken cooked with yams; "shaking" beef sautéed with onion and garlic; any of the terrific clay pot dishes; and, of course, Phan's special Vietnamese crepes. When business is booming the service gets slow, but if you order a pinot gris from the very good wine list, you won't mind so much. For dessert, the hands-down favorite is the all-American chocolate cake. *$$; MC, V; no checks; lunch, dinner Tues–Sun; beer and wine; reservations recommended; eat@slanteddoor. com; between 16th and 17th Sts.* &

Universal Cafe / ★★★

2814 19TH ST, SAN FRANCISCO; 415/821-4608

The Universal Cafe is the kind of place you would love to have on your block. First, the industrial-art decor is extremely sleek, suave, and chic, and the staff is refreshingly sans attitude. Second, you can actually find parking in this quiet section of the Inner Mission. And third, the food is both fantastic and reasonably priced. For lunch, try the salmon sandwich on focaccia, gourmet thin-crust pizza, or one of the wickedly good salads. Dinner gets more serious: braised duck leg on a bed of creamy polenta; sea bass served with risotto, spinach, and caramelized onions; pot roast with lumpy mashed potatoes and fresh veggies; pan-roasted filet mignon. If your dish doesn't come with it, ask for a side of the addictive mashed potatoes. If you're anywhere near the Mission or Potrero Hill, seek this place out and join the converted. *$$$; AE, DC, MC, V; no checks; breakfast, lunch Tues–Fri, dinner Tues–Sun, brunch Sat–Sun; beer and wine; reservations recommended; between Bryant and Harrison Sts.* &

The Castro

The multicolored flags hanging everywhere are not a throwback to a '70s rainbow craze; they're a symbol of gay pride, which flourishes in this animated enclave. Renovated Victorians and neatly trimmed gardens are nearly as bright as the banners flown from their walls. There's a buzz about this place. Striding down the street, checking out the scene, residents always seem to be going somewhere, and there are plenty of somewheres to head toward. Market, Castro, and 18th Streets are lined with eclectic purveyors of clothing and housewares, cafes and restaurants, bookstores, and gift shops. And nightlife in the Castro is never dull. If you find the bar scene a little too racy, relax in the Castro Theatre, with the Wurlitzer belting out *San Francisco, open your golden gate,* then disappearing into the floor before each movie.

RESTAURANTS

2223 Restaurant and Bar / ★★☆

2223 MARKET ST, SAN FRANCISCO; 415/431-0692
Also known as the No Name, this popular spot has been packing in the crowds because it's one of the first upscale restaurants in the area that offers serious food, friendly and professional service, and a terrific bar scene. You'll see only the restaurant's address on the outside of the building, so look for a red exterior and a lively crowd visible through large storefront windows. A long bar flanked by a mural dominates one side of the restaurant. You'll probably end up waiting there for a table, which will give you time to enjoy the great cosmopolitans and martinis. Across the room, the narrow dining area has wood tables, bistro chairs, and cushioned banquettes. The menu is as eclectic as the crowd—mostly American-Mediterranean, with Southwestern and Southeast Asian touches. The romaine salad is a great Caesar variation, with capers, thinly sliced cornichons, and smoky onions. Try one of the pizzas, such as the pancetta, onion confit, Teleme cheese, marjoram, and sun-dried tomato pesto version. For entrees, the kitchen serves generous portions of comfort food: juicy pan-roasted chicken with garlic mashed potatoes, grilled salmon with lemon-caviar fondue, and sliced lamb sirloin fanned on a ragout of fava beans and fresh artichoke hearts. Indulge in the Louisiana crème brûlée with pecan pralines for dessert. *$$$; AE, DC, MC, V; no checks; dinner every day, brunch Sun; full bar; reservations recommended; between Sanchez and Noe Sts.* &

LODGINGS

Inn on Castro / ★★☆

321 CASTRO ST, SAN FRANCISCO; 415/861-0321

This convivial bed-and-breakfast, catering to the gay and lesbian community for nearly two decades, has developed an ardent following—hence the intriguing collection of more than 100 heart-shaped boxes on the sideboard in the hallway, trinkets left behind by a legion of wistful patrons who can say they left their hearts in San Francisco. The restored Edwardian exterior is painted in a pleasing medley of blue, rose, and green, with gilded details and dentils. The interior is equally festive, with contemporary furnishings, original modern art, exotic plants, and elaborate flower arrangements. There are eight individually decorated guest rooms ranging from a small single to a suite with a deck; every room has a private bath and a direct-dial phone. Avoid the sunny but noisy rooms facing Castro Street. TVs are available (though noses tend to wrinkle if you ask for one). An elaborate breakfast, served in the dining room, may feature a fresh fruit salad, house-made muffins, fruit juice, and scrambled eggs, French toast, or pancakes. After your repast, relax in the cozy living room with its fireplace and deeply tufted Italian couches, or head out for a stroll in the colorful, ever-bustling Castro. $$$; AE, MC, V; checks OK; www.innoncastro.com; between Market and 16th Sts.

Noe Valley

Sunny Noe Valley sits west of wide, palm-lined Dolores Street and below Twin Peaks. 24th Street is the bustling commercial center for this mostly residential neighborhood, with plenty of places to grab a bagel or ice cream, as well as some great little restaurants. The street's shopping reflects the surrounding demographics (largely young families and couples): organic produce and groceries, children's clothing and supplies, shoes, and body and bath goodies. Primarily residential Church Street has restaurants for every palate—from American to German to Japanese to Thai to vegetarian—in the stretch between 24th and 30th Streets.

RESTAURANTS

Firefly / ★★★☆

4288 24TH ST, SAN FRANCISCO; 415/821-7652

Hidden in a cluster of homes on the west end of 24th Street is Noe Valley's best restaurant—just look for a giant metal sculpture of its namesake nocturnal insect perched above a lime green and sizzling yellow door. Inside, an eclectic array of modern art surrounds small tables laden with an equally eclectic display of food, which might include steaming bowls of bouillabaisse de Marseilles bubbling over with monkfish, prawns, scallops, and bass; shrimp-and-scallop pot stickers accompanied by a spicy sesame-soy dipping sauce (Firefly's signature appetizer); and a portobello mushroom Wellington served with linguine that's swirled with fresh vegetables. Chef/co-owner Brad Levy and co-owner Veva Edelson, both formerly of Embarko, dub it "home cooking with few ethnic boundaries." They also proudly announce on every menu that their meat comes from the well-known Niman Ranch, home of "happy, drug-free animals with an ocean view," which leaves politically correct Noe Valley carnivores smiling as they savor the spicy pork stew. The changing roster of desserts is as good as it looks, especially the not-too-sweet strawberry shortcake and the banana bread pudding with caramel anglaise. *$$$; AE, MC, V; no checks; dinner every day; beer and wine; reservations recommended; between Diamond and Douglas Sts.* &

Marin County

Visitors might lose their hearts in San Francisco, but they are bound to find much to love in Marin. The third smallest county in California, this little package is full of natural wonders, picturesque towns, and attractions. It is no wonder tourists from all over the world join the weary urbanites seeking respite and recreation who stream across the Golden Gate Bridge to visit Marin's secluded beaches, pristine mountain lakes, and virgin redwood forests.

Imagine Mount Tamalpais, elevation 2,064 feet, rising like a beloved giant near the county's center. Throw in 160,000 acres of protected land. This outdoor paradise is easily accessible from all directions. Outside of rush hour, you can drive from south to north in 30 to 45 minutes. The journey east to west is more time-consuming, given the undulating hills, unexpected cattle crossings, and scenic diversions at every turn—but it's relaxing to sit back and enjoy the meandering.

ACCESS AND INFORMATION

Two major airports provide access to Marin County. **SAN FRANCISCO INTERNATIONAL AIRPORT**, or SFO (650/876-2377), is 34 miles away, and **OAKLAND INTERNATIONAL AIRPORT** (510/577-4000) is 19 miles from Marin. **SHUTTLE SERVICE** to and from SFO is provided throughout the day by three carriers: **AIRPORTRIDE.COM** (707/523-0301 or 877/611-7433; www.airportride.com) services Sonoma and Marin Counties; **MARIN AIRPORTER** (Larkspur Landing Terminal, 415/461-4222; Novato Terminal, 415/884-2878) and **MARIN DOOR TO DOOR** (415/457-2717 or 800/540-4815) pick up and deliver in Marin. AIRPORTRide.com and Marin Door To Door also offer service to Oakland International Airport. **RADIO CAB** (415/485-1234 or 800/744-8294) services all of Marin County. Marin Door To Door is the only company that provides daily 24-hour service to San Francisco, Oakland, and San Jose Airports.

MARIN COUNTY THREE-DAY TOUR

DAY ONE: Indulge yourself. Start the day in **San Anselmo** with a down-home breakfast at **Bubba's Diner**. Browse the shops along San Anselmo Avenue. You'll find antiques and collectibles, vintage clothing, home and gardening delights, new and used books, and upscale attire. Stock up with picnic fixings at **Comfort's** (335 San Anselmo Ave; 415/454-9840). Head for the hills and points west via Sir Francis Drake Boulevard. You'll know the season by the ever-changing colors in the pastoral landscape—lush greens come with a rainy winter and spring; golden browns appear in the dry summer and fall. Make **Samuel P. Taylor State Park** (off Sir Francis Drake Blvd; 415/488-9897) your next stop. Picnic under a canopy of giant redwoods, and stretch your legs on the 1¼-mile self-guiding Pioneer Trail before heading back to San Rafael. It'll take about 30 minutes to reach the inviting **Gerstle Park Inn**. Check in and enjoy a late afternoon refreshment. How about dinner? Sausalito here we come—a scrumptious repast and views, views, views. It doesn't get much better than a window table at **Ondine**. Toast the end of a perfect day at the **Spinnaker Restaurant** (100 Spinnaker Dr, Sausalito; 415/332-1500).

DAY TWO: Past perfect. Linger over breakfast on the inn's sun porch, anticipating the discovery of nearby hidden places. Step into the past at **Mission San Rafael Arcangel** (1104 5th Ave, San Rafael; 415/457-4879), Marin's oldest historic site. Your next destination is North San Pedro Road and a beautiful loop drive around San Pablo

BUS and **FERRY SERVICE** is offered by the **GOLDEN GATE TRANSIT SYSTEM** (415/455-2000). Ferries run daily between the Larkspur Landing Terminal and Sausalito to San Francisco's Ferry Building and Fisherman's Wharf. The **BLUE & GOLD FLEET** (Pier 41, Fisherman's Wharf; 415/705-555) runs to and from Sausalito and Tiburon. The Angel Island–Tiburon Ferry (415/435-2131) provides service between downtown Tiburon and Angel Island.

Buses connect to the terminals and run daily throughout the county. However, it is generally not convenient to get around Marin on the bus. Schedules are focused on the commute to and from San Francisco. The service to West Marin is infrequent.

Two major bridges connect Marin to the greater Bay Area. The **GOLDEN GATE BRIDGE** provides access to and from San Francisco (pedestrians and bicyclists can use bridge sidewalks). The **RICHMOND–SAN RAFAEL BRIDGE** connects the county to the East Bay. Most Marin visitors travel north to south using Highway 101 (the central artery) or coastal Highway 1, with its near-legendary grades, narrow winding roads, and gorgeous views. Sir Francis Drake Boulevard, the longest east-

Bay. Stop at the Frank Lloyd Wright–designed **Marin Civic Center** (3501 Civic Center Dr, San Rafael; 415/499-6646) and stroll around the peaceful lagoon. Pause at quaint **China Camp** (see "China Camp" in this chapter) before heading for lunch at the **Buckeye Roadhouse**. Full and happy, set your compass for the **San Francisco Bay–Delta Model** (2100 Bridgeway Blvd, Sausalito; 415/332-3870). In addition to the amazing 1½-acre scale model operated by the U.S. Army Corps of Engineers, you'll enjoy exploring the world-class visitor center and Marinship, an exhibit on a World War II shipbuilding facility. Relax back at the **Gerstle Park Inn** and top off the evening with dinner at **Insalata's** or **Left Bank**.

DAY THREE: Lazy does it. Be sure to take a peek at neighboring Gerstle Park before leaving. Check in with the Italians at **Emporio Rulli**: Enjoy a cup of coffee or full-bodied espresso and load up on delectable treats for home and the road. Make your way to **Tiburon** and **Blackie's Pasture** park (located off Tiburon Blvd), where you'll access the popular multiuse path that traces the former railroad right-of-way. Join the local runners, bikers, walkers, and roller bladers headed for downtown (it'll take about an hour to walk there). You'll think this waterfront setting is postcard perfect, but wait until you arrive at **Sam's Anchor Cafe**. Head for the deck and lunch on a burger. Time permitting, you might want to say hello to **Mill Valley**. Hang out in the plaza, shop for a frame to showcase your favorite Marin photo, and dine at **Piazza D'Angelo** to complete your Mill Valley experience.

west artery in the county, extends from Interstate 580 (Richmond–San Rafael Bridge) to the Point Reyes Lighthouse. This route runs through the heart of scenic West Marin; it features pastoral settings and rolling hills. Highway 1 and Sir Francis Drake intersect at Olema.

Although Marin enjoys a temperate climate all year round, the **WEATHER** changes quickly from one location to the next. Expect cool, foggy mornings close to the bay and the ocean. The central part of the county is located in a sun belt. Spring and fall can be the best seasons of the year along the coast: southern Marin can be socked in with fog, but the sun will be shining brightly over West Marin beaches. Layers of clothing are recommended, along with comfortable walking shoes.

The **MARIN COUNTY CONVENTION & VISITORS BUREAU** (1013 Larkspur Landing Circle, Larkspur, CA 94939; 415/4999-5000; www.visitmarin.org) is an excellent county resource.

Sausalito

World travelers readily identify San Francisco as one of their favorite cities, just as they are quick to recall that enchanting little town just across the Golden Gate Bridge: Sausalito (Sausalito Visitor Center, 777 Bridgeway Blvd, Sausalito; 415/332-0505; info@sausalito. org). The name might escape them, but the Mediterranean-like setting and breathtaking views are sure to make a lasting impression. It's hard to imagine Rosie the Riveter here, much less victory ships rolling off assembly lines, but Sausalito was a major shipbuilding site during World War II. Most folks today are browsing the upscale boutiques or popular **ART GALLERIES** between gourmet dining and wine tasting.

RESTAURANTS

Alta Mira Restaurant / ★★★☆

125 BUCKLEY AVE, SAUSALITO; 415/332-1350

From scrumptious banquets to gourmet buffets and intimate dining, the Alta Mira restaurant has provided multiple options since 1954. A variety of gracious indoor settings, reminiscent of charming old European hotels, are enhanced with dramatic garden and bay views. The once tiny cocktail lounge was enlarged in 1954, the same year the inviting outdoor dining terrace was constructed. Luncheon choices on the regular menu include traditional salads, sandwiches, soups, pastas, and entrees. Seafood lovers often go for "Phyllis Green's World Famous Crab Louie." Hot and cold appetizers are offered on the dinner menu along with house specialties, such as herb-crusted roast rack of lamb and broiled Australian lobster tail. Weekend brunch, with a glass of bubbly or the famous Alta Mira gin fizz, is a Marin tradition—and one that locals enjoy sharing with out-of-town guests. The spectacular views from the terrace are sure to evoke oohs and ahs on a brilliant sunny day. $$$; AE, MC, V; no checks; breakfast, lunch, dinner every day; full bar; reservations recommended; off Princess St.

Ondine / ★★★★☆

558 BRIDGEWAY, SAUSALITO; 415/331-1133

Ondine, considered by many to be one of the finest restaurants in the Bay Area during the '60s, '70s, and '80s, has reopened in its former waterfront setting. The unsurpassed views remain the same, but everything else has been transformed into a contemporary wonder. The feeling of openness inside the restaurant highlights the dramatic design elements; swirls of dark polished wood, curved metals, and harmonious angles are everywhere. The innovative fusion menu was created by chef Seiji Wakababayashi, who trained in Japanese and classic French cuisine before emigrating to Southern California in 1989 (he was the opening sous-chef of Marina del Rey's Cafe Del Rey). Delicacies change with the season, but diners can expect an exotic blending of flavors—such as the saffron spaetzle, fava beans, tomato confit, and lotus chips that accompany the medallion of swordfish. The lobster salad, with chrysanthemum leaves,

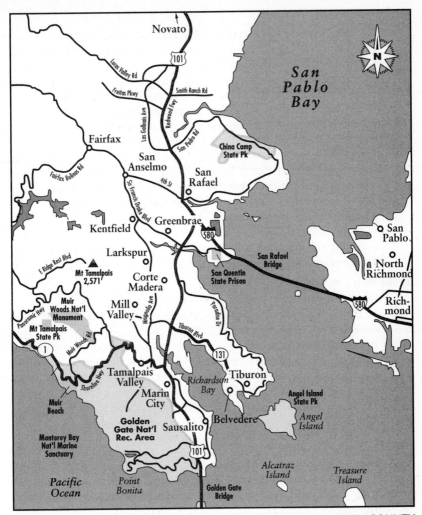

MARIN COUNTY

sweet ginger cream, smoked bacon, green papaya, and curry oil, is a favorite first course. Meat lovers will find at least one entree to enjoy, like the grilled filet mignon and crispy sweetbreads. For a little of everything, try the tasting menu. The popular weekend brunch features two courses, beginning with the likes of a salmon trio, crepes, or fruit salad, followed by scrambled eggs with lobster, a light pasta, or classic eggs Benedict. *$$$$; AE, DIS, MC, V; no checks; dinner every day, brunch Sat–Sun; full bar; reservations recommended; www.ondinerestaurant.com; located upstairs from Horizons.* &

Mikayla / ★★★

801 BRIDGEWAY, SAUSALITO; 415/331-5888 OR 800/567-9524

On the side of a terraced hill and just beyond the red-brick, rose-lined path of the Casa Madrona hotel stands sophisticated Mikayla. In a bright, pleasant interior designed by artist Laurel Burch, patrons are treated to the hotel's famous views of Belvedere and Angel Island. It's all very romantic and engaging, and fortunately there's a chef at the helm who is able to enhance the experience with his California Thai-influenced fare. Chef David Button, who was previously the executive chef of the Mark Hopkins Hotel, updates his menu based on the season's latest bounty. Memorable dishes have included the pan-roasted Chilean sea bass with horseradish whipped potatoes, pancetta, and beet vinaigrette, as well as the sweet-butter-roasted Maine lobster with parsnip whipped potatoes, sautéed tender greens, and warm whole-grain mustard sauce. *$$$; AE, DC, DIS, MC, V; no checks; dinner every day, brunch Sun; beer and wine; reservations recommended; casa@casamadrona.com; www.mikayla.com; downtown.* &

Sushi Ran / ★★★

107 CALEDONIA, SAUSALITO; 415/332-3620

To the loyal patrons of this southern Marin culinary landmark, sushi is not just food—it's a way of life. Hanging on the wall near the cash register is the smiling image of a portly gentleman who patronized the establishment more than 400 times in one year. (Folks, that's more than once a day.) The sushi served here is impeccable, prepared with aplomb and served with a flourish. The fish is glisteningly fresh, and the rice is warm and sticky. The kamikaze roll is stuffed with yellowfin tuna, bright flying-fish roe, and crunchy green onions; the spider roll enfolds a delicate tempura-fried soft-shell crab. Rice-wine lovers can choose from 17 sakes, including two from nearby Napa County, and, surprisingly for such a little restaurant, there is a mighty fine wine list offering 100 bottles. *$$$; AE, DIS, MC, V; no checks; lunch Mon–Fri, dinner every day; beer, wine, and sake; reservations recommended; managementoffice@sushi ran.com; www.sushiran.com; next to the Marin Theater.* &

LODGINGS

Alta Mira Hotel / ★★☆

125 BUCKLEY AVE, SAUSALITO; 415/332-1350

Bay Area residents and world travelers have been celebrating festive occasions at the Alta Mira, which means "high view" in Spanish, for almost 40 years. Don't be surprised if you see a small Japanese wedding party, the bride resplendent in white satin and lace, posing for photographs on a sunny terrace, the bay spreading out like a big mirror below. This Mediterranean hillside setting, which frames the lovely Alta Mira

Restaurant, and the pleasantly comfortable accommodations are ideal for those who love distinctive old-world charm. When the party is over, you'll want to relax in a room featuring a panoramic view of San Francisco, Angel Island, or Alcatraz. There are 30 rooms to choose from, as well as spacious suites with fireplaces, full baths, and balconies in the Victorian Mansion next door. Honeymooners might prefer the secluded Bridal Cottage or Bridal Suite. *$$; AE, MC, V; no checks; 2-night minimum stay on weekends; off Princess St.*

Casa Madrona Hotel / ★★★★

801 BRIDGEWAY, SAUSALITO; 415/332-0502 OR 800/567-9524

There are two Sausalitos—the tourist-trampled waterfront area and the exclusive residential region in the hills—and the Casa Madrona is where they meet. The entrance to this unique hotel complex is on boutique-lined Bridgeway, where natives never venture and visitors love to shop. Step into the Madrona's cramped elevator and you'll quickly be transported into Sausalito's enclave of multimillion-dollar mansions and panoramic bay views. The hotel offers everything you could possibly desire: sweeping bay vistas, an outdoor Jacuzzi, all the amenities of a citified hotel, plus a very good restaurant (see review of Mikayla, above). Each of Casa Madrona's 34 rooms is unique; the rooms in the Victorian cottages, which dot the landscaped hillside, and in the 110-year-old mansion on top of the hill are more rustic than those in the 15-year-old blue stucco building below. For greater privacy, choose one of the charming cottages; the Upper and Lower Bungalows have gigantic decks. The best room in the mansion is the Fireside Suite, which features a wood-burning fireplace and a private veranda. The rooms in the newer building tend to be more posh; the favorite is the Rose Chalet, which has rose-colored walls, pine furniture, a fireplace, a private deck, and a great view of the yacht harbor that you can enjoy from the comfort of your bed. Artists might request the Artist's Loft, which comes complete with an easel, paints, and brushes as well as a fireplace, a large deck, and a bay view. *$$$$; AE, DC, DIS, MC, V; no checks; 2-night minimum stay Nov–Apr, 3 nights May–Oct; casa@casamadrona.com; www.casamadrona.com; located downtown.* &

The Inn Above Tide / ★★★☆

30 EL PORTAL, SAUSALITO; 415/332-9535 OR 800/893-8433

The soothing ebb and flow of gentle tides is a natural attraction at this idyllic hideaway, the only hotel in the Bay Area built over the water. Every room faces the bay; 24 of the 30 rooms have balconies. Airy and spacious interiors, awash with soft aquatic blues and misty greens, enhance the sense of serenity. Check out the Vista Suite, a private world of luxury featuring a romantic, king-size canopied bed, wet bar, wood-burning fireplace, and spa tub. Water and views, the best that Sausalito has to offer,

THE CROOKEDEST RAILROAD IN THE WORLD

"It stands in Marin County—or rather it is Marin County; for take away Tamalpais and what is left would hardly fill a wheelbarrow." So wrote Albert Evans, editor of the *San Francisco Daily Alta,* in 1869. Mount Tam (as it's affectionately known), 2,064 feet at its highest peak, and according to Native American legend the sacred center, rises to claim the spiritual heart of Marin.

Early residents of San Francisco, in pursuit of balmy weather and recreational diversions, often enjoyed Sunday outings in Marin. They boarded the ferry at the foot of Market Street, decked out in hats and gloves, for a relaxing ride to Sausalito. From there a connecting narrow-gauge train would take them to Mill Valley, where forests of redwood trees awaited them. But the real goal of many North Bay visitors was Mount Tam. The brave of heart and lung set out on one of the rugged trails, anticipating sweeping vistas of the entire Bay Area from the summit.

And yet there had to be an easier and faster way to reach the top. In 1894 Sidney B. Cushing, who owned the Blithedale resort located just outside Mill Valley, took an interest in what was to become the **Mill Valley and Tamalpais Scenic Railway**. It took a year to complete the broad-gauge railroad. Workers were paid $1.75 for a 10-hour day.

In August 1896, a trainload of hand-waving passengers took off from Mill Valley Station on the inaugural run. A mighty engine pushed the packed cars 8¼ miles, over 22 trestles and around 281 scenic curves. The greatest thrill of all was the "double bowknot," where the track paralleled itself five times within a few hundred feet in order to gain elevation.

Advertisements promoting the **"Crookedest Railroad in the World"** lured tourists from all over the globe to Mill Valley for the thrill of ascending Mount Tam via rail (round-trip fare to and from San Francisco was only $1.90). Another daring engineering feat brought open-air gravity cars to the mountain in 1907. The "gravity man" occupied the front, right-hand seat, where he controlled a set of powerful double brakes with the aid of a huge handle beside him. Passengers could go on to Muir Woods from the summit or take the direct run back to Mill Valley. Either way, hurtling down the mountain at 10 miles an hour was a heart-stopping experience.

Alas, rails were to become another Mount Tam legend. The Great Depression and the advent of automobiles were factors in their demise, but the final blow was a natural force—a wildfire on the mountain in 1929. The "Crookedest Railroad in the World" was relegated to legendary status. **Gravity car # 9** found a home in deeply shaded Old Mill Park, and plans are under way to construct a **Gravity Car Barn** at the East Peak of Mount Tam.

—*Mary Brent Cantarutti*

are always beckoning. Grab the binoculars found in each room and head for the private balconies. Relax, enjoy the comings and goings of ferries, sleek sailboats, and oceangoing vessels. There's plenty to look forward to at this comfortably elegant inn: complimentary wine and cheese at sunset, evening turndown service, overnight shoe shine, morning newspaper delivery, and elaborate continental breakfast delivered to your room upon request. *$$$$; AE, DC, MC, V; no checks; 2-night minimum stay on weekends May–Nov; intide@ix.netcom.com; www.innabove.com; Portal is off Bridgeway—turn toward the water at downtown plaza.* &

Tiburon

Priceless views, waterfront dining, and shopping opportunities make Tiburon a popular destination for explorers arriving via ferry, car, or tour bus. Most folks head for picturesque Main Street and the **VILLAGE ARK ROW SHOPS**. The tiny downtown feels like a movie set, with touches of California Gold Country architecture highlighted against a nautical background.

RESTAURANTS

Guaymas / ★★

5 MAIN ST, TIBURON; 415/436-6300

Mexican food is as elaborate and nuanced as any of the world's great cuisines, with its mixture of indigenous, Spanish, and French flavors (French soldiers occupied Mexico from 1852 to 1857, and the only good that came of it was some new recipes). Guaymas's chef, Raudel Garcia, prepares Mexican classics such as posole, a hearty stew from his native Jalisco, as well as California-inspired variations like the *sopes con pato*—crisp, deep-fried corn shells filled with braised duck, pasilla peppers, onions, and garlic. The piping-hot white-corn tortillas are served with three sauces: a tangy salsa verde; a sweet and tantalizing salsa chipotle with smoked jalapeños, pineapples, and carrots; and a more pedestrian salsa cruda with tomatoes, onions, cilantro, and garlic. For an appetizer try the tender marinated slices of *nopales* (cactus) with onion and Mexican cheese or the pico de gallo, a large plate of fresh fruit served with wedges of lime and a dish of hot red pepper and other seasonings. Once your palate is warmed up, move on to the spicy tamales, the marinated shrimp, or the seafood platter of grilled octopus, squid, shrimp, and salmon. When the weather is favorable, dine on the deck and take in the incredible view of the bay, Angel Island, and the San Francisco skyline as you sip one of the mighty margaritas. *$$$; AE, DC, MC, V; no checks; lunch, dinner every day; full bar; reservations recommended; on Tiburon Harbor at the ferry landing.* &

Sam's Anchor Café / ★★

27 MAIN ST, TIBURON; 415/435-4527

Its another marvelous day in Marin. You want to relax with friends on a sun-drenched deck, enjoy a burger and fries, and relish views of neighboring San Francisco. Head for Sam's and a quintessential Marin experience. This is probably the only restaurant in the Bay Area that promises a refund if a marauding seagull spoils a meal. There's also lots of indoor space if you're looking for peace and quiet. The classic bar is a great spot to eavesdrop, spin your own tale, or ask about Sam, a bootlegger and colorful character. Seafood is a popular choice. Try the house specialty, cioppino, or stay with the tried-and-true oysters on the half shell. Or how about cracked Dungeness crab or a grilled halibut sandwich with pesto on focaccia? Weekend brunches feature eggs Benedict and a longtime favorite, Ramos gin fizzes. Oh yes, don't worry if you're arriving by private boat. There are two floating docks for guests. *$$; AE, DC, DIS, MC, V; no checks; lunch, dinner every day, brunch Sat–Sun; full bar; no reservations for outside seating (reservations recommended for inside dining Sat–Sun); sam@samscafe.com; www.samscafe.com; downtown.* &

Mill Valley

Everything in Mill Valley is either on or near Mount Tamalpais. Today's residents, including a bevy of famous musicians, writers, and actors, wouldn't dream of living anywhere else. The **MILL VALLEY BOOK DEPOT AND CAFE** (87 Throckmorton Ave; 415/383-2665), site of the town's last railway depot, is a favorite spot for locals to meet and greet. Brightly garbed bikers, hikers, and runners headed for the mountain add pops of color. Annual claims to fame include the **DIPSEA**, the oldest cross-country foot race on the West Coast, in June, and the **MILL VALLEY FILM FESTIVAL** in the fall. Seasoned shoppers will be happy to learn that the original Banana Republic still calls Mill Valley home. You never know who will be jamming at **SWEETWATER** (153 Throckmorton Ave; 415/388-2820) or enjoying a soothing massage at **TEA GARDEN SPRINGS** (38 Miller Ave; 415/389-7123). For more information, contact the Mill Valley Chamber of Commerce (85 Throckmorton Ave, Mill Valley, CA 94941; 415/388-9700; www.millvalley.org).

RESTAURANTS

Buckeye Roadhouse / ★★★

15 SHORELINE HWY, MILL VALLEY; 415/331-2600

The decor at the Buckeye Roadhouse combines a reserved elegance with over-the-top Marin kitsch—lofty ceilings, mahogany beams, glass chandeliers and sconces, a massive stone fireplace, a huge stuffed yellowfin tuna, and a moose head. The cuisine, likewise, is both classic and eclectic.

For an appetizer try oysters on the half shell served with a tasty cocktail sauce; Buckeye's memorable Caesar salad; a tangled mound of thin, sweet onion rings cooked in a feathery batter and served with house-made ketchup; or the house-smoked Atlantic salmon. Entrees include barbecued baby back ribs served with coleslaw; smoked Sonoma duck with wild rice and huckleberry sauce; and a sweet, tender, marinated grilled pork chop with to-die-for garlic mashed potatoes. Top off your meal with one of the old-time desserts such as warm gingerbread cake with Meyer lemon curd and whipped cream. *$$$; DC, DIS, MC, V; no checks; lunch Mon–Sat, dinner every day, brunch Sun; full bar; reservations recommended; e-mail@103064.245.com; from Hwy 101 take the Stinson Beach–Mill Valley exit.* &

Piazza D'Angelo

22 MILLER AVE, MILL VALLEY; 415/388-2000

When owners Paolo and Domenico Petrone renovated this restaurant in 1990, Piazza D'Angelo became one of Mill Valley's most popular restaurants—and it still is, with large (often noisy) crowds of Marinites packing the pleasant, airy bar. They don't necessarily come for the food, mind you, but for the charged atmosphere. D'Angelo's Italian menu abounds with familiar though not always well-executed fare, including numerous pasta plates—spaghetti sautéed with kalamata olives, chile pepper, baby spinach, onions, sun-dried tomatoes, white wine, and pecorino cheese is one of the better choices—and several juicy entrees from the rotisserie. The calzone, stuffed with fresh ingredients like ricotta, spinach, caramelized onions, mozzarella, and sausage, come out of the pizza oven puffy and light. Desserts are made fresh daily, and if there's a crème brûlée on the tray, pick that. The extensive wine list features a respectable selection of California and Italian labels (about 150 bottles), including 10 wines poured by the glass. *$$; AE, DC, MC, V; no checks; lunch Mon–Fri, dinner every day, brunch Sat–Sun; full bar; reservations recommended; located on the downtown square.* &

LODGINGS

Mill Valley Inn / ★★★

165 THROCKMORTON AVE, MILL VALLEY; 415/389-6608 OR 800/595-2100

Smack in the heart of trendy Mill Valley, you'll discover towering redwoods and a babbling creek just beyond the small reception area at this European-style inn. Accommodations, all designed with convenience, comfort, and California charm in mind, are secluded and quiet. There are 25 rooms, plus two cottages, each with a private bath, and king- or queen-size bed. Enjoy looking out at your own little redwood grove or indulge in the pleasures of a Zen spa at Tea Garden Springs. A complimentary continental breakfast, along with the morning paper, is served on the flower-filled Sun Terrace. Choose from a delectable assortment of pastries, breads, cereals, and fresh fruits. Would you like a double latte with low-fat milk and a sprinkling of chocolate? Make your request at the espresso bar before you head for the east peak of Mount Tam, test your running skills on the famous Dipsea Trail, or enjoy a picnic at Muir Beach. *$$$; AE, DC, MC, V; no checks; 2-night minimum stay on weekends; mgr@millvalleyinn.com; www.millvall.com; downtown.* &

Mountain Home Inn / ★★

810 PANORAMIC HWY, MILL VALLEY; 415/381-9000
Much has changed at the remote Mountain Home Inn since it opened in 1912 as a Bavarian restaurant, but what has stayed constant through the years is the stunning view. On clear days you can see the Marin hills, San Francisco Bay, the East Bay hills, and even Mount Diablo at the edge of the Central Valley. Perched high above Mill Valley on the side of Mount Tamalpais, the inn now has 10 guest rooms decorated in what might best be described as Marin modern, with plush carpeting and wood-paneled walls. All of the rooms have private baths. The standard rooms have small wooden balconies and a couple have wood-burning fireplaces, but your best bet is one of the three deluxe rooms with a fireplace, deck, king-size bed, and oversize tub with Jacuzzi jets. The New American cuisine served in the dining room is adequate, but you'd be better off bringing a picnic or making the winding 15-minute drive down the mountain to a restaurant in one of the neighboring towns. Mountain Home Inn becomes a madhouse on sunny weekends, when hikers and mountain bikers descend for après-trek drinks and snacks or a late brunch on the deck. A full breakfast is included with your stay. *$$$; AE, MC, V; no checks; innkeeper@mtnhomeinn.com; www.mtnhomeinn.com.* &

Larkspur

Larkspur got its name from the blue flowers that grew on nearby hillsides in the late 1800s. Today white larkspurs are found in the historic downtown village, adorning the blue banners that hang from the old-fashioned lampposts lining **MAGNOLIA AVENUE**. There's lots to discover within four short blocks: boutiques, restaurants, and splashes of European influence.

RESTAURANTS

Left Bank / ★★★

507 MAGNOLIA AVE, LARKSPUR; 415/927-3331
Roland Passot, chef/owner of La Folie (long regarded one of San Francisco's best restaurants), has transformed Larkspur's historic Blue Rock Inn into a fun, vibrant restaurant with a phenomenal French bistro-style menu. Sink your teeth into his leek and onion tart studded with apple-wood-smoked bacon or the roasted duck breast garnished with a sour

cherry sauce, and *le Tour Eiffel* looms. The menu changes seasonally, prompting Passot's happy patrons to return again and again for the latest rendition of his wonderful, traditionally prepared Gallic fare. And you'll love the mood as much as the food. Dine on the covered L-shaped veranda hugging the front of the restaurant and you just might believe you've been transported to Paris (especially if you've given the terrific fruit-infused vodkas a generous taste test). For the grand finale, indulge in the warm tarte Tatin topped with thick caramelized apple slices and a scoop of vanilla-bean ice cream. *$$$; AE, MC, V; no checks; lunch, dinner every day; full bar; reservations required Fri–Sat; at Ward St.* &

Lark Creek Inn / ★★☆

234 MAGNOLIA AVE, LARKSPUR; 415/924-7766

When famed Bay Area chef Bradley Ogden took over the Lark Creek Inn in 1989, he faced the unique task of creating a restaurant around a well-established local landmark. This beautiful century-old two-story Victorian inn, nestled in a stately redwood grove along Lark Creek, demanded a strong presence—and Ogden, fresh from worldwide acclaim at San Francisco's Campton Place, met the challenge. He soon opened what many have considered for years the best restaurant in Marin County; now that Ogden has launched several other Bay Area restaurants, however, Lark Creek has been suffering from his absence and food critics have been stripping the inn of its once-untouchable four-star status. Yet when things are going well in the kitchen, the dishes can still be wildly imaginative and successful, and they are always rooted in Ogden's superb mastery of basic American cooking. For instance, Ogden marries a tender Yankee pot roast with roasted vegetables and horseradish mashed potatoes; he roasts a free-range chicken with a tang of lemon and herbs and serves it with mashed red potatoes; and he grills the thickest, most perfect pork chop and enhances it with sweet braised red cabbage. Instead of potatoes au gratin, you might find root vegetables au gratin. For dessert, a devil's food cake is blessed with chocolate malt ice cream, and the classic strawberry shortcake gets a scoop of cheesecake ice cream for a kick. *$$$$; AE, DC, MC, V; no checks; lunch Mon–Fri, dinner every day, brunch Sun; full bar; reservations recommended; on the N edge of downtown.* &

Chai of Larkspur / ★★☆

25 WARD ST, LARKSPUR; 415/945-7161

Chai of Larkspur, widely recognized as a world-class tea salon, offers much more than dainty open-faced sandwiches and shortbread cookies. Begin your morning with one of the hearty breakfast specials, such as feather-bed eggs or farmhouse cheddar, broccoli, and potato high pie. Leave room for the tempting all-day dining specialties like the tea-marinated chicken and melon salad with gingery mango chutney dressing.

Then there's the international approach to the classic high tea. Try the Mediterranean Medley combo, featuring smoked provolone on a focaccia finger sandwich, roasted eggplant filo "flower," or sliced pear with prosciutto; top it off with a mocha kiss cookie and warm chocolate sandwich with the suggested herb and hibiscus tea. Or sample the hardy Huntsman's High Tea, offering a savory beef and vegetable pasty; crumpet with bacon and cheddar; tea scone with Devonshire cream, lemon curd, and preserves; chocolate meringue cookies; and a warm apple tartlet with chèvre. The appealing setting is transformed into an intimate cabaret ambience at night. As if all this weren't enough, you'll discover a selection of distinctive gift items. Teapot collectors will be in heaven. *$$; MC, V; local checks OK; breakfast, lunch, afternoon or evening teas Sun–Sat; wine and champagne; reservations recommended; www.chaioflarkspur.com; off Magnolia.* &

Emporio Rulli / ★★★

470 MAGNOLIA AVE, LARKSPUR; 415/924-7478

The rich aroma of full-bodied espresso wafts through the air. Gleaming glass display cases, set off by marble and finely polished wood, show off tantalizing Italian delicacies: panettone, gelato, panini, focaccia, marroni, panforte, and biscotti. Imagine Piazza Navona, but hurry to Emporio Rulli in downtown Larkspur. This authentic Italian experience was created by Gary Rulli, who apprenticed under master pastry chefs in Milan and Turin. The Larkspur pasticceria opened in 1989. Greeted with overwhelming success, the pastry shop soon expanded into two neighboring sites and reopened its doors in 1997 as Emporio Rulli—Bar, Pasticceria, Torrefazione, and Emporio. Worldwide sales of Rulli's signature Panettone Milanese, a holiday bread studded with fruit and nuts, skyrocketed after it was featured in the *New York Times*. (Would you believe that 9,000 pounds of the panettone is sold at Emporio Rulli in December?) *$; MC, V; local checks OK; light breakfast, lunch Tues–Sun; wine only; reservations recommended; emprulli@aol.com; www.Rulli.com; downtown Larkspur.* &

Kentfield

RESTAURANTS

Half Day Cafe / ★★

848 COLLEGE AVE, KENTFIELD; 415/459-0291

Breakfast in this beautifully renovated, plant-filled mechanic's garage features a number of first-rate dishes, including fluffy omelets stuffed with a variety of fresh fillings, jumbo orange-currant scones, and fine, dark espresso. The only complaint is that you may have to wait a stomach-growling hour for a table on a busy weekend morning, and even longer if you have your eye on the sunny patio. At lunchtime, the College of Marin's ravenous crowds pack the place for fresh salads, hearty sandwiches, and grilled specials. *$; MC, V; local checks only; breakfast, lunch every day; beer and wine; no reservations; across from the College of Marin.* &

San Anselmo

Most people don't set out for San Anselmo; they pass through it on their way to West Marin, via Sir Francis Drake Boulevard. The smart rows of **ANTIQUE STORES** situated along the boulevard are eye-catching enough, but they're only a preview of downtown attractions. You'll discover a diminutive version of a sophisticated city, a blending of old and new, on **SAN ANSELMO AVENUE**.

RESTAURANTS

Insalata's / ★★☆

120 SIR FRANCIS DRAKE BLVD, SAN ANSELMO; 415/457-7700

In a handsome, mustard-colored building large enough to be a car showroom, chef/owner Heidi Insalata Krahling (formerly of Square One in San Francisco and Butler's in Mill Valley) has chosen to showcase her dazzling Mediterranean fare behind her restaurant's floor-to-ceiling windows. At tables cloaked in white linen, diners bask in the spaciousness while noshing on the seven-vegetable Tunisian *tagine* served on a bed of fluffy couscous or the savory Genovese fish and shellfish stew simmering in a prosciutto broth seasoned with sage. You'll have no problem finding the perfect wine to accompany your meal from Insalata's good list, and don't hesitate to ask the staff for suggestions. Service is quite friendly and attentive, and once you've paid your bill, head to the back of the restaurant where goodies-to-go are sold and pick up a little bag of biscotti studded with plump golden raisins—a great treat for the drive home. *$$$; MC, V; no checks; lunch Mon–Sat, dinner every day, brunch Sun; beer and wine; reservations recommended; www.insalatas.com; at Barber St.* &

Bubba's Diner / ★★

566 SAN ANSELMO AVE, SAN ANSELMO; 415/459-6862

There's nothing on the menu at Bubba's that you probably couldn't make at home, but chances are you just couldn't make it as well. Lark Creek Inn alumna Elizabeth Casey offers classic diner food with decor to match: red Naugahyde booths, a black-and-white tile floor, colorful modern art, a big Bubba's clock, and a daily special board. People stand in line to get a taste of the hearty breakfast offerings, including chunky corned beef hash, honey whole-wheat flapjacks, and eggs prepared however you like 'em with home fries and a big, delicious, freshly baked biscuit. For lunch or dinner choose from a selection of salads, or order from an equally delicious if slightly less health-conscious list of sandwiches, such as the burger slathered with Swiss cheese or the terrific meat-loaf sandwich smothered in barbecue sauce. After 5:30pm you can indulge in chicken-fried steak with red-eye gravy, pot roast and mashed potatoes, crisp fried chicken, and similar fare. And since you've totally blown your diet by now, celebrate your newfound freedom with a real milk shake or malt, tapioca pudding, or a slice of banana-butterscotch pie. *$$; MC, V; no checks; breakfast, lunch, dinner Wed–Mon; beer and wine; reservations recommended for 6 or more; downtown.* &

San Rafael

San Rafael wins the prize for being the oldest, largest, and most culturally diverse city in Marin. **SAN RAFAEL ARCANGEL** (415/454-8141), the second-to-last in the California mission chain, was founded here in 1817. Masses in Haitian and Vietnamese are offered regularly at the mission chapel. Every second weekend in June the **ITALIAN STREET PAINTING FESTIVAL** (415/457-4879; www.youthinarts.org) takes place on Fifth Avenue and A Street in front of the mission. Scores of professional and student artists create chalk reproductions of old masterpieces or vivid original works.

The **MARIN COUNTY CIVIC CENTER** (415/499-6646; www.marin center.org) was the last design on **FRANK LLOYD WRIGHT**'s famous drawing board. Completed in 1969, the center is the seat of county government and has been designated a state and national historical landmark. Its 74-foot golden spire, rising above the azure roof, is a familiar beacon for those traveling north on Highway 101.

Fourth Street coffeehouses, trendy microbreweries, and restaurants with international cuisine offer popular choices night and day. Movie buffs will enjoy the **SAN RAFAEL FILM CENTER** (1118 4th St; 415/454-1222), a vintage art deco theater restored to perfection in 1998. Independent and art films from all over the world are showcased year-round.

RESTAURANTS

The Rice Table / ★★★

1617 4TH ST, SAN RAFAEL; 415/456-1808

Decorated with rattan screens and bright batik tablecloths, this small, popular, dimly lit restaurant offers dozens of wonderfully aromatic Indonesian dishes that are a treat for the soul as well as the palate. The menu here is deliberately simple: there are only 11 entrees. For a real Indonesian feast, order the Rice Table Dinner or the Rice Table Special. All meals begin with shrimp chips served with a trio of distinctly spiced sauces, followed by mint-tinged coleslaw, a raw vegetable salad, and

CHINA CAMP

China Camp State Park, featuring 1,640 acres of natural watershed, is one of Marin's best-kept secrets. Only 4 miles east of downtown San Rafael, a hundred years ago a quaint fishing village thrived on its quiet shores. Most of the residents came from the Kwangtung province of China and brought with them a heritage of fishing methods dating back thousands of years. Their first stop was San Francisco. Good fortune smiled on these hardworking immigrants who carved out a new life doing what they knew best. Business flourished, thanks in part to the Gold Rush frenzy and bounty from the bay (daily catches were as much as 3,000 pounds). By 1852 the enterprising immigrants were peddling fresh fish from door to door, but times were changing. Some resented the success of these first commercial fishermen. In 1860 the state legislature placed a heavy tax on commercial Chinese fishing. The Chinese, eager to avoid the tax collector and discrimination, relocated to Marin. Fishing camps, where residents lived and worked in isolation, soon dotted the shoreline along San Pablo Bay.

By 1887 China Camp had become a prosperous shrimp fishing village. Shrimp caught in the bay were dried and then exported to Hawaii, Japan, and China, where they were used to flavor and garnish traditional Asian dishes. Discarded shells were sold as fertilizer and feed for farm animals. The lucrative shrimp industry supported the community of 3,000 until 1910, when the State of California introduced sea bass into the San Pablo Bay. New regulations forced the Chinese to abandon their trap-nets. Without fishing, the population of the village dwindled. Finally only the well known Quan family remained at China Camp.

Leave it to Hollywood to capture the lovely cove setting and lasting impressions of China Camp on celluloid. *Blood Alley*, starring Lauren Bacall and John Wayne, was filmed there in 1955. Like a deserted movie set, remnants of the past greet visitors today. The old fan mill formerly used to winnow shrimp is displayed in a wooden building, along with a replica of a sampan used by Chinese fishermen and haunting photographs of early settlers.

China Camp State Park also features extensive intertidal, salt marsh, meadow, and oak habitats that are home to a variety of wildlife, including deer and red-tailed hawks. Visitors enjoy camping, hiking, swimming, boating, and windsurfing. Call for additional information (415/388-2070). —*Mary Brent Cantarutti*

lumpia (deep-fried Indonesian spring rolls stuffed with shrimp and pork). Favorite entrees include savory satays cooked with peanut sauce and an assortment of fork-tender curried meats in coconut milk. If you like your fare fiery hot, dip into the wonderful *sambals* (a paste of hot chile peppers mixed with various spices and lime juice), then cool the flames with an icy cold beer. For dessert, treat yourself to deep-fried bananas, accompanied by an Indonesian coffee or the floral jasmine tea. *$$; AE, MC, V; no checks; dinner Wed–Sun; beer and wine; reservations recommended; 4th and G Sts.* &

LODGINGS

Gerstle Park Inn / ★★★★

34 GROVE ST, SAN RAFAEL; 415/721-7611 OR 800/726-7611

One step onto the grounds of this inviting inn, and you'll want to stay, return often, and share the experience with family and friends. Tucked away on a quiet street in the charming old Gerstle Park neighborhood in San Rafael, it's like no other place in Marin—or almost anywhere. The owners, Judy and Jim Dowling, recognized the hidden possibilities when they purchased the run-down property in 1995. It feels like each lovingly restored room, nook, and cranny was created to complement an eclectic collection of family heirlooms, Asian treasures and European antiques. The bold patterned fabrics, worn polished wood, and sparkling glass all blend to please the eye and reflect elegant comfort. Each of the unique 12 suites in the wood-shingled main house has a private bath, individual patio, or deck; four suites have Jacuzzi tubs. The Lodge, or "Honeymoon Suite," comes with a separate parlor, private outside entrance, and double-size Jacuzzi tub with shower. Families and long-term guests might prefer one of the two separate apartments, complete with living room, bedroom, and kitchen. Business travelers especially appreciate the high-tech amenities and the comfortable balance between a full-service hotel and a homelike environment. All guests enjoy the idyllic 1½-acre setting and proximity to beautiful Gerstle Park. A full breakfast is served either in the glassed-in sunporch, outside on the terrace, or in suites. The kitchen, offering snacks and beverages, is open to guests all hours. *$$$; AE, DIS, MC, V; checks OK; innkeeper@gerstleparkinn.com; www. gerstlepark.com; off San Rafael Ave.* &

EAST BAY, SOUTH BAY, AND THE PENINSULA

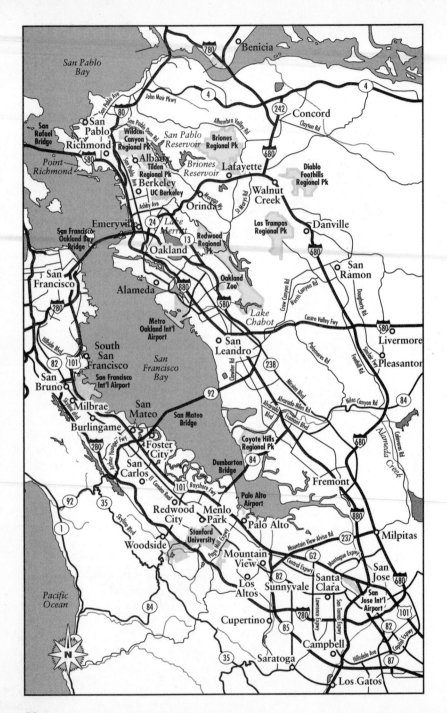

EAST BAY, SOUTH BAY, AND THE PENINSULA

It's been a long time coming, but the Bay Area is finally growing out of the restrictive name "the San Francisco Bay Area." It's as if the once lesser-known municipalities of the Bay Area, like younger siblings paying due respect to an older one, are saying to San Francisco, "Thank you very much for all you've done for us, but we've got our own identities now and would prefer to be called by our own names."

To the south of San Francisco on a verdant stretch of land referred to as the Peninsula, with the Pacific Ocean on one side and a grand bay on the other, lie the posh communities of Burlingame, Redwood City, Woodside, and San Carlos. Posher still, if that's even possible, is Atherton, as well as Menlo Park and most of Palo Alto, situated farther south.

Beyond the Peninsula, capping the bottom tip of the bay, is that massive and sometimes ambiguous stretch of land known as Silicon Valley—perhaps the only instance on earth in which a business moniker has redefined geography. Silicon Valley is a valley, true, but where it stops and starts is as difficult to track as its ever-burgeoning dot-coms. It includes, at present, Santa Clara, Sunnyvale, Mountain View, , and even Saratoga and Los Gatos, but keep an eye on it as it inches its way toward Morgan Hill to the south.

Working your way up the eastern side of the bay, banked by rolling hills, you'll find Milpitas—once the butt of Bay Area jokes because its only claim to fame was a sprawling dump site but now a blossoming residential city rising from the compost of its former reputation. North of Milpitas are Fremont, Newark, Hayward, and San Leandro. Across the bay from San Francisco is Oakland; once considered the bad stepchild of the Bay Area, it's now in the throes of a renaissance. Baby boomers will remember Berkeley, to the north of Oakland, for its legacy of sixties radicalism. Farther north still are Albany, Richmond, Pinole, and the charming Bencia.

East Bay

You've heard the comments about Californians: "Oh, those Californians are weird," or "Oh, those sprout-eating, tree-hugging Californians." When tightly wound outsiders refer to Californians as too "granola" or "woo-woo" or just plain old "touchy-feely," they don't realize they are unwittingly complimenting the East Bay from whence the perception came. There are good reasons for the perception.

First of all, the East Bay is cradled by the San Francisco Bay on one side and a range of beautifully undulating hills on the other—an enviable location for any segment of civilization. Who wouldn't feel a little "organic" living in such surroundings? The East Bay is also home to the largest regional park system in the United States. Founded in the 1930s, the system boasts 59 exquisitely maintained parks and untamed sanctuaries—each a haven for indigenous wildlife and plants as well as the East Bayers who cherish them.

Aside from being a topographical paradise, the region is also known for representing just about every ethnicity and major religion in the world. It's a place where Chinese, Ethiopian, Cambodian, or Brazilian cuisine is readily available; a locale where a mosque and a church can be happy neighbors; where you can hear the exuberant harmonies of a gospel choir on one corner, then cross the street and be mesmerized by chanting coming from an ashram. And, not to refute the rumors, it's a place where words like *karma, chakras, channeling, aromatherapy, reiki,* and *feng shui* are part of everyday mainstream vocabulary.

ACCESS AND INFORMATION

Not all that long ago, Northern Californians would scoff haughtily at the traffic and smog problems that plagued their Southern California neighbors. That is no longer the case. The dot-com-driven influx of people into the Bay Area has turned its freeway and bridge system into a baywide web. On these highways, there are only a few precious hours on a weekday—sometimes even on a weekend—when you actually get up to the speed limit. So if your destination is the East Bay, it's advisable to fly directly into **OAKLAND INTERNATIONAL AIRPORT** rather than its San Francisco or San Jose counterparts. **SHUTTLE SERVICES** such as Door to Door (888/-806-8463) or Bayporter Express (510/864-4000 or 877/467-1800) abound. Taxis are available, though not in unending streams, and charge a flat rate of $30 from the airport to downtown Oakland.

The Bay Area's public transit crown jewel is still Bay Area Rapid Transit, or **BART** (510/465-2278), but even though locals would agree it's in the Bay Area and it's transit, they'd likely take issue with the "rapid" part. Consider yourself warned. Occasional delays aside, it's still a relatively stress-free, quiet way to travel the greater part of the Bay Area. BART has several lines: Fremont/Richmond, Fremont/Daly City, Pleasanton/Daly City, Richmond/Colma, and Pittsburg/Colma. Hours of operation are weekdays 4am–midnight, Saturday 6am–midnight, and Sunday 8am–midnight. **AC TRANSIT** (Alameda/Contra Costa Transit; 510/817-1717 or 800/448-9790) is the bus system covering Alameda and western Contra Costa counties and also provides trans-bay service from those areas to San Francisco. If your travels take you into San Francisco from the East Bay, try slicing the waters of the bay via ferry; it's the most scenic and enjoyable way to get there. Just make sure you wear a jacket, as it's always several degrees colder than on land. The **OAKLAND/ALAMEDA FERRY** (510/522-3300) runs between Alameda, Oakland, and San Francisco on a daily basis, and the **HARBOR BAY MARITIME** (510/769-5500) provides commuter service from Harbor Bay Isle in Alameda to San Francisco.

Unlike its politics, the Bay Area's **WEATHER** is moderate most of the year, but there are several microclimates that vary by a few degrees. The Peninsula, like San Francisco, is generally the coolest because it's closest to the ocean; the East Bay is often two to four degrees warmer; and San Jose can run a couple of degrees warmer still. Savvy residents whose agendas will take them to more than one locale in the course of a day will not leave the house unlayered—ready to strip or cloak themselves at a moment's notice. Of course, the *El Niño* and *La Niña* cycles have made the weather a bit unpredictable over the past few years, but it's still safe to say that in winter and spring you can expect some rain, and summer will be temperate. The real treat comes in early fall, and it goes by the name Indian summer. Then you can expect temperatures to rise as if summer is offering everyone one last hurrah before disappearing into a mellow autumn.

The staff at the office of the **OAKLAND CONVENTION AND VISITORS BUREAU** (510/839-9000; 475 14th St, Ste 120, near Broadway) is cordial and helpful. The **BERKELEY CONVENTION AND VISITORS BUREAU AND FILM COMMISSION** (510/549-7040) is at 2015 Center Street, between Shattuck and Milvia.

Benicia

RESTAURANTS

Camellia Tea Room / ★★

828 1ST ST, BENICIA; 707/746-5293

If you've fallen under the spell of the recent tea trend, but are put off by the formality of the English ritual, you'll appreciate Camellia Tea Room. Located in historic Benicia in a sunflower-yellow Victorian storefront, this minute establishment pays homage to the afternoon tea tradition with a decidedly California-esque nod. The decor is spare in comparison to tearooms in Great Britain but not without beautiful antiques, like the long bar that lines the left side of the room. The ceiling is the eye-catcher—a masterpiece of molding and wallpaper in burgundy, pistachio green, and cream. Even if you didn't tilt your head back to admire it, the sugar rush from the chocolate cookies would induce the movement anyway. At once subtle and shocking, they're part of the lineup called "Traditional Tea," which includes finger sandwiches, scones, wickedly rich Devon cream, and sweets. But of course, the featured act is tea, and the 42-tea menu doesn't disappoint. Aside from the expected Earl Grey and English Breakfast offerings, selections include teas with exotic names

EAST BAY AREA THREE-DAY TOUR

DAY ONE: The historic hills of the East Bay. Check into your room at **Lord Bradley's Inn** in Fremont at the foot of Mission Peak, and start your day with a large continental breakfast. From there, it's just a few feet to Mission San Jose, 14th of the 21 world-famous Spanish missions in California. If you're feeling energetic, you can pack a picnic lunch, hike to the top of Mission Peak, and enjoy a breathtaking view of the Bay Area. If, however, the Mission has whetted your appetite for more history, including the kind you can purchase, drive down Mission Boulevard to Niles. Originally intended to be the moviemaking capital of the world—where Charlie Chaplin was filmed in his early movies—it's now a charming, refurbished enclave of antique shops and restaurants. Stop by the **Nile Fountain and Coffee House** (510/791-6049; 121 I St, Niles), a hip and artsy establishment for refreshments, or Thyme for Tea & Co. for a light lunch and tea. After you've returned to your room and freshened up, walk across the street to **Olive Hyde Art Gallery** (123 Washington Blvd, Fremont; 510/791-4357) and enjoy one of the many rotating exhibits featuring the first-rate work of local artists. For dinner, the best and only choice is **Pearl's Cafe** in Fremont.

DAY TWO: Shop till you drop day. After breakfast at the inn, put on comfortable shoes and drive up to Berkeley's famous **Fourth Street**. There you'll find an array of stores including the Gardener, which features the finest in ethnic antiques, contemporary home decor, and an olfactory delight of a bed and bath department. Other gorgeous boutiques dot the narrow street, including Sur La Table, Summer Store, Garden Home, and Miki's Paper for beautiful handmade papers. There's even an exotic pet store on **Fifth Street**, Vivarium—almost as educational as a trip to the zoo. If you really must buy an iguana, have it shipped. Enjoy lunch at **Bette's Oceanview Diner** but expect a wait and don't expect an ocean view because you won't be anywhere near the ocean. However, if you want to see the bay and distant San Francisco, go to the nearby **Berkeley Marina** for an after-lunch walk. Then, assuming you haven't had your fill of shopping, wander through **Ikea** (510/420-4532; 4400 Shellmound St), located in Emeryville. The Swedish home store opened in April 2000 to a crowd of approximately 15,000 and still attracts throngs of people on a daily basis. Be ready to drag your bag-laden self to your luxurious room at the **Claremont Resort and Spa**. Collapse poolside or schedule an afternoon massage to loosen your limbs. Then, having already made dinner reservations in advance, head over to **Chez Panisse**, the most notoriously divine restaurant in Northern California, for a meal you'll never forget.

DAY THREE: This is park-yourself-someplace day. After a luxurious breakfast and equally luxurious view at Jordan's, located in the Claremont Resort, you're pretty much on your own. The only requirement is that you choose one of the East Bay's 59 regional parks to visit—one cannot visit the East Bay without enjoying the natural beauty that comprises over 91,000 acres of its total mass. Lake Chabot is nestled in the hills and features boating and incredibly scenic walks. Mount Diablo is one of the most bucolic spots and, with its spectacular views, one of the most awe-inspiring. This, after all, is the point from which much of the Bay Area's early survey work was done because it was and is the highest peak for miles. The Diablo Foothills Park, entree to Mount Diablo, has no developed facilities but is perfect for hiking and wildlife watching. If you decide on Diablo, leave for the mountain early.

Tilden Park is thought of as the jewel of the East Bay park system. Some of its many attractions are the Botanic Garden, Lake Anza, and the Herschell Spillman merry-go-round, complete with intricately carved antique horses. Before you head out, pack a picnic lunch of delectables from **Whole Foods Market** (510/649-1333) in Berkeley on Telegraph Avenue. You might also want to pick up a book to read in the sun. To that end, there's no better place to go than **Cody's Books**. After communing with nature, end the day by indulging in a romantic dinner at **Bay Wolf Restaurant** in Oakland and settle in for a night at the Claremont Resort.

like Niligri, Russian Caravan, Gunpowder, and Haiku. If the three-tiered sandwich and cake presentation aren't your cup of tea, consider the reasonably priced, though minimal, lunch menu and follow with a decadent dessert like Chocolate-Orange Cloud Cake. *$$; DC, MC, V; checks OK; lunch, tea service Tues–Sun; champagne only; reservations recommended; near the corner of 1st and Military Sts.* &

Walnut Creek

RESTAURANTS

Lark Creek Cafe / ★★

1360 LOCUST ST, WALNUT CREEK; 925/256-1234
The Walnut Creek branch of the popular Lark Creek Cafe serves the same updated versions of American classics as the San Mateo branch. For a full review, see the Restaurants section of San Mateo. *$$; AE, DIS, MC, V; no checks; brunch Sun, lunch Mon–Sat, dinner every day; full bar; reservations recommended; near Mount Diablo.*

Le Virage / ★★★

2211 N MAIN ST, WALNUT CREEK; 925/933-8484
 Eating at Le Virage is just like dining at a bistro in Paris. Truly. Yes, the exterior is adorned with Lautrec-inspired murals—not especially Walnut Creek in sensibility—but it's the ambience inside that lulls you into

believing you're in the City of Lights. From the hearty handshake—or the kiss on the hand if you're female—you receive from the owner, Lolek Jasinski, to the warm wooden walls carved with Lautrec-ish images, the place exudes the charm of an authentic French restaurant. Jasinski's long and illustrious history as a restaurateur is evident in the classic menu—classic in the most literal sense, as the menu has barely changed in over 30 years. And in that 30 years, Le Virage has earned a list of awards too lengthy to mention. Chefs Gary Boyer and Rick Delamain have delivered consistently for a combined 27 years with appetizers like pâté maison, served with shallot marmalade and port wine reduction, and the ever-popular escargot bourguignonne, baked in plenty of garlic and shallot butter with Pernod. Some of the fantastic entrees you can expect are the canard aux fruits, roast duckling served with either an orange or cherry glaze, or steak au poivre flambé, a New York steak with black peppercorns flamed with brandy at your table. The desserts are equally sumptuous and include champagne-baked Alaska and, of course, crème brûlée. To complement your dinner, an extensive wine list captures the best of Europe and America. The only disappointment you'll experience is when the spell is broken as you leave the restaurant to find yourself on a busy intersection in Walnut Creek, a little too close to a freeway off-ramp, rather than Boulevard Saint-Germain in Paris. *$$$$; AE, DIS, MC, V; no checks; lunch Tues–Fri, dinner Tues–Sat; full bar; reservations recommended; near Pine St.* &

Prima / ★★

1522 N MAIN ST, WALNUT CREEK; 925/935-7780

When Italophiles Michael and Janet Verlander first offered sidewalk dining outside their restaurant on Walnut Creek's tree-lined Main Street, the city had laws against it. City politicos soon wised up, however, so now you can people-watch to your heart's content while savoring chef Peter Chastain's fine repertoire of northern Italian specialties. Start off with a generous hunk of thick rosemary focaccia dipped in olive oil, then move on to a perfectly al dente tagliolini with fresh seafood and house-dried organic tomatoes sautéed in a white wine sauce, or sample the risotto of the day. The grilled double-cut veal chop with a caramelized balsamic vinegar sauce and garlic mashed potatoes is worth waiting the extra 20 minutes for the preparation, and the wine list is encyclopedic—more than 1,500 California, Italian, and French bottles, with several available by the taste or the glass. Some can even be purchased in the adjacent wine shop. In addition to the high-quality, freshly made meals, Prima's patrons are treated to live jazz on the grand piano starting at 6:30pm Tuesday through Saturday. *$$; AE, DIS, MC, V; no checks; lunch Mon–Sat, dinner every day; full bar; reservations recommended; downtown, near Lincoln St.* &

Lafayette

RESTAURANTS

Miraku / ★★

3740 MOUNT DIABLO BLVD, LAFAYETTE; 925/284-5700
Don't let the drab blue-and-white exterior of this Japanese restaurant perched high on a hill fool you: inside there's an elegant, airy dining room lined with sea-blue padded booths and a sushi bar brightened by several large Oriental good luck statues. The sushi and other traditional Japanese dishes are top-notch—whether you indulge in the teriyakis, tempuras, or such specialties as the beef shabu-shabu, thinly sliced prime beef that's cooked tableside with fresh napa cabbage, spinach, bamboo shoots, mushrooms, green onions, tofu, and yam noodles and served with a pair of dipping sauces. A generous selection of combination plates is offered, too. And you can rest assured that no MSG enters any of the authentic cuisine at Miraku (Japanese for "joy of the taste"). *$$; AE, DC, DIS, MC, V; no checks; lunch Mon–Fri, dinner every day; full bar; reservations recommended; next to the Hillside Inn & Suites on the W side of town.*

LODGINGS

Lafayette Park Hotel / ★★

3287 MOUNT DIABLO BLVD, LAFAYETTE; 925/283-3700
Set at the end of a cobblestone drive on a hill on the east side of town, this golden ersatz French château is a briskly efficient operation catering to the booming Contra Costa corporate scene. In keeping with its upscale image, rates are steep for this part of the Bay Area (about $175 to $400). But the 139 rooms—all of which are designated nonsmoking—are suitably commodious. Wood-burning fireplaces and vaulted ceilings adorn the more luxurious rooms and suites. Bathrooms are equipped with Italian granite counters, hair dryers, ironing boards, and telephones (three in every room). An inviting 50-foot heated lap pool, a Jacuzzi, a redwood sauna, and a fitness center are also available to guests 24 hours a day. The hotel's cushy Duck Club Restaurant overlooks the pretty fountain courtyard and offers a small, pricey menu featuring filet mignon, fresh fish, pasta, and the namesake General Lafayette's roasted half duckling. The hotel's Bistro at the Park—reminiscent of an erudite men's club lounge—is a great place for a drink, especially when the weather is cool and you can cozy up to the roaring fireplace. *$$$; AE, DC, DIS, MC, V; checks OK; from Hwy 24, take Pleasant Hill Rd S exit and turn right on Mount Diablo Blvd.*

Danville

RESTAURANTS

Blackhawk Grille / ★★

3540 BLACKHAWK PLAZA CIRCLE, DANVILLE; 510/736-4295

In the exclusive community of Blackhawk, this glamorous, offbeat 7,000-square-foot restaurant is a testament to California's adoration of the automobile. There's almost always a vintage beauty displayed in the middle of the dining room (on loan from the Behring Auto Museum at the other end of the plaza). The Grille's exotic interior glows with brushed stainless steel, copper, and verdigris. Lighting fixtures are stylized hubcap sconces, and the bar is topped with etched glass. There's an eclectic but down-to-earth menu of wood-fired pizzas and satisfying and competently prepared entrees including the pan-seared Alaskan halibut with golden tomato gazpacho, bay shrimp, and sweet peppers. The wine list is vast and focuses on California vintners. Desserts, like everything else about this place, are excessive and fluctuate in quality: try the decadent Blackhawk peanut butter cup with roasted peanut fudge gelato and chocolate ganache or the blackberry-cassis granita with macerated berries and vanilla tuile. *$$$; AE, DC, DIS, MC, V; no checks; lunch Mon–Fri, dinner every day, brunch Sat–Sun; full bar; reservations recommended; from I-680, take Crow Canyon exit, head E on Crow Canyon, drive 7 miles to Camino Tassajara, and bear right to Blackhawk Plaza.* &

Bridges / ★★★

44 CHURCH ST, DANVILLE; 925/820-7200

Japanese businessman Kazuo Sugitani was so happy with the education his son received at Danville's famed Athenian prep school that he wanted to give something back to the town. Blending the best of East and West cuisine, Bridges is a pretty nifty gift. Beautifully landscaped grounds and an inviting outdoor terrace encircle a building that mingles the brown-shingled architectural influence of Morgan and Maybeck with soaring angles and interior spaces reminiscent of 17th-century Kyoto. Executive chef Mark Dantanavatanawong (no, that's not a typo), who took over in 2000, has continued the Bridges tradition of using fresh ingredients and ingenuity to create a wide array of savory dishes. The menu includes a grilled marinated pork tenderloin with a ginger–Fuji apple butter served with a crispy sweet-potato pancake; lemon and chive fettuccine with rock shrimp, wild mushrooms, baby tomatoes, and plum wine; and delicately pan-seared sea scallops with a pink grapefruit–vanilla sauce accompanied by braised greens, Chinese sausage, and garlic rice. The respectable wine list includes an extensive collection of dessert wines to match such sweet delights as the Tahitian vanilla-bean crème brûlée, the lemon-blueberry swirl ice cream with blueberry compote, or the popular go-ahead-and-splurge dessert sampler for two. *$$$; AE, DC, MC, V; no checks; lunch Fri only, dinner every day; full bar; reservations recommended; from I-680, take Diablo Rd exit, go W to Hartz Ave, turn left on Hartz, and drive 2 blocks to Church St.*

San Ramon

RESTAURANTS

Bighorn Grill / ★★

2410 SAN RAMON VALLEY BLVD, SAN RAMON; 925/838-5678

As the name suggests, this pleasant Western-themed restaurant attracts big beef eaters. They come for baby back pork ribs slathered with a watermelon barbecue sauce, meat loaf topped with country gravy and mashed sweet potatoes, and a 14-ounce garlic-roasted Black Angus New York steak, to name just a few of the meaty entrees. Freshly tossed salads and pasta and fish dishes are also on the menu. Designed by popular San Francisco Bay Area restaurateur Pat Kuleto (think Farallon, Kuleto's, and Boulevard), the Bighorn's large, airy, lodgelike dining room has antler chandeliers and horn-shaped hooks on the walls. A bronze bighorn sheep's head hangs over the long bar, where urban cowboys and business execs sip frosty beers or martinis with jalapeño-stuffed olives. Families love the Bighorn, too, and a Just for Kids menu caters to the young buckaroo wannabes. *$$; AE, DC, MC, V; no checks; lunch Mon–Fri, dinner every day; full bar; reservations recommended; near Crow Canyon Rd.* ᕁ

Mudd's Restaurant / ★★

10 BOARDWALK, SAN RAMON; 925/837-9387

Mudd's is about more than just food. The Mudd's experience conveys a sense of community from the minute you arrive. The wooden building exudes a sense of homey warmth, and a cat named Flower often sleeps in a planter box by the front door on a cluster of colorful rugs provided by staff. Beyond the restaurant spread 10 acres of municipal gardens, creeks, and open space. It's from the lush gardens, used as an educational tool for children, that Mudd's draws a third or so of its fruits, vegetables, and herbs. What it doesn't retrieve from the garden, it purchases from local farms. Chef Ron Ottobre is part of the Chefs Collaborative 2000 and is committed to supporting local sustainable food production. Chef de cuisine Josephine Segrave creates preserves, pickles, and relishes from her own organic garden as well as the restaurant's garden. Though the offering changes seasonally, some dependable items include the wine-barrel-smoked Niman Ranch pork chop, buttermilk Oregon russet mashed potatoes with house-canned spiced apples and sun-dried cranberries, or the grilled vegetable and portobello mushroom spinach lasagne. Portions are extremely generous, even by country cooking standards. *$$$; AE, DC, MC, V; no checks; lunch Mon–Fri, dinner every day, brunch Sun; full bar; reservations recommended; just off Crow Canyon Rd and Park Pl, 1 mile W of I-680.* &

Livermore

RESTAURANTS

Wente Vineyards Restaurant / ★★★

5050 ARROYO RD, LIVERMORE; 925/456-2450
The Wente family couldn't have devised a better way to showcase its wines than with this exquisite neo-Spanish colonial restaurant set among the vineyards and rolling hills of the 1,200-acre Wente estate. Chef Kimball Jones's daily-changing menu is a pleasant blend of traditional and experimental, showcasing fresh Hog Island oysters on the half shell served with a sparkling wine mignonette and roasted butternut squash soup with crème fraîche and sage. House-smoked meats and fresh fish are presented with intriguing, tangy sauces and exotic chutneys, and Wente's trademark beef dishes, such as rib-eye steak with a fire-roasted onion and portobello mushroom relish, are delicious. While it's unfortunate that the Wente wines don't usually measure up to the food, the good news is that the restaurant sells other wines, too. *$$$; AE, DC, MC, V; checks OK; lunch Mon–Sat, dinner every day, brunch Sun; wine and wine-based spirits; reservations recommended; follow L St until it turns into Arroyo Rd, about 4 miles S of town.*

Pleasanton

LODGINGS

Evergreen / ★★

9104 LONGVIEW DR, PLEASANTON; 925/426-0901
High in the emerald hills of Pleasanton stands the grand, flower-rimmed Evergreen. A contemporary bed-and-breakfast, this recently renovated two-story cedar house is lined with windows, decks, and skylights so you can see the sky and treetops at nearly every turn. Evergreen offers four comfortable, pretty guest rooms, including the coveted Grand View, with a private outdoor deck overlooking the garden and valley, a huge white-tiled bathroom with a Jacuzzi tub for two, a fireplace, and an antique king-size sleigh bed that overlooks the trees. Breakfast is served on bistro tables in the aptly named sunroom or on the deck, and after the morning repast guests can walk right out the door for a great hike through neighboring Augustin Bernal Park and along panoramic Pleasanton Ridge. *$$;*

AE, MC, V; checks OK; from Hwy 680, take the Bernal Ave exit, turn left on Foothill Rd and drive 1 mile, then turn left on Longview Dr.

Point Richmond

LODGINGS

Hotel Mac / ★★

10 COTTAGE AVE, POINT RICHMOND; 510/235-0010

Who would have thought there'd be a handsome hotel nestled in the quaint village of Point Richmond, a remote hamlet straddling the edge of the city of Richmond? Built in 1911, this imposing three-story, red-brick edifice on the National Register of Historic Places was remodeled in 1995 and now offers seven lovely guest rooms (including two deluxe suites) that cost half as much as what you'd pay for a similar room in San Francisco. Each unit is individually decorated with rich, colorful fabrics and brass light fixtures, and the windows are framed with handsome white plantation shutters. Every room also has a queen- or king-size bed, cable TV with a VCR, a small refrigerator, terry-cloth robes, and a safe for storing valuables; four rooms have gas fireplaces that you can turn on with the flick of a light switch. Colorful stained-glass windows line the Hotel Mac's dining room, where a respectable mix of cuisine—ranging from risotto with Florida rock shrimp to rack of lamb and chicken cordon bleu—is served. But the hotel's highlight is the spacious, high-ceilinged oak and mahogany bar, an ideal place for an apéritif. A continental breakfast is included in the room rate. *$$; AE, MC, V; checks OK; at Washington Ave.*

Albany

RESTAURANTS

Britt-Marie's / ★★

1369 SOLANO AVE, ALBANY; 510/527-1314

As inviting as a pair of favorite slippers, Britt-Marie's offers comfort food from many corners of the globe. Partisans of the Portuguese sandwich—garlic-rubbed toast topped with salt cod and potatoes—would revolt if it were to disappear from the menu, as would avid fans of the cucumbers in garlicky sour cream, the roast chicken with herbs, and the pork schnitzel with buttered noodles. Two Greek restaurateurs took over Britt-Marie's in 1987, six years after its founding, and enhanced a good thing by adding a few native dishes, including an incredible spanakopita as well as a California-style menu to supplement the roster of European classics (the fresh fish and risotto items are especially good). Sweet-toothed patrons can top off their meal with desserts like bourbon-pecan tart or chocolate cake with a thin layer of marzipan tucked under the chocolate frosting. *$$; no credit cards; checks OK; lunch Tues–Sat, dinner Tues–Sun; beer and wine; no reservations; between Ramona and Carmel Sts.* &

Berkeley

The minds of Berkeley's residents are almost audible. Try walking down Telegraph Avenue and looking into the faces of pedestrians. You can almost hear what they're thinking. Some look pensive, nagged, as though they can't get that pestering Nietzsche quote out of their heads; others appear to be in the silent throes of planning activist strategies; while still others look like they're communing with a presence invisible to mundane mortals. You'll conclude that Berkeley hasn't changed all that much since the sixties when it was the earth's axis for social change—things have simply become a bit more introspective.

That's not to say Berkeleyites aren't vocal. In some respects, the action has moved from the campus and People's Park to City Hall. There the town's residents—many of them former hippies, student intellectuals, and peace activists—seek to voice their opinions on issues from Columbus Day (Berkeley celebrates Indigenous People's Day instead) to the opening of a large video store downtown (too lowbrow and tacky). You can also find folks on a street corner, or hovering near a retail establishment's door, passing out flyers and taking petition signatures to defeat the latest unjust bill languishing on the state senate's floor. The *San Francisco Chronicle* recently called Berkeley the "most contentious of cities," and it's a mantle most of its inhabitants either wear with pride or shrug off like an uncomfortable suit.

Don't draw conclusions just yet. Berkeley is dichotomous. It's also known for its overwhelming plethora of fine restaurants, hip boutiques, and the best furniture stores in the Bay Area. Arguably, that could be why its residents often wear looks of consternation or deep concentration—it might be they're trying to justify the coexistence of conspicuous consumption and heightened consciousness in the same city. Or maybe they're trying to decide where to eat.

MAJOR ATTRACTIONS

If you're a newcomer to Berkeley, start your tour of the town at the world-renowned **UC BERKELEY** campus (also known as Cal), the oldest and second-largest of the nine campuses of the UC system. Driving through the university is virtually impossible, so park on a side street and set out on foot. The campus isn't so huge that you'd get hopelessly lost if you wandered around on your own, but without a guide you might miss some of the highlights, such as Sproul Plaza, Sather Gate, and the Hearst Mining Building. So pick up a self-guided walking packet at the

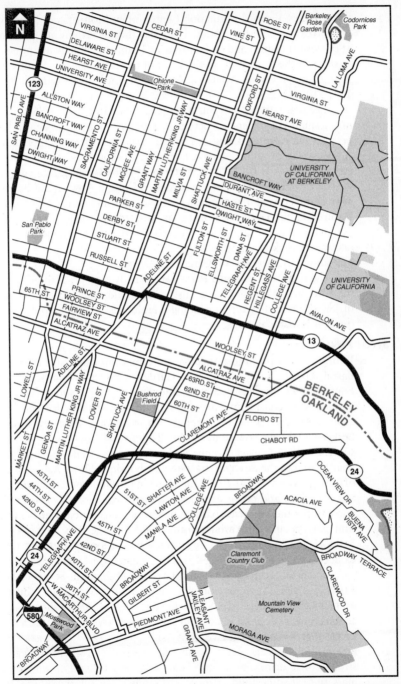

BERKELEY AND NORTH OAKLAND

UC Berkeley Visitor Information Center (open Mon–Fri), or attend one of the free one-hour tours offered Monday through Friday at 10am (meet at the visitor center) and on Saturday at 10am and Sunday at 1pm (meet in front of the Campanile in the heart of the campus); the visitor center is at 2200 University Avenue at Oxford Street, University Hall, Room 101, 510/642-5215 or 510/642-INFO.

The **UNIVERSITY ART MUSEUM** (2626 Bancroft Wy; 510/642-0808) has a small permanent collection of modern art and frequently hosts peculiar but riveting exhibitions by artists such as Robert Mapplethorpe. A vast array of anthropological artifacts is showcased at the **PHOEBE HEARST MUSEUM OF ANTHROPOLOGY** (510/643-7648), located in UC Berkeley's Kroeber Hall, at the corner of College Avenue and Bancroft Way. Hands-on exhibits exploring everything from bats to holograms are featured at the **LAWRENCE HALL OF SCIENCE** (510/642-5133). While you're there, duck outside to hear (and see) the giant, eerie wind chimes and take a peek at the Stonehenge-like solar observatory; located in the hills above UC Berkeley on Centennial Drive.

The **JUDAH L. MAGNES MUSEUM** (2911 Russell St; 510/849-2710), the third-largest Jewish museum in the West, offers numerous exhibitions of Jewish art and culture, including a Holocaust show and a display of modern Jewish paintings.

SHOPPING

With its recent profusion of chichi stores and upscale outlets (Crate & Barrel, Dansk, Sur La Table, the Gardener, Sweet Potatoes, etc.), the Fourth Street area has become a shopping mecca—a somewhat ironic development considering the city's traditional disdain for the bourgeoisie. Another favorite shopping area is in south Berkeley, near the Berkeley/Oakland border, in the small Elmwood neighborhood, which stretches along College Avenue and crosses over Ashby Avenue. Poke your head into the tiny **TAIL OF THE YAK** boutique (2632 Ashby Ave, W of College Ave; 510/841-9891) for a look at the fabulous displays of Central American and other art treasures, then stroll along College, where you can pet the lop-eared baby bunnies and squawk back at the beautiful parrots at **YOUR BASIC BIRD** (2940 College Ave, N of Ashby; 510/841-7617); dip into the huge candy jars at **SWEET DREAMS** (2901 College Ave at Russell; 510/549-1211); munch on fantastic fresh-fruit cheese danish at **NABOLOM BAKERY** (2708 Russell St at College; 510/845-BAKE); shop for clothes at numerous boutiques; and indulge in **BOTT'S** (2975 College Ave, S of Ashby; 510/845-4545) freshly made ice creams. For fresh pasta salads and sandwiches, try **ULTRA LUCCA DELICATESSEN** (2905 College Ave, N of Ashby; 510/849-2701) or **ESPRESSO ROMA** (2960 College Ave at Ashby; 510/644-3773), where you can sip strong coffee drinks, teas, fresh lemonade, beer on tap, or wine by the glass and eat some good calzones and sandwiches. On the other side of

Berkeley, where the northwest border meets the little town of Albany, is **SOLANO AVENUE**, a popular mile-long street lined with shops and cafes frequented by locals.

Most folks around here agree that if you can't find what you want at **CODY'S BOOKS** (2454 Telegraph Ave; 510/845-7872), Berkeley's best bookstore, it probably isn't worth reading. Almost every night, nationally known literary and political writers appear at Cody's and at **BLACK OAK BOOKS** (1491 Shattuck Ave; 510/486-0698), a popular purveyor of new and used books. The four-story **MOE'S BOOKS** (2476 Telegraph Ave; 510/849-2087) specializes in used tomes and remainders. And a **BARNES & NOBLE** megastore (2352 Shattuck Ave; 510/644-0861), complete with a high-tech fountain and park benches for on-the-spot reading, offers discounts on the *New York Times* best-sellers and hardcover books and stocks hundreds of periodicals.

For some of the best bread in the Bay Area, go to Steve Sullivan's famous **ACME BREAD COMPANY** (1601 San Pablo Ave; 510/524-1327) or the **CHEESE BOARD** (1504 Shattuck Ave; 510/549-3183), a collectively owned bakery and vast gourmet cheese shop. If you're a bagel lover, two Berkeley bagel shops rival Brooklyn's best: **NOAH'S BAGELS** (3170 College Ave, 510/654-0944; and 1883 Solano Ave, 510/525-4447) and **BOOGIE WOOGIE BAGEL BOY** (1281 Gilman St; 510/524-3104), formerly Brothers' Bagels.

Like many university towns, this one seems to run on coffee. **PEET'S COFFEE & TEA** (2124 Vine St, 510/841-0564; 2916 Domingo Ave, 510/843-1424; and 1825 Solano Ave, 510/526-9607), with its sizable selection of beans and teas, is the local favorite. For an outdoor latte beneath the trees, try **CAFFÈ STRADA** (2300 College Ave; 510/843-5282) or the hip, crowded, college-hangout **CAFE MILANO** (2522 Bancroft Wy; 510644-3100). **CAFFE MEDITERRANEUM** (2475 Telegraph Ave; 510/549-1128) churns out excellent cappuccinos and captures the bohemian flavor of Telegraph Avenue, still a favorite of students, street people, runaways, hipsters, professors, tarot readers, and street vendors. Or check out the homemade pastries and tasty lunch fare at **CAFÉ INTERMEZZO** (2442 Telegraph Ave; 510/849-4592), another popular Berkeley haunt. Some of the best beer in the Bay Area is brewed at the frat-packed **TRIPLE ROCK BREWERY** (1920 Shattuck Ave; 510/843-2739) and the hipper, more experimental **BISON BREWING COMPANY** (2598 Telegraph Ave; 510/841-7734), which has unusual offerings like honey-basil ale on tap and chocolate stout in magnums, not to mention hearty bistro food. In 1997, the **PYRAMID BREWERY & ALE HOUSE** (901 Gilman St; 510/528-9880) joined the fray with a state-of-the-art brewery and refined pub fare. For something completely different, treat your taste buds to a tour of **TAKARA SAKE USA** (708 Addison St; 510/540-8250), a sake factory that provides tastings of sake and plum wine.

PERFORMING ARTS

MUSIC: The Berkeley Symphony blends new and experimental music with the classics at ZELLERBACH HALL (510/841-2800) on the UC Berkeley campus. Modern rock, funk, and acid jazz are blasted at BLAKE'S (2367 Telegraph Ave; 510/848-0886). For Latin jazz and R&B, visit MR. E'S (2286 Shattuck Ave; 510/848-0260). If you're feeling a bit more mellow, take a seat at the FREIGHT & SALVAGE coffeehouse (1111 Addison St; 510/548-1761), a prime Euro-folkie hangout. In the mood to dance? Drop in at ASHKENAZ (1317 San Pablo, Ave; 510/525-5044). Live rock, jazz, folk, reggae, and other concerts are frequently held at UC Berkeley's intimate, open-air GREEK THEATRE (Gayley Rd off Hearst Ave; 510/642-9988), a particularly pleasant place for sitting beneath the stars and listening to music on warm summer nights. CAL PERFORMANCES (510/642-9988) presents up-and-coming and established artists of all kinds—from the Bulgarian Women's Chorus to superstar mezzo-soprano Cecilia Bartoli; the concerts are held at various sites on the UC Berkeley campus.

THEATER AND FILM: The BERKELEY REPERTORY THEATRE (2025 Addison St; 510/845-4700) has a national reputation for experimental productions of the classics and innovative new works, and the BLACK REPERTORY GROUP (3201 Adeline St; 510/652-2120) offers a range of plays, dance performances, and art by African Americans. Every summer the CALIFORNIA SHAKESPEARE FESTIVAL (100 Gateway Blvd; 510/548-3422) performs in an outdoor theater in the Berkeley hills near Orinda (bundle up 'cause it's usually freezing). Film buffs will appreciate the UC THEATER (2036 University Ave; 510/843-6267), a revivalist movie house where the flicks change every night, and the PACIFIC FILM ARCHIVE (2625 Durant Ave; 510/642-1412), which shows underground avant-garde movies as well as the classics. For up-to-date listings of cultural events, pick up a free copy of *The Express*, the East Bay's alternative weekly, available at cafes and newsstands throughout the area.

PARKS AND GARDENS

For more pastoral diversions, stroll through the BERKELEY ROSE GARDEN (Euclid Ave, between Bay View and Eunice Sts), a terraced park with hundreds of varieties of roses and a great view of San Francisco. Or visit the 30-acre UNIVERSITY OF CALIFORNIA BOTANICAL GARDEN (Strawberry Canyon on Centennial Dr; 510/642-3343), where you'll see a spectacular collection of cacti from around the world, a Mendocino pygmy forest, and a Miocene-era redwood grove. The gigantic TILDEN REGIONAL PARK (off Wildcat Canyon Rd; 510/843-2137), set high in the hills above town, offers miles of hiking trails plus a steam train, a merry-go-round, and a farm and nature area for kids. Tilden also boasts a beautiful BOTANICAL GARDEN (510/841-8732) specializing in California native plants.

RESTAURANTS

Ajanta / ★★

1888 SOLANO AVE, BERKELEY; 510/526-4373

This brightly lit and attractive restaurant was voted the Bay Area's best Indian restaurant in *San Francisco Focus* magazine's readers' poll back in 1996. The dining room is a serene and exotic space, with intricate woodwork, golden fabrics, and graceful reproductions of murals found in India's Ajanta cave temples. The lamb rib chops, *murg ularthu* (boneless chicken simmered in a sauce made with onions, mustard seeds, fennel, garlic, and ginger), and the prawn curry are a few of the standout dishes usually featured. There are always about half a dozen vegetarian dishes to choose from, including the wonderful *baigan ki boorani* (panfried eggplant slices topped with a garlic-lemon-yogurt sauce). *$$; AE, DC, DIS, MC, V; local checks only; lunch, dinner every day; beer and wine; reservations recommended; near the Alameda.*

Bette's Oceanview Diner / ★★

1807-A 4TH ST, BERKELEY; 510/644-3230

The charm of Bette's Oceanview Diner doesn't have anything to do with the ocean (there's not even a view here). What this small, nouveau-'40s diner does have is red booths, chrome stools, a checkerboard tile floor, a hip wait staff, the best jukebox around, and darn good breakfasts. On weekends expect a 45-minute stomach-growling wait but consider the payoff: enormous, soufflé-style pancakes stuffed with pecans and ripe berries, farm-fresh eggs scrambled with prosciutto and Parmesan, outstanding omelets, corned beef hash, and the quintessential huevos rancheros with black beans. If you can't bear the wait, pop into Bette's-to-Go (BTG) next door for a pre-breakfast snack. Later in the day, BTG offers superlative focaccia sandwiches and California pizzas. *$; MC, V; local checks only; breakfast, lunch every day; beer and wine; no reservations; between Virginia St and Hearst Ave.* &

Café Fanny / ★★

1603 SAN PABLO AVE, BERKELEY; 510/524-5447

Alice Waters's diminutive corner cafe can handle fewer than a dozen stand-up customers at once, but that doesn't deter anyone. On sunny Saturday mornings the adjacent parking lot fills with the overflow. Named after Waters's daughter, this popular spot recalls the neighborhood cafes so dear to the French, but Fanny's food is much better. Breakfast on crunchy Café Fanny granola, jam-filled buckwheat crêpes, or perfect soft-boiled eggs served on sourdough toast with a side of house-made jam, and sip a café au lait from a big authentic French handleless bowl. The morning meal is served until 11am and all day on Sunday. For lunch, order one of the seductive sandwiches, such as egg salad on sourdough toast with sun-dried tomatoes and anchovies or the simple but delicious grilled eggplant with olive paste. Many fans combine a visit here with a stop at Fanny's illustrious neighbors: Acme Bread Company on one side and Kermit Lynch Wine Merchant on the other. *$; MC, V; checks OK; breakfast, lunch every day; beer and wine; no reservations; between Cedar and Virginia Sts.*

Café Rouge / ★★

1782 4TH ST, BERKELEY; 510/525-1440

Opened in 1996, this Fourth Street bistro offers everything from duck braised in white wine and smoked trout with frisée and leeks to hot dogs and cheeseburgers. Maybe it all makes a little more sense when one realizes that those aforementioned burgers and franks are the creations of Niman Ranch, so they're the most upscale versions you're likely to have. In fact, chef/owner Marsha McBride, a Zuni Cafe alumnus, insists on high quality in all the ingredients, so it's hard to go wrong with anything on the small but beguiling menu. Her passions are oysters and charcuterie, but there are also creative salads and pastas, great grilled steaks, and juicy spit-roasted chicken. Desserts are absolute knockouts, including a seasonal warm quince bread pudding and a Jonathan apple puff pastry tartlet. Many of the house-smoked charcuterie items are available in the market in the back of the airy, bilevel restaurant, which boasts a long, curved zinc counter, skylights, and gold walls punctuated by red paper wall sconces and modern artwork. *$$$; AE, MC, V; no checks; lunch every day, dinner Tues–Sun; full bar; reservations recommended; between Hearst Ave and Delaware St.*

Cambodiana's / ★★

2156 UNIVERSITY AVE, BERKELEY; 510/843-4630

There aren't many Cambodian restaurants in Cambodia. It took a forward-thinking Assyrian priest—Father Nazarin—to convince the local immigrant community that a Cambodian restaurant could be a hot property. Cambodiana's is the best of the bunch. Owner Sidney Sok Ke and his wife, Carol Bopha Ke, the restaurant's talented chef, have assembled a menu organized around six regional sauces (based on tamarind, ginger, lemongrass, lamb juice, curry, and anchovy), each designed to complement delectable renditions of chicken, salmon, rabbit, lamb, prawns, quail, beef, and trout. Try the deboned quail stuffed with ground pork, shrimp, and garlic or the wonderful grilled lamb chops marinated in a mixture of garlic, lemongrass, galangal, paprika, and soy sauce. The country-style smoky eggplant, roasted and tossed with pork, shrimp, green onion, and garlic, also wins raves. *$$; AE, DC, MC, V; checks OK; lunch Mon–Fri, dinner every day; beer and wine; reservations recommended; between Shattuck Ave and Oxford St.*

Chez Panisse / ★★★★

1517 SHATTUCK AVE, BERKELEY; 510/548-5525

In the heart of Berkeley's gourmet ghetto, the most famous restaurant in Northern California is almost invisible from the street. Good-food lovers know where to find it, though; they just look for the small hand-carved sign in front of the vine-covered fence. Chef/owner Alice Waters has been at the forefront of the California cuisine revolution since 1971, when she started cooking simple French-influenced meals for groups of friends, then opened her legendary restaurant. Chez Panisse is divided into a fantastic (albeit expensive) prix-fixe dining room downstairs and a light-hearted (and more reasonably priced) upstairs cafe. Downstairs, the daily-changing dinner menu might begin with a bowl of olives and warm Acme bread, followed by aromatic, seasonal dishes such as an appetizer of thin-sliced salmon flash-cooked on a hot plate and served with an herbed flower butter, or a smooth corn-and-garlic soup flavored with a subtle touch of leek. An entree of boneless pigeon wrapped and grilled in vine leaves has a lovely smoky quality with a hint of mint and shallots, and a simple but sensational mixed-greens salad cleanses the palate before the appearance of a beautiful kirsch-infused Bavarian pudding. The warm, bustling upstairs cafe has a fine wine bar and seldom enough seats to go around. Its popular pizzas and calzones, baked in a wood-burning oven, often feature ingredients such as squid and roasted onion or simply mozzarella and the finest vine-ripened tomatoes in the state. Desserts include house-made ice creams and sherbets, fruit cobblers, tarts, and pies. *$$$; AE, DC, DIS, MC, V; local checks only; restaurant: dinner Mon–Sat; cafe: lunch, dinner Mon–Sat; beer and wine; reservations required; www.chezpanisse.com; between Cedar and Vine Sts.*

Kirala / ★★

2100 WARD ST, BERKELEY; 510/549-3486

A no-reservations policy often means a long wait at this small restaurant with the down-at-the-heels facade and plain-Jane decor. Expanded in 1999, it features an extensive sake bar—boasting more than 20 premium sakes from Japan—where you can enjoy a light meal. Once you snag a seat in the dining area or sushi bar, however, get ready to taste some of the best Japanese food in town. The sushi is fresh and ready in a flash of a knife, the *gyoza* and other appetizers are first rate, and the skewers of seafood, vegetables, and meats emerging from the robata grill are cooked to perfection and seasoned with a delicate hand. *$$; AE, MC, V; no checks; lunch Tues–Fri, dinner every day; beer and wine; no reservations; near Shattuck Ave.*

Lalime's / ★★

1329 GILMAN ST, BERKELEY; 510/527-9838

It's hard to pass Lalime's at night without stopping to stare at the goings-on through its fishbowl front window: the radiant yellow dining room boasts high ceilings, colorful collages on the walls, and a crush of sleek patrons leaning intimately over candlelit, white-linen-cloaked tables. The menu changes monthly, but if they're serving the soup made with Finn potatoes, golden beets, and ginger, or the roast garlic and shiitake mushroom ravioli, don't hesitate—they're always delicious. Desserts, such as the creamy house-made anise ice cream, mango flan, and chocolate cake with brandied cherries, are equally splendid. Lalime's prix-fixe dinners are often a good bet: one might feature seared spearfish marinated in fresh lime and curry and served with a blood-orange and fennel salad, followed by grilled chicken breast accompanied by crisp polenta triangles and a sweet onion, red pepper, and raisin relish, and, for dessert, a crisp candied pecan tart with a buttery crust. The witty, efficient, and exceptionally knowledgeable staff can direct you to the gems on Lalime's extensive beer and wine list. *$$$; AE, MC, V; dinner every day; beer and wine; reservations recommended; between Neilson and Peralta Sts.*

O Chamé / ★★★

1830 4TH ST, BERKELEY; 510/841-8783

Even jaded Berkeley food fanatics are bewitched by the fare in this exotic restaurant. Chef David Vardy spent years studying Buddhist-Taoist cooking in Taiwan, as well as Kansai and Kaiseki cuisine in Japan. (Kansai is the regional cuisine of Osaka; Kaiseki, created to complement the Japanese tea ceremony, consists of small dishes that can be consumed in a couple of bites.) Vardy developed an ardent local following when he opened the Daruma Teashop in North Berkeley in 1988, serving an intriguing assortment of teas, bento box lunches, and his popular Nambu tea cakes—thin, sesame-based biscuits flavored with nuts or seeds. These and more elaborate works of culinary art may now be found at O Chamé, a soothing cafe crafted in the style of a rustic wayside inn from Japan's Meiji period. The à la carte menu changes often, but typical dishes include a very fresh vinegared wakame seaweed, cucumber, and crab salad; tofu dumplings with burdock and carrot; grilled river eel with endive and chayote; and soba noodles with shiitake mushrooms and daikon sprouts. O Chamé also offers a range of delicately flavored teas and sakes as well as four good beers. *$$; AE, DC, MC, V; no checks; lunch, dinner Mon–Sat; beer and wine; reservations recommended; near Hearst Ave.*

Rivoli / ★★★

1539 SOLANO AVE, BERKELEY; 510/526-2542

Chef Wendy Brucker first came to the attention of East Bay diners in 1992 when she took over the kitchen of the dining room at Berkeley's Shattuck Hotel. That venue was too stiff and formal for her California sensibilities—honed at places such as San Francisco's now-shuttered Square One and the eclectic City Restaurant in L.A.—so she transferred her talents to a much more suitable place: her own, where she could have the freedom to present her relaxed yet refined ideas about California-Mediterranean cuisine. Start your meal with bruschetta topped with goat cheese, sun-dried tomatoes, and basil (a cliché, perhaps, but a wonderfully tasty one) or (definitely not a cliché) the expertly fried portobello mushrooms with arugula and aioli (superb!). Her braised lamb shank with white beans and rosemary aioli (offered in the winter) is the essence of good country cooking. Along with her husband and partner, Roscoe Skipper, Brucker deserves kudos for assembling a tantalizing menu that changes every two weeks and features numerous entrees for under $14; the wine list still offers several good choices under $20. *$$; MC, V; local checks only; dinner every day; beer and wine; reservations recommended; between Peralta Ave and Neilson St.*

Spenger's Fresh Fish Grotto / ★★

1919 4TH ST, BERKELEY; 510/845-7771

Weary of minimalist restaurants with painfully modern furniture, vying for the title "Most Tragically Hip Eating Establishment"? Tired of somber wait staff who look like Banana Republic poster children? Yet you still want great food? Spenger's Fresh Fish Grotto is confirmation that a classic never goes out of style. This unassuming restaurant is situated in Berkeley's famous Fourth Street shopping district and was there long before it was chic—since 1890, actually. The famous have dined there—Robin Williams, Joan Baez, Clark Gable, Spencer Tracy, and Ernest Hemingway, to name a few. The decor is restored rather than renovated and speaks to a seafaring time long gone. The wait staff is equally charming, having been chosen for their knowledge and dedication rather than their looks. But naturally, it's the food in which you're most interested and Spenger's will satisfy you on every level. The menu changes twice daily, based on fresh catch availability, but you can always expect simply prepared seafood with just the right amount of detail. Appetizers include tender fried calamari and stone crab claws with jalapeños, cilantro, and Key lime juice. Main courses may include such wonders as *monchong* blackened with Cajun spices, served with jasmine rice and Thai coconut curry sauce, or mahimahi, pan seared with a macadamia nut crust, served with mashed potatoes and spicy Jamaican hot rum butter. Regardless of what's on the menu for the day, you can be sure it will be fresh and beautifully prepared. After indulging in one of the homemade desserts, stroll on over to check out the proudly displayed Star of Denmark, a 34-carat diamond ring once given to Hawaii's Queen Kapiolani, and ponder the everlasting appeal of yet another classic. *$$$$; AE, MC, V; checks OK; lunch and dinner every day; full bar; reservations recommended; off University Ave.* &

Xanadu / ★★★

700 UNIVERSITY AVE, BERKELEY; 510/548-7880

No, it's not Hacienda de Hong Kong, and no, they don't play mariachi Chinese opera, though you might think that as you drive up and see the Spanish mission–style building you've been told houses some of the best Asian food in the Bay Area. The identity crisis ends as soon as you enter the front door. Swathed in aubergine-colored silk dupioni, this place features Chinese antiques—which are available for purchase—as part of its decor. The overall effect conjures images of dining in a pre-revolution Chinese restaurant in Shanghai—especially when the Amtrak train rumbles past, scant yards from the rear of the building. At first it can all be a bit unnerving, but you'll soon settle in, wishing you were wearing a smart fedora or finger-waves. Head chef Alex Ong, formerly of the Ritz-Carlton and the world-famous Stars, heats things up. For starters, try the Chairman Mao's Liberation Ribs tossed with roasted fennel seeds—so tender the meat nearly falls off the bone with a gentle push of your fork. And so delicious, you'll forget the alarming name. The large plates are for family-style eating. Wok-seared galanaga-spiced beef with crispy yams and watercress salad; Xanadu salt-and-pepper prawns; and crispy fried whole fresh fish with roasted pearl onions, Thai basil, and sambal chile sauce are a few of the exotic dishes featured. The Szechwan Pao-Wok chicken is buried under an angry red mound of chiles and garlic cloves, but don't worry—it's not as spicy as it looks. *$$$; AE, DC, MC, V; no checks; lunch Mon–Fri, dinner every day; full bar; reservations recommended; near 4th St.* &

LODGINGS

The Berkeley City Club / ★

2315 DURANT AVE, BERKELEY; 510/848-7800

Architect Julia Morgan called this lovely edifice with the grand Moorish flourishes her "little castle" (her "big castle" was San Simeon, the crowning achievement of her architectural career). The 1927 building, with its hallways graced by soaring buttresses and its tall lead-paned windows, garden courtyards, and handsome sandstone-colored facade, was designed as a women's club, and Morgan wanted it to rival the poshest male enclave. Today both genders are welcomed through its stately portals, not only as members who enjoy the club's fitness and social activities but as bed-and-breakfast guests. The club's 40 rooms are simply appointed, small, and old-fashioned (if the rooms were as grand as the public areas, this would be a three-star hotel), but all have private baths and many boast views of the bay, the nearby UC campus, or the Berkeley hills. If you need a bit more elbow room, try to book one of the two suites. Overnight guests have access to the club's dining room and fitness facilities, including a 25-yard-long indoor pool that even William Randolph Hearst wouldn't mind taking a dip in. Daily rates include a buffet breakfast; weekly and monthly arrangements are available, too. *$$; MC, V; checks OK; breakfast every day, lunch Mon–Fri, dinner Mon–Tues and Thurs–Sat for members and B&B guests only; full bar; between Dana and Ellsworth Sts.*

The Claremont Resort and Spa / ★★★

41 TUNNEL RD, BERKELEY; 510/843-3000 OR 800/551-7266

With its towers and cupolas gleaming white against the green and golden Berkeley hills, this proud prima donna of a hotel holds fast to its Edwardian roots. It's hard to hurry here: the posh lobby with its plush furniture and alabaster chandeliers is made for loitering and gaping, while the 22 acres of gorgeous grounds—with flower beds, rows of exotic palms, and even a modern sculpture garden—invite leisurely strolling. The only folks scurrying about are those rushing the net on the Claremont's 10 championship tennis courts or feeling the burn in one of the spa's aerobics classes. Amenities include everything you'd expect in a grand hotel, including concierge and room service, a fully equipped business center, and extensive spa facilities. Parking at the resort and transportation to the airports and San Francisco are available for a fee. In addition to the tennis courts, guests have access to fitness classes, beauty treatments, two heated pools, saunas, and a hot tub. Three restaurants grace the premises: the Presto Cafe for coffees, pastries, soups, salads, and sandwiches; the Bayview Cafe, which is located by the pool and serves sandwiches, salads, and grilled fare; and Jordan's, the Claremont's California–Pacific Rim flagship restaurant, which serves breakfast, lunch, and dinner in a casually elegant setting known for its stupendous views. *$$$; AE, DC, DIS, MC, V; checks OK; at the intersection of Ashby and Domingo Aves.*

Rose Garden Inn / ★★

2740 TELEGRAPH AVE, BERKELEY; 510/549-2145

This attractive bed-and-breakfast surrounded by beautifully landscaped lawns started out as a restored Tudor-style mansion furnished with wonderful old furniture and period antiques. Then it swallowed the house next door and added a couple of cottages and a carriage house, giving the Rose Garden Inn's empire enough space for 40 guest rooms. The best rooms are in the Fay House, which has glowing hardwood walls and stunning stained-glass windows. All of the rooms in the Garden and Carriage Houses have fireplaces and overlook the inviting English country garden in back (room 4 in the Carriage House is the best). Of course, the rooms facing away from Telegraph Avenue are the most tranquil. Each guest room has a private bath, a color TV, and a phone; some have balconies and views of San Francisco. *$$; AE, DC, DIS, MC, V; local checks only; between Ward and Stuart Sts.*

Emeryville

This tiny town slivered between Oakland, Berkeley, and the bay was once a dowdy industrial area, but a dozen years of manic redevelopment has turned it into one of the most intriguing urban centers in the Bay Area; computer jockeys, artists, and biotechies now abound here in their live-work spaces. Emeryville's town center is a nouveau ultramall called the **EMERYBAY PUBLIC MARKET**. The center offers great ethnic food stands, stores, a 10-screen cinema, and the hot **KIMBALL'S EAST** (510/658-2555), a jazz and blues club with national headliners; take the Powell Street exit from Interstate 80. Nearby is Emeryville's newest attraction: the Swedish home store **IKEA** (4400 Shellmound; 510/420-4532). You really can't miss it. The bright blue behemoth seems to have engulfed every previously undeveloped lot in town.

RESTAURANTS

Bucci's / ★★

6121 HOLLIS ST, EMERYVILLE; 510/547-4725

Located in a beautifully restored former warehouse, Bucci's is all brick and glass, with soaring ceilings, an open kitchen, and a small patio garden. At lunch biotech execs and multimedia artists nosh on rich focaccia sandwiches and crisp thin-crust pizzas topped with prosciutto, roasted peppers, provolone, mozzarella, and cherry tomatoes. Dinner offers more elaborate fare from a daily-changing menu, which might include a tender roast duck served with a rich butternut-squash risotto or delicate cannelloni stuffed with spinach, walnuts, roasted red peppers, and cheese and served in a lemon cream sauce. The desserts and espressos are topflight, and the full bar specializes in classic cocktails. *$$; MC, V; checks OK; lunch Mon–Fri, dinner Mon–Sat; full bar; reservations recommended; between 59th and 61st Sts.*

Hong Kong East Ocean Seafood Restaurant / ★★★

3199 POWELL ST, EMERYVILLE; 510/655-3388

With its green pagoda-style tile roof topped with writhing gold dragons and its white imperial lions guarding the front door, Hong Kong East Ocean looks more like a temple than a restaurant. Indeed, its worshippers are legion, thanks in large part to its superior dim sum. For the full dim sum treatment, come on the weekend, when the dining room swarms with dozens of carts pushed by Chinese waitresses who have a limited grasp of English, and when most of your fellow diners will be well-heeled Chinese. (During the week, you can order the dim sum from a menu—an efficient but boring departure from the traditional method.) Best bets are the crystal buns (delicate steamed dumplings filled with plump shrimp, chopped water chestnuts, cilantro, and ginger); crisp, baked *bao* (buns) filled with sweet red pork and topped with crunchy sesame seeds; and shrimp embedded in a noodle-dough crêpe served in a savory sauce. Besides dim sum, Hong Kong East Ocean offers authentic and exquisitely prepared Cantonese-style lunches and dinners: try the whole black cod dressed in a satiny soy-ginger-garlic sauce; the addictive, peppery deep-fried squid topped with chopped chiles and scallions; or anything that includes the feathery egg noodles. *$$; AE, MC, V; no checks; lunch, dinner every day; full bar; reservations recommended; at the end of the Emeryville Marina.*

Oakland

There's no question Oakland has gotten a bad and, in many respects, undeserved rap. After all, it was ranked 12th in *Money* magazine's Best Places to Live in the United States and third by the *Wall Street Journal* for fastest-rising real estate prices in the nation. But just ask Oakland residents what they love about their city—where to shop, where to eat—and you'll get a prideful response. They'll likely point you in the direction of charming yet somewhat eccentric **ROCKRIDGE**. They might give you directions to **PIEDMONT AVENUE** or Victorian Row. They'll tell you that if you follow Broadway to the bay, you'll hit Jack London Square. They may even let you know which neighborhoods boast some of the most amazing historic architecture in the Bay Area, or that the view from the Mormon Temple can't be bested. What they probably won't do is "dis" their city—Oaktown, as it is sometimes affectionately called.

With a resident celebrity list as diverse as its culture—Gertrude Stein, Maya Angelou, Bruce Lee, R & B group En Vogue, Amy Tan, and of course, Jack London, all of whom either called Oakland home or were born there—this city seems to have something about it that fosters self-expression. Even Mayor Jerry Brown—yes, the former California governor—has recognized the creative spirit that seems to run through the city's veins. He's declared promotion of the arts part and parcel of a city-wide renaissance and made it one of his primary focuses for his term in office.

In *Oakland: Story of a City* by Beth Bagwell, an anonymous Oaklander captured the mystique of the city best: "Oakland now is like a great old blues singer. She knows how to moan and cry, but the bad times behind her make her know how to savor the good times. The old-time Oaklanders, and the port, and the big corporations building new skyscrapers downtown are like instruments in a band, and all together now we're blowing some pretty good jazz."

MAJOR ATTRACTIONS

Oakland's premier tourist destination is **JACK LONDON SQUARE**, a sophisticated seaside spread of boutiques, bookstores, restaurants, hotels, cinemas, and saloons that is refreshingly void of the touristy schlock that pervades San Francisco's Pier 39. Must-see stops along the promenade include **HEINOLD'S FIRST AND LAST CHANCE SALOON** (56 Jack London Sq; 510/839-6761), a decidedly funky little bar crammed with faded seafaring souvenirs, and the recently overhauled **USS POTOMAC** (510/839-8256), the 165-foot presidential yacht that served as FDR's "floating White House."

The sunken building that holds the **OAKLAND MUSEUM** (1000 Oak St, between 10th and 12th Sts; 510/238-3401), a spectacular specimen of modern architecture designed by Kevin Roche in 1969, features innovative displays of the art, history, and ecology of California and also boasts beautiful terraced gardens.

Tots will get a kick out of **LAKE MERRITT'S CHILDREN'S FAIRYLAND** (off Grand Ave; 510/452-2259), a kid-size amusement park that supposedly inspired Walt Disney to construct Disneyland. Kids will also thrill to the beasts at the **OAKLAND ZOO** (9777 Golf Links Rd; 510/632-9525).

SHOPPING

In genteel North Oakland, the Rockridge neighborhood running along College Avenue boasts numerous bookstores, cafes, antique stores, expensive clothing boutiques, and a gourmet's paradise that rivals North Berkeley. Stroll through the **ROCKRIDGE MARKET HALL** (5655 College Ave at Shafter Ave, across from the Rockridge BART station; 510/655-7748), a chic multivendor market offering fresh pastas, gourmet cheeses, chocolates, fresh-cut flowers, delicious deli sandwiches and salads, breads from the great Grace Baking Company, exquisite produce, and a wide selection of wine. Grittier but just as interesting is downtown Oakland's **CHINATOWN** (tour the area between 7th and 10th Sts and Broadway and Harrison), which is not as congested (with cars or tourists) as San Francisco's Chinatown. An assortment of Mexican bakeries and taquerias tempt passersby along E 14th Street, between 2nd and 13th Avenues. The **PACIFIC COAST BREWING COMPANY** (906 Washington St; 510/836-2739) offers a lively bar scene and good microbrews. On the other side of town are your best bets for books and coffee near Oakland's downtown: **WALDEN POND BOOKS** (3316 Grand Ave; 510/832-4438) and the **COFFEE MILL** (3363 Grand Ave; 510/465-4224).

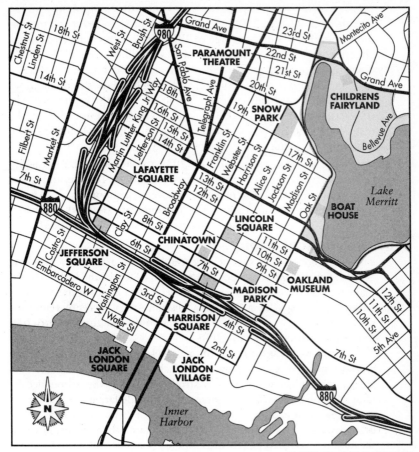

DOWNTOWN OAKLAND

PERFORMING ARTS

MUSIC: The highly regarded **OAKLAND SYMPHONY** (2025 Broadway; 510/444-0801) offers classical and choral concerts at the Paramount Theatre and the **CALVIN SIMMONS THEATER** (10 10th Street; call 510/238-7765 for symphony schedules). You can catch the hottest jazz in town at **YOSHI'S** (510 Embarcadero W; 510/238-9200; see review, below), the bluest blues at **ELI'S MILE HIGH CLUB** (3626 Martin Luther King Jr. Wy; 510/655-6661), and a little of both at the **FIFTH AMENDMENT** (3255 Lake Shore Ave; 510/832-3242). Gospel acts abound in the East Bay, but often they're hard to find; try calling **REID'S RECORDS** in Berkeley (510/843-7282), which has a bulletin board where folks post the latest local musical events.

THEATER AND FILM: Downtown's **PARAMOUNT THEATRE** (2025 Broadway at 21st St; 510/893-2300), a restored architectural masterpiece built in 1931 and restored in 1973, offers everything from organ concerts and rock concerts to plays and films from Hollywood's Golden Age. Guided tours of the 3,000-seat theater are given the first and third Saturday of each month, excluding holidays. No reservations are necessary—just show up at 10am at the box office entrance. The **GRAND LAKE THEATRE** (3200 Grand Ave; 510/452-3556), a beautifully restored Egypto-Deco movie palace, shows new films, which are kicked off on the weekends by a live organist's dazzling performance.

DANCE: The **OAKLAND BALLET** (2025 Broadway; 510/465-6400) jumps and twirls at the beautiful art deco Paramount Theatre, and at various Oakland venues dozens of innovative contemporary and African dance troupes kick up their heels, including **DIMENSIONS** (510/465-3363) and the **FUADIA CONGO DANCE COMPANY** (510/562-0831).

SPORTS AND RECREATION

Those hotshot boys of summer, the Oakland A's, are usually knocking 'em dead at the **OAKLAND COLISEUM** (from I-80 take the Coliseum exit or, better yet, avoid the freeway crawl by taking a BART train; 510/638-0500). And the sparkling Oakland Coliseum Arena—recently renovated to the tune of $102 million—is the home of the tall guys: the **GOLDEN STATE WARRIORS** (510/986-2200).

Pretty **LAKE MERRITT**, one of the largest saltwater tidal lakes in the world, is home to flocks of migrating ducks, geese, and herons and provides a great place for a leisurely stroll or jog; the lake is bounded by Grand Avenue, Lake Shore Avenue, and Lakeside Drive. For fun on the water, rent a sailboat, rowboat, paddleboat, or canoe at the lake's **SAILBOAT HOUSE** (510/444-3807). For the ultimate urban escape, head for the hills to **REDWOOD REGIONAL PARK** (off Joaquin Miller Rd; 510/635-0135), where miles of fern-trimmed trails wind through redwood groves and oak woodlands.

RESTAURANTS

Asmara Restaurant and Bar / ★

5020 TELEGRAPH AVE, OAKLAND; 510/547-5100

Asmara has a split personality: the comfortable restaurant is full of East African kitsch, while the adjacent bar—stark white and brightly lit—is a sterile jolt to the senses. Eritrean expatriates seem to prefer the bar, while locals enjoy the restaurant's African decor. Both groups, however, often get caught up in the communal spirit of the place, sharing their meals with fellow diners and using pieces of spongy injera bread to scoop up tasty *ziggni* (beef marinated in a surprisingly mild berbere sauce made with jalapeño and other chile peppers) and *yegomen alicha* (mustard greens simmered with spices). Make the most of this culinary adventure

THE CALL OF THE NOT-SO-WILD

Jack London Square is like a luxury SUV or a sailor in drag: gussied up, baubled, and bangled, when what it really wants to do is to load cargo. Beneath its tartish paint job lies the tattooed soul of a salty dog.

Back in the 1800s, when Oakland was little more than a township, the area at the end of Broadway was singled out to become a port that would rival—even surpass—the port of San Francisco; there was money to be made in the estuary muck. Soon docks sprang up, whaling ships lurched into Oakland, riverboats churned the water, and the locale gained a reputation as a rough and rowdy seafarer's gathering spot.

Nowadays there are a few places in Jack London Square where its beard stubble pokes through the blush. A ride on the Jack London Square Water Taxi or the Alameda/Oakland Ferry will take you past the real guts of the area: **the docks**. They were the places where, during the forties, scores of women lent their hands to the wartime effort and where massive shipments from far-off lands are received to this day. A walk through the nearby produce district will reveal the grittier side of the area—the raw inner workings of a diminished though still vibrant industry. Heinhold's First & Last Chance Saloon still stands; this is the bar where a young Jack London sold newspapers from a barstool and bent his ear to sailors' woolly tales.

It may not look as wild as it once was, thanks to the industrious efforts of makeup artist developers, but explore—answer the call, pull back the wig—and you'll find a weathered mariner, ready to hum a sea shanty.　　　　—*Brian Tacang*

by getting one of the combination dinners. *$; MC, V; no checks; lunch, dinner every day; full bar; reservations recommended; at 51st St.*

Bay Wolf Restaurant / ★★★
3853 PIEDMONT AVE, OAKLAND; 510/655-6004

Located in an attractive Victorian house with dark wood wainscoting and pale yellow walls, the Bay Wolf first became a local favorite under the direction of co-owner and executive chef Michael Wild. Don't look for bizarre flights of food fancy here; fresh ingredients and careful preparation take the place of culinary acrobatics. Typical first courses might include a spiced scallop and endive salad or a rich, smoky asparagus and hazelnut soup with lemon cream. Main courses vary from tender braised lamb shanks with white beans, artichokes, and rosemary to a flavorful seafood stew bubbling with cracked Dungeness crab, prawns, rockfish, and mussels. For dessert indulge in the sweetly spiced peach pie topped with a scoop of house-made cinnamon ice cream, or the chocolate-topped profiteroles stuffed with white moons of freshly made almond ice cream. The extensive, well-chosen wine list offers a number of moderately priced vintages. Service is efficient but a little stiff in the evening; the staff loosens up during the day. *$$$$; AE, MC, V; checks OK; lunch Mon–Fri, dinner every day; beer and wine; reservations recommended; between 40th St and MacArthur Blvd.*

Caffe 817 / ★★

817 WASHINGTON ST, OAKLAND; 510/271-7965

Visit the downtown Oakland farmers market on Friday morning, then rest your weary bag-laden arms at Caffe 817. This tiny restaurant bears the stamp of its design-conscious owner, Alessandro Rossi, an electrical engineer who saw potential in this high-ceilinged space and hired local craftspeople to fashion its avant-garde furnishings. Despite its lofty decor, the cafe has modest ambitions: cappuccino and pastries are mainstays in the morning, and Italian sandwiches, simple salads, and fresh soups and stews are on the midday menu. The sandwich fillings are what you might call contemporary Italian-American: roast beef with arugula, grilled mozzarella with artichokes, prosciutto with herb butter and pears. But the rice-and-borlotti-bean soup is a classic Tuscan dish. If all this good fare inspires you to make your own Italian classics at home, head next door to G. B. Ratto International Grocers, a favorite East Bay source for arborio rice, olive oil, beans, and other imported foodstuffs. *$; no credit cards; checks OK; breakfast, lunch Mon–Fri; beer and wine; no reservations; between 8th and 9th Sts.*

Citron / ★★★

5484 COLLEGE AVE, OAKLAND; 510/653-5484

An immediate hit when it opened in 1992, Citron has settled in for the long run. The intimate dining room, which, true to its French name, is bathed in soothing shades of lemon yellow, sets the stage for chef Chris Rossi's equally small menu of contemporary French-Mediterranean fare. Rossi's menu changes every two weeks. Recent appetizers included a roasted squash soup with apples and curry as well as a ceviche of rock shrimp with avocado and mango. One taste of the chicken with 40 garlic cloves and you'll think you've been transported to Provence. Then again, if it's Italian fare you're craving, look for Rossi's wild mushroom cannelloni with chanterelles, ricotta, and Swiss chard, or the lamb osso buco served on a bed of flageolet-bean and sun-dried tomato ragout with a sprinkling of pistachio gremolata garnish. Go Rossi! *$$; AE, DC, DIS, MC, V; local checks only; dinner every day; beer and wine; reservations recommended; between Taft and Lawton Sts.*

Jade Villa / ★★

800 BROADWAY, OAKLAND; 510/839-1688

Ever since Lantern restaurant closed, the title of Oakland's top dim sum house has been transferred to Jade Villa, a behemoth of a restaurant that takes up nearly a quarter block in Oakland's Chinatown. During the lunch hour the place is packed with Chinese families sitting at large, round tables. The ornate dining room offers a tempting array of dinners, but the real reason you should come here is for the dim sum, served from early morning to midafternoon. Sip a cup of aromatic tea as servers circulate through the room pushing carts laden with assorted delicacies. They'll pause by your table and lift the lids of tiered metal steamers to let you inspect the barbecued pork buns, stuffed dumplings, wedges of green pepper filled with shrimp, and lots of other tasty treats. Hold out for at least one order of the steamed prawns-in-shell, the best dish. You'll be charged by the plate, and you can afford to experiment here—two people can eat with abandon for about 20 bucks. *$$; MC, V; no checks; lunch, dinner every day; beer and wine; reservations recommended; at 8th St.*

Jojo / ★★★

3859 PIEDMONT AVE, OAKLAND; 510/985-3003

Any restaurant daring enough to set up shop next to Bay Wolf had better have some sturdy culinary legs to stand on—and like a farm-bred, French country milkmaid, Jojo has just the gams for the task. With its light Dijon mustard–colored walls, sage green wainscoting, and olive with black filigree chiffon curtains, it's a statement in subtlety. The menu is—you guessed it—French country. And, thankfully, it's not so pretentious as to be printed in French. The simple yet well-developed fare changes every three days or so and includes starters like warm crab-and-goat-cheese tart and seared scallops with calvados and apple, as well as wonderful entrees such as braised chicken with mushrooms and brandy sauce or grilled tuna with fennel-olive salad. For dessert, one simply must indulge in the chocolate soufflé cake with espresso crème anglaise and candied walnuts. Only eight months into their venture, co-owners and chefs Maryjo Thorsten and Kurt Coingman garnered *San Francisco* magazine's title of Best New Restaurant for Jojo. Aside from the food, the one other attribute Jojo shares with France is the way the wait staff glides across the room with immovable plaster-of-Paris expressions. Get one of them to crack a smile and your evening will be complete. *$$$; AE, DC, MC, V; no checks; dinner only Tues–Sat; beer and wine; reservations recommended; between 40th St and MacArthur Blvd.* &

Le Cheval / ★★

1007 CLAY ST, OAKLAND; 510/763-8957

With everyone in the restaurant shouting to be heard, the din in Le Cheval is impossible to ignore. The egg-carton acoustic material on the ceiling doesn't help since it's about three miles away from the dining room floor—it's like trying to sound-dampen a stadium with velvet curtains. Nevertheless, people still flock to Le Cheval in hoards for the best Vietnamese food in the Bay Area—a title bestowed upon it by *Bay Area*

Express newspaper. The menu is mind-bogglingly long, the seasonings are exotic, and the family-style portions are beyond generous. You could really pick just about anything off the menu and experience gastronomic euphoria, but be sure to sample some of the range of appetizers, which includes imperial rolls, roast quail, marinated beef in lemon, or "bun"— similar to imperial rolls but of the do-it-yourself variety. Whatever you choose from the main course menu—whether prawns stewed in a clay pot or chicken with bamboo shoots—you'll be so content it won't matter that you can't hear yourself chew. *$$; AE, MC, V; no checks; lunch, dinner every day; full bar; reservations recommended; near 10th St.* &

Mama's Royal Cafe / ★

4012 BROADWAY, OAKLAND; 510/547-7600

Die-hard regulars don't even question the 40- to 60-minute wait required on weekends to get a seat at this 20-year-old Oakland landmark known simply as Mama's. A combination of good food served in large portions and a schizo decor (picture a '40s-style diner/noodle house with pagoda door frames and Rosie-the-Riveter-era ads on Formica tabletops) attracts the bohemian/boomer crowd in Doc Martens and Tevas for some of the heartiest breakfasts in the East Bay. Unfortunately, the prices are kinda expensive, the service is suhloooow (leave the antsy kids at home), and the waiters sometimes serve up a little attitude with your home fries. But who cares when the menu includes 31 types of omelets and such breakfast specials as fresh fruit crêpes and burritos with chipotle tortillas? Of course, a place like this has to have its own lingo—"cowboy with spurs" is the name for a western omelet with fries, and "wax" is sliced American cheese—as well as a legend. Rumors abound of a ghost who haunts the third dining room, which purportedly was once a barbershop where a local mobster was cut down midshave. *$; cash only; breakfast, lunch every day; beer and wine; no reservations; at 40th St.* &

Nan Yang Rockridge / ★★

6048 COLLEGE AVE, OAKLAND; 510/655-3298

When Nan Yang opened in 1983, restaurants offering a full spectrum of Burmese delights were virtually nonexistent. Chef/owner Philip Chu assembled the menu for Nan Yang by tracking down recipes from monasteries, street vendors, festival food booths, and family homes to create the first Burmese restaurant in the Bay Area. His noble efforts have been rewarded with rave reviews and long lines of customers clamoring for his fare—especially his ginger salad, a crunchy, textural delight with 16 ingredients including split peas, fava beans, shredded cabbage, coconut slices, sun-dried shrimp, garlic oil, roasted peanuts, and shredded ginger. The generous curry dishes come with giant chunks of beef, chicken, or fish; there are also plenty of seductive vegetarian variations. On sunny days opt for a table on the front patio. *$$; MC, V; no* *checks; lunch, dinner Tues–Sun; beer and wine; reservations recommended; just S of Claremont Ave.*

Oliveto Cafe and Restaurant / ★★★

5655 COLLEGE AVE, OAKLAND; 510/547-5356

Oliveto has always been a top East Bay destination, thanks in part to chef Mike Tusk's and chef/owner Paul Bertolli's obvious passion for the Italian table and careful interpretations of Italy's rustic cuisine. Trimmed with granite, olive-wood, and custom ironwork, the restaurant has the air of a Florentine trattoria, and the well-dressed, well-heeled stockbroker-and-filmmaker crowd cements the impression. House specialties include the fresh fish dishes, such as petrale sole piccata served on a bed of sautéed spinach and topped with a caper, white wine, and butter sauce. Meats from the wood-fired rotisserie and grill range from Watson Farm lamb to the house-made pork sausage and grilled rabbit. Downstairs, the more casual cafe draws a crowd of commuters (a BART station is across the street) and neighbors from morning till night. You'll see tense-but-chic workaholic singles sizing each other up over small, crisp pizzas and sophisticated salads like the panzanella with cherry tomatoes and fresh mozzarella. A wood-burning oven rotisserie and high-end liquor cabinet (i.e., hard alcohol and a few mixed drinks) only add to Oliveto's popularity. *$$; AE, DC, MC, V; no checks; cafe: light breakfast, lunch, dinner every day; restaurant: lunch, dinner every day; beer and wine; reservations recommended; at Shafter Ave, across from the Rockridge BART station.*

Pho Anh Dao / ★

280 E 18TH ST, OAKLAND; 510/836-1566

Essentially a one-dish restaurant, Pho Anh Dao specializes in pho, the Hanoi anise-scented beef and noodle soup that many Vietnamese eat almost every day. This aromatic meal-in-a-bowl has everything in its favor: it's cheap (less than $4), delicious, plentiful, and healthful. The essential garnishes arrive on the side: Asian basil, sliced green chiles, a lime or lemon wedge, and bean sprouts. Add as much of them as you like and then, with chopsticks in one hand and a soup spoon in the other, dive in. Pho aficionados ask for raw beef so they can "cook" it in the hot broth a slice at a time. Good pho takes hours to make, and Pho Anh Dao does it right. *$; cash only; breakfast, lunch, dinner every day; beer only; no reservations; between 2nd and 3rd Aves.*

Pizza Rustica / ★

5422 COLLEGE AVE, OAKLAND; 510/654-1601

Housed in a salmon-colored postmodern building with blue Corinthian columns, this jazzy nouveau pizza joint has a cramped, noisy dining room with tiny, knee-bruising tables, bright pop art on the walls, and California pizzas made with a light, crunchy cornmeal crust or a traditional peasant-bread crust. The traditional Mediterranean-style pizzas are impeccable, but pizza adventurers should try one of the more exotic offerings: the Thai pizza is prepared with roasted chicken in a spicy ginger and peanut sauce, mozzarella, julienned carrots, scallions, daikon, peppers, and sesame seeds; and the Ambrosia features sun-dried tomatoes, artichoke hearts, roasted garlic, kalamata olives, and a mix of fontina, mozzarella, and Parmesan cheeses. *$; MC, V; local checks only; lunch, dinner every day; beer and wine; no reservations; between Kales and Manila Sts.*

Soizic Bistro-Cafe / ★★★

300 BROADWAY, OAKLAND; 510/251-8100

Just two blocks from Jack London Square in the produce and fishmonger districts, this handsome converted warehouse with 18-foot ceilings and a second-floor loft dining room is owned and operated by Hisuk and Sanju Dong, former owners of the now-closed (but it was wonderful) Cafe Pastoral in Berkeley. Hisuk is an architect, and Sanju is a painter and the head chef. They've created a Paris salon straight out of *The Moderns,* with warm, golden colors and rich details. Named after a French friend of the owners, Soizic (SWA-zik) offers a wonderful mix of Mediterranean-style cuisine: a terrific eggplant entree is layered with sun-dried tomatoes, goat cheese, and mushrooms and is served on a bed of polenta topped with a balsamic-kissed tomato sauce; tender smoked-chicken sandwiches are dressed with sun-dried tomatoes, watercress aioli, and spinach; and a hefty bowl of fresh New Zealand mussels is served steaming in a savory saffron broth with diced tomatoes. The fare is quite memorable and reasonably priced, too. Celebrate the occasion with the bistro's legendary dessert: a creamy ginger custard. *$$$; MC, V; local checks only; lunch Tues–Fri, dinner Wed–Sun; beer and wine; reservations recommended; near Jack London Sq.*

Spettro / ★★

3355 LAKESHORE AVE, OAKLAND; 510/465-8320

Would you consider it creepy to savor pasta and pizza amid the dearly departed? Well, welcome to Spettro (Italian for "spirit"). This restaurant's otherworldly theme is a bit unsettling at first (a skeleton, cigarette in hand, graces the entrance, warning patrons not to light up, and there is an assortment of macabre gravestone photography nearby), but your appetite will return once you get a whiff of the dishes being concocted in the kitchen. Run by the owners of the defunct Topless Pizza, Spettro has given rebirth to some of Topless's pies and added some Cajun and Brazilian dishes for variety, such as red beans and rice, smoked chicken and oyster gumbo, and Brazilian feijoada with black beans and linguiça on a bed of rice. But why the dead theme, you ask? Two of the owners, children of an anthropologist, used to get their kicks as tykes tracing gravestones. Whatever. The chatty staff is very much alive, and since the wait for a table can be as long as an hour on the weekend (reservations are not available), they will ply you with cider and wine to raise your own spirits. *$$; AE, DC, DIS, MC, V; no checks; dinner every day; beer and wine; no reservations; at Trestle Glen St.*

Tsing Tao / ★

200 BROADWAY, OAKLAND; 510/465-8811

A favorite Sunday-night destination for local Chinese-American families, Tsing Tao delivers high-quality Cantonese cooking. Avoid the standard dishes that seem aimed mostly at non-Chinese, and ask about the chef's specials of the day—that's where you'll find the good (i.e., authentic) stuff. For the Chinese equivalent of Mom's meat loaf, try the steamed pork patty flavored with heavily salted fish and pair it with the tender mustard-green hearts glazed with a rich broth. Another winning combo: stir-fried crab with scallions and ginger (ask the price first—it can be high here) and stir-fried baby pea shoots, a springtime delicacy. The fish tanks sometimes hold live sturgeon, a bony fish the kitchen subjects to a two-part preparation: the bones and head are turned into a milky broth, and the fillets are steamed. *$$; AE, MC, V; no checks; lunch, dinner every day; full bar; reservations recommended; at 2nd St.*

Yoshi's / ★★★

510 EMBARCADERO W, OAKLAND; 510/238-9200

Business at this jazz-club-cum-Japanese-restaurant—once a premier destination for live jazz on the West Coast—hit a sour note in the early '90s, and the owners were ready to permanently close its doors. Then along came the City of Oakland to the rescue. Fronting a sizable chunk of the $5.1 million construction bill, the Oakland Redevelopment Agency and the Port of Oakland lured Yoshi's from its humble though pleasant Rockridge neighborhood to a glitzy new spread at Jack London Square. Architect Hiroshi Morimoto has fused traditional Japanese materials and elements with a sleek, modern design, and the results are fantastic. Equal attention was paid to the separate 300-seat amphitheater, a semicircular room equipped with a state-of-the-art sound system—there's nary a bad seat in the house. And then there's the food: textbook Japanese all the way, including sukiyaki, tempura, seafood, vegetarian cuisine, and a sophisticated ash-wood sushi bar. Prices are reasonable, particularly for combo dinner specials that include an appetizer, rice, miso soup, and an entree. But let's be honest: you're here to hear America's top jazz and blues bands, as well as occasional big-name talents such as Herbie Hancock and John Lee Hooker, right? Right. Here's the scoop: there are typically two gigs every night at 8pm and 10pm, and ticket prices range from about $15 to $22. Monday-night headliners are local artists trying to hit the big time, which in the past have included jazz heavies Charlie Hunter,

Miles Perkins, and Joshua Redman. *$$$; AE, DC, DIS, MC, V; no checks; lunch, dinner every day; full bar; reservations recommended; 1 block W of Broadway.* &

Zatis / ★★★

4027 PIEDMONT AVE, OAKLAND; 510/658-8210

Zatis is a real find, discreetly tucked into a narrow spot near a bagel shop and Peet's coffeehouse on Piedmont Avenue. It's hardly noticeable during the day; only at night does the elegant ice-blue neon light entice you to step through the doors, where the aroma of roasted garlic and olive oil will certainly convince you to take a seat and stay for a while. The light seduces, and the jazz soothes. Think intimate (about 15 tables), and think Valentine's Day. Got the picture? Start with the smoked mozzarella and vegetable quesadilla spiced with a zingy guacamole, or dip into the roasted garlic with Gorgonzola and flatbread. Then try the vegetarian eggplant entree stuffed with kalamata olives, jalapeños, and artichoke hearts and baked in a spicy tomato sauce, the herb-crusted fillet of red snapper served with red potatoes and fresh seasonal vegetables, or any of the chef's specialties of the day. *$$$; AE, MC, V; no checks; lunch, dinner Mon–Sat; beer and wine; reservations recommended; between 40th and 41st Sts.* &

LODGINGS

Lake Merritt Hotel Clarion Suites / ★★

1800 MADISON ST, OAKLAND; 510/832-2300 OR 800/933-HOTEL

This art deco masterpiece standing right next to downtown Oakland looks out over Lake Merritt—a large, landscaped lake that's a mecca for joggers, walkers, and rowers. Built in 1927, the vintage white stucco hotel was restored in March 2000 to its original opulence with stunning light fixtures, richly patterned carpeting, plush furniture, and lush flower arrangements. Most of its 50 rooms are standard suites appointed in the charming manner of studio apartments circa 1930 (with a modern-day nod to microwaves and coffeemakers). The deluxe suites with separate living rooms are a bargain at less than $259 per night. Every room has satellite TV, a modern bathroom, a stocked mini-refrigerator, and a phone, and some units face the lake. Other amenities include fax and copy services, a concierge, weekly wine tastings, and a continental breakfast served downstairs in the Terrace Room, which is adorned with scenes of Lake Merritt during the mid-'50s. If you're a business exec, you'll be happy to know the hotel provides a complimentary shuttle to whisk you to the nearby Oakland Financial District. *$$$$; AE, DC, DIS, MC, V; no checks; at Lakeside Dr.* &

Waterfront Plaza Hotel / ★★

10 WASHINGTON ST, OAKLAND; 510/836-3800 OR 800/729-3638

This small luxury hotel perched on the water's edge at Jack London Square is not the fanciest hotel you'll ever stay in, but it comes with all the essential amenities at a reasonable price. And Jack London Square is brimming with great stores, restaurants, and attractions, including popular Yoshi's (see review, above). Heck, you can even catch a ferry to San Francisco or a shuttle to downtown Oakland from the lobby. Each of the 144 rooms is attractively outfitted with pinewood furnishings, pleasing prints, quilted comforters, and color schemes of beige, copper, and blue. Be sure to request a room with a deck and a view of the harbor (an extra $20), and in the winter months ask for a unit with a fireplace. Additional perks include business and fax services, a fitness center, and a heated pool and sauna overlooking the harbor. Adjacent to the hotel is Jack's Bistro, where you can munch on wood-fired meats in a dining room with a view of the marina. *$$$$; AE, DC, DIS, MC, V; no checks; in Jack London Sq.* &

Alameda

LODGINGS

Garratt Mansion / ★★

900 UNION ST, ALAMEDA; 510/521-4779

Surrounded by lush gardens and located just four blocks from the beach, this three-story 1893 colonial revival manse is a picture-perfect example of Victoriana, with gorgeous stained-glass windows, hand-carved interior woodwork, and a wealth of wonderful architectural details. All seven spacious guest rooms have sitting areas, and five have private baths and phones. Favored boudoirs include Diana's Room, a large second-floor suite with a fireplace, a separate sitting room, a bamboo canopy bed, and a private bath with a claw-footed tub and stall shower, and the Captain's Room, with a nautical motif in blue and gold, gold stars on the ceiling, a Venetian mask on the wall, leopard-print chairs, and a cigar-box collection. Innkeeper Betty Gladden serves guests a full breakfast with fresh orange juice and coffee and lays out platters of home-baked cookies in the late afternoon. *$$$; AE, MC, V; checks OK; between Encinal and Clinton Aves.*

Fremont

RESTAURANTS

Pearl's Cafe / ★★

4096 BAY ST, FREMONT; 510/490-2190

As you approach Pearl's Cafe, you wonder if you've taken a wrong turn or if you've fallen prey to some cruel guidebook joke. Located near a couple of mini-malls that are going through arduously slow resurrections, and housed in a converted '60s tract home that looks as though it were attacked by a band of marauding crayons, Pearl's is, well, a pearl in the rough. Once you're inside, though, you'll feel more at home—or garage—since that's what the front dining area once was. Oddly enough, the decor has an old-world feel with its beautifully crafted pine seating areas. The seasonal menu is an equally surprising turn of events. For starters there's the Brie, apples, onions, and thyme baked in pastry with roasted garlic and spiced walnuts, or the grilled spicy prawns and sweet potato–fennel fritters with roasted garlic aioli and caramelized tomato relish. Main course specials include such complex dishes as the grilled salmon with rosemary honey glaze, strawberry salsa, saffron basmati rice, and asparagus with orange-almond butter, or the herb-roasted baby chicken, sautéed green beans, roasted red potatoes and shallot with pancetta and shiitake mushroom jus. After you've finished off your meal with one of the wonderful homemade desserts, you'll wander back to your car, perhaps a bit disoriented, but certainly content. *$$$$; AE, MC, V; no checks; lunch Tues–Fri; dinner Tues–Sat; beer and wine; reservations recommended; near the intersection of Fremont Blvd and Washington Ave.* &

LODGINGS

Lord Bradley's Inn / ★★

43344 MISSION BLVD, FREMONT; 510/490-0520

Rebuilt after the devastating earthquake of 1868 that flattened large sections of the East Bay, this atmospheric Victorian-style hotel offers a good sense of what it must have been like to live in the Bay Area during the 19th century (though it's considerably more comfortable). The eight individually decorated guest rooms have antique bedsteads and private baths, and a few of them were recently redecorated from floor to ceiling. In the morning you'll be treated to a breakfast of fresh and dried fruit, croissants, and muffins with orange butter. During your stay, hike up Mission Peak—the highest prominence hereabouts, with panoramic views of the South Bay. Lord Bradley's also hosts outdoor weddings among the olive trees and roses, and in the Victorian next door there's a spacious second-floor room with a view, available for business meetings or special events. *$$; AE, DC, DIS, MC, V; checks OK; at Washington Blvd, next to Mission San Jose.*

San Jose and the South Bay

Nowadays, the answer to Dionne Warwick's question, "Do You Know the Way to San Jose?" might well be, "Dionne, honey, you've been away too long."

The rolling fields and orchards and the small-town spirit of the South Bay memorialized in Dionne's '60s hit song are gone—swallowed up by office complexes and shopping malls. The bumper crops San Jose peddles now are measured in gigabytes. With skyscrapers and stadiums springing up in unlikely places over the past few years, and traffic rerouted for construction, it's become somewhat the East Berlin of the Bay Area—constantly expanding its concrete girth—though nowhere near as bleak. There are a few undeveloped spots, rare and strangely beautiful against the backdrop of chrome and glass. And many of the ethnic neighborhoods—vibrant and alive with Latin rhythms or Asian austerity—remain intact.

ACCESS AND INFORMATION

Do yourself an enormous favor: fly into **SAN JOSE INTERNATIONAL AIRPORT** (408/501-7600) if your final destination is anywhere near San Jose. Silicon Valley's traffic problem is beyond monumental. Weary commuters—well, how weary can they be when they're sitting in climate-controlled, dot-com-stock-option-subsidized luxury sedans?— tell war stories of suffering petrification in rush hour traffic, languishing in the same spot for 45 minutes or longer. Even if your final destination is downtown, it still may take you forever to get there from the airport, but you'll have shaved off another two or more hours if you've arrived at San Jose International Airport instead of San Francisco International or Oakland International. **SHUTTLE SERVICES** include On Time Airport Shuttle (650/207-0221), San Jose Express (408/370-0701), and Silicon Valley Airporter (408/482-4415). There are plenty of **TAXIS** available.

The **VTA** (Valley Transportation Authority; 408/321-2300) runs the buses as well as the 24-hour light rail system that serves San Jose, Santa Clara, Sunnyvale, and Mountain View. **CALTRAIN** (800/660-4287) provides service from Silicon Valley to San Francisco.

San Jose enjoys the distinction of almost always being several degrees warmer than the rest of the Bay Area regardless of the season. Its valley location, with the Santa Cruz Mountains on the west and rolling hills to the east, locks in a temperate climate—and sometimes it's downright hot. You'd be safe dressing fairly lightly, even in winter when the barometer drops to a bone-chilling 64-or-so degrees. But be sure to bring a sweater or other layering piece any time of year, especially if your travels will take you to other parts of the Bay Area, as the evenings can be on the cool side.

The San Jose McEnery Convention Center is affiliated with the **VISITOR INFORMATION BUREAU** (150 W San Carlos St and 333 W San Carlos St, Ste 1000; 408/977-0900; www.sanjose.org).

San Jose

While some San Jose residents mourn the continuing loss of open space and grittiness to the onslaughts of new construction and gentrification, others seem puffed up with understandable pride at the city's energetic new look

SAN JOSE, SOUTH BAY, AND THE PENINSULA
THREE-DAY TOUR

DAY ONE: Afterlife day. Check in to your room at the predictably luxurious **Fairmont Hotel** in San Jose. You'll be glad you did since you'll be spending the day at some of the most peculiar sites in the Bay Area. Fuel up with a cappuccino at **Cafe Matisse** before your first stop at the **Egyptian Museum and Planetarium**. This attraction features incredible mummies, Egyptian artifacts, scale models of temples, and accurate reproductions of tombs. But that's not the unusual part. The unusual part is that the museum is run by the Rosicrucian Order—not unlike the Theosophic Society—which takes rather seriously the mysterious tenets of ancient Egypt. Don't worry, you won't be converted. Drop in at **71 Saint Peter** for lunch. From there, head on over to the **Winchester Mystery House** for more otherworldy fun. After you've been thoroughly spooked, go back to your accommodations at the Fairmont—where the doors do open up to rooms—and relax for a bit before heading off to **Orlo's**. Housed in a mansion built by faith healer Mary Hayes Chynoweth, it's the perfect place for an ethereal dinner.

DAY TWO: Day of the cat. Start your morning with breakfast at the hotel. No trip to the Silicon Valley would be complete without a side trip to Los Gatos. Located off Highway 17 just before the Santa Cruz Mountains, this enclave put both charming and chichi on the map. All you really need to do is find a place to park, which could take awhile, as there is primarily on-street parking, and start walking. Brimming over with stylish boutiques, exclusive gift stores, and home accessory shops, this town will keep

and feel. First-class restaurants, a state-of-the-art light rail system, a flourishing arts scene, and a dazzling sports arena have all contributed to the city's revitalization, furthering its emergence from the long cultural shadow cast by San Francisco, its cosmopolitan neighbor to the north.

MUSEUMS

The newly renovated **SAN JOSE MUSEUM OF ART** (110 S Market St; 408/294-2787) provides a handsome setting for contemporary European and American art. The **EGYPTIAN MUSEUM AND PLANETARIUM** (at the corner of Park Ave and Naglee St; 408/947-3636), run by the mystical Rosicrucian order, presents a collection of Egyptian artifacts, mummies, and re-creations of tombs in a pyramidlike structure (the British Museum it's not, but it's educational, funky, and fun). The lively and ever-so-loud **CHILDREN'S DISCOVERY MUSEUM** (180 Woz Wy; 408/298-5437), painted in Easter-egg purple, offers kids the opportunity to explore exhibits of urban life: traffic lights, fire engines, a post office, a bank, and even a sewer (spanking clean and minus any errant rats or Ninja turtles).

your credit card humming for some time. Try **I Gatti**—"the cats"—for lunch before sojourning through pesto-thick traffic to your room at the **Garden Court Hotel**. After you've had a chance to unwind from the drive, treat yourself to an amazing dinner at **Bistro Elan**. You will have earned it.

DAY THREE: The garden variety day. After breakfast of Italian pastries at Il Fornaio in the Garden Court Hotel, if you haven't yet done your share of shopping, you can start your day with more retail therapy in Palo Alto's **Stanford Shopping Center** (see Palo Alto, below). This shopping experience is a cut above the rest—the center retains its original outdoor layout, and its gardens are meticulously tended. For lunch, indulge in the exceptional fare at **Max's Opera Cafe** (650/323-6287), located in the shopping center. However, if gardens get your heart pumping, you could skip Stanford Shopping Center and go directly to Woodside and **Filoli Estate and Gardens** (86 Canada, pronounced *con-ya-da*, Rd; 650/364-8300). This palatial mansion and its surrounding gardens were built in 1915 by Mr. and Mrs. William Bouers Bourn II, founders of the Empire Gold Mine. Filoli stands for fight-love-live—to fight for just cause, to love your fellow man, to live a good life—just in case you were wondering. Both the sprawling house and the spectacular gardens are open for tours, but take your time and journey back to a way of life long gone. A light, casual lunch at the **Quail's Nest Cafe** on the Filoli grounds will be the perfect respite between tours and strolling. If all that fresh air has built you an appetite, head for Redwood City to dine at **2030**. This popular restaurant features generous portions. Try to be seated outdoors on the patio to properly round out your day. Head back to your room at the Garden Court Hotel to relax.

A Wells Fargo stagecoach, a farmhouse, and rural diversions like cornhusk doll-making help youngsters experience what the valley was like when it produced major crops instead of microchips. The **TECH MUSEUM OF INNOVATION** (201 S Market St; 408/274-8324) is a terrific hands-on science museum where adults and kids alike can play with robots, gain insight into genetic engineering, or design a high-tech bicycle; it's located across from the San Jose Museum of Art.

Fans of the supernatural might enjoy a tour of the **WINCHESTER MYSTERY HOUSE** (525 S Winchester Blvd; 408/247-2101), an odd, rambling mansion with an intriguing history: after inheriting $20 million from her husband's repeating-rifle company, Sarah Winchester became convinced that the ghosts of people killed by Winchester rifles were coming back to haunt her. Her paranoia led her to continually have additions built onto her home over a period of 38 years to house their restless spirits. The lovely—if somewhat unorthodox—Victorian mansion is a 160-room labyrinth of crooked corridors, doors opening into space, and dead-end stairways.

PERFORMING ARTS

San Jose has a thriving community of theater, ballet, and opera groups, most of which may be found at The **SAN JOSE CENTER FOR THE PERFORMING ARTS** (255 Almaden Blvd at Park Ave; 408/277-3900). The **SAN JOSE CIVIC LIGHT OPERA** (408/453-7108) puts on musicals and other frothy diversions, while **OPERA SAN JOSE** (408/437-4450), the **SAN JOSE CLEVELAND BALLET** (408/288-2800), and the **SAN JOSE SYMPHONY ORCHESTRA** (408/288-2828) offer more classical cultural enrichments. **LOS LUPEÑOS DE SAN JOSE** dance company (34 N 1st St; 408/292-0443) reflects the Spanish heritage of the city. For drama, the **SAN JOSE REPERTORY THEATRE** (1 N 1st St; 408/291-2255) offers innovative productions of new works and classics. The **SAN JOSE STAGE COMPANY** (490 S 1st St; 408/283-7142) primarily showcases American contemporary drama and comedy, while the **CITY LIGHTS THEATRE** (529 S 2nd St; 408/295-4200) follows the more experimental route.

PARKS AND GARDENS

KELLEY PARK is a pleasant place for a picnic and a stroll around the **JAPANESE FRIENDSHIP GARDEN** (corner of Senter Rd and Keyes St; 408/277-4193), complete with a koi pond and a teahouse. If you have little ones in tow, they're sure to be beguiled by the old-fashioned, low-tech charms of **HAPPY HOLLOW** next door, a zoo and amusement park aimed at the toddler-through-early-grade-school set. **GUADALUPE RIVER PARK** is undergoing extensive renovations to set up picnic areas and paved walkways that will stretch from the Children's Discovery Museum to near Highway 880 and the San Jose Airport; call the **SAN JOSE DEPARTMENT OF PARKS AND RECREATION** (408/277-4573) for more information.

NIGHTLIFE

Once the red-light district, the area around Market and First Streets has gradually developed into a clean, hip home for many nightclubs and a slightly more alternative scene. If you gotta dance, you'll find live rock and recorded dance tunes in the **CACTUS CLUB** (417 S 1st St, two blocks south of the Fairmont hotel; 408/491-9300) and in the **B HIVE** (372 S 1st St above Olympia Restaurant; 408/298-2529). For live jazz and a bit of alternative rock, head to **AGENDA** (at the NW corner of S 1st St and E San Salvador St; 408/287-4087). Live rock, dance classics, and cheap draft beer are featured at **TOONS** (52 E Santa Clara St at 2nd St; 408/292-7464). For a mix of music—modern rock, swing bands, DJ-spun rock, and '70s disco—check out **THE USUAL** (400 S 1st St; 408/535-0330; www.theusualnightclub.com). Coffee and attitude are dished out at **CAFE**

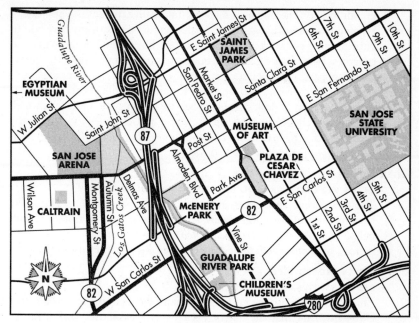

DOWNTOWN SAN JOSE

MATISSE (371 S 1st St; 408/298-7788). And if you want a little bit of everything, visit the **PAVILION** (150 S 1st St; 408/294-5483), where under one roof you'll find a deluxe, eight-screen movie theater, a virtual-reality theme park, and a smattering of shops, bars, and restaurants, as well as San Jose Live, a popular nightspot with two dance floors, a sports bar with 11 big-screen TVs, a cafe serving California fare, a cigar and martini bar, dueling piano players on baby grands, an arcade, pool tables, and even a basketball court.

RESTAURANTS

Agenda / ★★★

399 S 1ST ST, SAN JOSE; 408/287-3991

At this chic and beautifully designed restaurant in the city's SoMa district (yes, San Jose's got one, too), stylish types sip cosmopolitans at the sculptured wood bar, Silicon Valley execs talk IPOs at tables flanked by arty souls discussing the NEA, and jazz buffs check out the live (and very loud) band. A giant androgynous angel presides over all, stretching its da Vinci-esque flying-machine wings across an exposed brick wall. If you turn your attention away from your surroundings, however, you'll notice the eclectic food is what really takes flight here. That's apparent as soon as you spread a piece of feather-light focaccia with a delectable basil- and olive-infused tapenade, a secret recipe from chef Christian Raia's Sicilian grandmother. The kitchen displays impressive breadth, with dishes ranging from exotic vegetable empanadas to delicate seafood ravioli to barn-burning pot stickers to comfort food like to-die-for garlic mashed potatoes. Portions are generous, but try to save room for dessert; choices that seem passé on paper, such as cherries jubilee and crème caramel, turn out to be retro revelations, especially the air-spun milk chocolate mousse served in a tulip of dark chocolate. Service is savvy but a bit slow, which gives you a chance to soak up the scene and consider the rest of the evening. *$$; AE, MC, V; no checks; dinner Tues–Sat; full bar; reservations recommended; at San Salvador St.*

Chez Sovan Restaurant / ★★

2425 S 923 OLD OAKLAND RD, SAN JOSE; 408/287-7619
This restaurant specializes in Cambodian cuisine and exceptionally friendly service. For a full review, see the Restaurants section of Campbell. *$; AE, MC, V; no checks; lunch, Mon–Fri; beer and wine; reservations recommended; between Berryessa Rd and E Hedding St.*

Eight Forty North First / ★★

840 N 1ST ST, SAN JOSE; 408/282-0840
This restaurant with the no-nonsense name caters to the San Jose power elite—say, isn't that the mayor exchanging pleasantries with a justice from the municipal court? The food is eclectic, with Italian and Asian touches influencing the contemporary American menu. Starters include a spicy sauté of honey prawns nesting on a bed of Chinese cabbage; a vegetable quesadilla with pepper jack cheese, guacamole, and salsa; and a curried spinach salad with apples, peanuts, and golden raisins. Entrees include pastas (such as linguine with chicken and broccoli topped with a creamy sun-dried tomato sauce and a sprinkle of feta and walnuts), grilled sea scallops on wilted spinach, and other temptations from the deep. A panoply of meat and poultry dishes range from venison medallions to a chicken breast topped with goat cheese, spicy pecans, and a poached pear. By now, you've probably gotten the idea that chef/co-owner John Petricca takes chances here; sometimes he hits the mark and sometimes he misses. Still, his concoctions are always interesting, and you can wash them down with a selection from the extensive (and pricey) wine list *$$$; AE, DC, DIS, MC, V; no checks; lunch Mon–Fri, dinner Mon–Sat; full bar; reservations recommended; between Mission and Hedding Sts.*

Emile's / ★★★

545 S 2ND ST, SAN JOSE; 408/289-1960
Catering to an older, well-heeled crowd and expense-account execs, Emile's has been one of San Jose's finest restaurants for nearly three decades. Chef/owner Emile Mooser offers a California version of the cui-

sine he learned in his Swiss homeland, and his menu features classic French, Swiss, and Italian preparations as well as *cuisine minceur* (a somewhat leaner style of French cooking). Using fine stocks and the best seasonal ingredients available, the kitchen does a particularly good job with fish and game. Entrees on the seasonal menu may include a giant open-faced ravioli with prawns, scallops, and fish in a lobster-brandy sauce, fillet of beef with a roasted garlic and cabernet sauvignon sauce, or even such exotica as wild boar with fresh fruit compote. The *roesti*— a crunchy Swiss version of hash browns—is wonderful. Almost everything is made on the premises, from the house-cured gravlax to flawless desserts like the justly celebrated Grand Marnier soufflé. Emile's wine cellar contains more than 300 selections, ranging from the very reasonable to the very, very expensive. *$$$; AE, DC, DIS, MC, V; no checks; lunch Fri, dinner Tues–Sat; full bar; reservations recommended; between Williams and Reed Sts.*

Gombei Restaurant / ★★

193 E JACKSON ST, SAN JOSE; 408/279-4311

Among the many worthy restaurants in San Jose's Japantown, tiny, lively Gombei stands out with its unparalleled noodle dishes and the near-volcanic energy of its devoted patrons and youthful staff. The menu offers everything from teriyaki and domburi to Gombei's renowned udon—the Japanese equivalent of Jewish chicken soup, which arrives in a huge ceramic bowl filled with fat wheat noodles, loads of tender strips of chicken, ribbons of egg, green onion, and a sheaf of dried seaweed. Be sure to check the specials board for such irresistible nibbles as deep-fried oysters or cold chicken salad served on buckwheat noodles. *$; cash only; lunch Mon–Fri, dinner every day; beer and wine; reservations recommended; between 4th and 5th Sts.*

La Forêt French Restaurant / ★★★

21747 BERTRAM RD, SAN JOSE; 408/997-3458

Located in an old two-story hotel overlooking Los Alamedos Creek, this picturesque and pricey restaurant offers unusual wild game that's flown in daily. Chef Vazgen "Ken" Davoudi can always be counted on to create superb sauces for the day's special, which might be tender medallions of wild boar marinated in shallots, balsamic vinegar, brandy, and cumin and topped with an outstanding pink peppercorn sauce, paired with medallions of elk in an equally masterful tarragon cream sauce. Davoudi's prowess isn't limited to game; he also works well with seafood, including a perfectly poached salmon served with a port wine sauce. Appetizers might feature fusilli with olive oil, herbs, garlic, wild mushrooms, and Gouda cheese or escargot with garlic butter and Pernod. The dessert list features a selection of cakes, cheesecakes, and exotic soufflés. *$$$; AE, DC, DIS, MC, V; no checks; dinner Tues–Sun, brunch Sun; full bar;*

reservations recommended; from the Almaden Expwy, take the Almaden Rd exit, go S for 3 miles, turn left at Almaden Wy, and cross the small bridge to Bertram Rd.

Orlo's / ★★★

200 EDENVALE AVE, SAN JOSE; 408/226-3200

Faith healer Mary Hayes Chynoweth built a gorgeous 41,000-square-foot Mediterranean revival-style mansion in 1905 as a base of operations for her ministry. Unfortunately, the wealthy do-gooder passed away four months before the house was completed, and the grand estate fell into disrepair years later. These days, the restored and sensitively modernized mansion is a home-away-from-home for Silicon Valley professionals attending meetings at the Hayes Conference Center. Most of the healing going on here now takes place in the health spa, but one might also reap salubrious benefits from a meal at Orlo's, an innovative restaurant open to the public. Housed in the former family dining room, the elegant space has floral-fabric-and-wood-covered walls, green and maroon carpeting, ornate metal table bases, and built-in mission-style furniture. Service is a bit formal, which seems right for the setting, and the seasonal menu, which stresses fresh, first-rate ingredients, stops just short of fussy. Appetizers include Oyster Orlo's (oysters baked with house-made venison ham, crimini mushrooms, and sun-dried tomato pesto) and a splendid salad of baby greens with a walnut-balsamic vinaigrette and Amish blue cheese. Entrees are notable for unusual renderings of traditional fare, such as the mixed seafood grill with honey-lavender sauce or the Kona-coffee-roasted rack of lamb. Some of the bewitching items on the dessert tray look better than they taste (try the chocolate opera cake, which is ethereally light and boasts a liquory bite). *$$$; AE, DC, DIS, MC, V; no checks; lunch Mon–Fri, dinner every day; full bar; reservations recommended; from Hwy 101 turn W on Blossom Hill Rd, then right on Lean Ave, which turns into Edenvale Ave.*

Paolo's / ★★★

333 W SAN CARLOS ST, SAN JOSE; 408/294-2558

A longtime San Jose institution, Paolo's moved to expensive new digs in 1991, and while the handsome facility may have a bit of a corporate America feel, the flavorful food remains authentically Italian. Look for unexpected little flourishes that give even the most tried-and-true dishes an interesting twist: veal scaloppine, for example, is served on a bed of wilted spinach, while Paolo's gnocchi is baked with truffle butter and fontina Val D'ostra cheese. Other outstanding items include tortelli di zucca (pasta stuffed with pumpkin and cheese, tossed with brown butter and sage), roasted quail with white raisins and grappa, and an intriguing appetizer of grilled Tuscan cheese wrapped in chard served with roasted peppers and eggplant. Service can be a little brusque at times, especially if you're not a silver-haired CEO on his or her lunch hour, but it's always efficient. The wine list could bring a tear of joy to Bacchus's eye—the 50-page tome encompasses an outstanding variety of domestic and European selections. *$$$; AE, DC, DIS, MC, V; no checks; lunch Mon–Fri, dinner Mon–Sat; full bar; reservations recommended; between Woz Wy and Almaden Blvd.* &

71 Saint Peter / ★★

71 SAN PEDRO ST, SAN JOSE; 408/971-8523
Chef/co-owner Mark Tabak has attracted a loyal following with this tiny and romantic Mediterranean bistro. The Spanish floor tiles, flowers, exposed brick walls, and crisp linens help create a feeling of rustic elegance, a theme echoed by Tabak's robust yet refined cuisine. Outstanding starters include duck liver pâté with mustard and toast points, steamed New Zealand clams simply seasoned with tomato, basil, and garlic, and a bevy of interesting salads. For your entree, you'd do well to consider the roasted duck cloaked in a raspberry-black pepper demi-glace, the seafood linguine in a spicy tomato broth, or any of the fresh fish dishes. Tabak is justly proud of his crème brûlée, which was once voted the best in Santa Clara Valley. The sensibly priced wine list includes French and Italian selections as well as the usual California suspects. *$$; AE, DC, DIS, MC, V; checks OK; lunch Mon–Fri, dinner Tues–Sat; beer and wine; reservations recommended; between St John and Santa Clara Sts.*

LODGINGS

The Fairmont / ★★★

170 S MARKET ST, SAN JOSE; 408/998-1900 OR 800/527-4727
President Clinton's done it. So have Al Gore, Luciano Pavarotti, Neil Diamond, Mike Wallace, George Bush, and a host of other celebs—slipped between the Supercale cotton sheets of San Jose's Fairmont, that is. Twenty stories high in the heart of downtown, the city's most luxurious hostelry has become one of the best-known features of the skyline. The 541 guest rooms (as well as the public areas) recently have been refurbished and feature such niceties as marble bathrooms, plush robes, electric shoe polishers, desks, walk-in closets, custom-made mattresses, minibars, and nightly turndown service. In keeping with the Silicon Valley setting, they also contain an arsenal of tech toys such as high-speed modem links for computers and fax machines and interactive TV sets that let a guest do everything from ordering up a movie to checking out of the hotel. Three well-regarded restaurants stand ready to serve peckish travelers: the Pagoda serves Chinese food at lunch and dinner; the Fountain is a casual spot for breakfast, lunch, and dinner; the poolside Gazebo Bar and Grill offers cocktails and light fare in summer and fall, weather

permitting. In addition, an elegant afternoon tea is served in the hotel's lobby on weekends. *$$$; AE, DC, DIS, V; checks OK; between San Fernando and San Carlos Sts.* &

The Hensley House / ★★

456 N 3RD ST, SAN JOSE; 408/298-3537 OR 800/498-3537

Close to museums, theaters, and restaurants, this stately Queen Anne is a haven for corporate visitors and child-weary couples. Proprietors Toni Contreras and Ron Evans recently restored the landmark building. They added four more rooms, including three units in the lovely Craftsman-style house across the street. Each of the guest rooms has a queen-size featherbed, private bath, TV with VCR, and telephone. If you're ready to splurge, try the Judge's Chambers, with its wet bar, whirlpool bath for two, hand-painted ceiling and walls, and fireplace. (By the way, the ghost of the room's namesake, Superior Court Judge Perley Gosbey, one of the home's original owners, is rumored to pay a friendly visit now and then.) Guests are treated to a full breakfast. High tea is available to guests and the public on Thursday and Saturday afternoons by appointment only. *$$–$$$; AE, DC, DIS, MC, V; checks OK; at Hensley St.*

Hotel De Anza / ★★★

233 W SANTA CLARA ST, SAN JOSE; 408/286-1000 OR 800/843-3700

Renovations that took 10 months and $10 million brought this 1931 grande dame back to life after years of decay. The richly colored Moorish ceilings in the De Anza Room and the Hedley Club are art deco jewels, and the same design influence can be felt in the guest rooms. Each of the 99 rooms has a multiple-line desk phone with a dedicated data line and fax port, an armoire with an honor bar, and a TV with a VCR (you can check out movies gratis from the video library downstairs). Ask for one of the south-facing rooms to enjoy a sweeping view of downtown. The hotel's flagship restaurant, La Pastaia, serves some of the best Italian food in town, and the place is always packed with locals as well as hungry travelers. The stately Palm Court Terrace is a favorite place to meet for drinks in the warmer months, and a live jazz trio performs in the Hedley Club on Wednesday through Saturday nights. *$$$; AE, DC, MC, V; checks OK; at Almaden Blvd.*

Hyatt Sainte Claire / ★★★

302 S MARKET ST, SAN JOSE; 408/885-1234 OR 800/233-1234

This gracious Spanish revival–style hostelry was built in 1926 by the same architectural firm responsible for the design of the Mark Hopkins Hotel in San Francisco. The 170 refurbished guest rooms (including 14 one-bedroom suites and one grand suite boasting two fireplaces and a library) feature featherbeds, dual phone lines with high-speed modems, safes, and minibars among the other usual first-class amenities. In addi-

YOUR PC'S BIRTHPLACE

Two of the biggest babies on record were born in Silicon Valley—Microsoft and Apple—and this area continues to deliver software and dot-com start-ups at an alarming rate. Of course, where there are babies, there are albums to document their first steps, first words, what they might become. Such is the **Tech Museum of Innovation** (201 S Market St, San Jose; 408/294-8324) or, more simply, "The Tech"—a cache of technology's past, present, and future.

One look at the orange and cobalt blue museum building will make you chuckle at the now outmoded notion that "techie" was once synonymous with "geek"—this is not a gathering place for nerds with taped glasses and pocket protectors. Instead, its modern facade seems to beckon the tragically hip to enter and get in touch with their inner programmer. The interior architecture follows suit, drawing one in, then catapulting the attention upward via a dramatic curved staircase and a massive supporting column lathered in gold leaf.

The Tech is divided into three levels. The ground level features an **IMAX dome theater**—no museum is complete without one these days—and the Techstore, as interesting as the museum itself. The upper level contains the **Innovation area**, where you can, among other things, design and ride a virtual rollercoaster or tour a computer chip lab, and the **Life Tech area**—an utterly fascinating look at technology's role in studying, diagnosing, and treating the human body. The squeamish and the recently lunched should avoid the video display that shows how a computer-generated image of the human body and all its internal organs is created by using a cadaver. The upper level also includes an interactive area called Cyberplace, but skip it. Even though it contains 26 powerful desktop PCs, it's really no different than sitting at home plucking away at your own computer's keys. The lower level is where you can catch a glimpse of technology's future. From robotic dogs with amazingly realistic movement—you can buy one special-order if you're willing to pay $3,500—and a robotic submarine you can pilot to a model Mars rover you can ride, it's a techie playground. The Center of the Edge area showcases rotating exhibits of the newest, state-of-the-art technology.

If, after all this, you still haven't satisfied your techno-lust, there is hope; you can forgo a luxe room at the nearby Fairmont Hotel and, by advance reservation, spend the night at The Tech for 50 bucks. Yup, really. It's called **iCamp** (408/795-6105 or pubprograms@thetech.org). All you need to bring are kids (it's mainly designed for their benefit), a sleeping bag, and minimal toiletries. The package includes hands-on workshops, two IMAX films, a late-night snack, and a continental breakfast. If that doesn't tickle your fancy, you can snuggle up with your PC when you get back home and fall asleep to its electronic cooing and gurgling.   —*Brian Tacang*

tion, some of the rooms have whirlpool tubs and fireplaces, and 80 percent are equipped with laser printers and IBM-compatible computers with Internet access. A small exercise room with a treadmill and an exercise bike stands ready to help guests work out any knots or kinks resulting from sessions at those computers. And the Hyatt has a pleasant coffee shop, the Panetteria, serving Italian sandwiches and pastries, as well as a top-rated branch of Il Fornaio restaurant. *$$$; AE, DC, DIS, MC, V; checks OK; at San Carlos St.*

Santa Clara

RESTAURANTS

Birk's / ★★

3955 FREEDOM CIRCLE, SANTA CLARA; 408/980-6400
Despite its office-park setting and rather stern exterior, Birk's is a handsome American grill with a spirited atmosphere. Design features mark Birk's as a Pat Kuleto creation, and the hearty food reflects the vaguely men's-club feel of the place. Appetizers might include steak bits with béarnaise sauce, a grilled artichoke with garlic-lemon aioli, or oysters Rockefeller. For a main course, you can choose from all manner of grilled and smoked meat, fish, and fowl. Standouts include the popular smoked prime rib, the pan-seared duck breast with bourbon and maple-syrup sauce, and grilled lamb chops marinated in oregano, lemon, garlic, and olive oil. Lighter eaters might enjoy one of the imaginative salads, such as the teriyaki salmon with cabbage slaw, sprouts, noodles, and dried apricots served with a light sake dressing. If you still have room for dessert, Birk's offers a dynamite chocolate cake, berry crisp à la mode, and other oh-I'll-diet-tomorrow temptations. The wine list reflects a good range of California vintners, and you'll find an excellent selection of single-malt scotches and beers on tap, many from local microbreweries. *$$$; AE, DC, DIS, MC, V; no checks; lunch Mon–Fri, dinner every day; full bar; reservations recommended; at Hwy 101 and Great America Pkwy.*

Campbell

RESTAURANTS

Chez Sovan Restaurant / ★★

2425 S BASCOM AVE, CAMPBELL; 408/371-7711
An upscale cousin of the San Jose original, Chez Sovan's Campbell branch features the same authentic Cambodian cuisine and exceptionally friendly service. The stars of the menu are the *samlaws*, Cambodian stews. *Samlaw korko* is a brothy concoction that combines tender

chicken with an exotic array of vegetables. Several catfish dishes are offered, too, including a dynamite version with black beans, green onions, vinegar, and loads of fresh ginger. Skip the house specialty, *amok*—chicken or fish marinated in coconut milk and wrapped in a banana leaf (it may be a little too authentic for untutored Western palates). The fresh salads are packed with cilantro, mint, shredded Napa cabbage, bell peppers, and carrots, plus your choice of chicken, pork, or beef. *$; AE, DIS, MC, V; no checks; lunch, dinner every day; beer and wine; reservations recommended; near Dry Creek Rd.*

Los Gatos

RESTAURANTS

Café Marcella / ★★★

368 VILLAGE LN, LOS GATOS; 408/354-8006
This sophisticated little side-street bistro's flavorful California-Mediterranean cuisine has won a loyal following. The small but provocative menu features individual pizzas, pastas, and a handful of entrees, all supplemented by an ever-changing list of weekly specials. Starters range from duck pâté with whole-grain mustard and chutney to wild mushroom risotto. Entrees include such interesting fare as pork medallions with sundried cherries, swordfish steaks with celery cream and eggplant relish, and rabbit with orange-mustard sauce. And no matter how full you are, order dessert—many locals would argue that Café Marcella's are the best around (how about a terrine of three chocolates with raspberry coulis and crème anglaise, or perhaps rhubarb shortcake with hot caramel sauce?). The cafe is also known for its wine list, which offers a host of selections from both local vineyards and European boutique wineries. *$$$; AE, MC, V; no checks; lunch Tues–Sat, dinner Tues–Sun; beer and wine; reservations recommended; between Santa Cruz and University Aves.* &

Cafe Trio / ★★★

15466 LOS GATOS BLVD, LOS GATOS; 408/356-8129
Jack and Rosemary Edwards are the duo behind this engaging California bistro that opened in 1993. The black-and-white floor tiles, green marbleized wallpaper, and crisp table linens give the restaurant an uptown feel that triumphs over its shopping-center locale. Rosemary presides out front, ensuring friendly and knowledgeable service, while Jack, an alumnus of the Hotel De Anza's La Pastaia restaurant in San Jose, toils in the kitchen. He infuses the essentially California menu with French and Italian touches, and his predilection for spicy food keeps things interesting. Signature dishes include an appetizer of grilled Anaheim peppers stuffed with goat cheese, bread crumbs, and salsa, as well as entrees such as penne with chicken, tomatoes, pine nuts, and basil, and a delectable

pork loin stuffed with herbs, dried cranberries, and fresh horseradish. *$$$; AE, DC, MC, V; no checks; lunch Mon–Fri, dinner Mon–Sat; beer and wine; reservations recommended; in the Village Sq shopping center, between Lark Ave and Los Gatos–Amaden Rd.*

I Gatti / ★★★

25 E MAIN ST, LOS GATOS; 408/399-5180

With its sponge-painted mustard and red-brown walls, weathered wooden shutters, and terra-cotta floor tiles, I Gatti (the Italian counterpart to Los Gatos, Spanish for "the cats"—get it?) evokes a Tuscan patio on a sunny afternoon. Terrific appetizers are *scampi al vino blanco*, goat-cheese ravioli with a rich Chianti-wine glaze, and gnocchi (which can be a little doughy) with a first-rate creamy tomato-vodka sauce. There's a selection of both traditional and unusual salads (try the mixed greens with berries, leeks, and pistachios drizzled with a blackberry vinaigrette), well-prepared pizzas, and *secondi piatti* that include roasted filet mignon with a Barolo wine and wild mushroom sauce, braised lamb shank, and *pollo modo mio* (lightly breaded breast of chicken served with a champagne, lemon-herb, and caper sauce). *$$$; AE, MC, V; checks OK; lunch Tues–Fri, dinner Tues–Sun; beer and wine; reservations recommended; near University Ave.*

Los Gatos Brewing Company / ★

130-G N SANTA CRUZ AVE, LOS GATOS; 408/395-9929

This cheery, upscale techno-barn of a restaurant has something for everyone: good, house-made beers and ales for the thirsty, a lively singles scene for the action-oriented, crayons and coloring books for the wee ones, and, most important, good pub fare for the hungry. Executive chef Jim Stump (who formerly graced Le Mouton Noir in Saratoga and Birk's in Santa Clara) has created an ambitious menu encompassing everything from pizzas and fresh oysters on the half shell to rotisserie chicken. You can indulge in a dainty charred tuna carpaccio salad or give your arteries a workout with rib-eye steak in a red wine reduction sauce accompanied by garlic mashed potatoes, sautéed green beans, and buttermilk onion rings. In-house brewskis include special seasonal brews ranging from nut-brown ale to a German-style wheat beer. *$$; AE, DC, DIS, MC, V; no checks; lunch, dinner every day, brunch Sun; beer and wine; reservations recommended; at Grays Ln.* &

Pigalle / ★★

27 N SANTA CRUZ AVE, LOS GATOS; 408/395-7924

Playing off its name, some Los Gatos residents have affectionately dubbed this French bistro "Pig Alley" because of the generous, reasonably priced portions served here. Although the owners probably wouldn't appreciate that version of their moniker, they can't quibble with the loyalty their top-notch French country cuisine inspires. Named after Paris's red-light district (a mural of a Parisian street scene sets the mood), Pigalle offers a small, interesting menu that changes seasonally. Lunch offerings may range from a seafood fettuccine with scallops and prawns to a chicken pie made with artichoke hearts, mushrooms, and cream sauce. For dinner, crisp roast duck in a caramelized raspberry sauce, classic beef Wellington, or braised rabbit with a mustard cream sauce may be among the tempting entrees. Dessert specialties include soufflés and fruit concoctions such as poached pears drenched in a port wine sauce. *$$; MC, V; local checks only; lunch, dinner every day; beer and wine; reservations recommended; near Main St.*

Saratoga

RESTAURANTS

Le Mouton Noir / ★★★

14560 BIG BASIN WY, SARATOGA; 408/867-7017

For a small town, Saratoga has more than its fair share of good French restaurants, but the sheer inventiveness of Le Mouton Noir's kitchen has always set it apart from its competitors. A few years back there was an upheaval in both ownership and kitchen staff, but current chef Jason Siccone (an alumnus of San Francisco's La Folie and Los Gatos's Café Marcella) continues to turn out the superb French-California fare that has made Le Mouton Noir a destination restaurant. The menu changes seasonally, but specialties include such appetizers as escargots served on new potato skins, wild mushrooms and goat cheese encased in a pastry shell, and duck pâté with pistachios and sun-dried cranberries. Entrees may feature boneless, pan-roasted quail with pheasant sausage and risotto stuffing, salmon with an almond-citrus crust, and rack of lamb perched on a parsnip gratin. Duck remains a house specialty, with a rotating repertoire of preparations. Desserts may include such ethereal creations as a flourless mocha cake surrounded by crème anglaise, a banana-bread pudding with warm caramel sauce, and a frangipane pear tartlet. The pricey wine list features a wide range of French and California offerings, with a good selection from nearby wineries. *$$$; AE, DC, MC, V; no checks; lunch Sat, dinner every day; full bar; reservations recommended; between 4th and 5th Sts, near Hwy 9.*

Sent Soví / ★★★★

14583 BIG BASIN WY, SARATOGA; 408/867-3110

When Sent Soví opened in 1995, owners of many long-established and well-regarded Saratoga restaurants watched enviously as it inspired purple prose from the pens of dazzled restaurant critics and caused foodies from all over the Bay Area to clamor for reservations. Why all the fuss? Well, co-owner Aimee Hebert is one of those charming hostesses who treats every customer like a VIP, the service is big-city polished, and the dining room is a study in understated elegance. But Sent Soví's principal draw is the contemporary French cuisine of chef/co-owner David Kinch, whose résumé includes stints at Ernie's and Silks in San Francisco as well as some of the finest restaurants in Europe. The best way to sample Kinch's inspired cuisine is to order the six-course tasting menu; it changes nightly, but one menu included the following sumptuous lineup: an *amuse bouche* (a tiny taste to stimulate your palate) of chicken salad, duck foie gras with corn bread and quince sauce, creamy soup of wild mushrooms and black truffles, venison medallions with apples and dates, spiced cranberry soup with fresh fruit and granitas, and frozen passion fruit soufflé with champagne sabayon. If someone in your party balks at ordering the tasting menu (unfortunately, the entire table must elect this option), don't despair; à la carte selections might include such treasures as risotto with black truffles and turkey, braised lamb shank with a cumin-scented carrot confit, and duck breast glazed with a spiced honey, raspberry, and verbena sauce. *$$$; AE, MC, V; no checks; dinner Tues–Sun; beer and wine; reservations recommended; at 5th St.*

Sunnyvale

RESTAURANTS

Kabul Afghan Cuisine / ★★

833 W EL CAMINO REAL, SUNNYVALE; 408/245-4350
This family-run establishment re-creates the Mediterranean to Southeast Asian tastes of Afghanistan's national cuisine. For a full review, see the Restaurants section of San Carlos. *$$; AE, MC, V; checks OK; lunch Mon–Fri, dinner every day; beer and wine; reservations recommended; at Pastoira St.* &

Il Postale / ★★

127 WASHINGTON ST, SUNNYVALE; 408/733-9600
Set in Sunnyvale's old post office (hence the name), Il Postale is an airy, attractive trattoria with brick walls hung with large framed prints of Italian postal stamps, dark wood bistro furniture set with white linens, and an open kitchen. Although owner Joe Antuzzi insists that his welcoming little restaurant serves Italian-American bistro food, that designation doesn't begin to describe the ambitious menu. Sure, there are plenty of Italian classics (spaghetti puttanesca, linguine with clams, veal braciola, cheese pizza), but the kitchen seems to delight in putting its own twist on some of the standards, tossing grilled boar sausage in wild mushroom risotto, serving veal scaloppine with a sun-dried tomato, caper, and black-olive sauce, even stuffing agnolotti with garlic mashed potatoes (yikes!). And then there are dishes like grilled prawns with soba noodles,

defying inclusion on any Italian-American menu we've ever seen. Most of the time this iconoclastic approach works, resulting in a satisfying, interesting meal at a reasonable price. *$$; AE, DC, DIS, MC, V; no checks; lunch Mon–Fri, dinner every day; full bar; reservations recommended; near Murphy Ave.*

Mountain View

RESTAURANTS

Amber India Restaurant / ★★

2290 EL CAMINO REAL, MOUNTAIN VIEW; 650/968-7511

Opened in 1995 in a small, unprepossessing shopping center on busy El Camino Real, Amber India offers an escape into a serene, exotic realm. Soft light from brass sconces reflects off rough-textured white stucco walls, partitions and archways divide the space into a series of cozy areas, and wood-and-fabric awnings jut over the central dining room. The staff is solicitous and welcoming, and the food is a cut above the fare typically found in Bay Area Indian restaurants, in terms of both quality and variety. The menu derives its inspiration from several regions of India, resulting in an adventurous selection of exceptionally flavorful yet well-balanced dishes. Appetizers include deep-fried fish pakora, *shami kabab* (lamb patties mixed with lentils and onions), and *reshmi tikka* (marinated and barbecued chicken morsels seasoned with saffron and topped with mint). A large variety of distinctively spiced curries, tandoori selections, and rice dishes rounds out the menu; come with a group so you can order enough items to sample the kitchen's impressive breadth. Intrepid diners can top off their meal with *kulfi* (saffron-flavored ice cream with pistachios) or *gulab jamun* (deep-fried cheese balls drizzled with honey). *$$$; AE, DC, DIS, MC, V; no checks; lunch, dinner every day; full bar; reservations recommended; between Rengstorff and Ortega Aves.*

Hangen / ★★

134 CASTRO ST, MOUNTAIN VIEW; 650/964-8881

Mountain View's Castro Street is undeniably saturated with Asian restaurants of all descriptions, but chef Neng Wang's delicate and tasty Sichuan fare still has managed to carve out a distinctive niche. At lunch, Hangen caters to its workday crowd by offering multicourse menus entitled the Executive Lunch and the Business Lunch, both of which provide several choices. At dinner, the chef spreads his culinary wings, and the far-ranging menu includes delights such as Emerald Shrimp (shrimp with a spinach-wine sauce perched on a bed of orange slices and lettuce), deep-fried whole fish in a spicy sauce, beef satay, conch salad, tea-smoked duck, and mushrooms in a tangerine zest sauce. Some non-Asian customers grumble about being given a different, smaller menu than their

Chinese counterparts, but they're still assured of plenty of delicious options. *$$; AE, DC, MC, V; no checks; lunch, dinner every day; beer and wine; reservations recommended; just W of the Central Expwy.*

Los Altos

RESTAURANTS

Beauséjour / ★★★★

170 STATE ST, LOS ALTOS; 650/948-1382

A downtown gem, Beauséjour (bow-zay-ZHUR, French for "a beautiful visit") presents French cuisine in a charming old building with a European country-house feel. The atmosphere may be a little prim, but the food is executed with rare skill and precision. Traditional favorites are well covered, including escargots in puff pastry, sautéed sweetbreads, and beef bourguignon, but the menu also branches out into unusual, lighter fare. Starters might include pan-seared prawns on a bed of Parmesan mashed potatoes or duck mousse pâté with truffles. The soups are excellent, and the salads range from a very simple medley of mixed baby greens to a tiger prawn salad with grapefruit and red potatoes. The inviting entrees include medallions of venison with bok choy and curry-potato fritters, calamari steak in a lemon-caper sauce, and filet mignon with an herb sauce and goat cheese ravioli. Beauséjour is also known for its duck with raspberry sauce and lamb with mint sauce and potato timbale. A reasonably priced prix-fixe dinner is offered daily and includes soup or salad, entree, and dessert. *$$$; AE, DC, MC, V; no checks; lunch Mon–Fri, dinner every day; full bar; reservations recommended; between 3rd and 4th Sts.*

Chef Chu's / ★★

1067 N SAN ANTONIO RD, LOS ALTOS; 650/948-2696

Take a culinary tour of mainland China without ever leaving your table. Feast on dim sum from Guangzhou, banquet dishes from Shanghai and Beijing, dumplings and stretched noodles from Xian, and spicy favorites from Sichuan and Hunan—all from the kitchen of Lawrence Chu, a chef who's been expanding the culinary horizons of Los Altos for more than three decades. Chef Chu does all the standards well and offers some delicious innovations of his own, such as crisp salmon rolls (tender salmon mixed with Chinese herbs, wrapped in sheets of dried tofu and deep-fried). Munch on jumbo prawns with candied pecans in a mild mustard sauce. The Peking duck, which must be ordered in advance, is crisp and flawless, with virtually all the fat melted away. *$$; AE, DC, MC, V; no checks; lunch, dinner every day; full bar; reservations recommended; at El Camino Real.* ♿

The Peninsula

The Peninsula Q&A: Q: Are there houses for sale on the Peninsula under $700,000? A: Not unless you're looking for a one bedroom fixer-upper barely standing on its last leg. Q: Will I see one of those artsy, hand-painted VW vans driving the streets of the Peninsula? A: Only if one is visiting from Berkeley. Q: Will I be able to fly down Highway 101 at the speed limit any time I like? A: Not unless you're driving at midnight.

The Peninsula enjoys a prime location between cosmopolitan San Francisco and the booming Silicon Valley. As a result, living, eating, and playing there all come at a premium. From the stately mansions on University Avenue in Palo Alto to the sprawling ranch-style homes of Los Altos and the hillside estates of Woodside, the Peninsula wears its prosperity sometimes with restraint, other times shamelessly, but always with pride.

With the techno explosion, the Peninsula catapulted past its already posh aura to an almost astronomical exclusivity. A recent television news feature captured the Peninsula's air of privilege best; when viewers were asked to share their most outrageous real estate stories, this one came to the fore. A man was sitting in his house. A real estate agent rang the door-bell, introduced himself and said, "I have a client in my car. He wants to buy your house. He's willing to offer you $20 million for it." The home-owner, understandably flabbergasted, said, "Sorry, I'm not selling my house," or something to that effect. A few days later the real estate agent returned, telling the man, "My client is now willing to offer you $45 mil-lion." Escrow ensued shortly thereafter. That's the Peninsula for ya.

ACCESS AND INFORMATION

SAN FRANCISCO INTERNATIONAL AIRPORT (650/876-2377), or SFO, services both the Peninsula and San Francisco (of course) handily. Well, as handily as can be expected with traffic being what it is. Plan your appointments to allow for jockeying through traffic delays to your final destination. In fact, if at all possible, it would be best not to plan any-thing of importance to attend to once you arrive.

Sometimes—okay, frequently—SFO can be blanketed in fog as thick and as heavy as a down comforter, so don't be surprised if your takeoff from your point of departure or your landing at SFO is delayed. Espe-cially if you're arriving on a morning when the white stuff is spilling over the Peninsula hills. Once you've landed, though, you'll find a user-friendly airport layout and plenty of TAXIS to spare. SHUTTLE SERVICES include Bayporter Express (415/467-1800), Bay Shuttle (415/564-3400), and Super Shuttle (800/258-3826). CALTRAIN (800/660-4827) runs train service the length of the Peninsula from Silicon Valley to San Francisco.

Temperatures on the Peninsula are among the coolest in the Bay Area, often by several degrees, due to its close proximity to the chilly

Pacific Ocean, so it's advisable to bring a midweight jacket, even in summer; evenings can be on the cool side.

Palo Alto

The home of **STANFORD UNIVERSITY**, notable restaurants, fine-art galleries, foreign-movie houses, great bookstores, a thriving theater troupe, and some of the best shopping this side of heaven, Palo Alto is a beacon of cosmopolitan energy shining on the suburban sea. In spite of the fact that many of the Bay Area's rich-and-maybe-famous call Palo Alto home, much of the fuel for this cultural lighthouse comes from the university, which offers tours of its attractive campus on a fairly regular basis. Highlights of the university include the Main Quad, Hoover Tower (there are great views from its observation platform), the huge bookstore, and gorgeous Memorial Church; call the campus (650/723-2560) for more tour information. If you'd like to try to glimpse some atom smashing, visit the nearby **STANFORD LINEAR ACCELERATOR CENTER**; call (650/926-3300) to arrange a tour.

Moviegoers have a broad range of choices. The beautifully restored **STANFORD THEATER** (221 University Ave; 650/324-3700), which showcases classic flicks, is especially worth a visit. If you prefer your performances live, check out the local **THEATREWORKS** troupe (650/463-1950), the **LIVELY ARTS** series at Stanford University (650/725-2787), or the top-name talents currently appearing at the **SHORELINE AMPHITHEATER** (1 Amphitheater Pkwy, Mountain View; 650/967-3000).

If you have nothing to wear for the show (or, indeed, if you have any other shopping need), Palo Alto won't let you down. **UNIVERSITY AVENUE** and its side streets contain a plethora of interesting stores. The **STANFORD SHOPPING CENTER** (N of downtown on El Camino Real; 650/617-8585) is a sprawling, beautifully landscaped temple of consumerism (stores include Bloomingdales, Macy's, Nordstrom, Ralph Lauren, the Gap, Imaginarium, Crate & Barrel, the Disney Store, and many more). Good places to eat in this shoppers' paradise include Bravo Fono, Bok Choy, Max's Opera Cafe, and Cafe Andrea (avoid the handsome but substandard branch of Piatti).

Palo Alto and its neighbors provide many outlets for bibliophiles. **KEPLER'S BOOKS AND MAGAZINES** (1010 El Camino Real, Menlo Park; 650/324-4321) is a wonderland for serious bookworms, and you'll find a healthy selection of mind food at **PRINTER'S INC.** (310 California Ave; 650/327-6500), **BORDERS BOOKS** (456 University Ave; 650/326-3670), **STACEY'S** (219 University Ave; 650/326-0681), and **BOOKS INC.** (at the Stanford Shopping Center, on El Camino Real near University Ave; 650/321-0600).

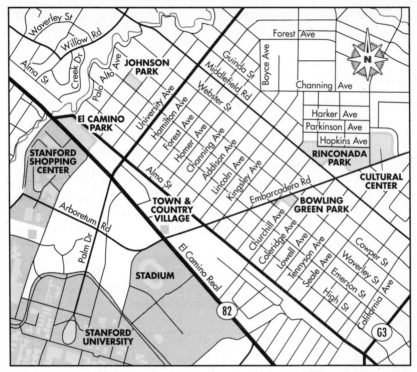

DOWNTOWN PALO ALTO

You'll probably need to follow that literary excursion with a cup of joe. Some of the bookstores, such as Printer's Inc. and Borders, serve coffee and light snacks, but for authentic coffeehouse atmosphere and great espresso try **CAFFÈ VERONA** (236 Hamilton Ave; 650/326-9942) or **CAFE BORRONE** (1010 El Camino Real, Menlo Park; 650/327-0830), located right next to Kepler's. If you'd like to surf the web while you sip your cappuccino, head to **CYBERSMITH** (353 University Ave; 650/325-2005), where you can hook up to the Internet, try out the latest software, or don helmet and gloves for a voyage into virtual reality.

RESTAURANTS

Beppo / ★

643 EMERSON ST, PALO ALTO; 650/329-0665

At one end of the Italian restaurant spectrum lie the sophisticated Northern Italian restaurants with their Euro-sleek decor; at the other stand the Southern Italian family-style restaurants with their posters of the Leaning Tower of Pisa and "Eat, you look too skinny" wait staffs. Then there's Beppo. Picture Alice in Wonderland meets the Knights of Columbus. Picture a place where you enter through the kitchen and wander through a maze of eating areas drenched in Christmas lights, statues glazed in neon colors, and hundreds and hundreds of photos of everything from the Spanish Steps to Sophia Loren in skimpy lingerie. Connie Francis, Dean Martin, and Ol' Blue Eyes himself belt out tunes over the sound system and the exuberant young wait staff often sing along as they plunk down huge serving platters on the red-and-white-checked tables. The small, traditional menu, inscribed on the walls, is as eccentric as the decor: the quantities are so huge and the prices so high ($16.95 for spaghetti with meatballs; $19.95 for chicken cacciatore), you had better come with a big group of people who all like to eat the same food—otherwise you end up with a shopping bag full of leftovers and a bill that's just as hefty. Even with this limited menu there are a few culinary land mines: the pasta is often overcooked and the eggplant Parmigiana tends to be dry and oddly seasoned. But the salads, wafer-thin-crusted pizza, green beans, veal piccata, and tortellini are usually quite good. Whatever you do, save room for the spumoni—it's so good, it almost makes you forgive the crazy reservations policy (too baffling to detail here; call and let the staff try to explain it to you). *$$; AE, DC, MC, V; local checks only; dinner every day; full bar; reservations recommended; between Forest and Hamilton Aves.*

Bistro Elan / ★★★

448 CALIFORNIA AVE, PALO ALTO; 650/327-0284

The Palo Alto restaurant explosion has spread from downtown to other sections of the city, and this natty little bistro, open since 1995, is one of the best and brightest to emerge in the California Avenue area. Although many of the offerings would be at home in any classic French bistro (duck confit, grilled pork tenderloin, lamb ragout), chef/co-owner Ambjörn Lindskog is not averse to taking cues from California cuisine. You'll find such seemingly disparate appetizers as sautéed Sonoma foie gras on brioche with oranges and arugula in hazelnut oil or fresh Maine crab with cucumber, mango, avocado, and a honey-and-coriander vinaigrette. Entrees might range from duck confit with porcini and parmesan risotto to oven-roasted chicken breast with shaved summer truffles, French green beans, prosciutto, and shallots. Desserts include such diverse creations as a stellar warm chocolate tart with whipped cream, a trio of tropical fruit ice creams topped with vanilla-butter sauce, and fresh-baked cookies and cupcakes. *$$$; AE, DC, MC, V; no checks; lunch Tues–Fri, dinner Tues–Sat; beer and wine; reservations recommended; just off El Camino Real.* &

Evvia / ★★★

420 EMERSON ST, PALO ALTO; 650/326-0983

This warm and welcoming restaurant has a sun-drenched, Mediterranean feel. Colored bottles, ceramic plates, and copper pots line the walls and the mantel of an imposing fireplace, beaded light fixtures cast a golden glow, and wooden beams and a planked oak floor add handsome rustic accents. Traditional Greek dishes have succumbed to California's culinary charms here, resulting in an emphasis on fresh produce and interesting twists on traditional dishes such as moussaka and Greek salad. Fish and pasta dishes are other good choices, and if leg of lamb is offered as a special, order it—the meat is exceptionally tender and juicy and comes flanked by some fine roasted potatoes and vegetables. Good desserts include the baklava and the chocolate torte. Order a traditional Greek coffee to top off your meal. *$$$; AE, MC, V; no checks; lunch Mon–Fri, dinner every day; full bar; reservations recommended; between Lytton and University Aves.* &

Higashi West / ★★
636 EMERSON ST, PALO ALTO; 650/323-9378
It's East meets West at this small, slick restaurant, where lamb chops are marinated in shallots and plum wine, mashed potatoes are infused with wasabi, and ravioli comes bathed in an herb-miso cream sauce. Some people will delight in the experimentation (the success of the wasabi mashed potatoes is an especially happy surprise); others might wonder what the heck they're smoking in the kitchen. The space is a bit loud and cramped and service can be slow, but adventuresome eaters will forgive all that. The murmur of the wall-mounted sculptural fountain, the stands of black bamboo, and the modern paintings help create a pleasing, sophisticated setting for the unusual fare. There's an excellent but expensive sushi bar and about a dozen varieties of sake to sip. *$$$; AE, DIS, MC, V; no checks; dinner Mon–Sat; beer and wine; reservations recommended; between Hamilton and Forest Aves.*

L'Amie Donia / ★★★
530 BRYANT ST, PALO ALTO; 650/323-7614
One of the first superstar chefs to desert San Francisco for the Peninsula, Donia Bijan, whose résumé includes the Sherman House and Brasserie Savoy, opened this amiable, bustling French bistro and wine bar in the summer of 1994. Expect traditional favorites such as onion soup, galantine of duck, and steak bordelaise with pommes frites, dished up in a pleasant space dominated by a zinc bar and a battery of banquettes covered in burgundy and green fabric reminiscent of a wine-country harvest. In keeping with her reputation, Bijan renders her traditional fare with a light touch, allowing diners to save room for one of her superb desserts, such as the celebrated tarte Tatin with vanilla ice cream. She has instituted an imaginative wine list, equally divided between California and French varietals, with about half of the well-priced choices offered by the glass. *$$$; AE, DIS, MC, V; no checks; dinner Tues–Sat; beer and wine; reservations recommended; between University and Hamilton Aves.*

Maddalena's Continental Restaurant / ★★★

544 EMERSON ST, PALO ALTO; 650/326-6082

If your mood is romantic, your culinary craving continental, and your wallet well padded, it's time to slip on your glad rags and head over to Maddalena's. This longtime favorite of Palo Alto's haves and have-mores is a splendid example of a dying breed: an unapologetically classic continental restaurant. The lush decor exudes an old-world formality, and waiters in tuxes hover about, ready to spring into service. Chef Jieme Maciel excels with veal dishes and such opulent fare as crisp duck with juniper berries and cassis, delicate poached salmon with a mustard-and-white-wine cream sauce, pheasant with Grand Marnier, and steak au poivre. If it's pasta you fancy, try the Fettuccine Chef Maciel (with smoked duck, spinach, and garlic in a light Roma tomato sauce) or fettuccine with lobster. The desserts, as rich and decadent as you'd expect, include a wonderful house-made cheesecake and a three-layer chocolate mousse cake. The wine list, tipped toward expensive vintages, offers mostly Italian and California selections. For a romantic surprise, book the beautifully appointed art deco private room for two upstairs. If you'd like to sample this Palo Alto classic but your bankroll is a little thin, try Cafe Fino, the less-expensive Italian bistro next door, which has the same management and shares Maddalena's kitchen. *$$$; AE, DC, MC, V; checks OK; lunch Tues–Fri, dinner Mon–Sat; full bar; reservations recommended; between University and Hamilton Aves.*

Spago Palo Alto / ★★★

265 LYTTON AVE, PALO ALTO; 650/833-1000

When Jeremiah Tower and his business partners opened Stars Palo Alto in 1995, it was an undeniable signal that the increasingly sophisticated Peninsula/South Bay restaurant scene had truly come of age. But plagued by management problems, poor service, uneven food, and a dizzying succession of short-lived head chefs (Tower left after just a few months), Stars Palo Alto never quite caught on. Enter Wolfgang Puck. Puck apparently took one look at the dazzling restaurant—and the bulging wallets of the Silicon Valley culinary cognoscenti—and declared that he at last had found the perfect site for his first Northern California outpost since unveiling the highly regarded Postrio in San Francisco in 1989. Spago Palo Alto opened in December 1997, boasting a new exhibition kitchen, a remodeled formal dining room, a separate casual cafe and bar area, and a menu featuring American cuisine with European and Asian influences. This is the seventh Spago in Puck's ever-expanding restaurant empire, which also contains a battalion of informal Wolfgang Puck Cafes and Expresses. And, as at most Puck enterprises, you won't see the celebrity chef in the kitchen very often; instead, Puck-trained executive chef Michael French, who was previously executive sous-chef at Postrio, is the man at the helm. French's menu changes daily; some of his standouts have included an appetizer of oven-roasted calamari stuffed with shrimp and Chinese black-bean sauce, and main courses such as Puck's popular Chinese-style duck with citrus-chile-glazed kumquats and curried vegetables, as well as an oven-roasted monkfish saddle with brussels sprouts and balsamic brown butter. Be sure to top off the memorable meal with the superb bittersweet-chocolate truffle cake. *$$$; AE, DC, DIS, MC, V; no checks; lunch Mon–Sat, dinner every day; full bar; reservations recommended; between Bryant and Ramona Sts.*

LODGINGS

The Garden Court Hotel / ★★★

520 COWPER ST, PALO ALTO; 650/322-9000 OR 800/824-9028
If you like elegance, pampering, and a happening location (well, some people may not), this is a darn good place to stay. A flower-laden courtyard, providing the balcony view for most of the 62 rooms, is surrounded by Italianate architecture draped with arches and studded with colorful tile work and hand-wrought-iron fixtures. The Mediterranean modern rooms are tinted in pastel shades of green, peach, and violet; all have four-poster beds, white faux-marble furniture, and thickly cushioned couches. The suites approach decadence; the penthouse, for example, has a fireplace, a whirlpool bath, and a wet bar. All the little details are covered in style, from an exercise room to terry-cloth robes to complimentary copies of the *Wall Street Journal*. The hotel is in a good shopping and nightlife area, just off University Avenue, and room service is available from Il Fornaio restaurant, which shares the building. *$$$$; AE, DC, MC, V; checks OK; between University and Hamilton Aves.* &

Menlo Park

RESTAURANTS

Bistro La Luna / ★★

1137 CHESTNUT ST, MENLO PARK; 650/324-3810
Flickering candlelight, not *la luna bonita*, illuminates the spare, golden-hued dining room, but the kitchen's what really shines at this small restaurant. The engaging owner, Ali Elsafy, constantly updates the globe-trotting fare, which melds Italian, French, and California flavors with a heavy dose of *sabor Latino*. The menu might include chicken flautas or shrimp soup with corn and potatoes for starters, followed by a simply prepared but tasty roasted trout or chile pepper linguine with chicken and green onions. Vegetarians (or anyone in the mood for a light dish) might try the transportingly delicious roasted red bell pepper with basmati rice and tomato-corn sauce, accompanied by expertly cooked and seasoned spinach and mushrooms. There's a good selection of wines by

the glass, but the dessert menu's limited, consisting mostly of basics like rice pudding, flan, and chocolate cake with vanilla ice cream. *$$; AE, MC, V; local checks OK; lunch Mon–Fri, dinner Mon–Sat; full bar; reservations recommended; between Oak Grove and Santa Cruz Aves.*

Carpaccio / ★★

1120 CRANE ST, MENLO PARK; 650/322-1211

Carpaccio was started by the same folks responsible for the wildly successful Osteria in Palo Alto, but a parting of the ways has left this restaurant to evolve along its own lines. Carpaccio holds tightly to its Northern Italian roots, as evidenced by such dishes as the grilled polenta with tomatoes and pesto and the restaurant's namesake dish, served with onions, capers, lemon, and mustard, plus a grating of grana cheese and a drizzle of olive oil. The real treat here is the free-range veal: the scaloppine features veal medallions and mushrooms, but those in search of the platonic veal ideal should choose the simple grilled chop. Also keep an eye out for the prosciutto-wrapped grilled prawns with garlic and shallots in a smooth lemon-cream sauce. The wood-burning oven (with bricks imported from Italy) turns out divine pizzas with premium toppings laced together with fresh mozzarella, Gorgonzola, and fennel sausage on wonderful smoke-flavored crusts. *$$; AE, DC, MC, V; no checks; lunch Mon–Fri, dinner every day; full bar; reservations recommended; between Oak Grove and Santa Cruz Aves.*

Dal Baffo / ★★

878 SANTA CRUZ AVE, MENLO PARK; 650/325-1588

A dignified fixture on the Peninsula dining scene for more than 20 years, Dal Baffo serves classic continental cuisine in a plush, old-fashioned setting. This is the type of place where tuxedo-clad waiters whip up Caesar salads tableside while the kitchen delights traditionalists with its competent renderings of classic French and Italian dishes. The pasta, lamb, and beef entrees tend to be especially good; if you're in the mood for a magnificent hunk of meat, knife into the filet mignon with foie gras and a black truffle–wine sauce. The award-winning wine list is four inches thick and contains rare (not to mention incredibly expensive) selections that will make a connoisseur's heart go pitter-pat. *$$$; AE, DC, MC, V; no checks; lunch Mon–Fri, dinner Mon–Sat; full bar; reservations recommended; at University Ave.*

LODGINGS

Stanford Park Hotel / ★★★

100 EL CAMINO REAL, MENLO PARK; 650/322-1234 OR 800/368-2468

Cedar shingles, dormer windows, serene courtyards, and a copper-clad gabled roof distinguish this gracious low-rise hotel near Stanford University, just a credit card's throw from the wonderful Stanford Shopping

Center. Some of the 163 rooms have fireplaces, balconies, vaulted ceilings, courtyard views, or parlors, and all are appointed with handsome English-style furniture and splashed with accents of green and mauve—a pleasant change from the timid beige-and-pastel color schemes found in so many other executive-class hotels. The Stanford Park provides a fitness room, a sauna, a heated pool, and a spa for its guests, as well as complimentary newspapers, morning coffee, turndown service, fresh-baked cookies, and shuttle service within the Menlo Park–Palo Alto area. The Duck Club restaurant serves good American regional cuisine and, appropriately enough, duck is the specialty of the house. *$$$$; AE, DC, DIS, MC, V; checks OK; just N of University Ave.* &

Woodside

RESTAURANTS

Buck's / ★★

3062 WOODSIDE RD; 650/851-8010

Since it opened in 1991, Jamis MacNiven's cheery and eccentric restaurant has become one of the most unlikely spots for power breakfasts in all of Silicon Valley and the Peninsula. Where else can you find high-profile execs, entrepreneurs, and venture capitalists cutting deals as they chow down on huevos rancheros and silver-dollar pancakes under brightly painted cowboy hat lamps while life-size marlin figurines, a 6-foot plaster Statue of Liberty, and a flying horse look on? Most of the design touches—including palomino-colored walls, rows of natty cowboy boots, and a portrait of Mona Lisa decked out in a Stetson and bandanna—play into a tongue-in-cheek Western motif, a good fit in this wealthy, horsey community. The food, however, is a cut above chuckwagon fare. Breakfast includes tasty and well-prepared renditions of the usual muffins, waffles, egg dishes, and the like; lunch ranges from chili to hot Dungeness crab sandwiches; and dinner features a freewheeling menu that has everything from Yankee pot roast to chicken piccata "so tender it will sing you to sleep" (it says so right on the mock-newspaper-style menu). *$$; AE, MC, V; no checks; breakfast, lunch, dinner every day; full bar; reservations recommended; near Canada Rd.*

John Bentley's Restaurant / ★★★

2991 WOODSIDE RD, WOODSIDE; 650/851-4988

Housed in Woodside's first firehouse, John Bentley's resembles a snug cabin inside and out. But this is a classy kind of rustic, with wood paneling on the ceiling and walls, a potbellied stove, dangling light fixtures with ribbed-glass shades, chair backs fashioned out of verdigris wrought-iron leaves, and a brown-and-green color scheme that heightens the mountain-retreat mood. In keeping with the atmosphere of backwoods elegance, chef/owner John Bentley serves fare that's bold yet refined and generously laced with rarefied ingredients: lobster-ginger wontons in a delicate broth, ravioli stuffed with artichokes and caramelized onions, medallions of venison with shiitakes and braised red cabbage. With options like apple tart with sun-dried-cherry ice cream and a milk chocolate crème brûlée so smooth it seemingly lacks molecules, desserts are a must here. *$$$; AE, MC, V; local checks only; lunch Tues–Fri, dinner Tues–Sun; beer and wine; reservations recommended; between Hwy 280 and Canada Rd.* &

The Village Pub / ★★★

2967 WOODSIDE RD, WOODSIDE; 650/851-1294

Don't let the name mislead you: this pub in the hills of Woodside is hardly typical of the genre—unless you're used to encountering a parking lot full of Mercedeses, Jaguars, and BMWs in front of your favorite watering hole. You won't exactly find bangers and mash on the menu either—think hearty California cuisine served in a classy, modern setting. Chef Kirke Byers's starters include Thai shrimp ravioli, wild mushrooms sautéed with pears served over goat cheese polenta with huckleberry essence, and raw tuna with wasabi coleslaw. Entrees cover a wide range of standards to suit the pickiest of eaters (seafood, steak, chicken, and pasta), and Byers goes out on a limb with a few creative specials every night. Some intriguing choices include fillet of salmon with a mustard-seed crust and brandy mashed potatoes, Australian lamb with figs and dried cherry pinot sauce, and wild mushroom pasta in a tarragon cream sauce. *$$$; AE, DC, DIS, MC, V; no checks; lunch Mon–Fri, dinner every day; full bar; reservations recommended; 1 mile W of Hwy 280.*

Redwood City

RESTAURANTS

The Redwood Cafe & Spice Company / ★★

1020 MAIN ST, REDWOOD CITY; 650/366-1498

This pretty blue Victorian house with lovely gardens is a welcome surprise in the midst of a rather gritty section of downtown. Celebrated for its wonderful breakfast dishes, the cafe serves soul-satisfying morning fare such as Swedish oatmeal pancakes with lingonberries or house-made applesauce; house-made muffins and scones; and 10 varieties of country egg scrambles, including a smoked salmon, spinach, and cream cheese mélange dubbed the Northern Lights. The cafe also attracts a sizable lunch crowd, drawn as much by the patio outside or the cozy atmosphere inside as by the home-made soups and tasty salads. Sandwiches range from comfortable old standards like chicken salad to more unusual offerings such as Nashelle's Shrimp Sandwich, which features tiny shrimp, creamy dill dressing, and cheddar cheese grilled on sourdough bread. On weekends, there's a well-priced prix-fixe brunch (you may bring your own champagne, if you're so inclined) offering a range of egg dishes as well as sweeter treats like Belgian waffles and pecan pancakes. Whatever the meal, the ingredients are always fresh, the service friendly, and the value outstanding. *$; AE, DC, DIS, MC, V; checks OK; breakfast Tues–Fri, lunch Tues–Fri, brunch Sat–Sun; no alcohol; reservations recommended; at Middlefield Rd.*

2030 / ★★

2030 BROADWAY, REDWOOD CITY; 650/363-2030
Wide, brick-parquet sidewalks, a bevy of attractive restaurants with outdoor cafe seating, and a parade of spiffed-up storefronts announce that gentrification has come to Redwood City, at least along this handsome stretch of Broadway. One of the best spots to grab a bite here is 2030, a stylish restaurant serving generous portions of California and American regional food. At lunchtime you'll find diners on the patio soaking up the rays along with imaginative salads, focaccia sandwiches, and entrees ranging from chicken potpie to agnolotti filled with chicken and prosciutto in an alfredo sauce. Dinners, which include a big bowl of soup and a salad, feature an exciting lineup of ever-changing entrees, which might include steak with a five-pepper crust and Cognac-chive butter, Dungeness crab cakes on linguine tossed with cayenne cream and corn, a double-thick pork chop with sweet potato sauce and pear ginger chutney, and smoked salmon ravioli with asparagus cream and sun-dried tomatoes. In the unlikely event you have room for dessert (portions are huge here), delicacies such as white chocolate cheesecake with warm chocolate sauce, almond brittle with Jamoca Almond Fudge ice cream, and berry shortcake with whipped cream await to sabotage any vestige of self-control. *$$; AE, DIS, MC, V; no checks; lunch Mon–Fri, dinner every day; full bar; reservations recommended; between Jefferson and Main Sts.* &

LODGINGS

Hotel Sofitel San Francisco Bay / ★★★

223 TWIN DOLPHIN DR, REDWOOD CITY; 650/598-9000 OR 800/763-4835
This gray behemoth perched in a corporate park is distinguished by its pretty setting on a man-made lagoon and Gallic touches provided by the French management: filigreed ironwork above the entrance, old-fashioned Parisian street lamps scattered throughout the property, and a staff endowed with charming accents. The 319 spacious guest rooms are decorated in a French country motif and feature blond-wood furniture and amenities like desks, TVs, voice mail, imported toiletries, minibars, and turndown service. The lobby and restaurants boast a large sweep of windows that take full advantage of the Sofitel's waterfront location, and the hotel is equipped with a workout room, a parcourse, a health and beauty spa, and an outdoor pool. French regional food is served all day at the casual Gigi Brasserie, while the formal and well-regarded Baccarat restaurant specializes in classic French cuisine. *$$$$; AE, DC, MC, V; checks OK; turn on Shoreline Dr to reach the hotel's entrance.* &

San Carlos

RESTAURANTS

Creo La. / ★★★

344 EL CAMINO REAL, SAN CARLOS; 650/654-0882

It took awhile for this restaurant serving terrific New Orleans–style food to catch on in San Carlos, but now that the food-savvy know to ignore its inauspicious El Camino Real location and humble facade, Creo La. is coming into its own. Chef/co-owner Bud Deslatte has four other, similar restaurants to his credit—two in Atlanta and one each in New Orleans and San Diego—and he knows how to craft a menu that ably represents the new, lighter side of Creole and Cajun cooking. Deslatte goes right to the source for many of his dishes, flying out andouille sausage, Gulf shrimp, and several other top-notch ingredients from Louisiana. For appetizers, try the Shrimp Bourbon Street (lightly battered, flash-fried prawns served with a tangy orange marmalade–horseradish sauce), Satchmo's Special (red beans and rice with andouille sausage rings), or the crawfish hush puppies with rémoulade. Interesting salads are served, too, including a Caesar topped with bacon-wrapped fried oysters, and the list of entrees includes everything from alligator piccata and pan-blackened catfish to chicken with corn-bread stuffing and crawfish étouffée. For a real taste of the bayou, go for the zesty Cajun Indulgence, a five-course sampler featuring red beans and rice, gumbo, salad, jambalaya, and bread pudding. Creo La.'s lineup of desserts includes a not-to-be-missed silky Cajun Velvet Pie with a light-as-air peanut butter mousse filling. *$$; AE, DC, DIS, MC, V; no checks; dinner Tues–Sat; beer and wine; reservations recommended; just N of Holly St.* &

Kabul Afghan Cuisine / ★★

135 EL CAMINO REAL, SAN CARLOS; 650/594-2840

Afghanistan's national cuisine has roots ranging from the Mediterranean to Southeast Asia. This family-run establishment re-creates these tastes for Northern California with the highest-quality ingredients, including well-marbled meats along with spices the owners procure on trips to Asia and the Middle East. Set in a corner of a small shopping center, Kabul's spacious interior is unexpectedly atmospheric, with glimmering, candlelit, whitewashed stucco walls studded with bright Afghani tapestries and costumes; pink and white tablecloths; and the low whine of sitar music discreetly in the background. The management and servers are charming and attentive (even when you wander in with children—the true test of a place's friendliness quotient). A few dishes shouldn't be missed: the fragrant charbroiled lamb chops marinated in yogurt, olive oil, fresh garlic, and black and white pepper; the splendid sautéed pumpkin topped with yogurt and a tomato-based ground-beef sauce; and *aushak* (leek-and-onion-filled dumplings topped with yogurt and a meat sauce). First-timers might enjoy Kabul's combination platter for lunch—a generous sampler of three popular appetizers. Another Kabul restaurant run by the same family is located in Sunnyvale. *$$; AE, MC, V; checks OK; lunch Mon–Fri, dinner every day; beer and wine; reservations recommended; in the San Carlos Plaza, between Holly St and Harbor Blvd.*

San Mateo

RESTAURANTS

Buffalo Grill / ★★

66 31ST AVE, SAN MATEO; 650/358-8777

Here a Kuleto, there a Kuleto, everywhere a Kuleto—sometimes it seems that no one designs restaurants in the Bay Area these days except Pat Kuleto. Still, there's no denying the appeal that his sophisticated and playful Southwestern decor lends to this mall-side restaurant. Good American regional cuisine—and plenty of it—is dished up in a friendly, high-voltage atmosphere. Chef Keith Lord, formerly of the Lark Creek Inn in Marin County, serves some interesting dishes, such as buffalo carpaccio, maple-cured pork chops with corn spoon bread, and other robust, neo-heartland fare (the roast chicken with garlic mashed potatoes is exceptional). Desserts are smashing: the 10-mile-high devil's food cake with white chocolate ice cream is one perpetual favorite—and so gigantic you'll need help polishing off a serving. For some reason the quality of the food at lunchtime can be uneven, but the kitchen almost always shines at dinner. *$$; AE, DC, MC, V; no checks; lunch Mon–Sat, dinner every day; full bar; reservations recommended; in the Hillsdale Mall off El Camino Real.*

Gibson / ★★★

210 E 3RD AVE, SAN MATEO; 650/344-6566

Named after the onion-garnished classic cocktail and owned by the same folks who run the popular Rumpus in San Francisco, Gibson opened its doors in late 1996 and immediately made the A-list of Peninsula gourmets. Inside, large oil paintings punctuate the peach-colored walls, banquettes and chairs are swathed in a tapestry-like fabric bearing images culled from the Golden Age of Hollywood (think preening starlets and reels of film), and a row of stylized leaded-glass windows and iron-and-glass light fixtures lend art deco touches. Head chef Benjamin Davis, whose credits include stints at San Francisco's Cypress Club and Burlingame's Tavern Grill, specializes in a gutsy brand of California cuisine enhanced by Mediterranean and Asian influences. On one of his seasonal menus, stellar starters included squash ravioli with cranberries, sage, pistachios, and spinach; oysters on the half shell with fennel mignonette; and spicy gulf prawns coyly poised on dollops of white-bean purée. The salads feature marvelously fresh produce, and the entrees included such unusual fare as a moist and tender fillet of halibut steamed in a fragrant broth infused with lemongrass, ginger, and Thai chiles (absolutely wonderful!); slices of perfectly seared tuna accompanied by simmered burdock root; and marinated duck breast flanked by mustard spaetzle and Swiss chard. Desserts run the gamut from a classic crème brûlée to a subtly flavored chèvre cheesecake. The far-ranging wine list is reasonably priced and as imaginative as the food. *$$$; AE, DC, MC, V; local checks only; lunch Mon–Fri, dinner every day, brunch Sun; full bar; reservations recommended; at Ellsworth St.* &

Lark Creek Cafe / ★★

50 E 3RD AVE, SAN MATEO; 650/344-9444

In 1996, uber chef Bradley Ogden expanded his Lark Creek Inn empire by opening this inviting, casual-chic cafe on San Mateo's main drag. Chef John Mitchell continues the Lark Creek tradition of serving what Ogden likes to call "seasonal farm-fresh American fare," a concept that translates into updated versions of such stick-to-your-ribs dishes as chicken and dumplings, meat loaf and mashed potatoes, and spiral pasta with green beans, pesto, and goat-cheese ricotta. You'll also find burgers, pizza, sandwiches, salads, and Ogden's justly celebrated onion rings with blue-cheese dipping sauce. Every evening, a different American classic is featured—grilled liver with bacon and onions on Wednesday, a New England lobster and shellfish bake on Friday, prime rib on Saturday, and so on. Portions are generous, and Lark Creek prides itself on scouring the local produce markets for the best raw ingredients. The smartly designed dining room, with its whimsical collection of gaily painted birdhouses, lark-bedecked light fixtures, roomy booths, and long bar counter, sports an inviting country-sophisticate look, and service is polished and friendly. The wine list is carefully chosen and concentrates on California selections. Another branch of this cafe is located in Walnut Creek. *$$; AE, DC, MC, V; no checks; lunch, dinner every day; full bar; reservations recommended; near El Camino Real, in the Benjamin Franklin Hotel.*

Ristorante Capellini / ★★

310 BALDWIN AVE, SAN MATEO; 650/348-2296

Opened in 1990, this dapper, trilevel restaurant designed by (who else?) Pat Kuleto was one of the first to bring big-city sophistication to San Mateo's dining scene. The antipasto, fried calamari, and *insalata con pera* (a seasonal salad of pears, endive, radicchio, arugula, pine nuts, and Gorgonzola in a champagne-shallot vinaigrette) make excellent starters. You might move on to one of the imaginative, thin-crusted pizzas or entrees such as sole piccata, veal Milanese, and steak with a merlot-mushroom sauce. The pasta is usually excellent here, light and cooked al dente; the long lineup includes linguine with assorted seafood, four-cheese ravioli in a lemon-pesto cream sauce, and penne with pancetta, tomatoes, garlic, mushrooms, and smoked mozzarella. The creamy tiramisu ranks as the most popular dessert, but the *torta di limone* and the warm bread pudding served with brandy hard sauce and a scoop of vanilla gelato are also winners. *$$$; AE, DC, MC, V; no checks; lunch Mon–Fri, dinner every day; full bar; reservations recommended; at the corner of South B St.*

Spiedo Ristorante / ★★

233 4TH AVE, SAN MATEO; 650/375-0818

Good Italian regional fare is served in an attractive, modern setting at this family-friendly restaurant. The owners are justly proud of their mesquite-fired rotisserie, from which emerge herb-kissed and succulent chicken, game hen, rabbit, and duck. Savvy choices from the grill include the salmon, lamb chops, and pork cutlets. The kitchen also has a pleasant way with pasta, turning out delicate noodles flavored by interesting sauces; the agnolotti with smoked salmon and the *tortelloni di ànitra* (hat-shaped pasta filled with duck and zucchini in a sun-dried tomato and wild mushroom cream sauce) are two winners. Pizzas are quite good here, too. When it's time for dessert, forsake the unremarkable gelato and opt for the tiramisu—the raspberry sauce gives this old standard an unexpected twist. *$$; AE, DC, MC, V; no checks; lunch, dinner every day; full bar; reservations recommended; between Ellsworth and B Sts.*

231 Ellsworth / ★★★

231 ELLSWORTH, SAN MATEO; 650/347-7231

This upscale restaurant caters to the refined palates of old-money Peninsulites from Hillsborough and other tony suburbs. The pink-and-aqua color scheme seems a little dated, but it's still a pleasant stage for the ever-changing predominantly French menu. Appetizers might include smoked rabbit with pear brûlée, oysters on the half shell with lemon-pepper ice and vodka, or a selection of forest mushrooms (a specialty here, since the owner also heads a mushroom company). A fillet of beef with hazelnut gnocchi, sweetbreads with black truffles and apple cider, and a roasted, marinated salmon topped with fresh chanterelle cream sauce are typical of the complex, compelling entrees. Primo desserts from celebrated pastry chef Phil Ogiela include an unusual and utterly delicious coriander soufflé and a delicate warm chocolate cake accompanied by a nest of chocolate curls holding a scoop of gelato and sorbet—heaven on a plate. The prodigious cellar offers more than 200 fine wines from Europe and California. Service is usually impeccable, although when the restaurant gets packed, the pace of the meal can sometimes be measured in geologic time. You'll also find a two-course prix-fixe lunch and a four-course dinner that are not outrageously priced. *$$$; AE, DC, MC, V; checks OK; lunch Mon–Fri, dinner Mon–Sat; beer and wine; reservations recommended; between 2nd and 3rd Aves.*

Viognier / ★★★

222 4TH ST, SAN MATEO; 650/685-3727

Among the many conundrums raised by the opening of Viognier—how to pronounce its name (roughly vee-on-YAY, a type of Rhône varietal), why an urbane, four-star chef like Gary Danko decided to set up a post in the 'burbs—perhaps none is more vexing than figuring out exactly what to wear to dinner. The stylish ambience, the refined cuisine, and Danko's stature (former chef at San Francisco's Ritz-Carlton, the James Beard Foundation's 1995 Best Chef in California) all point toward somewhat formal attire. But, darn it all, one does feel just a tad foolish puttin' on the ritz for a restaurant plopped right in the middle of a supermarket, even one as upscale as Draeger's Market Place. However, once you've decided an outfit and slid into one of Viognier's many comfortable booths, you'll settle down to matter at hand: choosing from the intriguing and wide-ranging menu. Danko drew upon his 27 years of cooking experience to design a vigorous and wide-ranging brand of cuisine for his restaurant—you'll find everything from the simple roasted chicken and mashed potatoes to more rarefied delights like chilled lobster salad with mustard-tarragon vinaigrette or grilled quail with creamy polenta, arugula, pine nuts, and wild mushroom sauce. There are usually a couple of lamb dishes, as well as a roster of imaginative vegetarian dishes and specialties from the wood-burning oven. You'll probably still have room for dessert, which may include a frozen almond soufflé with warm chocolate sauce or port-roasted figs and peaches with raspberries and vanilla gelato. Service is courteous and professional, and Viognier's award-winning sommelier, Joseph Stein, is happy to guide your selection from the extensive and extremely well-priced wine list. *$$$; AE, DIS, MC, V; local checks only; breakfast, lunch Mon–Fri, dinner every day, brunch Sat–Sun; full bar; reservations recommended; at B St.*

Burlingame

RESTAURANTS

Kuleto's / ★★

1095 ROLLINS RD, BURLINGAME; 650/342-4922

A spinoff of the popular San Francisco restaurant that bears the same name, this Burlingame branch immediately became one of the area's see-and-be-seen places when it opened in 1993. The sophisticated decor (which isn't, believe it or not, a product of the restaurant's namesake, designer Pat Kuleto) is bright and lively, with expanses of polished wood, a smattering of booths swathed in handsome fabrics, a large wood-burning oven, and a multilevel dining area. Alas, the Northern Italian food is not always as winning as the environment—it's not uncommon to see a diner swooning with ecstasy over a meal while her companion complains about his disappointing dish. Selections such as butternut squash and Mascarpone cheese ravioli with hazelnut and sage brown butter or roasted duck with soft polenta, braised cabbage, and Grappa-soaked cherry sauce are noteworthy. However, the staff is often helpful about steering you through the menu's shoals, and the pizzas, salads, and many of the roast meats and pasta selections are noteworthy. *$$; AE, DC, DIS, MC, V; no checks; lunch Mon–Fri, dinner every day; full bar; reservations recommended; just W of Hwy 101.*

Tavern Grill / ★★

1448 BURLINGAME AVE, BURLINGAME; 650/344-5692
This upscale bar and grill opened in 1995 and immediately won raves for its stylish ambience and chef Benjamin Davis's delicious Cal-Med-American fare. Davis left a year later to head up the kitchen at San Mateo's Gibson (see review, above), but his successor, Vince Nannini, is doing a fairly good job of maintaining the quality of the food. Nannini has shifted the menu's focus to American bistro dishes, with starters such as smoked salmon on a corn and green-apple pancake with chive crème fraîche, andouille-crusted prawns, and smoked chicken ravioli on sweet-onion confit. Main courses include jambalaya with prawns, chicken, and sausage; grilled flatiron steak with balsamic syrup and horseradish mashed potatoes; and herb-crusted lamb chops with apple-mint relish and Creole mustard. The mango crème brûlée and the bittersweet chocolate torte are two stars on the dessert roster. The dining room has a California-meets-England feel, with a two-story bar, a large stone fireplace, wainscoting, and a Victorian-style lantern at the entrance. The bar scene is always hopping, and a wide variety of both live and recorded music is offered most nights. Service can range from charming to downright surly, efficient to space-cadetish. *$$; AE, MC, V; no checks; dinner every day; full bar; reservations recommended; 4 doors E of El Camino Real.*

LODGINGS

Embassy Suites San Francisco Airport-Burlingame / ★★★

150 ANZA BLVD, BURLINGAME; 650/342-4600 OR 800/EMBASSY
This hotel's a towering pink-and-aqua spectacle more typical of the sunny Southland than Northern California. In front, a cobblestone drive encircles a Spanish-style fountain; just inside, another fountain gurgles in front of the junglelike atrium. Each of the 340 suites has a private bedroom and a separate living room complete with a refrigerator, wet bar, coffeemaker, microwave, two color televisions, two telephones, and a pull-out sofa bed. Ask for a room overlooking San Francisco Bay. You can amuse yourself by lounging in the indoor swimming pool or by checking out the action at Bobby McGee's, a popular singles bar and restaurant specializing in hearty fare like steaks, ribs, and chops. *$$$; AE, DC, DIS, MC, V; checks OK; just off Hwy 101.*

Millbrae

RESTAURANTS

Hong Kong Flower Lounge / ★★★

51 MILLBRAE AVE, MILLBRAE; 650/878-8108 OR 650/692-6666
1671 EL CAMINO REAL, MILLBRAE; 650/588-9972

Hong Kong, probably the world's most competitive culinary arena, has hundreds of excellent restaurants vying to produce the freshest, subtlest, and most exciting flavors. In 1987 Alice Wong, whose family owns four Flower Lounges in and around that city, expanded their empire to California with a small restaurant on Millbrae's main drag. Its success prompted her to open another fancier branch on Millbrae Avenue, followed by another location in San Francisco, although the city branch doesn't win quite the same raves (see review). Fortunately, the food at the Millbrae locations has remained legendary, thanks largely to the Hong Kong chefs, who continue to produce cuisine according to the stringent standards of their home city. The red, gold, and jade decor is pure Kowloon glitz (although the patrons are comfortably informal), and the service is outstanding. Among the best dishes on the vast menu are the exquisite minced squab in lettuce cups, the delicate crystal scallops in shrimp sauce, the fried prawns with walnuts, and any fish fresh from the live tank. An excellent Peking duck is served at a moderate price. *$$; AE, DC, DIS, MC, V; no checks; lunch, dinner every day; full bar; reservations recommended; at El Camino Real (Millbrae Ave); at Santa Clara Ave (El Camino Real).*

LODGINGS

Oyster Point Marina Inn / ★★

425 MARINA BLVD, MILLBRAE; 650/737-7633

This small, pleasant hotel works hard to accentuate the positive (attractive, well-appointed rooms, a spectacular bay setting) and diminish the negative (the fact that you have to wade through an industrial park to get here). In keeping with its marina setting, the modern, Cape Cod–style inn is decked out in a snappy nautical-looking blue-and-white color scheme, and the 30 guest rooms have bay views and tile fireplaces. Some rooms come equipped with saunas, featherbeds, and VCRs. A continental breakfast is included in the price of the room, and there's free shuttle service to nearby San Francisco International Airport (by prior arrangement). A branch of the popular Pasta Moon restaurant occupies part of the first floor, and its deck overlooks the marina and is a great place for lunch on a warm day (see review in the Half Moon Bay section of the Central Coast chapter). *$$$; AE, DC, DIS, MC, V; checks OK; take the Oyster Pt Blvd exit off Hwy 101, head toward the bay, and turn right at Marina Blvd.*

CENTRAL COAST

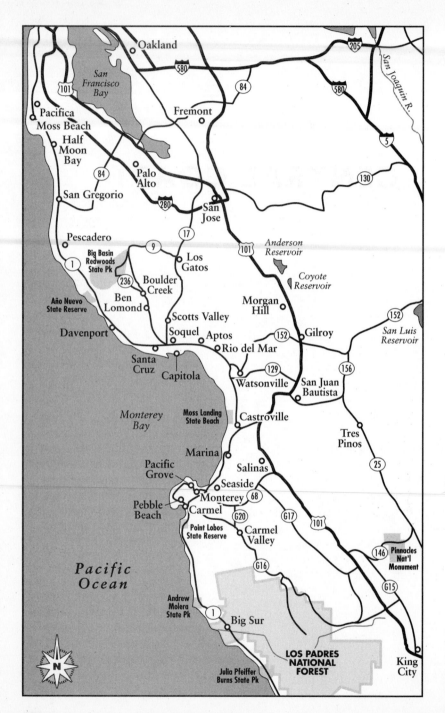

CENTRAL COAST

With its dramatic coastlines, farmlands, forests, and unique small towns, Northern California's Central Coast offers up breathtaking beauty with laid-back style. Even though it's easily accessible from either San Francisco or Southern California, the Central Coast feels as though it's taken a time-out from the rush and noise of the rest of the world. It's the perfect place to spend hours collecting seashells or listening to the silence of the redwood trees, and you won't have to worry about bumping elbows with anyone. With 16 state and national parks, there's more than enough nature to go around.

The largest park on the Central Coast is one you might not see up close, unless you take a fishing or whale-watching excursion from Half Moon Bay, Santa Cruz, or Monterey, but its influence and importance is felt everywhere here. The **MONTEREY BAY MARINE SANCTUARY**, established in 1992, is a vast biologic conservatory that stretches from the mouth of the San Francisco Bay in the north to the tip of Big Sur in the south, encompassing one-fifth of California's coastline and covering 5,300 square miles. Monterey Canyon, the most dramatic submarine feature of the sanctuary, is more than 10,000 feet deep and rivals the Grand Canyon in size and topographic complexity. The nutrient-enriched seawater that upwells from its steep walls draws in more than 30 species of marine mammals, making it one of the Northern Hemisphere's most diversified underwater areas. On land, the Central Coast is dotted with beach towns, farm communities, and vacation destinations; underwater, it's an international hub.

ACCESS AND INFORMATION

Northern California's Central Coast includes nearly 400 miles of shoreline, from Pacifica in the north to Big Sur in the south. **HIGHWAY 1**, also named the **CABRILLO HIGHWAY** after the first Spanish explorer to lay claim to the land, is a scenic two-lane highway that meanders all along the coast, connecting with **HIGHWAY 92** at Half Moon Bay, **HIGHWAY 17** at Santa Cruz, and **HIGHWAY 101** near Monterey. The Central Coast's inland valleys are served by Highway 101, but anyone traveling the inland route from San Francisco will want to take **HIGHWAY 280** to avoid commuter traffic on the 101 San Francisco–San Jose stretch.

SAN FRANCISCO INTERNATIONAL AIRPORT (650/876-2377; www.flysfo.com) is near the end of a $2.4 billion face-lift, which will offer passengers the largest international terminal in the nation, new parking garages, a consolidated rental car center, a BART station, and an airport rail system linking it all. Visitors to points south—Santa Cruz to Big Sur—will appreciate the convenience of **SAN JOSE INTERNATIONAL AIRPORT** (408/277-4759). It's smaller than SFO and less congested but offers many of the same flights as its larger cousin to the north. **CAR RENTALS** are available at both airports and in the larger cities, such as Santa Cruz and Monterey.

With a rainy season that lasts from November through March, and an average daily temperature of 60°F—that's year-round—no one's ever going to confuse the Central Coast with Malibu. During spring and summer, offshore breezes strip away the warm surface waters of the Pacific and bring frigid waters to the top. The result is a heavy marine layer (also known as fog) that settles over the coast morning and evening. It's always wise to carry a sweater, as summer can be just as blustery as winter. This might not be everyone's idea of perfect beach weather—but when summer temps scorch the valleys, there's a massive influx of cool-ocean-breeze worshippers. The best months are September and October, when the crowds disappear along with the fog.

Half Moon Bay Region

With the exception of Half Moon Bay, the picturesque stretch of shore between Moss Beach and Año Nuevo has been left undisturbed by development (thanks in part to the often blustery weather hereabouts). This lack of super-luxe lodgings is a boon to nature lovers, as many of the beaches are open to the public. Check out the more than 200 species of marine animals at Moss Beach's Fitzgerald Reserve, or pay a visit to the elephant seals' breeding ground at Año Nuevo.

ACCESS AND INFORMATION

Highway 92, which intersects Highway 280 and Highway 101 south of San Francisco, is the main route into Half Moon Bay. Highway 1 also offers direct access; turn east at Highway 92 to go downtown. The **HALF MOON BAY VISITORS BUREAU** (520 Cally Ave; 650/726-8380; www.coastsidelive.com; at Hwy 1) is open Monday though Friday 9am to 4pm, Saturday 10am to 3pm.

Moss Beach

RESTAURANTS

Moss Beach Distillery / ★★

BEACH WY AT OCEAN BLVD, MOSS BEACH; 650/728-5595

Used by bootleggers during Prohibition to store their illicit wares, this coastal grande dame was treated to a $2 million face-lift back in 1997, and the old gal's better for it. With its blue-painted walls, cozy dining alcoves, and massive patio and windows affording magnificent ocean views, the cliff-side landmark still has its beguiling 1920s beach-house atmosphere. The food has gotten considerably better, too, with new chef Greg Fedderse in charge of the kitchen. Gone is the pedestrian surf-and-turf fare; in its place are tasty, creative California-Mediterranean dishes such as grilled portobello mushrooms with cabernet sauce, shrimp tempura with a ginger vinaigrette, and a fork-tender pork chop enlivened by a mustard-shallot sauce and leek-buttermilk mashed potatoes. As if the views, historical setting, and good food weren't enough, the Distillery also lays claim to a couple of resident ghosts, including the famous Blue Lady, a flapper-era beauty who's said to haunt the place searching for her faithless lover. *$$; AE, DC, DIS, MC, V; no checks; lunch Mon–Sat, dinner every day, brunch Sun (patio menu available all day); full bar; reservations recommended; www.mossbeachdistillery.com; from Hwy 1, take the Cypress Ave turnoff and turn right on Marine Blvd, which turns into Beach Wy.*

LODGINGS

Seal Cove Inn / ★★★

221 CYPRESS AVE, MOSS BEACH; 650/728-7325
Karen Brown Herbert (of *Country Inns* guidebook fame) knows what makes a superior bed-and-breakfast, and she didn't miss a trick when she and her husband, Rick, set up their own. The result is a gracious, sophisticated B&B that somehow manages to harmoniously blend California, New England, and European influences in a spectacular seacoast setting. The large, vaguely English-style country manor has 10 bedrooms that overlook a colorful half-acre wildflower garden dotted with birdhouses. All the rooms have wood-burning fireplaces, fresh flowers, antique furnishings, original watercolors, grandfather clocks, hidden televisions with VCRs, and refrigerators stocked with free beverages. One thing's for sure: you won't starve here. Early in the morning, you'll find coffee and a newspaper outside your door, and later Herbert serves a full breakfast, wherever you prefer to eat. In the afternoon, wine and hors d'oeuvres are offered in the dining room. The inn's extravagant backyard garden fronts open parkland with seaside meadows and a miniforest of cypress trees. On the other side of the park is the Fitzgerald Marine Reserve, one of the area's best spots for exploring tide pools. Nearby are some interesting local restaurants, horseback riding on the beach, and a seaside bike trail. *$$$$; AE, DIS, MC, V; checks OK; sealcove@coast side.net; www.sealcoveinn.com; 6 miles N of Half Moon Bay on Hwy 1, then W on Cypress Ave.* &

Princeton-by-the-Sea

LODGINGS

Pillar Point Inn / ★★

380 CAPISTRANO RD, PRINCETON-BY-THE-SEA; 650/728-7377 OR 800/400-8281
Located on a bustling harbor with a commercial fishing fleet, sportfishing and whale-watching charters, a few popular restaurants, and a busy pier, this modern inn is surprisingly quiet. Cheery and reminiscent of Cape Cod, the inn's 11 sunny, smallish rooms have harbor views, private baths, gas fireplaces, featherbeds, and televisions with VCRs. Breakfast, served in the

CENTRAL COAST THREE-DAY TOUR

DAY ONE: Marine magic. Grab a latte and a bagel on the way and start the day by exploring the teeming tide pools of the **Fitzgerald Marine Reserve** at **Moss Beach**. Enjoy lunch at **Moss Beach Distillery**, then browse the shops along Half Moon Bay's quaint Main Street, or go to **Sea Horse Ranch** for a horseback ride along the beach. Drive south on Highway 1 to check into your deluxe tent bungalow at **Costanoa** in Pescadero. For an ocean view of the setting sun, take the Pampas Heaven Loop Trail. Start at the main trailhead at Costanoa, cross Whitehouse Creek Bridge, and follow Whitehouse Creek Trail to the loop. Try **Duarte's Tavern** in Pescadero for dinner, or bring your own fixins and fire up one of the barbecues in the camp.

DAY TWO: Sweet nature and spas. Rise early and walk the **Redwood Nature Trail** to commune with the flora and fauna in **Big Basin Redwoods State Park** (21600 Big Basin Wy; 831/338-8860). Return to Costanoa for continental breakfast, a shower, and a sauna; don't forget to stock up on gourmet goodies for the road at Costanoa's General Store. Take Highway 1 south and follow the signs to **Pacific Grove** and 17-Mile Drive for a tour of some of the world's most expensive real estate. Exiting 17-Mile Drive at Ocean Avenue will put you right in the center of **Carmel**'s many bou-

common room, includes coffee, tea, juice, house-made granola, fresh fruit, and a daily hot entree such as cheese-potato pie, quiche, or Belgian waffles. *$$$–$$$$; AE, MC, V; checks OK; www.pillarpointinn.com; 4 miles N of Half Moon Bay on Hwy 1, then W on Capistrano Rd.* &

Half Moon Bay

Victorian houses and boutiques line downtown Half Moon Bay, the oldest city in San Mateo County, while produce stands, U-pick farms, well-stocked nurseries, and flower farms ring its perimeter. Once a sleepy town whose main attraction was its annual Pumpkin Festival, Half Moon Bay has become a satellite city for neighboring Silicon Valley—and seen its real estate prices rise right along with the sale of microchips. At once chichi and funky, it has an old-time Americana ambience residents and visitors love; anyone witnessing its Fourth of July parade or annual Civil War Reenactment will get a kick out of the low-key, small-town hoopla. Half Moon Bay also has a history as a hippie haven: Rocker Neil Young lives in the mountains off Highway 92, and tie-dyed establishments such as Mystic Gifts and the Center for Contemporary Shamanism somehow fit right in with the flag-waving elders and cell-phoning commuters. Even though there's plenty to do and see, and enough good restaurants to keep you well fed from dawn to dusk, Half Moon Bay is

tiques and restaurants. After lunch at **Casanova Restaurant,** you can opt for a little shopping, or a walk along glorious Carmel Beach. Head to **Carmel Valley** to spend the night at **Bernardus Lodge**. Before dinner at the lodge's **Marinus Restaurant**, freshen up with a dip in the pool, or indulge in a massage or facial at the luxurious on-site spa.

DAY THREE: Big Sur-prises. After breakfasting on your private terrace, enjoy a game of tennis, boccie ball, or croquet at Bernardus, or a round of golf at one of Carmel Valley's championship courses. Travel south on Highway 1 for a look at literary memorabilia in the **Henry Miller Library** and lunch at Big Sur's **Nepenthe Restaurant**. Browse the **Phoenix Gift Shop** at Nepenthe for imported treasures and locally made jewelry, soaps, and aromatic oils before driving a few miles north to the **Post Ranch Inn**. After checking in to your mountain- or ocean-view cabin, take the walking trail down to the inn's Olympic-size pool for a late afternoon swim, or drink in an amazing view of the Pacific (and predinner cocktails, if you like) while relaxing in the giant hot tub known as the Basking Pool. End the day with dinner at Post Ranch's romantic **Sierra Mar Restaurant** and some stargazing from the restaurant patio.

the antithesis of bright lights, big city. From all indications it plans to stay that way—good news for those looking for a peaceful getaway.

The Half Moon Bay area offers some of the most scenic beaches north of Carmel, with long stretches of white sand and protected tide pools. **MONTARA BEACH** and **SAINT FRANCIS BEACH** are arguably the most beautiful; **VENICE BEACH** and **DUNE BEACH** are among the least crowded. Surfers hang-ten at (where else?) **SURFER'S BEACH** in El Granada and at **MAVERICK'S,** which is just south of Princeton-by-the-Sea and is famous for its challenging and sometimes lethal waves. For the best tide pools, explore the **FITZGERALD MARINE RESERVE** (650/726-2913) at nearby **MOSS BEACH**. Look for signs along Highway 1 for directions to the reserve.

PILLAR POINT HARBOR, 4 miles north of Half Moon Bay off of Highway 1, is the place to go for seasonal whale-watching and sportfishing tours. **CAPTAIN JOHN'S FISHING TRIPS** (650/726-2913 or 800/391-8787) and **HUCK FINN'S SPORTFISHING** (650/726-7133 or 800/572-2934) offer excursions for salmon and cod for approximately $50 per person. Huck Finn's also has a daily whale-watch outing January through March. **CALIFORNIA CANOE & KAYAK** (650/728-1803) offers rentals and lessons for those who like to paddle their own boat.

You can explore Half Moon Bay's beach on horseback or bicycle. **SEA HORSE & FRIENDLY ACRES RANCH** (Hwy 1; 650/726-2362 or 650/726-8550; 1 mile N of Hwy 92) offers trail and beach rides with or without guides for adults and children 5 and up; pony rides are available for children ages 1 through 4. At the **BICYCLERY** (432 Main St; 650/726-6000) you can rent mountain bikes for $8 an hour or $24 all day. Knowledgeable staffers will steer you toward the best biking trails in the area.

The Arnold Palmer–designed **HALF MOON BAY GOLF LINKS** (2000 Fairway Dr; 650/726-6384; at the S end of Half Moon Bay next to the Half Moon Bay Lodge) is rated among the top 100 courses in the country, with two 18-hole oceanside courses.

The **HALF MOON BAY ART & PUMPKIN FESTIVAL** (650/726-9652), held annually in October, is known for its acres of U-pick pumpkins, pumpkin-carving and pie-eating contests, and the very, very long line of cars creeping along Highway 92 into town. Unfortunately, the only way to avoid the worst of the gridlock is to make hotel reservations far in advance and arrive before the crowds.

RESTAURANTS

Pasta Moon / ★★

315 MAIN ST, HALF MOON BAY; 650/726-5125
Executive chef Matthew Kurze, formerly chef de cuisine at San Francisco's One Market, has updated Pasta Moon's traditional Italian-style menu with lighter, more creative fare. Kurze's new approach features lots of locally grown, organic produce, and fresh fish. Start with an appetizer of Half Moon Bay artichokes "à la greque," served with Italian butter beans, arugula, and lemon vinaigrette, or house-smoked salmon with pickled pearl onions and parsley salad. *Secondi piatti* include wood-oven-roasted veal chop stuffed with portobello mushrooms, parmesan polenta, and endive with thyme-infused olive oil, and pan-seared sea bass with asparagus and risotto with lemon, garlic, and shrimp vinaigrette. The focaccia is heavenly, the house-made pasta seldom disappoints, and pizza lovers can select from a wide range of thin-crust creations. Pastas, breads, and pastries are all made on the premises. *$$; AE, DC, DIS, MC, V; local checks only; lunch, dinner every day, brunch Sun; full bar; reservations recommended; in the Tin Palace, at the N end of Main St, near Hwy 92.*

San Benito House / ★★

356 MAIN ST, HALF MOON BAY; 650/726-3425
A pastel blue Victorian on Half Moon Bay's Main Street, San Benito House has a candlelit dining room that's one of the prettiest on the Central Coast, decorated with country antiques, vases of fresh flowers, and paintings by local turn-of-the-century artists. At lunch, the deli cafe turns out top-notch sandwiches on fresh house-made bread, perfect for a repast in the garden or on one of the nearby beaches. A trio of chefs—owner Greg Regan, Carol Mickelsen, and Lidia Machado—presides over the kitchen at dinnertime, turning out such interesting California-Mediterranean fare as homemade ravioli stuffed with fennel, fontina,

and toasted almonds with creamy leek sauce, fillet of beef with Gorgonzola and herb butter, and salmon topped with a lemon-caper vinaigrette on a bed of lentil ragout. Desserts are terrific here, and may include a strawberry-rhubarb crepe served with crème anglaise and strawberry sauce, chocolate-espresso custard with Chantilly cream, and a pear poached with ginger and port wine. Too stuffed to move? Consider spending the night upstairs in one of the dozen modest but cheerful guest rooms (the one above the garden is the best). *$$; AE, DC, MC, V; no checks in the restaurant, advance checks OK in the hotel; lunch (deli cafe only) every day, dinner (main restaurant only) Thurs–Sun; full bar; reservations recommended; www.sanbenito house.com.* &

Sushi Main Street / ★★

696 MILL ST, HALF MOON BAY; 650/726-6336
The food is Japanese, the decor is Balinese, and the background music might be anything from up-tempo Latin to bebop American. Hard to envision, yes, but these elements come together beautifully at Sushi Main Street, a funky yet tranquil oasis in the heart of town. The alluringly offbeat ambience blends Eastern elements with contemporary Western details like spot lighting and towering flower arrangements. Grab a seat at the L-shaped sushi bar, pull up a chair at one of the rust-colored asymmetrical slate tables, or, if you're feeling limber, plunk yourself down at the large, low table designed for traditional cross-legged dining. You might want to tickle your tonsils with a drop of the special sake (served room temperature in a traditional wooden box) or nosh on a kelp salad (a crisp, sesame-laden mixture of Japanese seaweeds) before diving into your main course. You can choose from a wide range of sushi and sashimi, from arctic surf clams to marinated mackerel. For a Zen sense of wholeness, top off your meal with green-tea ice cream or a dessert roll with papaya, plum paste, sesame seeds, and teriyaki sauce. *$$; MC, V; checks OK; lunch Mon–Sat, dinner every day; beer and wine; reservations recommended; www.SushiMainSt.com; just off Main St.*

LODGINGS

Beach House Inn at Half Moon Bay / ★★★

4100 COAST HWY 1, HALF MOON BAY; 650/712-0220 OR 800/315-9366
This three-story Cape Cod–style building overlooking Pillar Point Harbor offers 54 deluxe suites with enough amenities to make you feel right at home. Each guest room features a separate sleeping area, step-down living room with fireplace, private patio or balcony, wet bar, refrigerator, microwave, two TVs, and five-CD disk player. Oversize baths offer deep soaking tubs and separate showers. A small swimming pool and roomy Jacuzzi spa on the south-facing terrace afford views of Surfer's Beach and local surfers—a perfect place to warm up on a foggy morning. If the spa and the calming sound of surf aren't enough to work out those stress-related kinks, make an appointment

with the Beach House Day Spa for a massage or aromatherapy wrap; for a small extra charge, the massage therapists will perform their healing ministrations in your room. A complimentary continental breakfast is served in the lobby. *$$$$; AE, DC, DIS, MC, V; checks OK; view@beach-house. com; www.beach-house.com; 3 miles N of Half Moon Bay.*

Cypress Inn on Miramar Beach / ★★☆

407 MIRADA RD, HALF MOON BAY; 650/726-6002 OR 800/83-BEACH
With Miramar Beach literally 10 steps away, this wonderful modern inn is the place to commune with the ocean along the Peninsula coast. From each of its 12 rooms you not only see the ocean, you hear it, smell it, even feel it when a fine mist drifts in with the morning fog. The cheerful wooden building, set at the end of a residential block, has beamed ceilings, skylights, terra-cotta tiles, colorful folk art, and warm, rustic furniture made of pine, heavy wicker, and leather: sort of a Santa-Fe-meets-California effect. Each room has a featherbed, a gas fireplace, its own bath, and an ocean view. Most have private balconies, and the enormous penthouse also boasts a two-person soaking tub. The older rooms don't come with televisions, but the obliging innkeepers will put one in your room if you ask. Breakfast is far above the standard B&B fare; expect fresh juices, croissants, a fruit parfait, and made-to-order entrees such as eggs Benedict and the inn's signature peaches-and-cream French toast. In the afternoon you'll find an elaborate feast of wine and hors d'oeuvres (perhaps prosciutto and melon, freshly baked quiche, and fresh fruit pie) in the common room. And if the proximity to the sea, engaging decor, great food, and flawless service aren't enough to relax you, make a reservation with the in-house masseuse. *$$$$; AE, MC, V; checks OK; lodging@cypressinn.com; www.cypressinn.com; 3 miles N of the junction of Hwys 92 and 1, turn W on Medio Rd, and follow it to the end.* &

Mill Rose Inn / ★★

615 MILL ST, HALF MOON BAY; 650/726-8750
One of the oldest bed-and-breakfasts on the Peninsula coast, the Mill Rose Inn fancies itself an old-fashioned English country house, with an extravagant garden and flower boxes as well as all the requisite lace curtains, antique beds, and nightstands. Romantics may love it here, but the inn's profusion of fabric flowers and slightly garish wallpapers (think William Morris on LSD) take it over the top for many folks; frankly, the overall effect is more Harlequin romance than authentic British country manor. The rooms are spacious and chock-full of creature comforts, the hosts are friendly, and the Jacuzzi, tucked inside a frosted-glass gazebo, is quite enjoyable on a chilly coastal evening. The six guest rooms have private entrances and private baths, king- or queen-size featherbeds, fireplaces (with the exception of the Baroque Rose Room), and views of the garden. They also have telephones, tele-

visions with cable and VCRs, well-stocked refrigerators, fresh flowers, chocolates, and liqueurs. Two rooms, the Bordeaux and Renaissance Suites, have sitting rooms as well. In the morning, you'll find a newspaper outside your door and a full breakfast that you can enjoy in the dining area or in the privacy of your room. *$$$–$$$$; AE, DIS, MC, V; checks OK; www.millroseinn.com; 1 block N of Main St.*

Old Thyme Inn / ★★
779 MAIN ST, HALF MOON BAY; 650/726-1616
Located on the quiet southern end of Main Street, this 1898 Victorian B&B was sold in 1998 to Rick and Kathy Ellis, who refurbished it with style and grace. Each of the seven guest rooms—named after the herbs that grow in the inn's English garden—are painted in restful colors and decorated with well-chosen antiques. All offer a private bath, TV and VCR, and sumptuous queen-size featherbed topped with down comforter and imported linens. The Garden Room and the Thyme Room feature double whirlpool tubs and fireplaces. Every morning, Kathy serves gourmet breakfasts with delectable entrees such as lemon-rosemary or banana-coconut crumb cake, quiche du jour, lemon-cheese pancakes with strawberry syrup, chiles rellenos, zucchini souffle, or eggs Benedict. Wine and hors d'oeuvres are served daily in the parlor. *$$$–$$$$; AE, DC, DIS, MC, V; checks OK; innkeeper@oldthymeinn.com; www.old thymeinn.com; near Filbert St.*

The Zaballa House / ★★
324 MAIN ST, HALF MOON BAY; 650/726-9123
The oldest building in Half Moon Bay, this 1859 pastel blue Victorian offers a few amenities that go beyond the usual B&B offerings. Homey, pretty, and unpretentious, the nine guest rooms in the main house are decorated with understated wallpaper and country furniture. Some have fireplaces, vaulted ceilings, or garden views. None have telephones, but three rooms have TVs. A more recent addition that was designed and painted to mimic this historic structure houses three attractive (and costlier) private-entrance suites that feature kitchenettes, double Jacuzzis, VCRs, and private decks. Each is decorated differently: Casablanca-inspired number 10 is a charming, airy room with skylights, ceiling fans, and light wood-and-wicker furniture; number 11 has a French country look; room 12—the most opulent—uses red velvet and plaster pillars, busts, and cornices to create an over-the-top classical look that will thrill some and be Greek to others. Whether you're staying in the suites or in the original structure, in the evening you may partake of wine, hors d'oeuvres, and cookies by the fireplace in the main house's snug, antique-filled living room. Come morning, guests are treated to a lavish buffet breakfast. *$$–$$$; AE, DIS, MC, V; checks OK; www.zaballahouse.com; at the N end of town.*

Pescadero

LODGINGS

Costanoa / ★★★★

2001 ROSSI RD, PESCADERO; 650/879-1100 OR 877/262-7848

Ever dream of communing with the great outdoors without all the packing and unpacking, tent collapsing in the middle of the night, or pesky critters in your sleeping bag? Costanoa's lodge, cabins, and tent bungalows provide an ideal alternative. Set in a pristine wilderness bordering four state parks and 30,000 acres of hiking trails, Costanoa is a perfect place to get away from it all in grand style. With its wide variety of accommodations, you can choose exactly how rough you want to rough it. If you're a tenderfoot, stay in the lodge, a striking cabinlike structure with 40 superlative guest rooms. In keeping with Costanoa's eco-sensibilities, the rooms are decorated with a well-designed mix of natural materials: polished wood, slate tile, and pale, earth-toned hues. Room amenities include private baths, Bose stereo systems, refrigerators, robes, private decks, and access to the lodge's spa facilities and outdoor hot tub. Many rooms have fireplaces and soaking tubs. One step lower on the luxury ladder are the six duplex cabins. Each of the 12 cabin rooms features a vaulted ceiling, fireplace, and deck with porch swing that overlooks wild, lush terrain. The cabins don't have private baths, but one of six "comfort stations" (sleek and upscale, with heated floors, large showers, and dry saunas) is only a short walk away. Reserve one of the deluxe tent bungalows for Costanoa's most unique lodging experience. Their queen-size beds, down comforters, heated mattress pads, and retro-style furnishings will make you feel like Meryl Streep in *Out of Africa* (Robert Redford not included, alas). As with Costanoa's other accommodations, daily maid service and continental breakfast are part of the deal. A variety of less luxurious tent bungalows are also available, as is a small area for pitching your own tent or parking your RV. The General Store on the premises offers a coffee bar and deli with all the makings for a gourmet picnic; the small spa offers massage, sauna, and steam room. *$–$$$$; AE, DC, DIS, MC, V; no checks; www.costanoa.com; Hwy 1 between Pigeon Point Lighthouse and the Año Nuevo State Reserve, 9 miles S of Pescadero.*

Año Nuevo State Reserve

You're not the only one having fun in the sun. For a seaside sex show, pull off Highway 1 between the coastal towns of Pescadero and Davenport (22 miles north of Santa Cruz) at Año Nuevo State Reserve (800/444-4445, tickets; 650/879-0227, information; www.anonuevo.org), a unique and fascinating breeding ground for **NORTHERN ELEPHANT SEALS**. A close encounter with a 16-foot-long, 2-ton male elephant seal waving his humongous schnoz is an unforgettable event. The seals are named after the male's dangling proboscis, which can grow up to a couple of feet long. The reserve is open year-round, but you'll see hundreds of these marine mammals during their mating season, which starts in December and continues through March. To access the reserve during the mating season, you must have a reservation for one of the 2½-hour naturalist-led tours (offered Dec 15–Mar 31). The tours are terrific and tickets are cheap, but they sell out fast, so plan about two months ahead (and don't forget to bring a jacket).

Santa Cruz and the Monterey Bay Area

Although the Santa Cruz Boardwalk gets the lion's share of visitors, there's much more to do in the Santa Cruz region than ride the country's oldest roller-coaster. For adventures off the beaten track, try the redwood-studded valley setting of Ben Lomond, the historic mission at San Juan Bautista, or the tiny hamlet of Tres Pinos.

Back before the wine boom of the '70s and '80s, going on a **WINE-TASTING TOUR** was something of an adventure. Napa and Sonoma have become major-league tourist stops in recent decades, but it's still possible to find smaller, boutique wineries along Northern California's Central Coast. **RIDGE VINEYARDS** (17100 Montebello Rd, Cupertino; 408/867-3233) earned its reputation with superb zinfandels and cabernets. It's easy to get lost on your way to **ROUDON-SMITH WINERY** (2364 Bean Creek Rd, Santa Cruz; 831/438-1244), but its estate-grown chardonnay is worth the risk. If you want to find out why wine maker Randall Graham named his Rhône-style red wine after a "flying cigar," visit **BONNY DOON VINEYARD** (10 Pine Flat Rd, Santa Cruz; 831/425-3625).

ACCESS AND INFORMATION

HIGHWAY 1 and scenic but highly trafficked **HIGHWAY 17** lead right into the center of Santa Cruz. Just "over the hill" is **SAN JOSE INTERNATIONAL AIRPORT**, with plenty of major airlines and **CAR RENTAL COMPANIES. GREYHOUND** (800/231-2222) provides service to Santa Cruz's downtown bus terminal (425 Front St, Santa Cruz; 831/423-1800). The excellent **VISITORS INFORMATION CENTER** (1201 Ocean St, Santa Cruz; 800/833-3494; www.santacruzca.org) boasts a friendly staff and lots of info about area attractions and events.

Highway 1 continues on with direct access to Monterey. From **HIGHWAY 101**, take the **HIGHWAY 156–MONTEREY EXIT**, which merges with Highway 1. The **MONTEREY PENINSULA AIRPORT** (831/648-7000; www.montereyairport.com; Hwy 68 off Holsted Rd, 4 miles from Monterey) has nearly 100 arrivals and departures daily, with connections to all domestic and foreign airlines. **CAR RENTAL** offices of Avis, Budget, and National are located here. **AMTRAK'S** (800/USA-RAIL) Coast Starlight route stops in Salinas; free bus service is provided for the 30-minute ride into downtown Monterey. The **MONTEREY PENINSULA VISITORS AND CONVENTION BUREAU** (831/649-1770; Lake El Estero at Franklin and Camino El Estero; www.monterey.com) is open seven days a week year-round.

Ben Lomond

RESTAURANTS

Ciao! Bella!! / ★★

9217 HWY 9, BEN LOMOND; 831/336-9221

This exuberant restaurant, nestled in a mountain redwood grove, serves what owner Tad Morgan describes as "new California-Italian" cuisine. In addition to nightly specials, Ciao! Bella!! serves up delectable pasta dishes, ranging from Tutto Mare (prawns, clams, calamari, and fresh fish sautéed in cream and white wine) to Penne alla Napoletana (penne with tomatoes, basil, garlic, and mozzarella tossed in a marinara sauce). *Secondi piatti* include scampi as well as chicken with prosciutto, mozzarella, and spinach, topped with a sauce of basil, tomatoes, and garlic. Be sure to save room for the yummy house-made desserts: zabaglione, tiramisu, and bread pudding. *$$; AE, DIS, MC, V; no checks; dinner every day; beer and wine; reservations recommended; just S of town.*

Santa Cruz

Most of Santa Cruz's 3 million annual visitors flock to the Santa Cruz Beach Boardwalk, but there's much more to this beachside city than thrill rides, hot dogs, and T-shirt shacks—just ask any one of the 54,000 folks who call it home. Keep in mind, however, that you'll get a different answer from each person you query. Wet-suit-clad surfers will point to the best waves on the West Coast; tweedy intellectuals might mention Santa Cruz's University of California campus and excellent bookstores; well-dressed matrons love the gracious neighborhoods near West Cliff Drive; dot-com entrepreneurs thrive on the proximity to Silicon Valley and the growing number of upscale eateries; and dreadlocked Deadheads will give an enthusiastic nod to the city's active nightlife and ultraliberal politics.

Santa Cruz (Spanish for "holy cross") was founded by the ubiquitous Father Junípero Serra when he built the **MISSION OF THE HOLY CROSS** (corner of Emmet and High Sts; 831/426-5686) here in 1791. The mission was destroyed by earthquakes in 1857 and 1858, but in 1931 a half-size replica was built and is open to the public. Every day except Monday you can take part in a morning mass and view some of the mission's original books and vestments.

The half-mile-long, 100-year-old **SANTA CRUZ BEACH BOARDWALK** (400 Beach St; 831/423-5590) is the last remaining beachfront amusement park on the West Coast. Take a spin on the famous Giant Dipper, one of the best and oldest wooden roller coasters in the country (with a great view at the top), then grab a seat on one of the intricately hand-carved horses on the 1911 Looff Carousel (both rides are listed on the National Register of Historic Places). Of course, the Boardwalk (now a cement walk) also caters to hard-core thrill-seekers who yearn for those whirl-and-twirl rides that do their best to make you lose your lunch. If you're among the crowds here on a Friday night in the summer, don't miss the Boardwalk's free concerts, which feature retro rock 'n' roll from groups such as the Shirelles, the Drifters, and the Coasters.

Beaches are Santa Cruz's other crowning glory. On the north end of West Cliff Drive is **NATURAL BRIDGES STATE BEACH**, named after arch-ways carved into the rock formations here by the ocean waves (only one of the three original arches still stands). The beach is popular with surfers, windsurfers, tide-pool trekkers, and sunbathers, as well as fans of the migrating monarch butterflies that roost in the nearby eucalyptus grove from late October through February. On the south end of West Cliff Drive is **LIGHTHOUSE FIELD STATE BEACH**, the reputed birthplace of American surfing. This beach has several benches for sitting and gazing, a jogging and bicycling path, and a park with picnic tables, showers, and even plastic-bag dispensers for cleaning up after your dog (it's one of the few public places in town where canines are allowed). The nearby brick light-house is now home to the tiny **SANTA CRUZ SURFING MUSEUM** (West Cliff Dr at Lighthouse Point; 831/420-6289), the first of its kind in the world, which is chock-full of hang-ten memorabilia (admission is free).

Between the lighthouse and the Boardwalk is that famous strip of the sea known as **STEAMERS LANE**, the summa cum laude of California surfing spots (savvy surfers say *this*—not Southern California—is the place to catch the best breaks in the state). Watch the dudes ride the gnarly waves, then head over to the marvelous (but often crowded) white-sand Santa Cruz Beach fronting the Boardwalk. The breakers are tamer here, and free volleyball courts and barbecue pits make this a favorite spot for sunbathing, swimming, picnicking, and playing volley-ball on the sand courts. In the center of the action is the 85-year-old **MUNICIPAL WHARF**, where you can drive your car out to the shops, fish markets, and seafood restaurants.

The **PACIFIC GARDEN MALL** (a.k.a. Pacific Avenue), Santa Cruz's main shopping district, was hit hard by the Loma Prieta earthquake in 1989, but the entire area has been rebuilt, and it's shinier and spiffier than before. Major retailers such as the Gap and Starbuck's have settled in alongside book, antique, and vintage clothing stores; movie theaters; and sidewalk cafes. As you make your way down the mall, look for the **OCTAGON BUILDING**, an ornate, eight-sided Victorian brick edifice built in 1882. The building once served as the city's Hall of Records and is now part of the **MCPHERSON CENTER FOR ART AND HISTORY** (705 Front St; 831/429-1964; at Cooper St), where museums showcase 10,000 years of the area's past as well as contemporary art of the Pacific Rim.

The nearby **BOOKSHOP SANTA CRUZ** (1520 Pacific Ave; 831/423-0900) has an inventory worthy of any university town, with a particularly good children's section, an adjacent coffeehouse, and plenty of places to sit, sip, and read a bit of your prospective purchase. For great organically grown produce and other picnic-basket goodies, shop at the **FARMER'S MARKET** (Lincoln St, between Pacific Ave and Cedar St), held Wednesday from 2:30pm to 6:30pm.

Another town highlight is the newly constructed **SEYMOUR MARINE DISCOVERY CENTER** (100 Shaffer Rd; 831/459-4308; www2.ucsc.edu/seymourcenter; at the end of Delaware Ave). The center's exhibit galleries, aquariums, and teaching laboratories provide an inside look at a marine research laboratory and the work of researchers at UC Santa Cruz's Institute of Marine Sciences. Can't-miss spectacles include the 87-foot blue whale skeleton and superb vistas of the bay.

For some serious hiking and mountain biking, drive about 23 miles north to the 18,000-acre **BIG BASIN REDWOODS STATE PARK** (21600 Big Basin Wy; 831/338-8860; off Hwy 236, 9 miles N of Boulder Creek), California's first state park and its second-largest redwood preserve. Big Basin is home to black-tailed deer and mountain lions, and 80 miles of trails wind past 300-foot-high redwoods and many waterfalls.

Locomotive lovers, kids, and fans of Mother Nature should hop aboard one of the trains at **ROARING CAMP AND BIG TREES NARROW-GAUGE RAILROAD** (5355 Graham Hill Rd, Felton; 831/335-4400). The Roaring Camp Train is a narrow-gauge, steam-powered train that makes a 6-mile round-trip excursion through stately redwood groves to the summit of Bear Mountain; Big Trees Railroad offers an 18-mile round-trip ride through mountain tunnels and along ridges with spectacular views of the San Lorenzo River before stopping at the Santa Cruz Beach Boardwalk. Train schedules vary seasonally.

RESTAURANTS

El Palomar / ★★

1336 PACIFIC AVE, SANTA CRUZ; 831/425-7575

Even on a rainy day, this lovely, vibrant restaurant hidden at the back of a former '30s hotel has a sunny atmosphere. Maybe it's the tall vaulted-and-beamed ceiling painted in the Spanish manner, the huge mural depicting a Mexican waterfront village scene, or all the plants in big ceramic urns, but something about the place puts you in a good frame of mind even before the food shows up. El Palomar is known for its seafood dishes, which are topped with exotic sauces, but traditional Mexican favorites such as bur-

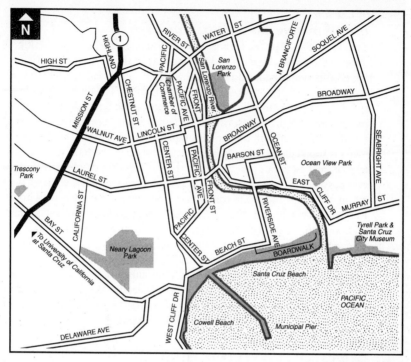

SANTA CRUZ

ritos and tacos are also outstanding. A casual new sister restaurant, Cafe El Palomar (222 E Cliff Dr; 831/462-4248), serves breakfast, lunch, and "taco cafe" fare beside the Santa Cruz harbor from 7am to 7pm. *$$; AE, DIS, MC, V; local checks only; lunch, dinner every day; full bar; reservations recommended; in the Pacific Garden Mall, near Soquel Ave.* &

O'mei Restaurant / ★★★

2316 MISSION ST, SANTA CRUZ; 831/425-8458
Named after a mountain in the Sichuan province of China, this acclaimed Chinese restaurant is a wondrous little paradox tucked into one of Santa Cruz's many strip malls. Chef/owner Roger Grigsby is not Chinese, nor are any of his cooks, but his food caters less to American sensibilities than do most Chinese restaurants. While you may order predictable northern Chinese offerings such as Mongolian beef and mu shu pork, those with adventurous palates are better served if they forgo the old standbys. Pushing the envelope of Chinese cuisine, O'mei offers tasty provincial curiosities such as litchi chicken and an enchanting black sesame ice cream. Another plus: O'mei boasts a limited but well-chosen wine list, with most wines available by the glass. *$$; AE, MC, V; no checks; lunch Mon–Fri, dinner every day; beer and wine; reservations recommended; near Fair Ave.*

Oswald / ★★★

1547 PACIFIC AVE, SANTA CRUZ; 831/423-7427

Thanks to chef Damani Thomas's adept cooking, reverence for fresh produce, and restrained spicing and saucing that let the flavors of the principal ingredients sing out loud and clear, this small California-French bistro will remind you of Berkeley's celebrated Chez Panisse. The dining room has a spare, arty look, with bold still-life paintings on the brick and pale-yellow-painted walls, high ceilings, wooden banquettes, and a petite wrought-iron-railed balcony set with a couple of tables. Chef Thomas's small seasonal menu is supplemented nightly by a roster of specials that take good advantage of the best meats and veggies in the markets that day (organic whenever possible). Expect starters such as pecan-encrusted chèvre coquette with marinated beets and white truffle oil or Belgian endive salad with apple, Roquefort cheese, and walnuts. Entrees might include steamed Atlantic salmon with lentils and gremolata, rack of lamb with potato gratin and tapenade, or seared day boat scallops over asparagus risotto dressed with black trumpet mushroom vinaigrette. The servers are knowledgeable and solicitous, and the wine list features a good lineup of both California and French offerings. *$$; AE, DC, MC, V; local checks OK; dinner every day; beer and wine; reservations recommended; use the parking lot on Cedar St and enter the restaurant through the courtyard.* &

Ristorante Avanti / ★★★

1711 MISSION ST, SANTA CRUZ; 831/427-0135

Newcomers who take one look at this unpretentious restaurant set in a humble strip mall may be forgiven for thinking, "Three-star restaurant? I don't think so." Ah, but wait until they've tasted the food and experienced the considerate, professional service. In keeping with the Santa Cruz lifestyle, Avanti prides itself on serving "the healthiest meal possible" (think fresh, organic produce and free-range chicken, veal, and lamb). The modern, casual decor, with a long wooden counter dominating one of the small rooms and Italian ceramics scattered throughout, provides a welcome setting for aromatic, seasonal dishes such as sweet squash ravioli with sage butter, lasagne al forno, spaghetti with wild-mushroom and shallot duxelles, and orecchiette with salmon, Italian greens, mushrooms, and sun-dried tomatoes. The ample and reasonably priced wine list contains selections from California, France, Spain, and Italy. Don't even think about skipping dessert: any one of the ever-changing selections is worth an extra 20 minutes on the Stairmaster. *$$; AE, MC, V; local checks only; breakfast, lunch, dinner every day; beer and wine; reservations recommended; near Bay St.* &

LODGINGS

The Babbling Brook Inn / ★★

1025 LAUREL ST, SANTA CRUZ; 831/427-2437 OR 800/866-1131

Set in a fantastical garden with waterfalls, wishing wells, gazebos, and, of course, a babbling brook, Santa Cruz's oldest B&B offers 13 rooms, most named after famous artists. The mauve-and-blue Van Gogh Room has a private deck, a fireplace, a beamed ceiling, and a whirlpool tub for two. Peach and ivory predominate in the Cézanne Room, with its generous bath and canopy bed. The blue-and-white Monet Room has a corner fireplace, a canopy bed, a private deck, and a view of the waterfall and footbridge. In the morning, you can choose from a delectable spread of fruit compote, muffins, croissants, fresh-squeezed orange juice, yogurt, fresh coffee, and more. *$$$; AE, DC, DIS, MC, V; checks OK; www.babblingbrookinn.com; near California St.*

Casablanca Inn / ★★

101 MAIN ST, SANTA CRUZ; 831/423-1570 OR 800/644-1570; 831/426-9063 (RESTAURANT)

Right across the street from the beach and wharf, the Casablanca Inn has a close-up view of the ongoing street carnival that is the Santa Cruz Boardwalk. The 39 comfortable rooms are divided between the four buildings of the Cerf Mansion, a multilevel Spanish-style structure with red-tile roof. Because the Cerf Mansion is a historic building, each room has a slightly different configuration, and rooms on the upper end of the rate scale have decidedly more personality. All guest rooms come with telephones, cable TV, microwaves, and refrigerators; a good number feature fireplaces, kitchens, or private terraces; and 33 of the 39 have ocean views. If you're in the mood for a party, reserve a room facing Beach Street; if you'd rather stay in a less boisterous environment, opt for a room in the Guest House or Carriage House. There's nothing very Moroccan about the hotel's Casablanca Restaurant, a boardwalk bastion of California-continental cuisine, except, perhaps, the palpable air of romance. Starters include fried calamari with a spicy lime dipping sauce and Blue Point oysters on the half shell. Entrees range from grilled salmon with citrus vin blanc to filet mignon with wild mushroom whole grain demi-glace. Local wines share a book-length wine list with selections from Italy, Germany, France, and Australia. *$$$; AE, DC, DIS, MC, V; checks OK; www.casablanca-santacruz.com; at Beach St, on the waterfront.*

Cliff Crest Bed and Breakfast Inn / ★

407 CLIFF ST, SANTA CRUZ; 831/427-2609

History, the allure of an antique-laden Victorian house, and views of the Santa Cruz Boardwalk and the bay beyond are all a part of this welcoming five-room B&B. With grounds designed by Golden Gate Park architect John McLaren, this 1887 Queen Anne inn is the former home of Lieutenant Governor William Jeter and his formidable wife, Jenny. Mrs. Jeter, who lived here until her death at age 99, reportedly used her cane to keep unruly nieces and nephews in line and insisted on driving her horse and buggy into town until the authorities prevailed upon the 89-year-old dowager to desist in 1949. These days, guests are greeted by the charming and, rest assured, far more easygoing hosts Bruce and Sharon Taylor. Some painting and minor carpentry wouldn't be amiss, but the lack of these doesn't really detract from the feeling of old Santa Cruz charm fostered by the inn's intricate woodwork, stained glass, intriguing nooks, and converted gaslight fixtures. The Rose Room boasts bay views, a sitting area, and an Eastlake bed, while the more modest Jenny's Room offers a window seat and a shower reputedly large enough for three (Aunt Jenny must be turning in her grave). Two other guest rooms have fireplaces. All the rooms are equipped with telephones, TVs are available upon request, and the complimentary full breakfast may be served in bed or on the garden terrace outside. *$$–$$$; AE, DIS, MC, V; checks OK; innkpr@cliffcrestinn.com; www.cliffcrestinn.com; near 3rd St.*

Capitola-by-the-Sea

Just east of Santa Cruz sits Capitola-by-the-Sea, a tiny, very popular resort town nestled around a small bay. The small downtown is a quaint, jumbled mix of restaurants, gift shops, and beachwear boutiques reminiscent of resort towns of yesteryear. Capitola's broad, sandy beach attracts lots of sun worshipers, primarily because it's sheltered from the wind; it's also bordered by a charming promenade. At the west end of town is the bustling 867-foot-long **CAPITOLA PIER**—a great place to hang out, admire the view of the town, and, on weekends, listen to live music. Many anglers come here to try their luck at reeling in the big one (and you don't need a license to fish from a pier in California). If you'd rather try your luck out at sea, visit **CAPITOLA BOAT & BAIT** (1400 Wharf Rd; 831/462-2208; closed Jan–mid-Feb) at the end of the pier. Rates are reasonable and include fuel, safety equipment, and a map of the hot fishing spots. You can also rent fishing gear and purchase one-day licenses, so there's no excuse not to brave the open ocean—if only just for the halibut.

RESTAURANTS

Gayle's Bakery & Rosticceria / ★★

504 BAY AVE, CAPITOLA-BY-THE-SEA; 831/462-1200

Take a number and stand in line. It's worth the wait at this wildly popular place, which is packed with local folk on weekend mornings. A bakery and deli, Gayle's offers numerous imaginative sandwiches, pastas, casseroles, roasted meats, salads, cheeses, appetizers, breads, and treats. The variety is staggering and the quality first-rate. There's a good selection of wine, beer, bottled water, and espresso drinks, too. Once you've fought your way to the counter, you'll have the makings of a first-class picnic to take to one of the nearby parks or beaches. You can also eat your feast in the cafe's small dining area or on the heated patio. *$; MC, V; checks OK; breakfast, lunch, snacks (6:30am–8:30pm) every day; beer and wine; no reservations; by Capitola Ave.*

LODGINGS

The Inn at Depot Hill / ★★★

250 MONTEREY AVE, CAPITOLA-BY-THE-SEA; 831/462-3376 OR 800/572-2632

The Inn at Depot Hill is a dream of a place, with trompe l'oeil paintings on the walls and soft, sophisticated lighting that bathes everyone in an angelic glow. The 12 guest rooms, lavishly designed to evoke international ports of call, seem to have sprung directly from the pages of *Architectural Digest*. The terra-cotta-walled Portofino Room sports a stone cherub, ivy, frescoes, and a brick patio. No less charming is the Stratford-upon-Avon, a faux English cottage with a cozy window seat. The Railroad Baron is an opulent yet tasteful study in red and gold, with a large marble bath that features a deep soaking tub. Every room has a TV and a VCR, a built-in stereo system, and a marble bathroom with mini-TV and coffeemaker. In the morning, there's a buffet of pastries, cereal, and fruit, as well as a hot dish such as French toast or potato frittata. In the evening, you'll find homemade desserts and wine in the downstairs parlor. *$$$$; AE, MC, V; checks OK; lodging@innatdepothill.com; www.innatdepothill.com; near Park Ave, next to railroad tracks.*

Aptos

RESTAURANTS

Cafe Sparrow / ★★

8042 SOQUEL DR, APTOS; 831/688-6238

Owner Bob Montague opened this quaint French country restaurant in June 1989. Then along came the Loma Prieta earthquake on October 17th (whose epicenter lay just a short distance away), and Montague had little more than a pile of rubble on his hands. Fortunately, he didn't throw in the trowel, and the remodeled restaurant is indeed a gem of a dining spot, acting as a magnet for local gourmets. Two charming rooms, decorated in a casual yet elegant style with custom-painted walls and a tentlike expanse of French printed fabric, provide an enchanting backdrop for chef Josh Elliott's spirited culinary creations. Start with a pâté of fresh chicken livers seasoned with fresh herbs and Cognac, grilled prawns with orange beurre blanc, or a fondue of white wine, herbs, and cheeses, served with fresh fruits, vegetables, and croutons. Then progress to such entrees as a grilled chicken breast and pears topped with Brie, oven-roasted rack of lamb with an herbed Dijon mustard crust, or pan-sautéed calamari steak with lemon, butter, and capers. Desserts are as decadent as you'd expect from a place that seems intent on spoiling its customers rotten. One unexpected touch: This sophisticated restaurant isn't afraid to be kid-friendly, and dishes tailored to tots are available. The wine list is far-ranging and agreeably priced, and the service is amiable. *$$; MC, V; checks OK; breakfast, lunch Mon–Sat, dinner every day, brunch Sun; beer and wine; reservations recommended; www.cafesparrow.com; near Trout Gulch Rd.*

LODGINGS

Seascape Resort / ★★

I SEASCAPE RESORT DR, APTOS; 408/688-6800 OR 800/929-7727

This new condo-resort complex on 45 cliff-side acres offers spacious accommodations and plenty of creature comforts. The more than 250 guest suites are arranged in a cluster of three-story stucco buildings and are available in studio or one- or two-bedroom configurations. Each suite is outfitted with identical beach-house-style furnishings—not especially luxurious but pleasant enough—and comes with a fireplace, a private balcony or patio, a TV, a kitchenette, sitting and dining areas, a modem port, and an ocean view. A paved path leads down to the beach, and guests enjoy member privileges at a nearby PGA-rated golf course and the Seascape Sports Club, which offers tennis, swimming, and a fully equipped gym. There's 24-hour room service, a children's program during the summer, and a spa offering massage and beautician services. Fresh seafood is the specialty at Sanderlings, the resort's airy, Florida-style restaurant with patio dining and gorgeous ocean vistas. *$$$$; AE, DC, MC, V; checks OK; www.seascaperesort.com; at Sumner Blvd 9 miles S of Santa Cruz.* &

Rio Del Mar

RESTAURANTS

Bittersweet Bistro / ★★

787 RIO DEL MAR BLVD, RIO DEL MAR; 831/662-9799

In its earlier incarnation as Cafe Bittersweet, this sleek restaurant and wine bar was embraced by Santa Cruz foodies. Now in spacious new digs a few miles down the road in the old Deer Park Tavern, and six times the size of the previous cafe, the restaurant features a patio for dining alfresco and a stylish mahogany, lacquer, and black granite bar area. Chef/owner Thomas Vinolus is still at the kitchen's helm, creating appetizers such as the tasty grilled shrimp served over a bed of greens and white beans or Monterey Bay calamari. Pasta offerings include seafood puttanesca and five-cheese ravioli. For a main course, order the grilled lamb sirloin with a rosemary-cabernet demi-glace or the Bitter-sweet Paella. The seasonal menu also features a range of pizzas from the wood-fired oven. The pretty-as-a-picture desserts are scrumptious—no surprise, given that the chef's last gig involved whipping up pastries at Carmel's Casanova restaurant. The wine list is extensive and varied, with some interesting if pricey older vintages among its treasures. *$$$; AE, MC, V; local checks only; late lunch 3pm–6pm, dinner every day, brunch Sun; full bar; reservations recommended; www.bittersweet-bistro.com; take Hwy 1 south of Santa Cruz to the Rio Del Mar exit.* &

Gilroy

Will Rogers called Gilroy the only town in America where you can marinate a steak just by hanging it out on the line—and, yes, when the wind's blowing in the right direction, the aroma from the area's garlic fields is just about that strong. So it only made sense that the people of Gilroy decided in 1979 to celebrate their odoriferous claim to fame with the now-famous **GARLIC FESTIVAL** (408/842-1625; www.gilroy garlicfestival.com), held the last weekend in July. The three-day-long festivities attract throngs of people eager to try such oddities as garlic ice cream and garlic chocolate and to enter their own stinking-rose recipes in the Great Garlic Cook-Off. You may also buy any number of garlic-based foodstuffs and doodads. To find out about Gilroy before the age of garlic, visit the **GILROY HISTORICAL MUSEUM** (5th and Church Sts; 408/848-0470). If bargain hunting, not garlic, happens to set your heart aflutter, be sure to stop at the newly expanded **PRIME OUTLETS** (Leavesley Rd; 408/847-4155; just east of Hwy 101), with 150 attractive outlets for big-name retailers.

San Juan Bautista

This sunny little town is home to one of the most beautifully restored missions in California. Built just 2 feet away from the main trace of the San Andreas Fault, **MISSION SAN JUAN BAUTISTA** (831/623-2127) was nearly destroyed by the 1906 quake, but locals raised the money to rebuild it. With its pretty chapel and gardens, the mission sits on a broad plaza surrounded by other well-preserved Spanish colonial buildings. On the first Saturday of the month, docents dress in period costume and give tours; fans of Alfred Hitchcock's *Vertigo* will want to explore the bell tower from which Kim Novak's character fell to her death. San Juan Bautista is also home to the world-famous theater troupe **EL TEATRO CAMPESINO** (705 4th St; 831/623-2444). Director Luis Valdez left the San Francisco Mime Troupe in the '60s to form this political theater group composed of migrant farmworkers. The group puts on plays throughout the year and is most famous for its Christmas plays, *La*

Virgen del Tepeyac and *La Pastorela*, presented at the mission. Hikers, rock climbers, bird-watchers, and other nature lovers will want to explore the cliffs and caves of nearby **PINNACLES NATIONAL MONU-MENT** (831/389-4485), a glorious 16,000-acre volcanic park located high in the hills above the Salinas Valley off Highway 101.

RESTAURANTS

Felipe's California & Mexican Cuisine / ★

313 3RD ST, SAN JUAN BAUTISTA; 831/623-2161
One of several Mexican places on San Juan Bautista's main street, this crowded storefront restaurant serves all the standard Mexican fare—good chicken mole, pork burritos, and light, freshly made tortilla chips—but its Salvadoran dishes are what set it apart from its neighbors. Especially delicious are the handmade *pupusas* (fat corn tortillas stuffed with cheese) and the *plátanos fritos* (fried plantains) served on a bed of rich, nicely textured, refried pinto beans. The Salvadoran dishes are served with an appropriately tangy pickled-cabbage dish called *curtido*. Felipe's also has several good Mexican beers. Don't leave without trying the fried ice cream, a house specialty. Vegetarians take note: Felipe's uses no lard. *$; MC, V; no checks; lunch, dinner Wed–Mon; beer and wine; no reservations; between Mariposa and Polk Sts.*

Tres Pinos

RESTAURANTS

Inn at Tres Pinos / ★★

6991 AIRLINE HWY, TRES PINOS; 831/628-3320
Tres Pinos is one of those blink-and-you'll-miss-it towns, but it's worth keeping your peepers wide open to catch this intriguing restaurant. "Keep it fresh and keep it simple" is owner Mike Howard's philosophy, a credo that executive chef Rob Stevens translates into a continental menu with an Italian accent. Popular dishes include filet mignon with green peppercorn sauce, Fettuccine Fantasia (chicken, artichoke hearts, sun-dried tomatoes, olives, herbs, and garlic with a white-wine and cream sauce), and calamari sautéed in chardonnay and butter. Rustic but surprisingly elegant, the inn wins high praise for both its desserts and its romantic atmosphere. *$$$; AE, MC, V; local checks only; dinner Tues–Sun; full bar; reservations recommended; 5 miles S of Hollister.* &

Moss Landing

Nature lovers have long revered Moss Landing's **ELKHORN SLOUGH** as a prime spot to study egrets, pelicans, cormorants, terns, great blue herons, and many other types of aquatic birds, not to mention packs of frolicking harbor seals and otters. Besides hiking or kayaking, one of the best ways to explore this scenic coastal wetland is to embark on an **ELKHORN SLOUGH SAFARI** (831/633-5555; www.elkhornslough.com). Naturalist guides provide expert and enthusiastic commentary aboard a 27-foot-long pontoon boat, and special activities (such as Bird Bingo) are provided for children. Binoculars are available for rent, and coffee, soda, and cookies are served on the way back. The two-hour tours operate every day, year-round.

RESTAURANTS

The Whole Enchilada / ★

7902 HWY 1, MOSS LANDING; 831/633-3038

Fresh seafood is the focus of this upbeat restaurant on Highway 1. Gaily painted walls, folk-art decorations, and leather basket chairs lend an engaging south-of-the-border ambience. You'll find the usual lineup of burritos, tacos, chiles rellenos, and enchiladas on the comprehensive menu, but go for one of the more exotic regional specialties, such as Tamal Veracruz or Sundried Tomato Castroville Chimichangas. Service is warm and efficient, and little touches like crayons and plastic mermaids clinging to the drink cups make this a place your kids will like, too. *$$; AE, DC, DIS, MC, V; no checks; lunch, dinner every day; full bar; reservations recommended; at Moss Landing Rd.*

Monterey

Since the late 1900s, when the luxurious Hotel Del Monte hosted Victorian-garbed ladies and gents who arrived by carriage or rail, Monterey has attracted more tourists than any other California city except San Francisco. For the past 100 years, visitors have been flocking to the Monterey Peninsula as numerously as the monarch butterflies that arrive en masse each spring, delighting in the breathtaking coastal vistas and the sheltering pines. Along the way, Monterey has had its ups and downs: its whaling-based economy went bust before the 20th century began, and the sardines that fueled a 30-year fishing boom mysteriously disappeared in the late 1940s. The gritty, working-class village of John Steinbeck's *Cannery Row* is no longer here, but shapes and shadows of Monterey's indigenous, Spanish, and early California history still remain in the form of historic adobes, Victorian homes, and bounteous natural beauty.

Along with its neighboring cities of Pacific Grove, Pebble Beach, and Carmel, Monterey is considered a romantic destination, and it may surprise you to learn that it's also a terrific town for a family vacation. In fact, this is one place where you might have a better time if you bring the kids. The Monterey Bay Aquarium (see below) is the flagship for family fun, and adjacent **CANNERY ROW** (831/649-6690; www.canneryrow.com) and **FISHERMAN'S WHARF** (831/649-6544; www.montereywharf.com)

have joined in the regatta, offering kid-friendly activities such as kayaking, biking, roller blading, or simply watching in amazement as hundreds of seals have a raucous party in the marina. Numerous annual events, from the **HISTORIC ADOBE TOUR** to **WHALEFEST**, provide something new and interesting almost every week. There's enough cultural and natural history in Monterey for you to feel that you're doing something educational for your children, and enough tacky thrills in the way of video arcades and souvenir shops to keep them from ever getting bored.

Attracting nearly 2 million visitors each year, the **MONTEREY BAY AQUARIUM** (866 Cannery Row; 831/648-4888 or 800/756-3737; www.montereybayaquarium.org; reservations recommended) is Monterey's jewel in the crown. At 322,000 square feet, it's the largest aquarium in the United States, with more than 300,000 marine animals and plants on display in over 100 galleries and exhibits. The Outer Bay exhibit boasts one of the world's largest indoor aquarium tanks, where you'll see life as it's lived in the open ocean. Other popular exhibits include the towering kelp forest and the sea otter "playground": Be sure to stop by for the daily feedings at 10:30am, 1:30pm, and 3:30pm. The newly opened Splash Zone caters to the little ones, with hands-on, interactive tours through two shoreline habitats.

To get the flavor of Monterey's heritage, follow the 2-mile **PATH OF HISTORY**, a walking tour of the former state capital's most important historic sites and splendidly preserved old buildings—remember, this city was thriving under Spanish and Mexican flags when San Francisco was still a crude village. Free tour maps are available at various locations, including the **CUSTOM HOUSE** (at the foot of Alvarado St, near Fisherman's Wharf), California's oldest public building, and **COLTON HALL** (on Pacific St, between Madison and Jefferson Sts), where the California State Constitution was written and signed in 1849. Call **MONTEREY STATE HISTORIC PARK** (831/649-7118) for more information.

Nautical history buffs should visit the **MARITIME MUSEUM OF MONTEREY** (5 Custom House Plaza; 831/373-2469; near Fisherman's Wharf), which houses ship models, whaling relics, and the two-story-high, 10,000-pound Fresnel lens used for nearly 80 years at the Point Sur lighthouse to warn mariners away from the treacherous Big Sur coast.

The landmark **FISHERMAN'S WHARF**, the former center of Monterey's cargo and whaling industry, is awash in mediocre restaurants and souvenir shops—although, with its seaside-carnival ambience, it's a place the kids might like. The best time to visit is in the winter or spring, when **WHALE-WATCHING TRIPS** sail regularly from the wharf. You'll have a number of tour companies to choose from; a popular choice is **MONTEREY SPORT FISHING AND WHALE WATCHING CRUISES** (96 Fisherman's Wharf; 831/372-2203 or 800/200-2203; www.monterey

baywhalecruises.com). Serious shoppers will be better off strolling **ALVARADO STREET**, a pleasantly low-key, attractive downtown area with a much less touristy mix of art galleries, bookstores, and restaurants. Alvarado Street is also the site of the popular **OLD MONTEREY FARMER'S MARKET AND MARKETPLACE**, a good spot for free family entertainment and picnic-basket treats; it's held Tuesday year-round from 4pm to 8pm in the summer and 4pm to 7pm in the winter.

Children will love the **DENNIS THE MENACE PLAYGROUND** (Camino El Estero and Del Monte Ave, near Lake El Estero). Designed by cartoonist Hank Ketcham, it has enough climbing apparatuses to please a monkey. For fun on the water, take your Curious Georges on a paddleboat and pedal around **LAKE EL ESTERO** (831/375-1484). You can rent bicycles and inline skates at the **MONTEREY BAY RECREATION TRAIL**, which runs along the Monterey shore for 18 miles to Lover's Point in Pacific Grove. More adventurous sorts should get a sea kayak at one of the rental outlets along **DEL MONTE AVENUE** and explore the coast.

The **MONTEREY COUNTY VINTNERS ASSOCIATION** (831/375-9400; www.wines.com/monterey) offers a wine-tasting and touring map of Monterey County's excellent vineyards and wineries, many of which have public tasting rooms and picnic grounds.

For a terrific, toe-tappin' time, visit Monterey on the third weekend in September, when top talents such as Wynton Marsalis, Etta James, and Ornette Coleman strut their stuff at the **MONTEREY JAZZ FESTIVAL** (800/307-3378 for tickets; 831/373-3366 for information; www.montereyjazzfestival.org), one of the country's best jazz jubilees and the oldest continuous jazz celebration in the world. Tickets and hotel rooms sell out fast, so plan early—die-hard jazz fans make reservations at least six months before show time. Monterey also hosts a **BLUES FESTIVAL** (831/649-6544; www.montereyblues.com) in late June, which attracts a respectable but smaller crowd.

RESTAURANTS

Fresh Cream / ★★★

99 PACIFIC ST, MONTEREY; 831/375-9798

One of the most highly rated restaurants on the California coast, Fresh Cream has a veritable mountain of rave reviews to its credit. It's easy to see why. From the delightful complimentary caviar-and-onion tartlet that starts each meal to the divine dessert at the end, the food here is exquisitely prepared and presented. Specializing in French cuisine with hints of California, Fresh Cream has appetizers ranging from lobster ravioli with gold caviar to escargots in garlic butter with Pernod to a smooth-as-silk goose liver pâté with capers and onions. Executive chef Gregory Lizza's luscious entrees include roasted duck with black currant sauce, the definitive rack of lamb Dijonnaise, and a delicate poached salmon in saffron-thyme sauce. Vegetarians needn't feel left out; the tasty grilled seasonal

STEINBECK COUNTRY

"I think I would like to write the story of this whole valley, of all the little towns and all the farms and the ranches in the wilder hills. I can see how I would do it so that it would be the valley of the world," John Steinbeck wrote in 1933 to his friend George Albee.

In many of his novels and short stories, Salinas-born Nobel and Pulitzer Prize–winning author Steinbeck did exactly that. From the Salinas Valley to Big Sur, "Steinbeck country" provided memorable settings for *East of Eden, Cannery Row, The Red Pony, Of Mice and Men,* and *Tortilla Flat.* Although time has changed many of the places Steinbeck described, you can still get a glimpse of the towns, the farms, and even the wilder hills he knew and loved so well.

Salinas's **Old Town Main Street** figures prominently in *East of Eden.* Many of the original buildings were razed due to damage from the 1989 Loma Prieta earthquake, but Old Town still retains its turn-of-the-century charm. Other sites in Salinas include **Central Avenue,** where *East of Eden*'s Adam Trask family lived, and the **Steinbeck House** (132 Central Ave; 831/424-2735), where Steinbeck was born and raised.

Monterey's **Cannery Row** was immortalized in 1945. Steinbeck's famous opening line, "Cannery Row is a stink, a poem, a grating noise," doesn't exactly hold true anymore; the smell left when the canneries closed down in the 1950s. However, a few of Cannery Row's monuments remain, most notably the **Wing Chong Grocery** (835 Cannery Row), which now houses Alicia's Antiques. Stand across the street to see its vintage facade and imagine the Chinese immigrants who lived upstairs in its 22 hotel rooms; inside, be sure to check out the Steinbeck memorabilia room and the collection of authentic Chinese lanterns. If you'd like a personal escort through Steinbeck Country, **Carol Roble & Associates** (831/751-3666) offers tours, slide presentations, and lectures by appointment.

One of the best places to get a feel for Steinbeck's life and work is at Salinas's fascinating **National Steinbeck Center** (1 Main St; 831/775-4720; www.steinbeck.org). Opened in 1998, the center contains a theater with a short biographical film, multimedia exhibits, and gallery with Steinbeck-themed art. This fun, family-oriented museum is no dusty shrine: kids (especially those who can read) will have a blast exploring the colorful interactive exhibits, which allow them to touch clothing and tools in a replica of the bunkhouse from *Of Mice and Men,* smell the sardines at a Monterey cannery, and try washing laundry as the Joads did in *Grapes of Wrath.* If they get too rowdy, have them chill out in the refrigerated boxcar à la *East of Eden.* The on-site gift shop has a comprehensive collection of Steinbeck's works, and the museum's One Main Street Cafe offers breakfast and lunch with regionally inspired dishes such as Gilroy Garlic Fries, Chicken Castroville, and Tortilla Flat Black Bean Soup.　　　　—*Christi Phillips*

vegetable plate is a cut above most veggie entrees. For dessert try the Grand Marnier soufflé or the amazing *sac au chocolat*, a dark chocolate sack filled with a mocha milk shake. Service tends to be a bit on the formal side; the wine list is extensive and expensive. *$$$; AE, DC, DIS, MC, V; checks OK; dinner every day; full bar; reservations recommended; dining@freshcream.com; www.freshcream.com; Ste 100C in the Heritage Harbor complex, across from Fisherman's Wharf.* ⅙

Montrio / ★★★

414 CALLE PRINCIPAL, MONTEREY; 831/648-8880

It's rare indeed to find a haven where all the rough edges have been smoothed off, but that's the delightful state of affairs at this downtown Monterey hot spot. All's welcoming here, from the curved lines and soft-sculpture clouds that define the decor of this converted 1910 firehouse to the insightful, cordial wait staff. The only thing even slightly edgy is the food, which has the lusty, rough-yet-refined flavors characteristic of Rio Grill and Tarpy's, two other local favorites founded by Montrio co-owners Tony Tollner and Bill Cox. Indulge in such eloquent dishes as Dungeness crab cakes with spicy rémoulade and duckling with dried plum–juniper reduction. The Tuesday-night special is another standout: a fork-tender fillet of beef over garlic whipped potatoes in a red wine reduction that one must taste to comprehend. The wine list, which received *Wine Spectator* magazine's Award of Excellence, includes a passel of vintages by the glass. Surprisingly for such a stylish place, a kid's menu and crayons are available, which should keep junior diners as content as their parents. *$$$; AE, DIS, MC, V; no checks; lunch Mon–Sat, dinner every day; full bar; reservations recommended; www.montrio. com; near Franklin St.* ⅙

Stokes Adobe / ★★★

500 HARTNELL ST, MONTEREY; 831/373-1110

A historic peach-colored adobe built in 1833 for the eponymous town doctor is the setting for one of Monterey's most engaging restaurants. Co-proprietors Dorothea and Kirk Probasco (Kirk formerly managed Carmel's Rio Grill and Pacific's Edge at the Highlands Inn) didn't miss a trick when they opened Stokes in 1996. They snagged Brandon Miller as head chef (think Campton Place and Tra Vigne), assembled a well-trained, friendly staff, and redesigned the building with a skillful blend of old and new. The two-story adobe and board-and-batten house is surrounded by lovely gardens and reflects the Spanish character of Old Monterey. Inside, the large space has been divided into several airy dining rooms, with terra-cotta floors, bleached-wood plank ceilings, Southwestern wooden chairs and tables, and white walls dotted with paintings. It's a soothing and lovely showcase for Miller's terrific food, which he describes as contemporary rustic Mediterranean fare. Offerings include butternut squash soup with apple cider and maple crème fraîche; roasted spinach gratin with mussels and herbed bread crumbs; grilled lavender-infused pork chops with savory bread pudding and pear chutney; and cassoulet of duck confit and homemade currant sausage with chestnut beans. Desserts are wonderful here and include such winners as a warm apricot clafouti, chocolate espresso crème brûlée, and warm banana-rum bread pudding with vanilla crème anglaise. A prix-fixe dinner is offered on weekends; it's a real bargain at about $26 (and for another $20 you can get a carefully orchestrated selection of wines). *$$; AE, MC, V; no checks; lunch Mon–Sat, dinner every day; full bar; reservations recommended; www.stokesadobe.com; at Madison St.* &

Tarpy's Roadhouse / ★★★
2999 MONTEREY-SALINAS HWY, MONTEREY; 831/647-1444
Worth a hop in the car for a spin on Highway 68, this exuberant restaurant features a broad, sunny patio shaded by market umbrellas out front and a handsome Southwestern decor inside, with rustic, bleached-wood furniture, golden stone walls, and whimsical art. The menu indulges in a creative approach to traditional American food. Lunch emphasizes well-prepared sandwiches and salads, but dinner is when Tarpy's really excels. Appetizers might include grilled polenta with mushrooms and Madeira, fire-roasted artichokes with lemon-herb vinaigrette, and Pacific oysters with red wine–jalapeño mignonette. Entrees run the gamut from a bourbon-molasses pork chop or a Dijon-crusted lamb loin to sea scallops with saffron penne or a grilled vegetable plate with succotash. Desserts include lemon and fresh ginger crème brûlée, a triple-layer chocolate cake, and olallieberry pie. The wine list has received the *Wine Spectator* Award of Excellence for the past four years. *$$$; AE, DIS, MC, V; no checks; lunch, dinner every day, brunch Sun; full bar; reservations recommended; www.montrio.com/tarpys.htm; at Hwy 68 and Canyon Del Rey.*

LODGINGS

Hotel Pacific / ★★★
300 PACIFIC ST, MONTEREY; 831/373-5700 OR 800/554-5542
Like a Modigliani in a gallery full of Fra Angelicos, this modern, neo-hacienda hotel stands out in the midst of Monterey's authentic old adobes. A sparkling fountain burbles beside the entrance; inside you'll find handwoven rugs, muted Southwestern colors, terra-cotta tiles, and beamed ceilings. Connected by tiled courtyards, arches, and flowered pathways, the hotel's condo-style buildings hold 105 suites. All rooms have private patios or terraces, fireplaces, goose-down featherbeds, three telephones, and two TVs (one in the bathroom). Ask for a room on the fourth level, or a room facing the inner courtyard with its large fountain. A continental breakfast is provided in the morning, and guests may

indulge in afternoon tea. Complimentary underground parking is available, too. *$$$$; AE, DC, DIS, MC, V; checks OK; www.hotel pacific.com; between Scott St and Del Monte Blvd.* &

Monterey Plaza Hotel & Spa / ★★★

400 CANNERY ROW, MONTEREY; 831/646-1700 OR 800/368-2468
Situated right at the edge of Monterey Bay, the Monterey Plaza Hotel brings big-city style and services to Cannery Row. In contrast to the California beach-house decor often found in waterfront hotels, the Monterey Plaza strikes a note of classic, sleek traditionalism, with a spacious lobby that gleams with Brazilian teakwood walls, Italian marble, and red, Oriental-style carpeting. Beidermeier-style armoires and writing desks, cozy duvet bedspreads, and sumptuous marble baths carry the classic look into the hotel's 290 guest rooms and suites. And 24-hour in-room dining, a well-stocked honor bar, On-Command videos, and nightly turndown make guest rooms especially nice to cocoon in. Many of the rooms face the bay and feature sliding glass doors and private balconies that place you right above the lapping surf. The recent addition of the Plaza's 16,000-square-foot European-style spa has transformed it from simply a nice to place to stay to something of a destination. Although the spa services are extra, a well-equipped fitness room is complimentary and available to guests 24 hours a day. The hotel's Duck Club Restaurant enjoys an enviable location right on the water and serves American regional cuisine with an emphasis on wood-roasted specialties, including duck, beef, lamb, chicken, and fresh seafood. The adjacent Schooner's Bistro serves lighter fare, with a tasty range of starters, salads, sandwiches, and pastas. *$$$$; AE, DIS, MC, V; checks OK; www.woodsidehotels.com; at Drake St.*

Old Monterey Inn / ★★★

500 MARTIN ST, MONTEREY; 831/375-8284 OR 800/350-2344
Even those who feel they've seen it all on the bed-and-breakfast circuit are likely to be awed by the elegantly appointed Old Monterey Inn. Nestled among giant oak trees and gardens filled with rhododendrons, begonias, impatiens, and ferns, this Tudor-style country inn built in 1929 positively gleams with natural wood, skylights, and stained-glass windows. The 10 beautifully decorated guest rooms, each with a private bath, are filled with lovely antiques and comfortable beds with plump down comforters and huge, fluffy pillows. Most rooms have fireplaces and telephones; TVs can be supplied in a few of the cable-equipped rooms upon request. For the utmost privacy, request the lacy Garden Cottage, which has a private patio, skylights, and a fireplace sitting room. Another standout: the handsome Library guest room, with its book-lined walls, stone fireplace, and private sundeck. Breakfast, taken in the dining room or in your suite, might include berry cobbler, French toast, crepes, cheese rolls, and curiosities such as coconut-lime muffins.

You'll also find delightful afternoon refreshments and evening hors d'oeuvres. *$$$$; MC, V; checks OK; omi@oldmontereyinn.com; www.oldmontereyinn.com; near Pacific St.*

Spindrift Inn / ★★★

652 CANNERY ROW, MONTEREY; 831/646-8900 OR 800/841-1879

With its soaring four-story atrium and rooftop garden, the Spindrift is an unexpected and elegant refuge amid the hurly-burly tourist world of Cannery Row. Downstairs, plush Oriental carpets muffle your footsteps, and a tall pair of attractive, if politically questionable, Italian blackamoor statues keep you company in the fireside sitting room. Upstairs, all 42 rooms have featherbeds (many with canopies) with down comforters, fireplaces, hardwood floors, telephones, and tiled bathrooms with marble appointments. The corner rooms, with their cushioned window seats and breathtaking ocean views, are the best in the house. In the morning there will be a newspaper, a dewy rose, and a delicious breakfast of fruit, orange juice, croissants, and sweet rolls waiting outside your door on a silver tray. In the afternoon you're invited to partake of tea, pastries, wine, and cheese. *$$$$; AE, DC, DIS, MC, V; checks OK; www.spindriftinn.com; at Hawthorne St.*

Pebble Beach and the 17-Mile Drive

How much are a room and a round of golf at Pebble Beach these days? Let's put it this way: if you have to ask, you can't afford it. This exclusive gated community of 5,000 or so residents even requires a $7.50 levy to drive on its gilded avenues. If you have no strong desire to tour corporate-owned hideaways and redundant—albeit gorgeous—seascapes along the famous **17-MILE DRIVE**, save your lunch money; you're not really missing anything that can't be seen elsewhere along the Monterey coast. Then again, some folks swear that cruising past Pebble Beach's mansions and manicured golf courses is worth the admission just to contemplate the lifestyles of the very rich.

If you decide to pay the toll, you'll see everything from a spectacular Byzantine castle with a private beach (the **CROCKER MANSION** near the Carmel gate) to several tastefully bland California Nouvelle country-club establishments in perfectly maintained forest settings. Other highlights include the often-photographed gnarled **LONE CYPRESS** clinging to its rocky precipice above the sea; miles of hiking and equestrian trails winding through groves of native pines and wildflowers, with glorious views of Monterey Bay; and **BIRD ROCK**, a small offshore isle covered with hundreds of seals and sea lions (bring binoculars). Self-guided nature tours are outlined in a variety of brochures, available for free at the gate entrances and at **THE INN AT SPANISH BAY** and **THE LODGE AT PEBBLE**

BEACH (see reviews, below). And then there are the golf courses. This area is heaven to golfers, who flock to such famous courses as **SPYGLASS HILL**, named after a location in Robert Louis Stevenson's *Treasure Island*.

ACCESS AND INFORMATION

The Pebble Beach area and 17-Mile Drive have five guarded entrance gates, and the entire drive takes about 1 to 2 hours (though you can whiz by the highlights in 30 minutes). Your best bet is to avoid the busy summer weekends and come midweek. Visitors may enter the 17-Mile Drive for free on foot or bike, although **CYCLISTS** are required to use the Pacific Grove gate on weekends and holidays—and must dust off the wheels of their bikes, of course. For more information, contact **PEBBLE BEACH SECURITY** at 831/624-6669.

The **CARMEL BUSINESS ASSOCIATION** (San Carlos St; 831/624-2522 or 800/55-4330; between 5th and 6th Aves) runs the **CARMEL VISITOR INFORMATION CENTER**, which is amply stocked with brochures on area attractions and lodgings.

Pacific Grove

Established in 1889 as a retreat for pious Methodists, this beautiful Victorian seacoast village retains its decorous old-town character, though it's loosened its collar a bit since the early days, when dancing, alcohol, and even the Sunday newspaper were banned. Less tourist-oriented than Carmel, less commercial than Monterey, P.G. (as locals call it) exudes peace and tranquillity—there's no graffiti, no raucous revelers, and not even an unleashed dog in sight. Introduce yourself to the town by strolling the 4 miles of trails that meander between the white-sand beaches and rocky tide-pool-dotted coves at **LOVER'S POINT BEACH** (off Ocean View Blvd on the east side of Point Piños) and **ASILOMAR STATE BEACH** (off Sunset Dr on the west side of Point Piños). Be sure to sit and enjoy the view from the landmark Lover's Point (named for lovers of Jesus Christ, not the more carnal kind).

At the tip of Point Piños (Spanish for "Point of the Pines") stands the Cape Cod–style **POINT PIÑOS LIGHTHOUSE** (Asilomar Blvd at Lighthouse Ave; 831/648-3116), the oldest continuously operating lighthouse on the West Coast, built in February 1855. This National Historic Landmark is open to the public Thursday through Sunday, from 1pm to 4pm, and admission is free.

P.G. is famous for its Victorian houses, inns, and churches, and hundreds of them have been declared historically significant by the Pacific Grove Heritage Society. Every October, some of the most artfully restored are opened to the public on the **VICTORIAN HOME TOUR**; for details contact the **PACIFIC GROVE CHAMBER OF COMMERCE** (584 Central Ave; 831/373-3304; www.pacificgrove.org). If you can't make the tour, you can at least admire the ornate facades clustered along Lighthouse Avenue, Central Avenue, and Ocean View Boulevard.

Pacific Grove bills itself as Butterfly Town, USA, in honor of the thousands of monarchs that migrate here from late October to mid-March. Two popular places to view the alighting lepidoptera are the **MONARCH GROVE SANCTUARY** (at Lighthouse Ave and Ridge Rd) and **GEORGE WASHINGTON PARK** (at Sinex Ave and Alder St). To learn more about the monarchs, visit the charmingly informal and kid-friendly **PACIFIC GROVE MUSEUM OF NATURAL HISTORY** (Forest and Central Aves; 831/648-3116), which has a video and display on the butterfly's life cycle, as well as exhibits of other insects, local birds, mammals, and reptiles (admission is free). For good books and coffee, amble over to the nearby **BOOKWORKS** (667 Lighthouse Ave; 831/372-2242), which also has an extensive array of magazines and newspapers.

RESTAURANTS

Fandango / ★★

223 17TH ST, PACIFIC GROVE; 831/372-3456
Fandango, the name of a lively Spanish dance, is the perfect moniker for this kick-up-your-heels restaurant specializing in Mediterranean country cuisine. It's a big, sprawling, colorful place with textured adobe walls and a spirited crowd filling five separate dining rooms; the glass-domed terrace in back, with its stone fireplace and open mesquite grill, is especially pleasant. Start with a few tapas—perhaps spicy sausage, roasted red peppers, or a potato-and-onion frittata. If you're feeling adventurous, order the Veloute Bongo Bongo, an exotic creamy soup with oysters, spinach, and Cognac, or the Couscous Algerois, a 130-year-old family recipe featuring lamb, vegetables, and North African spices. Other selections include the flavorful Paella Fandango (served at your table in a huge skillet), pasta puttanesca, bouillabaisse Marseillaise, osso buco, and a 26-ounce porterhouse steak. Fandango's wine list is one of the best in the area, with an impressive selection of French, California, Spanish, and Italian varietals. For dessert, try the profiteroles filled with coffee ice cream and topped with hot fudge sauce. *$$$; AE, DC, DIS, MC, V; no checks; lunch, dinner every day, brunch Sun; full bar; reservations recommended; www.fandango.com; near Lighthouse Ave.*

Gernot's Victoria House / ★★

649 LIGHTHOUSE AVE, PACIFIC GROVE; 831/646-1477
Located in the beautiful Hart Mansion, Gernot's Victoria House has the kind of quiet charm and gracious service that the town's trendier restaurants can't match, and at comparatively modest prices. All of chef Gernot Leitzinger's continental entrees come with soup, a salad made with local greens in an herby vinaigrette, and hot country rolls. Popular selections

include Wiener schnitzel with lingonberry compote, rack of lamb Dijon with bread crumbs, herbs, and garlic, and salmon with mango salsa. Daring sorts may want to sample Gernot's wild boar bourguignon. For dessert, there's a luscious Sacher torte and delicate meringue shells topped with ice cream and chocolate sauce. *$$; AE, MC, V; checks OK; dinner Tues–Sun; beer and wine; reservations recommended; at 19th St.*

Old Bath House Restaurant / ★★★

620 OCEAN VIEW BLVD, PACIFIC GROVE; 831/375-5195
Although many locals are quick to dismiss the Old Bath House as a pricey tourist restaurant (and it is indeed guilty on both counts), the food is meticulously prepared and the setting is undeniably romantic. This former bathhouse at Lover's Point has a fine view of the rocky coast and a wonderful wood interior with a low, carved ceiling. Chef Sheri O'Connor, formerly at Fresh Cream and Tarpy's Roadhouse in Monterey, has breathed new life into the continental menu. Expect starters such as lobster ravioli with diced asparagus and lemon beurre blanc, or carpaccio of filet mignon with extra-virgin olive oil, Dijon mustard, and capers. Entrees may feature prawns crowned with crab and orange hollandaise, or dayboat scallops, oak grilled and topped with pancetta, served on lemon risotto with snow peas and tomato concassé. Tempting desserts include hot pecan ice-cream fritters and the aptly named Oceans of Chocolate (chocolate ice cream on chocolate pudding cake cloaked in chocolate fudge and white-chocolate chunks). The service is impeccable and the wine list extensive. *$$$; AE, DC, DIS, MC, V; no checks; dinner every day; full bar; reservations recommended; www.oldbathhouse.com; at Lover's Point Park.*

Pasta Mia / ★★

481 LIGHTHOUSE AVE, PACIFIC GROVE; 831/375-7709
A century-old Victorian house provides a homey backdrop for Pasta Mia's hearty Italian fare. The soup and appetizers include tried-and-true standards such as minestrone, cream of artichoke, mozzarella fresca, and carpaccio, as well as fried calamari and garlic mussels. The house-made pastas include intriguing choices such as black-and-white linguine with scallops, caviar, cream, and chives, or half-moon pasta stuffed with pesto in a lemon-zest cream sauce dotted with chicken and sun-dried tomatoes. The corkscrew pasta with sausage and chicken is satisfying and flavorful, as is the scampi in a light champagne cream sauce. *Secondi piatti* include veal marsala; certified Angus rib eye steaks or prime rib of beef, both served with crab ravioli; and a daily fish char-grilled and served with pasta or polenta. Portions are generous in this friendly, informal restaurant. *$$; AE, MC, V; no checks; dinner every day, Sun brunch; beer and wine; reservations recommended; www.pastamiatrattoria.com; near 13th St.*

Red House Café / ★★

662 LIGHTHOUSE AVE, PACIFIC GROVE; 831/643-1060

A trim, 103-year-old brick-red house in downtown Pacific Grove is the deceptively modest setting for some of the most adroit cooking on the Monterey Peninsula. Opened in 1996 by Laura and Chris D'Amelio (both formerly of Taste Cafe & Bistro), the Red House offers a handful of humble-sounding dishes at breakfast and lunch: items such as Irish oatmeal, Belgian waffles, pastries, a mixed green salad, roast beef on sourdough, a BLT, and eggs any way you like them as long as they're scrambled. Order at the counter, then take a seat on the porch with its smattering of wicker chairs and tables-for-two or in one of the snug, country-cottage dining rooms. After your food is served and you tuck into your warm pine-nut tart or chicken sandwich, you'll realize how even the simplest fare can be transporting if it's prepared by the right hands. The Red House has been a locals' favorite ever since it opened, and its popularity is the only rub; traffic can back up at the counter as people wait to place their orders, creating some cramped conditions in the dining areas. A small dinner menu with two to three items is offered Thursday through Saturday. *$; no credit cards; no checks; breakfast, lunch Tues–Sun, dinner Thurs–Sat; beer and wine; reservations recommended; info@redhousecafe.com; www.redhousecafe.com; at 19th St.*

Taste Cafe & Bistro / ★★★

1199 FOREST AVE, PACIFIC GROVE; 831/655-0324

When it opened several years ago, Taste Cafe quickly developed a loyal and enthusiastic word-of-mouth following that remains the envy of several more established restaurants in town. You'll be hard-pressed to find higher-quality food for the same price anywhere else on the coast. Chef/owners Bill Karaki and Huss Hamade describe their preparations as a combination of rustic French, Italian, and California cuisines, and they work hard to glean the best and freshest produce, seafood, and meats from local suppliers. Start your meal with house-cured salmon carpaccio, butternut squash agnolotti, or an organic red oak leaf salad with crumbled blue cheese, balsamic dressing, sliced pears, and glazed pecans. Move on to entrees such as tortellini Florentine, marinated rabbit with braised red cabbage, and grilled pork medallions on mashed potatoes with shiitake sauce. Be sure to save room for one of Taste's wonderful desserts: warm brioche pudding with apricot coulis and crème fraîche, a hazelnut-chocolate torte, or a country-style apple galette with vanilla-bean ice cream and caramel sauce. The word is out on this terrific restaurant, so be sure to call well ahead for reservations, especially for weekend dinners. *$$; AE, MC, V; checks OK; lunch, dinner Tues–Sun; beer and wine; reservations recommended; at Prescott Ave.* &

LODGINGS

Gatehouse Inn / ★★

225 CENTRAL AVE, PACIFIC GROVE; 831/649-8436 OR 800/753-1881
When State Senator Benjamin Langford built this ocean-view Victorian mansion in 1884, Pacific Grove was less a town than a pious Methodist meeting ground. Swathed in rules and regulations, it was separated from wicked, worldly Monterey by a white picket fence. Langford's domain is now an enticingly eccentric B&B. Decorated in an interesting mix of Victoriana and art deco, the inn's nine guest rooms have private baths and queen-size beds, with the exception of the Cannery Row Room, with its king-size bed. The Langford Suite ranks as the inn's most luxurious, with an ocean-view sitting room, fireplace, and a claw-footed bathtub that's just a step away from the bed and commands a stunning view of the coast. You'll find delicious hors d'oeuvres, tea, and wine every evening and a full breakfast buffet in the morning. You can even help yourself to cookies and beverages from the kitchen any time of day or night. *$$$; AE, DIS, MC, V; checks OK; at 2nd St.*

Grand View Inn / ★★★

557 OCEAN VIEW BLVD, PACIFIC GROVE; 831/372-4341
Even in a town as rich in resplendent Victorians as Pacific Grove, this pristine and romantic inn stands out. Built in 1910 as the residence of Dr. Julia Platt, a marine biologist who became Pacific Grove's first female mayor, the Grand View was bought by the family that owns the Seven Gables Inn next door (the two inns share the same garden). A bit more casual and restrained in decor than its ornate sister, this charmer with its cheerful blue exterior has 10 guest rooms, all with bay views, high plaster ceilings with decorative detailing, eclectic antique furniture and light fixtures, queen-size beds, sitting areas, and beautifully appointed marble bathrooms. A full breakfast is served in the elegant first-floor dining room with its breathtaking view of Lover's Point; later in the day, the same room is the setting for a pleasant afternoon tea. Complimentary off-street parking is available, too. *$$$$; MC, V; checks OK; www.7gables-grandview.com; at Grand Ave.*

Lighthouse Lodge and Suites / ★★

1150 AND 1249 LIGHTHOUSE AVE, PACIFIC GROVE; 831/655-2111 OR 800/858-1249
Less than a block from the ocean, the Lighthouse Lodge and Suites is really two entities with rather distinct personalities. The lodge offers a heated pool and 64 motel-like rooms, which have been newly remodeled with large-screen TVs, refrigerators, and microwaves; many have fireplaces. Those seeking more luxurious accommodations should spring for one of the 31 newer suites down the road. The Cape Cod–style suites feature beamed ceilings, fireplaces, vast bathrooms with marble Jacuzzis, large-

screen TVs, minikitchens, and king-size beds. After a made-to-order breakfast in the fireside lounge, take a morning stroll around the grounds, nicely landscaped with native plants and fountains. *$$ (lodge), $$$$ (suites); AE, DC, DIS, MC, V; no checks; www.lhls.com; at Asilomar Blvd.*

The Martine Inn / ★★

255 OCEAN VIEW BLVD, PACIFIC GROVE; 831/373-3388 OR 800/852-5588
Perched like a vast pink wedding cake on a cliff above Monterey Bay, this villa with a Mediterranean exterior and a Victorian interior was built in 1899 for James and Laura Parke (of Parke-Davis Pharmaceuticals fame). The inn has 23 spacious guest rooms, all with private baths and gloriously unfussy antiques. Most rooms have fireplaces; all have views of the water or the garden courtyard with its delightful dragon fountain. If you feel like splurging, the Parke Room at the very top of the house is outstanding. Originally the master bedroom, it has a magnificent picture window, a four-poster canopy bed, and a massive white brick fireplace. No matter which room you choose, you'll find a silver basket of fruit and a rose waiting for you upon arrival, and a newspaper at your door in the morning. Several intimate sitting rooms offset three large common areas: the library, the main dining room (with a dazzling view of the bay), and the breakfast parlor. There's also a pool table and an eight-person Jacuzzi in the old conservatory. The Martine serves an elaborate and well-prepared breakfast and offers wine and hors d'oeuvres in the late afternoon. *$$$–$$$$; AE, DIS, MC, V; checks OK; www.martineinn.com; 4 blocks from Cannery Row.*

Seven Gables Inn / ★★★

555 OCEAN VIEW BLVD, PACIFIC GROVE; 831/372-4341
Set in an immaculate yellow Victorian mansion built in 1886 and surrounded by gardens, this family-run inn commands a magnificent view of Monterey Bay. Chock-full of formal European antiques, Seven Gables will seem like paradise to those who revel in things Victorian. Once you're ensconced in one of the 14 guest rooms, which are divided among the main house, a guest house, and a smattering of cottages, the warm and welcoming Flatley family will see to your every comfort. The beautifully appointed rooms feature ocean views, private baths, and queen-size beds. A pull-out-all-the-stops breakfast is served in the imposing dining room, and tea is set out every afternoon. *$$$$; MC, V; checks ok; www.7gables-grandview.com; at Fountain Ave.*

Pebble Beach

LODGINGS

The Inn at Spanish Bay / ★★★★

2700 17-MILE DR, PEBBLE BEACH; 831/647-7500 OR 800/654-9300

Set on the privately owned 17-Mile Drive, this sprawling modern inn defines deluxe. Its 270 luxuriously appointed rooms and suites perched on a cypress-dotted bluff have gas fireplaces, quilted down comforters, and elegant sitting areas. Most have private patios or balconies affording gorgeous views of the rocky coast or the Del Monte cypress forest. Three of the most deluxe suites even come with grand pianos. The bathrooms, equipped with all the modern conveniences you could want, are appropriately regal. Hotel guests have access to the world-famous Pebble Beach, Spanish Bay, and Spyglass Hill golf courses, as well as eight championship tennis courts, a fitness club, a swimming pool, and miles of hiking and equestrian trails. At sunset a Scottish bagpiper strolls along the golf course and serenades the guests. Relax over a repast at the newly opened Peppoli, which serves fashionable Tuscan fare, or at Roy's, where Hawaiian master chef Roy Yamaguchi serves an artful blend of Asian-Pacific and European cuisine. *$$$$; AE, DC, MC, V; checks OK; www.pebblebeach.com; near the Pacific Grove entrance.* &

The Lodge at Pebble Beach / ★★★

17-MILE DR, PEBBLE BEACH; 831/624-3811 OR 800/654-9300

Despite greens fees that top $300, Pebble Beach remains the mecca of American golf courses, and most avid golfers feel they have to play it at least once before retiring to that Big Clubhouse in the Sky. Until the rooms in the Lodge were renovated several years ago, this scattered cluster of accommodations surprised many guests with its rather run-down appearance—it was clear that golf and the spectacular natural setting, not the rooms, were the big draw. The guest rooms have been tastefully revamped, however, swathed in soothing earth tones and outfitted with a sophisticated, modern decor. There are 161 rooms and suites, most with private balconies or patios, brick fireplaces, sitting areas, and gorgeous views. All the usual upscale amenities are provided, from phones by the commode and honor-bar refrigerators to robes and cable TVs. The whole effect is very East Coast country club. Four restaurants cater to visitors, most notably Club XIX, which has been drawing raves since signing up Hubert Keller of San Francisco's Fleur de Lys as executive chef, and the Stillwater Bar & Grill. *$$$$; AE, DC, DIS, MC, V; checks OK; www.pebblebeach.com; near the Carmel Gate.* &

Carmel

Carmel prides itself on its charm and eccentricity, and there's no denying it's got plenty of both. How many other towns have no street addresses, require a permit to wear high heels, and even, for a time, had a law against eating ice cream cones on the street? How many cities once elected a mayor who's known around the world as .45-toting vigilante cop Dirty Harry, or have a movie-star-owned hotel that caters to canines? Yes, it's unique, and that, combined with its spectacular setting, have changed what was once a quaint little seaside town into a sometimes overcrowded tourist attraction, with all the attendant drawbacks: too much traffic, too many T-shirt stores, and stratospheric prices.

But if you hit Carmel on the right day—preferably midweek in the off season, when the sun is shining and a good, stiff breeze is blowing in from the sea—you'll discover all the charm that made the burg so famous. Stroll the streets in the early morning or early evening to avoid the crowds and admire the varied architecture that gives the town its unique look: Hansel-and-Gretel cottages abut Italian villas, and Spanish haciendas nudge tiny Tudor-style houses that would be right at home in a remote English hamlet. Flowers abound in every season, in pretty little courtyards complete with benches for weary travelers, in window boxes, and even on traffic islands. And then there's the setting: even the city's firmest detractors have to admit that Carmel boasts one of the most beautiful curves of beach on the Central Coast.

Without doubt, the best way to see Carmel is on foot. **CARMEL WALKS** (831/642-2700) offers a two-hour tour of the town's most interesting haunts, including Hugh Comstock's storybook cottages and the homes of famous former denizens such as feminist Mary Austin, photographer Edward Weston, and poet Robinson Jeffers. Tours are offered Tuesday through Friday at 10am, Saturdays at 10am and 2pm; meet in the courtyard of the Pine Inn (Lincoln St, at Ocean Ave).

The restored Mission San Carlos Borromeo del Río Carmelo, better known as the **CARMEL MISSION** (3080 Rio Rd; 831/624-3600; at Lasuén Dr, several blocks W of Hwy 1) is located next to **MISSION TRAILS PARK**, with 5 miles of winding paths dotted by wildflowers, willows, deer, and redwoods. Established in 1770, the Carmel Mission was the headquarters of Father Junípero Serra's famous chain of California missions—and his favorite (Serra is buried in front of the altar in the sanctuary, which is marked with a plaque). The vine-covered baroque church with its 11-bell Moorish tower, completed in 1797, is one of California's architectural treasures. Be sure to see the main altar, with its Gothic arch and elaborate decorations, and Serra's restored cell, where he died in 1784. The mission houses three extensive museums, and its surrounding 14 acres are planted with native flowers and trees. The cemetery has more than 3,000 graves of Native Americans who worked and lived in the mission; in place of a gravestone, many plots are marked by a solitary abalone shell.

TOR HOUSE (26304 Ocean View Ave; 831/624-1813; www.tor house.org; at Stewart Wy), the former home of poet Robinson Jeffers, is a rustic granite building that looks as though it were transplanted from the British Isles. Constructed over several years beginning in 1914, today it's the residence of one of Jeffers's descendants. Even more intriguing is the nearby four-story **HAWK TOWER**, which Jeffers built for his wife, Una, with huge rocks he hauled up from the beach below. Guided tours of the house and tower are available for a fee on Friday and Saturday by reservation only (no children under 12 admitted).

Are you ready for a good dose of Mother Nature's great wonders? Then visit one of the town's two beautiful beaches. **CARMEL CITY BEACH**, at the foot of Ocean Avenue and the town's shopping district, tends to be overcrowded in the summer (though its chilly aquamarine water is unsafe for swimming), but the gorgeous white sand and towering cypresses are worth the price of sunbathing among the hordes. Or head a mile south on Scenic Drive to spectacular **CARMEL RIVER STATE BEACH**, where the locals go to hide from the tourists (though swimming is unsafe here, too). The Carmel River enters the Pacific at this point, and you'll see a bird sanctuary frequented by pelicans, hawks, sandpipers, kingfishers, willets, and the occasional goose. **MIDDLE BEACH** and **MONASTERY BEACH** lie beyond. These areas are remarkably scenic, but Mother Nature saved her best efforts for the 1,276-acre **POINT LOBOS STATE RESERVE** (831/624-4909 for park information; 831/624-8413 for scuba-diving reservations; pt-lobos.parks.state.ca.us/; on Hwy 1 approximately 3 miles S of Carmel). More than a dozen Point Lobos trails lead to ocean coves, where you might spy sea otters, harbor seals, California sea lions, large colonies of seabirds, and, between December and May, migrating California gray whales. Some trails will even take you to one of the two naturally growing stands of Monterey cypress remaining on earth; the other stand is in Pebble Beach on the 17-Mile Drive. For more nearby hiking recommendations, see the Big Sur section in the following pages.

Shopping is a popular pastime in Carmel. Not only is its downtown packed with interesting little stores, but just outside of town lie two luxe suburban malls: **THE BARNYARD** (831/624-8886; on Hwy 1 at Carmel Valley Rd) and **THE CROSSROADS** (831/624-9492; on Hwy 1 at Rio Rd). **OCEAN AVENUE** has its share of tourist-schlock shops, it's true, but hit the side streets for some fine adventures in consumerland. Intriguing stores include **LADYFINGERS** for jewelry (831/624-2327; on Dolores St between Ocean and 7th Aves), the **SECRET GARDEN** for pretty garden accessories (831/625-1131; on Dolores St between 5th and 6th), and **THE WHITE RABBIT** for the world's largest variety of *Alice*

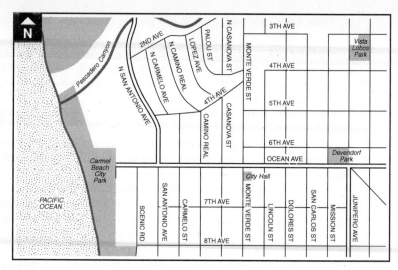

CARMEL

in Wonderland collectibles (831/624-2556; Dolores St; ½ block S of Ocean Ave). Numerous quality art galleries are located between Lincoln and San Carlos Streets and Fifth and Sixth Avenues. Particularly noteworthy is the **WESTON GALLERY** (831/624-4453; 6th Ave, at Dolores St), which showcases 19th- and 20th-century photographers' works, including a permanent display featuring such famous Carmelites as Edward Weston, Ansel Adams, and Imogen Cunningham.

Carmel has an active theater scene, perhaps best represented by the **PACIFIC REPERTORY THEATRE COMPANY** (831/622-0700 or 831/622-0100; www.pacrep.org), which puts on an outdoor musical and Shakespeare festival each summer and performs other classics such as *Amadeus* and *Death of a Salesman* in its indoor theater year-round.

The annual monthlong **CARMEL BACH FESTIVAL** (831/624-2046; www.bachfestival.com) offers numerous concerts, recitals, lectures, and discussion groups—some are even free. In addition to Bach masterpieces, you'll hear scores by Vivaldi and Scarlatti, and some by those young whippersnappers Beethoven and Chopin. The classical music celebration begins in mid-July; series tickets are sold starting in January, and single-event tickets (ranging from $10 to $50) go on sale in April.

RESTAURANTS

Anton & Michel / ★★

MISSION ST, CARMEL; 831/624-2406

This longtime Carmel favorite overlooks the Court of the Fountains with its Louis XV lions and verdigris garden pavilions. Anton & Michel's elegant dining room has pink walls, white wainscoting, and tall, slender pillars topped by elegant curlicue cornices. Despite the interesting decor, the continental cuisine isn't very daring, but chef Max Muramatsu trained at Maxim's in Paris and Tokyo, and his food is delicious and extremely well prepared. Standouts include the rack of lamb with an herb-Dijon mustard au jus, grilled veal with a spinach-Madeira sauce, and medallions of ahi tuna with a black-pepper-and-sesame-seed crust and a wasabi-cilantro sauce. Anton & Michel also offers traditional French desserts such as crepes suzette, cherries jubilee, and chocolate mousse cake with sauce anglaise. Service is courtly, and the extensive wine list has garnered many *Wine Spectator* magazine awards. *$$$; AE, DC, DIS, MC, V; no checks; lunch, dinner every day; full bar; reservations recommended; www.carmelsbest.com; between Ocean and 7th Aves.*

Casanova Restaurant / ★★

5TH AVE, CARMEL; 831/625-0501

The former home of Charlie Chaplin's cook, this sunny cottage with a Mediterranean feel attracts happy throngs of locals and tourists alike. Casanova specializes in Italian and French country-style dishes. Lunch on the big patio out back is informal and fun, with heaters keeping patrons warm on chilly afternoons. Inside, the cottage is a jumble of nooks and crannies decked out in rustic European decor. Casanova prides itself on its extensive and reasonably priced wine list, including the well-received Georis merlot and cabernet, produced by one of the restaurant's owners. Cap off your meal with one of Casanova's superb desserts; the many choices include a Basque-style pear tart and a chocolate custard pie with whipped cream, nuts, and shaved dark and white Belgian chocolates. *$$; MC, V; no checks; lunch, dinner every day, brunch Sun; full bar; reservations recommended; www.casanovarestaurant.com; between San Carlos and Mission Sts.* &

Flying Fish Grill / ★★

MISSION ST, CARMEL; 831/625-1962

Hidden on the ground level of the Carmel Plaza shopping center, Flying Fish Grill is worth seeking out for its fun, stylish atmosphere and its delicious Pacific Rim seafood. The interior is a maze of booths and tables flanked by an expanse of warm, polished wood and crisp blue-and-white banners. Chef/owner Kenny Fukumoto offers such creative dishes as Yin-Yan Salmon (roast salmon on angel hair pasta sprinkled with sesame seeds and served with a soy-lime cream sauce); catfish fillets with fermented Chinese black beans, ginger, and scallions steamed in paper pouches; pan-fried Chilean sea bass with almonds, whipped potatoes, and a Chinese cabbage and rock shrimp stir-fry; and his specialty, rare peppered ahi tuna on angel hair pasta. A few meat dishes and a couple of flavorful clay pot dishes that you cook at your own table round out the menu. There's also a tempting lineup of desserts, including Chocolate Decadence, a warm banana sundae, and an assortment of delicate sorbets. *$$; AE, DIS, MC, V; no checks; dinner Wed–Mon; beer and wine; reservations recommended; between Ocean and 7th Aves, in Carmel Plaza.*

Grasing's / ★★★

6TH AVE, CARMEL; 831/624-6562

Noted chefs Kurt Grasing and Narsai David teamed up to open this eponymous restaurant (formerly the 6th Avenue Grill), which serves a more casual version of the contemporary California-Mediterranean cuisine Grasing previously turned out at tony eateries like San Mateo's 231 Ellsworth. At lunch, you'll find superb pastas, salads, sandwiches, and entrees such as bronzed salmon with grilled portobellos, roasted potatoes, and garlic. Dinner starters might include potato, wild rice, and zucchini pancakes with house-cured salmon and crème fraîche or a savory three-onion tart with a fennel sauce and balsamic syrup; main courses range from wild-mushroom stew with creamy polenta to roast duck with an orange-port glaze. The dining room is a cheerful stage for Grasing's inspired cooking, with Milano-modern furnishings, textured ocher walls, cathedral ceilings, and witty sculptures and art. The wine list is ample and thoughtfully selected, desserts are diet-busting delights, and there's a small patio for dining alfresco. *$$; AE, MC, V; local checks only; lunch, dinner every day; beer and wine; reservations recommended; www. grasings.com; at Mission St.* &

La Bohême / ★★

DOLORES ST, CARMEL; 831/624-7500

La Bohême is very small, very cute, and—depending on your luck—very good. The walls of this heart-flutteringly romantic restaurant are painted a pale blue and dotted with cream-puff clouds. Two of the most sought-after tables are tucked inside a topsy-turvy little toy house, part of a whimsical street scene mural. The restaurant serves only a prix-fixe menu, which changes nightly. Calendars list the entrees for an entire month, and patrons in the know make it a point to pick up this schedule as soon as they hit town. The three courses include a salad, a bowl of soup, and a main course: perhaps duck with a sherry sauce, filet mignon with a Roquefort-wine sauce, or prawns and scallops in a champagne sauce. The soups, such as salmon bisque, and the salads, with Carmel Valley organic greens, are universally wonderful. When everything works, La Bohême's cuisine ranks among the best in Carmel, at bargain prices to boot. Desserts include the rich but fluffy chocolate mousse and a velvety crème brûlée. *$$; AE, MC, V; no checks; dinner every day; beer and wine; reservations recommended; at 7th Ave.*

La Dolce Vita / ★★

SAN CARLOS ST, CARMEL; 831/624-3667

Those in the mood for authentic Italian food in a casual atmosphere will enjoy this restaurant, a local favorite. Decorated in an Italian-flag color scheme—green chairs and plastic red-and-white tablecloths—it's a wonderfully unassuming place to sit back, sip a glass of wine, and revel in *la dolce di far niente*—the joy of doing nothing. The main dining room resembles a cozy trattoria with slate floors, light wood furniture, and peach-toned walls bedecked with garlic braids. Specialties include the transporting ravioli alla Rachele (homemade spinach ravioli stuffed with crab and cheese in a champagne cream sauce, topped with scallops and sun-dried tomatoes) and gnocchi della nonna (fresh potato dumplings in either a tomato or Gorgonzola-sage-cream sauce). A variety of individual-size pizzas is also available, along with *secondi piatti* ranging from traditional osso buco to calamari steak drizzled with sun-dried tomato pesto, lemon juice, and crisp Orvieto wine. *$$; AE, MC, V; local checks only; lunch, dinner every day; beer and wine; reservations recommended; between 7th and 8th Aves.* ♿

Pacific's Edge / ★★★

HWY I (HIGHLANDS INN); 831/622-5445 OR 800/682-4811

Pacific's Edge, the Highlands Inn's flagship restaurant, is one of the best (and most expensive) dining establishments in the area, serving inspired California cuisine in a luxe setting blessed with panoramic views (reserve well in advance for a table at sunset). Starters might include farm-fresh artichokes with basil mayonnaise, potato-wrapped ahi tuna, or grilled quail with creamy rosemary polenta. Entrees range from grilled Monterey Bay salmon in an onion-rosemary sauce to roasted rack of lamb with white truffle potatoes. Chef Jeff Rogers also offers a nightly Sunset Dinner, a hand-picked selection of courses designed to create a truly memorable meal. *$$$; AE, DC, DIS, MC, V; checks OK; lunch, dinner every day, brunch Sun; full bar; reservations recommended; www. highlands-inn.com; 4 miles S of Carmel.*

Piatti Ristorante / ★★

6TH AVE, CARMEL; 831/625-1766

Part of a popular chain of chic nouvelle Italian restaurants. For a full review, see the Restaurants section of Sonoma in the Wine Country chapter. *$$; AE, MC, V; no checks; lunch, dinner every day; full bar; reservations recommended; at Junipero Ave.*

Rio Grill / ★★

101 CROSSROADS BLVD, CARMEL; 831/625-5436

This noisy Southwestern-style grill is packed with a lively, young crowd from opening to closing. The salads, such as organic mixed greens with aged goat cheese, seasoned walnuts, and curry vinaigrette, are wonderfully fresh, and appetizers like the ever-popular onion rings and fried Monterey Bay squid with orange-sesame dipping sauce draw raves. The tasty barbecued baby back ribs and the herb-crusted chicken with crispy broccoli-corn risotto cakes are good bets for the main course, as is the pumpkin-seed-crusted salmon with chipotle-lime vinaigrette and roasted red-pepper potato cakes. Desserts include a killer olallieberry pie and caramel-apple bread pudding. While the atmosphere may be chaotic, the service isn't, and the grill boasts a large wine list, with many selections available by the glass. *$$; AE, DIS, MC, V; no checks; lunch, dinner every day, brunch Sun; full bar; reservations recommended; in the Crossroads Shopping Village, at Hwy 1 and Rio Rd.* &

Robert's Bistro / ★★★

217 CROSSROADS BLVD, CARMEL; 831/624-9626

The master chef who created Monterey's ever-popular Fresh Cream restaurant returned to the area in 1995 to open this charming temple to earthy haute cuisine. Wooden beams adorned with hanging dried flowers, golden-hued stucco walls, provençal furnishings, and not one but two roaring stone hearths beckon visitors to relax. The older, mon-eyed clientele isn't here for the French farmhouse atmosphere, though—they've come to sample Robert Kincaid's culinary magic. His updated bistro fare includes such appetizers as an exceptionally creamy (and delicious) onion tart; delicate and delectable crab dumplings in two sauces (a honey-mustard and a dill sauce); and a baked Brie in white wine–butter sauce that may leave you feeling dangerously like Henry VIII after a state banquet. Main courses include sautéed red snapper Grenobloise (with bay shrimp, capers, and lemon) and a fillet of beef seared with green peppercorns, cream, and brandy. The *San Francisco Chronicle* deemed the roast duckling the best on the Monterey Peninsula. Desserts include delicious treats such as the signature chocolate bag with chocolate shake as well as pithivier, a wonderfully light and tasty marriage of flaky puff pastry and almond cream. The service is both warm and impeccable, a rare combination, but the wine list disappoints: it's not as extensive as one would expect at a restaurant of this caliber and it's tipped toward pricier vintages. *$$$; AE, DIS, MC, V; local checks only; lunch Mon–Fri, dinner Mon–Sun; beer and wine; reservations recommended; in the Crossroads Shopping Village, at Hwy 1 and Rio Rd.* &

Sans Souci / ★★★

LINCOLN ST, CARMEL; 831/624-6220

True to the name, the folks at Sans Souci (French for "without worry") are determined that you'll never have to fret about the food or the service at their charming restaurant, which specializes in both classic and contemporary French cuisine. Despite the traditional white linens, silver, china, and crystal, Sans Souci isn't a bit stuffy. Chef Aaron Welsh's changing menu offers a large selection of appetizers, including escargots encased in filo pastry with white wine and garlic butter, and Sonoma foie gras on toasted brioche with Belgian endive and cassis. Entrees on the seasonal menu might include pan-seared Muscovy duck breast with sun-dried cherries and pinot noir sauce, a Roquefort-crusted filet mignon in cabernet sauce, or oven-roasted Chilean sea bass with mango and grapefruit relish and jasmine rice. The desserts here put the "d" in decadent: try one of the luscious soufflés, the classic crème brûlée, or the crepes filled with fresh fruit and ice cream. *$$$; AE, MC, V; no checks; dinner Thurs–Tues; full bar; reservations recommended; between 5th and 6th Aves.*

LODGINGS

Cypress Inn / ★★

LINCOLN ST, CARMEL; 831/624-3871 OR 800/443-7443

This charming Mediterranean-style inn in the center of town was treated to a much-needed renovation that brought it up to date while preserving its Old Carmel charm. The 33 guest rooms received new paint, furniture, carpets, and TVs, and the bathrooms have been outfitted in new ceramic or marble tile. Movie star and animal-rights activist Doris Day owns the inn, and pets, naturally, are more than welcome; the hotel even provides dog beds for its four-footed guests. Service is uniformly professional and courteous, and the rooms contain some thoughtful touches: fresh fruit, bottles of spring water, a decanter of sherry, and chocolates on the pillow at night. Some have sitting rooms, wet bars, private verandas, and ocean views. There's a spacious Spanish-style living room with a comforting fire and a friendly bar that dishes out coffee and a continental breakfast in the morning, as well as libations of a more spirited kind at night. Posters of Doris Day movies add a touch of glamour and fun to the decor. *$$$$; AE, DIS, MC, V; checks OK; www.cypress-inn.com; at 7th Ave.*

Highlands Inn / ★★★

HWY 1, CARMEL; 831/622-5450 OR 800/682-4811

This exquisite luxury hotel began as a clutch of cabins in 1916, but its rustic days are long gone. Set high above the rocky coastline south of Carmel with fine views of Yankee Point, the Highlands Inn is now a sprawling modern complex of glowing redwood and soaring glass. In the main lodge, a skylit promenade leads to a series of glass-walled salons built for watching sunsets. In the fireside lobby you'll find deep leather settees, a granite fireplace, a grand piano, and elaborate floral displays. Outside, flower-lined walkways connect the cottagelike collection of rooms and suites. Every suite and town house unit features a living room with fireplace, kitchen, and bath with a massive spa tub. Most rooms have fireplaces, private decks, and fabulous views of the ocean, landscaped grounds, and evergreen-draped hills. Another perk is the inn's elegant three-star restaurant, Pacific's Edge (see review, above), and the less formal California Market, which boasts lovely coastline views and serves casual, well-prepared California fare. *$$$$; AE, DC, DIS, MC, V; checks OK; www.highlands-inn.com; 4 miles S of town.* &

La Playa Hotel / ★★★

CAMINO REAL, CARMEL; 831/624-6476 OR 800/582-8900

Almost regal in its splendor, this imposing 1904 luxury hotel spills down a terraced, bougainvillea-and-jasmine-strewn hillside toward the sea. Paths lit by antique street lamps wind among lush gardens with cast-iron gazebos and past a heated swimming pool festooned with mermaids, La Playa's mythical mascots. The hotel's 75 guest rooms were remodeled in January 1997, and everything from the carpeting and bedspreads to the pillows and window fixtures was replaced. The rooms are lighter now, with Spanish-style furnishings and refinished headboards hand-carved with the hotel's signature mermaids. To do La Playa right, invest in one of the five cottages, some of which are nestled in the gardens. These have varying numbers of rooms, and four of them offer full kitchens, fireplaces, and private patios. The hotel's restaurant, the Terrace Grill, has a fine view of the gardens and serves such tasty seasonal fare as artichoke ravioli, grilled local Monterey prawns, or chicken carbonara. *$$$–$$$$; AE, DC, MC, V; checks OK; www.laplayacarmel.com; at 8th Ave.* &

Lincoln Green Inn / ★★

CARMELO ST, CARMEL; 831/824-1880

If you're looking for a place far from the madding crowd, one of Lincoln Green Inn's four cottages may be the perfect solution. Located at Carmel Point just across the road from picturesque River Beach, the white, green-shuttered cottages occupy a bucolic English garden setting. Each cottage features a living room with cathedral ceiling and stone fireplace; three cottages have full-size kitchens. The Lincoln Green Inn is about as close as you can get to your own Carmel summer house without spending a fortune; it's a nice place for families or groups, affording closeness and privacy in equal measure. One caveat: Although the vintage-style kitchens are spotlessly clean, the cottage furnishings aren't particularly stylish or new. While some might consider the decor "homey," others may think that the rooms are due for a few upgrades. *$$$–$$$$; AE, MC, V; checks OK; at 15th Ave.*

Mission Ranch / ★★★

26270 DOLORES ST, CARMEL; 831/624-6436 OR 800/538-8221; 831/625-9040 (RESTAURANT)

When Clint Eastwood—director, movie star, and former mayor of Carmel—was a young recruit stationed at Fort Ord over 50 years ago, he happened to venture onto the Mission Ranch, and it was love at first sight. Once a working dairy farm, the ranch had become a humble road-house restaurant and motel—nothing special, perhaps, except for its magnificent natural setting. Nestled in back of the Carmel Mission, the Ranch overlooks a carpet of pastureland that gives way to a dramatic view of Carmel River Beach, with the craggy splendor of Point Lobos stretching just beyond. Alas, over the years, termites, erosion, and lack of management took their toll on the ranch, and a developer was all set to raze the buildings in the late 1980s when Eastwood rode in to the rescue. Determined to remain true to the original spirit of the place, he poured a ton of money and a lot of love into restoration of the Victorian farmhouse, cottages, bunkhouse, and other buildings. The result is simply wonderful. The peaceful, Western-style spread opened in 1992, offering everything a guest needs to feel comfortable. The 31 rooms, dis-tributed among a clutch of pretty, immaculately maintained buildings, are sparsely but tastefully appointed, with props from Eastwood's films, such as the clock from *Unforgiven*, nonchalantly scattered among the furnishings. Handmade quilts grace the custom-made country-style wooden beds that are so large you literally have to climb into them, and each guest room has its own phone, TV, and bathroom. Rates include a continental breakfast served in the tennis clubhouse. The informal and Western-themed Restaurant at Mission Ranch, which operates under separate management, serves hearty American-style fare. The place's only flaw is that the piano bar can get a little rowdy, and guests in the struc-tures closest to the restaurant may find themselves reaching for earplugs in the middle of the night. *$$–$$$; MC, V; checks OK; at 15th Ave.* &

Carmel Valley

LODGINGS

Bernardus Lodge / ★★★★

415 CARMEL VALLEY RD, CARMEL VALLEY; 831/659-3131 OR 888/648-9463
You'll sigh with satisfaction the moment you enter Bernardus Lodge, Carmel Valley's newest boutique resort. The lodge is the vision of Bernardus Vineyard and Winery owner Ben Pon, who spared no expense getting everything just right. Situated on a terraced hillside dotted with ancient oaks and pines and affording grand vistas of the sur-rounding Santa Lucia mountains, the lodge offers 57 guest rooms and suites, two restaurants, two tennis courts, boccie and croquet courts, a swimming pool, and a full-service spa and salon. Understated elegance is a key theme here, since Pon has mercifully deleted the *nouveau* from the *riche*. Generously sized guest rooms feature stone fireplaces, antique wardrobe armoires, a sitting area with sofa and chairs, vaulted ceilings, French doors, private patios, and king-size featherbeds with down com-forters and soft-as-silk Frette linens. Portable phones allow you to take

calls even when you're by the pool or on the courts; the silk-covered terry robes are so sensuously comfortable you'll want to do a Hugh Hefner and hang around in them for days on end. The lodge spa is a restorative haven; be sure to reserve spa treatments when you make your lodging reservation—weekend appointments fill up far in advance. Under the direction of award-winning chef Cal Stamenov, formerly of Highlands Inn and, before that, Domaine Chandon in Yountville, Marinus restaurant offers French-inspired wine-country cuisine. Wickets Bistro, a less formal environment, also draws upon Bernardus's extensive wine list and penchant for local, fresh ingredients. Although jacket and tie are optional in both establishments, a slightly snooty wait staff may make you wish you'd worn your Sunday best. Showing up in your robe, however tempting, is an absolute no-no. *$$$$; AE, CB, DC, DIS, MC, V; no checks; www.bernardus.com; at Los Laureles Grade.* &

Carmel Valley Ranch / ★★★

I OLD RANCH RD, CARMEL VALLEY; 831/625-9500 OR 800/422-7635
Nestled on a 1,700-acre spread in bucolic Carmel Valley, this haven for golf and tennis enthusiasts (and corporate retreaters) is about as plush a ranch as you're ever likely to encounter. Outfitted in earth tones, burgundies, and greens, the 144 guest suites are arranged in low-lying, condo-like clusters on the rolling hills; each comes equipped with cathedral ceilings, a wood-burning fireplace, a well-stocked refreshment center, two TVs, a trio of phones, a private deck, and a richly appointed bathroom. Some of the pricier suites come with a dining area, a kitchenette, and a private outdoor whirlpool tub (discreetly enclosed, of course). You might need that whirlpool after partaking of the ranch's activities: golf at a newly renovated Pete Dye 18-hole course, tennis on one of a dozen clay and hard-surface courts, guided nature hikes, biking, horseback riding, workouts with a personal trainer at the fitness club, or a dip in one of two swimming pools. When you're ready to relax, indulge in a facial or a manicure, a soak in one of six whirlpool spas, or perhaps a couple's massage followed by champagne and chocolate-covered strawberries. The ranch also offers three restaurants, including the elegant Oaks, which serves refined American regional cooking in a formal room graced by Old California antiques, a towering stone fireplace, and a phalanx of windows affording a panoramic view of the oak-covered hills. *$$$; AE, MC, V; checks OK; www.grandbay.com; off Carmel Valley Rd.* &

Quail Lodge / ★★★

8205 VALLEY GREENS DR, CARMEL VALLEY; 831/624-2888 OR 888/828-8787
This posh resort catering to golfers and tennis players has 100 guest rooms set along winding paths flanking a meticulously kept 18-hole course and a series of pretty little ponds. Comfort, not ostentatious luxury, is the byword here, and Quail Lodge does comfort very well

indeed. Decorated in nature-inspired shades of green, yellow, and red, even the least expensive rooms are spacious and have private balconies or patios. Higher-priced units feature fireplaces, Jacuzzis, and separate living rooms. Nice touches abound: all rooms have a coffeemaker, robes, room service, a minibar, a refrigerator, cable TV, and a bathroom equipped with every amenity. Two pools and a large hot tub stand ready for your dipping pleasure. The Covey Restaurant offers Wine Country cuisine, such as venison osso buco, sweetbread salad, crab-crusted halibut, and other fare that reflects an emphasis on fresh local products. Hearty, well-prepared, reasonably priced breakfasts and lunches are served at the clubhouse, a pleasant quarter-mile stroll away. Guests are entitled to reduced greens fees at the private club and use of the tennis courts. *$$$$; AE, DC, MC, V; checks OK; info@quail-lodgeresort.com; www.quail-lodge-resort. com; 3½ miles E of Hwy 1, just off Carmel Valley Rd.* &

Stonepine / ★★★★

150 E CARMEL VALLEY RD, CARMEL VALLEY; 831/659-2245

This exquisite Mediterranean villa (the former country home of the Crocker banking family) rises in terraced splendor against the oak-covered hills of the Carmel Valley. Surrounded by cypress, imported stone pines, and wisteria trailing from hand-carved Italian stone pillars, the inn has 16 guest rooms divided among Château Noel (named after owner Noel Hentschel), the Paddock House, and the idyllic (and astronomically expensive) Briar Rose Cottage, a two-bedroom affair with a private rose garden, living room, dining room, kitchen, and bar. The suites in the main house are studies in formal splendor; all have French antique furnishings, Jacuzzis, down comforters, and fluffy robes, and five of them feature fireplaces. The cost of your room includes a big breakfast; for an additional charge you may partake of a wine reception followed by an elegant five-course estate dinner in the Château's dining room. During the day, float in the jewel-like swimming pool, play tennis, explore the ranch's 330 acres, or horse around at the Stonepine Equestrian Center. Beware: The equestrian staff takes horseback riding mighty seriously, and more than one city slicker has suffered a bruised ego as well as a sore derriere after a turn on the trails. *$$$$; AE, MC, V; checks OK; www.stonepinecalifornia.com; 13 miles E of Hwy 1.* &

Big Sur

Originally "el pais grande del sur" (Spanish for "the big country to the south"), Big Sur encompasses 90 miles of rugged, spectacular coastline that stretches south from Carmel to San Simeon. A narrow, twisting segment of

HIGHWAY 1 (built with convict labor in the 1930s) snakes through this coastal area, and the mist-shrouded forests, plunging cliffs, and cobalt sea bordering the road make the drive one of the most beautiful in the country, if not the world. The region is so scenic that some folks favor giving it national park status; others, however, recoil in horror at the thought of involving the federal government in the preservation of this untamed land and have coined the expression "Don't Yosemitecate Big Sur."

Whether you're cruising through for the day or have booked a few nights at a resort, be sure to spend some time hiking in the gorgeous **POINT LOBOS STATE RESERVE** (for more details on the reserve, see Carmel in the previous pages). Farther south, Highway 1 crosses Bixby Creek via the 268-foot-high, 739-foot-long **BIXBY BRIDGE** (also known as the Rainbow Bridge), a solitary, majestic arch built in 1932 that attracts lots of snap-happy photographers. Nearby is the automated **POINT SUR LIGHTHOUSE** (off Hwy 1; 831/625-4419; 19 miles S of Carmel), built in 1889 and situated 360 feet above the surf on **POINT SUR**, a giant volcanic-rock island. Inexpensive (though physically taxing) three-hour guided lighthouse tours are offered on weekends year-round, with additional tours on Wednesdays during the summer and full-moon tours every month (be sure to take a jacket, even in the summer months).

Hikers and bicyclists often head farther south to navigate the many trails zigzagging through the sycamores and maples in 4,800-acre **ANDREW MOLERA STATE PARK**, the largest state park on the Big Sur coast. A mile-long walk through a meadow laced with wildflowers leads to the park's 2-mile-long beach harboring the area's best tide pools. A few miles down Highway 1 on the inland side is one of California's most popular parks, **PFEIFFER–BIG SUR STATE PARK**. Here, 810 acres of madrona and oak woodlands and misty redwood canyons are criss-crossed with hiking trails, and many paths provide panoramic views of the sea. The **BIG SUR RIVER** meanders through the park, too, attracting anglers and swimmers who brave the chilly waters. Nearby, the unmarked **SYCAMORE CANYON ROAD** (the only paved, ungated road west of Hwy 1 between the Big Sur Post Office and Pfeiffer–Big Sur State Park) leads to beautiful but blustery **PFEIFFER BEACH** (follow the road until it ends at a parking lot, about 2 miles from Hwy 1) with its white-and-mauve sands and enormous sea caves.

If your idea of communing with nature is a comfy chair in the shade, grab a seat on the upper deck of the fabled Nepenthe bar and restaurant (see review in Restaurants, below), perched 800 feet above the roiling Pacific. Four miles south of Nepenthe is the **COAST GALLERY**, a show-place for local artists and craftspeople featuring pottery, jewelry, and paintings, including watercolors by author Henry Miller, who lived nearby for more than 15 years. The author's fans will also want to seek out the **HENRY MILLER LIBRARY** (831/667-2574; just beyond Nepenthe restaurant on the E side of Hwy 1). In addition to a great collection of Miller's books and art, the library serves as one of Big Sur's cultural centers and features the art, poetry, prose, and music of locals; it's open Thursday through Sunday. Seekers of other sorts flock to **ESALEN INSTITUTE** (831/667-3000; see "Free Your Mind, Soak Your Feet" in this chapter), the world-famous New Age retreat and home of heavenly massages and hot springs that overlook the ocean.

At the southern end of Big Sur is beautiful **JULIA PFEIFFER BURNS STATE PARK**, with 4,000 acres to roam. You'll find some excellent day hikes here, but if you just want to get out of the car and stretch your legs, take the quarter-mile **WATERFALL TRAIL** to 80-foot-high McWay Waterfall, one of the few falls in California that plunges directly into the sea. Keep an eye open for the silly sea otters that play in **MCWAY COVE**. But wherever you trek through Big Sur, beware of the poison oak—it's as ubiquitous as the seagulls hovering over the coast.

ACCESS AND INFORMATION

Despite Big Sur's popularity, the area miraculously has remained sparsely populated, and most people journey here for only a few days to camp, backpack, or luxuriate in the elegant (and, in some cases, exorbitantly priced) resorts hidden in the hills. The bumper-to-bumper traffic on summer weekends can be reminiscent of LA's rush hour. Avoid the crowds by arriving midweek or in the spring, when the gold, yellow, and purple wildflowers brighten the windswept landscape. To order an audiotape with a guided tour of the region, call the **BIG SUR LAND TRUST** (831/625-5523).

RESTAURANTS

Nepenthe Restaurant / ☆

HWY 1, BIG SUR; 831/667-2345

This venerable Big Sur institution recently celebrated its 50th anniversary and still draws in the crowds. Locals will remark that people come for the setting more than the food. It's true that this is a place where the environment takes precedence over the cuisine, but once you're staring out at the Pacific, you may decide that it doesn't really matter. Located 800 feet above the ocean, Nepenthe commands views of the Big Sur coastline that must make hotel developers sigh with envy. Happily, there's little chance that corporate money will ever be welcome here. Nepenthe is a friendly, family-owned and managed place, and therein lies part of its appeal. Originally a log cabin that housed Lolly and Bill Fassett and their five children, Nepenthe was born when they realized that the only way to keep their family amply fed was to open a restaurant. The log cabin remains, but over the years Nepenthe has grown to encompass the entire bluff it rests upon. The restaurant boasts a full bar, and two outdoor areas offer lots of room for alfresco dining. Even after warnings about overpriced meals, locals insist visi-

FREE YOUR MIND, SOAK YOUR FEET: HOW ESALEN GOT
EVERYONE INTO HOT WATER

Before Grace Slick sang "feed your head," before Ram Dass urged us to "be here now," and before Timothy Leary coined the slogan "turn on, tune in, drop out," the Esalen Institute in Big Sur encouraged esoteric thought and avant-garde therapies. In the jargon of the day, it was a primo place to blow your mind.

It all began with a bath. Or baths, to be more precise. In 1910 Dr. Henry C. Murphy, a physician from Salinas, purchased 375 acres of majestic Big Sur coastline fed by mineral springs. He intended to build a European-style spa, constructing bathhouses and installing large concrete tubs, but died before the spa could come to fruition.

Fast-forward to 1960. Michael Murphy, Dr. Murphy's grandson, and friend Richard Price, both Stanford grads with an interest in Eastern religions, envisioned an institute that integrated Eastern and Western ideas and inspired personal transformation. Murphy's family property provided the perfect locale. The cofounders offered their first series of programs, called the Human Potentiality, in 1961; what followed sowed the seeds of the 1960s and '70s "consciousness revolution." Esalen held seminars led by some of the most forward-thinking philosophers, psychologists, writers, and theologians of the time, including Aldous Huxley, Abraham Maslow, Fritz Perls, Alan Watts, Susan Sontag, Linus Pauling, Ken Kesey, Carlos Castaneda, Fritjof Capra, Timothy Leary, and Joseph Campbell.

tors to Big Sur should try Nepenthe at least once. The fare tends toward standard American, but the menu's got something for everyone. Starters include Cajun poached shrimp and Castroville artichoke; entrees offer a choice of fresh fish, steaks, and broiled or roast chicken. Burgers and salads should keep kids and vegetarians happy. Be sure to check out Nepenthe's Phoenix Gift Shop on your way out. This magical little store harbors wonderful imported treasures, books, jewelry, kids' toys, and locally made soaps, lotions, and body oils. *$$; AE, MC, V; no checks; lunch, dinner every day; full bar; reservations required for parties of 5 or more; www.nepenthebigsur.com; 27 miles S of Carmel.*

LODGINGS

Post Ranch Inn / ★★★★

HWY 1, BIG SUR; 831/667-2200 OR 800/527-2200; 831/667-2800 (RESTAURANT)

Travel & Leisure magazine has hailed the 98-acre Post Ranch Inn as "the most spectacular hotel on the Pacific Coast," and that might not be hyperbole. Discreetly hidden on a ridge 1,300 feet above the crashing surf, architect Mickey Muennig's redwood complex was completed in

Soaking up the intoxicating, idea-filled atmosphere and the healing waters of the sulfurous baths became a rite of passage for many. To Esalen we can give thanks—or blame—for bringing terms like *self-actualization, peak experience, encounter group,* and *Gestalt therapy* into the popular lexicon, and for that essential contribution to instant enlightenment—the hot tub.

Originally located at the ocean's edge, the baths were a source of controversy during Esalen's first two decades, generating rumors of drug use and public sex. Murphy and Price tried to keep the lid on, so to speak, by declaring the baths chastely separate-sex, but the demand for coed nudity eventually overruled them. In 1998, El Niño storms caused extensive damage to the baths and the towering slope that rises above them. The baths were moved to the top of the bluff, where they'll remain until the hillside and the baths are repaired. They're still coed and clothing-optional and continue to be popular with Esalen guests, but the wild antics are long gone. Hey, it's not the '60s anymore.

Almost 40 years have passed since the heady days when Alan Watts and Joseph Campbell debated the mysteries of the universe, Joan Baez gave impromptu concerts, and George and Ringo flew in with the Maharishi in tow, but Esalen continues to be a countercultural enclave for spiritual seekers. A smorgasbord of workshops such as "Mindfulness Meditation," "Quantum Decision Making," and "Shamanic Shapeshifting and Medicine" offer enough options to keep anyone's body, mind, and spirit in proper working order. Workshops are either two-day (Fri–Sun) or five-day (Sun–Fri) and cost $485 and $885 respectively. Shared lodgings and all meals are included. For more information, call Esalen (831/667-3000) or visit www.esalen.org.   —Christi Phillips

April 1992. Muennig supposedly camped out on the property for five months before setting pencil to paper for his design, which had to conform to the strict Big Sur Coastal Land Use Plan. He propped up seven of the inn's units (known as the Tree Houses) on stilts to avoid disturbing the surrounding redwoods' root systems and sank others into the earth, roofing them with sod. The inn's deceptively simple exteriors harmonize with the forested slopes, while windows, windows everywhere celebrate the breathtaking vista of sky and sea that is Big Sur's birthright. Environment, in fact, is a word you'll hear a lot around this place, which was named after William Post, one of the area's early settlers. The Post Ranch Inn is one of the new breed of eco-hotels, where the affluent can indulge in sumptuous luxury and still feel politically correct. The water is filtered; visitors are encouraged to sort their paper, glass, and plastic garbage; and the paper upon which guests' rather staggering bills are printed is recycled. The 30 spacious rooms have spare—but by no means spartan—decor, including fireplaces, king-size beds, and sideboards made of African hardwoods (nonendangered, naturally). Slate-tile Jacuzzi tubs for two adorn the well-equipped bathrooms, and stereo systems fill the air with ethereal New Age music. A continental breakfast, guided nature hikes, and yoga classes are included in the room rates; the massages, facials, and herbal wraps are not. The Ranch also boasts a gorgeous, cliff-hugging restaurant that has been hailed as one of the best on the Central Coast. Sierra Mar serves a sophisticated brand of California cuisine in a serene expanse of wood and glass that lets you drink in the incredible views along with the wine. The dinner menu, which changes daily, features such sumptuous starters as pine-smoked squab with ginger and cilantro, mussel soup with saffron and potatoes, and perhaps a salad of lettuces (organic, of course) mixed with shaved fennel, oranges, Parmesan, and a Campari vinaigrette. Main courses include such bounty as roast rack of venison with glazed chestnuts and huckleberries, truffled fettuccine with asparagus and English peas, and roasted Guinea fowl with potato gnocchi and pearl onions. *$$$$; AE, MC, V; checks OK; www.postranchinn.com; 30 miles S of Carmel.*

Ventana Inn & Spa / ★★★★
HWY I, BIG SUR; 831/667-2331 OR 800/628-6500

If one casts the Post Ranch as the brash newcomer, the Ventana must be the revered granddaddy of the eco-hotel scene. Not that this stunning resort is showing its age; the Ventana is as fresh and up with the times as it was when it made its debut nearly 25 years ago. Set on the brow of a chaparral-covered hill in the Santa Lucia Mountains, this modern, weathered cedar inn is almost too serene and contemplative to be called decadent, yet too luxurious to be called anything else. Its spacious 62 rooms, decorated in an upscale country style and divided among 12 low-rise buildings, look out over the plunging forested hillsides, wildflower-laced meadows, and roiling waters of the Big Sur coast. Three houses are also available to rent; the rooms in the Sycamore and Madrone Houses have large private balconies and some of the best views of the ocean. Several rooms have fireplaces, hot tubs, and wet bars; rates climb in accordance with the amenities offered (peak-season prices range from approximately $300 to a whopping $900). A sumptuous breakfast is included. The inn's other big draw is Cielo Restaurant, which delivers panoramic patio views of 50 miles of coastline at prices that can be equally breathtaking. A revolving-door parade of chefs has kept critics uncertain about the quality of the food since Jeremiah Tower did his star turn here years ago, however. The current chef, Jerry Regester, serves rustic "New American"–style dishes such as seared ahi tuna with asparagus, porcini mushroom, and leek sauce; lavender-grilled lamb chops; or oak-grilled Angus New York steak. *$$$$; AE, DC, DIS, MC, V; checks OK; www.ventanainn.com; 28 miles S of Carmel, 2 miles S of Pfeiffer–Big Sur State Park.*

WINE COUNTRY

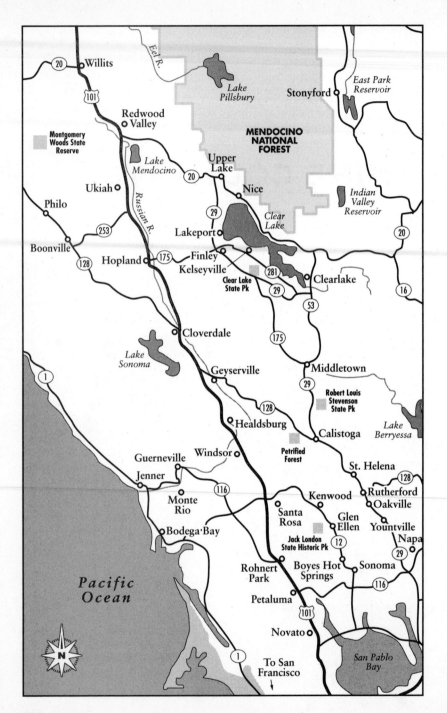

WINE COUNTRY

Napa and Sonoma are two of the top tourist attractions in the United States, with little wonder. When you combine supernatural scenic beauty with nearly year-round excellent weather, top-notch restaurants, and world-class wines, what's not to like? These qualities have made the region, which includes pastoral Anderson Valley and its fringe of Mendocino County towns, a popular destination for oenophiles and gourmets alike. And for the nature lover who comes along for the ride, the Wine Country delivers some of America's most stunning vistas. Like competitive siblings of the same robust family, these areas contain many similarities, but each also retains its individual personality.

ACCESS AND INFORMATION

There are two main options for those arriving in the Wine Country BY AIR. Fly into SAN FRANCISCO INTERNATIONAL AIRPORT (located off Hwy 101, just S of San Francisco; 650/876-2377) or OAKLAND INTERNATIONAL AIRPORT (1 Airport Dr; 510/577-4000), and then rent a car, since that is by far the best way to tour this largely rural area. Driving from San Francisco, you will likely hit more traffic, and the route can be tricky: from the airport, head north on Highway 101 toward San Francisco. Take the 101 North/Duboce/Mission Street exit, stay right, then turn right onto Mission Street/US 101 North. Turn left onto South Van Ness, which will take you north across the city. Turn left onto Lombard and follow signs to the Golden Gate Bridge. Cross the bridge, then continue on Highway 101 North.

Just past Novato, exit onto Highway 37. For the town of Sonoma, head east on 37 for about 8 miles. Take a left onto Highway 121 North (Sears Point Raceway will be on your left). You are now in the Sonoma Valley. Stay on 121 and take Highway 12 North.

For Napa, follow the directions above, but stay on 121, following signs for Napa until you reach Highway 29, which will then take you the length of the valley to your destination. Travel time from SFO is approximately 2 hours; double that for rush hour. For other Sonoma County destinations, stay on 101 and continue north.

Napa is easily accessible from the East Bay side of the Bay Area, and that makes the OAKLAND AIRPORT a good choice (Oakland flights can also be cheaper and less inclined to be delayed by fog than flights to and from SFO). From Oakland, take Highway 80 North to Vallejo, then take the Highway 37/Marine World exit going west. This will take you to Highway 29, where you will go right (north) to Napa. As you approach Napa, the road will split; for downtown Napa, stay to the right and follow the signs that say Lake Berryessa/Downtown Napa. For the rest of the Napa Valley, stay to the left and follow signs for 29 North.

If you want to rent a car, but would rather skip the horrific Bay Area traffic, you can take a **SHUTTLE BUS TO SANTA ROSA** and rent a car there. **SANTA ROSA AIRPORTRIDE.COM** (formerly Santa Rosa Airporter; 707/523-0301; www.airportride.com) connects to both airports. **CAR RENTALS** available in Santa Rosa include Avis, Budget, Enterprise, and Hertz.

If driving is simply not an option, your choices are limited. You can take one of the airport shuttles to different points in the region. For Napa: take the **EVANS SHUTTLE** (707/255-1559) from either airport, then take a taxi from the Evans parking lot to downtown Napa. Use Napa city as your base, which will allow you to access most necessities on foot. The **NAPA CONFERENCE AND VISITORS BUREAU** (1310 Town Center Mall, Napa; 707/226-7459; www.napavalley.com) can arrange bicycle, van, and limousine tours of the wineries.

Pedestrians visiting Sonoma can take the **SONOMA AIRPORTER** (800/611-4246) and stay in the town of Sonoma in the plaza area. Sonoma Airporter service is available from SFO only. The **SONOMA VALLEY VISITORS BUREAU** (453 1st St E, Sonoma; 707/996-1090; www.sonomavalley.com) has winery tour information.

The Napa Valley

When the words "wine country" come up, the picture that most likely comes to mind is one of the Napa Valley, a place that is a phenomenon in every sense of the word. It's only about 30 miles long and a few miles wide, but its natural beauty has been documented by countless photographs celebrating every season: late winter's glowing fields of yellow mustard; spring's emerald hills and blossoming fruit trees; summer's vines weighted with luscious green and purple grapes; and autumn's crimson and gold vineyards curving to the horizon.

Napa is an economic phenomenon as well, as the region has exploded in 30 years to become the nation's second-largest tourist attraction and the world's most visited wine region. This popularity and the subsequent influx of capital has changed the valley in numerous ways, producing a quality of glamour that is not evident in any other wine region—including Sonoma. Ubiquitous white limousines cruise the well-worn wine routes, and a profusion of upscale inns, spas, restaurants, and hot-air balloon charters cater to the moneyed traveler. The rapid change has produced an odd mix wherein celebrities rub shoulders with vineyard workers. But whether traveling by BMW convertible or GMC pick-up, your reward for making the journey to Napa will be a taste of some of the best wines in the known universe. Popularity has also resulted in most wineries charging a tasting fee, which can range from $2 for a series to $25 for a single glass at Opus One.

Lodging information, winery maps, and details about parks, hot-air balloon rides, and other recreational pastimes like the **NAPA VALLEY WINE TRAIN** (707/253-2111), a dining train that traverses the valley floor, are available at the **NAPA VALLEY CONFERENCE AND VISITORS BUREAU** (1310 Town Center Mall, off 1st St, Napa; 707/226-7459; www.napavalley.com).

Napa Wineries

Staff at most wineries assume that the folks who walk through their doors are not wine connoisseurs and welcome questions. During the congenial process of touring their facilities and sampling various vintages, they try to show visitors what makes their product unique. So if you've ever had a dream of entering a French restaurant and wiping that smirk off the sommelier's face, this is the place to learn how to do it—and what fun the learning is!

Although most vintners now charge you to taste their wines, tours are usually free (some require reservations, but don't let that deter you—establishments simply need to control the number of visitors at any one time). Since Napa has over 250 wineries, it's safe to say you won't see them all in a weekend. A good plan of attack is to choose the ones you most want to visit and then tour three a day—with a leisurely lunch break somewhere in between. Leave room in your schedule for the serendipitous detour, because this is the best way to make new discoveries. Napa's wineries are mainly clustered along Highway 29 and the Silverado Trail, two parallel roads running the length of the valley. On summer weekends, the traffic on 29 slows to a standstill, so the wise traveler will look for alternatives. One very important thing to remember: *never speed along these roads.* While the local law enforcement officers have no desire to harass winery visitors, they vigilantly monitor speeding; if you're pulled over after having one too many glasses of cabernet, you'll have more than a hangover ahead of you.

Here's a roster of some of the Napa Valley's most popular wineries, many of which offer free tours of their facilities:

S. ANDERSON (1473 Yountville Crossroad, Yountville; 707/944-8642). S. Anderson is the only family-owned champagne house in the United States. Lively candlelight tours of the caves educate the visitor on *méthode champenoise*—the method for making premium sparkling wines.

BEAULIEU VINEYARDS (1960 St. Helena Hwy, Rutherford; 707/963-2411). Nicknamed "BV," this winery is housed in a historic estate and is famous for its cabernet sauvignon.

BERINGER VINEYARDS (2000 Main St, St. Helena; 707/963-7115). The Napa Valley's oldest continuously operating winery features a

WINE COUNTRY THREE-DAY TOUR

DAY ONE: Glamorous Napa. The ultimate Napa experience begins at **Auberge du Soleil** hotel with a leisurely breakfast on the patio overlooking the valley (also available to nonguests). Drive your convertible south down **Silverado Trail**—taking in the vineyard views—and make a right onto Yountville Crossroad to catch the 10:30am tour at **S. Anderson Vineyard**. Buy a bottle of Diva to take home. Cruise west along Yountville Crossroad to downtown Yountville for a 12:30 lunch reservation at **Bistro Jeanty**. Next head north on Highway 29 to the **Niebaum-Coppola Estate Winery**. Try the claret, buy wine paraphernalia in the gift shop, and peruse Frances Ford Coppola's movie memorabilia collection upstairs. Continue north along 29 to **Beringer Vineyards** and investigate the lovely Rhine House, then visit the tasting room. Stroll along St. Helena's Main Street before heading on to have a Tuscan-inspired dinner down the road on the patio at **Tra Vigne**. Then head back to your room at Auberge du Soleil for a good night's rest.

DAY TWO: Scenic Sonoma. From Napa, begin your day with a woodsy drive along the hairpin curves of Oakville Grade (which, closer to Sonoma, will become first Dry Creek Road, then Trinity Road). At Glen Ellen, turn left and follow Highway 12 south to the town of Sonoma. Grab a cappuccino and pastry at **Cucina Viansa**, then begin

stately, old Rhineland-style mansion and good tours of the vineyards and caves. It's well known for its chardonnay and cabernet sauvignon.

CHÂTEAU MONTELENA WINERY (1429 Tubbs Ln, Calistoga; 707/942-5105). This stunning French château-style winery is built of stone and is celebrated for its chardonnay. The beautiful setting includes a lake with two islands and wonderful gazebos.

CLOS PEGASE (1060 Dunaweal Ln, Calistoga; 707/942-4982; www.clospegase.com). Designed by architect Michael Graves, this stunning, modern facility offers grand outdoor sculpture, a "Wine in Art" slide show, and good guided tours of the winery, caves, and art collection.

DOMAINE CHANDON (1 California Dr, Yountville; 707/944-2280; www.dchandon.com). Excellent sparkling wines come from this winery's handsome building. There's a four-star dining room (see the restaurant's review, below) and fantastic guided tours, too.

THE HESS COLLECTION WINERY (4411 Redwood Rd, Napa; 707/255-1144). A stone winery in a remote, scenic location, the Hess Collection is well known for its cabernet sauvignon and chardonnay. Contemporary American and European art is showcased in a dramatic building, as part of an informative self-guided tour.

MERRYVALE VINEYARDS (1000 Main St, St. Helena; 707/963-7777). Within Merryvale's historic stone building the winery offers daily tastings

BEST PLACES®

You don't have to stop with just one Best Places® guidebook.

We offer a complete line of guides to Alaska, the Northwest, and California, as well as regional favorites in cooking, gardening, and literature.

Call toll-free 1-800-775-0817

or visit us on the web at www.SasquatchBooks.com

Yes, please send me a FREE copy of the Sasquatch Books catalog.

Name _____

Address _____

City _____ State ____ Zip _____

Phone _____ Email address _____

I bought this book at: _____

I wish Best Places would publish a guide for: _____

       I've bought Best Places® guides for ____ years.

Subjects I'm interested in: ☐ Food & Wine ☐ Outdoors ☐ Children's Books
      ☐ Travel ☐ Gardening ☐ Other

BPNC4

BUSINESS REPLY MAIL
FIRST-CLASS MAIL   PERMIT NO. 998   SEATTLE WA

POSTAGE WILL BE PAID BY ADDRESSEE

SASQUATCH BOOKS

615 2ND AVE STE 260
SEATTLE WA 98104-9841

SASQUATCH BOOKS
SEATTLE

shopping in the gourmet deli for the day's picnic lunch. Walk around the plaza and continue gathering goodies from the **Sonoma Cheese Factory** and whatever else strikes your fancy. Drive north of town to **Ravenswood Winery** for some of the best zinfandels around. Take your picnic to **Bartholomew Park Winery**, and after tasting the wines and visiting the museum, lunch on the 400-acre grounds and walk the trails. Next stop is historic **Buena Vista Winery** (try the cream sherry), followed by a visit to **Gundlach Bundschu Winery**, where you can hike up the hill to view the valley below. Drive back into Sonoma for dinner on the vine-covered patio at **Della Santina's** before heading back to the hotel.

DAY THREE: Calistoga Mud Baths. Breakfast again at Auberge du Soleil, then begin the day with the breathtakingly beautiful tram ride up the mountain to **Sterling Vineyards**, where you can taste wines on the patio. Next head south to **Wine Spectator Restaurant** at Greystone and while away a couple of hours with lunch, a tour of the building, and a visit to the basement cookware marketplace. Head back to Calistoga for an afternoon of sybaritic pleasures at **Indian Springs**, the region's historic Victorian spa. Have a mud bath or facial, then soak up the sun in the enormous mineral-springs-fed swimming pool. Enjoy a relaxed dinner at **Cin Cin** before heading out of town. Drive south along Silverado Trail, savoring the final vineyard views in the last dying rays of the sun.

and, by appointment only, informative, thorough tasting classes on Saturday and Sunday mornings. The winery is best known for its chardonnay.

NIEBAUM-COPPOLA WINERY (1991 St. Helena Hwy, Rutherford; 707/963-9099). Filmmaker Francis Ford Coppola now owns the former Inglenook grand château, built in the 1880s. The winery features displays on Coppola's film career and Inglenook's history, plus an enormous gift shop stocked with wine, gifts, books, gourmet foods, and even Coppola's favorite cigars. Daily wine tastings; tours by appointment only.

OPUS ONE (7900 St. Helena Hwy, Oakville; 707/944-9442). Robert Mondavi started this extraordinary venture in collaboration with France's Baron Rothschild. In a dramatic bermed neoclassical building, tours and expensive wine tastings ($25 for a 4-ounce glass of wine) are offered by appointment.

ROBERT MONDAVI WINERY (7801 St. Helena Hwy, Oakville; 707/963-9611; www.robertmondavi.com). This huge, world-famous winery, housed in a mission-style building, offers excellent tours of the facilities, a famous cooking school, and numerous special events.

SCHRAMSBERG VINEYARDS (1400 Schramsberg Rd, Calistoga; 707/942-4558). Schramsberg's first-rate sparkling wines are showcased in attractive, historic facilities and extensive caves. Interesting guided tours are available by appointment only.

STERLING VINEYARDS (1111 Dunaweal Ln, Calistoga; 707/942-3300). Sterling offers an excellent self-guided tour through its sleek, white Mediterranean-style complex perched on a hill. Access is via an aerial tramway offering splendid views, and there's a vast tasting room with panoramic vistas.

Napa

The downtown area of Napa is currently undergoing a renaissance that includes the renovation of historic structures, the building of a new museum, and the opening of several restaurants on Main Street. Along the Napa River, the historic Hatt Building has been recreated as the NAPA MILL (500 Main St; 707/251-8500), a center featuring a boutique hotel, shops, restaurants, and a weekend farmer's market. Across the river, the AMERICAN CENTER FOR WINE, FOOD, AND THE ARTS (500 1st St; 707/257-3606) is scheduled to open on Thanksgiving 2001. It will be a cultural museum with offerings ranging from cooking demonstrations and wine-tasting classes to art lectures and an exhibition organic garden. In 2002, the old opera house where Jack London once gave readings will reopen, after a complete restoration, with its first performance since 1914. The 116-year-old structure will be known as the MARGRIT BIEVER MONDAVI OPERA HOUSE (1030 Main St; 707/226-7372).

For the traffic-weary traveler, downtown Napa provides a base where a plethora of Victorian bed-and-breakfasts and nearby restaurants, as well as the attractions listed above, can all be accessed on foot. Lodging reservations and walking tour maps are available through the NAPA VALLEY CONFERENCE AND VISITORS BUREAU (1310 Town Center Mall, Napa; 707/226-7459; www.napavalley.com). For a break from seeing the sights, stop at ABC BAKING COMPANY (1517 3rd St; 707/258-1827) and enjoy goodies like espresso and chocolate-caramel cake. Or browse the large selection of books on the Wine Country at COPPERFIELD'S (1303 1st St; 707/252-8002), then walk down to NAPA VALLEY ROASTING COMPANY (948 Main St; 707/224-2233) to read your selections over a latte. On the same block, DOWNTOWN JOE'S (902 Main St; 707/258-2337) serves breakfast, lunch, and dinner along with fine house-brewed ales.

RESTAURANTS

Bistro Don Giovanni / ★★★

4110 ST. HELENA HWY, NAPA; 707/224-3300

As the name suggests, Donna and Giovanni Scala (who also opened the wonderful Scala's Bistro in San Francisco's Sir Francis Drake hotel) bring a touch of French bistro to their friendly Italian trattoria. Although the kitchen has been known to stumble in years past, the food is now consistently well prepared, whether you order the penne with green beans and pesto, the ravioli stuffed with fresh basil and ricotta, the juicy "chicken under a brick," or even the side dish of grilled corn on the cob with red pepper butter. The wine list, although skewed toward expensive California vintages, is extensive and imaginative, and such offerings as watermelon granita and a delectable fresh fruit crisp beckon from the dessert menu. *$$; AE, DC, DIS, MC, V; local checks only; lunch, dinner every day; full bar; reservations recommended; on Hwy 29, just N of Salvador Ave.*

Celadon / ★★

1040 MAIN ST, STE 104, NAPA; 707/254-9690

By the time you find this restaurant, hidden behind a downtown office building and overlooking the creek, you will have worked up an appetite. And that's good news, because you'll be in the right place to satisfy it. Chef Greg Cole fuses an eclectic blend of spicy international flavors into a small, rotating menu. Some of the constants are grilled tuna salad with macadamia nuts and spicy sesame greens; an udon noodle bowl with shiitake mushroom broth; and a "Jamaican-inspired" pork chop with black beans and grilled pineapple salsa. The impressive wine list is not surprising

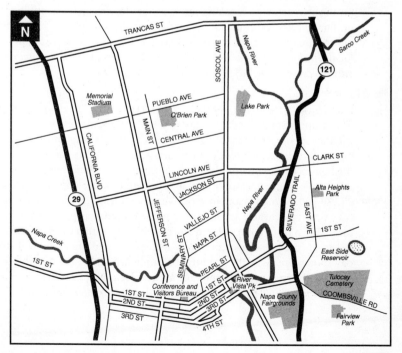

when you know that Cole once worked at Robert Sinskey Vineyards in order to learn all he could about wine. His by-the-glass prices are some of the more reasonable in the area. The decor of this small indoor restaurant is unpretentious and serene; outdoor creekside dining is an option in warm weather. Celadon does not accept reservations, a deliberate if unusual strategy to accommodate the locals and the spontaneous traveler. To find the restaurant, take the outdoor walkway to the rear of the Main Street Exchange Building. *$$$; AE, V, MC, DC; local checks only; lunch Mon–Fri, dinner Mon–Sat; beer and wine; no reservations; at Pearl St.*

La Boucane / ★★

1778 2ND ST, NAPA; 707/253-1177

Housed in a restored Victorian, Napa Valley's bastion of classic French cuisine has a small teal-and-rose dining room that glows with candles. The wine list, with its healthy mix of Bordeaux and Burgundian varietals from California's top vintners, is perfectly matched to chef/owner Jacques Mokrani's traditional French fare: crisp roasted duck in a zesty, bittersweet orange sauce; perfect poached salmon in a delicate champagne-cream sauce; and thick, flavorful tournedos forestière in a reduction of game and beef stock with fresh herbs and red wine. All entrees come with a richly flavored soup such as crawfish bisque or cream of turnip, artfully arranged vegetables, a salad, and a divine dessert such as soufflé glacé praline, *mousse au chocolat*, or crème caramel. Despite the restaurant's old-fashioned decor, the atmosphere is delightfully unstuffy. *$$$; MC, V; local checks only; dinner Mon–Sat (closed in Jan); beer and wine; reservations recommended; 1 block E of Jefferson St.*

Pearl / ★★

1339 PEARL ST, STE 104, NAPA; 707/224-9161

This homey establishment is a favorite with locals, mainly because of the friendly service and reliably good fare. Owners Nickie and Pete Zeller divide duties; Nickie presides over the kitchen, and Pete runs the front of the house. The menu offers something for all tastes and budgets, running the gamut from an array of raw and prepared oyster appetizers to goat cheese pizzas to an Asian-inspired ahi tuna sandwich with red cabbage cole slaw to a hearty triple pork chop with mashed potatoes. Pearl is located in a terra-cotta-colored stucco building, with a cute patio on the street. Inside, hex signs scare away evil spirits, and hopefully will some day soon scare away the restaurant's chipboard tables, because this food deserves a better presentation. *$$; MC, V; local checks only; lunch and dinner Tues–Sat; beer and wine; reservations recommended; at Franklin.*

ROBERT LOUIS STEVENSON'S TIME IN NAPA

The Scottish author Robert Louis Stevenson came to California in search of Fanny, a married woman, ten years his senior, whom he'd met and fallen in love with in France. By the time he arrived by ship in San Francisco, he was half dead from bronchitis, his condition worsening as he waited for Fanny to obtain a divorce. By then he was penniless and critically ill.

The couple married in May of 1880, and in an attempt to restore the groom's health, spent their last $10 on a honeymoon cabin at a hot springs resort in Calistoga—a region even then famed for its restorative powers. With their money gone, they spent the summer in the old bunkhouse of an abandoned silver mine on **Mount St. Helena**. Their neighbors were grizzly bears, mountain lions, and rattlesnakes.

Dry weather and sunshine did, in fact, restore Stevenson's health. He describes his adopted home in a memoir, *Silverado Squatters:*

"The house, after we had repaired the worst of the damages, and filled in some of the doors and windows with white cotton cloth, became a healthy and a pleasant dwelling-place, always airy and dry, and haunted by the outdoor perfumes of the glen. Within, it had the look of habitation, the human look. . . . And yet our house was everywhere so wrecked and shattered, the air came and went so freely, the sun found so many portholes, the golden outdoor glow shone in so many open chinks, that we enjoyed, at the same time, some of the comforts of a roof and much of the gaiety and brightness of alfresco life. A single shower of rain, to be sure, and we should have been drowned out like mice. But ours was a California summer, and an earthquake was a far likelier accident than a shower of rain."

The writer admits more than the weather was a draw to Napa: "I was interested in California wine. Indeed, I am interested in all wines, and have been all my life. . . ." To this end, he spent time with Jacob Schram, who founded **Schramsberg Vineyards**.

While Stevenson idled on the mountain with Fanny, his family accepted the news of his marriage. The couple returned to Scotland, where Stevenson wrote *Treasure Island.* Mount St. Helena is said to be the inspiration for Spyglass Hill.

Today, at **Robert Louis Stevenson State Park**, you can hike up rugged, solitary Mount St. Helena to the site where the newlyweds squatted; a stone monument of a book marks the spot. In St. Helena, the **Silverado Museum** houses one of the world's largest collections of Stevenson memorabilia. Documentary filmmakers from Scotland have, ironically, made the pilgrimage to Napa to research one of their most distinguished native sons.

—*Cathleen Miller*

LODGINGS

Churchill Manor / ★★

485 BROWN ST, NAPA; 707/253-7733

Churchill Manor is an elegant, meticulously maintained mansion, incongruously set in a modest neighborhood. Built in 1889 by a local banker, it is listed on the National Register of Historic Places. The colonial revival house, which rises three stories above an expanse of beautiful gardens, is graced by stately pillars and a large, inviting veranda. Each of the 10 immaculate guest rooms features antique furnishings, ultra-plush carpeting, and an elegant private bath; among the favorites are Victoria's Room (imposing and spacious, with a king-size bed and a claw-footed tub perched by the fireplace), Rose's Room (with a scattering of French antiques including a carved-wood, king-size bed), and Edward's Room (the largest room, Mr. Churchill's former sanctuary also boasts magnificent French antiques and a lavish bath with hand-painted tiles). Rates include a full breakfast served in the marble-floored sun room, fresh-baked cookies and coffee or tea in the afternoon, and a wine-and-cheese reception in the evening. When you're not out touring the local wineries, you may tickle the ivories of the grand piano in the parlor, play croquet on the lovely side lawn, or tour Old Town Napa on the inn's tandem bicycles. Owners Brian Jensen and Joanna Guidotti are attentive and welcoming hosts. *$$; AE, DIS, MC, V; checks OK; www.churchill manor.com; at Oak St.*

La Residence / ★★

4066 ST. HELENA HWY, NAPA; 707/253-0337

Set back in the trees along busy Highway 29, this multimillion-dollar creation of partners David Jackson and Craig Claussen has twenty guest rooms scattered throughout two houses separated by a heated swimming pool and an elaborate gazebo. The main house, a Gothic revival mansion built in 1870 by a former New Orleans riverboat captain, contains nine comfortable guest rooms beautifully decorated with designer fabrics and American antiques. Most have sitting rooms, fireplaces, and private baths. Airier accommodations can be found in the modern French-style barn across the plaza. Filled with simple pine antiques, these spacious rooms have fireplaces, private baths, and French doors that open onto small patios or balconies. A delicious gourmet breakfast is served downstairs in the barn in a cheery, sunny dining room. Although La Residence is undeniably one of the region's loveliest small inns, its location next to the highway detracts from the away-from-it-all feel that B&Bs usually try to cultivate. *$$$; AE, DC, DIS, MC, V; checks OK; on Hwy 29, next to Bistro Don Giovanni.*

Silverado Country Club & Resort / ★★

1600 ATLAS PEAK RD, NAPA; 707/257-0200

Golfers and tennis players flock to this 1,200-acre estate, and it's easy to see why. The Silverado boasts two perfectly maintained 18-hole golf courses designed by Robert Trent Jones Jr. and the largest tennis complex in North America, with 20 championship courts rimmed with flowered walkways. If you're not into golf or tennis, however, there's little reason to stay here; the 280 unprepossessing rooms seem to have been designed for people who don't plan to spend much time indoors. The standard rooms, in a condo-like warren, start at about $165. The one- and two-bedroom suites overlooking the golf course are prettier but equally soulless; they're gleamingly modern with black-marble fireplaces and well-appointed kitchens. A few minutes' drive from the main complex are the more secluded Oak Creek East accommodations, street after street of mind-numbingly similar houses and condominiums owned by country-club members and rented out to guests. Numerous swimming pools dot the extensive grounds—popular spots to cool off on the valley's sweltering summer days. The resort's clubhouse and restaurants are located in the magnificent colonnaded Southern Gothic mansion at the heart of the main complex. Vintners Court, a formal dining room dominated by a glittering chandelier and a white grand piano, offers decent Pacific Rim fare. For a more casual meal, order a club sandwich or a hamburger at the Silverado Bar & Grill. The Royal Oak restaurant is a luxurious throwback to the days of elegant club grills. *$$$; AE, DC, DIS, MC, V; checks OK; www.silveradoresort.com; from Hwy 29, turn right onto Trancas St (Trancas St will become Hwy 121), then turn left onto Atlas Peak Rd.*

Yountville

Sleepy little Yountville has suddenly emerged as the dining capital of the valley, with the opening of several new restaurants, including two impressive French bistros, **BOUCHON** and **BISTRO JEANTY**. They join the other tried-and-true standbys, which run the gamut of styles from the casual **PACIFIC BLUES CAFE** (located in the Vintage 1870 shopping center, 6525 Washington St), with a wonderful outdoor patio, to the dining summit of the **FRENCH LAUNDRY**, where capturing a reservation is regarded on par with climbing Mount Everest. Yountville contains several posh inns and small hotels, spas, boutiques, antique shops, and the historic **PIO-NEER CEMETERY** (at the north end of Lincoln St), making it a fruitful stop for the traveler.

RESTAURANTS

Bistro Jeanty / ★★★

6510 WASHINGTON ST, YOUNTVILLE; 707/944-0103

Philippe Jeanty was a culinary pioneer in Napa. He came from France to head Domaine Chandon's now-legendary kitchen back when the region was known more for cattle and prunes than for four-star wines. After 20 years at Chandon, he left to open his own place in Yountville, and it's been a success ever since, with the James Beard Foundation nominating it for the title of Best New Restaurant in the United States. Bistro Jeanty represents the rare perfect marriage of setting and cuisine, perhaps because Jeanty designed the whole thing himself, modeled on the small French bistros from his childhood. The details are flawless—from the window boxes with geraniums outside to the antiques and specials chalkboard inside. A large "community table" by the front door seats the diners without partners or reservations and is a favorite of locals who drop by. The food remains true to Jeanty's heritage: lamb tongue salad, *haricot verts*, sole meunière, steak tartare, and a dreamy coq au vin—all of which are well followed by a sinfully luxurious chocolate mousse. *$$$; MC, V; no checks; lunch, dinner every day; full bar; reservations recommended; at Mulberry St.*

Bouchon / ★★

6534 WASHINGTON ST, YOUNTVILLE; 707/944-8037

Thomas Keller opened this small bistro to handle the overflow business from the French Laundry and as a late-night gathering place for the valley. Bouchon looks like a miniature Paris nightclub—one with such a sophisticated, elegant atmosphere that you immediately feel stylish simply by walking through the door. A zinc bar is put to good use serving raw seafood specialties such as oysters, mussels, and langoustines. The fare is traditional *bistro français*: foie gras, quiche du jour, charcuterie plates, onion soup gratin, steak frites, mussels marinières, and for dessert, tarte Tatin and profiteroles with ice cream and chocolate sauce. A short menu of appetizers, entrees, and desserts is served till 1:30am daily. *$$$; AE, MC, V; local checks only; lunch, dinner every day; full bar; reservations recommended; across from the Vintage 1870 shopping center.*

Domaine Chandon / ★★★★

I CALIFORNIA DR, YOUNTVILLE; 707/944-2892

Napa Valley's culinary reputation was born at this elegant restaurant with its rough-textured walls and wood archways overlooking the winery's manicured gardens and vineyards. Rooted in traditional French techniques enlivened by California innovation, executive chef Robert Curry's creative and delicate cooking style is perfectly matched to Domaine Chandon's sparkling wines. Past winners from the ever-changing menu have included an exquisite appetizer of alder-smoked trout served on a bed of curly endive, and a Japanese eggplant soup that arrives not as the customary purée but as a multicolored mélange streaked with basil and red and yellow peppers. Anything from the grill—such as beef, rabbit, or the divine pancetta-wrapped salmon—packs a salt-and-peppery punch, followed by a flavorful unfolding of meltingly tender meat. Grand desserts have included such jewels as a ground-almond shortcake with strawberries and a polenta pudding saturated with grappa and topped with fresh raspberries and mascarpone. The extensive wine list features some interesting (mainly California) vintages at surprisingly reasonable prices. Service is gracious and impeccable. Domaine Chandon also offers patio dining during the warm months, making it one of the most pleasant places to lunch in the Wine Country. *$$$; AE, DC, DIS, MC, V; no checks; lunch every day, dinner Wed–Sun May–Oct; lunch, dinner Wed–Sun Nov–Apr (closed first 2 weeks of Jan); wine only; reservations recommended; www.dchandon.com; just W of Hwy 29.*

The French Laundry / ★★★★

6640 WASHINGTON ST, YOUNTVILLE; 707/944-2380

This is the place you dream of stumbling upon in the French countryside: an unassuming old stone house (with no sign announcing its purpose) draped in ivy and surrounded by herb gardens, occupied by a brilliant chef offering magnificent meals, stellar wines, and faultless service. There is nothing accidental about the French Laundry, however. Since taking over the helm in 1994, chef Thomas Keller has created one of the finest— and most expensive—dining experiences in the Napa Valley. His prix-fixe tasting menu offers a choice of five or seven courses that change daily and are always memorable. On one evening, dinner commenced with a chilled English pea soup infused with white truffle oil, followed by Maine lobster poached in sweet butter, pan-seared white quail with braised Adriatic figs and a Mission fig coulis, and an incredible saddle of venison. In true French style the meal was topped off by a cheese course with French butter pears poached in white wine, followed by a divine yellow nectarine sorbet. The service is subtle and perfectly timed, but such perfection doesn't come quickly *or* cheaply. The French Laundry (the place was indeed a laundry when it was constructed in the 1890s) also serves a four-course lunch, which is best enjoyed on the patio next to the flower and herb gardens. Reservations are accepted up to two months in advance. *$$$$; AE, MC, V; local checks only; lunch Fri–Sun, dinner every day; beer and wine; reservations required; at Creek St.*

Mustards Grill / ★★★

7399 ST. HELENA HWY, YOUNTVILLE; 707/944-2424

Some critics call Mustards' feisty American regional cuisine comfort food, but that's too complacent a description for the vigorous, spicy, vaguely Asian-influenced bistro fare served here. Part of the Cindy

Pawlcyn dynasty (which includes such highly successful restaurants as St. Helena's Tra Vigne and Mill Valley's Buckeye Roadhouse), this wildly popular restaurant has a big open kitchen, pale yellow walls, dark wood wainscoting, and a black-and-white checkerboard floor. Appetizers range from wild mushroom toast with goat cheese to Chinese chicken noodle salad with spicy peanut dressing. The menu changes frequently, but is anchored by long-standing favorites such as the giant Mongolian pork chop with braised sweet-and-sour cabbage and garlic mashed potatoes. Mustards specializes in entrees from the wood-burning grill; try the tea-smoked Peking duck with almond-onion sauce, or barbecued baby back ribs. The desserts often change, but they're always worth the splurge, especially if they include the fresh blueberry crisp with lemon ice cream. Mustards' voluminous international wine list includes a vintage chart, and the restaurant pours a selection of domestic microbrews including a "sassy beer of the day." *$$; DC, DIS, MC, V; no checks; lunch, dinner every day; full bar; reservations recommended; on Hwy 29, just N of town.*

Ristorante Piatti / ★★

6480 WASHINGTON ST, YOUNTVILLE (AND BRANCHES); 707/944-2070
Piatti is a deservedly popular chain of chic nouvelle Italian restaurants with outlets in touristy towns throughout Northern California. And it all started right here in tiny Yountville. Chef Peter Hall (of Tra Vigne and Mustards Grill fame) took over from Renzo Veronese in 1997, bringing his own touch to the kitchen with such dishes as Peter's Rabbit Sausage and homemade potato gnocchi. Kick off your meal with the melt-in-your-mouth sweetbreads sautéed with mushrooms or perfectly grilled vegetables with whole roasted garlic. For a main course, try any of the plump, delicately flavored cannelloni or the risotto of the day: favorites include a creamy risotto packed with artichoke hearts, chicken, and sun-dried tomatoes, and a delicious variation with smoked salmon and fresh asparagus. Grilled items, such as the chicken and rabbit, are also consistently top-notch. Piatti sometimes goes overboard with the seasonings, forsaking balance for blasts of flavor, so select a wine with a lot of backbone. The Italian/Napa Valley wine list is extensive. *$$; AE, DC, MC, V; no checks; lunch, dinner every day; full bar; reservations recommended; S of the Vintage 1870 shopping center.*

LODGINGS

Maison Fleurie / ★★

6529 YOUNT ST, YOUNTVILLE; 707/944-2056

Built in 1873, this beautiful, ivy-covered brick-and-fieldstone hotel was a bordello and later a 4-H clubhouse before it opened in 1971 as the Napa Valley's first bed-and-breakfast inn. Purchased by the owners of the Four Sisters Inns company (who also run the charming Petite Auberge in

San Francisco and Pacific Grove's Gosbey House), the old Magnolia Hotel was reborn as Maison Fleurie in 1994 and endowed with a new, French country feel. Seven of the guest rooms are located in the main house, with its thick brick walls, terra-cotta tiles, and vineyard views; the remaining six are divided between the old bakery building and the carriage house. All have private baths, and some feature fireplaces, private balconies, sitting areas, and patios. After a long day of wine tasting, unwind at the pool or soak your tired dogs in the outdoor spa tub. The inn also provides bicycles for tooling around town. *$$$; AE, DC, MC, V; no checks; www.foursisters.com; at Washington St.*

Vintage Inn / ★★

6541 WASHINGTON ST, YOUNTVILLE; 707/944-1112 OR 800/351-1133
Spread throughout a 23-acre estate and designed by the same architect who created Big Sur's Ventana Inn, the Vintage Inn provides the Napa Valley traveler with a host of creature comforts in a modern setting. The 80 large, cheery rooms, bathed in soothing earth tones and wood accents, are all equipped with fireplaces, Jacuzzi tubs, refrigerators, patios or verandas, ceiling fans, and plush private baths. Guests may take a dip in the heated pool or outdoor spa, play a game of tennis, order room service, sip a spirit at the bar, or rent the inn's bikes, hot-air balloon, or private limo for a tour of the Wine Country. You'll also be treated to a continental breakfast served with glasses of bubbly. *$$$; AE, DC, DIS, MC, V; checks OK; www.vintageinn.com; just E of Hwy 29.*

Oakville

Other than several world-class wineries, Oakville's main claim to fame is the **OAKVILLE GROCERY** (7856 St. Helena Hwy at Oakville Cross Rd, 707/944-8802), a local icon disguised as an old-fashioned country market complete with a fading "Drink Coca-Cola" sign outside. It's not a scene for the claustrophobic; any given noontime will find this homey establishment clogged with tourists lined up to buy gourmet deli treats. But those who brave the scene will find a fine variety of local wines (including a good selection of splits), a small espresso bar tucked in the corner, and pricey but delicious picnic supplies ranging from pâté and caviar to sliced-turkey sandwiches and several freshly made sweets.

Rutherford

LODGINGS

Auberge du Soleil / ★★★★

180 RUTHERFORD HILL RD, RUTHERFORD; 707/963-1211 OR 800/348-5406
This exclusive 33-acre, 52-unit resort, inspired by the sunny architecture of southern France, is nestled in an olive grove on a wooded hillside

above the Napa Valley. Its 11 original cottages have rough-textured adobe-style walls, white French doors and windows, and smashing views of the valley. Set on a winding street on a terraced hillside, each cottage is divided into four guest rooms and suites that have private entrances and balconies designed for maximum privacy. The upstairs rooms with their vaulted, exposed-beam ceilings are particularly posh, but even the humblest accommodations here are sinfully hedonistic, with fireplaces, artful and comfortable furnishings, candles, sitting areas, and tiled floors. Two additional rooms on the top floor of the main building lack fireplaces but have king-size beds and French doors that open onto private terraces. Two new cottages offer you a true 1,800-square-foot home-away-from-home—that is, if your home has a Jacuzzi on the terrace, two fireplaces, a living room, den, and master bedroom and bath, not to mention a $2,500-a-night price tag. The gorgeous Southwestern-style dining room has soaring lodgepole accents, carved wooden chairs, and a kiva fireplace. Look for classic Wine Country cuisine such as wild mushroom sauté in an herb-garlic filo nest with black peppercorn sauce, or sautéed Sterling salmon with crisp vegetables and pinot noir sauce, followed by an almond tulip filled with Grand Marnier ice cream, fresh berries, and bittersweet chocolate sauce. The bar serves a light menu on the deck from 11am to 11pm. $$$$; AE, DIS, MC, V; checks OK; www.aubergedu soleil.com; N of Yountville—from the Silverado Trail, turn right on Rutherford Hill Rd.

St. Helena

For many years St. Helena has been entrenched in a never-ending battle to preserve its exclusive, small-town way of life—instead of becoming one more tourist haven for Wine Country visitors. Citizens have filed injunctions against everything from the Napa Valley Wine Train (forbidding it to stop in town) to Safeway (the grocery giant wanted to build a larger supermarket). Needless to say, Wal-Mart was out of the question.

As a result, **MAIN STREET** has retained its Victorian Old West feel, and historic structures like **STEVE'S HARDWARE** (1370 Main St; 707/963-3423) coexist with the trendy **1351 LOUNGE** (1351 Main St; 707/963-1969), located in a former bank complete with vault. Just off the main drag you can find more down-home pleasures at the **NAPA VALLEY OLIVE OIL MANUFACTURING COMPANY** (835 Charter Oak Ave; 707/963-4173), an authentic Italian deli and general store stuffed to the rafters with goodies like dried fava beans, biscotti, salami, and fresh mozzarella. For great gifts, be sure to pick up a bottle or two of the top-notch extra-virgin olive oil or the olive oil soap. Just south of town, the notorious New York deli **DEAN & DELUCA** (607 S St. Helena Hwy; 707/967-9980) has opened a huge store selling a mind-boggling array of cheeses, wines, deli items, and cookware. For a picnic, take your treats to **LYMAN PARK** (on Main St between Adams and Pine) and sit on the grass or in the beautiful little white gazebo where bands sometimes perform summer concerts. A more bucolic picnic spot is **BALE GRIST MILL STATE HISTORIC PARK** (Hwy 29, 3 miles N of St. Helena).

RESTAURANTS

Brava Terrace / ★★

3010 ST. HELENA HWY, ST. HELENA; 707-963-9300

Brava Terrace offers lively French-Mediterranean cuisine in an idyllic setting: the beautiful dining room has vaulted ceilings with exposed wood beams, white walls with bright modern art, glowing hardwood floors and furniture, and a big stone fireplace. Even better are the large, beautifully landscaped terraces—the perfect place for a lazy lunch, a late afternoon snack, or dinner on a warm evening. Owner Fred Halpert breathes life into old classics like cassoulet, but he also has an inviting menu of daily pastas and risottos. The grilled portobello mushrooms with spinach and artichokes topped by a roasted garlic–walnut vinaigrette is a first-rate appetizer, and the pan-roasted chicken with "garlic-smashed" potatoes and rosemary-infused pan juices is a soul-satisfying choice for the main course. Finish with a chocolate chip crème brûlée or one of the exquisite house-made sorbets. There's a lengthy, reasonably priced wine list to boot. *$$$; AE, DC, DIS, MC, V; no checks; lunch, dinner every day May–Oct; lunch, dinner Thurs–Tues Nov–Apr; full bar; reservations recommended; fredbrava@aol.com; on Hwy 29, between St. Helena and Calistoga, next to Freemark Abbey.*

Pinot Blanc / ★★

641 MAIN ST, ST. HELENA; 707/963-6191

Celebrity chef Joachim Splichal (owner of LA's Patina and a trio of other Pinots in Los Angeles) migrated north to open this "country bistro." With executive chef Sean Knight in the kitchen, the food usually shines. Don't miss his salmon with a shallot- and apple-smoked-bacon crust, marinated pork chop with horseradish mashed potatoes, or any of the *plats du jour* (for example, braised Calistoga pig with homemade sauerkraut is served on Sunday, and provençal-style bouillabaisse with saffron rouille is offered on Friday). The wine list suggests trying a bottle of pinot blanc, but it also features more than 350 other possibilities, including a lengthy list of whites for those suffering from chardonnay burnout. *$$$; AE, DC, DIS, MC, V; no checks; lunch, dinner every day; full bar; reservations recommended; off Hwy 29.*

Terra / ★★★

1345 RAILROAD AVE, ST. HELENA; 707/963-8931

Housed in a historic stone building with high ceilings and arched windows, Terra's subdued dining rooms have an ineffable sense of intimacy about them. Fervid tête-à-têtes, however, are more likely to revolve around Terra's fine Southern French/Northern Italian food than around *amore*. Yet this isn't the sort of food that screams to be noticed; chef Hiro Sone's cuisine never grandstands. Unusual combinations such as mild duck-liver wontons with an earthy wild mushroom sauce may sound a little forced, but they don't play that way on the palate. Recommended dishes include broiled sake-marinated Chilean sea bass with shrimp dumplings; spaghettini with fresh tomatoes and white bean stew; a grilled veal chop with pinot noir sauce; and strawberries drenched in a cabernet-and-black-peppercorn sauce served with vanilla ice cream. *$$$; DC, MC, V; local checks only; dinner Wed–Mon; beer and wine; reservations recommended; between Adams and Hunt Sts, 1 block E of Main St.*

Tra Vigne & Cantinetta Tra Vigne / ★★★★

1050 CHARTER OAK AVE, ST. HELENA; 707/963-4444 (RESTAURANT) OR 707/963-8888 (CANTINETTA)

The Tuscan-inspired food at Tra Vigne is exceptionally fresh, and almost everything is made on the premises, including the anise-flecked bread, pasta, cheese, olive oils, smoked meats, and desserts. Appetizers are chef Michael Chiarello's forte. The menu changes seasonally, but you can usually find delicately crisp polenta rounds topped with meaty wild mushrooms in a rich, gamy vinaigrette; wonderfully fresh mozzarella and tomatoes drizzled with basil oil and balsamic vinegar; and a daily seafood selection fried crisp in arborio rice flour with mustard seed vinegar. Pastas run the gamut from traditional to outrageous—such as ravioli stuffed with puréed pumpkin and sprinkled with fresh cranberries—and pizzas are delicately and expertly rendered. Entrees might include grilled Sonoma rabbit with Teleme-cheese-layered potatoes, oven-dried tomatoes, and mustard sauce; ahi tuna grilled on a rosemary skewer and served on a roasted-pepper salad with pea sprouts; and a crisp leg of duck confit on a pea-and-potato purée with spring onion sauce. Desserts are stellar: try the velvety espresso custard with a thin layer of fudge-like chocolate dusted with powdered sugar, served with a crisp hazelnut cookie. Service is knowledgeable, witty, and efficient. The wine list, though not large, includes a carefully chosen array of Italian and Napa Valley bottles. The vast, exquisitely designed dining room has soaring ceilings and taupe walls covered with big, bright Italian poster art. If you'd prefer a light lunch or want your food to go, amble over to the less-expensive Cantinetta Tra Vigne. The cantinetta sells several varieties of focaccia pizza, gourmet sandwiches, interesting soups and salads, pastas topped with smoked salmon and other delights, and a variety of sweets. *$$$; DC, DIS, MC, V; local checks only; lunch, dinner every day (restaurant); lunch every day (catinetta); full bar; reservations recommended; off Hwy 29.*

Wine Spectator Restaurant at Greystone / ★★★★

2555 MAIN ST, ST. HELENA; 707/967-1010

When you first spot Greystone perched high atop a hill, you'll catch your breath, as it's the closest thing the United States has to a castle. The building, which formerly housed the Christian Brothers winery, was constructed in 1889 out of local tufa stone. The restaurant is on the first floor of the Culinary Institute of America (it's named for *Wine Spectator* magazine, which donated $1 million to the school's scholarship fund) and is in a large, noisy room with a fireplace and a display kitchen surrounded by a bar. The CIA's cooking students play an integral role in restaurant preparations, led by talented chef Todd Humphrey. Humphrey has steered the menu away from the Mediterranean theme of former restaurateur/chef Joyce Goldstein into New American territory. Diners have two choices for appetizers: raw oysters or a chef's tasting menu. Choose both. Begin with oysters and the CIA's own reasonably priced house champagne, then move on to the tasting menu, which offers small morsels of indescribable variety and pleasure. Some examples from one offering: carpaccio, smoked salmon on a bed of shredded beets, potato balls, and scallops in crème fraîche. The main course brings other unique mouthwatering combinations: venison served with a confit of autumn vegetables and huckleberry sauce; seared sea scallops with saffron gnocchi, asparagus and morel sauce, and so on. A fine finish to the meal is the velvety crème brûlée accompanied by vin santo. The wine list is extensive, offering something for every taste and price range. Tours of the building are also available, as are cooking demonstrations on weekends (707/967-1100). The basement houses a huge cookware emporium, complete with every gadget and cookbook imaginable. *$$$$; AE, DC, MC, V; local checks only; lunch, dinner every day; full bar; reservations recommended; www.ciachef.edu; at Deer Park Rd.*

LODGINGS

The Ink House Bed and Breakfast / ★

1575 ST. HELENA HWY, ST. HELENA; 707/963-3890

This gorgeous Italianate Victorian inn, built in the shape of an ink bottle by Napa settler Theron Ink in 1884, would merit three stars if it weren't for its no-star location along a busy, noisy stretch of Highway 29. The three-story yellow-and-white home has seven sumptuously decorated guest rooms, plus a lavish living room and parlor with an old-fashioned pump organ and a grand piano. The B&B's most interesting architectural feature is the glass-walled belvedere that sits atop the house like the stopper of an inkwell and offers a sweeping 360-degree view of the Napa Valley hills and vineyards. The best (and quietest) room is the spacious, high-ceilinged French Room, with its richly carved mahogany bed graced by an elegant half-canopy. The rooms at the front of the house are for sound sleepers only. Innkeepers David and Diane Horkheimer are incredibly friendly and helpful, and they'll nourish you with a full country breakfast, plus wine and appetizers in the afternoon. *$$; MC, V; checks OK; inkhousebb@aol.com; www.napavalley.com/inkhouse/; at Whitehall Ln.*

Inn at Southbridge / ★★★

1020 MAIN ST, ST. HELENA; 707/967-9400 OR 800/520-6800
This new sister to the swanky Meadowood Resort fills the gap between Napa's ultra-luxe digs and its ubiquitous bed-and-breakfast inns. Designed by the late William Turnbull Jr. the 21-room inn is part of a terra-cotta-hued complex that dominates a long block on St. Helena's main drag. Inside, the guest rooms are almost Shaker in their elegant simplicity, with white piqué cotton comforters, candles, fireplaces, vaulted ceilings, and French doors opening onto private balconies. Guest privileges are available at the exclusive Meadowood Resort, though the on-site Health Spa Napa Valley offers a plethora of spa treatments, plus its own swimming pool and exercise equipment. In the courtyard, a big red tomato sets the mood at Tomatina, the inn's stylish pizzeria. Sit on one of the tomato-red bar stools facing the open kitchen and order the clam pie, a winning pizza combo. *$$$$; DC, MC, V; checks OK; www.slh. com; between Charter Oak Ave and Pope St.*

Meadowood Resort / ★★★★

900 MEADOWOOD LN, ST. HELENA; 707/963-3646 OR 800/458-8080
Rising out of a surreal green sea of fairways and croquet lawns, Meadowood's pearl-gray, New England–style mansions are resolutely Eastern. Winding landscaped paths and roads connect the central buildings with smaller lodges scattered over 256 acres; the lodges are strategically situated near an immaculately maintained nine-hole golf course, two croquet lawns (with a full-time croquet pro on hand), seven championship tennis courts, and a 25-yard lap pool. The 85 exorbitantly priced accommodations range from one-room studios to four-room suites, each with a private porch and a wet bar. The suites tucked back in the woods are the most private, but the Lawnview Terrace rooms are the best, with their vaulted ceilings, massive stone fireplaces, and French doors opening onto balconies that overlook the croquet green. The vast bathrooms have hair dryers, magnified makeup mirrors, thick bathrobes, and floors inset with radiant heating to keep your toes cozy as you pad to the cavernous shower. All guests have access to the swimming pool, the outdoor whirlpool, and the well-equipped health spa that offers a weight room, aerobics classes, massages, and numerous other ways to pamper your body. The octagonal Restaurant at Meadowood has a high ceiling and a

beautiful balcony overlooking the golf course. Appetizers, like the sweet-bell-pepper ravioli with wild mushrooms in a browned sage butter or the Miyagi oysters on the half shell with champagne sauce and caviar, are consistently very good, though the expensive entrees vary in quality. The more informal Grill at Meadowood offers an elaborate breakfast buffet and sandwiches and salads for lunch. *$$$$; AE, DC, DIS, MC; checks OK; www.meadowood.com; off the Silverado Trail.*

Calistoga

Mud baths, mineral pools, and massages are still the main attractions of this charming little spa town, founded in the mid-19th century by California's first millionaire, Sam Brannan. Savvy Brannan made a bundle of cash supplying miners in the Gold Rush and quickly recognized the value of Calistoga's mineral-rich **HOT SPRINGS**. In 1859 he purchased 2,000 acres of the Wappo Indians' hot springs land, built a first-class hotel and spa, and named the region Calistoga (a combination of the words California and Saratoga). He then watched his fortunes grow as affluent San Franciscans paraded into town for a relaxing respite from city life.

Generations later, city slickers are still making the pilgrimage to this city of spas. These days, however, more than a dozen enterprises touting the magical restorative powers of mineral baths line the town's Old West–style streets. You'll see an odd combo of stressed-out CEOs and earthier types shelling out dough for a chance to soak away their worries and get the kinks rubbed out of their necks. While Calistoga's spas and resorts are less glamorous than the Sonoma Mission Inn & Spa (see review in the Sonoma section), many offer body treatments and mud baths you won't find anywhere else in this part of the state. Among the most popular spas are **DR. WILKINSON'S HOT SPRINGS** (1507 Lincoln Ave; 707/942-4102; www.napavalley.com/drwilkinson.html), where you'll get a great massage and numerous other body treatments in a rather drab setting; **CALISTOGA SPA HOT SPRINGS** (1006 Washington St; 707/942-6269; www.napavalley.com/Calistoga), a favorite for families with young children that boasts four mineral pools in addition to several body-pampering services; **INDIAN SPRINGS** (1712 Lincoln Ave; 707/942-4913) for pricey spa treatments in a historic setting and the best (and largest) mineral pool in the area (you can even see—and hear—the steam from one of the geysers feeding hot mineral water into the pool); and **LAVENDER HILL SPA** (1015 Foothill Blvd/Hwy 29; 707/942-4495; www.lavenderhillspa.com), which provides aromatherapy facials, seaweed wraps, mud baths, and other sybaritic delights in one of the most attractive settings in town.

After you've steamed or soaked away all your tensions, head over to the **CALISTOGA INN**'s (1250 Lincoln Ave; 707/942-4101) pretty outdoor patio for a tall, cool drink. Try one of the house-brewed beers or ales, but save your appetite for one of the better restaurants in town. Once you're rejuvenated, stroll down the main street and browse through the many quaint shops marketing everything from French soaps and antique armoires to silk-screened T-shirts and saltwater taffy. For a trip back in time to Calistoga's pioneer past, stop by the **SHARPSTEEN MUSEUM AND BRANNAN COTTAGE** (1311 Washington St; 707/942-5911). Just outside of town you can marvel at **OLD FAITHFUL GEYSER** (1299 Tubbs Ln, 2 miles N of Calistoga; 707/942-6463), which faithfully shoots a plume of 350°F mineral water 60 feet into the air at regular intervals.

Other natural wonders abound at the **PETRIFIED FOREST** (4100 Petrified Forest Rd, off Hwy 128, 6 miles N of town; 707/942-6667), though if you aren't a trained geologist, it might be hard to appreciate those towering redwoods turned to stone when Mount St. Helena erupted three million years ago. For a splendid view of the entire valley, hike through the beautiful redwood canyons and oak-madrona woodlands in **ROBERT LOUIS STEVENSON STATE PARK** (off Hwy 29, 8 miles N of Calistoga; 707/942-4575) to the top of Mount St. Helena.

RESTAURANTS

All Seasons Cafe / ★★

1400 LINCOLN AVE, CALISTOGA; 707/942-9111

Many restaurants in the Napa Valley have elaborate wine lists, but none compare to this cafe's award-winning roster. The rear of the restaurant— a retail wine store with a tasting bar—stocks hundreds of first-rate foreign and domestic selections at remarkably reasonable prices. If nothing catches your fancy on the restaurant's regular wine list, ask to see the shop's enormous computerized catalog. The All Seasons menu is even structured around wine: the appetizers, such as crisp, herby bruschetta and creative salads, are recommended to accompany sparklers, chardonnay, and sauvignon blanc; respectable California pizzas and pastas are paired with sauvignon blanc, zinfandel, and Rhône wines; and entrees such as delicate roast quail with walnut-studded polenta, grilled lamb with fresh sprigs of dill, and fish with fruity sauces are matched with an excellent selection of chardonnay, cabernet, and pinot noir. So much emphasis is placed on wine, in fact, that the food sometimes suffers. However, the enthusiastic and opinionated servers can usually steer you safely to the better choices on the changing menu. *$$; DIS, MC, V; local checks only; lunch Thurs–Tues, dinner every day; beer and wine; reservations recommended; at Washington St.*

Catahoula / ★★

1457 LINCOLN AVE, CALISTOGA; 707/942-2275

By playfully dubbing his Wine Country restaurant Catahoula, the name of the Louisiana state dog, chef/owner Jan Birnbaum served notice that he was returning to his Southern roots—a surprise move, since Birnbaum's reputation had been built at such bastions of haute cuisine as New York's Quilted Giraffe and San Francisco's Campton Place restaurant. The discrepancy between his formal training and Catahoula's down-home fare turns out to be serendipitous, resulting in a glorious, spirited brand of nouvelle Southern cuisine. Hominy cakes served hot off the griddle are paired with fennel, potatoes, endive, and other veggies coated with a smoked-onion vinaigrette. The cornmeal-fried catfish is laced with lemon-jalapeño meunière and served with slaw, and a thin-crusted pizza is crowned with crayfish and andouille sausage. Catahoula is located in the Mount View Hotel, with its homey lobby featuring a huge hearth and overstuffed couches. The hotel saloon offers Catahoula's appetizers and light dinners on weekends and serves other tidbits on the poolside patio in the summer. If you overindulge, you can always relax at the Mount View's well-appointed spa, or sleep it off in one of the hotel's guest rooms. *$$$; DIS, MC, V; checks OK; breakfast, lunch Sat–Sun, dinner every day; full bar; reservations recommended; near Washington St.*

Cin Cin / ★★★

1440 LINCOLN AVE, CALISTOGA; 707/942-1008

Cin Cin's soulful Mediterranean food satisfies more than mere appetite. Dishes like melt-in-your-mouth gnocchi, served in a deep, flavorful ragout of duck, porcini mushrooms, and pancetta, offer a comfort akin to a nice warm blanket on a chilly night. The changing menu showcases delicacies of the season; one spring visit found a delicious salad of warm grilled asparagus combined with tart and juicy blood oranges. An inspired lavender and honey crème brûlée provided the perfect finish to the meal. The wine list features an international selection, with unusual vintages from France, Italy, and even New Zealand added to the usual California suspects. While the restaurant is located on Calistoga's main drag, the interior has a sophisticated big-city bistro feel, probably explained by the fact that chefs John Gillis and Gina Armanini both worked in San Francisco before opening their own place. *$$$; MC, V; no checks; dinner Wed–Sun, brunch Sat–Sun; beer and wine; reservations recommended; next to the Ace Hardware store.*

NAPA VALLEY'S WINE HISTORY

Napa's famous wine region began with a bang. **Mount St. Helena** was once an active volcano, and its eruptions left the valley with the loamy soil in which grapes thrive. The first person to take advantage of this development was also Napa's first American settler; George Yount planted vineyards in 1838 and shared the fruits of his labor with other thirsty pioneers.

By the latter half of the 19th century, European immigrants began making their mark, establishing a wine industry in the valley. Many of their names can still be seen on today's vintages: Charles Krug (**Charles Krug Winery**); Jacob Schram (**Schramsberg Vineyards**); Gustave Niebaum (**Niebaum-Coppola Estate Winery**); and Frederick and Jacob Beringer (**Beringer Vineyards**).

By the 1890s, the industry was thriving, with more than 140 wineries in operation, when disaster struck in the form of phylloxera, a louse that destroys the grapes' roots. (A hundred years later, phylloxera would strike again—causing grape growers to replant the majority of their vineyards.) Then, in 1919, a disease more deadly than any parasite finished off Napa's wine industry: Prohibition. Only a handful of wineries survived—by making blessed sacramental altar wine.

By 1960, only 25 wineries remained in Napa Valley. Instead of grapes, the sleepy farming community raised cattle, walnuts, and prunes. But the next three decades would witness an amazing resurrection of Napa's wine industry.

Wappo Bar & Bistro / ★★

1226-B WASHINGTON ST, CALISTOGA; 707/942-4712

Husband-and-wife chefs Aaron Bauman and Michelle Matrux opened this zesty bistro in 1993 and immediately began collecting accolades for what Bauman describes as "regional global cuisine." Confused? Well, even Bauman admits the cuisine is hard to pinpoint, merrily skipping as it does from the Middle East to Europe to Asia to South America to the good old USA. The small menu changes often, but this culinary United Nations has embraced such diverse dishes as chicken potpie with a cornmeal-herb crust, fresh sea bass dipped in chick-pea flour served with mint chutney and lentil crepes, and Moroccan lamb stew with dried fruit and couscous. One dish that turns up often due to popular demand: chiles rellenos stuffed with basmati rice, crème fraîche, currants, and fresh herbs, dipped in a blue cornmeal batter, deep-fried, and served on a bed of walnut-pomegranate sauce. This is ambitious, imaginative cooking, and the talented chefs usually pull it off with aplomb. *$$; AE, MC, V; local checks only; lunch, dinner Wed–Mon; beer and wine; reservations recommended; off Lincoln Ave.*

Through a dedication to quality, a handful of wine makers gradually began to elevate the stature of Napa's wines, attracting international attention. Still, California vintages were always considered second-rate to France until a landmark event occurred in 1976, known as the Paris Tasting. Organized to coincide with the American Bicentennial, the blind tasting was held in Paris, with French judges. And to every Napa Valleyite's joy and amazement, Napa Valley wines won—in both the white and red categories. The French judges cried foul and demanded to see their tasting notes again. But when they dried their eyes, the facts remained: a **Château Montelana** chardonnay and a **Stag's Leap** cabernet sauvignon had beaten all the grand crus from France. *Time* magazine immediately dispatched a team of journalists to Napa to cover the story, and wine makers and oenophiles alike headed to the valley to find out what all the fuss was about.

Today the region boasts more than 250 wineries, and no one is surprised when Napa vintages garner international awards. A fitting monument to local accomplishments is to be unveiled in 2001, when the $50 million **American Center for Wine, Food, and the Arts** opens in downtown Napa. This museum and cultural institute celebrates America's unique contributions to food and wine; its board of directors features some of the key players who helped shape the nation's appetites: Robert Mondavi, Julia Child, and Alice Waters. At the center, visitors can dine in Julia's Kitchen, learn how to taste wine, or examine a demonstration vineyard—because, after all, that's where the valley's fame and fortune began.

—Cathleen Miller

LODGINGS

Cottage Grove Inn / ★★

1711 LINCOLN AVE, CALISTOGA; 707/942-8400 OR 800/799-2284

If B&B quarters are a little too cozy for comfort, you can't beat the privacy of your very own cottage tucked in a grove of elm trees. Too bad Calistoga's busiest street is a little too close to some of the cottages at this new resort along Lincoln Avenue (though the walls have double layers of Sheetrock to cut down on noise). Still, the 16 gray clapboard structures are storybook sweet, with white wicker rockers and firewood on the porches, two-person Jacuzzi tubs, fireplaces, hardwood floors, TVs with VCRs, CD players, and quaint quilts on the beds. An expanded continental breakfast of pastries, fresh fruit, cereal, coffee, and juice (included in the rate) is served in the guest lounge, and wine and cheese are offered in the evening. *$$$$; AE, DC, DIS, MC, V; checks OK; www.cottage grove.com; at Wappo Ave.*

237

Indian Springs Resort / ★

1712 LINCOLN AVE, CALISTOGA; 707/942-4913

This historic inn was built in 1860 by Sam Brannan, the founder of Calistoga, on a site where Native Americans used to erect sweat lodges to harness the region's thermal waters. A procession of 60 palm trees leads to the accommodations—17 rustic and casually furnished wooden cottages with partial kitchens, which appeal to families eager to cavort in the resort's huge hot-springs-fed swimming pool. Indian Springs also offers a playground and the full gamut of spa services (massages, facials, mud baths, and more). The spa is open to the public, but the wonderful pool is now restricted to spa and hotel guests only. *$$$; DIS, MC, V; checks OK; between Wappo Ave and Brannan St.*

Quail Mountain Bed and Breakfast / ★★

4455 ST. HELENA HWY, CALISTOGA; 707/942-0316

Quail Mountain is a good choice for people who want to escape the bustle of the valley floor but still want to be near the action. Decorated with contemporary furnishings, artwork, and a smattering of antiques, the inn's three rooms open onto the outside balcony through sliding glass doors. During the day, you can read in the glass-enclosed solarium, swim in the small lap pool out back, warm up in the hot tub, nap in the hammock tucked in the trees on the hill above the house, or stroll through the fruit orchard and nibble on the amazing bounty. Innkeepers Don and Alma Swiers encourage guests to pick their own apricots, apples, peaches, cherries, figs, oranges, kumquats, and more. Some of the harvest always turns up at the table for breakfast, perhaps fresh with yogurt or in a brandy-wine sauce over French toast. The bad news is that this idyllic place is almost always booked; you'd be wise to make reservations several months in advance. *$$$; MC, V; checks OK; from Hwy 29, turn left just after Dunaweal Ln and follow the signs.*

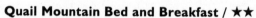

Clear Lake Area

California's largest freshwater lake, Clear Lake once had more than 30 wineries ringing its shore. Prohibition put an end to all that in 1919. The land was converted to walnut and Bartlett pear orchards, and only in the past few decades have the grapes (and the wineries) been making a comeback. This area may one day become as celebrated as Napa and Sonoma, but unlike these trendy stepsisters to the south, there ain't nothin' nouveau about Clear Lake. Country music wafts from pickup trucks, bored (and bared) youths wander the roads aimlessly (perhaps in search of their shirts), and there's generally not a whole lot going on until the weekend boaters and anglers arrive.

Middletown

If you're traveling north from the Napa Valley to Clear Lake, stop at the well-regarded **GUENOC WINERY** (21000 Butts Canyon Rd, 6 miles E of Middletown; 707/987-2385; www.guenoc.com), a 23,000-acre estate once owned by British actress **LILLIE LANGTRY** in the 1880s. In Langtry's memory, the current owners grace their wine labels with her portrait. Take a tour of the winery and taste the buttery chardonnays and the trendy blend of reds called Meritage. For the lowdown on what to expect up ahead in the Clear Lake region, visit the small branch office of the **LAKE COUNTY INFORMATION AND VISITOR CENTER** (21159 Calistoga St/Hwy 29, Middletown; 707/987-0359), open Monday through Friday, 10am to 2pm.

Clear Lake

Clear Lake's big annual blowout is the **FOURTH OF JULY FESTIVAL** (contact the Lake County Visitor Information Center, 707/263-9544), when thousands of born-again patriots amass (and timorous locals split) for a three-day sunburnt orgy of flag-waving, fireworks, and waterskiing. If you want to dive into the aquatic activities, boats of all shapes and sizes, as well as Jet Skis and Wave-Runners, can be rented at **MIKE'S WATERSPORTS** (6035 Old Hwy 53, Clearlake; 707/994-6267) or from **ON THE WATERFRONT** (60 3rd St, Lakeport; 707/263-6789).

Clear Lake also draws crowds eager to snag some of its largemouth bass, catfish, perch, and crappie. Although the lake has earned the title of **BASS CAPITAL OF THE WEST**, there aren't any shops renting fishing equipment, so you'll have to tote your own. For a stunning view of the lake and the surrounding mountain peaks, hop aboard a **GLIDER PLANE** or, if you're a true daredevil (or truly nuts), **SKYDIVE** into the scenery; air tours and skydiving trips are available through **CRAZY CREEK SOARING** (18896 Grange Rd, 3 miles N of Middletown; 707/987-9112). For more information on Clear Lake and its surrounding towns and wineries, call or drop by the **LAKE COUNTY VISITOR INFORMATION CENTER** (875 Lakeport Blvd, Vista Point, Lakeport; 707/263-9544 or 800/LAKESIDE).

Lakeport

With its small, old-fashioned downtown, Lakeport is the prettiest town on Clear Lake. Formerly known as Forbestown (after early settler William Forbes), the area is usually very peaceful until people from outlying cities pack up their Jeeps and station wagons and caravan out here in the summer for fishing, camping, swimming, and wine tasting. **CLEAR LAKE STATE PARK** (off Soda Bay Rd, S of Lakeport; 707/279-4293) is one of the area's main draws, with its campgrounds, miles of hiking trails, and beaches. Folks also flock to Lakeport every Labor Day weekend for the **LAKE**

COUNTY FAIR, featuring 4-H exhibits, livestock auctions, horse shows, and a carnival; it's held at the fairgrounds (401 Martin St; 707/263-6181).

RESTAURANTS

Park Place / ★★

50 3RD ST, LAKEPORT; 707/263-0444
Ever since the Loon's Nest restaurant in nearby Kelseyville closed, there hasn't been much debate over Lake County's best restaurant. It's Park Place—a small lakeside cafe serving very good Italian food. Owners Barbara Morris and Nancy Zabel make fettuccine every day and serve it with simple, fresh sauces such as creamy alfredo, zingy marinara, pesto, or *quattro formaggi*. Also highly recommended are Nancy's made-from-scratch soups (particularly the chunky Italian vegetable) and the gourmet pizzas. Save room for the superb cheesecake. *$$; MC, V; checks OK; lunch, dinner every day; beer and wine; reservations recommended; off Main St, near the lake.*

Nice

LODGINGS

Featherbed Railroad Company / ★

2870 LAKESHORE BLVD, NICE; 707/274-8378 OR 800/966-6322
Nine cabooses that look as though they would be right at home in Disneyland are spread out underneath a grove of oak trees at this gimmicky but fun bed-and-breakfast. The freight-train cars are burdened with cutesy names, but they're equipped with quilt-covered featherbeds, private baths (some with Jacuzzi tubs), and other amenities that make up for the silliness. Favorite train cars include two new cabooses, the Orient Express (with a private deck) and the Casablanca (complete with a piano and bar), but it's the black-and-maroon La Loose Caboose, tackiest of them all, with a bordello decor and a mirror over the bed, that's always booked. The Rosebud Caboose has two small bunk beds for the kids, and there's only a $10 extra charge per child. Breakfast is served at the Main Station, a century-old ranch house, in front of a cozy fire or on the porch overlooking the lake. A small pool and spa adjoin the house. Boat and Jet Ski rentals available. *$$; AE, MC, V; checks OK; www.feather bedrailroad.com; off Hwy 20, at the SW end of town.*

The Sonoma Valley

Many would argue that when it comes to comparing Sonoma Valley's Wine Country with Napa's, less is definitely more: Sonoma is less congested, less developed, less commercial, and less glitzy than its rival. Smitten with the bucolic charm of the region, oenophiles delight in wandering the area's backroads, leisurely hopping from winery to winery and exploring the quaint towns along the way. There are moments when—sitting in the sunshine at some of the beautifully landscaped wineries, inhaling the hot camphor smell of the eucalyptus trees, listening to a gurgling brook and the serenade of songbirds as you sip a glass of chilled sauvignon blanc—you think that even Eden would be a disappointment after Sonoma.

Before setting out for this verdant vineyard-laced region, stop at the **SONOMA VALLEY VISITORS BUREAU** (453 1st St E; 707/996-1090; www.sonomavalley.com) for lots of free, helpful information about the area's wineries, farmers markets, historical sites, walking tours, recreational facilities, and seasonal events.

Sonoma Wineries

California's world-renowned wine industry was born in the Sonoma Valley. Franciscan fathers planted the state's first vineyards at the Mission San Francisco Solano de Sonoma in 1823 and harvested the grapes to make their sacramental wines. Thirty-four years later, California's first major vineyard was planted with European grape varietals by Hungarian Count Agoston Haraszthy at Sonoma's revered Buena Vista Winery. Little did the count know that one day he would become widely hailed as the father of California wine—wine that is consistently rated as some of the best in the world. Today more than 100 wineries dot the Sonoma Valley, most offering pretty picnic areas and free tours of their winemaking facilities. Here's a roundup of some of Sonoma's best:

BARTHOLOMEW PARK WINERY (1000 Vineyard Ln, Sonoma; 707/935-9511). The winery sits in the midst of 400-acre Bartholomew Memorial Park, making it one of the most beautiful settings in the valley and an exceptional picnic spot, complete with hiking trails. A museum provides photos by Victorian photographer Eadweard Muybridge documenting viticulture practices from the 19th century.

BENZIGER FAMILY WINERY (1883 London Ranch Rd, Glen Ellen; 707/935-3000 or 800/989-8890). Tram ride tours take visitors through the vineyards here, and tastings are held in the wine shop. Home to good chardonnay and cabernet sauvignon, Benziger also operates the nearby Sonoma Mountain Brewery.

BUENA VISTA WINERY (18000 Old Winery Rd, Sonoma; 707/938-1266). California's oldest premium winery (founded in 1857) is a large estate set in a forest with picnic grounds. Tours of the stone winery and the hillside tunnels are available, and a gallery features locals' artwork.

CHÂTEAU ST. JEAN (8555 Sonoma Hwy/Hwy 12, Kenwood; 707/833-4134). Beringer purchased Château St. Jean in 1996; since that time the mansion and 250-acre estate have undergone a dramatic renovation. So did the tasting room, which is now reminiscent of a Napa corporate winery, as opposed to its previous intimate atmosphere.

FERRARI-CARANO VINEYARDS AND WINERY (8761 Dry Creek Rd, Healdsburg; 707/433-6700). This cutting-edge facility features five acres of spectacular gardens. Ferrari-Carano made its reputation with its chardonnay but also offers top-notch fumé blanc and cabernet sauvignon.

GEYSER PEAK WINERY (22281 Chianti Rd, Geyserville; 707/857-9463). In a stone facility covered with ivy, Geyser Peak produces pleasant gewürztraminer and riesling. There are beautiful hiking trails and a great picnic area, available by reservation.

GLORIA FERRER CHAMPAGNE CAVES (23555 Hwy 121, Sonoma; 707/996-7256). This champagne house's subterranean cellars make for an excellent tour. Spanish cooking classes are occasionally offered.

GUNDLACH BUNDSCHU WINERY (2000 Denmark St, Sonoma; 707/938-5277). Located in a grand, historic building set on impressive grounds, Gundlach Bundschu is known primarily for its zinfandel but also makes several interesting German-style whites. Picnic facilities are available.

KENWOOD VINEYARDS (9592 Sonoma Hwy/Hwy 12, Kenwood; 707/833-5891). Kenwood is renowned for its quaint wooden barns and red wines. The best of its zinfandel and cabernet grapes come from Jack London's old vineyard on Sonoma Mountain.

KORBEL CHAMPAGNE CELLARS (13250 River Rd, Guerneville; 707/887-2294). In an ivy-covered brick building set in a redwood forest with a view of the Russian River, Korbel hosts informative tours. The extensive and beautiful flower gardens are open for tours from May through September.

KUNDE ESTATE WINERY (10155 Sonoma Hwy/Hwy 12, Kenwood; 707/833-5501). The Kunde family has been growing grapes for more than five generations, and today they're one of Sonoma County's largest suppliers. Their century-old winery sits in the middle of this lovely 2,000-acre setting.

LEDSON WINERY & VINEYARDS (7335 Sonoma Hwy, Santa Rosa; 707/833-2330). Ledson is a new addition to the Sonoma wine scene, located in a modern-day castle complete with formal gardens and fountains. The winery offers a large array of wines for tasting and a well-stocked deli.

MATANZAS CREEK WINERY (6097 Bennett Valley Rd, Santa Rosa; 707/528-6464). A beautiful drive leads to this winery's attractive facilities. Matanzas offers outstanding chardonnay and merlot as well as guided tours and picnic tables.

QUIVIRA VINEYARDS (4900 W Dry Creek Rd, Healdsburg; 707/431-8333). Quivira is housed in a postmodern barn in a quiet vineyard setting. The winery is known for its zinfandel, but the superbly spicy Sauvignon Blanc Fig Tree Vineyard is worth trying as well.

RAVENSWOOD WINERY (18701 Gehricke Rd, Sonoma; 888/669-4679). Home of some of the tastiest zinfandels made, Ravenswood's vintages run the full range of styles from jammy to peppery. The winery offers the perfect accompaniment—barbecue—on weekends, Memorial Day through Labor Day.

SEBASTIANI VINEYARDS (389 4th St E, Sonoma; 707/938-5532 or 800/888-5532). Sonoma's largest premium-variety winery, Sebastiani Vineyards provides tours of its fermentation room and aging cellar, which includes an interesting collection of carved-oak cask heads. There's also a tasting room and picnic tables.

VIANSA WINERY AND ITALIAN MARKETPLACE (25200 Hwy 121, Sonoma; 707/935-4700). Modeled after a Tuscan village, these buildings and grounds are owned by the Sebastiani family. They produce several fine Italian-style wines, like dolcetto and nebbiolo. Grilled meats, gourmet Italian picnic fare, and local delicacies are available for enjoying on the beautiful hillside picnic grounds.

Sonoma

Sonoma, one of the most historic towns in Northern California, is a good place to experience the region's Mexican heritage. Designed by General Mariano Vallejo in 1835, Sonoma is set up like a Mexican town, with an 8-acre park-like plaza in the center—complete with a meandering flock of chickens and crowing roosters. Several authentic adobe buildings hug the perimeter, most of which now house an assortment of boutiques, restaurants and also the vintage **SEBASTIANI THEATER** (476 1st St E; 707/996-2020). **MISSION SAN FRANCISCO SOLANO DE SONOMA** (on the corner of 1st St E and E Spain St; 707/938-1519), a.k.a. the Sonoma Mission, is the northernmost and last of the 21 missions built by the Spanish fathers.

A stroll around the plaza area offers interesting shopping, including two excellent bookstores, **READER'S BOOKS** (127 and 130 Napa St E; 707/939-1779) and **PLAZA BOOK SHOP** (40 W Spain; 707/996-8474) for used and rare volumes. Or find everything for a wine-country feast: cheeses and deli fare galore from the **SONOMA CHEESE FACTORY** (2 W Spain St; 707/996-1931) or pâtés, hams, bratwurst, and sausages from the **SONOMA SAUSAGE COMPANY** (414 1st St E; 707/938-1215). If you didn't have time to hit all the wineries you wanted, or if you're ready for a beer instead, stop by the **WINE EXCHANGE** (452 1st St E; 800/938-1794). Wine and beer tastings are available in the rear, and you can choose from an enormous selection of each to complete your picnic. **CUCINA VIANSA** (400 1st St E; 707/935-5656), which has the same take-out gourmet fare as Viansa Winery, also features wine tasting, an espresso bar, a lively cafe, and music on weekend nights. Listen to acoustic music at **MURPHY'S IRISH PUB** (435 1st St E; 707/935-0660), hidden in the courtyard behind the Sebastiani Theater.

RESTAURANTS

Cafe La Haye / ★★

140 NAPA ST E, SONOMA; 707/935-5994

Located just off the main plaza, this light-filled cafe blends two sensual pleasures: art and food. Paintings in the bold California Colorist style cover the walls, and larger-than-life fantasy nudes float across the bathroom walls. Not to be outdone, the food is also a unique work of art. Brunch dishes offer surprising twists, like a poached egg with ham bobbing in a sea of white cheddar grits. Or try the ubiquitous eggs Benedict, updated here with roasted red peppers and shiitake mushrooms, served on an herb biscuit. Dinner offers a short menu of rustic European dishes, like seared black pepper–lavender fillet of beef with Gorgonzola potato gratin, or risotto and fish specials that change daily. The wine list is three times as long as the menu and, in keeping with the theme, offers some unusual Sonoma specialties, such as Crane Canyon Cellars's Viognier and Cline Cellars's Cotes d'Oakley. *$$; MC, V; local checks only; dinner Tues–Sat, brunch Sat–Sun; beer and wine; no reservations for brunch, reservations recommended for dinner; just E of the Plaza.*

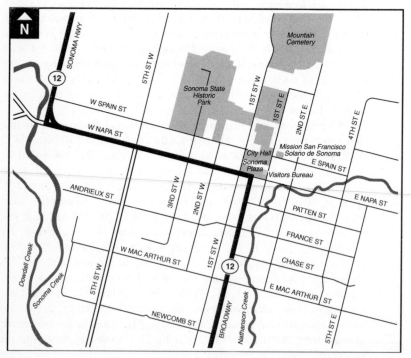

SONOMA

Della Santina's / ★★★

133 NAPA ST E, SONOMA; 707/935-0576

A fixture on the plaza for years, this popular local outpost of the Joe's restaurant dynasty in San Francisco was smart to move down the block into the digs vacated by the late Eastside Oyster Bar & Grill. In addition to the small, trattoria-style dining room, Della Santina's inherited the wonderful vine-laced brick patio tucked in back—the place to dine when the weather is warm. The menu includes a good selection of light to heavy house-made pastas (the Gnocchi della Nonna with a tomato, basil, and garlic sauce would impress any Italian grandmother) and wonderful meats from the *rosticceria* (the chicken with fresh herbs is tender and perfectly spiced). Be sure to inquire about the *pasticceria*—and if *panna cotta* (a vanilla cream custard flavored with Italian rum) is among the offerings, nab it. Paired with an espresso, it's the perfect finale to a fine meal. *$$; AE, DIS, MC, V; local checks only; lunch, dinner every day; beer and wine; reservations recommended; off 2nd St.*

Ristorante Piatti / ★★

405 1ST ST W (EL DORADO HOTEL), SONOMA (AND BRANCHES); 707/996-2351

Another pleasant link in a chain of chic nouvelle Italian restaurants with outlets in touristy towns throughout Northern California. For a full review, see the Restaurants section of Yountville. *$$; AE, MC, V; local checks only; lunch, dinner every day; full bar; reservations recommended; in El Dorado Hotel, at W Spain St, facing the plaza's W side.*

LODGINGS

El Dorado Hotel / ★★

405 1ST ST W, SONOMA; 707/996-3030 OR 800/289-3031

If you've had it with cutesy B&Bs, El Dorado Hotel is a welcome respite, offering 26 moderately priced rooms modestly decorated with terra-cotta tile floors, handcrafted furniture, and down comforters. Renovated by the team that created the exclusive Auberge du Soleil, each room has French doors leading to a small balcony overlooking the town square or the hotel's private courtyard—a pleasant, sunny spot where you can enjoy the complimentary continental breakfast. There's also a heated outdoor lap pool and concierge service to help you arrange your next Wine Country excursion. *$$$; AE, MC, V; checks OK; at W Spain St, on the plaza's W side.*

Sonoma Chalet / ★★

18935 5TH ST W, SONOMA; 707/938-3129

So close, and yet so far: every room in this secluded Swiss-style farmhouse overlooks the grassy hills of a 200-acre ranch, giving you the impression that you're way out in the country. Fact is, you're at the edge of a suburban neighborhood—three-quarters of a mile from Sonoma's town square.

There are four rooms in the two-story 1940s chalet (two of them share a bath) and three adorable private cottages, each with its own little sitting area, featherbed, fireplace or wood-burning stove, and kitchen. All of the rooms have decks or balconies with views, and each boasts an assortment of Western antiques, quilts, and collectibles that complement the rustic surroundings. In the morning, proprietor Joe Leese serves pastries, juices, yogurt, and granola in the country kitchen or, if you prefer, in the privacy of your cottage. *$$; AE, MC, V; checks OK; www.sonomachalet.com; follow 5th St W to the end, then continue W on the gravel road.*

Victorian Garden Inn / ★

316 NAPA ST E, SONOMA; 707/996-5339

This 1870s Greek revival farmhouse with a wraparound veranda has one of the most inviting small gardens you'll ever see: lush bowers of roses, azaleas, and camellias encircle wonderful little tables and chairs, while flowering fruit trees bend low over Victorian benches. The inn's four guest rooms, decorated in white wicker and florals, are pretty, if a bit cloying. The most requested room is the Woodcutter's Cottage, favored for its comfy sofa and armchairs facing the fireplace and its private entrance and bath. In the evening, owner Donna Lewis pours glasses of wine and sherry to enjoy in front of the parlor fireplace. Breakfast, served at the dining table, in the garden, or in your room, consists of granola, croissants, gourmet coffee, and fruit picked right from the garden. A big bonus is the large swimming pool in the backyard—a blessing during Sonoma's typically hot summer days—and a therapeutic spa located in the gardens. *$$$; AE, DC, MC, V; checks OK; VGardeninn@ aol.com; www.victorian-gardeninn.com; between 3rd St E and 4th St E, 2 blocks from the plaza.*

Boyes Hot Springs

LODGINGS

Sonoma Mission Inn & Spa / ★★★

18140 SONOMA HWY, BOYES HOT SPRINGS; 707/938-9000 OR 800/862-4945

With its ethereal, serene grounds and elegant pink stucco buildings, the Sonoma Mission Inn feels a bit like a convent—except that novitiates wear white terry-cloth bathrobes or colorful running suits instead of nuns' habits. And that indulgence, in body and spirit, is the order of the day. The recently renovated European-style spa offers everything from aerobics classes and Swedish massages to aromatherapy facials, seaweed wraps, and tarot card readings in perfectly groomed surroundings (the likes of Barbra Streisand, Tom Cruise, and Harrison Ford come here to get pampered). You'll also find exercise rooms, saunas, Jacuzzis, a salon, yoga and meditation classes, and a swimming pool filled with artesian mineral water. While the luxurious spa is the main draw, the inn also recently reacquired its historic golf course, which had been sold during the Depression. Thirty new suites were added in 2000; they offer every amenity, including mission-style decor, and views of the gardens and fountain. Bathed in shades of light peach and pink, each of the more than 230 rooms features plantation-style shutters, ceiling fans, and down comforters. Some units have wood-burning fireplaces and luxe granite or marble bathrooms big enough for an impromptu tango. Also pleasing are the rooms overlooking the inn's swimming pool (a favorite, room 232, is in a turret), which are in the historic building. The inn's two restaurants, the recently remodeled Restaurant at Sonoma Mission Inn & Spa and the Big 3 Diner, are both basic Californian. The restaurant is one of the most expensive in Sonoma; the less-expensive Big 3 Diner offers such California-Mediterranean fare as light pastas, pizzas, and grilled items, as well as hearty breakfasts. *$$$$; AE, DC, MC, V; checks OK; www.sonomamission.com; on Hwy 12, at Boyes Blvd.*

Glen Ellen

There are more places and things named after Jack London in Sonoma County than there are women named María in Mexico. This cult reaches its apex in Glen Ellen, where the writer built his aptly named Beauty Ranch, an 800-acre spread now known as **JACK LONDON STATE HISTORIC PARK** (2400 London Ranch Rd, off Hwy 12; 707/938-5216). London's vineyards, piggery, and other ranch buildings are here, as well as a house-turned-museum containing his art collection and mementos (including a series of rejection letters London received from several publishers, who must have fallen over backwards in their cushy chairs the day they learned London had become the highest-paid author of his time). Ten miles of trails lead through oaks, madrones, and redwoods, including a grove of oaks shading London's grave. If you'd rather ride than walk through London's land, let the friendly folks at the **SONOMA CATTLE COMPANY** (located in Jack London State Historic Park; 707/996-8566) saddle up a horse for you. Call for the lowdown on their **GUIDED HORSEBACK TRIPS** (reservations are required).

The tiny town of Glen Ellen was also the longtime home of the late celebrated food writer **M. F. K. FISHER**. It offers a couple of good restaurants, plus wine-tasting and antiquing excursions. The **WINE COUNTRY FILM FESTIVAL** (707/996-2536), a three-week summer splurge of screenings and parties throughout Napa and Sonoma, is headquartered here.

RESTAURANTS

Glen Ellen Inn / ★★

13670 ARNOLD DR, GLEN ELLEN; 707/996-6409
If you're staying in Glen Ellen, it's nice to know you don't have to go far to find a good meal. In fact, Christian and Karen Bertrand's tiny, romantic

restaurant is worth a drive from farther afield. The menu changes frequently but always features local cuisine at its freshest and in beautiful preparations. Dinner might include a jambalaya of prawns, bay shrimp, chicken, sausage, and honey-smoked ham, simmered in vegetables and fresh-from-the-garden herbs; expertly seared ahi tuna in a wasabi cream sauce with pickled ginger; or tender ricotta and pecorino cheese dumplings in a roasted bell pepper sauce with a garlic-infused tomato-basil salsa. The wine list features strictly Sonoma Valley labels. With just six white-clothed tables in the dining room and eight more outside in the herb garden, service is personal and attentive, almost as if you've been invited into the Bertrands' home. *$$; AE, MC, V; local checks only; dinner Thurs–Tues; beer and wine; reservations recommended; at O'Donnell Ln.*

LODGINGS

Beltane Ranch / ★★★

11775 SONOMA HWY, GLEN ELLEN; 707/996-6501

Surrounded by vineyards at the foot of the Mayacamas Mountains, this century-old buttercup yellow and white clapboard farmhouse was a bunkhouse long before it was a bed-and-breakfast—but certainly the cowhands of old never had it so good. Each of the inn's five rooms is uniquely decorated; all have sitting areas, private baths, separate entrances, and a family antique or two. Ask for one of the upstairs rooms that opens onto the huge wraparound doubledecker porch equipped with hammocks and a swing. Innkeeper Deborah Mahoney serves a full country breakfast in the garden or on the porch, which overlooks Sonoma's hillsides. Blissfully calm and beautiful, the whole place makes you feel as though you should be wearing a wide-brimmed hat and sipping a mint julep. Should you tire of lolling Southern-belle-style, knock a few balls around the tennis court near the house, pitch horseshoes in the garden, or hike the trails through the estate's 1,600 acres of vineyards and hills. *$$$; no credit cards; checks OK; on Hwy 12, 2.2 miles past the Glen Ellen turnoff.*

Gaige House Inn / ★★★

13540 ARNOLD DR, GLEN ELLEN; 707/935-0237 OR 800/935-0237

From the outside, the Gaige House looks like yet another spiffed-up Victorian mansion, inevitably filled with the ubiquitous dusty antiques and family heirlooms. Inside, however, the Victorian theme comes to a screeching halt. All eleven rooms are spectacular, and each is individually decorated in an Indonesian plantation style with an eclectic mix of modern art. Owners Ken Burnet Jr. and Greg Nemrow have added three new guest rooms, including one with a private Japanese garden and waterfall. An old favorite is the Gaige Suite, which features a king-size four-poster canopy bed; it's also known as the Oh Wow! Room (since that is what everyone instantaneously gasps as they enter the bathroom). The suite has an enormous blue-tiled bathroom centered by a whirlpool tub that could easily fit a party of six (and probably has), as well as a huge wraparound balcony. The three Garden Rooms, slightly smaller and less expensive, open onto a shaded deck and are within steps of a beautiful brick-lined 40-foot swimming pool surrounded by a large, perfectly manicured lawn. Included in the room rate—which is surprisingly affordable considering the caliber of the accommodations—is a two-course gourmet breakfast served at individual tables in the dining room. *$$$; AE, DIS, MC, V; checks OK; gaige@sprynet.com; www.gaige. com; from Hwy 12, take the Glen Ellen exit.*

Kenwood

LODGINGS

Kenwood Inn / ★★★

10400 SONOMA HWY, KENWOOD; 707/833-1293

This posh inn, owned by Roseann and Terry Grimm, resembles a centuries-old Italian pensione. The 12 guest rooms are beautifully decorated, each with a fluffy featherbed, a fireplace, and a sitting area. Room 3, bathed in shades of burgundy and green paisley, has a pleasant private patio, and room 6 sports a sitting room with a stereo, Jacuzzi, and balcony overlooking the vineyards and the swimming pool. The six-room, full-service spa pampers guests with such special treatments as a Mediterranean scrub of lemon rind, rosemary, and salt followed by a massage. The Grimms serve an ample breakfast with fresh fruit, polenta with poached eggs, and buttery house-made croissants. *$$$; AE, MC, V; checks OK; www.kenwoodinn.com; on Hwy 12, 3 miles past Glen Ellen.*

Santa Rosa

Santa Rosa is the closest thing Sonoma County has to a big city, but it's more like a countrified suburb. Oddly enough, it's got more than its share of offbeat museums. Botanists, gardeners, and other plant lovers will want to make a beeline for the popular gardens and greenhouse at the **LUTHER BURBANK HOME & GARDENS** (corner of Santa Rosa and Sonoma Ave; 707/524-5445). Burbank was a world-renowned horticulturist who created 800 new strains of plants, fruits, and vegetables at the turn of the century. Pop culture fans will get a kick out of **SNOOPY'S GALLERY & GIFT SHOP** (1665 W Steel Ln; 707/546-3385), a "Peanuts" cartoon museum with the world's largest collection of Snoopy memorabilia, thanks to donations by the beagle's creator, Charles Schulz, who lived in Santa Rosa. The tacky but fun **ROBERT L. RIPLEY MEMORIAL MUSEUM** (492 Sonoma Ave; 707/524-5233), housed in the historic Church Built from One Tree, is filled with wacky displays and information about the late Santa Rosa resident who created the world-famous "Ripley's Believe It or Not" cartoon strip.

For music, magicians, and a plethora of fresh-from-the-farm food, head over to the wildly successful **THURSDAY NIGHT FARMERS MARKET** on downtown Santa Rosa's Fourth Street, which is closed to traffic every Thursday night for this festive event and draws folks from far and near from Memorial Day through Labor Day (707/542-2123). Another local crowd-pleaser is the annual **SONOMA COUNTY HARVEST FAIR** (1350 Bennett Valley Rd; 707/545-4200), a wine-tasting, food-gobbling orgy held at the fairgrounds from late July to early August.

RESTAURANTS

John Ash & Co. / ★★★★

4330 BARNES RD, SANTA ROSA; 707/527-7687

This casually elegant restaurant, founded by Wine Country cuisine guru John Ash, has topped the list of Santa Rosa's best restaurants for many years. It's pricey, but the service is expert, the food is fabulous, and the serene dining room with cream-colored walls, tall French windows, and a crackling fire will entice you to settle in for a good long time. The menu, under

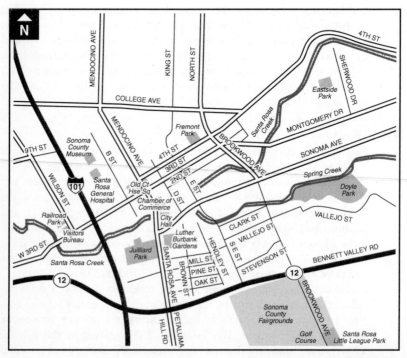

SANTA ROSA

the direction of executive chef Jeffrey Madura, is a classic California hybrid of French, Italian, Asian, and Southwestern cuisines. A meal might include such glorious dishes as rich corn chowder with firecracker rock shrimp, followed by a sautéed breast of chicken with mango-avocado salsa and orzo pasta with spinach, oranges, and macadamia nuts; a perfectly pink roast loin of lamb in a nutty walnut-thyme sauce; or an expertly poached Bodega Bay salmon with fresh ginger sauce. For dessert, pastry chef Theresa Di Falco makes diners swoon with her signature tiramisu served in a chocolate cup or her port wine crème brûlée with house-made walnut cookies and fresh Sonoma figs. The large, reasonably priced wine list, showcasing Napa and Sonoma wines, also includes a good selection of ports, sherries, and dessert wines. For a taste of Ash's superb cuisine at one-third the regular price, sit at the bar or on the patio and order from the Vineyard Cafe menu. *$$$; AE, MC, V; local checks only; lunch Tues–Sun, dinner every day, brunch Sun; full bar; reservations recommended; www.johnashco. com; next door to Vintners Inn, off River Rd, at Hwy 101.*

Lisa Hemenway's / ★★
714 VILLAGE CT, SANTA ROSA; 707/526-5111
Don't let the rather drab shopping center setting fool you—within that boxy brown shrine to the '70s is a refreshingly light, airy restaurant with alfresco dining and an inviting menu. With cooking skills honed at the venerable John Ash & Co. restaurant, combined with working vacations in Asia and Europe, chef/owner Lisa Hemenway has created an expansive and varied menu: triàngoli with a wild mushroom filling and an eggplant pesto sauce; a skewer of grilled shiitake mushrooms served on sun sprouts and buckwheat noodles with a spicy ginger dressing; vegetable tamales with smoked California chile sauce; Hungarian tortes; and chutney burgers. If all this is too daunting for you, pass on the main menu and ponder the appetizer selection at the wine bar, which proudly boasts numerous Awards of Excellence from *Wine Spectator* magazine. *$$; DC, DIS, MC, V; checks OK; lunch Mon–Sat, dinner every day, brunch Sun; full bar; reservations recommended; in the Village Court Mall/Montgomery Village at Farmers Ln and Sonoma Ave.*

Willowside Cafe / ★★★
3535 GUERNEVILLE RD, SANTA ROSA; 707/523-4814
Hiding out in a funky roadhouse a few miles from downtown Santa Rosa, Willowside may be Sonoma County's best-kept dining secret. Inside, the mood is simple yet sophisticated, with pale yellow walls, copper-topped tables, and fresh flowers—the perfect match for chef/co-owner Richard Hale's highly personal rendition of California-French cuisine. Hale rewrites the menu every week, but it always includes five starters (such as duck breast with red onion marmalade or mussels in mustard sauce) and five entrees (quail with portobello mushrooms, lamb

with fava beans and pecorino cheese). Rounding out the trio of culinary talents behind Willowside are co-owners Mike Hale, the maitre d', and his wife, Carole Hale, the pastry chef (don't miss her first-rate cobblers and tarts). A favorite with local wine makers, Willowside offers 200 labels on its wine list, including hard-to-find California, French, and Australian bottles. *$$; MC, V; local checks only; dinner Wed–Sun; beer and wine; reservations recommended; at Willowside Rd.*

LODGINGS

Vintners Inn / ★★

4350 BARNES RD, SANTA ROSA; 707/575-7350 OR 800/421-2584

The Vintners Inn combines the charm of a country inn with the conveniences of a modern hotel. Its four provençal-style buildings are clustered around a central courtyard set amid vineyards. The inn's 44 newly refurbished rooms have pine beds, plush carpets, antique armoires and desks, and separate sitting areas; many have wood-burning fireplaces, too. French doors open onto a balcony or patio with a view of the vineyards or the landscaped grounds (ask for a room with a vineyard view facing away from Highway 101). The young, courteous staff is very attentive, providing first-class room service. A complimentary breakfast is served in the main building's sunny dining room until 10am on weekdays and 11am on weekends. Though there's also a fine deck for sunning and a Jacuzzi, the inn's best feature is its adjoining four-star restaurant, John Ash & Co. (see review, above). *$$$; AE, DC, MC, V; checks OK; www. vintnersinn.com; off River Rd, at Hwy 101.*

Healdsburg

This is one tourist town whose charm seems completely unforced. Boutiques and bakeries surround a pretty, tree-lined plaza where you can sit and read the newspaper while munching on pastries from the marvelous **DOWNTOWN BAKERY & CREAMERY** (308-A Center St; 707/431-2719). In the summer, nothing beats paddling down the glorious **RUSSIAN RIVER** past vineyards and secret swimming holes in a canoe rented from W. C. "Bob" Trowbridge Canoe Trips (20 Healdsburg Ave; 707/433-7247 or 800/640-1386). If you're in need of a respite from your activity-packed day trips, catch a flick at the **RAVEN THEATER** (115 North St, 707/433-5448), the Wine Country's best movie house for new releases and art films.

RESTAURANTS

Bistro Ralph / ★★★

109 PLAZA ST E , HEALDSBURG; 707/433-1380

In a town where restaurants have been afflicted with the revolving door syndrome, simple yet stylish Bistro Ralph continues to thrive. Housed in a slender storefront on the square, Ralph Tingle's intimate bistro serves consistently excellent food, with a focus on local ingredients. Choice starters include grilled portobello mushrooms with white truffle oil and crispy Sichuan pepper calamari. The lamb dishes are always good, particularly the hearty spring lamb stew à la provençal, and the lamb shanks with crème fraîche–horseradish mashed potatoes. The lunch menu sticks to upscale salads and sandwiches, such as the grilled ahi or salmon sandwich and the popular lamb burger on a fresh roll, all three served with a pile of irresistible shoestring fries. The decor has a cozy, slightly industrial feel, with a dozen or so linen-topped tables, white brick walls, and a long concrete counter where you can watch chef Tingle perform culinary magic in the small open kitchen. *$$; MC, V; local checks only; lunch Mon–Sat, dinner every day; beer and wine; reservations recommended; on the plaza.*

Zin / ★★

344 CENTER ST, HEALDSBURG; 707/473-0946

Located just off Healdsburg's main plaza, Zin opened in 1999 and has been a welcome addition to the local food scene. The menu specializes in updated versions of American classics, and each day features a blue plate special, such as meat loaf or St. Louis–style barbecued ribs. The dishes are particularly well-suited to pairing with zinfandels, and the wine list features a whole page of them—a fitting tribute, considering Sonoma is prime zin country. The hush puppies with red pepper make a great starter—a mountain of them served hot and fluffy and grease-free. Entrees include a succulent sliced duck breast served on a bed of garlic mashed potatoes topped by sautéed spinach. Grilled lamb chops come with asparagus and a giant helping of roasted new potatoes. This is a great place for those with hearty appetites, because portions are huge. Feel free to indulge, because, frankly, desserts can be a disappointing conclusion to the meal, with flavorless sorbets and a gritty mud pie that resembles its name a little too closely. Zin's architecture is Postmodern California Bomb Shelter—a concrete bunker trimmed in redwood— which, thankfully, has little to do with the aesthetic of the food. *$$$; AE, MC, V; local checks only; lunch Mon–Fri, dinner Wed–Mon; beer and wine; reservations recommended; 1 block from the plaza.*

LODGINGS

Belle de Jour Inn / ★★★

16276 HEALDSBURG AVE, HEALDSBURG; 707/431-9777

In a region where rampant Victoriana is all the rage, Belle de Jour's four romantic hillside cottages and large carriage house have a refreshingly spare, uncluttered feel. From the bedroom of the cottage called the Terrace Room, you can savor a fine view of the valley from the comfort of a giant Jacuzzi. Also recommended is the Caretaker's Suite with its lace-canopied four-poster bed, private deck with a vine-covered trellis, and blue-tiled whirlpool tub. All of the accommodations have a fireplace or a wood-burning stove, ceiling fans, and refrigerators and are air-conditioned—a big plus around here in the summer. Innkeepers Tom and Brenda Hearn whip up a bountiful country breakfast in their beautiful state-of-the-art kitchen and serve it on the deck of the main house. Also available to guests for an hourly fee is a chauffeured backroads winery tour in the Hearns' 1925 Star touring car—something to consider if wine tasting makes you tipsy. *$$$; MC, V; checks OK; 1 mile N of Dry Creek Rd, across from Simi Winery.*

Haydon Street Inn / ★★

321 HAYDON ST, HEALDSBURG; 707/433-5228

This pretty blue 1912 Queen Anne Victorian inn with a large veranda set behind a white picket fence offers eight cheery guest rooms, a few with private baths. But your best bet is to rent one of the two larger rooms in the Victorian Cottage tucked behind the main house. Owner Joann Claus lives on the first floor of the cottage; the upstairs has been turned into two spacious rooms with vaulted ceilings, queen-size beds, high dormer windows, big whirlpool tubs, and loads of charm. In the morning you'll find a full country breakfast featuring such treats as green chile frittatas with basil and cilantro, fresh fruit or baked apples, and plenty of house-made muffins and croissants. *$$; MC, V; checks OK; www.haydon.com; at Fitch St.*

Healdsburg Inn on the Plaza / ★★★

110 MATHESON ST, HEALDSBURG; 707/433-6991 OR 800/431-8663

Originally built as a Wells Fargo Express office in 1900, this surprisingly quiet inn on the plaza has high ceilings and a lovely old staircase leading from the ground-floor art gallery to the 10 attractive guest rooms upstairs. The four rooms facing the plaza have beautiful bay windows; particularly engaging is the spacious pale yellow and white Song of the Rose Room, which has a queen-size white iron and brass bed, as well as a comfy oak rocker set in front of the fireplace. The largest room is the Garden Suite, with its Jacuzzi, king-size bed, and private patio bedecked with flowers. All rooms have private baths with showers, TVs with VCRs, and air conditioning, and all but three have gas-log fireplaces and claw-footed bathtubs. A full breakfast and afternoon wine and snacks are served at tables for two in the glass-enclosed solarium. *$$$; MC, V; checks OK; www.healdsburginn.com; on the plaza's S side.*

Geyserville

LODGINGS

Hope-Bosworth House / ★★

21238 GEYSERVILLE AVE, GEYSERVILLE; 707/857-3356 OR 800/825-4233

Across the street from its showier cousin, the Hope-Merrill House, the 1904 Hope-Bosworth House provides a cheery, informal, and less expensive place to stay. This Queen Anne–style Victorian inn has four bedrooms, three of which have full baths, including one with a Jacuzzi tub. The downstairs Sun Porch Room has the dry, woody fragrance of a summer cottage, and it reverberates each morning with birdsong from the backyard. Everyone's favorite, however, is the sunny and spacious Wicker Room with its old-fashioned white and pink flowered wallpaper. Guests are treated to the same elaborate breakfast as their neighbors, and they have access to the pool and other facilities at the Hope-Merrill House. *$$; AE, MC, V; checks OK; from Hwy 101, take the Geyserville exit.*

Hope-Merrill House / ★★★

21253 GEYSERVILLE AVE, GEYSERVILLE; 707/857-3356 OR 800/825-4233
Since nearly every mediocre shack built in the late 19th century gets dubbed "Victorian," it's easy to forget the dizzying architectural and design heights reached during that period. This beautifully restored 1870 Eastlake Gothic will remind you: the three-story brown and cream Hope-Merrill House has expansive bay windows and a back veranda furnished with comfortable cane chairs. The landscaping is formal and strictly symmetrical, with box hedges and weeping mulberries. The inn offers eight individually decorated guest rooms with private baths and queen-size beds. The fairest is the Peacock Room: images of gold, rose, and gray-blue peacocks strut around a ceiling border, a wood-burning fireplace dominates one wall, and French doors open into a bathroom with an immense marble-topped whirlpool tub. For the best views, ask for the Vineyard View Room or the Bradbury Room, which have fireplaces, two-person showers, and views of the swimming pool and the pretty gardens. A hearty breakfast is included in the rates. *$$; AE, MC, V; checks OK; from Hwy 101, take the Geyserville exit.*

Cloverdale

LODGINGS

Vintage Towers Bed and Breakfast Inn / ★★

302 N MAIN ST, CLOVERDALE; 707/894-4535
Listed on the National Register of Historic Places, this beautiful mauve mansion located on a quiet residential street has seven air-conditioned guest rooms. The three corner suites have tower sitting rooms (one round, one square, and one octagonal), separate sleeping quarters, and private baths. Particularly unique is the Vintage Tower Suite, which has its own private porch complete with a telescope for stargazing and a spiral staircase that descends to the yard. Scarlet's Room and the Sunroom share a bath. Downstairs you'll find a large dining room with a fireplace, a parlor, and a library. In the morning, friendly innkeepers Cindy and Gus Wolter serve a full gourmet breakfast in the dining room; the

veranda is the spot for lemonade and homemade cookies in the afternoon. *$$; AE, DIS, MC, V; checks OK; www.vintagetowers.com; at 3rd St, off Cloverdale Blvd.*

Anderson Valley and Mendocino County Wine Region

For a glimpse of what the Napa Valley looked like 30 years ago, visit the quiet, bucolic Anderson Valley. Once noted only for sheep, apples, and timber, the Anderson Valley has become the premier producer of cool-climate California wines such as chardonnay, gewürztraminer, and riesling. The enological future of this valley, whose climate is almost identical to that of the Champagne region of France, may also reside in the production of sparkling wine, now that some of France's best champagne makers have successfully set up shop here.

Anderson Wineries

Most of the Anderson Valley's wineries line the narrow stretch of Highway 128 that winds through this gorgeous, verdant 25-mile-long valley before it reaches the Pacific Coast. Here are some of Anderson's premier wineries:

GREENWOOD RIDGE (5501 Hwy 128, Philo; 707/895-2002). Known for its white riesling (and cabernet and zinfandel produced in another region), Greenwood is the site of the annual California Wine Tasting Championships (for novices and pros) held on the last weekend of July; it also has a picnic area by a pond and a tasting room.

HANDLEY CELLARS (3151 Hwy 128, Philo; 707/895-3876; www.avwines.com). Popular for its chardonnay, Handley has a tasting room full of exotic artifacts from around the world, and a picnic area in a garden courtyard.

HUSCH VINEYARDS (4400 Hwy 128, Philo; 707/895-3216). The oldest winery in the Anderson Valley (founded in 1971), Husch produces chardonnay, pinot noir, and gewürztraminer, along with wines from its Ukiah vineyards. It offers a small, rustic redwood tasting room and picnic tables.

NAVARRO VINEYARDS (5601 Hwy 128, Philo; 707/895-3686). This small, family-owned winery pioneered the region's trademark wine (dry, fruity, spicy Alsatian-style gewürztraminer) and produces excellent chardonnay, pinot noir, and white riesling. Navarro wines are sold only by mail order and at the winery, which offers a surprisingly large tasting menu.

ROEDERER ESTATE (4501 Hwy 128, Philo; 707/895-2288). This winery was established by one of France's most prestigious champagne producers. Inside the quietly elegant hillside facility, visitors can take tours to learn about the sparkling wine–making process. The tasting room has an antique French bar topped with zinc where you can sip high-quality sparkling wines.

PACIFIC ECHO CELLARS (8501 Hwy 128, Philo; 707/895-2957). In 1991 Scharffenberger Cellars was sold to Moët Hennessey, which has since begun bottling its traditional French sparkling wine under the generic-sounding label "Pacific Echo Cellars." The company still produces excellent brut, blanc de blancs, brut rosé, and crémant. The tasting room is in a remodeled farmhouse. Tours are available.

Boonville

This speck of a town in the heart of the Anderson Valley is best known for a regional dialect called Boontling, developed by townsfolk at the beginning of the century. No one really speaks Boontling anymore, though a few old-timers remember the lingo. As in most private languages, a large percentage of the words refer to sex, a fact glossed over in most touristy brochures on the topic. Most people don't know what the Boontling word for beer is, but the folks at the **ANDERSON VALLEY BREWING COMPANY & BUCKHORN SALOON** (14081 Hwy 128; 707/895-BEER), a fine little microbrewery across from the Boonville Hotel, probably do. While you're in town, grab a copy of the *Anderson Valley Advertiser,* a rollicking, crusading (some say muckraking), small-town paper with avid readers from as far away as San Francisco and the Oregon border. **BOONT BERRY FARM** (13981 Hwy 128; 707/895-3576), an organic-produce market and deli in a small, weathered-wood building, turns out terrific treats.

LODGINGS

The Boonville Hotel and Restaurant / ★★★

HWY 128, BOONVILLE; 707/895-2210

After a roller-coaster history of highs and lows, the Boonville Hotel languished for a few years until current owner John Schmitt brought it back to life as a small restaurant and inn. The decor of the Old West–style hotel is pleasantly austere, but feels more like New Mexico than Northern California. Half of the rooms have private balconies, although two of them overlook the busy highway. Two newer suites offer spacious separate sitting areas, making them well-suited to those with kids in tow. (The staff hasn't seemed to figure out that the bare hardwood floors of the old hotel are not suited to the clomping of small children, a fact that can make sleeping near-impossible for the other guests.) The smaller rooms at the back of the hotel are quieter and less expensive, but here the inn's minimalist decor heads toward bleak. Medium-size room 3, with its unique iron bed, is a good compromise of price, spaciousness, and peacefulness. Guests are treated to a continental breakfast in the sunny dining room. A deck overlooks the beautiful 2-acre vegetable and herb garden behind the hotel.

The restaurant, a gathering spot for local wine makers, is still one of the best north of the Napa Valley. Chef Schmitt (who for years cooked with his mother when she owned the French Laundry restaurant in Yountville) offers a fresh mix of California, Southwestern, and backwoods regional cuisine, such as sliced pork tenderloin with cumin, cilantro, and oranges, and chicken breast with roasted tomato–mint salsa. From May through October, the hotel parking lot becomes the site of the festive Boonville Farmers Market, held every Saturday from 9am to noon; here you can purchase wonderful produce, handmade soaps, wool, and even the occasional billy goat. Reservations are recommended for the restaurant, especially in summer. *$$$; MC, V; checks OK; usually closed Jan; at Lambert Ln, in the center of town.*

The Toll House Inn / ★★
15301 HWY 253, BOONVILLE; 707/895-3630
Located high in the oak-covered hills on the twisting road between Boonville and Ukiah, this wonderful 1912 Victorian farmhouse set on a 360-acre ranch feels far away from everything. The five individually decorated guest rooms have a modern flair, softened by a few attractive antiques (you won't find any Victorian clutter here). Unfortunately, as with every other roadside inn in the Anderson Valley, the rooms toward the front of the house are plagued by truck noise at night. Proprietors Betty Ingram and Barbara McGuinness serve a full breakfast made from the fruit and vegetables grown in their organic garden. Guests are welcome to roam the property, which is also home to two llamas and six sheep. *$$$; DIS, MC, V; checks OK; 5 miles N of town.*

Philo
There's not much to see in this hamlet, but about two miles west you'll find **GOWAN'S OAK TREE** (6350 Hwy 128; 707/895-3353), a great family-run roadside fruit-and-vegetable stand with a few picnic tables in back and a swing for road-weary tots.

LODGINGS
Philo Pottery Inn / ★★
8550 HWY 128, PHILO; 707/895-3069
This 1888 redwood farmhouse is pure and authentic country—no frilly ruffles, no overdressed dolls, just a lavender-filled English garden in the front yard and bright handmade quilts and sturdy frontier furnishings in each of the five guest rooms. You may linger in the library downstairs or snooze in the bent-willow loungers on the rustic front porch. Evaline's and Donna's Rooms are the lightest and most spacious, but the favored unit is the cozy one-room cottage with a detached private bath, a woodburning stove, and a back porch. Owner Sue Chiverton will direct you to all the best hiking and biking trails (ask her about the great 12-mile

mountain bike route) and will happily arrange private tastings at the valley's many small private wineries. She also serves a full breakfast, featuring many homemade treats, in the dining room. For a great snack, ask for her freshly made biscotti. *$$; MC, V; checks OK; in town.*

Hopland

This small town's name originated from hops, an herb used to flavor beer. Hop vines once covered the region from the 1860s until mildew wiped out the crop in the 1940s. The only legacy left of that era today is the hops growing in the beer garden of Mendocino Brewing Company, a location that's also home to several award-winning microbrews. Today, Hopland's rich alluvial soil is dedicated to the production of wine grapes and Bartlett pears.

RESTAURANTS

Hopland Brewery Pub & Restaurant at the Mendocino Brewing Company / ★

13351 HWY 101, HOPLAND; 707/744-1015

California's first brew pub since Prohibition (and the second in the nation), the Hopland Brewery is a refreshing break from the crushed-grape circuit. This quintessential brew pub has tasty grub, foot-stomping live music on Saturday (everything from the blues to Cajun), and eight fine beers brewed on the premises. The classic beer garden has long tables shaded by trellised hops, as well as a sandbox to keep the kids amused while you chow down on the large burgers served on house-made buns or the Red Tail Chili—a heavenly mash of fresh vegetables, sirloin steak, and a generous splash of Red Tail Ale. *$; MC, V; no checks; lunch, dinner every day; beer and wine; reservations recommended; www.mendobrew.com; downtown.*

LODGINGS

Thatcher Inn / ★

13401 HWY 101, HOPLAND; 707/744-1890 OR 800/266-1891

Built as a stage stop in 1890, this haughty cream-colored combination of Gothic spires and gabled windows still looks like a luxurious frontier saloon-hotel, thanks to an $800,000 restoration in 1990. The lobby is dominated by a long, mirrored, polished wood bar; and the gorgeous, dark, wood-paneled library is filled with interesting old books, velvet settees, and shiny brass reading lamps. A wide, curving wood stairway leads from the lobby to 20 charmingly decorated guest rooms on the second and third stories—all with private baths. The quietest rooms with the best views are on the south side of the hotel overlooking the backyard patio with a fountain, wrought-iron lampposts, and a giant oak tree. A full breakfast, usually served alfresco, is included in the rate. The hotel's Thatcher Inn Restaurant serves acceptable but uninspired California cuisine. *$$$; AE, MC, V; checks OK; downtown.*

Ukiah

Located in the upper reaches of the California Wine Country, Ukiah is still what Napa, Sonoma, and Healdsburg used to be—a sleepy little agricultural town surrounded by vineyards and apple and pear orchards. Peopled by an odd mix of farmers, loggers, and back-to-the-landers, Ukiah is a down-to-earth little burg with few traces of Wine Country gentrification. That doesn't mean there isn't any wine, however. **JEPSON VINEYARDS** (10400 Hwy 101; 707/468-8936) produces chardonnay, sauvignon blanc, and sparkling wine, as well as brandy, which is distilled in a copper alembic. Mendocino County's oldest winery, founded in 1932, is **PARDUCCI WINE ESTATES** (501 Parducci Rd; 707/462-WINE), an enterprise that produces a variety of reds and whites. And if you continue up the road a bit to the Redwood Valley, you'll find **FREY VINEYARDS** (14000 Tomki Rd, off Hwy 101, Redwood Valley; 707/485-5177 or 800/760-3739), one of the few wineries in the state that doesn't add sulfites to its wines and uses certified organically grown grapes. Sample the Frey family's petite sirah, cabernet, and sauvignon blanc.

Soak away the aches and pains of your long drive (Ukiah is a long drive from almost anywhere) at the clothing-optional **ORR HOT SPRINGS** (13201 Orr Springs Rd; 707/462-6277), or in North America's only warm and naturally carbonated mineral baths at **VICHY SPRINGS RESORT** (see review, below). Hikers will want to stretch their legs at **MONTGOMERY WOODS STATE RESERVE** (on Orr Springs Rd, off Hwy 101, 15 miles NW of Ukiah); it features 1,142 acres of coastal redwoods with a self-guided nature trail along Montgomery Creek. In town, the main attraction is the **GRACE HUDSON MUSEUM AND SUN HOUSE** (431 S Main St; 707/467-2836), housing Hudson's paintings of Pomo Indians and a collection of beautiful Pomo baskets.

RESTAURANTS

Schat's Courthouse Bakery and Cafe / ★

113 W PERKINS ST, UKIAH; 707/462-1670

Schat's Courthouse Bakery has been open in Ukiah since 1990, but its history dates back to Holland in the early 1800s—which is as far back as the fifth-generation baker brothers Zach and Brian Schat can trace the roots of a very long line of Schat bakers. In 1948, the Schat clan emigrated to California, bringing with them the hallowed family recipe for their signature Sheepherder's Bread, a semisour, dairy- and sugar-free round loaf that's so popular it's been featured in *Sunset* magazine's "Best of the West" column. What really separates Schat's Courthouse Bakery from the rest are the huge, more-than-you-can-possibly-eat lunch items: made-to-order sandwiches, build-your-own baked potatoes, house-made soups, tangy Caesar salad, and huge slices of vegetarian quiche (served with bread and a salad), all for around five bucks. Located just off Highway 101, this is a great spot to load up on munchies while exploring the local wine country. Schat's stays open for lunch until 6pm during the week and 4:30pm on Saturday. *$; no credit cards; local checks only; light breakfast, lunch Mon–Sat; from Hwy 101 take the Perkins St exit W; ½ block W of State St, across from the courthouse.*

LODGINGS

Sanford House Bed and Breakfast / ★★

306 PINE ST S, UKIAH; 707/462-1653
There's something indisputably small-town about this tall, yellow Victorian inn on a tree-lined street just west of Ukiah's Mayberry-like downtown. Peaceful, unhurried, and bucolic, Sanford House boasts only one Gothic turret, but it does have a big front porch dotted with white wicker chairs and an old-fashioned baby buggy, plus an English garden complete with a koi pond. Inside, antiques grace every room and everything is freshly painted, but it's far too comfortable and unpretentious to be called a showplace. The five guest rooms are named after turn-of-the-century presidents; the Taft Room, with its dark four-poster bed, floral fabrics, and a sort of spooky Princess Di doll in a wedding dress, is the most elegant, but equally pleasant is the spacious cream-and-green Wilson Room with its floral wallpaper, beautiful armoire, and sunny turret sitting area. Innkeeper Dorsey Manogue serves a breakfast feast every morning in the dining room using fresh, mostly organic ingredients, and in the evening she offers homemade biscotti (dipped in white and dark chocolate) and wine in the parlor. *$$; MC, V; checks OK; from Hwy 101, take the Perkins St exit, head W, and turn left on Pine.*

Vichy Springs Resort / ★

2605 VICHY SPRINGS RD, UKIAH; 707/462-9515
Although the rejuvenating effect of the naturally carbonated mineral pools at Vichy Springs had been known by the Pomo Indians for hundreds of years, it wasn't until the mid-1800s that others caught on to the idea. Since then, this California Historic Landmark has attracted the likes of Ulysses S. Grant, Teddy Roosevelt, Mark Twain, and Jack London, who all soaked their famous bones in North America's only naturally carbonated mineral baths—baths that have a mineral content identical to the famed pools in Vichy, France. With such a remarkable distinction and luminous history, one would expect the resort to be ringed by four-star accommodations and fancy bathhouses. Ironically, the estate was practically a disaster area for years, littered with rusting cars and machinery, until proprietors Gilbert and Marjorie Ashoff completely refurbished the 700-acre property and reopened it in 1989. Even with its face-lift, the resort is far from posh, though five new creekside rooms, all with private

baths, and the new two-bedroom Jack London Cottage bring the accommodations up a notch. Twelve more small, simply decorated guest rooms—all with private baths and most with queen-size beds—line a long ranch house–style building. If you're visiting with children, consider staying at one of the three private cottages, each fully equipped with a kitchen, a wood-burning stove, and a shaded porch. Built more than 130 years ago, the eight indoor and outdoor baths remain basically unchanged (bathing suits required). Also on the grounds are a nonchlorinated Olympic-size pool filled with the therapeutic bubbly, a modern whirlpool bath, a playground, a barbecue, a small cabin where Swedish massages are administered, and 6 miles of ranch roads available to hikers and mountain bikers. Room rates include an expanded continental breakfast and unlimited use of the pools, which are rarely crowded. The baths are available for day use, too, and the resort has basic services for business travelers. $$$; AE, DC, DIS, MC, V; checks OK; from Hwy 101, take the Vichy Springs Rd exit and head W.

Redwood Valley

RESTAURANTS

Broiler Steak House / ★★

8400 UVA DR, REDWOOD VALLEY; 707/485-7301
The Broiler is more than a steak house—it's a temple to meat. If you arrive without a reservation, expect to wait awhile in the giant cocktail lounge—a good place to catch up on the latest Western fashions. Eventually you'll be ushered into the inner sanctum, where, if you're a true believer, you'll order a juicy steak grilled (to your exact specifications, of course) over an oak wood pit. All entrees include a mammoth baked potato with butter, sour cream, and chives, plus a garden-fresh dinner salad the size of your head. $$; AE, DIS, MC, V; checks OK; dinner every day; full bar; reservations recommended; from Ukiah, drive 7 miles N on Hwy 101, take the West Rd exit, and turn left. &

NORTH COAST

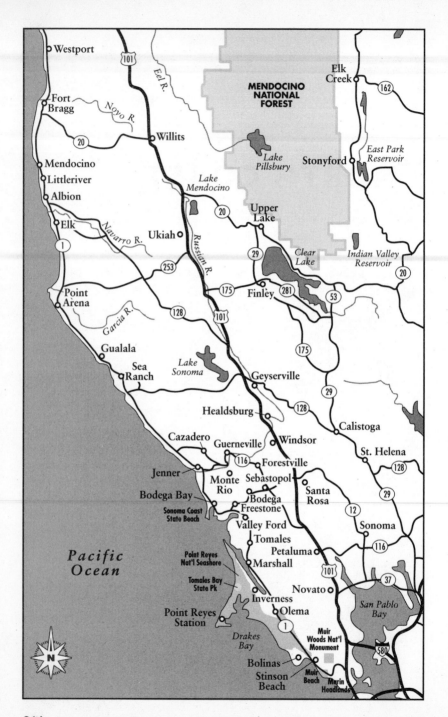

NORTH COAST

From the point at which the Golden Gate Bridge touches the sunny shores of Marin County to the ruggedly beautiful timber- and trawler-dotted land and seascapes of Fort Bragg, the North Coast offers sophisticated stops for the traveler where nature is the star performer. Informal yet elegant restaurants, charming B&Bs, and a spectacular setting make this the perfect getaway.

ACCESS AND INFORMATION

Two major highways provide access to the North Coast: **HIGHWAY 1**, the only route that runs along the coast, and **HIGHWAY 101**, the central artery that connects to Highway 1 via three main scenic roads. To enjoy the full-blown coast experience, take the Stinson Beach/Highway 1 exit from Highway 101 north and head west. Driving is always slow along the coast; on a good day it'll take you five hours to reach Mendocino. Here are three alternative Highway 1/Highway 101 combo routes to consider, depending on time constraints and the fear factor (think of the coast road as a roller-coaster ride, with you doing the driving). First: Exit from Highway 101 at Sir Francis Drake Boulevard, which will take you through West Marin to Olema, where Highway 1 and Sir Francis Drake Boulevard intersect. Second: Traveling north on Highway 101, exit at Sebastopol/Highway 12 west, which connects with the Bodega Highway. Third: Traveling north on Highway 101, exit at Petaluma/Highway 116 west. Follow Bodega Ave to Petaluma Valley Ford Road and continue on to Bodega Highway. Once you exit Highway 101—avoid commute hours like the plague—you will be rewarded with scenic drives through idyllic pastoral settings and little traffic.

Expect more fog, wind, and cold weather as you travel north along the coast. The **NATIONAL WEATHER SERVICE** (831/656-1725) provides updated weather reports. Call **CALTRANS** (800/427-7623) for **HIGHWAY CONDITIONS**. Stock up on provisions for the drive and bring layers of clothing. Oh yes, and don't forget the binoculars and wide-angle lens.

The **MARIN COUNTY CONVENTION & VISITORS BUREAU** (1013 Larkspur Landing Circle, Larkspur, CA 94939; 415/4999-5000; www.visitmarin.org) is an excellent Marin County information resource. Contact the **FORT BRAGG–MENDOCINO COAST CHAMBER OF COMMERCE** (332 N Main St, Fort Bragg, CA 95437; 707/961-6300 or 800/726-2780; www.mendocinocoast.com) for information about the Mendocino area.

The Marin Coast

When you consider that the San Francisco Bay Area has more people than the entire state of Oregon, and that Marin County has one of the highest per-capita incomes in the nation, you would expect its coastline to be lined with gated communities and fancy resorts. Truth is, you won't find even a Motel 6 along the entire Marin coast, due partly to public pressure but mostly to the inaccessibly rugged, heavily forested terrain (it may look like a 15-minute drive from San Francisco on the map, but 90 minutes later you'll probably still be negotiating hairpin curves down the side of Mount Tamalpais). The only downside to the Marin coast's underdevelopment is the scarcity of affordable lodgings; expensive B&Bs reign supreme, which is fine if you don't mind spending $150 a night or more for a bed and a bagel. Note that most lodgings on the coast have a two-night minimum on weekends. Otherwise, the Marin coast is just short of Eden, a veritable organic playground for weary commuters and adventure-bound tourists.

Marin Headlands

On a sunny San Francisco day, there's no better place to spend time outdoors than in the Marin Headlands. For more than a century following the Civil War, this vast expanse of grass-covered hills and rocky shore was off-limits to the public, appropriated by the U.S. Army as a strategic base for defending the bay against invaders. Remnants of obsolete and untested defense facilities—dozens of thick concrete bunkers and batteries recessed into the bluffs—now serve as viewing and picnic sites for the millions of tourists who visit each year.

There's a wealth of scheduled activities offered daily within the 15-square-mile **GOLDEN GATE NATIONAL RECREATION AREA (GGNRA)**, including birding clinics, bunker tours, wildflower hunts, and geology hikes. The **MARIN HEADLANDS VISITOR CENTER** (GGNRA Bldg 948, Fort Barry, Sausalito; 415/331-1540; www.nps.gov/goga) houses plenty of information, including maps and pertinent facts about all the locations listed below. The center is open daily from 9:30am to 4:30pm.

The **MARINE MAMMAL CENTER** (415/289-SEAL), a popular Marin Headlands attraction, is a volunteer-run hospital for injured and abandoned mammals of the sea. Signs list each animal's adopted name, species, stranding site, and injury—the latter of which is usually human-caused. The center, located at the east end of Fort Cronkhite near Rodeo Lagoon, is open daily from 10am to 4pm. Admission is free (donations appreciated).

Closed to the public for several years due to storm damage, the precariously perched 1877 **POINT BONITA LIGHTHOUSE** (415/331-1540) is once again thrilling those tourists brave enough to traverse the long, dark tunnel and seven small footbridges leading to the beacon. The reward for such bravery is, among other things, a rare and sensational view of the entrance to the bay. The story goes that one 19th-century lighthouse keeper rigged ropes around his children to prevent them from slipping into the raging sea below. Call for tour times, and be sure to inquire about the full-moon tours, which take place twice a month by reservation only.

Also within the Marin Headlands is **HAWK HILL** (located above Battery 129, where Conzelman Rd becomes one-way), one of the most remarkable avian sites in the western United States and the biggest hawk lookout in western North America. Record count in 1992 was more than 20,000 birds, including 21 species of hawk. The best time to visit is during September and October, when thousands of birds of prey soar over the hill each day.

Muir Woods

When you stand in the middle of Muir Woods (415/388-2595; www.nps.gov/muwo; from Hwy 101 in Sausalito, take the Stinson Beach/Hwy 1 exit heading W and follow the signs) surrounded by a canopy of ancient redwoods towering hundreds of feet skyward, it's hard to fathom that San Francisco is less than 6 miles away. It's a den of wooden giants; tourists speak in hushed tones as they crane their necks in disbelief, snapping photographs that don't begin to capture the immensity of these living titans.

Muir Woods can get absurdly crowded on summer weekends. Admission is $2 per person, 17 years and older. Picnicking is not allowed, but there is a snack bar and gift shop at the entrance. It's typically cool and damp, so dress appropriately. Open 8am to sunset.

Three miles west of Muir Woods, along Highway 1, is a small crescent-shaped cove called **MUIR BEACH**. Strewn with bits of driftwood and numerous tide pools, Muir Beach is a more sedate alternative to the beer 'n' bikini crowds at the ever-popular Stinson Beach up north. If all you're looking for is a sandy, quiet place for some R&R, park your car right here and skip the trip to Stinson.

RESTAURANTS

The Pelican Inn / ★★

10 PACIFIC WY, MUIR BEACH; 415/383-6000
One of the better ways to spend a Sunday afternoon in the Bay Area is to take a leisurely drive to this homey little English pub, grab a table at the glassed-in patio or by the fireplace, and gorge yourself proper on a steaming shepherd's pie. Rack of lamb, prime rib, and a few fish dishes are also on the menu, and in the bar you'll find a goodly number of British, Irish, and Scottish beers on tap. After lunch, burn a few calories with a stroll down Muir Beach. *$$$; MC, V; no checks; lunch, dinner every day May 1–Oct 31 and holidays year-round (lunch, dinner Tues–Sun Nov 1–Apr 30); beer and wine; reservations recommended; innkeeper@pelicaninn.com; www.pelicaninn.com; at the entrance to Muir Beach.* &

NORTH COAST THREE-DAY TOUR

DAY ONE: Meet the giants. Fuel up at the Dipsea Cafe (200 Shoreline Hwy, Mill Valley; 415/381-0298). Follow the curves on Highway 1 to **Muir Woods**, home of the giant redwoods. Grab your jacket, pick up a trail guide at the entrance, and look up—always look up. Take the 1-mile main trail loop to Cathedral Grove, where you might be inspired to grow a tree of your own. Live redwood burls are sold at the gift shop. Back on Highway 1, expect winding roads aplenty and gigantic views. Pull off at Muir Beach Overlook. That's San Francisco to the south, **Duxbury Reef** to the north. Wind down to **Stinson Beach**. Get your toes wet in the sand, join in a fast game of volleyball, or search for an elusive sand dollar. Refuel at the **Parkside Cafe**, then move on to the **Point Reyes National Seashore**. Check in at the **Olema Inn** and enjoy a refreshing respite. Round 'em up and head for **Main Street** at **Point Reyes Station**. Dinner's served at the **Station House Cafe**. Be sure to mosey over to the Old Western Saloon before you hit the hay.

DAY TWO: Earth-shaking events. The continental breakfast at the inn didn't quite do it? If you're dying for biscuits and gravy or Celia's Chilaquiles, set out for the **Pine Cone Diner** in Point Reyes Station. Time to see what's shaking at the **Bear Valley Visitor Center**: Stop at the seismograph station and check out the status of "the big one." Walk through the large picnic area in back of the visitor center and follow the signs to the half-mile-long Earthquake Trail. Walk along the San Andreas fault and examine the epicenter of the 1906 San Francisco earthquake. Then check out the Morgan Horse Farm and drop into the sweat house at Kule Loko, a re-created Coast Miwok Indian Village. For a great

LODGINGS

The Pelican Inn / ★★

10 PACIFIC WY, MUIR BEACH; 415/383-6000

Romantic intentions of a homesick expatriate led to the creation of this 16th-century English Tudor country inn, and by God if it isn't filled with convivial dart-playing chaps chugging pints of bitter as lovebirds snuggle in front of the hearth's glowing fire in the inn's pub (see review, above). The inn, named after Sir Francis Drake's ship the *Pelican*, has seven small yet cozy rooms with canopied beds, leaded-glass windows, heavy brocade curtains, and English antiques (the top pick is room 3 with its authentic Half-Tester bed). In the morning guests are treated to an authentic English breakfast of bangers and eggs, toast and marmalade, and—but of course—a cuppa. *$$$; MC, V; no checks; innkeeper@pelicaninn.com; www.pelicaninn.com; off Hwy 1 at entrance to the beach.*

picnic, buy your provisions at **Tomales Bay Foods** and set out on Highway 1, bound for **Tomales** and **Dillon Beach**. Spread out your blanket and soak up the fresh air and sweet sound of the surf. You'll be camping tonight, Tuscan style, at the **Sonoma Coast Villa**. Hang up your gear and prepare to be pampered. If you're still raring to go after watching the sunset, have dinner at the **Duck Club**, or call it a day with a massage.

DAY THREE: Night beams, day sparkles. Let the fog burn off while you linger over a full breakfast at the Villa. Set your compass north; take it easy on the curves. Cruise through **Bodega Bay**. The first pit stop is **Jenner**, home of **Goat Rock Beach**. You can stand on the cliffs by the road and, with the aid of binoculars, get close-up views of the harbor seals congregated on the sandbar below. Lunch is on the way—the **Sea Ranch Lodge and Restaurant** is the spot. Hug the curves to Point Arena. Find out about those ships of the night and mysterious lights when you tour the **Point Arena Lighthouse and Museum** (707/882-2777). On to **Mendocino**. Fortified with a sugar rush from the **Tote Fête Bakery**, stroll through the galleries and shops before making your way to Mendocino's postcard-perfect headlands. So you've seen beach after beach and rock after rock, now go for the sparkly stuff in **Fort Bragg**, your final stop. To reach Glass Beach, site of the former city dump, go west on Elm Street; at the end of the street is a path that leads to the ocean. The cove setting is a treasure trove of shards and colored glass. Search to your heart's content for the ocean-polished souvenir of your dreams. Let it catch the light while you enjoy dinner at the **North Coast Brewing Company** before settling in for the night at the **Grey Whale Inn**.

Stinson Beach

On those treasured weekend days when the fog has lifted and the sun is scorching the Northern California coast, blurry-eyed Bay Area residents grab their morning paper and beach chairs, pile into their SUVs, and scramble to the sandy shores of popular Stinson Beach—the North Coast's nice-try answer to the fabled beaches of Southern California.

A 3½-mile stretch of beige sand provides elbow room for everyone to spread out beach blankets, picnic baskets, and toys. Swimming is allowed, and lifeguards are on duty from May through mid-September, though notices about riptides (plus the sea's toe-numbing temperatures and the threat of sharks) tend to discourage folks from venturing too far into the water. Call 415/868-1922 for recorded **WEATHER AND SURF CONDITIONS**.

Joined at the hip with *la playa* is a village filled with art galleries, specialty shops, and informal cafes. There are plenty of adventurous things to do in the area. For example, Scott Tye, a kayak instructor for **OFF THE BEACH BOATS** (15 Calle del Mar; 415/868-9445) offers three-hour lessons on the basics of sea and surf kayaking. Rentals are surprisingly cheap (about $25 for four hours for surf kayaks), and they even rent a kayak that can hold an entire nuclear family. You'll find the shop next to the Stinson Beach Post Office.

The most famous of all bards livens up weekend evenings May through October. Dress warmly, grab your blanket, and head for **SHAKE-SPEARE AT STINSON** (Hwy 1 at Calle del Mar; 415/868-9500). Enjoy *Much Ado About Nothing, Twelfth Night*, or *Macbeth* in the damp sea breeze beneath the stars.

Skinny-dipping is the trend at **RED ROCK** (www.redrockbeach.com), one of the few nude beaches on the Marin coast. Located about 1 mile south of Stinson Beach on Highway 1, it's easy to miss since you can't see it from the road. Park at the first dirt pull-off on your right after leaving Stinson and look for a steep path leading down to the water.

RESTAURANTS

The Parkside Café / ★★☆

43 ARENAL AVE, STINSON BEACH; 415/868-1272

The interior of this popular neighborhood cafe has been completely renovated, and the new dinner menu featuring contemporary American cuisine plays to rave reviews. Morning favorites are the omelets, blueberry pancakes, and the not-to-be-missed raisin-walnut bread. For lunch there are basics like burgers, grilled sandwiches, and soups, as well as a few daily specials. Once the beach crowd departs, chef John Gilbert starts preparing the seasonal evening menu, which might include oven-roasted Sonoma squab, pan-seared Alaskan halibut, or grilled filet mignon. On sunny days dine alfresco on the brick patio; otherwise, cozy up to the fire. For a quick bite to go, the cafe's snack bar sells great burgers, fries, and shakes daily from March through September, and on weekends from October through February. *$$$; AE, MC, V; local checks only; breakfast, lunch every day, dinner Thurs–Mon; beer and wine; reservations recommended for dinner; www.parksidecafe.com; off Calle del Mar.* &

LODGINGS

Casa del Mar / ★★★

37 BELVEDERE AVE, STINSON BEACH; 415/868-2124

After stints as a lawyer and a fisherman, proprietor Rick Klein jumped headfirst into the B&B business by designing, building, and running the Casa del Mar, a beautiful Mediterranean-style haven that overlooks Stinson Beach. Each of the six sun-drenched rooms has large windows—featuring views of Mount Tamalpais, the ocean, or the spectacular terraced garden—French doors that open onto a private balcony, and a private bath. The comfortable furnishings include a few cushy chairs and platform beds topped with down comforters and piles of pillows. Fresh flowers from the garden and whimsical works by local artists brighten the rooms; the sound of the ocean provides the ambience. Breakfast features an ever-changing array of wonders such as fresh fruit compote, spinach and mushroom quiche, Spanish frittata, and fresh baked breads. *$$$$; AE, MC, V; checks OK; Inn@StinsonBeach.com; www.Stinson Beach.com; heading N into Stinson Beach, turn right at the fire station.*

Bolinas

The beach town of Bolinas, a tight-knit community of free-spirited individuals, is one of the most reclusive towns in Northern California. Residents regularly take down highway signs pointing the way to their rural enclave, an act that ironically has created more publicity for Bolinas than any road sign ever did. As a tourist, you don't have to worry about being chased out of town by a band of machete-wielding Bolinistas, but don't expect anyone to roll out the welcome mat either. The trick is not to *look* like a tourist, but more like a Bay Area resident who's only here to buy some peaches at the **PEOPLE'S STORE** (14 Wharf Rd, Bolinas; open every day 8:30am–6:30pm; 415/868-1433).

What's the People's Store, you ask? It's a town landmark that's famous for its locally grown organic produce and exceptional service—the antithesis of the corporate supermarket. It's a little hard to find, hidden at the end of a gravel driveway next to the Bolinas Bakery (don't confuse it with the much larger general store down the street), but it's worth searching out just to see, and taste, the difference between Safeway and the Bolinas way.

Three side trips offer surprise discoveries. Just before entering downtown Bolinas, turn right (west) on Mesa Road, left on Overlook Road, and right on Elm Road, and you'll dead-end at the **DUXBURY REEF NATURE RESERVE** (415/499-6387), the largest intertidal reef in North America. Rich tide pools harbor an array of starfish, lacy purple plants, sea anemones, and kelp. Check the tide conditions and wear appropriate shoes; the rocks are slippery. If you continue west on Mesa Road you'll reach the **POINT REYES BIRD OBSERVATORY** (415/868-1221, ext. 40), where ornithologists keep an eye on more than 400 feathered species. Admission to the visitors center and nature trail is free, and visitors are welcome to observe the tricky process of catching and banding the birds. It's open daily from dawn to dusk. Banding hours vary; call for information. At the very end of Mesa Road is the **PALOMARIN TRAILHEAD**, which accesses beautiful coast and inland trails that stretch for more than 12 miles. The 6-mile round-trip trek passes several small lakes and meadows before it reaches **ALAMERE FALLS**, a freshwater stream that cascades down a 40-foot bluff onto **WILDCAT BEACH**.

BOLINAS LAGOON, a placid saltwater expanse that serves as refuge for numerous shorebirds and harbor seals, is just south of the town of

Bolinas on Highway 1. Across from the lagoon is the **AUDUBON CANYON RANCH'S BOLINAS LAGOON PRESERVE** (415/868-9244; www.egret.org), a 1,014-acre wildlife sanctuary that supports a major population of **GREAT BLUE HERONS** and **WHITE GREAT EGRETS**. This is the premier spot along the Pacific Coast to watch these immense, graceful seabirds as they court, mate, and build huge nests at the top of towering redwoods. Baby birds are usually in the nests by late April. The trails leading to the overlook are steep and often slippery. Wear sturdy shoes or boots. Admission is free; donations are appreciated. It's open mid-March through mid-July on Saturdays, Sundays, and holidays, 10am to 4pm, and by appointment for groups.

LODGINGS

Thomas's White House Inn / ★★

118 KALE RD, BOLINAS; 415/868-0279
This inn is Bolinas personified—charming, offbeat (e.g., the bathroom doubles as an aviary), and surrounded by incredible vistas. Lounging on the immense and beautifully landscaped front lawn—it alone is worth the room rate—you get a sweeping view of the Bay Area coastline from Marin to Half Moon Bay. The two guest rooms are located upstairs and boast cathedral ceilings and window seats ideal for gazing out at the sea. The larger room has a more rustic feel, with old pine furnishings and an antique steamer trunk, while the smaller room is decorated in softer tones with lace and white wicker. Owner Jackie Thomas serves a simple continental breakfast. $$; *no credit cards; checks OK; www.coastallodging. com; call for directions.*

Point Reyes National Seashore

Hiking, biking, swimming, sailing, windsurfing, sunbathing, camping, fishing, horseback riding, bird-watching, kayaking—all are fair game at this 71,000-acre sanctuary of forested hills, deep green pastures, and undisturbed beaches. Point Reyes is hardly a secret anymore—more than 2 million visitors arrive each year—but the land is so vast and varied that everyone finds a space.

There are four towns in and around the Point Reyes National Seashore boundary: **OLEMA, POINT REYES STATION, INVERNESS PARK,** and **INVERNESS.** Choose one and you'll be within a stone's throw of the park. While the selection of lodging in Point Reyes is excellent, it's also expensive, with most rooms well over $150 per night. Be sure to make your reservation far in advance for the summer and holidays, and bring layers of clothing: Point Reyes gets chilly at night regardless of the season. If you're having trouble finding a vacancy, call the **WEST MARIN NETWORK** (415/663-9543) for information on available lodgings.

Your first stop is the **BEAR VALLEY VISITOR CENTER** (Bear Valley Rd; 415/663-1092; www.nps.gov/pore/), located at the entrance to the Point Reyes National Seashore; follow the signs from Highway 1 in Olema. Pick up a free map and trail guide and chat with a friendly ranger about overnight campsites, weather forecasts, tide conditions, and special programs. The center is open weekdays 9am to 5pm and weekends 8am to 5pm. Drive out to the **POINT REYES LIGHTHOUSE** (415/669-1534; open 10am–4:30pm, Thurs–Mon, weather permitting) at the westernmost tip of the Point Reyes Peninsula. It's a 45-minute scenic excursion through windswept meadows and working dairy ranches—watch out for cows on the road. When the fog burns off, the lighthouse and the headlands provide a fantastic lookout point for spying **GRAY WHALES** and thousands of **COMMON MURES** that inundate the rocks below. Visitors have free access to the lighthouse via a windy .4-mile walk with a thigh-burning 308-step staircase.

If bivalves are your thing, stop off at **JOHNSON'S OYSTER FARM** (off Sir Francis Drake Blvd, about 6 miles W of Inverness; 415/669-1149). It may not look like much—a cluster of trailer homes, shacks, and oyster tanks surrounded by huge piles of oyster shells—but that certainly doesn't detract from the taste of fresh-out-of-the-water oysters dipped in Johnson's special sauce. Eat 'em on the spot, or buy a bag for the road—either way, you're not likely to find California oysters as fresh or as cheap anywhere else. The oyster farm resides within Drakes Estero, a large saltwater lagoon on the Point Reyes peninsula that produces nearly 20 percent of California's commercial oyster yield. It's open 8am to 4pm Tuesday through Sunday.

A popular Point Reyes pastime is **OCEAN KAYAKING**. Don't worry, the kayaks are very stable and there are no waves to contend with because you'll be paddling through placid Tomales Bay, a haven for migrating birds and marine mammals. Rental prices at **TOMALES BAY SEA KAYAKING** (415/663-1743) start at about $35 for a half-day. You can sign up for a guided day trip, a sunset cruise, or a romantic full-moon outing. Instruction, clinics, and boat delivery are available; all ages and levels welcome. The launching point is located on Highway 1 at the **MARSHALL BOATWORKS**, 8 miles north of Point Reyes Station. It's open in summer, Friday through Sunday from 9am to 6pm, and by appointment.

As most ardent Bay Area mountain bikers know, Point Reyes National Seashore boasts some of the finest **MOUNTAIN BIKE TRAILS** in the world. Narrow dirt paths wind through densely forested knolls and end with spectacular ocean views. A map is a must (available for free at the Bear Valley Visitor Center) since many of the park trails are off-limits to bikes. To rent a bike, call David Barnett at **CYCLE ANALYSIS** (415/309-7694; www.cyclepointreyes.com).

Olema

RESTAURANTS

Olema Inn Restaurant / ★★★

10000 SIR FRANCIS DRAKE BLVD, OLEMA; 415/663-9559

The stagecoach used to stop here in the late 1800s, and stories about the wild times enjoyed in the old saloon and brothel are legendary in these parts. During World War II the U.S. Army commandeered the inn for barracks, investors saved it from rack and ruin in the '70s, and in 1999 the inn changed hands again. Longtime diners will be happy to know that Randy Libby, the chef for eight years, stayed on along with the rest of the staff. The current logo, a simple woodblock print of four wild blackberries—one for each season—captures the commitment to use the freshest local ingredients available. Luncheon choices range from Hog Island oysters to salad Lyonnaise or a tasty hamburger served with smoked tomato onion relish and fries (cheese or bacon available on the side). The dinner entrees read like the catch of the day: cioppino prepared with local rock cod, Dungeness crab, mussels, clams, and crostini; a roasted halibut served with risotto and salsa verde. The succulent meats come from neighboring Niman Ranch. Try the lamb chops with ratatouille and mashed potatoes and, of course, a good bottle of Northern California wine. Sunday brunch at the Olema Inn is a tradition in the San Francisco Bay Area. There is something for everyone, from a smoked chicken omelet to tortilla español and corned beef hash. *$$$; AE, MC, V; checks OK; breakfast (guests only), lunch every day except Thurs and Sun, dinner every day, brunch Sun; beer and wine; reservations recommended; corner of Sir Francis Drake Blvd and Hwy 1.* &

LODGINGS

An English Oak / ★★

88 BEAR VALLEY RD, OLEMA; 415/663-1777

When Sharyn Trevillyan and Ken Eichstaedt purchased the rustic Bear Valley Inn in 1999, they changed the name to An English Oak in honor of Sharyn's British heritage, lovingly refurbished the two-story house (built by Italian-Swiss dairy farmers in 1917), and rejuvenated the neglected gardens. The location—half a mile from the Bear Valley Visitor Center—provides a perfect base for exploring nearby trails and secluded beaches. There are three cozy bedrooms in the main house. Each has a queen-size bed, private bath, and eclectic mix of comfortable furnishings. The Welsh Poppy Room, overlooking the creek, is the most spacious. If you're traveling with family or friends, ask about the separate Acorn Cottage, complete with breakfast-making facilities, private shower room, queen-size bed, two futon couches in the living space, and a wheelchair ramp. Most guests begin the morning with a hearty, complimentary breakfast served in the farmhouse dining room and look forward to relaxing by the wood fireplace with a cup of tea or coffee after a day of discovery. *$$$; MC, V; checks OK; sharyn@anenglishoak.com; www.anenglishoak.com; at intersection of Hwy 1 and Bear Valley Rd.* &

Olema Inn / ★★★

10000 SIR FRANCIS DRAKE BLVD, OLEMA; 415/663-9559

This historical Shaker-style inn, dating back to 1876, feels simple, straightforward, and real—from the clapboard exterior to the wrap-around veranda and the crossroads location. Step through the front door, painted a warm red, and you'll be in another world. The inn and restaurant (see review, above) have been completely renovated since Jennifer and Dana Sulprizio bought the property in 1999. Their passion for classic Americana is expressed in every detail. Would you believe the old pine floors were reclaimed from a tobacco warehouse in Virginia? There are six well-appointed rooms on the second floor, each with a private bath, queen- or king-size bed, and antique wardrobes that serve as closets. The rooms are light and airy; floral prints enhance polished woods, iron bed frames, and hand-painted light fixtures. First choice is room 3, outfitted in patriotic red, white, and blue plus a few bold stripes. Guests are also treated to a complimentary continental breakfast. *$$; AE, MC, V; checks OK; corner of Sir Francis Drake Blvd and Hwy 1.*

Point Reyes Seashore Lodge / ★★☆

10021 HWY 1, OLEMA; 415/663-9000 OR 800/404-5633

For folks who want the beauty of the countryside combined with the creature comforts of the city, this is the place. Built in 1988, the three-story cedar inn has 21 guest rooms, most of which offer a fireplace, telephone, down comforter, whirlpool bath, and view of the exquisite garden. If price is no object, opt for one of the two-story suites with a sleeping loft, refrigerator, and the perk of having breakfast delivered to your room. One note of caution: the lodge is located on Highway 1, next to a restaurant that does a brisk (read noisy) business. For peace and quiet, ask for a room in the north wing, or reserve the Casa Olema Retreat, a detached cottage that sleeps up to eight and has a hot tub with room for eight as well. A continental breakfast, included in the nightly rate, is served in the lodge's common room. *$$$; AE, DIS, MC, V; checks OK; prsl@worldnet.att.net; www.placestostay.com; at Hwy 1 and Sir Francis Drake Blvd.* &

Point Reyes Station

It feels like time stood still in this West Marin community that was a rail town in the 1890s, is steeped in dairy-farming tradition, and boasts a population of 675. Maybe that's why so many weary Bay Area commuters flock to Point Reyes Station on weekends. The three blocks everyone calls **MAIN STREET** are actually on Highway 1. It's worth waiting in line to sample the breads and pastries at the renowned **BOVINE BAKERY** (415/663-9420); if gourmet picnic goodies are on your list, head for **TOMALES BAY FOODS** (415/663-9335)—also home of the **COWGIRL CREAMERY**. Those western gals sure know how to make ice cream and cheeses. **TOBY'S FEED BARN** (415/663-1223) is the place to buy farmfresh fruits and vegetables, seeds, sunbonnets, local arts and crafts, and souvenir postcards. The **PINE CONE DINER** (415/663-1536) rustles up made-from-scratch biscuits and gravy every morning.

RESTAURANTS

The Station House Cafe / ★★

11180 SHORELINE HWY, POINT REYES STATION; 415/663-1515

For more than two decades the Station House has been a favorite stop for West Marin residents and San Francisco day-trippers. The menu changes weekly, but you can count on chef Denis Bold to work daily wonders with local produce, seafood, and organic beef from Niman Ranch. Breakfast items range from French toast to buckwheat pancakes to roasted vegetable frittatas. For dinner, start with a platter of local oysters and mussels, followed by a braised lamb shank (made with Guinness Stout) or one of the Station House standbys, such as fish-and-chips with cole slaw. There's a good selection of wines, too. In summer, barbecued oysters are often served on the patio. *$$; DIS, MC, V; local checks only; breakfast, lunch, dinner every day; full bar; reservations recommended; on Main St.* ⅚

Inverness Park

The most familiar landmark in this little community, which originated in 1909 as a subdivision of Inverness, is **PERRY'S DELICATESSEN** (12301 Sir Francis Drake Blvd). Visitors bound for **DRAKE'S BEACH** (415/669-1250), the **POINT REYES LIGHTHOUSE**, and **TOMALES BAY STATE PARK** (415/669-1140) stock up on provisions here.

LODGINGS

Blackthorne Inn / ★★★

266 VALLEJO AVE, INVERNESS PARK; 415/663-8621

With its four levels, five rooms, multiple decks, spiral staircase, sky bridge, and fire pole, the Blackthorne Inn is more like a tree house for grown-ups than a B&B. The octagonal Eagle's Nest, perched on the top level, has its own sundeck and a 360-degree view of the forest (the bath, however, is located across the sky bridge—something of a nuisance on blustery nights); the spacious Forest View and Hideaway Rooms, which share a bath, have sitting areas facing the woods; the outdoor treetop-level hot tub offers a great view of the stars. A country buffet breakfast is included in the room rate and is served on the upper deck when the sun is shining. *$$$; MC, V; checks OK; susan@blackthorneinn. com; www. blackthorneinn.com; from Inverness Park, go 1¼ mile up Vallejo Ave.*

Holly Tree Inn / ★★★

3 SILVERHILLS RD, INVERNESS PARK; 415/663-1554

Hidden within a 19-acre valley with a meandering creek and wooded hillsides is the blissfully quiet Holly Tree Inn. This family-owned B&B has four cozy guest rooms, each with a private bath (one with a fireplace) and decorated with Laura Ashley prints and country antiques. The large, airy living room has a fireplace and comfortable chairs where guests converse over afternoon tea. If privacy is what you're after, tucked in a far corner of the estate is the Cottage-in-the-Woods, a two-room hideaway with a small fireplace, a king-size bed, and an old-fashioned bathtub from which you can gaze at the garden. Families or honeymooners should inquire about the separate Sea Star Cottage—built on stilts over Tomales Bay—and the two-bedroom Vision Cottage; both have hot tubs. In the morning enjoy a bountiful country breakfast. *$$$; AE, MC, V; checks OK; off Bear Valley Rd.*

Inverness

Affluent San Franciscans built summer homes in Inverness at the turn of the century; sailors have always been attracted to the misty waters. Today expensive B&Bs are hidden in the wooded hillsides, kayaks glide on Tomales Bay, and it's as serene and peaceful as ever. If you want to paddle around for yourself, check in at **BLUE WATERS KAYAKING** (415/669-2600; www.bwkayak.com).

RESTAURANTS

Manka's Inverness Lodge / ★★★

ARGYLE ST, INVERNESS; 415/669-1034 OR 800/58-LODGE

Half the fun of dining at Manka's is waiting for your table. Sit in the lobby's plush high-backed chairs, warm your toes by the small wood-burning fireplace, and watch in fascination as one of the cooks kneels beside you to grill the house-made wild boar sausages over the fire: it's like being in a freaking Jack London novel. To complement the hunting lodge illusion, Manka's serves "unusual game, local line-caught fish, oysters pulled from the bay, and bounteous greens from down the road and over the hill." Appetizers range from grilled California quail with wild-mushroom sauce to fire-roasted figs with black-pepper syrup. And the entrees? How about pan-seared elk tenderloin, black buck antelope chops with sweet corn salsa, and wild Canadian pheasant with mashed potatoes? The divine desserts—such as the cinnamon-croissant pudding with warm caramel sauce—are made from scratch, and the wine list is longer than the drive to get here. *$$$; MC, V; checks OK; dinner Thurs–Mon; beer and wine; reservations recommended; mankas@ best.com; www.mankas.com; on Argyle St, off Sir Francis Drake Blvd.*

LODGINGS

Manka's Inverness Lodge / ★★★★

ARGYLE ST, INVERNESS; 415/669-1034 OR 800/58-LODGE

What a difference a Grade makes. For years Manka's was a mediocre Czech restaurant, but when Margaret Grade and family took over in 1989, things changed. This former hunting and fishing lodge soon became one of the most romantic places to stay in California, as well as a wonderful place to eat (see review, above). Manka's offers a dozen accommodations, including four upstairs guest rooms that look as though they came out of a Hans Christian Andersen fairy tale—small and cozy, with tree-limb bedsteads, down comforters, high ceilings, and old-fashioned bathrooms. Rooms 1 and 2 extend out to large private decks overlooking Tomales Bay and have fireplaces and double tubs with showers open to the sky. Manka's also offers four handsome rooms in its Redwood Annex, and two spacious one-bedroom cabins with living rooms, fireplaces, and hot tubs. For the ultimate romantic—or family— retreat, reserve either the fantastic two-level/two-bedroom/two-bath boathouse built out over the bay (equipped with a fireplace, deck, and kitchenette) or the Chicken Ranch, a private 19th-century hunting cabin. *$$$; MC, V; checks OK; www.mankas.com; on Argyle St off Sir Francis Drake Blvd.*

Dancing Coyote Beach / ★★★

12794 SIR FRANCIS DRAKE BLVD, INVERNESS; 415/669-7200

The local Miwok Indians called falling stars "dancing coyotes"—something to ponder as you stare at the heavens through the skylit sleeping lofts of this bayside bed and breakfast. Hidden in a pine-covered cove and within easy walking distance of downtown Inverness, the four adjoining natural-wood cottages are painted in Southwestern pastels and equipped with simple furniture, private decks, fireplaces, and full kitchens. The Beach Cottage, with its small upper deck overlooking Tomales Bay, should be your first choice; Acacia Cottage, which gets a fair amount of traffic noise, should be your last, although you're allowed to bring your pooch to this one. The private lawn, beach, and sun deck are perfect spots for settling down with a good book. *$$$; no credit cards; checks OK; www.coastaltraveler.com; just N of Inverness.*

Tomales

Most people don't even know the town of Tomales exists. Consisting of not much more than a general store, two churches, and a superb little bakery, the tiny ranching community looks pretty much as it did a hundred years ago. It's in a prime location, though—only 30 minutes' drive from **POINT REYES NATIONAL SEASHORE,** yet far enough away to avoid the traffic and commotion. The 4-mile drive from Tomales to **DILLON BEACH** (via Dillon Beach Rd) is one of the most scenic routes on the Marin coast. There is a $5 day-use fee at the beach. The fishing pier and dune campgrounds at **LAWSON'S LANDING** (707/878-2443) also attract visitors.

Tomales is a popular stop for fresh raw and barbecued oysters. The **TOMALES BAY OYSTER COMPANY** (15479 Hwy 1; 415/663-1242; open daily 9am–5pm) has been in business since 1909. They sell them by the dozen or in a sack of 100. Those in the know bring their own knife, lemons, cocktail sauce, and even bags of charcoal for the nearby barbecue pits.

The Sonoma Coast

While many people associate Sonoma County with fine wines, few seem aware that it also commands more than 50 miles of largely undeveloped California coast, and judging from the sparsely visited parks and beaches, they're obviously missing the boat. True, a quiet and undeveloped stretch of shoreline isn't for everyone, but scenic vistas minus hordes of visitors might put it high on many travelers' lists.

Valley Ford

This sleepy little community, a charming bend in the road for most coastal travelers, has a population of 126. The Northern Pacific Railroad steamed through here in 1876, potato farming flourished in the 1920s, and today most of the 126 residents are ranchers of cows or sheep. There were traffic jams in 1976 when the artist Christo installed his **RUNNING FENCE,** 18 feet high and 24.5 miles long, through Valley Ford. Created from pure white silk, the undulating fence snaked over green rolling hills straight into the Pacific.

LODGINGS

Valley Ford Hotel / ★★

14415 HWY 1, VALLEY FORD; 707/876-3600

The pleasant, old-fashioned Valley Ford Hotel, built in 1864 and refurbished under new ownership in 1999, is a good choice for travelers who prefer the privacy of a hotel to the more intimate quarters of a B&B. The seven rooms are clean, spacious, and comfortably furnished. Each has a private bath; bed sizes range from twin to king. The Bernardoni Suite is the most luxurious accommodation, with a sitting room, gas fireplace, satellite TV, and videos. For those who love sports and company, there is a full bar with satellite TV in the cocktail lounge. Many move into the adjoining restaurant after the game, choosing dinner entrees like chicken saltimbocco or filet Madagascar. Guests also enjoy a full breakfast. *$$$; AE, MC, V; checks OK; info@valleyfordhotel.com; www.valleyford hotel.com; downtown.* &

Bodega Bay

When it comes to fancy restaurants, accommodations, and boutiques, Bodega Bay has a long way to go. There is only one three-star lodge and restaurant, and the town's most venerable store sells taffy and kites. This is odd, considering Bodega Bay is only a few hours' drive from the Bay Area, a good two to three hours closer than Mendocino, and has all the beautiful scenery and golden beaches you could possibly hope for. Spend a few hours meandering through town and it becomes apparent that Bodega Bay is, for the most part, still a working-class fishing village. Most people start their day before dawn—mending nets, rigging fishing poles, and anticipating the catch of the day.

The **BODEGA BAY AREA CHAMBER OF COMMERCE** (850 Hwy 1; 707/875-3422; www.bodegabay.com) is a good place to load up on free maps, guides, and brochures, including the "Bodega Bay Area Map & Guide." The latter gives the exact locations of all the town's attractions, including nearby **BODEGA HEAD** (from downtown Bodega Bay, turn W on Eastshore Rd, go right at the stop sign onto Bay Flat Rd, and follow it to the end), the small peninsula that shelters Bodega Bay. You'll discover two superb **WALKING TRAILS** that follow the ocean at the Head. The first, a 4-mile round-trip trail, starts from the west parking lot, leads past the **BODEGA BAY MARINE LABORATORY** (707/875-2211; www. bml.ucdavis.edu), and ends at the sand dunes of **SALMON CREEK BEACH**. An easier, 1½-mile round-trip walk begins in the east parking lot and encircles the edge of Bodega Head. From December through April, Bodega Head also doubles as one of the premier **WHALE-WATCHING** points along the California coast.

A great way to spend a lazy afternoon in Bodega Bay is at the **DOCKS**, watching the rusty fishing boats unload their catches. **TIDES WHARF RESTAURANT** (835 Hwy 1 in Bodega Bay; 707/875-3652) has the most active dock scene, including a viewing room near the processing plant that allows you to witness a fish's ultimate fate—a swift and merciless gutting by deft hands, followed by a quick burial in ice. Just outside, sea lions linger by the dock hoping for a handout.

Linking Bodega Bay and the nearby town of Jenner are the **SONOMA COAST STATE AND COUNTY BEACHES**, 16 miles of pristine sand and gravel beaches, tide pools, rocky bluffs, hiking trails, and one heck of a gorgeous drive along Highway 1. Although all the beaches are pretty much the same—divine—the safest for kids is **DORAN PARK BEACH**, located just south of Bodega Bay. When the water's rough everywhere else, Doran is still calm enough for swimming, clamming, and crabbing (an added bonus: the adjacent Doran mud flats are a favorite haunt of egrets, pelicans, and other seabirds). The best tide pools are at the north end of **SALMON CREEK BEACH** (off Bean Ave, 2 miles N of town) or **SHELL BEACH**, a small low-tide treasure trove 10 miles north of Bodega Bay. If all you want to do is get horizontal in the sand, deciding which of the 14 beaches along Highway 1 looks the best will drive you nuts; just pick one and park.

RESTAURANTS

The Duck Club / ★★★

103 HWY 1 (BODEGA BAY LODGE AND SPA), BODEGA BAY; 707/875-3525 OR 800/368-2468

Bodega Bay sure took its sweet time coaxing a premier chef to the coast, but now that Jeff Reilly (formerly the executive chef at Lafayette Park in Walnut Creek) is in town, gastronomes up and down the coast are coming to the Bodega Bay Lodge and Spa to sample his wares. "Sonoma County cuisine" best describes Reilly's penchant for local yields, with creations such as roasted Petaluma duck with Valencia orange sauce or a Sonoma farm-fresh asparagus strudel bathed in a mild curry sauce. *Le poisson du jour* comes straight from the docks down the street. Large windows overlook the bay, so be sure to beg for a table-with-a-view when making the required reservations. The Duck Club offers a lengthy wine list with an extensive selection of Sonoma County labels. *$$$; AE, DC, DIS, MC, V; no checks; breakfast, dinner every day; beer and wine; reservations required; bbl@woodsidehotels.com; www.woodsidehotels.com; S end of town.* &

LODGINGS

Bodega Bay Lodge and Spa / ★★★

103 HWY 1, BODEGA BAY; 707/875-3252 OR 800/368-2468

Granted, the competition isn't very fierce, but it's safe to say that the Bodega Bay Lodge and Spa provides some of the Sonoma Coast's finest accommodations. It's the view that clinches it: all 79 rooms—recently remodeled in handsome hues of cardinal red and forest green, with wood-burning fireplaces and stocked minibars—have private balconies with a wonderful panorama of Bodega Bay and its bird-filled wetlands. Plus, the lodge has added five suites, featuring Jacuzzi tubs for two. Should you ever leave your balcony, a short walk through elaborate flower gardens leads to an outdoor fieldstone spa and heated swimming pool overlooking the bay. A fitness center, sauna, and complimentary morning newspaper are part of the package. Ask about the on-site facials, massages, and body treatments that are now among the extra offerings. More proof of Bodega Bay Lodge and Spa's top standing is its Duck Club restaurant (see review, above), easily the Sonoma Coast's best. *$$$$; AE, DC, DIS, MC, V; checks OK; bbl@woodsidehotels.com; www.wood sidehotels.com; S end of town.* ⅃

Inn at the Tides / ★★

800 HWY 1, BODEGA BAY; 707/875-2751 OR 800/541-7788
In Bodega Bay the architectural style of most structures is nouveau Californian—wood-shingled boxes with lots of glass—and the Inn at the Tides is no exception. Perched on a hillside overlooking Bodega Bay, it offers 86 units with bay views, spacious interiors, and contemporary (albeit *dated* contemporary) decor, and all with the usual amenities of an expensive resort: terry-cloth robes, coffeemakers, hair dryers, cable TV, refrigerators, minibars, fresh flowers, continental breakfasts, and access to the indoor/outdoor pool, sauna, and whirlpool tubs. A few of the rooms have king-size beds, and most have fireplaces. The Inn at the Tides's restaurant, the Bay View, is open for dinner only. It offers ocean views and has a romantic, somewhat formal ambience. *$$$; AE, DIS, MC, V; checks OK; iatt@monitor.net; www.innatthetides.com; across from the Tides Wharf.* ⅃

Bodega

A quick trip to the town of Bodega, a few miles southeast of Bodega Bay off Highway 1, is a must for any Hitchcock fan. The attraction is a bird's-eye view of the hauntingly familiar **POTTER SCHOOL HOUSE** and **ST. TERESA'S CHURCH**, both immortalized in Hitchcock's *The Birds*, filmed here in 1961. The two or three boutiques in downtown Bodega manage to entice a few visitors to park and browse, but most people seem content with a little rubbernecking and finger-pointing as they flip U-turns through the tiny town.

LODGINGS

Sonoma Coast Villa / ★★★⯪

16702 COAST HWY 1, BODEGA; 707/876-9818 OR 888/404-2255

So you have pampering and comfort in mind. How about a Mediterranean footbath, rejuvenating body massage, or soothing facial in a 60-acre Tuscan setting? It's all yours at Sonoma Coast Villa, plus a nine-hole putting green, swimming pool, and indoor whirlpool spa. Built in the mid-1970s by the owners of the San Francisco Blue Boar restaurant, the property was purchased by Susan and Cyrus Griffin in 1992. They spent a year lovingly refurbishing every inch of the country estate, added six new rooms, and settled into the role of innkeepers with a zestful hospitality that charms guests today. There are 12 spacious rooms, featuring exposed wooden beams, wood-burning fireplaces, Italian slate floors, large marble walk-in showers or jetted tubs, well-stocked mini-refrigerators, and private patios. Phones are not featured in this quiet refuge, but there are board games aplenty, and movies for VCR fans. Don't miss the all-glass Tower Library Room perched at the top of the winding wrought-iron staircase in the reception area. Choose a book tailored to your reading pleasure, or aim the resident telescope toward the sea. Cyrus will have been busy in the kitchen long before you rise, rustling up a hot country breakfast accompanied by fresh baked goods. Guests who like to stay in on a Friday or Saturday evening are invited to partake of a complimentary supper buffet. Typical menus include a tasty entree, green salad, pasta salad with roasted vegetables, rice or potatoes, and fresh Sonoma rolls. Oh yes, and don't forget the house wine. All meals are enjoyed in the dining room with its vaulted wood-beamed ceiling, fireplace, and windows overlooking the lush gardens. *$$$$; AE, MC, V; checks OK; reservations@scvilla.com; www.scvilla.com; 2 miles past Valley Ford.* &

Occidental

LODGINGS

The Inn at Occidental / ★★★

3657 CHURCH ST, OCCIDENTAL; 707/874-1047 OR 800/522-6324
Innkeeper Jack Bullard has done a fantastic job remodeling this stately 1887 Victorian into one of the finest country inns anywhere. Covered porches, wainscoted hallways, antique wicker furniture, walled-in English gardens, and a comfortable sitting parlor are all elegant reminders of the historic days when Occidental was a stopping point on the railroad between San Francisco and the Northwest. The sixteen individually decorated rooms have private baths and are furnished with the innkeeper's vast collection of heirlooms, antiques, and original artwork. Overlooking the courtyard is the Marble Room, sumptuously furnished with an antique pine queen bed, a large separate sitting area with a fireplace, comfortable chairs, and a spa tub for two overlooking the hill and woods behind the inn. Guests are treated to a full gourmet breakfast of fresh fruit, juices, homemade granola, freshly baked pastries, and hot entrees such as orange-thyme pancakes or French toast with jam—all served in the dining room or outdoors. Inquire about the inn's Saturday dinners, reserved for guests only. *$$$$; AE, DIS, MC, V; checks OK; innkeeper@innatoccidental.com; www.innatoccidental.com; off the Bohemian Hwy.* &

Sebastopol

Situated at the crossroads of Highway 116 and Highway 12, Sebastopol is the gateway between western Sonoma County and the North Coast. Gravenstein apples, the area's greatest claim to fame, were introduced in the late 1800s. The **APPLE BLOSSOM FESTIVAL** is held every April, and **CHRISTMAS TREE FARMS** bustle during the holidays. Antique shopping is a popular pastime year-round. Stop at **TEA & TAROT** (2661 Gravenstein Hwy S; 707/823-3882) for a taste of old England and glimpse into the future. Gardeners will enjoy a walking tour of **GOLD RIDGE FARM** (7781 Bodega Ave; 707/829-6711). This is where **LUTHER BURBANK**, the world-renowned horticulturist credited with developing the Shasta Daisy, conducted plant-breeding experiments at the turn of the century. Hungry? Try **LUCY'S CAFE** (110 N Main St; 707/829-9713), a local favorite for breakfast, lunch, and dinner. For more information, contact the Sebastopol Visitor Center (165 S Main St; 707/823-3032; www.sebastopol.org).

RESTAURANTS

Chez Peyo / ★★

2295 GRAVENSTEIN HWY, SEBASTOPOL; 707/823-1223

Pierre and Rose Marie Lagourgue, chef and hosts of this homey restaurant, have been serving savory French California cuisine to satisfied diners since 1977. Pierre (Peyo is the Basque form of his name) is well-known for the fare he dishes up, like the braised lamb shanks dressed in a pinot noir sauce. Another favorite is the baked salmon coated in an almond-and-black-pepper crust and topped with a citrus beurre blanc. The restaurant's Sunday champagne brunches, featuring the likes of eggs basquaise and vegetarian Benedict, are a popular tradition in Sebastopol. *$$; MC, V; local checks OK; lunch, dinner Wed–Sat, brunch Sun; beer and wine; reservations recommended; chezpeyo@sonic.net; www.sterba. com/chezpeyo; on Hwy 116, 2 miles S of town.* &

101 Main Bistro & Wine Bar Restaurant / ★★★

101 S MAIN ST, SEBASTOPOL; 77/829-3212

City folks will be pleasantly surprised to discover this sophisticated setting and innovative menu in downtown Sebastopol. The vintage 1907 building's exterior contrasts dynamically with the bistro's 25-foot ceilings, sienna-colored walls, and hand-forged wine bar. No wonder this bistro swept award categories in the recent *Sonoma County Independent* Readers Poll: best local chef, best wine list, and best Sunday brunch. It's also a heartwarming success story for husband-and-wife owners Volodia and Laura Crettol. They opened the 101 Main Bistro & Wine Bar in 1995, immediately after he graduated from the California Culinary Academy. The couple works side by side, providing friendly service while satisfying the expectations of discriminating palates. You'll find more than 100 wines, carefully selected to complement the eclectic country cuisine. The menu, featuring fresh local ingredients, offers lots of seasonal choices, plus daily specials. For starters, try the white corn–pasilla pepper chowder, or seared Nova Scotia scallops atop a crispy risotto cake with a Thai yellow curry–coconut sauce. You'll have a hard time choosing when it comes to entrees. How about portobello mushroom schnitzel served with basil Israeli couscous and fall vegetable ratatouille? Meat lovers will go for the grilled marinated rib-eye steak topped with crispy shoestring onions, served with garlic mashed potatoes and sautéed vegetables. At Sunday brunch, try the Roman's Blue Max, a potato pancake topped with grilled Black Forest Gruyère, poached eggs, and hollandaise. *$$$; AE, DIS, MC, V; local checks OK; dinner Tues–Sun, brunch Sun; beer and wine; reservations recommended; at Bodega Hwy.*

Stella's Cafe / ★★★

4550 GRAVENSTEIN HWY N, SEBASTOPOL; 707/823-6637

Foodies will think they have died and gone to heaven when they discover this little gem. Originally part of the 1930s World Trade Fair, the small restaurant—it seats 50, including the bar space—opened in October 1999. Gregory Hallihan, the gregarious owner, graduated from the California Culinary Academy in 1992. He brings years of experience, including a stint with the Ritz-Carlton in Hawaii, to Stella's Cafe. There is something for everyone on the ever-changing menu, from vegan, vegetarian, and seafood to old-fashioned rib-eye steak. Try the likes of coconut lentil soup or spicy grilled prawns with red jalapeño mango purée and pineapple couscous salad. You'll soon know why locals fill the place night after night. Wine connoisseurs will also be pleased with the excellent choices, many from nearby vineyards. If you're still hankering after a sweet road treat after the divine strawberry shortcake, try Mom's Apple Pie, located next door. *$$; MC, V; checks OK; call to confirm lunch schedule, dinner Wed–Mon; beer and wine; reservations recommended; just before Forestville, adjacent to Mom's Apple Pie (look for the green awning imprinted with Stella's Cafe).* &

LODGINGS

Avalon / ★★★

11910 GRATON RD, SEBASTOPOL; 707/824-0880 OR 877/3AVALON

The secluded entrance to Avalon, a luxury bed-and-breakfast, conjures up images of a magical forest reminiscent of the knights of the round table. And yes, soft mists often hug the old bay trees and towering redwoods. Hilary and Gary McCalla, the engaging owners and hosts, fulfilled a cherished dream when they opened this charming Tudor-style B&B in early 2000. Avalon—a family name—coupled with a love of old English legends inspired the themes and unique decor of the three well-appointed suites. Try the Magician's Suite, featuring a spacious steam room shower, sleek three-sided fireplace, bright-blue-glass vessel sinks, and a tranquil forest view. Sweet dreams are yours in the Enchanted Forest Suite: soak in the full-size outdoor hot tub before sinking into the elegant king-size bed and being lulled to sleep by a splashing creek. Honeymooners should choose Guenevere's Tower, complete with a spacious sitting area, antique claw-footed soaking tub, and two Romeo and Juliet–style balconies. Each suite features a separate entrance, gas fireplaces with thermostats, king-size beds, fine linens, large private baths, and local handmade soaps. Indoor exercise facilities are available for those who miss the gym, while the brave of heart might enjoy an invigorating plunge in the nearby swimming hole. Tea is an afternoon ritual, and Hilary whips up a yummy breakfast every morning. "French Babies," scalloped puff pastries filled with Brie and fresh strawberries, are a specialty, along with baked pears or apples and homemade scones. *$$$$; AE, DC, MC, V; checks OK; 2-night minimum stay on weekends, 3-night minimum stay on holiday weekends; Hilgar@aol.com; www.avalonluxuryinn.com; 3.3 miles off Graton Rd.*

The Sebastopol Inn / ★★

6751 SEBASTOPOL AVE, SEBASTOPOL; 707/829-2500

Guests at the Sebastopol Inn enjoy comfortable new accommodations in a historic setting. Located behind the restored vintage Gravenstein Railroad Station in downtown Sebastopol, the inn exudes small-town–country charm. Constructed with vertical board- and batten-siding and topped with a verdigris copper roof, it has 31 rooms and suites to choose from. You can expect all the amenities of a boutique hotel, including queen- or king-size beds, coffeemakers, TVs, and full concierge service. Some rooms have fireplaces, whirlpool tubs, microwaves, and refrigerators. Ask about the balcony rooms looking out on pristine wetland preserves, and don't miss the heated pool and spa in the garden courtyard. *$$$; AE, DC, MC, V; checks OK; sean@thesebastopolinn.com; www.thesebastopolinn.com; downtown, look for the old train barn.* &

Vine Hill Inn / ★★

3949 VINE HILL RD, SEBASTOPOL; 707/823-8832

The rolling vineyards will remind you of *bella* Tuscany, but this beautifully restored 1897 Victorian farmhouse and its rambling country gardens belong in western Sonoma. You'll feel right at home, too, when you snuggle up in one of the four upstairs bedrooms. Furnished with charming antiques, each has a private bath; choose from a whirlpool tub or claw-footed bath with shower. An inviting porch or deck, with comfortable seating and glorious views, is never far away. How about a cool dip in the pool, nap in the hammock, or a fast game of ping pong? Guests are welcome to store their favorite snacks and beverages in the kitchen.

The owner and hospitable hostess, Kathy Deichmann, is especially proud of the recently constructed barn with stable accommodations for one or two boarding horses. Wake up to the clucking of hens and the aroma of a hearty country breakfast coming from the kitchen. Frittata is a specialty, but Deichmann has been known to turn out a mean rhubarb pie. *$$$; AE, DIS, MC, V; checks OK; innkeeper@vine-hill-inn.com; www.vine-hill-inn.com; follow Hwy 116 W to Vine Hill Rd.*

Forestville

From this tiny hamlet surrounded by redwoods you can launch an all-day **CANOE TRIP** down the gentle Russian River. Set forth from **BURKE'S CANOE TRIPS** (707/887-1222) from May through September, and someone there will pick you up 10 miles down the scenic river—a haven for turtles, river otters, egrets, and great blue herons—and take you back to your car. On Forestville's itty-bitty main drag is **BROTHER JUNIPER'S BAKERY** (6544 Front St; 707/542-9012), the home of the Russian River Valley's best breads. Also worth a detour is **KOSLOWSKI FARMS** (5566 Gravenstein Hwy; 707/887-1587), a family farm that has turned into a gourmet-food business. The Koslowskis' apple butter, jams, and vinegars are sold in specialty shops throughout Sonoma County and beyond.

RESTAURANTS

Topolos Russian River Vineyards Restaurant & Winery / ★★

5700 GRAVENSTEIN HWY, FORESTVILLE; 707/887-1562
Delectable Greek food on the Russian River? Well, why not—chefs Bob Engel and Christine Topolos prepare the food the same way you'd get it on the Mediterranean. Every meal at this family-owned restaurant and winery comes with *tzatziki*, a garlic-laden cucumber-yogurt dip for bread, and a tomato stuffed with aromatic ratatouille. Follow that with an order of *mezes*: a plate of *dolmas*, *tiropita* (a cheese-and-egg pie wrapped in scrumptious, flaky filo pastry), marinated eggplant, and feta. Then choose from such main courses as prawns Santorini, prepared with tomato, feta, and dill, roast Petaluma duckling with a black currant–Madeira wine sauce, or roast rack of baby lamb. Topolos wines, made here, and other local wines are served with dinner. Dessert, naturally, is a hunk of honey-drenched baklava. *$$$; AE, DC, MC, V; checks OK; lunch, dinner every day, brunch Sun; wine only; reservations recommended; topolos@topolos.com; www. topolos. com; on Hwy 116, ¼ mile S of town.*

LODGINGS

Farmhouse Inn / ★

7871 RIVER RD, FORESTVILLE; 707/887-3300
Don't let the outside of the Farmhouse Inn's eight guest cottages fool you. At first glance these buildings tucked within a grove of trees look like

nothing more than your everyday roadside motel cabins. But step inside and you'll see that these little lodges are actually quite luxurious, with plush carpets, fireplaces, saunas, and jumbo Jacuzzis. The grounds—six acres of hills and redwoods—include a large swimming pool, a croquet course, and formal English gardens. Guests gather for a hearty breakfast in the restored turn-of-the-century farmhouse, which features country-style furniture and a giant fireplace. Expect to be treated to fruit, cereal, and hot dishes such as huevos rancheros or eggs Florentine. The inn's restaurant is also open to the public for dinner. *$$$; AE, MC, V; checks OK; innkeep@farmhouseinn.com; www.farmhouseinn.com; River Rd (at Wohler Rd).* ♿

Guerneville

The longtime residents of Guerneville—one of the busiest logging centers in the West during the 1880s—have seen their town undergo a significant change of face in every recent decade. Once it was a haven for bikers—the leather, not the Lycra, sort—then it became a hangout for hippies. Now it's a summer mecca for Bay Area gays and for naturalists attracted by the beauty of the redwoods and the **RUSSIAN RIVER**. The town is a good launching spot for nature expeditions and touring the area's wineries. **KORBEL CHAMPAGNE CELLARS** (13250 River Rd; 707/887-2294), overlooking the vineyards and the Russian River, is one of the region's most popular wineries and offers free tastings of its bubbly. **ARMSTRONG WOODS STATE RESERVE** (17000 Armstrong Woods Rd; 707/869-2015) boasts a peaceful grove of spectacular ancient redwoods and a variety of hiking trails. Equestrians should saddle up at **ARMSTRONG WOODS PACK STATION** (707/579-1520), which offers 1½-hour and half- and full-day horseback rides with gourmet lunches as well as overnight camping rides. From May through October, you can rent canoes, kayaks, and paddleboats at **JOHNSON'S BEACH** (707/869-2022) just under the main bridge. Johnson's Beach is also home to the wildly popular **RUSSIAN RIVER JAZZ FESTIVAL** (707/869-3940), held every September. Another crowd-pleaser is the annual **STUMPTOWN DAYS PARADE AND RODEO** (707/869-1959), which takes place on Father's Day weekend. For a good, simple meal, grab a bite at **BURDON'S** (15405 River Rd; 707/869-2615) or **SWEET'S RIVER GRILL** (16521 Main St; 707/869-3383). For more information, check out the Russian River Chamber of Commerce & Visitors Center (16209 1st St, Guerneville; 877/644-9001; www.russianriver.com).

RESTAURANTS

Applewood Restaurant / ★★★

13555 HWY 116, GUERNEVILLE; 797/869-9093

Folks at the nearby inn are apt to describe the new Applewood Restaurant's design as rustic-barn architecture, but don't be fooled. When was the last time you saw a barn with lofty beam ceilings, two river-rock fireplaces, and spacious windows looking out to towering redwoods? Guests are invited to arrive in casual attire and linger over a romantic candlelit dinner impeccably prepared by executive chef Brian Gerritsen. Formally trained at the New England Culinary Institute, he also brings his enriching experiences in the French countryside to the Russian River Valley. In keeping with Applewood's culinary history, Brian uses only the freshest ingredients, with a strong focus on the organic bounty from the inn's own 2-acre garden and fruit orchard. For starters you'll find treats like the lightly curried cauliflower soup with duck prosciutto or hazelnut-crusted sweetbreads on a celery root and Asian pear rémoulade. Entrees range from a hearty veal osso buco braised in cabernet with white beans and Spanish olives, to grilled Pacific swordfish on a warm cabbage, watercress, and citrus salad. Save room for the warm roasted pear fritters with ginger and vanilla cream, or chocolate graham pound cake with cocoa hazelnuts and cinnamon ice cream. Wine lovers will be in heaven: there are 247 selections—many from local vineyards—to choose from. *$$$; AE, MC, V; no checks; dinner Tues–Sat; beer and wine; reservations recommended; stay@applewoodinn.com; www.applewoodinn. com; 1 mile S of Guerneville.* &

LODGINGS

Applewood Inn / ★★★☆

13555 HWY 116, GUERNEVILLE; 707/869-9093
A grand old 1922 California mission revival mansion, formerly the country home of a wealthy banker, is the centerpiece of this tranquil inn (see review of Applewood Restaurant, above). The 16 secluded rooms and suites, each individually decorated with stylish antiques and attractive artwork, look out onto the surrounding redwoods, apple trees, and vineyards. All the rooms have TVs, fresh flowers, and private baths. Seven come with either a spa tub or shower-for-two. Everyone feels pampered with lush Turkish cotton towels, European down comforters, and hand-pressed linens. Room 1, decorated in soothing forest green colors and English oak, features French doors that open onto a private patio and garden; room 4 has a Louis Philippe cherry-wood sleigh bed and a sitting room framed by huge, curved bay windows. The Gate House, completed in 1999, offers three contemporary deluxe suites featuring bedside fireplaces, whirlpool baths, couples showers, and private decks. You'll discover cozy sitting areas, some with fireplaces, throughout the inn. The Mediterranean-style garden is always beckoning. There's a large outdoor swimming pool and spa beyond the stone courtyard and bubbling lion's-head fountain. Guests welcome the day with a breakfast of eggs Florentine, French toast, or other well-prepared dishes, served in the airy Applewood Restaurant. *$$$$; AE, MC, V; no checks; 2-night min-*

imum stay July–Sept; stay@applewoodinn.com; www.applewoodinn.com; 1 mile S of Guerneville. &

Jenner

About 16 miles north of Bodega Bay on Highway 1 is what seems to be every Northern Californian's "secret" getaway spot: Jenner. Built on a bluff rising from the mouth of the Russian River, the tiny seaside town consists of little more than a gas station, three restaurants, two inns, and a deli, which means the only thing to do in town is eat, sleep, and lie on the beach—not a bad vacation plan. It is also two hours closer to the Bay Area than Mendocino, yet offers the same spectacular coastal scenery and a far better selection of beaches.

The sandbar at beautiful **GOAT ROCK BEACH** (707/875-3483), a breeding ground for **HARBOR SEALS**, becomes a major seasonal attraction during pupping season—March through May. Seals give birth on land, and orange-vested volunteers are usually around to protect the playful mammals, answer questions, and even lend binoculars for a closer look.

A serpentine 12-mile drive north of Jenner on Highway 1 takes you to the **FORT ROSS STATE HISTORIC PARK** (707/847-3286), a fortress built by Russian fur traders in 1812. The fort's distinctive structures, including a stockade, a Russian Orthodox chapel, and the commandant's house, have been replicated and restored. Short history lessons are offered in the Fort Compound (11:30am, 1:30pm, and 3:30pm in summer; noon and 2pm in winter). Be sure to walk down to the cove and beach. The day-use parking fee is $6.

A great day trip from Jenner is the scenic drive along Highway 101 to **SALT POINT STATE PARK**. There are 3,500 acres to explore and all kinds of things to do, including **SKIN DIVING** off rocky beaches, **TIDE-POOLING**, and **HIKING** through coastal woodlands. Simply pull the car over anywhere along Highway 1 and start walking. At the north end of the park on Kruse Ranch Road is the 317-acre **KRUSE RHODODENDRON PRESERVE** (707/847-3221), a forested grove of plants that grow up to 18 feet tall under a vast canopy of redwoods. Masses of vivid pink and purple flowers appear in early spring. Peak blooming time varies, but April is usually the month to see the world's tallest *Rhododendron californicum*.

RESTAURANTS

River's End / ★★

1104A HWY 1, JENNER; 707/865-2484
Longtime fans of this popular restaurant and former chef/owner Wolfgang Gramatzki will be glad to know that the place is still bustling. Dave Dahlquist, who worked with Gramatzki for 15 years, has taken over as chef. The menu is still decidedly eclectic, with entrees ranging from

Indian curries to beef Wellington, seafood, and steaks. Lunch is more down to earth, with reasonably priced burgers and sandwiches. Most tables have a wonderful view of the ocean, as does the small outside deck—the perfect spot for a glass of Sonoma County wine. *$$; MC, V; no checks; lunch, dinner Fri–Sun; full bar; reservations recommended; bert@river'send.com; www.sterba.com/bodega/river; just N of town.* &

Sizzling Tandoor / ★

9960 HWY 1, JENNER; 707/865-0625

When the weather is warm and sunny, Sizzling Tandoor is the best place on the Sonoma coast to have lunch. This Indian restaurant is perched high above the placid Russian River, and the view, particularly from the outside patio, is fantastic. Equally great are the inexpensive lunch specials: huge portions of curries and kebabs served with vegetables, soup, pilau rice, and superb naan (Indian bread). Even if you don't have time for a meal, drop by and order some warm naan to go. *$; AE, DIS, MC, V; no checks; lunch, dinner every day (closed Tues in winter); beer and wine; reservations recommended; at S end of the Russian River Bridge, S of Jenner.* &

Sea Ranch

The Sea Ranch is undoubtedly one of the most beautiful seaside communities in the nation, due mostly to rigid adherence to environmentally harmonious architectural standards. Approximately 300 homes, some quite grand, are available as **VACATION RENTALS**. There are eight or nine rental companies, charging prices ranging from as low as $165 to as high as $550 for two nights—rates are generally lower on the east side of Highway 1. The **SEA RANCH LODGE AND RESTAURANT** (800/732-7262; www.searanchlodge.com) offers the only hotel accommodations. Return visitors often sample different locations—woods, meadows, ocean bluffs. For rentals contact **SEA RANCH RENTALS** (707/785-2579; www.searanchrental.com) or **RAMS HEAD REALTY** (800/785-3455; www.ramshead-realty.com). Rentals also include use of the community's three outdoor heated swimming pools, tennis courts, and recreation center. The award-winning **SEA RANCH GOLF LINKS** (located along Sea Ranch's northern boundary at the entrance to Gualala Point Regional Park; 707/785-2468), a challenging Scottish-style 18-hole course, was designed by Robert Muir Graves and is open daily to the public.

The Mendocino Coast

There are four things first-time visitors should know before heading to the Mendocino coast. First, be prepared for a long, beautiful drive; there are no quick and easy routes to this part of California, and there's no public transportation, so traveling by car is your only option. Second, make your hotel and restaurant reservations as far in advance as possible because everything involving tourism books up solid during summers and holidays. Third, bring warm clothing. A windless, sunny, 80-degree day on the Mendocino coast is about as rare as affordable real estate. Fourth and finally, bring a lot of money and your checkbook. Cheap sleeps, eats, and even banks are few and far between along this stretch of shoreline, and many places don't take credit cards (though personal checks are widely accepted).

So where exactly is the Mendocino coast? Well, it starts at the county line in the town of Gualala and ends a hundred or so miles north at the sparsely populated stretch known as the Lost Coast. The focal point is the town of Mendocino, but the main center of commerce—and the region's only McDonald's (if you can believe it)—is in Fort Bragg, 15 miles up the coast. Compared with these two towns, every other part of the Mendocino coast is relatively deserted—something to consider if you're looking to escape the masses. Spring is the best time to visit, when the wildflowers are in full bloom and the crowds are still sparse. Then again, nothing on this planet is more romantic than cuddling next to the fireplace on a winter night, listening to the rain and thunder pound against your little cottage. For more information on visiting the area, contact the **FORT BRAGG–MENDOCINO COAST CHAMBER OF COMMERCE** in Fort Bragg (800/726-2780).

Gualala

The southernmost town in Mendocino County, Gualala also happens to have the most mispronounced name in Mendocino County. Keep the G soft and you end up with "wah-LAL-ah," the Spanish version of *walali*, which is Pomo Indian patois for "water coming down place." The water in question is the nearby Gualala River, a placid year-round playground for kayakers, canoers, and swimmers.

Once a lively logging town, Gualala has tamed considerably since the days loggers literally climbed the saloon walls with their spiked boots. Though a few real-life lumberjacks still end their day at the Gualala Hotel's saloon, the coastal town's main function these days is providing gas, groceries, and hardware for area residents. On the outskirts, however, are several excellent parks, beaches, and hiking trails; combine this with the region's glorious seascapes, and suddenly little mispronounced Gualala emerges as a serious contender among the better vacation spots on the North Coast.

One of the most enjoyable activities on the California coast is river and sea kayaking, and the **GUALALA RIVER** is ideal for beginner kayakers. **ADVENTURE RENTS** (downtown Gualala; 888/881-4386) provides the necessary gear, instruction, and transportation of the kayaks and canoes to and from the river.

SEA RANCH STYLE

The Sea Ranch cries out to weary commuters, lures helpless romantics, and soothes the stressed. It's no wonder, given a master development plan based on the belief that humans and nature can achieve a harmonious relationship, and that buildings can blend into the landscape rather than intrude upon it.

Oceanic Properties, a division of Castle and Cooke in Hawaii, bought 10 miles of wild Northern California coast in the early '60s. The property was divided by Highway 1, with wooded hills to the east and meadows to the west. Environmental consultants were engaged to study the area, and several San Francisco design firms were commissioned to create model buildings that would establish guidelines for future development. Design of the Hedgerow Houses, named after a nearby cypress hedgerow, and the early lodge went to architect Joseph Esherick, while the first condominiums were awarded to the architectural firm Moore Lyndon Turnbull Whitaker. Lawrence Halprin was the site planner for the designated 1,800 acres.

The resulting natural-wood structures—with distinctive shed roofs to deflect the wind, no eaves, and large windows adorned only by the view—almost immediately became famous worldwide. In fact, the original Sea Ranch condominium is recognized as one of the most influential American buildings of the period; it won the American Institute of Architects (AIA) 25-Year Award in 1991.

The concept of clustered hedgerow houses and densely sited condominiums gave way to more traditional lot-by-lot sites and fewer, smaller common areas. But proposed structures still had to be approved by the Sea Ranch Style/Design Committee and review board. Today there are 1,500 homes; only 25 percent of them are occupied year-round. Forty percent are vacation homes, and the remaining 35 percent are available for rent. Sea Ranch, like every organic community, is facing the challenge of how to deal with the ongoing forces of change.

But some things haven't changed. Seize the moment; treat yourself to a weekend, or a week, at this hauntingly beautiful place. You'll take away visions of spring wildflowers carpeting windswept meadows, the sounds of a mighty sea that never rests, and the smell of salty air laced with the scent of fresh cypress.   —*Mary Brent Cantarutti*

Of the six public beach access points along Highway 1 between Sea Ranch and Gualala, the one that offers the most bang for the $3 parking fee is the 195-acre **GUALALA POINT REGIONAL PARK** (707/785-2377). The park has 10 miles of trails through coastal grasslands, redwood forests, and river canyons, as well as picnic sites, camping areas, and excellent bird- and whale-watching along the mostly deserted beaches.

RESTAURANTS

St. Orres Restaurant / ★★★

36601 HWY 1, GUALALA; 707/884-3335

St. Orres Restaurant is one of Gualala's star attractions and one of the main reasons people keep coming back to this region. The constantly changing prix-fixe dinner menu focuses on wild game: dishes range from wild turkey tamales to tequila-marinated quail or sautéed medallions of venison. Self-taught chef Rosemary Campiformio's dark and fruity sauces and sublime soups are perfectly suited to the flavorful game, a distinctly Northern California rendition of French country cuisine. St. Orres's wine cellar stores a sizable selection of California wines. *$$$; MC, V for hotel guests only, otherwise no credit cards; checks OK; breakfast (guests only), dinner every day; beer and wine; reservations required; rosemary@mcn.org; www.saintorres.com; 2 miles N of Gualala on the E side of Hwy 1.* &

The Old Milano Hotel Restaurant / ★★

38300 HWY 1, GUALALA; 707/884-3256

If you can get over the odd feeling that you're dining in somebody's former living room (which you are), you're bound to enjoy a candlelight dinner in the Old Milano's small, wood-paneled, Victorian dining room. The executive chef serves his guests such tantalizing entrees as spice-crusted rack of Sonoma spring lamb, seared sea scallops in a ruby red vinaigrette, and a wonderful puff pastry appetizer filled with sautéed wild mushrooms. The menu changes weekly, but always includes fresh seafood, thick steaks, and fancy fowl. Come early and spend some time basking on the sun porch overlooking the ocean, and be sure to request a table by the fireplace. *$$$; MC, V for hotel guests only, otherwise no credit cards; checks OK; breakfast (guests only), dinner every day; beer and wine; reservations recommended; coast@oldmilanohotel.com; www.oldmilanohotel.com.* &

LODGINGS

The Old Milano Hotel / ★★

38300 HWY 1, GUALALA; 707/884-3256

Overlooking the sea above Castle Rock Cove, this picturesque Victorian bed-and-breakfast, built by the Lucchinetti family in 1905, is featured on the National Register of Historic Places. If you can drag yourself away from the veranda with the knockout ocean view and through the front door, you'll find six small yet elegant bedrooms upstairs (all with shared baths) and a downstairs suite replete with antique furnishings and a private bath. Elsewhere on the 3-acre estate are the Vine Cottage, located in the gardens and furnished with a brass bed, reading loft, wood-burning stove, and private bath; the Caboose, a genuine railroad caboose converted into the quaintest, coziest, and most private room at the inn (if not on the coast) with its wood-burning stove and small deck; four new cottages with fireplaces, ocean views, and hot tubs or showers for two; and a cliff-side Jacuzzi reserved for only two at a time. A full breakfast, included in the room rate, may be served in your room, on the garden patio, or by the fire in the parlor. *$$$; MC, V; checks OK; 2-night minimum on weekends and holidays; coast@oldmilanohotel.com; www.oldmilanohotel.com; 1 mile N of town, just N of the Food Company.* &

St. Orres / ★★★

36601 HWY 1, GUALALA; 707/884-3335

In the early '70s, a group of young architects and builders, inspired by the Russian architecture of the early Northern California settlers, took their back-to-the-land dreams to Gualala and created this dazzling copper-domed inn from redwood timbers scrounged from old logging mills and dilapidated bridges. Located just off Highway 1 and within walking distance of a sheltered, sandy cove, St. Orres consists of eight small, inexpensive rooms in the main lodge (two with great ocean views and all with shared baths) and eleven private cottages scattered throughout the 42 acres of wooded grounds. The best cottage is the ultra-rustic and surprisingly affordable Wild Flower Cabin, a former logging-crew shelter furnished with a cozy sleeping loft, a wood-burning stove (topped with cast-iron skillets), an adorable outside shower overlooking the woods, and even a gaggle of wild turkeys waiting for handouts at your doorstep. Another top choice: the gorgeous Sequoia Cottage, a solid-timbered charmer tucked into the edge of the forest. Start the day with a complimentary full breakfast (delivered to the cottages in baskets), spend the next few hours lolling around the nearby beaches, and have dinner at St. Orres's superb restaurant (see review, above). Reserve a table for dinner when you make your room reservation; breakfast comes with the room, but dinner doesn't, and the restaurant is almost always booked. *$$$; MC, V; checks OK; rosemary@mcn.org; www.saint orres.com; 2 miles N of Gualala on the E side of Hwy 1.* &

Point Arena

Fifteen miles north of Gualala is one of the smallest incorporated cities in California, Point Arena. This former bustling shipping port now has a population of 400; many residents are transplants from larger cities, and some have set up shop along the three-block **MAIN STREET**.

The **POINT ARENA LIGHTHOUSE** (707/882-2777; www.mcn.org/1/ palight) is the biggest attraction in the area. Built in 1870 after 10 ships ran aground here on a single stormy night, the fully operational light-house had to be rebuilt after the 1906 earthquake, but now it's solid enough for visitors to trudge up the 6-story tower's 145 steps for a standout view of the coast—if the fog has lifted. The dazzling 6-foot-wide, lead-crystal lens is worth the hike alone. The lighthouse is open 11am to 3:30pm weekdays, 10am to 3:30pm weekends in the summer (11am–2:30pm daily in the winter), and is located at the end of scenic Lighthouse Road, about 5 miles northwest of downtown Point Arena off Highway 1. The parking/tour/museum fee is only a few bucks.

Virtually isolated is the 5-mile sweep of shore, dunes, and meadows of **MANCHESTER STATE BEACH** (707/882-2463 or 707/937-5804). Though several access roads off Highway 1 lead to the shore, the closest one to Point Arena also happens to be the best—the 15-minute walk across the dunes from the parking lot is a leg-burner, but it's a small price to pay for your own private beach. Take the Stoneboro Road exit west off Highway 1; the beach is 2 miles north of the turnoff to Point Arena Lighthouse.

RESTAURANTS

Pangaea / ★★★

250 MAIN ST, POINT ARENA; 707/882-3001
When local chef Shannon Hughes decided to sell her restaurant, the community wondered what would become of their beloved haunt. They wonder no more. Current owners Rob and Jill Hunter are well suited to Pangaea's eclectic reputation. Chef Rob uses locally grown, organic products, specializes in seasonal cooking, and highlights cuisines from the couple's travels to Italy, Australia, Africa, and India. He shows his love of diversity with such dishes as the kung pao calamari, served with soba noodles, vegetables, and peanuts. Brined and grilled double-thick pork chops, accompanied with grilled peaches and goat cheese polenta, is another favorite. The Hunters have also expanded the restaurant to include the Green Room, a less-expensive alternative featuring dishes like soup, salad, Asian noodles, and pork carnitas. The rotating local art remains, as does the warm, comfortable ambience. *$$$; MC, V; checks OK; dinner Wed–Sun (winter hours may vary); beer and wine; reservations recommended; downtown just S of the post office.*

LODGINGS

Coast Guard House Historic Inn / ★★

695 ARENA COVE, POINT ARENA; 707/8882-2442 OR 800/524-9320
Poised high above Arena Cove, this historic Cape Cod–style inn was originally built by the Life-Saving Service in 1901 to lodge crew members. Beacon lamps, anchors, and a sea captain's hat tossed haphazardly on a table evoke memories of Point Arena's seafaring past, but the inn's Arts and Crafts interiors remain simple and uncluttered. The six guest rooms have all-cotton linens and fluffy down comforters and are stocked with organic soaps, shampoo, conditioner, and body lotion. The Surfman Cove Room, with windows on three sides, has a beautiful view of the

RIVERS MEET THE SEA

Imagine for a moment that there's a mighty matchmaker in the sky, bringing together powerful natural forces to flow as one. Mother Nature sprinkles in a generous potion of dynamic tension—unfolding seasons, capricious weather, and phases of the moon. The stage is set for a best-ever natural attraction: the meeting of the river and the sea. California's rugged Northern Coast offers not one but six easily accessible spots to observe the confluence of fresh and salt water.

Each of the settings is unique—from a commercial harbor to windswept beaches and sandy spits—but some environmental similarities exist. The blending of fresh river water and salty sea water produces an ecosystem called an estuary, complete with salt marshes, tidal flats, and creeks. Nutrients washed down from the river and, trapped in the estuary, support a diverse community of animals and plants. Oysters, crabs, scallops, and fish live under the water. When the tide goes out, shorebirds hunt for food on the beaches and mudflats. Migratory birds, such as pintails, mallards, and canvasbacks, appear in fall and spring.

The ever-changing environment brings magic to every moment. Land that is covered with cool water in the morning can be hot and dry in the afternoon. Ocean tides and river currents battle moment by moment. Visit one, visit them all, and enjoy another of nature's miracles.

Six spots on the North Coast well worth visiting are the **Russian River** at Goat Rock State Beach (707/865-2391), **Gualala River** at Gualala Point Regional Park (707/785-2468), **Big River** at Mendocino Headlands State Park (707/937-5397), **Navarro River** at Navarro River State Park, **Little River** at Van Damme State Park, **Noyo River** at Noyo Harbor, and **Ten Mile River** at MacKerricher State Park (707/937-5804 for the last four parks).   —*Mary Brent Cantarutti*

ocean and cove, a wood-burning stove, and a sunken Japanese tub. Top choice is the separate Boathouse Cottage, a replica of the original Generator House (except for the spa tub for two, Swedish wood-burning stove, and private patio overlooking the cove). An ocean-view hot tub is available for guests. A full breakfast, served by amiable innkeepers Mia and Kevin Gallagher, is included in the room rate. *$$$; MC, V; checks OK; coast@mcn.org; www.coastguardhouse.com; off Iversen Ave, 1 mile W of downtown Point Arena.*

Elk

Once known as Greenwood, this tiny former logging town was renamed Elk by the postal service when someone realized there was another town in California called Greenwood. For a such a small community (population 250), it sure has a booming tourist trade: six inns, four restaurants, and one authentic Irish pub. Its close proximity to the big tourist town of Mendocino, a mere 30-minute drive up the coast, is one reason for its popularity. Elk's paramount appeal, however, is its dramatic shoreline; the series of immense sea stacks here creates one of the most awesome seascapes on the California coast.

RESTAURANTS

The Harbor House Restaurant / ★★★

5600 S HWY 1 (HARBOR HOUSE INN), ELK; 800/720-7474

The four-course prix-fixe dinners served at the Harbor House Restaurant change nightly, but they always begin with a small, hot-from-the-oven loaf of bread that's perfect for sopping up the chef's delicious soups, such as the tomato-basil or Indian spice-spinach. The salad, made from homegrown vegetables, might be a combination of greens tossed with an herb vinaigrette or sprouts mixed with olives, water chestnuts, and a toasted sesame-seed dressing. The seafood is harvested from local waters, and the meats and cheeses come from nearby farms. Expect to find entrees such as ravioli stuffed with crab, fennel, and shiitakes in a Pernod cream sauce or seared sea scallops on roasted-yellow-pepper rouille with Spanish basmati pilaf. Many of the fine wines offered are locally produced. To take full advantage of the restaurant's spectacular view, beg for a window table (alas, you can't reserve a particular table). The only seating (which is very limited when the inn is full) is at 7pm. $$$$; MC, V; checks OK; dinner every day; beer and wine; reservations required; harborhs@mcn.org; www.theharbor houseinn.com; in the Harbor House Inn, at the N end of Elk.

LODGINGS

Greenwood Pier Inn / ★★★

5926 HWY 1, ELK; 707/877-9997

What separates this cliff-top wonder from the dozens of other precariously perched inns along Highway 1 are its rooms' fantastic interiors and the brilliant flower gardens gracing the property. The inn offers 12 guest rooms, including three detached cliff-hanging suites (Cliffhouse and the two Sea Castles) and the separate Garden Cottage. All the units have private decks with stunning views of Greenwood Cove, and all guests have access to a hot tub on the cliff's edge. The whimsical avant-garde decor and tile and marble detailing in most of the rooms are the work of proprietor/artist Kendrick Petty. Some units also feature Petty's colorful airbrush collages, and all the rooms have private baths, fireplaces or wood-burning stoves, and stereos. The elegantly rustic Cliffhouse is a favorite, with its expansive deck, marble fireplace, whirlpool tub, and Oriental carpets. While the suites and castles are rather expensive, the rooms in the main house are moderately priced. Room rates include a continental breakfast delivered to your doorstep, and you can even have dinner from the cafe brought to your room. *$$$$; AE, MC, V; local checks only; gwpier@mcn.org; www.green pierinn.com; center of town.* &

The Harbor House Inn / ★★★

5600 S HWY 1, ELK; 800/720-7474
Constructed in 1916 in the classic Craftsman style, the majestic Harbor House was originally an executive lodge for lumber company executives. Purchased by Elle and Sam Haynes in 1998, the inn has recently been refurbished. There are six rooms in the main house, with classic and antique furnishings, fireplaces, decks, and private baths throughout. The names of the rooms, such as Cypress, Harbor, and Lookout, reflect the inn's magical natural setting. And should you want a cottage nestled among the redwoods, there are four to choose from, intimate and tastefully appointed. Down comforters, featherbeds, luxurious robes, and CD players come with each of the 10 rooms. Fine dining is a tradition at the Harbor House Inn; a full breakfast and four-course dinner for two are included in the rates. *$$$$; MC, V; checks OK; harborhs@mcn.org; www.theharborhouseinn.com; N end of Elk.*

Albion

A renowned haven for pot growers until an increase in police surveillance and property taxes drove most of them away, **ALBION** is more a free-spirited ideal community than an actual town. A white wooden bridge, the last of its kind on Highway 1, marks the entrance to town.

RESTAURANTS

Albion River Inn Restaurant / ★★

3790 HWY 1, ALBION; 707/937-1919 OR 800/479-7944
Chef Stephen Smith has presided over the Albion Inn's ocean-view dining room for seven years, and contented diners keep coming back for more of his consistently good cooking. Fresh local produce complements such dishes as braised Sonoma rabbit, grilled sea bass, and rock shrimp pasta. The extensive award-winning wine list—more than 500 choices—includes hard-to-find North Coast labels. Arrive before nightfall to ooh and aah over the view. *$$$; AE, DIS, MC, V; checks OK; dinner every day; beer and wine; reservations recommended; on the NW side of the Albion bridge.* &

The Ledford House Restaurant / ★★

3000 HWY 1, ALBION; 707/937-0282
It's rare when an ocean-view restaurant's food is as good as the view, but owners Lisa and Tony Geer manage to pull it off, serving provençal-style cuisine in a wonderfully romantic cliff-top setting. The menu, which changes monthly, offers a choice of bistro dishes, such as Antoine's Cas-

soulet (lamb, pork, garlic sausage, and duck confit slowly cooked with white beans), rack of lamb, and roast duckling. Vegetarian entrees and soups are always featured as well. With a view like this, a window table at sunset is a must. After dinner, sidle up to the bar and listen to the live music, featured nightly. *$$$; AE, DC, MC, V; checks OK; dinner Wed–Sun (closed for 3–4 weeks last of Feb–Mar 1); full bar; reservations recommended; tony@ledfordhouse.com; www.ledfordhouse.com; exit W off Hwy 1 at Spring Grove Rd.* &

LODGINGS

Albion River Inn / ★★★

3790 HWY 1, ALBION; 707/937-1919 OR 800/479-7944

This seaside inn, poised high above Albion Cove where the Albion River meets the sea, is one of the finest on the California coast, and guests return again and again. Under the same ownership for a couple of decades, each of the 20 New England–style cottages feature distinctive antique and contemporary furnishings, private decks, king- or queen-size beds, fireplaces, and lots of potted plants. Check out the six rooms that have a spa tub for two. All the accommodations come with colorful pocket gardens and out-of-this world views. Breakfast, served in the restaurant (see review, above), is included in the rates. *$$$$; AE, DIS, MC, V; checks OK; ari@mcn.org; www.albionriverinn.com; on the NW side of the Albion bridge.* &

Little River

Once a bustling logging and shipbuilding community, Little River is now more like a suburb of Mendocino. The town does a brisk business handling the tourist overflow from its neighbor 2 miles up the coast; vacationers in the know reserve a room in serene Little River and make forays into Mendocino only for dining and shopping.

The town is near **VAN DAMME STATE PARK** (707/937-5804), a 2,337-acre preserve blanketed with ferns and second-growth redwoods. One of the finest state parks on the Mendocino coast, it has a small beach, visitor center, and campground, but its main attraction is the 15 miles of spectacularly lush trails—ideal for a stroll or a jog—that start at the beach and wind through the redwood-covered hills. **FERN CANYON TRAIL** is the park's most popular, an easy and incredibly scenic 2½-mile hiking and bicycling path that crosses over the Little River. You can also hike or drive (most of the way) to Van Damme's peculiar **PYGMY FOREST**, an eerie scrub forest of waist-high stunted trees. To reach the Pygmy Forest by car, follow Highway 1 south of the park and turn up Little River Airport Road, then head uphill 2¾ miles.

RESTAURANTS

Heritage House Restaurant / ★★★

5200 HWY 1 (LITTLE RIVER INN), LITTLE RIVER; 707/937-5885 OR 800/235-5885

The Heritage House offers high-quality cuisine served in several dining rooms, with alfresco seating for breakfast and brunch on sunny days. The menu, which changes seasonally, may include such appetizers as local cod cakes and grilled polenta with wild mushroom ragout. Main-course selections vary from braised lamb shank with Basque white beans to pan-roasted pork chops, grilled salmon, and roast Peking duck breast. The extensive wine list ranks among the highest-rated in the country. *$$$$; MC, V; checks OK; breakfast Mon–Fri, dinner every day, brunch Sat–Sun (closed briefly in Dec and Jan 2–right before Valentine's Day); full bar; reservations required for dinner; heritage@mcn.org; www. innaccess.com/hhi/; just S of Van Damme State Park.* &

Little River Inn Restaurant / ★★

7750 HWY 1, LITTLE RIVER; 707/937-5942 OR 888/466-5683

The Little River Inn Restaurant is a casual place for breakfast or dinner but, oddly enough, is the only room at the inn without an ocean view. Chef Silver Canul maintains the house tradition of using mostly local products: fresh fish from nearby Noyo Harbor; lamb, beef, and potatoes from the town of Comptche; and greens and vegetables from local gardens. For breakfast try the popular Ole's Swedish Pancakes. *$$$; AE, MC, V; checks OK; breakfast, dinner every day; full bar; reservations recommended; lria@mcn.org; www.littleriverinn.com; across from the Little River Market and Post Office.* &

LODGINGS

Glendeven Inn / ★★★

8221 HWY 1, LITTLE RIVER; 707/937-0083 OR 800/822-4536

Some years ago Glendeven was named one of the twelve best inns in America by *Country Inns* magazine, and rightly so. This stately 19th-century farmhouse resides among 2½ acres of well-tended gardens and heather-covered headlands that extend all the way to the blue Pacific. The ten spacious rooms and suites feature an uncluttered mix of country antiques and contemporary art. For the ultimate in luxury, stay in the Pinewood or Bayloft Suites in the Stevenscroft Annex—each has a sitting parlor, a fireplace, and a partial ocean view. The cozy East Farmington Room, with its private garden deck and fireplace, is another good choice. Above the Glendeven Gallery, the inn's fine-arts boutique, sits the fabulous Barn House Suite, a two-story, redwood-paneled house ideal for families or two couples. After breakfast, which is included with your room, walk to the beautiful fern-rimmed canyon trails in nearby Van

Damme State Park. *$$$$; AE, MC; checks OK; innkeeper@glen deven.com; www.innaccess.com/gdi/; 2 miles S of Mendocino.*

Heritage House / ★★★

5200 HWY 1, LITTLE RIVER; 707/937-5885 OR 800/235-5885
Immortalized as the ultimate bed-and-breakfast lodge in the movie *Same Time, Next Year*, Heritage House has a history well suited to Hollywood melodrama: its secluded farmhouse was used as a safe house for smugglers of Chinese laborers during the 19th century, for rumrunners during Prohibition, and for the notorious bandit "Baby Face" Nelson during the '30s. Since 1949, however, the hotel has catered to a considerably tamer crowd. The inn is situated on a bluff overlooking a rocky cove and is surrounded by 37 acres of cypress trees, bountiful flower and vegetable gardens, and expansive green lawns. Lodging consists of three guest rooms in the main building, 63 cottages, and a detached 1877 farmhouse. The best rooms are the cliff-hanging Same Time and Next Year Cottages with their king-size beds, fireplaces, and extraordinary ocean views (the Next Year Cottage also has a whirlpool tub). Unlike in years past, room rates no longer include breakfast and dinner at the restaurant. *$$$$; AE, MC, V; checks OK; closed briefly in Dec and Jan 2–right before Valentine's Day; heritage@mcn.org; www.innaccess.com/ hhi/; just S of Van Damme State Park.* &

The Inn at Schoolhouse Creek / ★★

7051 N HWY 1, LITTLE RIVER; 707/937-5525 OR 800/731-5525
Whereas most small inns located along the Mendocino coast have to make do with an acre or less, the Inn at Schoolhouse Creek has the luxury of spreading its nine private, immaculate cottages amidst 10 acres of beautiful flower gardens, lush meadows, and cypress groves. As a result, the instant you pull into the driveway you feel like you've gotten away from it all and have entered a more tranquil environment. Most of Schoolhouse Creek's cottages sleep two, though a few can fit small families. The turn-of-the-century cottages are quaint and lovely, particularly the Cypress Cottage with its own private yard graced by an inviting pair of Adirondack chairs. *$$$; MC, V; checks OK; innkeeper@schoolhousecreek.com; www.innatschoolhousecreek.com; just S of Little River.* &

Little River Inn / ★★

7750 HWY 1, LITTLE RIVER; 707/937-5942 OR 888/466-5683
Set on a 225-acre parcel of oceanfront land, the Little River Inn is an ideal retreat for those North Coast travelers who simply can't leave their golf clubs or tennis rackets at home; it's often jokingly referred to as the poor man's Pebble Beach. Susan McKinney, her husband, Mel, and brother Danny own and operate the inn and restaurant (as well as the nine-hole golf course, driving range, putting green, and two lighted championship tennis courts). All the estate's 65 rooms and cottages offer spectacular

ocean views, many feature fireplaces, and some also have whirlpool tubs (if you prefer to relax indoors, check out the inn's extensive video library). The antique-filled rooms in the main Victorian house are preferable to the north wing's motel-style units, which suffer from uninspired decor. In addition to lodging, the restaurant (see review, above) offers breakfast and dinner every day. *$$$$; AE, MC, V; checks OK; lria@mcn.org; www.littleriverinn.com; across from the Little River Market and Post Office.* &

Rachel's Inn / ★★

8200 N HWY 1, LITTLE RIVER; 707/937-0088 OR 800/347-9252
Strategically sandwiched between Van Damme State Park and the Mendocino headlands is Rachel Binah's 1860s Victorian farmhouse, one of the best bed-and-breakfasts on the Mendocino coast. Each of the seven rooms and three suites has a queen-size bed with a fluffy comforter, a private bath, and original artwork (including some by Binah); six rooms also have fireplaces. Gardeners will especially like the Blue Room, complete with a balcony overlooking the back garden, meadow, and trees. The Parkside Cottage, nestled in a stand of cypress trees, comes with a private back porch, wet bar with coffeemaker and refrigerator, whirlpool bathtub, gas fireplace, and window seat. The inn's main attraction is Binah, a vivacious innkeeper who spends her time campaigning to protect our nation's coastline from offshore oil drilling when she's not busy welcoming guests or preparing one of her grand breakfasts. *$$$$; MC, V; checks OK; www.rachelsinn.com; 1½ miles S of Mendocino.* &

Stevenswood Lodge / ★★★

8211 HWY 1, LITTLE RIVER; 707/937-2810 OR 800/421-2810
Stevenswood Lodge is for people who want the comforts of a modern hotel—cable television, telephone, refrigerator, honor bar—without feeling like they're staying at a Holiday Inn. As it works out, not many Holiday Inns are surrounded on three sides by a verdant 2,400-acre forest, or located just a quarter of a mile from the Mendocino shoreline, or embellished with sculpture gardens and contemporary art displays throughout the grounds. Built in 1988, the lodge's one wheelchair-accessible room and nine suites are outfitted with handcrafted burl-maple furniture, large windows with striking vistas (some with a partial ocean view), private bathrooms, and access to several shared decks. The Pullen Room has a particularly pleasant view of the forest and gardens. Recent additions to the lodge include a restaurant offering gourmet breakfasts and dinners to guests and the public, as well as two spas set within the forest canyon (one spa is available to all guests and the other is private and may be reserved by guests on an hourly basis). *$$$$; AE, DIS, MC, V; checks OK; info@stevenswood.com; www.stevenswood.com; 2 miles S of Mendocino.* &

Mendocino

The grande dame of Northern California's coastal tourist towns, this refurbished replica of a New England–style fishing village—complete with a white-spired church—has managed to retain more of its charm and allure than most North Coast vacation spots. Motels, fast-food chains, and anything hinting of development are strictly forbidden here (even the town's only automated teller is subtly recessed into the historic Masonic Building), resulting in the almost-passable illusion that Mendocino is just another quaint little coastal community. Try to find a parking space, however, and the illusion quickly fades; even the four-hour drive fails to deter hordes of Bay Area residents.

Founded in 1852, Mendocino is still home to a few anglers and loggers, although writers, artists, actors, and other urban transplants now far outnumber the natives. Spring is the best time to visit, when parking spaces are plentiful and the climbing tea roses and wisteria are in full bloom. Start with a casual tour of the town, and end with a stroll around Mendocino's celebrated headlands. Suddenly the long drive and inflated room rates seem a trivial price to pay for visiting one of the most beautiful places on earth.

To tour Mendocino proper, lose the car and head out on foot to the **TOTE FÊTE BAKERY** (10450 Lansing St; 707/937-3383). Fuel up with a double cappuccino and cinnamon bun, then throw away your map of the town and start walking—the **SHOPPING DISTRICT** of Mendocino is so small it can be covered in less than an hour, so why bother planning your attack? One must-see shop is the **GALLERY BOOKSHOP & BOOK-WINKLE'S CHILDREN'S BOOKS** (45098 Main St; 707/937-BOOK), one of the best independent bookstores in Northern California, with a wonderful selection of books for kids, cooks, and local-history buffs. Another is **MENDOCINO JAMS & PRESERVES** (440 Main St; 707/ 937-1037 or 800/ 708-1196), a town landmark that offers free tastings—à la cute little bread chips—of its luscious marmalades, dessert toppings, mustards, chutneys, and other spreads.

As with many towns that hug the Northern California coast, Mendocino's premier attractions are provided by Mother Nature and the Department of Parks and Recreation, which means they're free (or nearly free). **MENDOCINO HEADLANDS STATE PARK**, the grassy stretch of land between the village of Mendocino and the ocean, is one of the town's most popular sites. The park's flat, 3-mile trail winds along the edge of a heather-covered bluff, providing spectacular sunset views and good lookout points for spotting seabirds and California gray whales. The headlands' main access point is at the west end of Main Street—or skip the footwork altogether and take the scenic motorist's route along Heeser Drive off Lansing Street. Mendocino State Park Visitor Center is located at Ford House (735 Main St; 707/937-5397).

About 2 miles north of Mendocino, off Highway 1, is the worst-kept secret on the coast: **RUSSIAN GULCH STATE PARK** (707/937-5804), a veritable paradise for campers, hikers, and abalone divers. After paying a $5 entry fee, pick up a trail map at the park entrance and find the path to **DEVIL'S PUNCH BOWL**—a 200-foot-long, sea-carved tunnel that has partially collapsed in the center, creating an immense blowhole that's particularly spectacular during a storm. Even better is the 5½-mile round-trip hike along **FALLS LOOP TRAIL** to the **RUSSIAN GULCH FALLS**, a misty 35-foot waterfall secluded in the deep old-growth forest.

If you have a passion for plants and flowers, spend a few bucks on the admission fee to the **MENDOCINO COAST BOTANICAL GARDENS** (18220 Hwy 1; 707/964-4352; www.gardenbythesea.org), located 2 miles south of Fort Bragg. The nonprofit gardens feature 47 acres of plants—ranging from azaleas and rhododendrons to dwarf conifers and ferns—as well as a picnic area, retail nursery, and gift store.

The black sheep of Mendocino's hiking trails is **JUG HANDLE STATE RESERVE'S ECOLOGICAL STAIRCASE TRAIL** (707/937-5804). This 5-mile round-trip trail is a wonderful hike and gets surprisingly little traffic. The attraction is a series of naturally formed, staircase-like bluffs—each

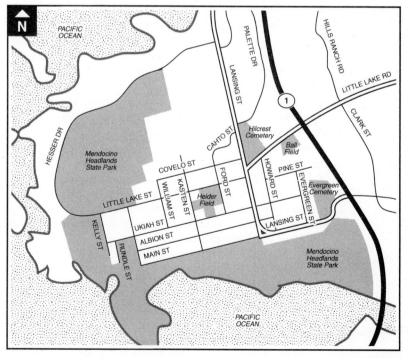

about 100 feet higher and 100,000 years older than the one below it—that differ dramatically in ecological formation: from beaches to headlands to an amazing pygmy forest filled with waist-high, century-old trees. The trail entrance is located on Highway 1, 1½ miles north of the town of Caspar, between Mendocino and Fort Bragg.

After a full day of adventuring, why not top off the evening with a little nightcap and music? If you appreciate classical tunes and warm snifters of brandy, take a stroll down Mendocino's Main Street to the elegant bar and lounge at the **MENDOCINO HOTEL AND RESTAURANT** (see review, below). If blue jeans and baseball caps are more your style, hang out with the guys at **DICK'S PLACE** (45080 Main St; 707/937-5643), which has the cheapest drinks in town and the sort of jukebox 'n' jiggers atmosphere you'd expect from this former logging town's oldest bar. For a rowdy night of dancing and drinking, head a few miles up Highway 1 to **CASPAR INN** (Caspar Rd exit off Hwy 1, ¼ mile N of Mendocino and 4 miles S of Fort Bragg; 707/964-5565), the last true roadhouse in California, where everything from rock and jazz to reggae and blues is played live Thursday through Saturday nights starting at 9:30pm.

RESTAURANTS

MacCallum House Restaurant / ★★★

45020 ALBION ST, MENDOCINO; 707/937-5763

Using the freshest ingredients—seafood straight from the coast, organic meats and produce from neighboring farms and ranches—chef/owner Alan Kantor whips up some wonderful North Coast cuisine. Entrees on the seasonally changing menu may range from roasted wild salmon with saffron-pistachio risotto and arugula pesto to pan-seared duck breast with huckleberry-honey vinegar sauce. Lighter and less expensive fare, such as the delicious pan-charred rock-cod tacos with handmade corn tortillas, are served at the adjoining Grey Whale Bar & Cafe, a nice alternative for those who wish to forgo a formal dinner in the elegant dining room. Your room will be steps away if you're staying at the MacCallum House Inn, Mendocino's finest Victorian landmark. *$$$; MC, V; no checks; dinner every day (closed Jan–mid-Feb); full bar; reservations recommended; macmendo@mcn.org; www.maccallumhousedining.com; between Kasten and Lansing Sts.* ᚼ

The Mousse Café / ★★☆

390 KASTEN ST, MENDOCINO; 707/937-4323

Rising triumphantly from its ashes—literally—this small, popular cafe has made an amazing comeback after burning to the ground a few years back. Formerly known as the haunt for Mendocino's confessed chocoholics, the Mousse has switched to a more substantial (read healthier) menu that makes the most of local and organic meats, herbs, and vegetables (the

Caesar salad, fashioned with a perfect balance of Parmesan and a robust smack of garlic, is particularly good). Popular entrees are the fresh mixed seafood cakes served over basmati rice with a roasted red pepper rémoulade and the lavender-smoked double-thick pork chop served with roasted yam and apple puree. Make a reservation, because there's usually a waiting list for dinner. Of course, dessert (especially the wicked Blackout Cake) is as good as it ever was. *$$$; MC, V; checks OK; lunch Mon–Sat, dinner every day, brunch Sun (closed in Jan); beer and wine; reservations recommended; at the corner of Kasten and Albion Sts.* &

955 Ukiah Street Restaurant / ★★★

955 UKIAH ST, MENDOCINO; 707/937-1955

This relatively unknown Mendocino restaurant is described by local epicureans as "the sleeper restaurant on the coast." The powers behind the restaurant's doors are Jamie and Peggy Griffith, who have managed to turn 955 Ukiah into a serious (and slightly less expensive) rival to its recently sold neighbor, Cafe Beaujolais. The dramatic interior, with its split-level dining room, 20-foot ceilings, rustic wood-trimmed walls, and elegant table settings, sets the mood for the haute cuisine, which might include seared pork loin stuffed with prosciutto, crispy duck served with ginger-apple brandy sauce, and a thick swordfish steak resting in a red chile–tomatillo sauce. The upstairs section can get cramped and a little noisy, so try to sit downstairs—preferably at the corner window table— where the vaulted ceiling imparts a comfortable sense of space. *$$$; MC, V; checks OK; dinner Wed–Sun; beer and wine; reservations recommended; Ukiah and Evergreen Sts, E end of town.* &

The Stanford Inn by the Sea Restaurant / ★★★

HWY 1 AND COMPTCHE-UKIAH RD, MENDOCINO; 707/937-5615 OR 800/331-8884

To complement their environmentally friendly lodge (see review, below), Joan and Jeff Stanford have taken a huge gamble and opened the region's only fancy vegetarian/vegan restaurant. The menu varies monthly to take advantage of seasonal organic produce, some of which derives from the lodge's own gardens. Dishes range from lighter fare—herbed asiago polenta cakes sauteed in a roasted garlic–chardonnay sauce with local organic shiitake mushrooms (fantastic)—to hearty entrees such as tarragon roasted acorn squash filled with wild rice, shiitake mushrooms, roasted garlic, and caramelized apples. Truly, these are masterfully crafted dishes that explode the myth that it takes meat to make a meal. Though the dining room exudes a rustic elegance, dining attire is anything but formal. *$$; AE, DC, DIS, MC, V; checks OK; breakfast, lunch Mon–Sat, dinner every day, brunch Sun; full bar; reservations recommended; 1 mile S of Mendocino at Hwy 1 and Comptche-Ukiah Rd.*

LODGINGS

Agate Cove Inn / ★★★

11201 N LANSING ST, MENDOCINO; 707/937-0551 OR 800/527-3111
Completely renovated in 1995 with light pine furnishings and "casual country" decor, the cottages at Agate Cove offer seclusion, privacy, and views that in-town B&Bs just can't match. All but one of the 10 cottages have good views of the ocean, king- or queen-size beds, down comforters, CD players, TVs with VCRs (and a free video and CD library), wood-burning stoves or gas fireplaces, and private decks. In the morning you'll find the *San Francisco Chronicle* on your doorstep, and you can peruse the paper at your leisure over a bountiful country breakfast in the main house's enclosed porch. *$$$$; AE, MC, V; checks OK; agate@mcn.org; www.agatecove.com; ½ mile N of downtown.*

Cypress Cove / ★★★

CHAPMAN DR, MENDOCINO; 707/937-1456 OR 800/942-6300
Hidden among the cypress trees that encircle the bluff across the bay from Mendocino is Suzanne and Jim Hay's Cypress Cove, a pair of bright, modern suites stacked atop each other in a way that results in one of the best views of the Mendocino coast. Each abode is lavishly appointed with a wood-burning fireplace, fully equipped kitchen, spa tub, separate shower, stereo, and TV with a VCR, but it's the stellar view from the large bay windows and private deck that will make you fall instantly in love with this place. Trust us: if you're looking for a romantic weekend retreat, this is where you want to be. *$$$$ MC, V; checks OK; jimbay@mcn.org; www.cypresscove.com; off Hwy 1 at the S end of Mendocino Bay (call for directions).*

John Dougherty House / ★★

571 UKIAH ST, MENDOCINO; 707/937-5266 OR 800/486-2104
This classic saltbox is a wonderful example of why so many movies supposedly set in New England (*The Russians Are Coming, Summer of '42*) are actually filmed in Mendocino. The John Dougherty House features authentic Early Americana throughout: stenciled walls, Early American furniture, and all-cotton linens on the beds. Innkeepers Marion and David Wells have given each of the six rooms touches of individual charm, but your first choice should be one of the spacious two-room suites: the Starboard Cottage, Port Cottage, or everyone's favorite, Kit's Cabin—a small private cottage hidden in the flower garden. All the rooms have a private bath, and most have a TV, a small refrigerator, and a wood-burning stove. An expansive breakfast including homemade bread and scones is served next to a crackling fire. *$$$; DIS, MC, V; checks OK; jdhbmw@mcn.org; www.jdhouse.com; Ukiah St just W of Kasten St.*

Joshua Grindle Inn / ★★★
44800 LITTLE LAKE RD, MENDOCINO; 707/937-4143 OR 800/GRINDLE
The most authentic of Mendocino's many New England–style B&Bs, this masterpiece was built in 1879 by the town's banker, Joshua Grindle. Startlingly white against a backdrop of wind-whipped cypress trees, the two-story beauty has lovely bay windows and a wraparound front porch trimmed with gingerbread arches. There are five Early American rooms in the clapboard house (including one with a whirlpool tub and fireplace), two in the cottage, and three in an old-fashioned water tower set back in the trees. Top picks are any of the cute water-tower rooms or the Library Room with its country-pine furnishings, four-poster bed, and 19th-century hand-decorated tiles encircling the fireplace. All of the rooms have sitting areas and private baths. The large front lawn and garden, equipped with a pair of Adirondack chairs and a redwood picnic table, is an ideal place to relax in the sun. *$$$$; MC, V; no checks; stay@joshgrin.com; www.joshgrin.com; E end of Little Lake Rd.*

Mendocino Farmhouse / ★★
43410 COMPTCHE RD, MENDOCINO; 707/937-0241 OR 800/475-1536
Once you emerge from deep within the redwood forest surrounding Marge and Bud Kamb's secluded estate, you know you're going to be very happy here. First to greet you is one of the Kambs' friendly farm dogs, followed by their can't-pet-me-enough cats, and finally the instantly likable Kambs themselves. All five rooms—filled with antique furnishings and fresh flowers from the surrounding English gardens—have private baths, queen- or king-size beds, and, if you listen carefully, echoes of the nearby ocean; all but one have fireplaces as well. A real country breakfast (straight from the chicken coop) is served each morning at tables-for-two in the sitting room, after which the dogs give free lessons in the meadow on how to loll around in the sunshine. *$$; MC, V; checks OK; mkamb@mcn.org; www.mendocinofarmhouse.com; off Olson Ln.*

Mendocino Hotel and Restaurant / ★★
45080 MAIN ST, MENDOCINO; 707/937-0511 OR 800/548-0513
The Mendocino Hotel, built in 1878, combines modern amenities—telephones, full bathrooms, room service—with turn-of-the-century Victorian furnishings to create a romantic yesteryear setting with today's creature comforts. The hotel's 51 rooms—all decorated with quality antiques, patterned wallpapers, and old prints and photos—range from inexpensive European-style rooms with shared baths to elaborate garden suites with fireplaces, king-size beds, balconies, and parlors. Suites 225A and 225B, on the hotel's third floor, have wonderful views of Mendocino Bay from their private balconies. Other favorites are the deluxe rooms with private baths, particularly rooms 213 and 224, which face the water. Breakfast and lunch are served downstairs in the verdant Garden Cafe.

For dinner, chef Colleen Murphy's California-style cuisine, which might include pan-seared ahi tuna, double-baked pork chops, and prime rib au jus, is offered in the adjacent Mendocino Hotel Restaurant's Victorian dining room. Budding sommeliers should inquire about the hotel's Winemaker Dinners, featured occasionally on Sundays October through May. *$$$$; AE, MC, V; checks OK; reservations@mendocinohotel.com; www. mendocinohotel.com; between Lansing and Kasten Sts.* &

The Stanford Inn by the Sea/Big River Lodge / ★★★★

HWY I AND COMPTCHE-UKIAH RD, MENDOCINO; 707/937-5615 OR 800/331-8884

Hats off to Joan and Jeff Stanford, the environmentally conscious couple who turned this parcel of prime coastal property and the former Big River Lodge into something more than a magnificent resort. It's a true ecosystem, a place where plants, animals, and people coexist in one of the most unforgettable lodging experiences in California. Upon entering the estate you'll see several tiers of raised garden beds, where a wide variety of vegetables, herbs, spices, and edible flowers are organically grown for local grocers and restaurants. Watching your every move as you proceed up the driveway are the Stanfords' extended family of 14 curious llamas, which, besides providing an endless source of entertainment, do their part in fertilizing the gardens. Guests may also bring along their own menagerie of critters, be they pet dogs, cats, parrots, or iguanas. Also on the grounds is a gigantic, plant-filled greenhouse that encloses a grand swimming pool, sauna, and spa. And if all this doesn't provide you with enough diversions, there's also a mountain bike and canoe shop on the property. The inn's 23 rooms and 10 suites display a mixture of styles, from units with dark wood walls, deep burgundy furnishings, and four-poster beds to sun-streaked suites with pine-wood interiors, country antiques, and sleigh beds topped with down comforters. All of the rooms feature decks with ocean views, fireplaces or Waterford stoves, TVs with VCRs, telephones, and sitting areas. The isolated, utterly romantic River Cottage sits right on the water's edge—an ideal honeymooners' hideaway. A cooked-to-order full breakfast, served in the restaurant (see Restaurants, above), afternoon snacks, and evening wine and hors d'oeuvres are included in the price. *$$$$; AE, DC, DIS, MC, V; checks OK; stanford@stanfordinn.com; www.stanfordinn. com; ½ mile S of Mendocino.* &

Whitegate Inn / ★★★

499 HOWARD ST, MENDOCINO; 707/937-4892 OR 800/531-7282

The Whitegate Inn is billed as a setting that fast "catches the eye and then captures the heart." You'll agree, from the moment you see the rambling gardens scarcely contained behind a white picket fence, enter the elegant drawing room showcasing ocean views, and sink into a comfy European featherbed. When you decide to get up, there'll be a scrumptious morning repast waiting in the dining room, featuring such delicacies as caramel-apple French toast served on bone china. Not to rush—there's plenty of time for everything in this beautifully executed Victorian setting master-minded by Carol and George Bechtloff. Just ask the stars—Julia Roberts, Mel Gibson, Bette Davis, and Angela Lansbury all stayed at the inn while shooting movies. Choose from six rooms individually decorated with classic antiques, featuring fireplaces, immaculate private baths, luxurious bedding, TVs, and garden or ocean views. The Enchanted Cottage, secluded in the garden, has a private entrance and deck, king-size bed, and claw-footed tub and shower. The gracious staff brings warmth and casual elegance to your entire lodging experience. *$$$; MC, V; checks OK; innkeeper@whitegateinn.com; www.whitegateinn.com; corner of Howard and Ukiah Sts.*

Fort Bragg

Originally built in 1855 as a military outpost to supervise the Pomo Indian Reservation, Fort Bragg is still primarily a logging and fishing town proud of its century-old timber-and-trawler heritage. But not a year goes by in Fort Bragg without yet another commercial fishing vessel being converted into a whale-watching boat or an unemployed logger trading in his chain saw for a set of carving knives.

Two popular festivals are celebrated annually: **PAUL BUNYAN DAYS** on Labor Day weekend features a big Labor Day parade and log-cutting races, and the annual **WHALE FESTIVAL**, held the third Saturday of March, includes ranger-led talks about the cetaceans, a Whale Run, and a beer and chowder tasting.

If you've visited all of Mendocino's boutiques and still haven't shrugged the shopping bug, head over to **HISTORIC DOWNTOWN** Fort Bragg. The facades of buildings have been restored to their early 1900s look; inside you'll find shops, galleries, and restaurants—all within walking distance of each other. Two dangerous places for a credit card are the **UNION LUMBER COMPANY STORE** (corner of Main and Redwood Sts), and **ANTIQUE ROW** (Franklin St between Laurel and Redwood).

One of the prettiest—and largest—public beaches on the Mendocino coast is **MACKERRICHER STATE PARK** (707/937-5804), located 3 miles north of Fort Bragg off Highway 1. The 8-mile shoreline is the perfect place to while away an afternoon, and it's free-admission to boot. The highlight of the park is the **LAGUNA POINT SEAL WATCHING STATION**, a fancy name for a small wooden deck that overlooks the harbor seals sunning themselves on the rocks below.

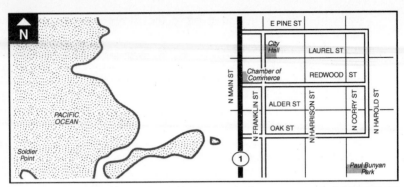

FORT BRAGG

All aboard: Fort Bragg's popular **SKUNK TRAIN** (100 Laurel St Depot, Fort Bragg; 707/961-2940) is leaving the station. The intriguing name is derived from the odoriferous mix of diesel fuel and gasoline once used to power the train—you could smell it coming. Depending on which day you depart, a steam-, diesel-, or electric-engine train will take you on a scenic 6- to 7-hour round-trip journey through the magnificent redwoods to the city of Willits and back again (or you can take the 3½-hour round-trip excursion to Northspur). Reservations are recommended, especially in summer.

If you're passing through between December and April, be sure to watch the migrating California gray whales and humpback whales make their annual appearances along the North Coast. Although they're visible from the bluffs, you can practically meet the 40-ton cetaceans face to face by boarding one of the **WHALE-WATCHING** boats in Fort Bragg. **ALL ABOARD ADVENTURES WITH TIM** (707/964-2079) offers two-hour tours for $25 per adult, departing from the Old Fish House on North Harbor Drive in Fort Bragg. Another great way to get out on the ocean is to book a trip on one of the numerous **FISHING CHARTERS** that depart from Noyo Harbor. For approximately $45 per person, which includes pole and bait, **TELSTAR CHARTERS** (707/964-8770) will take you on a five-hour salmon- or rock-cod-fishing trip (whale-watching excursions are also available Jan–Mar). No experience is necessary; gear, instruction, and fish-cleaning services are provided.

RESTAURANTS

North Coast Brewing Company / ★★

444 N MAIN ST, FORT BRAGG; 707/964-3400
If Norm Peterson of *Cheers* died and went to heaven, he'd end up here, permanently hunched over the bar within easy reach of his own ever-flowing tap of the North Coast Brewing Company's Scrimshaw Pilsner

(a Gold Medal winner at the Great American Beer Fest, the Super Bowl of beer tastings). To his right would be a bowl of the brewery's tangy Route 66 Chili, on his left a hearty plate of beef Romanov (made with braised sirloin tips, fresh mushrooms, and Russian Imperial Stout), and in front of his brewski would be a big platter of fresh Pacific oysters. This homey brew pub is the most happening place in town, especially at happy hour, when the bar and dark wood tables are occupied by boisterous locals. The pub is housed in a dignified, century-old redwood structure, and the beer is brewed on the premises, in large copper vats displayed behind plate glass. A pale ale, wheat beer, stout, pilsner, and a seasonal brew are always available, though first-timers should opt for the inexpensive four-beer sampler—or, heck, why not indulge in the eight-beer sampler?—to learn the ropes. You'll like the menu, too, which offers above-average pub grub as well as more exotic fare ranging from Mayan roast pork to seafood crepes. *$$; DIS, MC, V; checks OK; lunch, dinner every day; beer and wine; no reservations; on the corner of Pine and Main Sts.* &

Viraporn's Thai Cafe / ★

500 S MAIN ST, FORT BRAGG; 707/964-7931
When Viraporn Lobell opened this tiny Thai cafe in 1991, Asian-food aficionados on the North Coast breathed a communal sigh of relief. Born in northern Thailand, Viraporn attended cooking school and apprenticed in restaurants there before coming to the United States. After moving to the North Coast with her husband, Paul, she worked for a while at Mendocino's renowned Cafe Beaujolais. A master at balancing the five traditional Thai flavors of hot, bitter, tart, sweet, and salty, Viraporn works wonders with refreshing Thai classics such as spring rolls, satays, phad thai, lemongrass soup, and a wide range of curry dishes. *$; no credit cards; checks OK; lunch Mon, Wed–Fri, dinner Wed–Mon; beer and wine; reservations recommended for parties of 4 or more; across from RiteAid.* &

LODGINGS

Grey Whale Inn / ★★

615 N MAIN ST, FORT BRAGG; 707/964-0640 OR 800/382-7244
Wide doorways and sloped halls are the only vestiges of this popular inn's previous life as the town hospital. Owners Colette and John Bailey have successfully transformed the stately four-story building into one of the more comfortable and distinctive inns on the coast. Decorated with quilts, heirlooms, and antiques, the 14 large guest rooms have private baths and wonderful views of town or sea. Reserve one of the two penthouse rooms: Sunrise offers a view of the town, pretty wicker furniture, and a double whirlpool bath, while Sunset opens onto a private deck

overlooking the ocean. Another good choice is the spacious Campbell Suite, which comes with a marble gas-log fireplace. The full buffet breakfast (with trays for carrying your food back to bed, if you prefer) is included in the rates. *$$$; AE, DIS, MC, V; checks OK; stay@grey whaleinn.com; www.greywhaleinn.com; corner of Main and 1st Sts.* &

Willits

RESTAURANTS

Purple Thistle / ★★☆

50 S MAIN ST, WILLITS; 707/459-4750

The Purple Thistle is the successor to the popular Tsunami restaurant, in the same location, and the new menu retains many of the favorite old items. The current owners continue the Tsunami dedication to organic ingredients and the freshest fish around. Red snapper, prawns, chicken breast, or tofu can be served up grilled, Cajun-style, or in a tempura batter. In deference to unrepentant carnivores, however, Harris Ranch steaks have been added to the bill of fare. The service is a bit tentative, and on a recent visit for dinner the fruit dessert listed on the menu was still in the oven, apparently for the foreseeable future. Darn. Even so, it's a homey spot with a loyal following, good food, and friendly faces. *$; no credit cards; checks OK; lunch Mon–Fri, dinner every day; beer and wine; reservations recommended; on Hwy 101, near Commercial St.* &

LODGINGS

Emandal Farm / ★

16500 HEARST POST OFFICE RD, WILLITS; 707/459-5439 OR 800/262-9597

Since 1908 this thousand-acre working farm situated along the Eel River has been a popular summer getaway for Bay Area families who long for a stint on the farm. The second and third generations of the Adams family own and run Emandal Farm, and they happily let children and their parents assist with the daily chores, such as feeding the pigs, milking the goats, tending the garden, and gathering eggs in the chicken coop. The fruits of their labor are often presented hours later at meals. In addition to helping out on the farm, guests may enjoy the Adamses' private sandy beach on the river or explore trails meandering through the valley. At night a campfire circle inevitably forms, where parents struggle to remember old skits, ghost stories, and campfire songs. The 13 rustic, redwood one-bedroom cabins and seven two-bedroom cabins are nestled under a grove of oak and fir trees. They're not equipped with much—just single and queen-size beds, cold spring water, and electricity (and that's it). The bathrooms and showers are housed in a separate, communal facility. The Adamses prepare a healthy, hearty breakfast, lunch, and dinner, all included in the price of rooms. Expect fare like omelets stuffed with garden-fresh vegetables, garden lasagne with homemade noodles, barbecued chicken (most likely the bird your child befriended earlier in the day), and homemade bread that's baked fresh daily. Although no alcohol is permitted at tables, guests may bring beer and wine into the cabins. The farm is usually open to guests for weeklong stays in August and for weekend trips only in September; the schedule occasionally changes, so call for an update. *$$$$; MC, V; checks OK; open late July–late Sept; 16 miles E of town; call or write for directions.*

Westport

If you've made it this far north, you're either lost or determined to drive the full length of Highway 1. If it's the latter, then you'd best stock up on a sandwich or two at the **WESTPORT COMMUNITY STORE & DELI** (37001 N Hwy 1; 707/964-2872) because this is the northernmost town on the Mendocino coast, and you still have a loooong way to go.

LODGINGS

DeHaven Valley Farm / ★★★

39247 HWY 1, WESTPORT; 707/961-1660 OR 877-DEHAVEN

This remote 1875 Victorian farmhouse, with its sublime rural setting and access to a secluded beach, comes complete with a barnyard menagerie of horses, sheep, goats, and donkeys. If the animals aren't enough to keep you amused, try a game of croquet or horseshoes, do a little bird-watching or horseback riding, or take a meditative soak in the hot tub set high on a hill overlooking the ocean. The inviting parlor has deep, comfortable couches, while the five guest rooms in the house and the three nearby cottages are decorated with colorful comforters and rustic antiques; some even have fireplaces. In the morning, you'll wake to such treats as apple pancakes or potato-artichoke frittata. The small DeHaven Valley Farm Restaurant offers a commendable prix-fixe four-course dinner menu (served every Saturday, or for groups of 6, reserve any day) that might include entrees like roasted pork tenderloin with apple horse-radish or seafood baked in filo dough with roasted pepper aioli, and a killer apple strudel for dessert. *$$$; AE, MC, V; checks OK; www. dehaven-valley-farm.com; 1½ miles N of Westport.*

Howard Creek Ranch / ★★★

40501 N HWY 1, WESTPORT; 707/964-6725

Located off a remote stretch of Highway 1 near the tiny town of West-port, this isolated 40-acre ranch appeals to travelers who really want to get away from it all. You'll revel in the peace and quiet of this rustic retreat, which Mendocino County has designated a historic site. For more than two decades, proprietors Sally and Charles Grigg have been renting out three cabins, four guest rooms in the farmhouse, and six rooms in the renovated carriage barn. Set back just a few hundred yards from an ocean beach, the farmhouse and barn are on opposite sides of Howard Creek, connected by (among other routes) a 75-foot-long swinging footbridge. The rooms in the farmhouse feature separate sitting areas, antiques, and homemade quilts, while the barn units—each one handcrafted by Charles, a master builder with a penchant for skylights— have curly-grain redwood walls and Early American collectibles. The separate Beach House, with its freestanding fireplace, skylights, king-size bed, large deck, and whirlpool tub, is a great romantic getaway. A hot tub and sauna are perched on the side of a hill, as are Sally's guardian cows, sheep, llama, and horses. In the morning, Sally rings the breakfast bell to alert her guests that it's eatin' time—and the fare is definitely worth getting out of bed for. Note: Pet dogs are welcome with prior approval. *$$$; AE, MC, V; checks OK; www.HowardCreekRanch.com; 3 miles N of Westport.*

REDWOOD EMPIRE

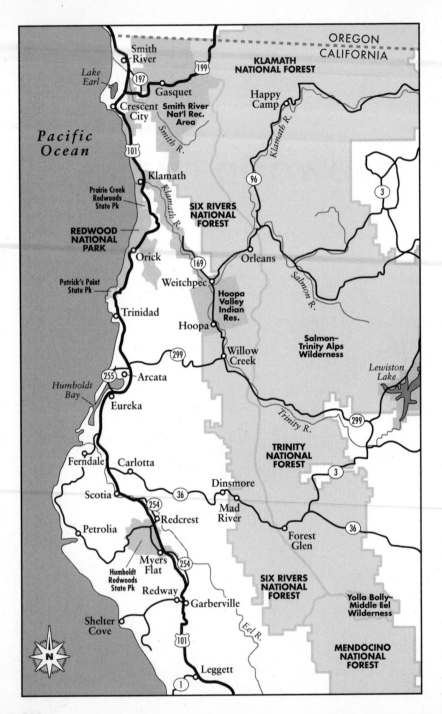

REDWOOD EMPIRE

This far corner of California contains some of the most beautiful parks the state has to offer. The Redwood Empire encompasses thousands of acres of old-growth forests, and if you move just a few feet away from the tacky tourist attractions, you will find yourself profoundly alone among the world's tallest trees, *Sequoia sempervirens*, or California coast redwoods. Clustered in misty, silent groves, these trees are typically several hundred years old when mature and 200 feet tall. Some are over 360 feet—comparable to a 30-story building—and can live more than 2,000 years. *Sempervirens*, as a matter of fact, means forever living.

On the other hand, a few of the places where humankind congregates hereabouts will bring you back to earth with a thud. Guaranteed, you will never again see as much burl statuary for sale as you will along some of these roads. The decline in the timber and fishing industries hit the local populace hard, and while tourism is growing, the area is a little too far away from major population centers for spur-of-the-moment weekend trips. There are lots of visitors in summer months, but the rest of the year you can have the place practically to yourself. For many folks, that's precisely its charm: you can camp, hike, fish, cycle, kayak, beachcomb, whale watch, or bird-watch—and relatively inexpensively, too—without making reservations a year in advance. Typical California prices haven't made it here—yet.

For those who can't survive without good restaurants, interesting boutiques, and a few bookstores to browse, Eureka, the largest town in northwestern California (population 27,000), has all those hallmarks of civilization in and around its picturesque Old Town. Located on historic Humboldt Bay, it also has a number of bed-and-breakfast accommodations that are as fine as any in far more expensive locales in the state. Just 16 miles away, the entire village of Ferndale has been designated a State Historical Landmark for its well-preserved Victorian architecture. If your perfect bliss is the total absence of civilization, however, the romantically named Lost Coast is as remote and empty as the most confirmed misanthrope could desire. This 850-square-mile area south of Ferndale and north of Westport, with more than 75 miles of coastline, has few roads, and though several towns are shown on maps, it is almost uninhabited. Backpackers love the beaches with their pristine tide pools, abundant wildlife, remnants of legendary shipwrecks, and miles and miles of solitude.

ACCESS AND INFORMATION

US Highway 101 is the only highway worthy of the name in California's redwood country. It stretches north from Willits in northern Mendocino County to Humboldt County and Eureka on the coast, then farther north to Crescent City and into Oregon. The seldom-visited **LOST COAST** can be reached by the **MATTOLE ROAD**, which starts just north of Weott at the southern boundary of the Avenue of the Giants, runs north and west to the hamlets of Honeydew and Petrolia, and reaches the coast just south of Cape Mendocino. From there it continues north to Ferndale.

Three other roads for the adventuresome lead east over the mountains: California 36 runs from Fortuna along the Van Duzen River to Dinsmore and Mad River, ending at Interstate 5 in Red Bluff (past Mad River the going gets really rough, and the road is sometimes closed in winter); California 299 follows the Klamath and Trinity Rivers to Weaverville and Lewiston, then continues on to Interstate 5 in Redding; and California 199 parallels the Smith River (nationally designated a wild and scenic river, and California's only undammed river system) north and east to Oregon and Interstate 5 at Grants Pass.

The Arcata/Eureka airport in McKinleyville (11 miles N of Eureka) is served by Horizon Air (800/547-9308) and United Express (800/241-6522). Rental cars are available there. Greyhound Bus (800/231-2222) offers service along Highway 101; there are two buses each way daily for travelers from San Francisco and Oregon.

Tourism is the area's number-two revenue generator, gaining fast on timber, and information about tourist destinations is plentiful. Contact the **EUREKA/HUMBOLDT CONVENTION AND VISITORS BUREAU** (1034 2nd St, Eureka; 707/443-5097; www.redwoodvisitor.org) or the **DEL NORTE COUNTY CHAMBER OF COMMERCE** (1001 Front St, Crescent City; 707/464-3174; www.northerncalifornia.net) for information.

The Lost Coast

The Lost Coast isn't really lost, it's just little frequented. Without a coastal road, this untamed and undeveloped stretch of California shoreline is mainly occupied by ranchers, retirees, and alternative lifestylers (a.k.a. hippies). The good life goes on here with few interruptions, although hints of gentrification in certain towns (like Shelter Cove) suggest that the Lost Coast is gradually being found.

Garberville

RESTAURANTS

Woodrose Cafe / ★

911 REDWOOD DR, GARBERVILLE; 707/923-3191

This late-blooming flower-child coffee shop is the social center of Garberville—a place to eavesdrop on local gossip from a booth, table, or counter stool. Colorful artwork by local artists hangs on the plain white walls, and in back there's a small outdoor patio perfect for basking in the sun and wolfing down healthy (some would say hippie) fare such as omelets, granola, vegetarian garden burgers, organic-fruit shakes, and chunky, vegetable-based soups served with sourdough garlic bread. Organic produce is used whenever possible. Everything is skillfully and tastefully prepared, and you'll certainly leave feeling well nourished. *$; no credit cards; checks OK; breakfast every day, lunch Mon–Fri; beer and wine; no reservations; from Hwy 101, take the Garberville exit.*

LODGINGS

Benbow Inn / ★★★

445 LAKE BENBOW DR, GARBERVILLE; 707/923-2124

From its sophisticated afternoon tea to its beautifully cultivated gardens of primroses, narcissus, tulips, and roses, this elegant Tudor-style inn built in 1926 is a little slice of England nestled in the redwoods. A National Historic Landmark, the inn (named after the family who built it) has hosted such luminaries as Herbert Hoover, Eleanor Roosevelt, and Charles Laughton. The 55 guest rooms vary in size and amenities; the deluxe accommodations include private patios and Jacuzzis, fireplaces readied with kindling, and VCRs (there's a large movie library at the front desk). The least expensive rooms are small but comfortable, and while they don't have the frills of the other rooms, they are tastefully decorated with antiques. The aristocratic dining room is lined with carved-wood and marble sideboards, and the large-paned windows provide a great view of the river and gardens. The menu changes frequently but always features seafood, beef, pasta, and poultry dishes. Dinner entrees might include fresh salmon, grilled chicken breast marinated in lime and herbs, and honey-miso-roasted pork loin served with black-eyed peas. Breakfast and lunch are served daily, and on Sunday the Benbow offers a sumptuous champagne brunch. Of course, as British etiquette dictates, tea and scones are also served daily from 3pm to 4pm. The inn hosts many special events throughout the year, including a Nutcracker Christmas celebration, a New Year's dinner dance, a summer Shakespeare on the Lake festival, and a fall Murder Mystery Weekend. *$$–$$$$; AE, DIS, MC, V; checks OK; breakfast, lunch Mon–Sat, dinner every day, brunch Sun (lunch is not served mid-Sept–mid-May, except on holidays); open mid-Apr–Dec 31; full bar; reservations recommended; from Hwy 101, take the Benbow Dr exit.*

Redway

RESTAURANTS

The Mateel Cafe / ★★

3342 AND 3344 REDWOOD DR, REDWAY; 707/923-2030

With its delicious, healthful food and lively atmosphere, the Mateel has become a social and cultural magnet for the southern Humboldt region (SoHum to the natives). Lunch and dinner are served in three areas: the

REDWOOD EMPIRE THREE-DAY TOUR

DAY ONE: Eureka, you've found it! The best way to explore the area's many charms is to make Eureka your hub, with visits and overnights at nearby attractions. After a quick bagel and a latte at **Los Bagels** in Eureka's Old Town, your first stop is 20 miles north of Eureka at Trinidad, a tiny fishing village of white clapboard houses overlooking **Trinidad Bay**. Admire the view, pick up some smoked salmon at **Katie's Smokehouse**, and if you like colorful local eateries, munch on some of the freshest seafood in this neck of the coast at the **Seascape Restaurant** (707/677-3762), beside the pier at the foot of Bay Street. Continue on Highway 101 north along the coast through Orick, the burl capital of the world. Watch out for artists with chain saws. About 5 miles farther, take the **Newton B. Drury Scenic Parkway**—a 10-mile trip through the unspoiled scenery of **Prairie Creek Redwoods State Park** with herds of Roosevelt elk, giant trees, fern canyons, and beaches along the way. As beautiful as it is, you can't dawdle too long, because you have to go back the way you came, following the signs to 640-acre **Patrick's Point State Park**, 5 miles north of Trinidad. Here you can look for whales, hunt for stones on Agate Beach, and wander through Sumeg, a Yurok Indian village with redwood houses and a sweat lodge still used for ceremonial purposes. Check into the charming **Lost Whale Bed and Breakfast Inn** and enjoy a sherry on the deck at sunset before you finish the day with dinner at the nearby **Larrupin' Café**.

DAY TWO: All about town. After breakfast at the inn, head back to Eureka, stroll the **Old Town** with its restored Victorian shops; gawk at the **Carson Mansion**, possibly the finest Victorian anywhere (but you can't go in, as it's privately owned). After lunch at **Tomaso's Tomato Pies** (don't eat too much if you are a candidate for *mal d'mer*),

main dining room, which has high-backed wooden booths and a modest collection of watercolors by local artists; the African-style Jazzbo Room, decked out in giraffe decor; and the covered patio, the preferred spot on warm days and nights. A worldly selection of food is served here, ranging from roast rack of lamb to seafood linguine, Louisiana tiger prawns, Thai tofu, and fresh seafood specials of the day. All entrees are served with appetizers, soup or salad, and house-made pita bread. If you're not up to one of the full meals, try a stone-baked pizza (there are more than 20 toppings to choose from) or a gourmet salad, such as the Napa cabbage, spinach, and chicken salad topped with tomatoes and almonds and a curry dressing. *$; MC, V; checks OK; lunch, dinner Mon-Sat; beer and wine; no reservations; from Hwy 101, take the Redway exit to downtown.* &

hop aboard the **Madaket**, the oldest passenger vessel on the Pacific Coast, for a tour of Humboldt Bay. For dinner you can choose between gobs of basic, rib-stickin' food at the historic **Samoa Cookhouse** (see "Please, Sir, May I Have Samoa") or an elegant dinner at **Restaurant 301**, the best restaurant on the North Coast. Then it's off to the Victorian village of **Ferndale**, just a hop away, for a performance at the Ferndale Repertory Theater. Spend the night in the village's most elegant B&B, the fabled **Gingerbread Mansion**, where you can wind down with a soak in matching claw-footed tubs.

DAY THREE: Among giants. After a lavish B&B breakfast, you're on the road to **Scotia** for a glimpse of a real company town, built entirely of redwood, owned by the Pacific Lumber Company. It's so clean and tidy, it's almost surreal. Take the self-guided tour through one of the last sawmills in the area, and the world's biggest to boot. It will give you a perspective on your next destination, the **Avenue of the Giants**. The Avenue was originally a stagecoach road, and it winds some 32 miles along the Eel River through stunning groves of coast redwoods. For lunch, grab a bite in the down-home **Eternal Treehouse Cafe** in tiny Redcrest, complete with country or gospel music coming from the kitchen. Don't dally, though, because you're going to want to check into the historic **Benbow Inn** as early as possible so you can catch a few rays on its private beach before dinner in the restaurant. Afterward, see what's happening across the road at Lake Benbow's outdoor stage—jazz, pop, reggae, or Shakespeare—under the stars and the redwoods, with the lake as a backdrop.

Shelter Cove

RESTAURANTS

Cove Restaurant / ★★

210 WAVE DR, SHELTER COVE; 707/986-1197

At the north end of a small runway for private planes, this rather remote restaurant—selected by *Private Pilot* magazine as one of the nation's premier fly-in lunch spots—is situated in an A-frame beach house with two-story-high picture windows, an outdoor dining area, and a spectacular view of this untamed region of California known as the Lost Coast. The menu's offerings are wide ranging and well prepared: charbroiled steak cut to order, Cajun-style fish (we're talking right out of the water), grilled chicken, juicy hamburgers, and piles of fresh shellfish. All meals are served with a choice of a creamy clam chowder; shrimp salad or green salad; and house-made bread. Desserts range from fresh fruit pies (snatch a slice of the wonderfully tart wild blackberry if it's available) to chocolate mousse and cheesecake. *$$; MC, V; checks OK; lunch, dinner Thurs–Sun; full bar; reservations recommended; off Lower Pacific Dr.*

LODGINGS

Shelter Cove Ocean Inn / ★★

148 DOLPHIN DR, SHELTER COVE; 707/986-7161

Snoozing seals, grazing deer, and migrating whales are just some of the sights you'll see in Shelter Cove, the Lost Coast's only oceanside community. Once you leave Highway 101 in Garberville, prepare to navigate along 24 miles of steep, twisting tarmac that passes through rocky grasslands and patches of forest before reaching the cove (good brakes are a must). At the end of the journey you'll reach the Shelter Cove Ocean Inn, a handsome Victorian-style facility built smack-dab on the shoreline. The inn, which is popular with recreational pilots who can park their planes within walking distance, offers two spacious suites with sitting rooms and Jacuzzi tubs. Two smaller rooms upstairs have private baths and balconies. All rooms have an ocean view, but the panorama from the suites is definitely worth the extra expense. Since the B&B is in such a remote location, a home-cooked breakfast, lunch, and dinner may be delivered to your room on request. *$$; AE, MC, V; checks OK; turn right off Lower Pacific Dr.* &

Petrolia

LODGINGS

The Lost Inn Bed and Breakfast / ★

OLD MATTOLE RD, PETROLIA; 707/629-3394

As you wind along Old Mattole Road through the sleepy hamlet of Petrolia, keep a lookout for an old green tractor with a hand-painted sign that reads, "Welcome! You have just found the Lost Inn." Once you've spotted it, drive up the circular driveway lined with flowers, fruit trees, and rustic antiques, and prepare to be greeted by a friendly entourage of cats, dogs, and chickens. They belong to Gail and Phil Franklin, the friendly keepers of this remote country inn, the only B&B in the Mattole Valley. There's just one guest room at present (plans are under way for another): a large two-room suite with a queen-size bed, glassed-in porch, and private entrance. Breakfast, including eggs from the Franklins' chickens and organic fruit from their trees, is served either in your room or on the porch. You can even bring your pooch, and the Pacific Ocean is only 5 miles away. *$$; no credit cards; checks OK; 1 block from the Petrolia General Store.*

Myers Flat

Just outside of Myers Flat you'll find the magnificent **AVENUE OF THE GIANTS**, located in Humboldt Redwoods State Park. In spite of tacky tourist attractions such as the Chimney Tree and the Shrine Drive-Thru Tree, this awesome 32-mile stretch of coastal redwoods, some of which are more than 340 feet high and over 2,000 years old, is a detour worth taking. It's hard to think of these giants as ephemeral, but get a good, long look; there aren't that many left.

LODGINGS

Myers Inn / ★

12913 OLD REDWOOD HWY/AVE OF THE GIANTS, MYERS FLAT; 707/943-3259

The two-story, wood-framed Myers Inn, constructed in 1860 and restored in 1906, sits just outside Humboldt Redwoods State Park in Myers Flat, a hamlet reminiscent of a cardboard-cutout saloon town. Ten comfortable, sparkling clean guest rooms—all with private baths—have been renovated with an eye toward upscale country charm. Verandas encircle the building on both floors, providing every room with a balcony that has a view of the town, mountains, and forest. Although the inn is close to the highway, the nearby Eel River and redwoods seem to absorb most of the noise. The forest also provides plenty of superb hiking and biking trails. A continental breakfast is served to B&B guests, and for dinner many dine at the popular Knights Restaurant (707/943-3411) across the street, which serves reasonably priced classic American fare such as steak, prime rib, and fresh seafood, including lobster. *$$$; AE, MC, V; no checks; in the center of town.*

Redcrest

RESTAURANTS

Eternal Treehouse Cafe / ★

26510 AVE OF THE GIANTS, REDCREST; 707/722-4247

Located in the tiny town of Redcrest on the scenic Avenue of the Giants, the Eternal Treehouse is an all-American cafe right down to the house-made pies and country-and-western music flowing out of the kitchen. This family-run cafe serves the best biscuits and gravy in the county, as well as wholesome daily specials such as corned beef and cabbage served with potatoes, carrots, and a choice of soup or salad—all for less than the price of a movie. *$; MC, V; checks OK; breakfast, lunch, dinner every day; no alcohol; no reservations; from Hwy 101, take the Redcrest exit.*

Scotia

LODGINGS

Scotia Inn / ★★✩

MAIN ST, SCOTIA; 707/764-5683

This landmark three-story hotel constructed entirely of redwood is the pride of Scotia, one of the last company-owned towns in America. In fact, the whole town is built of redwood—no surprise once you discover the town's owner is the Pacific Lumber Company. The Scotia Inn has two guest rooms downstairs and 20 spacious rooms on the second floor, each gussied up with antiques and balloon drapery. The inn's private bathrooms are equipped with showers and claw-footed tubs. The elaborate dining room, handsomely decorated in rust, green, and burgundy, is lit by brass chandeliers. The well-prepared dinners feature locally grown vegetables, berries, and fowl. Traditional American fare such as steak, prime rib, elk, and seafood is offered alongside Mexican, Italian, and French entrees like chicken breast marinated in chipotle chiles served with freshly made house salsa. Sundays generally feature ethnic specials like Greek-style mustard lamb or Thai-roasted pork loin. The wine list is excellent. For classic, hearty steak house grub, dine at the inn's Steak n' Potato Pub. *$$–$$$$; AE, DIS, MC, V; checks OK; at Mill St, directly across from the mill; from Hwy 101, take the Scotia exit.*

Bridgeport

RESTAURANTS

The Weekender Cafe / ★

HWY 36, BRIDGEPORT; 707/574-6521

All the proceeds of this homey, volunteer-run cafe support the local fire department and its four secondhand engines. Neighbors donate the homemade rolls, muffins, breads, pies, cakes, cookies, soups, relishes, salads, and even the fresh flowers decorating every table, and the fire chief answers the phone. Most of the ingredients come from local pastures, chicken coops, and gardens (including sun-ripened tomatoes and sweet, freshly picked carrots and celery) and are prepared in a family-size kitchen behind the eight-stool counter (newly expanded from five). For breakfast the staff whips up waffles, pancakes, freshly made Danish pastries, homemade biscuits and gravy, and a variety of egg dishes. This is the kind of place where you help yourself to the coffee, and if the vinyl chairs get too uncomfortable you can always take a seat on the couch in front of the fire. *$; no credit cards; checks OK; breakfast, lunch Tues–Sun; no alcohol; no reservations; 1½ miles E of Dinsmore, between Bridgeville and Mad River.*

Mad River

LODGINGS

Journey's End Resort / ★

200 MAD RIVER RD, MAD RIVER; 707/574-6441

This remote resort is settled on the edge of little-known Ruth Lake, a well-hidden man-made lake that's a 1½-hour winding drive from the coast. Created in 1962, the lake is frequented by serious anglers in search of its sizable trout and black bass, which explains why a good number of guests at Journey's End are fisher folk (and the rest are typically water-skiers and jet-skiers). The motel's four no-frills guest rooms are clean and warm, equipped with two firm double beds and a bathroom with a shower. A cabin on the premises sleeps up to eight people and is supplied with a dishwasher, stove, refrigerator, and towels—all you need to bring is food. Evening entertainment is left to the imagination rather than the networks, and if that doesn't suffice, there's a game-filled pub with a satellite TV. The resort also has a grocery store, a laundry, and basic fishing and boating supplies. New owners took over in 1999. They have upgraded the food at Journey's End Restaurant. The fare is still simple, but no frozen, packaged, or pretend nourishment is served here, and the pizza is made from scratch. The majority of the dinners are range-fed—rib-eyes, 16-ounce New York steaks, and prime rib every Friday—and served with housemade fries, sautéed mushrooms, and grilled onions. *$$; AE, DIS, MC, V; no checks; at the NE end of Ruth Lake, 10 miles S of Hwy 36.*

Ferndale

Even if Ferndale isn't on your itinerary, it's worth taking a detour off Highway 101 to stroll for an hour or two down the colorful Main Street, browsing through the art galleries, gift shops, and cafes strangely reminiscent of Disneyland's "old town." Ferndale, however, is for real, and hasn't changed much since it was the agricultural center of Northern California in the late 1800s. In fact, the entire town is a National Historic Landmark because of its abundance of well-preserved Victorian storefronts, farmhouses, and homes. What really distinguishes Ferndale from the likes of Eureka and Crescent City, however, is the fact that Highway 101 doesn't pass through it—which means no cheesy motels, liquor stores, or fast-food chains.

For a trip back in time, view the village's interesting memorabilia—working crank phones, logging equipment, and a blacksmith shop at the **FERNDALE MUSEUM** (515 Shaw St at 3rd Street; 707/786-4466). Not officially a museum, but close enough, is the **GOLDEN GATE MERCANTILE** (421 Main St). Part of this general store hasn't been remodeled (or restocked) in 50 years, giving you the feeling that you're walking through some sort of time capsule or movie set. Far less historic but equally engrossing are the pedal-powered, amphibious entries in the wacky three-day **WORLD CHAMPIONSHIP GREAT ARCATA TO FERNDALE CROSS-COUNTRY KINETIC SCULPTURE RACE** on display at the **KINETIC SCULPTURE MUSEUM** (580 Main St at Shaw St; no phone). The dusty, funky museum is unlike anything you've ever seen, but it seems a fitting tribute to a race that gives eccentricity new meaning.

Another worthy Ferndale attraction is the leisurely drive along scenic **CENTERVILLE ROAD**. The 5-mile excursion starts at the west end of Main Street downtown and passes through several ranches and dairy farms on the way to the **CENTERVILLE BEACH COUNTY PARK**. If you continue beyond the park and past the retired naval facility, you'll be rewarded with an incredible view of the Lost Coast to the south. On the way back, just outside of town on the north side of the road, keep an eye out for **FERN COTTAGE**, a restored 1865 Victorian farmhouse built by the late state senator Joseph Russ, one of the first Ferndale settlers. Tours of the farmhouse are by appointment only; call caretaker Greg Martin (who's also an accomplished organic gardener) at 707/786-4835.

In keeping with its National Historic Landmark status, Ferndale has no movie theaters. It has something better: the **FERNDALE REPERTORY THEATRE** (447 Main St; 707/786-5483). Converted in 1972 from a movie theater, the 267-seat house hosts live performances by actors from all over Humboldt County. The revolving performances run pretty much year-round and range from musicals to comedies, dramas, and mysteries. Tickets are reasonably priced and, due to the popularity of the shows, reservations are advised. For more information on Ferndale's upcoming events and activities, visit the town's Web site (www.victorianfern dale.org/chamber).

RESTAURANTS

Curley's Grill / ★★☆

400 OCEAN AVE (VICTORIAN INN), FERNDALE; 707/786-9696
Longtime restaurateur and Ferndale resident Curley Tait decided it was finally time to open his own business. So in April 1995 he opened Curley's Grill in a little hole in the wall on Main Street, and it was a big hit—so much so that Curley recently relocated to fancy, spacious digs in the Victorian Inn several blocks down the street. The reason Curley's place is considered the best in town? He doesn't fool around: the prices are fair, the servings are generous, the food is good, and the atmosphere is bright and cheerful. Sure bets are the grilled polenta with Italian sausage, fresh mushrooms, and sage-laden tomato sauce, and the moist tortilla-and-onion cake served with a tangy onion salsa. Indulge in the house-made breads and desserts, and take a look at Curley's collection of Marilyn Monroe memorabilia, including Marilyn Merlot wine. *$$; DIS, MC, V; checks OK; lunch, dinner every day; beer and wine; reservations recommended; corner of Ocean Ave and Main St.* ✔

LODGINGS

The Gingerbread Mansion / ★★★

400 BERDING ST, FERNDALE; 707/786-4000 OR 800/952-4136
The awe-inspiring grande dame of Ferndale, this peach-and-yellow Queen Anne inn is a lavish blowout for Victoriana buffs. Gables, turrets, English gardens, and architectural gingerbread galore have made it one of the most-photographed buildings in Northern California. The man-

sion has been through several reincarnations since 1899, including stints as a private residence, a hospital, a rest home, an apartment building, and even an American Legion hall before Ken Torbert converted it into a B&B in 1983. All 11 guest rooms have queen- or king-size beds and private baths. For the ultimate in luxury, though, reserve the new Empire Suite, an orgy of marble and columns with twin fireplaces and a lavish bathing area. In the morning all guests awaken to a sumptuous breakfast in the formal dining room that overlooks the garden. An extravagant afternoon tea is served in one of five parlors, each handsomely furnished with Queen Anne, Eastlake, and Renaissance revival antiques. *$$$–$$$$; AE, MC, V; checks OK; at Brown St, 1 block S of Main St.*

The Victorian Inn / ★★☆

400 OCEAN AVE, FERNDALE; 707/786-4558 OR 999/589-1808
If you can get your honey past the jewelry store on the first floor, you'll love the romantic rooms at this conveniently located bed-and-breakfast and country inn in the heart of Ferndale. Built in 1890 of North Coast/Humboldt County redwood, the spacious inn has 12 guest rooms to choose from, all with private baths and some with fireplaces and sitting areas. The high-ceilinged rooms are individually decorated with charming wallpaper, antiques, formal draperies, and period fixtures. If you're traveling with the family, several of the rooms have extra beds and the friendly proprietors don't mind a kid in a sleeping bag on the floor, either. Breakfast is served at Curley's Grill, also located in the inn. During the week it's a buffet of hot quiche, cereals, fruit, and beverages, and on weekends you choose from a guest menu. *$$–$$$; AE, DIS, MC, V; checks OK; corner of Ocean Ave and Main St.*

Eureka and the Redwood Coast

Granted, the weather this far north is known to be a bit on the soggy side, but that makes for happy trees and humans, if tastes run toward little visited, fabulously scenic terrain. Delightful inns with personable landlords and fresh, healthy, sometimes homegrown foods complete the recipe for a good time. The coastal fog usually burns off by late afternoon, but do remember the umbrella.

Eureka

The town is named after the popular gold-mining expression "Eureka!" (Greek for "I have found it"). The heart of Eureka is **OLD TOWN**, a 13-block stretch of shops, restaurants, and hotels, most of them housed in painstakingly preserved Victorian structures. It's bordered by First and Third Streets, between C and M Streets. One of the finest Victorian architectural masterpieces is the multigabled-and-turreted **CARSON MANSION**

PLEASE, SIR, MAY I HAVE SAMOA?

Visiting the Eureka area without a stop at the **Samoa Cookhouse** (from Eureka on Hwy 101, take the Samoa Bridge to the end, turn left on Samoa Rd, then left on Cookhouse Rd; 707/442-1659) is like visiting Paris without seeing the Eiffel Tower. This venerable dining spot is the last surviving cookhouse in the West (it's been in operation for more than a century) and a Humboldt County institution. When logging was king in redwood country, every mill operation had a cookhouse that was the hub of life in the community. Lumbermen worked six days a week, 12 hours a day, and got three hot meals daily. Waitresses rushed back and forth from kitchen to tables keeping the platters filled. Guests today are served lumber-camp-style in the enormous barnlike building at long tables covered with checkered oil cloths. Few decisions are required—just sit down, and the food will come until you say "uncle." Breakfast typically features sausages, biscuits, scrambled eggs, and potatoes as well as a choice of French toast, hash browns, or pancakes (not to mention all the coffee and OJ you can drink). Lunch and dinner include soup, salad, potatoes, and the meat-of-the-day, which might be ham, fried chicken, pork chops, roast beef, barbecued chicken, or fish. Mind you, the food isn't haute cuisine (except for the delicious bread, which is baked on the premises), but there's plenty of it, and prices are modest. And just when you think you're about to burst, along comes the fresh-baked pie. After your meal, spend a few minutes waddling through the adjoining **logging museum** to see a wonderful collection of logging tools and photographs of early lumber and shipping activities in Eureka. The cookhouse name, by the way, comes from the old company town of Samoa, so-called because Humboldt Bay resembles the harbor at Pago Pago. —*Mary Anne Moore*

(on the corner of 2nd and M Sts), built of redwood in 1886 for lumber baron William Carson, who initiated the construction to keep mill workers occupied during a lull in the lumber business. Although the three-story, money-green mansion is closed to the public (it's now a snooty men's club), you can stand on the sidewalk and click your Kodak at one of the state's most-photographed houses. For more Old Town history, stroll through the CLARKE MEMORIAL MUSEUM (240 E St at 3rd St; 707/443-1947), which has one of the top Native American displays in the state, showcasing more than 1,200 examples of Hupa, Yurok, and Karok basketry, dance regalia, and stonework. A block away, there's more Native American artwork, including quality silver jewelry, at the INDIAN ART & GIFT SHOP (241 F St at 3rd St; 707/445-8451), which sells many of its treasures at reasonable prices.

If you need a good book at a great price, stop by the **BOOKLEGGER** (402 2nd Street; 707/445-1344), a marvelous bookstore in Old Town with thousands of used paperbacks (especially mysteries, westerns, and science fiction), as well as children's books and cookbooks. If purple potatoes, cylindra beets, and other fancy foods are on your shopping list, you're in luck, because you'll find them at the **FARMERS MARKETS** held weekly from June through October in Eureka and Arcata. Most of the produce is grown along the local Eel and Trinity Rivers and is sold at bargain prices at the Henderson Center (Henderson and E Sts) on Thursdays from 10am to 1pm; in Eureka's Old Town on Tuesdays from 10am to 1pm; and at Arcata Plaza on Saturdays from 9am to 1pm. Better yet, why not spend the day picking produce directly from the North Coast's small farms? Call the **NORTH COAST GROWERS ASSOCIATION** (707/441-9999) for a free copy of the "Farmer's Market Directory & Farm Trails Guide," an annotated map of 13 local family-run farms that encourage visitors to drop by and purchase their products—vegetables, fruit, herbs, flowers, plants, and more—directly from the dirt.

Before you leave Eureka, be sure to take a bay cruise on skipper Leroy Zerlang's **MADAKET**, the oldest passenger vessel on the Pacific coast. The 75-minute narrated tour—a surprisingly interesting and amusing perspective on the history of Humboldt Bay—departs daily from the foot of C Street in Eureka, and gets progressively better after your second or third cocktail. For more information, call **HUMBOLDT BAY HARBOR CRUISE** (707/445-1910). Afterward, stroll over to the **LOST COAST BREWERY** (617 4th St, between G and H Sts; 707/445-4480) for a fresh pint of Alleycat Amber Ale and an order of buffalo wings.

RESTAURANTS

Los Bagels / ★

403 2ND ST, EUREKA; 707/442-8525

 Simply put, this is Eureka's best bagel shop. For a full review of the original Los Bagels, see the Restaurants section of Arcata. *$; no credit cards; local checks only; breakfast, lunch Wed–Mon; no alcohol; no reservations; at E St in Old Town.* ♿

Restaurant 301 / ★★★★

301 L ST (HOTEL CARTER), EUREKA; 707/444-8062 OR 800/404-1390

Chef Robert Szolnoki, who prides himself on using ultrafresh ingredients, collects many of the herbs and vegetables he uses at this eatery on the first floor of Hotel Carter from the hotel gardens, and he gets his seafood direct from local fisheries. Diners, seated at windowside tables overlooking the bay, may order from either the regular or the prix-fixe five-course dinner menu. A favorite meal started with a savory satay of grilled marinated quail, followed by a garden-fresh salad topped with warmed chèvre, roasted hazelnuts, and a pear vinaigrette, and then an entree of tender grilled medallions of filet mignon served with smoked oyster dressing and a green peppercorn glaze. For dessert, Christi Carter's fresh rhubarb tart drizzled with lemon-curd sauce is superb. Restaurant 301's impressive 1,200-bottle wine list received an award of excellence from *Wine Spectator* magazine in 1998 and 1999. *$$–$$$; AE, DC, DIS, MC, V; checks OK; breakfast, dinner every day; full bar; reservations recommended; at 3rd St in Old Town.* &

Tomaso's Tomato Pies / ★★☆

216 E ST, EUREKA; 707/445-0100

This family-style Italian pizza parlor reeks so divinely of baked garlic and olive oil that you can smell it a block away. Top of the list of Tomaso's favored fare are the calzone and the spinach pies, both guaranteed to make garlic lovers (and their dining partners) swoon. Be prepared for a 30-minute wait—it's the price you pay for such fresh ingredients. Other popular plates include the chicken cannelloni and the square pizza with a whole-wheat crust. For a proper Italian finale, order a cremosa: a blend of milk, soda water, and whipped cream infused with a fruity Torani Italian syrup. *$; AE, DIS, MC, V; local checks only; lunch Mon–Sat, dinner every day; beer and wine; reservations recommended; between 2nd and 3rd Sts in Old Town.* &

LODGINGS

Abigail's Elegant Victorian Mansion / ★★★

1406 C ST, EUREKA; 707/444-3144

This inn is a jewel—a National Historic Landmark lovingly maintained by owners Doug "Jeeves" Vieyra and Lily Vieyra. If you're a fan of Victoriana, be prepared for a mind-blowing experience. Each of the four guest rooms upstairs has furnishings reflecting a different period, place, or personage. The light-filled Lillie Langtry Room, named for the famed 19th-century chanteuse who once sang at the local Ingomar Theatre, has an impressive four-poster oak bed and a private bath down the hall. The French country–style Governor's Suite sleeps up to three, has a private bath, and offers a distant view of the bay. The Vieyras have a great array of old (1905–40) movies and a collection of popular music from the same era, which guests often enjoy in the common room. Then there's Doug's obsession with antique autos—he's frequently seen motoring around (with guests on board) in his 1928 Model A Ford or one of his two other old Fords. Doug and Lily are incredibly attentive hosts; they'll lend you bicycles, show you the way to their Finnish sauna and Victorian flower garden, pore over road maps with you, and make your dinner reservations. Lily, trained as a French chef (and Swedish masseuse), prepares a morning feast. *$$–$$$; MC, V; no checks; at 14th St.*

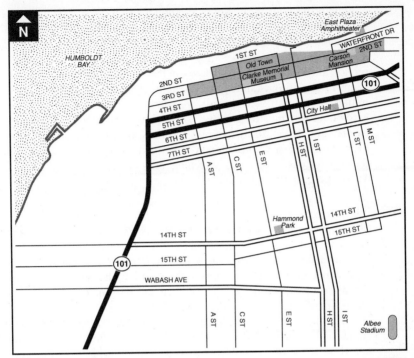

EUREKA

Carter House, Hotel Carter, Bell Cottage, Carter Cottage / ★★★★

301 L ST, EUREKA; 707/444-8062 OR 800/404-1390

What is now one of the finest accommodation-and-restaurant complexes on the upper North Coast started serendipitously in 1982, the year Eureka residents Mark and Christi Carter converted their newly built dream home—a four-story, five-bedroom Victorian reproduction—into an inn. Not only did they turn out to be some of the area's best hosts, but the Carters actually reveled in their newfound innkeeper roles. Once word got around that the Carter House was *the* place to vacation, they were flooded with folks who wanted a room. In 1986, Mark, a former builder, added the 23-room Hotel Carter across the street (its design is based on the blueprints of a historic 19th-century Eureka hotel), and four years later he refurbished the Bell Cottage, an adjacent three-bedroom Victorian mansion built in 1890. A year later, in 1991, next door to the other two, he added Carter Cottage, perhaps the most romantic of all—with just one suite, lavishly furnished as a honeymoon getaway. The foursome of inn, hotel, and two cottages offers a contrasting array of luxury accommodations, ranging from rooms with classic Victorian dark-wood antique furnishings in the house and cottage to a softer, brighter, more contemporary look in the hotel. Amenities include baskets filled with wine and specialty foods, concierge services, overnight dry cleaning and shoe shining, a videotape and CD library, tea-and-cookie bedtime service, and wine and hors d'oeuvres in the evening. Also included in the room rate is an outstanding full breakfast featuring fresh-baked tarts, muffins, cinnamon buns, breads, fresh fruit, an ever-changing array of entrees, juices, and strong coffee. The highly acclaimed Restaurant 301 (see review, above), formerly known as the Carter House Restaurant, is located on the first floor of Hotel Carter and is widely regarded as one of the North Coast's top spots for dining. *$$$–$$$$; AE, DC, DIS, MC, V; checks OK; at 3rd St in Old Town.* &

Arcata

Home to the **CALIFORNIA STATE UNIVERSITY AT HUMBOLDT**, a liberal arts school, Arcata is like most college towns in that everyone tends to lean toward the left. Environmentalism, artistry, good breads, and good bagels are indispensable elements of the Arcatian philosophy, as is a cordial disposition toward tourists, making it one of the most interesting and visitor-friendly towns along the North Coast.

The heart of this seaside community is **ARCATA PLAZA**, where a statue of President McKinley stands guard over numerous shops and cafes housed in historic buildings. A walk around the plaza—with its perfectly manicured lawns, hot dog vendor, and well-dressed retirees sitting

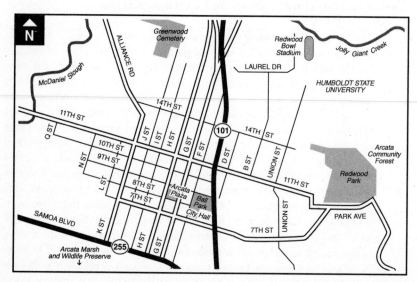

ARCATA

FROM NIGHT SOIL TO NIGHT HERONS—ARCATA CLEANS UP

The small town of Arcata, just north of Eureka, has garnered international praise for turning an abandoned industrial and landfill site into the beautiful 154-acre **Arcata Marsh and Wildlife Sanctuary**, with miles of trails, over 100 varieties of plants, and thousands of birds—more than 200 species, to be exact—including egrets, osprey, hummingbirds, and night herons. Not so unusual, you say? It wouldn't be, except that this natural splendor contains the 49 acres of oxidation ponds that treat Arcata's wastewater. Time, water, plants, bacteria, and fungi purify the wastewater that circulates through six marsh systems before it is finally released into Humboldt Bay. Natural processes in the marshes simultaneously purify the wastewater and feed marsh plants that attract birds, fish, and other wildlife. Get the free self-guided walking tour map of the preserve, available at the **Arcata Chamber of Commerce** (1062 G St at 11th St; 707/822-3619). Each Saturday at 8:30am and 2pm, local docents give free one-hour guided tours of the preserve—rain or shine—at the cul-de-sac at the foot of South I Street. Reservations are not required. The community has received many awards and lots of press for the marsh, leading to its slogan "Arcata residents flush with pride."

—Mary Anne Moore

on spotless benches—is enough to restore anyone's faith in small-town America. At the plaza's southwest end is its flagship structure, **JACOBY'S STOREHOUSE** (791 8th St at H St), a handsomely restored 1857 brick pack-train station that now holds shops, offices, and restaurants. If you need a new book, the **TIN CAN MAILMAN** (1000 H St at 10th St; 707/822-1307) is a terrific used-book store with 130,000 hard- and soft-cover titles, including a few collector's items.

You can see (and touch!) 3-billion-year-old fossils and view various California flora and fauna exhibits at Humboldt State University's **NATURAL HISTORY MUSEUM** (13th and G Sts, downtown; 707/826-4479). For a wide range of first-run and classic college flicks, queue up at the **ARCATA THEATRE** (1036 G St at 10th St; 707/822-5171) or the **MINOR THEATRE** (1013 H St at 10th St; 707/822-5171), both of which offer a wide range of films at starving-student prices (the daily matinees are particularly cheap). After the flick, savor a pitcher of Red Nectar Ale at the **HUMBOLDT BREWING COMPANY** (corner of 10th and G Sts next to the Minor Theatre; 707/826-BREW); brewery tours are offered, too.

Once you've toured the downtown area, it's time to explore Arcata's numerous parks and preserves. A 2-minute drive east of downtown on 11th Street will take you to Arcata's beloved **REDWOOD PARK**, a beautiful grassy expanse—ideal for a picnic—complemented by a fantastic playground that's guaranteed to entertain the tots. Surrounding the park is the **ARCATA COMMUNITY FOREST**, 600 acres of lush second-growth redwoods favored by hikers, mountain bikers, and equestrians; before you go, pick up a free guide to the forest's mountain-biking or hiking trails at the **ARCATA CHAMBER OF COMMERCE** (1635 Heindon Rd at Janes Rd; 707/822-3619).

The best way to spend a summer Sunday afternoon in Arcata is at the **ARCATA BALLPARK** (707/822-3619), where only a few bucks buys you nine innings of America's favorite pastime hosted by the **HUMBOLDT CRABS** semipro baseball team. With the brass band blasting and the devoted fans cheering, you'd swear you were back in high school. Most games are played Wednesday, Friday, and Saturday (doubleheader) evenings and Sunday afternoons in June and July. The ballpark is located at the corner of Ninth and F Streets in downtown Arcata, but don't park your car anywhere near foul-ball territory.

RESTAURANTS

Abruzzi / ★★

791 8TH ST, ARCATA; 707/826-2345

Named after a region on the Italian Adriatic, Abruzzi is located on the bottom floor of the historic, 140-year-old Jacoby Storehouse, an old brick complex that's been converted into the Arcata Plaza shopping and dining complex. If you have trouble finding the place, just follow your nose: the smell of garlic and fresh bread will soon steer you to Chris Smith and Bill Chino's friendly spot, where you'll be served an ample amount of artfully arranged food. Meals begin with a basket of warm breads from a local bakery, followed by such highly recommended dishes as pasta carbonara, *linguine pescara* (prawns, calamari, and clams tossed in a light Sicilian tomato sauce), or any of the fresh seafood specials. The standout dessert is the Chocolate Paradiso—a dense chocolate cake set in a pool of champagne mousseline. Smith and Chino also own the Plaza Grill on the third floor of the same building—a great place to finish off the evening by sipping a glass of wine in front of the fireplace. *$$; AE, DIS, MC, V; checks OK; dinner every day; full bar; reservations recommended; at H St in the Arcata Plaza.* &

Folie Douce / ★★

1551 G ST, ARCATA; 707/822-1042

To say Folie Douce just serves pizza is like saying Tiffany's just sells jewelry. *Designer* pizza is more like it. Try the Thai chicken pizza—marinated bits of breast topped with fontina, mozzarella, bean sprouts, and mushrooms—which is cooked in a wood-fired oven. Other toppings you won't find in your standard Pizza Hut include chèvre, Brie, and wild mushrooms. If pizza doesn't set your heart aflutter, indulge in brandy-flambéed filet mignon topped with Roquefort cheese and green peppercorns or the moist Monk's Chicken, a full boneless breast sautéed in butter, flambéed in brandy, and simmered in white wine, mustard, and cream. Locals love this festive, brightly painted place, so reservations, even for early birds, are strongly recommended. *$$; DIS, MC, V; checks OK; dinner Tues–Sat; beer and wine; reservations recommended; between 15th and 16th Sts.* &

Los Bagels / ★

1061 I ST, ARCATA; 707/822-3150

In 1987 bagel companies all over the country sent their doughy products to NBC's *Today Show* to vie for the title of Best Bagel. The verdict: the best bagel outside of New York City was made by Los Bagels in Arcata. This emporium is a popular town hangout, where you'll see lots of folks scanning the morning paper while they munch on bagels layered with smoked salmon, smoked albacore, or lox. Try some fresh-baked challah or, if you're feeling particularly adventurous, a poppy seed bagel topped with jalapeño jam and cream cheese, or a multigrain bagel smeared with hummus or guacamole. Owing to Los Bagels's brisk business, the owners opened a second location in Eureka (403 2nd St; 707/442-8525; see review). *$; no credit cards; local checks only; breakfast, lunch Wed–Mon; no alcohol; no reservations; between 10th and 11th Sts.* &

LODGINGS

The Lady Anne / ★★

902 14TH ST, ARCATA; 707/822-2797

Just a few blocks from Arcata Plaza in a quiet residential neighborhood, this exquisite example of Queen Anne architecture has been painstakingly restored by innkeepers Sharon Ferrett and Sam Pennisi (who, by the way, was once Arcata's mayor). Five large and airy guest rooms are decorated with antiques, burnished woods, English stained glass, Oriental rugs, and lace curtains. The inn's two parlors are stocked with several games, as well as a grand piano and other musical instruments that you're welcome to play. When the weather is warm, relax on the Lady Anne's veranda or head out to the lawn for a game of croquet. Breakfast (beg for the Belgian waffles) is served in the grand dining room, which is warmed by a roaring fire in the winter. *$$; MC, V; checks OK; at I St.*

Trinidad

In the early 1850s Trinidad was a booming supply town with a population of 3,000; now it's one of the smallest incorporated cities in California, encompassing a little rocky bluff that a handful of anglers, artists, retirees, and shopkeepers call home. A sort of Mendocino-in-miniature, cute-as-a-button Trinidad is known mainly as a sportfishing town: trawlers and skiffs sit patiently in the bay, awaiting their owners or tourists eager to spend an afternoon salmon fishing. Scenery and silence, however, are the town's most desirable commodities; if all you're after is a little R&R on the coast, Trinidad is among the most peaceful and beautiful areas you'll find in California.

There's plenty to see and do in the Trinidad region. Five miles north of Trinidad off Patrick's Point Drive is **PATRICK'S POINT STATE PARK**, a 640-acre oceanside peninsula with lush, fern-lined trails that wind through foggy forests of cedar, pine, and spruce. The park was once a seasonal fishing village of the Yurok Indians. Nowadays it's overrun with campers in the summer, but it's still worth a visit. Stroll down **AGATE BEACH** (keep an eye out for the semiprecious stones), climb the stone stairway up to the house-size **CEREMONIAL ROCK**, and admire the vistas from the **RIM TRAIL**, a 2-mile path along the cliffs where you can sometimes spot sea lions, harbor seals, and gray whales. In 1990 descendants of the original Native American settlers reconstructed an authentic Yurok village within the park, and visitors are welcome. A map and guide to all of the park's attractions are included in the $5-per-vehicle day-use fee; call 707/677-3570 for more details.

The **HUMBOLDT STATE UNIVERSITY MARINE LABORATORY** (Edwards and Ewing Sts; 707/826-3671) features various live marine life displays, including a touch tank and tide pools; it's open to the public daily. Then again, why not catch your own sea critters? A day spent **SPORTFISHING** off Trinidad's bounteous coast is more fun and much easier than you probably think. You simply drop your prerigged line into the water, reel it in when something's tugging on the other end, and throw your catch in the burlap sack at your feet. The crew does all the dirty work of cleaning and cutting your fish, and **KATY'S SMOKEHOUSE** (740 Edwards St; 707/677-0151) will take care of the rest. Trinidad's two sportfishing charter boats are the 36-foot **JUMPIN' JACK** (707/839-4743 or 800/839-4744) and the 45-foot **SHENANDOAH** (707/677-3625). Both charters offer morning and afternoon trips daily from Trinidad Pier, and walk-on customers are welcome. The five-hour salmon or rockfish hunt costs about $60 per person, which includes all fishing gear. One-day fishing licenses can be purchased on board the *Jumpin' Jack*. If you're lucky enough to reel in a lunker salmon, haul it to Katy's Smokehouse just up the road from the pier. Katy herself will smoke it up and wrap it to go—or even send it via UPS to your home. Her salmon jerky isn't bad, either.

RESTAURANTS

Larrupin' Café / ★★★

1658 PATRICK'S POINT DR, TRINIDAD; 707/677-0230

Trinidad's finest restaurant—looking very chic with its colorful urns full of exotic flowers—draws crowds with its creative seafood dishes and fantastic pork ribs doused in a sweet and spicy barbecue sauce. Often, oysters, mussels, and crab are served the same day they're plucked from Humboldt Bay. Every meal comes with a red- and green-leaf salad tossed with a gorgonzola vinaigrette and an appetizer board stocked with gravlax, pâté, dark pumpernickel, apple slices, and the house mustard sauce. For your choice of a starch, order the tasty twice-baked potato stuffed with house-made cheese, sour cream, and scallions. Finish off your feast with a slice of pecan-chocolate pie topped with hot rum sauce. *$$; no credit cards; checks OK; dinner every day in summer (Thurs–Sun only from Labor Day to Memorial Day); beer and wine; reservations recommended; from Hwy 101, take the Trinidad exit and head N on Patrick's Point Dr.* &

LODGINGS

The Lost Whale Bed and Breakfast Inn / ★★★

3452 PATRICK'S POINT DR, TRINIDAD; 707/677-3425 OR 800/677-7859
The Lost Whale isn't just a place to stay overnight; it's a destination in itself—particularly for families with small children. The traditional Cape Cod–style building, constructed in 1989, stands alone on a 4-acre grassy cliff overlooking the sea, with a private stairway leading down to miles of deserted rocky beach. Proprietors Suzanne Lakin and Lee Miller manage to give romancing couples lots of space and solitude, yet they also have created one of the most family-friendly inns on the California coast. Five of the inn's eight soundproof rooms have private balconies or sitting alcoves with views of the Pacific, two rooms have separate sleeping lofts, and all have private baths and queen-size beds. Lakin and Miller also rent out a charming farmhouse set on 5½ acres that can accommodate up to six people. It's equipped with a whirlpool tub, a fireplace, a kitchen, and a laundry room. After a day on the inn's beach or at neighboring Patrick's Point State Park, relax in the outdoor hot tub while listening to the distant bark of sea lions or looking out for whales. Kids can romp around on the playground—which has a small playhouse with its own loft—or play with the menagerie of pygmy goats and rabbits. Lakin and Miller take great pride in their huge breakfasts—casseroles, quiches, home-baked muffins, fresh fruit, locally smoked salmon served with vegetables from the garden—and provide plenty of snacks throughout the day and evening. *$$–$$$; AE, DIS, MC, V; checks OK; from Hwy 101, take the Seawood Dr exit and head N for 11 miles on Patrick's Point Dr.*

Trinidad Bay Bed and Breakfast / ★★

560 EDWARDS ST, TRINIDAD; 707/677-0840
Perched on a bluff overlooking Trinidad's quaint fishing harbor and the rugged California coast, this Cape Cod–style inn is the dream house of innkeepers Cor and Don Blue (known to their friends as Cordon Bleu), Southern California transplants who fell in love with the area while vacationing here. They offer four guest rooms and two great suites. Both suites

have private entrances, comfortable sitting rooms, spectacular views of Trinidad Bay, and breakfast-in-bed service. The full breakfast features entrees such as French toast puff and Italian egg pie served with fresh and baked fruit and homemade breads. *$$$; MC, V; checks OK; from Hwy 101, take the Trinidad exit to Main St and turn left on Trinity St.*

Orick and Redwood National and State Parks

The burl art capital of the world, Orick looks more like a huge outdoor gift shop than a town. What's burl art, you ask? Well, take a sizable chunk of redwood, do a little carving here and there with a small chain saw, and when it resembles some sort of mammal or rodent, you have yourself a piece. There are thousands of burl pieces to choose from here, ranging from the Abominable Burlman to Sasquatch and the Seven Dwarfs. Several roadside stands have viewing booths where mesmerized tourists watch the redwood chips fly. Orick is also the southern entry to **REDWOOD NATIONAL AND STATE PARKS**; one mile south of town off Highway 101 is the **REDWOOD INFORMATION CENTER** (707/464-6101, ext. 5265; www.nps.gov/redw), where visitors can pick up a free park map and browse through geologic, wildlife, and Native American exhibits; open every day 9am–5pm.

Of course, the best way to experience the parks and their magnificent redwoods is on foot. The short **FERN CANYON TRAIL** leads through an incredibly lush fern grotto. The **LADY BIRD JOHNSON GROVE LOOP** is an easy, one-hour self-guided tour that loops 1 mile around a gorgeous grove of redwoods. Closer to shore is the **YUROK LOOP NATURE TRAIL** at Lagoon Creek, located 6½ miles north of the Klamath River bridge on Highway 101; the 1-mile self-guided trail gradually climbs to the top of rugged sea bluffs—with wonderful panoramic views of the Pacific—and loops back to the parking lot. Perhaps the summa cum laude of trails is the **BOY SCOUT TREE TRAIL**, a 6-mile round-trip hike through a cool, damp forest brimming with giant ferns and majestic redwoods.

RESTAURANTS

Rolf's Park Café / ★

HWY 101, ORICK; 707/488-3841

After decades of working as a chef in Switzerland, Austria, San Francisco, and even aboard the presidential ship SS *Roosevelt*, the trilingual Rolf Rheinschmidt decided it was time to semiretire. He wanted to move to a small town to cook, and towns don't get much smaller than Orick—population 650. So here, among the redwoods, Rheinschmidt serves up good bratwurst, Wiener schnitzel, and crepes suzette. His specialty is marinated rack of spring lamb, and he has some unusual offerings such as wild boar, buffalo, and elk steak (the truly adventurous should get the combo platter featuring all three). Each dinner entree includes lots of extras: hors d'oeuvres, salad, vegetables, farm-style potatoes, and bread. And ever since the debut of Rheinschmidt's German Farmer Omelet—an open-faced concoction of ham, bacon, sausage, mushrooms, cheese, potatoes, and pasta, topped with sour cream and salsa and garnished with a strawberry crepe—breakfast in Orick has never been the same. *$$; MC, V; local checks only; breakfast, lunch, dinner every day in summer (typically open Mar–Nov); beer and wine; no reservations; 2 miles N of Orick.* ♿

Klamath

From the looks of it, the town of Klamath hasn't recovered much since it was washed away in 1964, when 40 inches of rain fell within 24 hours. All that remains are a few cheap motels, trailer parks, tackle shops, and boat rental outlets, kept in business by the numerous anglers who line the mighty Klamath River, one of the finest salmon and steelhead streams in the world. The scenery around the river is extraordinary; **REDWOOD NATIONAL PARK** and **KLAMATH NATIONAL FOREST** have some incredible coastal drives and trails that even the timid and out-of-shape can handle with aplomb.

Stretch out your legs at the lofty **KLAMATH OVERLOOK**, which stands about 600 feet above an estuary at the mouth of the Klamath River. A short but steep trail leads down to a second overlook that's ideal for whale-watching and taking photographs. To get there, take the Requa Road turnoff from Highway 101, north of the Klamath River bridge. For more hiking recommendations, read about Redwood National and State Parks in Orick (above).

One of the premier coastal drives on the Redwood Coast starts at the mouth of the Klamath River and runs 8 miles south toward **PRAIRIE CREEK REDWOODS STATE PARK**. If you're heading south on Highway 101, take the Alder Camp Road exit just south of the Klamath River bridge and follow the signs to the river mouth. North-bound travelers should take the Redwood National and State Parks Coastal Drive exit off the **NEWTON B. DRURY SCENIC PARKWAY**. Campers and cars with trailers are not advised. The narrow, partially paved road winds through stands of redwoods, with spectacular views of the sea and numerous turnouts for picture-taking (sea lions and pelicans abound) and short hikes. Keep an eye out for the World War II radar station, disguised as a farmhouse and barn.

LODGINGS

The Klamath Inn / ★

451 REQUA RD, KLAMATH; 707/482-1425

The Klamath Inn (formerly Requa Inn) was established in 1885, and since then it has gone through several owners, three name changes, one relocation, and a major fire that burned it to the ground in 1914 (it was rebuilt the same year). In 1985 innkeeper Paul Hamby discovered the inn abandoned and in foreclosure. He and his wife brought it back to life, and this venerable riverside inn is still going strong. The 10 spacious guest rooms are modestly decorated with antique furnishings and have private baths with showers or claw-footed tubs; four offer views of the lower Klamath River. Aside from being the only decent lodge in the greater Klamath area, the inn also has one of the best restaurants in the region. The bad news is that it's for guests only, though if it's not too busy, the management tries to accommodate a drop-in or two. From April through September breakfast is included with the room. Call for winter specials that include both breakfast and dinner. *$–$$; DIS, MC, V; checks OK; breakfast and dinner (guests only); beer and wine; from Hwy 101, take the Requa Rd exit and follow the signs.* &

Crescent City

Because it's the northern gateway to the popular **REDWOOD NATIONAL AND STATE PARKS** (for park highlights, see Orick, above), one might assume Crescent City would be a major tourist mecca, rife with fine restaurants and hotels. Unfortunately, it's not. Cheap motels, fast-food chains, and mini-malls are the main attractions along this stretch of Highway 101, as if Crescent City exists only to serve travelers on their way someplace else. The city is trying, however, to enhance its image, and if you know where to go (which is anywhere off Hwy 101), there are actually numerous sites worth visiting in the area and several outdoor-recreation options that are refreshingly nontouristy. You won't want to make Crescent City your primary destination, mind you, but don't be reluctant to spend a day lolling around here, either; you'd be surprised what the town has to offer besides gas and groceries.

For starters, take a side trip to the **NORTH COAST MARINE MAMMAL CENTER** (at the N end of Crescent City Harbor, at 424 Howe Dr in Beach Front Park; 707/465-MAML). This nonprofit organization was established in 1989 to rescue and rehabilitate stranded or injured marine mammals. Staffed by volunteers and funded by donations, the center is the only facility of its kind between San Francisco and Seattle, providing emergency response during environmental disasters and assisting marine researchers by collecting data on marine mammals. The center is open to the public every day year-round, and visitors are welcome to watch the volunteers in action, make a donation, and buy a nature book or two at the gift shop.

Other interesting local sites include the operational **BATTERY POINT LIGHTHOUSE** (707/464-3089), built in 1856 on a small island off the foot of A Street. Guided tours of the lighthouse and the light-keeper's living quarters are offered Wednesday through Sunday from 10am to 4pm, April through September, tide permitting (you have to cross a tide pool to get there). Next, head to the **B STREET PIER** (at the S foot of B St), rent a crab net ($5) and fishing pole ($5 including tackle) from Popeye's bait shop, and do some fishing and crabbing off the city's 800-foot-long pier. Crabbing is simple: throw the prebaited net into the water (don't forget to tie the other end to the pier), wait about 10 minutes, then pull it up and see what's for supper. Because it's a public pier, you don't even need a fishing license.

If you're not one to get your hands dirty, take a shoreline tour along **PEBBLE BEACH DRIVE** from the west end of Sixth Street to Point St. George. You're bound to see a few seals and sea lions at the numerous pullouts. End the tour with a short walk though a sandy meadow to **POINT ST. GEORGE**, a relatively deserted bluff that's perfect for a picnic or beach stroll. On a clear day, look out on the ocean for the **ST. GEORGE REEF LIGHTHOUSE**, reportedly the tallest (146 feet above sea level), deadliest (several light-keepers died in rough seas while trying to dock), and most expensive ($704,000) lighthouse ever built.

One of the prettiest picnic sites on the California Coast is along **ENDERTS ROAD** at the south end of town. Drive 3 miles south on Highway 101 from downtown, turn right on Enderts Road (across from the Ocean Way Motel), and continue 2⅓ miles. Park at the Crescent Beach Overlook, lay your blanket on the grass, and admire the ocean view. Type-A personalities can drive to the end of Enderts Road and take the 1.2-mile round-trip hiking trail to **ENDERTS BEACH**. In the summer, free 1½- to 2-hour ranger-guided tide pool and seashore walks are offered when the tides are right, starting at the beach parking lot. For specific tour times, call 707/464-6101, ext. 5265.

Crescent City's best-kept secret, however, is the **LAKE EARL WILDLIFE AREA**, a gorgeous habitat replete with deer, rabbits, beavers, otters, red-tailed hawks, peregrine falcons, bald eagles, songbirds (some 80 species), shorebirds, and migratory waterfowl who share these 5,000 acres of pristine woodlands, grasslands, and ocean shore. Hiking and biking are permitted, but you'll want to make the trip on foot with binoculars in hand to get the full effect of this amazing patch of coastal land. To get there, take the Northcrest Drive exit off Highway 101 in downtown Crescent City and turn left on Old Mill Road. Proceed 1½ miles to the park headquarters at 2591 Old Mill Road (if it's open, ask for a map) and park in the gravel lot. Additional trails start at the end of Old Mill Road. For more information, call the Department of Fish and Game (707/464-2523).

RESTAURANTS

Beachcomber Restaurant / ★

1400 HWY 101 S, CRESCENT CITY; 707/464-2205

Although several trendy eateries have made a brave stand in Crescent City, they've all fallen by the wayside. The Beachcomber is the most-nominated spot for a reliably decent meal. If you can get past the nautical theme and blue Naugahyde booths, it does a fair job of providing fresh seafood—halibut, red snapper, lingcod, chinook salmon—at reasonable prices. Set right on the beach, the Beachcomber also specializes in flame-broiled steaks, cooked to your specification on an open barbecue pit. Ask for a booth by the window, and start the evening with the steamer-clam appetizer: 1½ pounds of the North Coast's finest. *$$; MC, V; local checks only; dinner Thurs–Tues; beer and wine; reservations recommended; 2 miles S of downtown.* &

LODGINGS

Crescent Beach Motel / ★

1455 HWY 101 S, CRESCENT CITY; 707/464-5436

Crescent City has the dubious distinction of being the only city along the coast without a swanky hotel. There is, however, an armada of inexpensive accommodations, the best of which is the Crescent Beach Motel. A new color scheme of brown, beige, and green has improved the interiors considerably, and all but four of the 27 rooms are within steps of the beach. Most units have queen-size beds and color TVs. The small lawn area and large sundecks overlooking the ocean are great venues for kicking back and enjoying some true R&R. Another perk: you can get a seafood dinner at the Beachcomber Restaurant (see review, above), which is right next door. *$; AE, DIS, MC, V; no checks; 2 miles S of downtown.* &

NORTH MOUNTAINS

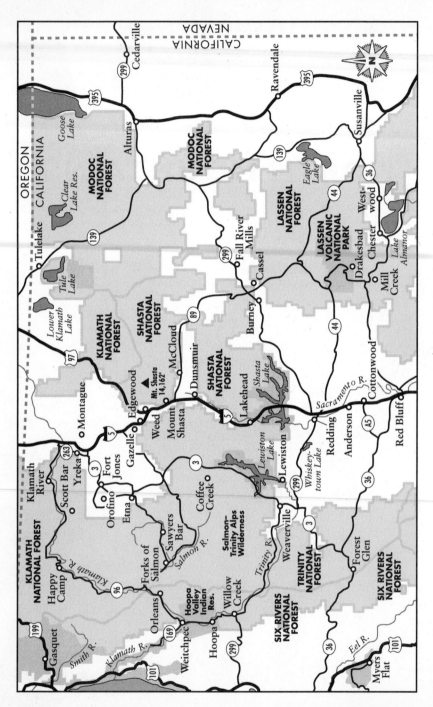

NORTH MOUNTAINS

As you drive north toward Redding up the flat, uninspiring Interstate 5 corridor, snow-topped Mount Shasta appears as a white smudge at the end of the highway. Venture a little closer and the imposing volcano soon dominates the horizon. This unforgettable sight heralds your approach to California's northern mountains. Step out of your car, and you'll feel as though you've stepped back in time to a simpler (and, frequently, less expensive) way of life. This area offers everything a pleasure-seeking visitor could hope for: prime fishing, bird-watching, boating, waterskiing, mountain biking, rock climbing, camping, hiking, river rafting, kayaking, golfing, and, in winter, every kind of snow sport.

You can detoxify in one of the many gorgeous mineral springs; hang out on a houseboat on Shasta Lake; explore the tortured lava caves and steaming thermal vents in Lassen Volcanic National Park; take a scenic ride on the dinner train departing from the adorable little town of McCloud; bike or cross-country ski the 10-mile paved path at Lake Almanor; get-along some little doggies at a dude ranch; or, if you're in really good shape, climb the magic mountain itself.

Accommodations in this part of the state range from wonderful wood cabins lit by kerosene lanterns to luxurious bed-and-breakfasts. Some very good restaurants are tucked away in places you've probably never heard of—Weaverville, Etna, Dunsmuir, and Chester—as well as in places you have. The town of Mount Shasta offers fine cuisine. This little piece of California is nature's unspoiled, uncrowded playground. And if you are friendly and play nicely, maybe the locals will let you keep coming back.

ACCESS AND INFORMATION

The region is predominantly medium-high mountain ranges (the Cascades, the Salmon, and Siskiyou Mountains), with high desert and rangeland to the east. The three major highways run north-south. INTERSTATE 5 from Los Angeles and Sacramento leaves the Central Valley at Redding (the largest town in the northern mountains region) and continues to Dunsmuir, Mount Shasta City, Weed, and Yreka, then on to Oregon. US 395 heads north from Reno, Nevada, through high desert and not much else until it gets to Alturas, then leaves California via its lonely northeastern corner. HIGHWAY 89, the curviest of the three north-south routes, starts from US 395 north of Reno and heads northwest to Lake Almanor and Chester. It then winds its way through Lassen Volcanic National Park past Burney and McCloud, skirting the great mountain, then joins Interstate 5 just south of Mount Shasta City.

East-west roads through this country are mostly mountainous. HIGHWAY 299 from Arcata to Redding via Weaverville is officially described as going "from the Redwood Coast to the Valley Oaks," neglecting any mention of the roller-coaster curves. From Redding it continues east to Alturas. **HIGHWAY 44** is the best route to Lassen Volcanic National Park from Redding.

The only airport in the region is the **REDDING MUNICIPAL AIRPORT**, served by two airlines, Horizon Air (800/547-9308) and United Express (800/241-6522). Car rentals are available there. The closest major airport is **SACRAMENTO INTERNATIONAL AIRPORT** (916/929-5411; 150 miles S of Redding; www.sacramentoairports.org).

GREYHOUND BUS (800/231-2222; www.greyhound.com) serves the towns along Interstate 5, and **AMTRAK'S COAST STARLIGHT TRAIN** (800/USA-RAIL; www.amtrak.com) from Seattle to Los Angeles makes two stops a day (one each way) at Dunsmuir and Redding.

For additional information, contact the **REDDING CONVENTION AND VISITORS BUREAU** (777 Auditorium Dr, Redding; 800/874-7562; ci.redding.ca.us/cnvb/cnvbhome.htm) or the **SHASTA CASCADE WONDERLAND ASSOCIATION** (800/474-2782; www.shastacascade.org), which offers info on Lassen, Modoc, Plumas, Siskiyou, Shasta, and Trinity Counties.

Redding and the Shasta Lake Area

About 20 minutes north of Redding, Shasta Lake, the largest reservoir in California, is a perfect introduction to the pleasures of the region and the ideal place for fishing, waterskiing, or just lounging with a good book in the sun on a houseboat. Be sure to stop in Redding for homey pleasures and a bit of local history.

Redding

A popular attraction here is the **REDDING MUSEUM OF ART AND HISTORY** (56 Quartz Hill Rd; 530/243-8801), which has local-history exhibits and a fine collection of Native American baskets. Next door is the **CARTER HOUSE NATURAL SCIENCE MUSEUM** (48 Quartz Hill Rd; 530/243-5457), a funky, spirited place that houses live animals as well as those that have spent some time with a taxidermist (rest assured that only animals that died accidentally or of natural causes got the glass-eye treatment). Kids will also find plenty of hands-on activities to keep them amused. For an extensive selection of newspapers, magazines, and other good reading material, the **REDDING BOOKSTORE** (1712 California St; 530/246-2171) is second to none in this part of the state. The bookstore also houses the **DOWNTOWN ESPRESSO AND COFFEE ROASTING COMPANY**, so you can get a good cup of joe to go along with that terrific travel tome you're now reading.

The 6-mile-long **SACRAMENTO RIVER TRAIL** meanders along the town's riverbanks and over a stress-ribbon concrete bridge—the only bridge of its kind in the country. This section of the river also offers good year-round urban fishing for steelhead, trout, and salmon; for information about where to cast your line, call Redding's world-class fly-fishing store, the **FLY SHOP** (800/669-3474). **WHISKEYTOWN LAKE**, west of Redding, offers great beaches and windsurfing and sailing opportunities; for information, call the lake's visitors center (530/246-1225).

RESTAURANTS

Buz's Crab / ★

2159 EAST ST, REDDING; 530/243-2120

Every day the bounty of the North Coast is hauled over the hills into California's parched interior to Buz's seafood market. With Naugahyde booths and Formica tables, this ain't no pretty place for a romantic dinner for two, but Buz's earns its star for doing what it does perfectly. The seafood baskets offer much more than your standard fish-and-chips: you'll find everything here—from stuffed prawns, oysters, scallops, and clam strips to calamari, catfish, Cajun halibut, and crisp potato rounds. From December through May, order the fabulous crab (just plucked from the boiling crab pots on the patio), along with a slab of Buz's fresh-baked sourdough bread. *$–$$; MC, V; local checks only; lunch, dinner every day; beer and wine; no reservations; N of W Cypress Ave and Pine St.*

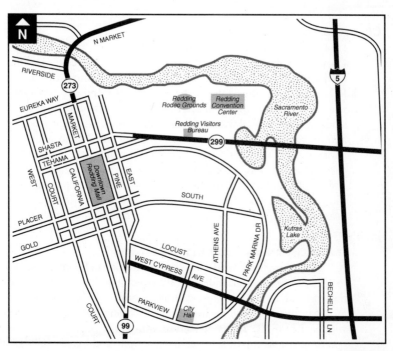

NORTH MOUNTAINS THREE-DAY TOUR

DAY ONE: Trail and rail. Spend the first night in Chester. Have dinner under the aspens (and by the creek) on the deck of the **Creekside Grill** and stay at the **Bidwell House Bed and Breakfast**. In the morning, grab breakfast at the B&B and then stop at one of the grocery stores downtown and get picnic fixings before you head out to **Lassen Volcanic National Park**, where you can stretch your legs by walking the **Bumpass Hell Trail** past wildflowers, hissing fumaroles, steam vents, and assorted mud pots. Back in the car, continue north on Highway 89 around Mount Lassen, briefly stopping at 129-foot-high **McArthur-Burney Falls** to watch some of the 200 million gallons of water that fall there daily. A short trip through the pines will get you to **McCloud** to board the **Shasta Sunset Dinner Train** for a fine dinner with **Mount Shasta** as a backdrop. Repair to the **McCloud Bed and Breakfast Hotel** for the night.

DAY TWO: Up a mystic mountain. Fuel up at the B&B, then move on to **Mount Shasta**, stopping at **Mount Shasta Ski Park** to rent a mountain bike and gear. Take the ski lift to the top (elevation: 6,600 feet) and bike back down to the lodge. Repeat this as many times as your nerves and muscles will allow. Then, make the short drive to

Cheesecakes Unlimited & Cafe / ★★

1344 MARKET ST, REDDING; 530/244-6670

Cory Gabrielson and Nicholas Parker started Cheesecakes Unlimited as a wholesale cheesecake business, then opened a small cafe that offers light meals—so now you can have your cake and eat croissant sandwiches and freshly made salads, too. A couple of winners are the house-smoked salmon salad with tomatoes, cucumbers, asparagus, red peppers, and oregano vinaigrette, and the prawn and pasta salad with a roasted garlic and herbed vinaigrette dressing. Of course, the New York–style cheesecakes (lemon, chocolate-chocolate, raspberry, almond amaretto, and mocha Baileys) are the kind you'd never want to pass up—or even share with your mate. *$; AE, DIS, MC, V; checks OK; lunch Mon–Fri; beer and wine; no reservations; just N of the downtown mall.*

Jack's Grill / ★★

1743 CALIFORNIA ST, REDDING; 530/241-9705

A 1930s tavern, Jack's Grill is a beloved institution in Redding—so beloved, in fact, that few even grumble over the typical two-hour wait for a table on the weekend. But be forewarned: this is a carnivores-only club, specializing in huge, juicy 1-pound steaks, tender brochettes, and thick steak sandwiches. The meaty meals are served with garlic bread, a green salad, a potato, and coffee. Jack starts cooking at 5pm, and hungry folks get there

Mount Shasta City, stopping at Lily's for a lunch on the deck before you check in at the **Mount Shasta Ranch Bed and Breakfast**. Do some serious lounging on the front lawn for late afternoon views of America's most photogenic mountain before you get back in the car for a short jaunt to Dunsmuir for a Sardinian dinner at **Cafe Maddalena**. Afterward, take a walk in the town's restored historic railroad section along Sacramento Avenue.

DAY THREE: Nature's temple. After scrumptious breakfast at the inn, head for the beautiful **upper Sacramento River** (it's more of a stream here) down to **Shasta Lake**, stopping first for a ferry ride across the lake to visit the **Lake Shasta Caverns** with 20-foot-high stalactites/mites, followed by a stop at **Shasta Dam**. Take the tour of the dam, descending 600 feet into its bowels to view its dynamos and turbines. Then it's on to **Redding**, with a stop at **Buz's Crab** for a quick Louie and a beer before heading west into the **Trinity Alps** to **Weaverville**. Walk around this 1850s gold mining town that reeks of history, being sure to peek in at the old Chinese miners' **Taoist temple** on Main Street. End your tour with one of Sharon Heryford's great dinners at the **La Grange Cafe**, two short blocks from the temple before heading to the **Old Lewiston Inn** in Lewiston to unwind.

early. *$$; AE, DIS, MC, V; local checks only; dinner Mon–Sat; full bar; no reservations; S of the downtown mall, between Sacramento and Placer Sts.*

La Gondola / ★★

630 N MARKET ST, REDDING; 530/244-6321

La Gondola is so popular in Redding that when it moved to its current location, loans from loyal customers kept it going until the new place was up and running. The restaurant specializes in Northern Italian cuisine, which features creamier, less spicy sauces than Southern Italian food. Some of the most popular entrees are chicken stuffed with prosciutto cooked in white wine and cream; filet mignon topped with roasted garlic, caramelized onions, and Madeira wine; and spinach- and cheese-filled agnolotti. The restaurant's version of tiramisu, a layered confection of chocolate, mascarpone cheese, and Kahlua, is justifiably famous. *$$; AE, DIS, MC, V; local checks only; lunch Tues–Fri, dinner Tues–Sat; beer and wine; reservations recommended; a few blocks N of the Sacramento River.* &

LODGINGS

Tiffany House Bed and Breakfast Inn / ★★

1510 BARBARA RD, REDDING; 530/244-3225

 Perched on a hill above town, Brady and Susan Stewart's beautifully refurbished Cape Cod–style home offers three guest rooms and a cottage, a swimming pool, and a fine view of Mount Lassen. The Victorian Rose

Room, dressed in black-and-mauve rose-print walls, features charming cupola windows and a claw-footed bathtub. If you're an early bird, you'll appreciate the blue and white Tierra Room and the larger Oak Room, which both offer great sunrise views. All three rooms have a queen-size bed and a private bath. Guests are welcome to lounge in the antique-filled music parlor, where old-time sheet music is stacked on the piano. Another parlor houses a game table and a fireplace, an ideal retreat on cool nights. If you prefer total privacy (and can fork over a few more bucks), rent the attractive guest cottage, where you can bask in the luxurious indoor spa. $$–$$$; AE, DIS, MC, V; checks OK; off Benton Dr.

Shasta Lake

To fully appreciate Shasta Lake's 370 miles of shoreline, view the lake by boat. And while you're at it, keep your eye on the sky for a glimpse of the mighty **BALD EAGLE**, the largest bird of prey in North America. Shasta Lake is currently the home of at least 18 pairs of the endangered bird—the largest nesting population of bald eagles in California. For information about other lake attractions and **HOUSEBOAT RENTALS**, call the Redding Convention and Visitors Bureau (800/874-7562).

If you're heading up to Shasta Lake on I-5, the monolithic 3,640-foot-long **SHASTA DAM** (from I-5, take the Shasta Dam Blvd exit and follow the signs; 530/275-4463) is a great place to pull over for a lengthy pit stop. Shasta is the second-largest and second-tallest concrete dam in the United States (it contains enough concrete to build a 3-foot-wide sidewalk around the world) and one of the most impressive civil engineering feats in the nation. The visitors center and viewing area are rather ho-hum, but the free 45-minute tour of the dam is outstanding. It kicks off with a speedy elevator ride into the chilly bowels of the 15-million-ton, 602-foot-high structure—definitely not recommended for claustrophobes. Dam tours are held from 9am to 4pm every day; call for information and winter and holiday hours.

About 10 miles north of the dam is another popular attraction: guided tours of the impressive, crystal-studded stalagmites and stalactites in the **LAKE SHASTA CAVERNS** (from I-5, take the Shasta Caverns Rd exit and follow the signs; 530/238-2341). Getting there is an adventure in itself; after you pull off the highway and check in at cavern headquarters, you'll have to hop aboard a ferry for a 15-minute trip across Shasta Lake, then climb onto a bus for a white-knuckle ride up to the caverns (open every day, year-round). And anglers take note: the stretch of the **SACRAMENTO RIVER** between Shasta Lake and Mount Shasta is one of the top spots in the country for trout fishing, so don't forget to pack the rod and reel. For tips on touring the area north of Shasta Lake, see the Mount Shasta section in this chapter.

The Trinity Alps Region

National forest blankets 70 percent of Trinity County, which includes the stunning Trinity Alps north of Highway 299. The area is chock-full of good fishing spots, especially on the **TRINITY RIVER, TRINITY (A.K.A. CLAIR ENGLE) LAKE, AND LEWISTON LAKE**. Mountain bikers, hikers, and horseback riders flock to the scenic 50-mile **WEAVER BASIN TRAIL**, which circles Weaverville.

Lewiston

LODGINGS

Old Lewiston Inn / ★★

ON DEADWOOD RD, LEWISTON; 530/778-3385 OR 800/286-4441

This B&B on the banks of the Trinity River's fly-fishing-only section caters—surprise—to fly fishermen (and women). It has seven guest rooms: three small rooms in the 1875 Baker House and four rooms in the adjoining inn. All have private baths. A favorite is the Baker House's Herbert Hoover Room, where the 31st president once slept. The inn accommodations have less history but more elbow room, with private entrances and decks overlooking the Trinity River. The Old Lewiston Inn also has a hot tub for unwinding after a hard day of touring the area or fishing for trout. New innkeepers Cynthia Stack and Rich Doty prepare a hearty country breakfast, and you can eat and keep an eye out for fish rising in the river out the back door. *$$; DIS, MC, V; checks OK; ½ block from the bridge.* ૬

Weaverville

Founded nearly 150 years ago by gold miners, the little rural town of Weaverville, population 4,000, is the largest town in Trinity County (an area the size of Rhode Island and Delaware combined). While cruising through the historic downtown district, keep your peepers open for the peculiar outdoor spiral staircases that grace many of the homes—they're remnants of the days when each floor was owned by a different person. For a bit of Gold Rush and Weaverville history, stroll down Main Street and visit the small **JAKE JACKSON MUSEUM** (508 Main St; 530/623-5211). Adjacent to the museum is **JOSS HOUSE STATE HISTORIC PARK**, site of the oldest **CHINESE TEMPLE** (530/623-5284) in the United States. The well-preserved temple was built by immigrant Chinese miners in 1874 and is worth a peek (and the nominal entrance fee); call for information on temple tours.

Another town highlight is the grueling **LA GRANGE CLASSIC MOUNTAIN BIKE RACE**, typically held the first weekend in June. To find out more about this mountain town's activities, call the **TRINITY COUNTY CHAMBER OF COMMERCE** (530/623-6101 or 800/487-4648). For infor-

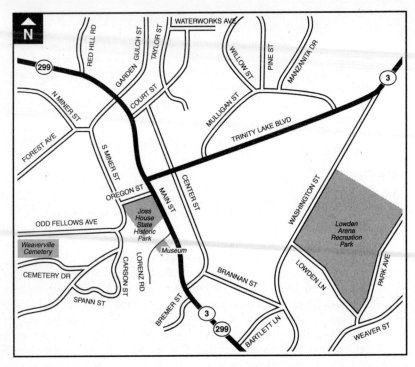

WATERWORKS AVE

299

3

WEAVERVILLE

mation about hunting, fishing, and backpacking in the area, visit the helpful staff at **BRADY'S SPORT SHOP** (201 Main St; 530/623-3121), located on the ground floor of the Weaverville Hotel.

RESTAURANTS

La Grange Cafe / ★★★

226 MAIN ST, WEAVERVILLE; 530/623-5325

Named after a nearby mine, La Grange Cafe serves the best food in the county. Start your dinner with chef/owner Sharon Heryford's exceptionally fresh salad tossed with an Italian dressing and chunks of blue cheese. Then sink your teeth into her charbroiled marinated steak served with black bean chili, or try one of the game dishes such as venison loin chops or buffalo burger steak. There are lots of choices of seafood, chicken, and pasta dishes, too. An excellent and moderately priced wine list boasts more than 100 selections. And then there's the sweet stuff: divine desserts, such as berry cobbler, banana cream pie, and old-fashioned bread pudding, are made on the premises. La Grange recently relocated into a big, airy brick building in the town's historic area, with lots of room for the folks who flock to the place. *$$; AE, DIS, MC, V; checks OK; breakfast, lunch, dinner every day; full bar; reservations recommended; on Hwy 299.* ⅋

Noelle's Garden Cafe / ★★

252 MAIN ST, WEAVERVILLE; 530/623-2058

This snug, cheerful cafe in an old two-story house has a phalanx of windows and a sunny outside deck. Proprietor Noelle Roget's specialties include Austrian strudel (a flaky puff pastry filled with shrimp, veggies, and cheeses) and a hefty veggie melt served with her home fries spiced with garlic and onion. The seasonal dinner menu may include such dishes as a perfectly cooked lime-marinated halibut or a stir-fry prepared with jumbo shrimp, chicken, or fresh vegetables. She also offers an array of baked desserts, and if the espresso cake is up for grabs, grab it. *$; no credit cards; checks OK; breakfast, lunch every day Memorial Day–Labor Day (Tues–Sat Labor Day–Memorial Day), dinner Fri–Sat year-round; no alcohol; no reservations; 1 block W of Oregon St.*

LODGINGS

Red Hill Motel / ★

RED HILL RD, WEAVERVILLE; 530/623-4331

The Red Hill's 14 well-maintained auto-court units (cabins with small covered garages) would have made a great set for a '40s film noir starring Ida Lupino and Humphrey Bogart. (If you've forgotten your film history lessons, auto-courts were a prominent feature of flicks in those days.) So put on your best Bogart fedora and step back in time by booking a night or two at these one- or two-bedroom cabins, decorated with authentic pre–World War II furnishings (except for the remote-control cable TV and in-room phones, of course). Owners Patty and Willie Holder are doing a good job of restoring and refurbishing this jewel, surrounded by a rolling green lawn and ponderosa pines. Spend the day reeling in rainbow trout on the Trinity, then prepare your catch for supper at the Red Hill's fish-cleaning station. Or kick back in a lawn chair under the pines and think about the good ol' days, when life was simpler, the fish were bigger, and folks were named Claudette, Clark, Ida, and Humphrey. The friendly Red Hill folks permit pets, too. *$; AE, DIS, MC, V; no checks; across from the U.S. Forest Service station on Main St, at the W end of town.*

Weaverville Hotel

201 MAIN ST, WEAVERVILLE; 530/623-3121

This hotel has been in operation since 1861—a few fiery interruptions notwithstanding (it burned to the ground several times in the town's early days). The eight guest rooms, located on the second floor, are a bit spare, but they're a good choice for the budget-conscious traveler who likes historic surroundings with that morning cup of coffee. All rooms have private baths; most have TVs. Register at Brady's Sport Shop on the ground floor, a gold mine of information about hunting, backpacking, and fishing in the area. *$; MC, V; checks OK; in the center of town.*

Willow Creek

RESTAURANTS

Cinnabar Sam's / ★

19 WILLOW WY, WILLOW CREEK; 530/629-3437

If you travel between the Pacific coastline and Redding, be sure to stop for a bite at Cinnabar Sam's. A popular hangout for rafters and kayakers, this restaurant is decked out in Western memorabilia: antique gas pumps, old photographs, and movie posters from the golden days—even the salad bar is in a claw-footed tub. A favorite breakfast dish is the Claim Jumper: ham, scrambled eggs, hash browns, onions, bell peppers, sausage, and cheese. For lunch or dinner, try the popular do-it-yourself fajitas, the behemoth burger, the sirloin steak, or the barbecued ribs. *$; AE, DIS, MC, V; checks OK; breakfast, lunch, dinner every day; no reservations; beer and wine; at Hwy 299, at the E end of town.*

Forks of Salmon

LODGINGS

Otter Bar Lodge / ★★★

ON SALMON RIVER RD, FORKS OF SALMON; 530/462-4772

Surrounded by a pond and acres of mowed green grass, this seven-bedroom ranch-style lodge features oak floors, French doors, and lots of glass—all in an effort to bring the outdoors indoors. Two living rooms, two kitchens, a sauna, and a hot tub are also available to guests. The cedar-roofed, whitewashed rooms have private decks and down comforters on the beds, and some are stocked with good books. Reserve the romantic Tower Room, an upstairs retreat lined with windows offering views of the fir trees, or try one of the three cabins. Otter Bar Lodge doubles as a world-class kayaking school and offers some of the most beautiful mountain biking trails in the state. The food is terrific—no ranch-style meat and potatoes here. Instead, look for paella, snapper Veracruz, and other sophisticated delights on the ever-changing menu. Breakfast offerings include veggie omelets, homemade granola, and berry pancakes. Weeklong stays are required. All meals are included in the weekly rate. *$$$$; MC, V; checks OK; open mid-Apr–Sept 30; 15 miles E of Somes Bar.*

Coffee Creek

South of Etna on Highway 3 is the postage-stamp-size town of Coffee Creek, which supposedly got its name from a miner's pack train that

BIGFOOT STEPPED HERE

Consider yourself forewarned . . . California's North Mountains are Sasquatch territory. Also known as Bigfoot, this huge, hairy, ape-like mammal has been the subject of hundreds of reports in and around Trinity County, including three sightings within 10 miles of each other (by different people) in the Shasta-Trinity National Forest in 1999. There's a new Bigfoot Wing in the **Willow Creek/China Flat Museum** (corner of Hwys 299 and 96 in Willow Creek; 530/629-2653) that commemorates the elusive creature. You'll know you're in the right place when you see the 23-foot redwood carving of Bigfoot out front. The museum contains dozens of plaster casts of large footprints discovered in the Northern California wilderness as well as a Bigfoot research center.

The legend of the man-beast has been around forever, known in many countries and by many names: as Yeti, the abominable snowman; as one of the Mound People; as Sasquatch, a name that comes from an ancient tribal language in British Columbia; and as Bigfoot. Information compiled from thousands of reputed sightings in North America has been organized into a composite description. Bigfoot is typically described as being between 7 and 12 feet tall and as weighing between 250 to 400 pounds. Experts on the subject maintain that there are 133 such creatures living in 16 family groups in North America, and that an average family group consists of 8 members. Bigfoot is nocturnal, lives in caves, and has enhanced night vision, smell, and hearing. You will be relieved to know that the California Sasquatch is a vegetarian, while in the southern part of the United States, Bigfoot is a carnivore. This creature swims well, runs fast, is painfully shy—although curious—and apparently smells really, really bad.

The search for Sasquatch has gone high-tech in recent years, with investigators carrying tape recorders, motion detectors, infrared cameras, and nightscopes into the wild. Sharing information on the Internet has enabled searchers to pursue patterns and similarities among the reported encounters. In spite of the footprints, sightings, blurry photographs, and tapes, however, no verifiable physical remains of Sasquatch have been found. A California Department of Fish and Game spokesman in Redding declared that while Bigfoot sightings do occur in Trinity County, the agency probably won't investigate the most recent ones. "We don't have a management plan for Bigfoot," he explained.

—*Mary Anne Moore*

spilled coffee into the town's creek, although some claim the name came from the spring runoff, which colors the creek brown. Whatever the case, this town dates back to the Gold Rush days of the 1850s. There aren't many places to dine around here, but your best bet is the **FOREST CAFE** (Hwy 3 at Coffee Creek Rd; 530/266-3575). Venture a little farther south, and you'll see **TRINITY LAKE** (also known as Clair Engle Lake in honor of an environmentally conscious local politician), a popular haunt of anglers and other lovers of the great outdoors.

LODGINGS

Ripple Creek Cabins / ★★

EAGLE CREEK LOOP, COFFEE CREEK; 530/266-3505 OR 510/531-5315
Set amid tall pines and cedars where Ripple Creek enters the Trinity River, all seven of Jim and Michele Coleman's well-furnished cabins have amply stocked kitchens (wow! corkscrews and garlic presses!) and private baths. Most of the cabins accommodate two to six people. There's also a four-bedroom house for rent—ideal for a family reunion or group retreat. Diversions include table tennis, bicycles, a volleyball and badminton court, and a swimming hole. For a $10 fee, you can even bring your pooch along. *$–$$; no credit cards; checks OK; off Hwy 3.*

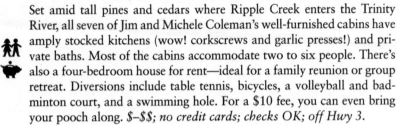

Mount Shasta and the Yreka Area

Magnificent, snowcapped Mount Shasta, soaring 14,162 feet into the sky, is the largest volcano (by mass) in the contiguous 48 states. Shasta is a dormant volcano; it's not dead, just sleeping until it decides to blow its snowy stack—something it hasn't done since the late 1700s. Nestled about the peak are the railroad, mill, and lumber towns of Dunsmuir, McCloud, and Weed, along with Mount Shasta City. Traveling north toward the Oregon border, you'll discover the rustic treasures and rough-and-tumble pleasures of more small towns set in the great outdoors.

Dunsmuir

When a Southern Pacific train ran off the tracks in 1991 and spilled an herbicide in the Sacramento River, it killed all aquatic life for 45 miles along the river. And it darn near killed Dunsmuir. But this pretty, historic railroad town has a population of 2,300 resilient residents who are bringing the place back with a vengeance. Using a financial settlement from Southern Pacific, the townsfolk have gussied up their community and hope to make Dunsmuir a major California tourist destination. They may just succeed. In addition to the beautiful natural surroundings, stylish gift shops and restaurants have sprung up on the city's streets (particularly on Dunsmuir and Sacramento Avenues). Furthermore, **TROPHY-SIZE WILD TROUT** now abound in the Sacramento River, and the community slogan is "Home of the best water on earth." Fortunately, not all of the tourists are coming to Dunsmuir by car, thanks to the Amtrak train that stops here daily. Call the **DUNSMUIR CHAMBER OF COMMERCE AND VISITORS CENTER** (800/DUNSMUIR) for the nitty-gritty.

RESTAURANTS

Cafe Maddalena / ★★★★

5801 SACRAMENTO AVE, DUNSMUIR; 530/235-2725
Had chef/owner Maddalena Sera built her restaurant in San Francisco, it would have been a great success among the city's culinary cognoscenti. Thank goodness she didn't, because Dunsmuir is a perfect (though surprising) place for her cafe. Sera is from Sardinia, an island west of the southern Italian peninsula, so expect superb Italian cuisine with subtle differences in flavors and ingredients from what you'd find on the Italian mainland. For example, Sardinians are particularly fond of using fish in their fare, and instead of incorporating Parmesan cheese into many of their dishes they prefer to use the sharper-flavored pecorino (cheese made from sheep's milk). Sera cooks everything herself from behind a counter in the corner of her cafe, which only holds a dozen tables. The small scale of her restaurant enables Sera to consistently whip up delicious fare night after night. Her seasonal one-page menu is always satisfying but quite simple: appetizers, salads, pizza, pasta, and a fresh fish and meat dish of the day. Don't pass up the menu's mainstays: the Gallega Salad—made with shrimp, parsley, garlic, and thinly sliced potatoes with a lemon dressing—and the Pasta Marco— fresh fettuccine with shrimp, tomatoes, herbs, and cream, wrapped in dough and baked in the pizza oven. Everything is made daily, including the breads and desserts. The wine list is small but carefully selected and reasonably priced. Cafe Maddalena is, unfortunately, only open half the year. *$$; MC, V; local checks only; dinner Thurs–Sun, open May–mid-Dec; beer and wine; reservations recommended; one block W of Dunsmuir Ave.*

LODGINGS

Railroad Park Resort/The Caboose Motel

100 RAILROAD PARK RD, DUNSMUIR; 530/235-4440
A must for railroad buffs but a maybe for everyone else, the Railroad Park Resort's funky Caboose Motel offers quiet, comfortable lodgings in a boxcar and 23 refurbished cabooses from the Southern Pacific, Santa Fe, and Great Northern Railroads. Most have king- or queen-size beds with small bay windows or rooftop cupolas. The Boxcar (room 20) is decorated in country antiques and has a small private patio. Motel management also rents out four cabins. All guests have access to the pool and Jacuzzi—not to mention a great view of nearby Castle Crags. Guests may bring along their small pets for an extra $10. And if you're a big prime rib fan, you're in luck: that's the specialty of the Railroad Park Resort Restaurant. *$–$$; AE, DIS, MC, V; checks OK; 1 mile S of town.* &

McCloud

A company-built mill town, McCloud bills itself as "the quiet side of Mount Shasta." And true to its motto, this is a relatively sleepy place, but its many sumptuous B&Bs attract a lot of anglers, hikers, and other nature lovers who spend their waking hours outdoors, as well as those bleary-eyed city folk who long for little more than a warm bed and some solitude. Whatever your attraction to this neck of the woods, you can introduce yourself to the area in style by hopping aboard the **SHASTA SUNSET DINNER TRAIN** (530/964-2142 or 800/733-2141), which follows a historic turn-of-the-century logging route. Now, as then, the steep grades, sharp curves, and a unique switchback at Signal Butte are still part of the route, though today's passengers ride in cars handsomely restored in wood and brass. As you nosh on a very good dinner in your railcar, you'll be treated to views of Mount Shasta, Castle Crags, and the Trinity Alps. The 40-mile, 3-hour journey is run by the McCloud Railway Company year-round and costs $75, which includes dinner. Special-event train trips are scheduled throughout the year.

In the summer, you can watch—or, better yet, join—the McCloud locals as they kick up their heels every night from May to September in the town's air-conditioned dance hall. **DANCING**—especially square dancing—is a favorite pastime here, so if you want to promenade your partner or swing to the beat, call 530/964-2578 for the latest schedule. This part of the North Mountains is also extraordinarily rich in outdoor recreational opportunities; see the Mount Shasta section for details.

LODGINGS

Hogin House / ★★★

424 LAWNDALE CT, MCCLOUD; 530/964-2882 OR 877-964-2882
Many innkeepers try, but few have managed to create the relaxing ambience and charm of a country B&B as well as Angie and Rich Toreson have. Located just outside downtown McCloud, their small, delightfully cluttered two-story Victorian house was built in 1904 for the town doctor. The four guest bedrooms are decorated with antique toys, colorful quilts, calico fabrics, and country-style wallpaper. An expanded continental breakfast of fresh fruit, cereal, homemade breads and muffins, juice, coffee, and tea may be served in the dining room, on the porch, or on the lush lawn that sweeps down toward the center of town. It's just a short, one-block walk from here to the popular Sunset Dinner Train. *$; AE, MC, V; checks OK; at W Colombero Dr.*

McCloud Bed and Breakfast Hotel / ★★★★

408 MAIN ST, MCCLOUD; 530/964-2822 OR 800/964-2823
Built in 1916, the McCloud Bed and Breakfast Hotel has earned a highly coveted spot on the National Register of Historic Landmarks. Its meticulous restoration was completed in 1995, and now the hotel offers 17 beautiful guest rooms gussied up with antiques, decorator fabrics, and, in many cases, tall four-poster beds. Each room also has a private bath. Gourmet

breakfasts of fresh fruit, house-made bread, and a hot dish are served in the lobby area (though if you're staying in a suite, you can have the meal delivered to your room). Lunch and dinner are also available for guests. If you happen to tire of McCloud's numerous outdoor attractions, kick back in the hotel lobby's comfortable chairs and sofas and borrow one of the many books, games, and puzzles stashed here. A new conference center has recently been opened. *$$–$$$; AE, DIS, MC, V; checks OK; from exit off Hwy 89, follow signs to the historical district.* &

McCloud Guest House / ★★★

606 W COLOMBERO DR, MCCLOUD; 530/964-3160 OR 877-964-3160
Built in 1907 for McCloud timber baron J. H. Queal, this stately two-story mansion became the McCloud River Lumber Company's guest house after Queal's death in 1921. Herbert Hoover, Jean Harlow, and various members of the Hearst family dallied here in the '20s and '30s, but soon afterward the house fell into disrepair. Restored as a country inn and restaurant, McCloud Guest House reopened its doors in 1984. In 1999, new ownership brought new life to this wonderful inn. Downstairs in the lobby and dining room are delicately wrought cabinetry, beveled glass, antique wallpaper, and a massive stone fireplace. The inn's spacious five guest rooms have four-poster beds and antique furnishings. A multicourse spa breakfast is served with offerings like fresh fruit smoothies, Belgian waffles, potato pancakes, and, sometimes, freshly baked scones with Devonshire cream. *$$; AE, MC, V; no checks; at the W end of town.*

McCloud River Inn / ★★★

325 LAWNDALE CT, MCCLOUD; 530/964-2130 OR 800/261-7831
Yet another of the delightful bed-and-breakfasts in charming McCloud, the innkeepers knock themselves out to make sure their guests have a good time. Built at the turn of the century as headquarters for the McCloud River Lumber Company, this inn has been beautifully restored, and its five guest rooms are filled with period-style furnishings. All have private bathrooms (one with a spa tub and one with a claw-footed soaking tub). Breakfast is a big attraction, with fresh fruit, pastries, and frittata. The inn has massage therapists on call and a gift shop specializing in German folk art and toys on the premises. *$–$$$; AE, DIS, MC, V; checks OK; at the N end of town.*

Mount Shasta

Mount Shasta is only the fifth-highest peak in the state, but unlike its taller cousins, which are clustered with other large mountains, this volcano stands alone, a position that seems to intensify its grandeur. "Lonely as God and white as a winter moon" is how author Joaquin Miller described this solitary peak in the 1870s. The mountain dominates the horizon from every angle, and on clear days it's visible from as far away as 150 miles.

Some Native Americans who lived in its shadow believed Mount Shasta was the home of the Great Spirit and vowed never to climb its sacred slopes, which they viewed as an act of disrespect. Today, men and women from around the world pay tribute to the volcano by making the spectacular trek to the top. This is not a mountain for novice hikers, however; its many tremendous crevasses have swallowed careless climbers, and its extreme, unpredictable weather at high altitudes makes expert equipment a must. But with some **BASIC MOUNTAIN CLIMBING** instruction and a good study of Shasta's various routes, physically fit adventurers can safely reach its stunning summit ("It's just like climbing stairs nonstop from 9 to 5," says one veteran climber). You can buy a good map of the mountain and rent crampons, an ice ax, and sturdy, insulated climbing boots at the **FIFTH SEASON** (300 N Mount Shasta Blvd at Lake St; 530/926-3606 store and 530/926-5555 mountain report), staffed by experienced and helpful mountaineers. If you're eager to climb Mount Shasta but you don't know a crampon from a tampon, take an all-day lesson in basic mountain-climbing skills from the folks at **SHASTA MOUNTAIN GUIDES** (530/926-3117), who also lead three- and four-day guided climbs. And whether you're a beginner or an expert climber, visit the **MOUNT SHASTA RANGER DISTRICT OFFICE** (204 W Alma St off N Mount Shasta Blvd; 530/926-4511), which provides up-to-date climbing literature as well as friendly advice. Get your free (and mandatory) **HIKING PERMIT** while you're there, so the rangers will know how long you'll be on the mountain. Permits are located in a small booth outside the front door. You also must sign off on your permit after you return from your climb so a rescue team won't be sent out to find you.

If all this climbing sounds a wee bit intimidating, there is an easier way. For the past decade, many folks have made their way up Mount Shasta via a chairlift (though it doesn't reach the peak) and their way down on skis. **MOUNT SHASTA SKI PARK** (at the end of Ski Park Hwy, off Hwy 89, 10 miles E of I-5; 530/926-8610 ski resort and 530/926-8686 snow report) offers mostly intermediate runs with nary a mogul in sight, and the lift tickets won't require taking out a second mortgage on your home. Ski Park also has a ski and snowboard rental/repair shop, restaurant, snack bar, and ski school. In the summer, the resort provides naturalist-led walks, mountain biking trails accessible by chairlift (bike rentals are available, too), and an indoor recreational climbing wall for people of all ages and abilities. About a quarter-mile down the highway is the **NORDIC LODGE** (on Ski Park Hwy; 530/926-8610), a cross-country ski center with several miles of groomed tracks.

If you prefer to admire Mount Shasta from afar, visit **CASTLE CRAGS STATE PARK** (from I-5, take the Castle Crags State Park exit, about 13 miles S of Mount Shasta; 530/235-2684), one of California's geologic wonders.

MYSTIC MOUNTAIN

Indigenous Native Americans have always considered Mount Shasta a holy mountain, the home of the Great Spirit. Over the years, spiritual seekers, New Age believers, and other metaphysical folk have also pronounced it one of the most powerful sacred sites in North America; organizations like the Creative Harmonics Institute, the Ascended Master Teaching Foundation, the Temple of Cosmic Religion, I AM Activity, Planetary Citizens, and the Radiant School of Seekers and Servers have, at one time or another, made the base of the mountain their temporal home. And then there are the people *inside* the mountain. Lemurians, believed by some to be highly evolved beings descended from an ancient civilization called Lemuria, can supposedly materialize at will and may (it is said) occasionally show themselves to the faithful. Strange lights and noises on Mount Shasta are sometimes attributed to these folk. There is also an Indian legend that says ancient lizard people once built a city beneath the mountain. And, indeed, a "lizard person" was allegedly spotted by one visitor in 1972.

The most famous metaphysical assembly in recent years was the 1987 Harmonic Convergence, a gathering of 5,000 people who met at Mount Shasta to create a cosmic consciousness providing "attunement to the planet and to higher galactic intelligences." Four UFOs and an angel announcing the beginning of heaven on earth reportedly appeared. The UFOs could be attributed to the saucer-shaped clouds that form around the mountain, emanating beams of light—a perfectly feasible explanation, scientists say. The angel remains a mystery.

Today around Mount Shasta, you can take workshops employing sweat lodges, ceremonial circles, and Peruvian whistling vessels to awaken your inner warrior or to retrieve your soul (special discounts for dot-com types). Locals not of the New Age persuasion have occasionally been heard to refer to their spiritual neighbors as "cosmic muffins," but for the most part, all is peace and harmony here. At the very least, you can get really good vegetarian food in town.

If you're interested in learning about the mountain's alleged mystical powers, visit the delightfully funky **Golden Bough Bookstore** (219 N Mount Shasta Blvd at Lake St, Mount Shasta City; 530/926-3228), where the staff can give you the lowdown and direct you to tapes, books, and all matter of spiritual info. —*Mary Anne Moore*

The park's enormous 6,500-foot spires of ancient granite are visible from the highway, but they deserve a much closer look. If you're anxious to really stretch your legs, hike up the park's moderately strenuous 2.7-mile SUMMIT DOME TRAIL to the base of the crags—the view of Mount Shasta alone is worth the trip. Less adventurous souls can stroll along the 1-mile ROOT CREEK or INDIAN CREEK TRAILS or picnic among the pines and wildflowers.

For another unforgettable experience, splurge on a guided **WHITE-WATER-RAFTING** trip down the mighty **KLAMATH RIVER**. Daredevils can soar down the narrow, steep chutes appropriately called Hell's Corner and Caldera, while saner souls (including children) can navigate the much-less-perilous forks. Trips are also available on the upper Sacramento, the Trinity, and other nearby rivers. Prices for one-day trips range from $85 to $120 (multiday trips are also available). Call the **TURTLE RIVER RAFTING COMPANY** (530/926-3223) for more details.

The town of Mount Shasta offers two good (and safe) attractions that won't even make a dent in your billfold: the free **SISSON MUSEUM** (530/926-5508) showcases changing exhibits on local history, nature, geology, and Native American life, and its adjacent **MOUNT SHASTA FISH HATCHERY** (take Lake St across the freeway, turn left on Hatchery Rd, and head to 3 N Old Stage Rd; 530/926-2215), the oldest hatchery in the West, keeps thousands of rainbow and brown trout, including a few biggies, in the holding ponds. For only a quarter you can get some fish food and incite a fish-feeding frenzy. For more information, contact the **MOUNT SHASTA VISITORS BUREAU** (300 Pine St at Lake St; 530/926-4865).

RESTAURANTS

Lily's / ★★

1013 S MOUNT SHASTA BLVD, MOUNT SHASTA; 530/926-3372
Even with new owners at the helm, this popular place offers very good California cuisine with an ethnic flair. Start your dinner with spicy jalapeño pasta or baked Brie and follow that with an entree of prime rib, Chicken Rosie (a chicken breast browned in butter and simmered with raspberries, hazelnut liqueur, and a hint of cream), or the terrific enchiladas suizas stuffed with crab, shrimp, and fresh spinach. Lunch offerings are equally varied and imaginative, and if you're looking for something a little different from the usual breakfast fare, try Lily's cheesy polenta fritters. *$; AE, DIS, MC, V; local checks only; breakfast Mon–Fri, lunch Mon–Fri, dinner every day, brunch Sat–Sun and holidays; beer and wine; reservations recommended; from I-5, take the Central Mount Shasta exit.*

Michael's Restaurant / ★

313 MOUNT SHASTA BLVD, MOUNT SHASTA; 530/926-5288

Michael and Lynn Kobseff have been running this estimable little restaurant since 1980, which makes them old-timers on the ever-changing Mount Shasta restaurant scene. Some of their best lunchtime offerings are the crisp, greaseless fried zucchini appetizer, the french fries, and a terrific Cajun turkey melt. Their Italian dinners will satisfy those with lumberjack-size appetites, especially the combination ravioli and linguine plate. Lynn makes all the desserts. The small but varied wine list features several bargains. *$;*

AE, DIS, MC, V; local checks only; lunch, dinner Tues–Sat; full bar; reservations recommended; from I-5, take the Central Mount Shasta exit.

Serge's Restaurant / ★★★

531 CHESTNUT ST, MOUNT SHASTA; 530/926-1276

This classical French-continental restaurant framed with lace curtains is one of Mount Shasta's best—and it's even more memorable because of the view of the grand volcano from the deck. The menu changes seasonally, and starters often range from garlicky escargots and prawns sautéed with Pernod to a classic Caesar. Entrees might include a perfectly grilled 9-ounce New York steak with provençal herbs or scallops and prawns in a light Chablis sauce served over a puff pastry shell. Mount Shasta is a hotbed of vegetarianism, so meatless dishes always make an appearance, such as the manicotti stuffed with toasted walnuts, mushrooms, and eggplant and drizzled with a lemon-thyme tomato sauce. Desserts are whipped up daily and often include a rich, heavenly chocolate mousse and a cheesecake topped with a savory berry sauce. *$$; AE, DIS, MC, V; checks OK; dinner Wed–Sun; beer and wine; reservations recommended; 1 block E of Mount Shasta Blvd.*

Trinity Cafe / ★★★★

622 N MOUNT SHASTA BLVD, MOUNT SHASTA; 530/926-6200

The small town of Mount Shasta has always been blessed with some fine restaurants, and now it has another one. Transplanted San Franciscans Nancy and Brett LaMott took a small Arts and Crafts–style bungalow and turned it into a very pleasant dining space with an open kitchen, where Brett, trained in traditional French cooking, turns out everything, including the house-made breads and desserts. The menu changes weekly depending on what's fresh in the area; raved-about entrees have included red rock cod with a spicy red pepper sauce, halibut with mashed potatoes and a corn salsa, and filet mignon in a bordelaise sauce. There's always a vegetarian entree and a game item, as well. The wine list is varied and imaginative. Both locals and visitors love this place, so make reservations well in advance. *$$–$$$; MC, V; checks OK; dinner Wed–Sun; beer and wine; reservations recommended; between Jessie and Ivy Sts.* &

LODGINGS

Mount Shasta Ranch Bed and Breakfast / ★★★

1008 W. A. BARR RD, MOUNT SHASTA; 530/926-3870

This striking 70-year-old bed-and-breakfast inn with gabled windows and hip roofs offers large rooms, large baths, large views, and even large breakfasts. In addition to five guest rooms in the main building, the Mount Shasta Ranch B&B has five rooms in a carriage house and a two-bedroom cottage. The main house, decorated with antiques and Oriental rugs, has the largest guest rooms (four of them sleep up to four people each), plus huge private bathrooms sporting original 1920s fixtures. The carriage house's five units are smaller and share two bathrooms but have great views of Mount Shasta and the rugged Siskiyous. Come morning, indulge in a hearty breakfast that might include cream-cheese-filled waffles with fresh fruit toppings, crepes bursting with local blackberries, plump sausages, a fresh fruit salad, and good strong coffee. Afterward, curl up with a book in front of the main lodge's gargantuan stone fireplace, or work off those waffles by hiking, swimming, playing a few rounds of table tennis or pool, or soaking in the inn's hot springs spa. Children are welcome. *$–$$; AE, DIS, MC, V; checks OK; S of the fish hatchery.* &

Mount Shasta Resort / ★★★

1000 SIKIYOU LAKE BLVD, MOUNT SHASTA; 530/926-3030 OR 800/958-3363

If you think people who live to hit little golf balls should get a life, you'll have second thoughts when you see the incredibly scenic Mount Shasta Resort. The prospect of spending all day on a rolling green lawn and breathing in clean air under the towering presence of Mount Shasta is alluring—even to those who have never heard of Tiger Woods. The 50 one- and two-bedroom Craftsman-style chalets have all the creature comforts, and they're located on the forested shore of Lake Siskiyou, where you can swim, fish, sailboard, kayak, canoe, or rent paddleboats. What? Left your putter at home? Don't despair. You can buy a new one here or consider such pastimes as fishing, hiking, mountain biking, or skiing—they're all within putting distance of the resort. Two-night minimum stays are required for Friday and Saturday in the summer and on major holidays. Chalet rentals vary seasonally. Ask about the special golf packages offered from May through September (weather permitting), the ski packages in the winter, or the romantic getaway deals year-round. The clubhouse restaurant serves good California cuisine, and there are several great restaurants nearby, in town and in Dunsmuir. *$$–$$$; AE, DC, DIS, MC, V; local checks only; from I-5, take the Central Mount Shasta exit, go W, turn left on Old Stage Rd, veer onto W. A. Barr Rd, and turn left on Siskiyou Lake Blvd.* &

Strawberry Valley Inn / ★★

1142 S MOUNT SHASTA BLVD, MOUNT SHASTA; 530/926-2052

Hosts Chuck and Susie Ryan have combined the privacy of a motel and the personal touches of a B&B to create this terrific 14-room inn surrounded by a lush garden and towering oaks. Guest rooms are individually decorated with color-coordinated fabrics; if you prefer lots of room to romp, ask for a two-room suite. A buffet breakfast featuring fresh fruit, granola, oatmeal, waffles, and pastries is set up next to the inn's stone fireplace (those who want to dine in private may take a tray to their room).

Complimentary wine is poured at the cocktail hour every evening. $; AE, DIS, MC, V; no checks; from I-5, take the Central Mount Shasta exit. &

Weed

Nestled on the north flank of Mount Shasta, this little lumber town doesn't offer much to the tourist, except, perhaps, the popular "I got high on Weed, California" T-shirt.

LODGINGS

Stewart Mineral Springs / ★

4617 STEWART SPRINGS RD, WEED; 530/938-2222

Hidden in a forested canyon at the end of a twisting country road, Stewart Mineral Springs is a great place to commune with nature and unwind from the rigors of daily life. To ensure you get the R&R you deserve, start off with a visit to the bathhouse, located across the creek at the end of the footbridge, for a detoxifying mineral bath, a sauna, and maybe even a plunge in the creek or the large pond. You can sleep in one of the two inexpensive but spiritually enriching tepees (bring your own bedding) or in one of the five more comfortable (though spartan) little cabins with kitchens. If you plan to cook in your cabin, buy food before you get to this remote locale—convenience stores and burger emporiums are (thankfully) not a part of the scenery here, though the resort does have a new restaurant now serving breakfast, lunch, and dinner. The five-bedroom A-frame is perfect for large groups of up to 10 people, and there are 10 modest motel rooms. Camping and RV sites are available, too. $; DIS, MC, V; checks OK; open Mar 1–Nov 15; about 7 miles NW of Weed; call for directions.

Gazelle

LODGINGS

Hollyhock Farm Bed & Breakfast / ★★★

18705 OLD HWY 99, GAZELLE; 530/435-2627

Mount Shasta looms beyond this B&B's front yard like some giant ghostly apparition, giving Hollyhock Farm one of the most impressive views in the area. Though this 1902 Normandy-style stone farmhouse is easily overlooked, its charm and setting make it a required stop for visitors to the North Mountains. The upstairs suite includes a queen-size bed, a daybed in the sunroom, and a private bath. For the ultimate in privacy, stay in the guesthouse behind the inn, equipped with a queen-size bed, twin bed, kitchenette, and private bath. The rooms have been tastefully furnished with antiques and lace curtains. The new owners, Britta and Terry Price, will even house your canine companions in their kennel and your horses at the farm. Breakfast is served whenever you'd like it.

$–$$; MC, V; checks OK; just W of I-5; from Yreka, take the Grenada/Gazelle exit; from Weed, take the Edgewood/Gazelle exit.

Etna

RESTAURANTS

Sengthong's / ★★★

434 MAIN ST, ETNA; 530/467-5668

Folks from Redding to Yreka sing the praises of this unpretentious restaurant hidden in one of the most remote areas of California. Born in Vietnam, Sengthong Phelps lived in Laos and Thailand before making her way to this sparsely populated corner of Siskiyou County. Now she and her husband, Don, run this small restaurant and work hard at blending the cuisines of the three countries Sengthong left behind. You can see (and taste) the Laotian influence in the savory sticky-rice balls. Also don't miss the Thai hot-spiced beef and the thick seafood stew bubbling with fresh fish, clams, scallops, and prawns. *$–$$; no credit cards; checks OK; dinner Wed–Sun; beer and wine; reservations recommended; off Hwy 3, in the center of town.*

LODGINGS

Bradley's Alderbrook Manor / ★★

836 MAIN ST, ETNA; 530/467-3917

Recently restored, this Victorian mansion set on three acres of oaks and alders has been lovingly furnished by Dr. Joyce Bradley with memorabilia from her travels around the world. The downstairs guest room has a private bathroom, the two rooms on the second floor share a bath, and a four-bed dorm shares a bath with Bradley. Alder Creek runs through the property, and downtown Etna is just a short walk away. Equestrians can board their horses here, and Diana, the assistant innkeeper, will take care of other manageable pets at her house nearby. *$; no credit cards; checks OK; near Church St.* &

Fort Jones

LODGINGS

The Wild Goose / ★★

11624 MAIN ST, FORT JONES; 530/468-2735

Furnished with family heirlooms and antiques, this 1890 country Victorian house has been rebuilt from the ground up by owners Terry and Cindy Hayes. The two rooms on the second floor were designed for the care and comfort of guests, and each has an antique double bed and a private bathroom. Step out onto the second-story veranda for a view of the village of Fort Jones and the distant Marble Mountains. The Wild

Goose goes wild over breakfast, so bring your appetite to the table and prepare yourself for Belgian waffles with champagne and fruit sauté, homemade granola, and fresh-squeezed juice. *$; no credit cards; checks OK; off Hwy 3.*

Yreka

Once a boomtown, Yreka now mines gold from tourists who visit the town's historic district; city maps are available at the **YREKA CHAMBER OF COMMERCE** (117 W Miner St; 530/842-1649). In the summer, take a scenic round-trip train ride on the **YREKA WESTERN RAILROAD** (530/842-4146) to the historic town of Montague, where you can poke around the museum in the 1887 railroad depot and get a snack at the **1904 OPERA RESTAURANT** (170 S 11th St; 530/459-5794).

RESTAURANTS

The Old Boston Shaft / ★

1801 FORT JONES RD, YREKA; 530/842-5768
You won't get the shaft at this Yreka restaurant, where a generous three- to four-course meal costs about $35 for two. What a deal! Swiss chef/owners Erich Gisler and Max and Erich Schuler specialize in hearty beef and veal dishes. Try their Veal Zingara, prepared with tomato, ham, and mushrooms, or the Veal à la Swiss, made with tomato, Swiss cheese, asparagus, and hollandaise. The wine list is basic but won't blow your budget. *$; AE, DC, DIS, MC, V; local checks only; lunch Mon–Fri, dinner Mon–Sat; full bar; reservations recommended; W of I-5 at the Fort Jones/Hwy 3 exit.*

Happy Camp

Happy Camp used to be a lot more, well, happy. Nowadays, the town is dependent on the uncertain fortunes of lumbering, fishing, and tourism; some locals jokingly suggest a different adjective might be in order.

RESTAURANTS

Indian Creek Cafe / ★

106 INDIAN CREEK RD, HAPPY CAMP; 530/493-5180
It may be a small cafe in one of the most sparsely populated corners of California, but Indian Creek has one of the state's largest menus. Young-sters in tow will definitely be happy campers, because there's something for everyone here—from breakfast sandwiches and subs to chicken, steak, and seafood platters. Still not satisfied? Take a look at the separate Mexican and vegetarian menus, and ask about the daily specials. *$; AE, DC, DIS, MC, V; local checks only; breakfast, lunch, dinner every day; beer and wine; no reservations; near 2nd Ave.*

Lassen Volcanic National Park and the Northeast

Surprisingly, many Californians have never even *heard* of Lassen Volcanic National Park, much less been there. In fact, it's one of the least crowded national parks in the country, forever destined to play second fiddle to its towering neighbor, Mount Shasta. This is reason enough to go, since the park's 108,000 acres (including 50 beautiful wilderness lakes) are practically deserted, even on weekends. But don't stop here. From Drakesbad to Mill Creek, this area of panoramic vistas, aspen-lined creeks, and popular lakes is worth exploring.

Lassen Volcanic National Park

The heart of the park is 10,457-foot **LASSEN PEAK**, the largest plug-dome volcano in the world (its last fiery eruption was in 1915, when it shot debris 7 miles into the stratosphere). For decades Lassen held the title of the most recently active volcano in the continental United States; it lost that distinction in 1980, when Washington's Mount St. Helens blew her top. The volcano also marks the southernmost end of the Cascade Range, which extends to Canada. A visitors' map calls the park "a compact laboratory of volcanic phenomena"—an apt description of this pretty but peculiar place. In addition to wildflower-laced hiking trails and lush forests typical of many national parks, parts of Lassen are covered with steaming thermal vents, boiling mud pots, stinky sulfur springs, and towering lava pinnacles—constant reminders that Mount Lassen is still active.

Lassen Park's premier attractions in the summer and fall are sightseeing, hiking, backpacking, and camping (sorry, no mountain bikes allowed). The $10-per-car entrance fee, valid for a week, gets you a copy of the "Lassen Park Guide," a handy little newsletter listing activities, hikes, and points of interest. Free naturalist programs are offered daily in the summer, highlighting everything from flora and fauna to geologic history and volcanic processes. If you have only a day here, spend it huffing up the mountain on the **LASSEN PEAK HIKE**, a spectacular 2½-mile zigzag to the top. Most hikers can make the steep trek in four to five hours—just don't forget to bring water, sunscreen, and a windbreaker. Another great—and much easier—trail is the 3-mile **BUMPASS HELL HIKE**, named after a mid-19th-century tour guide. Poor ol' Kendall Bumpass lost a leg on this one, but that was long before park rangers built wooden catwalks to safely guide visitors past the pyrite pools, steam vents, seething mud pots, and noisy fumaroles that line the trail.

Mount Lassen Park attracts a hardier breed of tourists in the winter, when the park's main thoroughfare is closed and the chief modes of transportation are snowshoes and cross-country skis. Smaller roads are plowed only from the north and south park entrances up to the ranger stations, and on sunny weekends parking lots are filled with families enjoying every kind of snow toy imaginable. On Saturday afternoons from January through March, a loquacious naturalist will take anyone who shows up at the **LASSEN CHALET** (at the park's south entrance, 5 miles north of the junction of Hwys 36 and 89) by 1:30pm on a free, two-hour eco-adventure across the park's snowy dales. You must be at least eight years old, warmly dressed, and decked out in boots. Free snowshoes are provided (although a $1 donation for shoe upkeep is requested) on a first-come basis. Pack a picnic lunch. For more details, call park headquarters (530/595-4444).

For the best lodgings and restaurants near the park, see the Drakesbad, Chester, Lake Almanor, and Mill Creek sections in this chapter.

Drakesbad

LODGINGS

Drakesbad Guest Ranch / ★★★★

HWY 36, DRAKESBAD; 530/529-1512 EXT. 120

Hidden in a high mountain valley inside Lassen Volcanic National Park, the Drakesbad Guest Ranch is probably the worst-kept secret in California. Demand for this mountain retreat's 19 rooms is so high that it's often booked several months (and sometimes a year or two) in advance. Fortunately, plans made that far ahead often change, and February through June are good times to call to take advantage of cancellations. At night, kerosene lamps cast a warm yellow glow over the rustic accommodations; there's no electricity, except in the lodge. The tables, chairs, and bedsteads are made of smooth-sanded logs and branches. There are a half-dozen pleasant rooms upstairs in the main lodge, but you might

prefer one of the four quieter cabins at the edge of the woods, a good place to watch wildlife. The lodge's guest rooms and each of the cabins have

their own sinks and toilets, but showers are in a shared facility. If you want a private bathroom, inquire about the two-room duplex (rented to a minimum of four people) or one of the six rooms in the bungalows at the edge of the meadow. One of the ranch's star attractions is the thermal swimming pool, fed by a natural hot springs and open 24 hours a day. Breakfast, lunch, and dinner (included in the price of lodging) are better than what you might expect in a national park. The breakfast buffet includes fresh fruit, hot and cold cereals, buttermilk pancakes, and excellent sausages. For lunch you can eat at the buffet or order a sack lunch. Dinner is a fancier affair, starting with soup or a fresh wild greens salad, followed by an entree such as roasted rosemary chicken with Monterey Jack polenta or vegetarian eggplant napoleon; dessert might be a white chocolate mousse cake. The popular Wednesday-night cookouts feature barbe-cued steak and chicken, plus pasta and an assortment of salads. *$$$$; DIS, MC, V; checks OK; closed mid-Oct–mid-June, depending on weather conditions; about 17 miles N of Chester, call for directions.* &

Cassel

LODGINGS

Clearwater House / ★★★★

HAT CREEK AND CASSEL/FALL RIVER RDS, CASSEL; 415/381-1173 OR 530/335-5500

This fine turn-of-the-century farmhouse is nestled right next to some of the finest trout waters in the United States. Created by former wilderness and fishing guide Dick Galland, the inn features seven rooms (all with private baths) decorated in the style of an English angling lodge, with fish and game prints on the walls, Oriental rugs on the hardwood floors, and cherry-wood tables set for family-style meals. Pick up pointers on the art of fly-fishing at a three-day (Sun–Tues) fishing class, or attend Galland's "Mastering the Art of Fly-Fishing" five-day program. Meals are included in the room rate—and they're the best you'll find for miles around. Expect traditional breakfasts, picnic lunches, and well-prepared country-style dinners. A tackle shop and tennis courts round out the amenities. *$$$$; MC, V; checks OK; open Apr 30–mid-Nov; at the intersection of Hat Creek and Cassel/Fall River Rds.* &

Fall River Mills

LODGINGS

Lava Creek Lodge / ★★★

EASTMAN LAKE, FALL RIVER MILLS; 530/336-6288

The panoramic view of the southern Cascades from Mount Lassen to Mount Shasta is Lava Creek's trump card. Set well back from the main road at the end of a country lane, the lodge has eight modest guest rooms with private baths, and most have lake views. But the best accommodations are actually in the woods: seven small, comfortable cabins were recently renovated, and all have private baths. Rates include a continental breakfast served in the knotty pine dining room of the lodge's restaurant. Lava Creek is located in one of the country's best trout-fishing areas, so take advantage of this golden opportunity: rent one of the lodge's boats and hire its fishing guide so you can tell the folks back home how you reeled in the big one. Hunting guides are generally available during duck season. Also nearby is the Fall River Golf Course, one of Northern California's best. The lodge is sometimes rented out to private parties or groups, so make sure you call ahead. *$$–$$$; MC, V; checks OK; at the end of Island Rd.*

Alturas

RESTAURANTS

Nipa's California Cuisine / ★

1001 N MAIN ST, ALTURAS; 530/233-2520
You won't find seared tuna in loquat sauce here. Nipa's version of California cuisine is actually spicy Thai food—and it's the finest fare of any kind in Modoc County. Located in an old drive-in burger joint that's been transformed into a contemporary cafe decorated with Thai artifacts, Nipa's serves such classic favorites as *tom yum kung,* a fragrant soup packed with prawns and mushrooms; phad thai, the satisfying pan-fried-noodle dish with prawns, chicken, egg, bean sprouts, green onions, and a sprinkling of ground peanuts; and a spicy, succulent red curry made with prawns, chicken, or beef simmered in coconut milk. Wash it all down with a deliciously sweet Thai iced tea. *$; MC, V; local checks only; lunch, dinner every day; beer and wine; no reservations; 1 block S of Hwys 299 and 395.*

LODGINGS

Dorris House / ★

COUNTY RD 57, ALTURAS; 530/233-3786
A room with a view is a standard feature of this two-story, turn-of-the-century ranch house, named for the brothers who founded Alturas in 1870. Set on a sage-covered plain at the edge of Dorris Lake, just below the towering Warner Mountains, the property is a favorite stop for migratory birds (not to mention patrons who migrate here for a respite). Hosts Karol and Mary Woodward have decorated their immaculate inn's four guest rooms with family antiques and comfortable furnishings, making the rooms a pleasant home-away-from-home. Longtime residents of Alturas, the Woodwards know all the choice spots for hiking, fishing, bird-watching, and picnicking, so be sure to ask them for touring tips. Breakfast, served in the homey kitchen, is simple but very good, and might include moist zucchini nut bread, sweet bran muffins, or a dazzling fruit platter. *$; no credit cards; checks OK; 3 miles E of Hwy 395, on County Road 56, turn right at County Road 57 and drive 1 mile.*

Cedarville

North of Alturas, Highway 299 turns east and crosses the narrow, little-known, and seldom visited **WARNER MOUNTAINS**, where antelope often graze. Then the highway descends into the aptly named **SURPRISE**

VALLEY, a onetime oasis for Overland Trail emigrants after the rigors of the Nevada desert, and Cedarville, a little old-fashioned town of a bygone time. As one local poet put it, Cedarville is "where the pavement ends, and the West begins."

Isolated by the Warner Mountains on one side and the western edge of the Great Basin on the other, Cedarville attracts an interesting mix of travelers: in addition to the usual hunters, fly fishers, history buffs, and bird and wildlife watchers, you'll find paleontologists and paleobiologists drawn to the plentiful animal and plant fossils found in this part of the Great Basin. Whatever lured you here, there are lots of hot springs to help rejuvenate those weary bones after a day of exploring. To find out what's currently happening in the area, visit the friendly folks at **GREAT BASIN BOOKS** (540 Main St; 530/279-2337).

RESTAURANTS

Country Hearth Restaurant & Bakery

551 MAIN ST, CEDARVILLE; 530/279-2280

The Country Hearth should be called the Country Heart for all the love owner Janet Irene puts into the meals served in her homey, pine-paneled dining room with its wood-burning stove. Bite into her good hamburgers served on toasted, fresh-baked rolls, or try the nightly special "country-cooked meal," which might feature pork chops or chicken-fried steak. Irene makes all the breads, rolls, pastries, and desserts, which are included in the price of dinner. You can also purchase baked goods for the trip home. *$; MC, V; checks OK; breakfast, lunch, dinner every day; beer and wine; no reservations; S of Hwy 299.*

LODGINGS

J. K. Metzker House Bed and Breakfast / ★★

520 MAIN ST, CEDARVILLE; 530/279-2650 OR 530/279-2337

Built in 1860 by town founder William Cressler, this pretty clapboard house with its white picket fence and rose-lined walkway was the residence of Cressler's descendants until 1990, when Judy Metzker Topol acquired it. She named the B&B in honor of her great-great-great grandfather who followed the Oregon Trail and settled in the Surprise Valley. After that long trek, Mr. Metzker surely would have appreciated snoozing in the comfort of one of the three upstairs guest rooms. Each room has a private bath and a queen-size bed. Innkeeper Linda Naomi fixes a real country breakfast each morning with bacon and eggs, fruit and muffins, and special items for guests with particular dietary needs and desires. *$; no credit cards; checks OK; turn right onto Main St from Hwy 299.*

Ravendale

LODGINGS
Spanish Springs Ranch / ★★★

HWY 395, RAVENDALE; 530/234-2150 OR 800/272-8282

Buckaroo wannabes should pack up their cowboy boots and head on out to this 3,800-acre cattle ranch. Authentic Western lodgings are scattered across the property, and whether you want to slumber in ultimate comfort or rough it on the range, the choice is yours: accommodations vary from log cabins to Western-style suites. You can saddle up and ride the trails, fish in stocked ponds, hike and camp in the wilderness, or swim in the pool. The smallest cowpokes should check out the ranch's "dudeo," a junior rodeo where kids can learn to ride those easier-to-mount four-legged creatures—sheep. Of course there are such traditional ranch activities as barbecues and campfires, plus a petting zoo for the kids. Meals, included in the room rate, are served family style in the ranch's dining room, and you can sip a cocktail in the lounge, or hoist a cold one in the Old West Beer and Wine Bar. Inquire about the special vacation packages. Children under age three stay for free. *$$–$$$; MC, V; checks OK; closed Oct 15–Apr 1; 40 miles N of Susanville and 6 miles S of Ravendale.* ♿

Susanville

RESTAURANTS
St. Francis Cafe / ★

830 MAIN ST (ST. FRANCIS HOTEL), SUSANVILLE; 530/257-4820

You won't hear anybody asking "Where's the beef?" in this cafe. Located in the 80-year-old St. Francis Hotel, the St. Francis Cafe specializes in prime rib, indisputably the best (and the largest servings) in the area. If you're not at the door by 6pm on Friday and Saturday, you may be out of luck, because the prime rib sells quickly. There's also a hearty 10-ounce New York steak sandwich, and freshly made soups and salads are served Basque-style in tureens and large bowls. The adjacent hotel bar, the Round-Up Room, features Picon Punch on its list of spirits—a tasty Basque drink that transforms even the grumpiest cowboy into a very friendly dude. *$$; MC, V; no checks; lunch, dinner Mon–Sat; full bar; no reservations; at Union St.*

Grand Cafe / ★

730 MAIN ST, SUSANVILLE; 530/257-4713

The art deco light fixtures in this time warp of a restaurant are the real McCoy. Owned by the Sargent family since 1921, this green stucco building is furnished with green-and-black tiles, dark wooden booths, and a long Formica counter. There's also a nickel jukebox (it doesn't work, so save your nickel) and a small lamp with a pull chain in each booth. At the counter, wooden chairs on ornate iron bases have clips to hold diners' hats. The mounted deer staring from the walls were shot by a Sargent in the '30s—back when a tuna sandwich was a mere 35 cents (even now, they're not charging a whole lot more). For breakfast, try the sweet buckwheat hotcakes. At lunchtime, soup, house-baked bread, and a chocolate malt are your best bets. *$; no credit cards; checks OK; breakfast, lunch Mon–Sat; full bar; no reservations; near Gay St.*

Chester

RESTAURANTS

Creekside Grill / ★★★

278 MAIN ST, CHESTER; 530/258-1966

This fine restaurant has upped the ante in the Chester cuisine game. Owners Don and Tracy Darue have taken a comfortable place with lots of natural wood and a great stone fireplace and fashioned it into a restaurant that attracts tourists and locals alike. A graduate of the prestigious California Culinary Academy in San Francisco, Tracy does the cooking (all dishes are prepared fresh daily) while her husband Don does everything else. One menu featured a crisp baby greens and romaine salad tossed with red onions, Gorgonzola, and a red wine vinaigrette; grilled prawns marinated in rosemary and garlic; seared scallops and angel hair pasta with a porcini-cream mushroom sauce; and a tender grilled pork tenderloin seasoned with rosemary, garlic, and sage and served with roasted garlic mashed potatoes and glazed carrots. The wine list is substantial, thanks to a newly added wine bar, and a quintet of microbrews is on tap. The changing dessert list is small but select: tiramisu, an exceptional carrot cake, and Tracy's signature diet-busting delight—alternating layers of white chocolate–walnut cake and chocolate cake, filled with a mocha mousse and glazed in a dark chocolate ganache. *$–$$; MC, V; local checks only; dinner Thurs–Sun in summer, Wed–Sat in winter; beer and wine; reservations recommended.* &

LODGINGS

The Bidwell House Bed and Breakfast Inn / ★★★

1 MAIN ST, CHESTER; 530/258-3338

The beautifully restored Bidwell House, fronted by a yard of aspens and cottonwoods, looks out over mountain meadows and the broad expanse of Lake Almanor. The former home of Chico pioneer John Bidwell, it opened as a B&B in 1991. The 14 guest rooms are furnished with antiques and a few have wood-burning stoves; most have private baths, and seven units are equipped with Jacuzzi tubs. A cottage that sleeps up to six makes an ideal family retreat. Be sure to show the kids the Bidwell House's pretty, enclosed downstairs porch fancied up with wicker furniture, a Gibson girl sketchbook, and antique doll buggies and tricycles. The inn's manager is a creative pastry chef, so guests are treated to delicious breakfast dishes such as fresh fruit crepes as well as frothy frappés, served in the airy dining room. If you're around in September, don't miss the popular cowboy poetry reading—it's a hoot. *$$–$$$; MC, V; checks OK; E end of town.*

Lake Almanor

RESTAURANTS

BJ's Bar-B-Que & Deli / ★

3881 HWY A-13, LAKE ALMANOR; 530/596-4210

Barbecue basics—beef, pork, and chicken—reign at this unassuming roadside spot. The baby back ribs are thick, tender, meaty, and slathered with a tangy sweet sauce, and the baked beans and barbecued pork sandwiches are good, too. Get plenty of napkins for this deliciously messy fare and eat it on the sunny, enclosed porch to the left of the front door. Prime rib takes a turn on the rotisserie Friday and Saturday nights, and it's so popular you'll need reservations. *$; no credit cards; checks OK; lunch, dinner Tues–Sun, closed Nov–Mar; beer and wine; reservations recommended; Hamilton Branch.*

Wilson's Camp Prattville & Carol's Cafe / ★

2932 ALMANOR DR W, LAKE ALMANOR; 530/259-2464

Certainly the oldest and funkiest place at Lake Almanor, Camp Prattville has been around since 1928, when it was founded by Frank and Nettie Wilson. Daughter-in-law Carol Wilson Franchetti, along with her new partner, Ken Wilson (one of four generations of Wilsons who have worked here), now runs the restaurant, which offers breakfast, lunch, and dinner in a small dining room crowded with knickknacks. The menu is prodigious, and breakfasts are served until 1pm. Sandwiches and french fries are among the better offerings, but save room for dessert, especially the terrific bread pudding with applejack hard sauce and the house-made pies with delicate, flaky crusts. When the weather is warm, eat lunch at one of the picnic tables on the deck overlooking the lake. *$; MC, V; checks OK; breakfast, lunch, dinner every day (closed mid-Oct–Apr); beer and wine; reservations recommended; on the lake's W shore.*

LODGINGS

Dorado Inn / ★★

4379 HWY 147, LAKE ALMANOR; 530/284-7790

What sets the Dorado apart from the other resorts along Lake Almanor's commercialized east shore are the spectacular Mount Lassen and lake views from the decks outside the cottages. All of the Dorado's six cottages (four two-bedroom cottages and two one-room units) are near the water's edge, and they have fully equipped kitchens, private bathrooms, electric heat, and wood-burning stoves. In addition to soaking in the view, most visitors spend their time either sunbathing and lounging lakeside, or boating, fishing, and swimming. *$$; no credit cards; checks OK; on the lake's E shore.* &

Mill Creek

RESTAURANTS

St. Bernard Lodge / ★★

44801 HWY 36 E, MILL CREEK; 530/258-3382

In 1912, the St. Bernard Lodge was constructed to house workers building the dam at Big Meadows (now known as Lake Almanor), and in 1929 it was picked up and moved to its present location, where it started a new life as a public lodge. There are seven comfortable rooms upstairs. However, most Mill Creek residents come here for the famous St. Bernard Burgers: a three-quarter-pound patty of lean chuck served on a fresh-baked bun (all breads are baked on site). You can also sink your teeth into prime rib, steak, fried chicken, and fried or sautéed fish. Before your meal, sip a cocktail in the antique bar with painted glass windows; afterward, head outside for a stroll along the deck and around the trout pond. *$$–$$$; MC, V; checks OK; breakfast, lunch Sat–Sun, dinner Thurs–Mon (Fri–Sun in winter); full bar; reservations required; on the S side of Hwy 36, 10 miles W of Chester.*

LODGINGS

Mill Creek Resort / ★★

I HWY 172, MILL CREEK; 530/595-4449

If it's peace and solitude you're after, look no further. The Mill Creek Resort makes you feel as though you've stepped back in time to a quieter, gentler, and infinitely more affordable era (somewhere around 1925). A picture-postcard general store and coffee shop serve as the resort's center, and nine housekeeping cabins are rented on a daily or weekly basis. The units are clean and homey, with vintage '30s and '40s furniture. Seclusion is one of the main charms of the place, though it's not far from cross-country skiing trails and Lassen Volcanic National Park. Pets are welcome. *$; no credit cards; checks OK; 3 miles S of Hwy 36.* &

SIERRA NEVADA

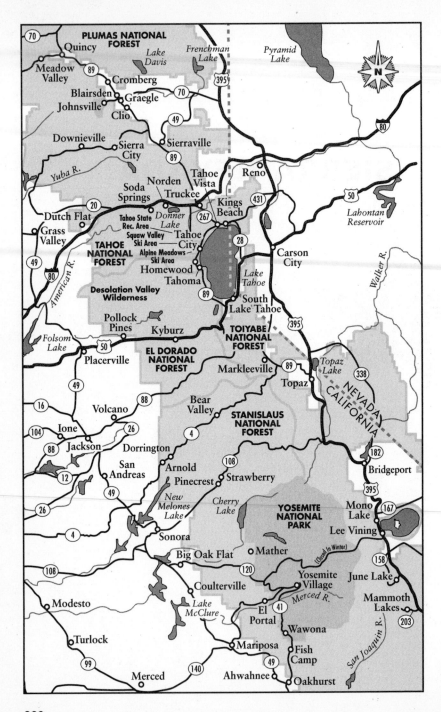

SIERRA NEVADA

The Sierra Nevada is home to two of the state's most popular destinations—Lake Tahoe and Yosemite. Keep in mind, however, that these mountains also harbor lots of other spots that are almost as gorgeous and much less crowded. If you have your heart set on the Lake or the Valley, remember, lots of other folks do, too.

Lake Tahoe and Yosemite are gradually being loved to death, although ambitious steps are being taken to slow the environmental damage to two of the most beautiful places on earth. Preservation of the water clarity of cobalt-blue Lake Tahoe and its crisp mountain air has become a priority for both the community and state legislators. A plan to drastically cut back the number of cars allowed in Yosemite Valley (using reasonably priced low-polluting or zero-emission motor coaches from outlying parking lots) is in the public hearing stage. Try to plan your visit to either area for the spring or fall, when there are far fewer cars and people.

If you're after a more peaceful, but not primitive, communion with nature, take a peek at the Lakes Basin (about an hour's drive north of Truckee). The area has an assortment of lakeside lodges so sweetly simple and pleasant you'll remember them forever. On the eastern side of the Sierra Nevada, the haunting Mono Lake, a 60-square-mile desert salt lake with strangely beautiful limestone tufa spires, is like nothing you've ever seen before. Nearby Bodie is the most eerily authentic ghost town in California, kept in a state of "arrested decay" by park rangers. The Mammoth Lakes area, farther south, offers every kind of snow sport in winter, plus hiking, biking, and world-famous fishing in summer. It also has the Devil's Postpile National Monument, 60-foot-tall rock columns formed 100,000 years ago from molten lava. And if you're feeling frisky, the 211-mile John Muir Trail, which connects Yosemite with Kings Canyon and Sequoia National Parks, is accessible here.

ACCESS AND INFORMATION

The 400-mile-long Sierra Nevada Mountains begin northwest of Quincy with 6,500-foot peaks, eventually rising to 14,494 feet at Mount Whitney, the highest summit in the continental United States. From there, going south, they decrease in height, ending in the desert near the town of Mojave.

The **HIGHWAY SYSTEM** through the Sierra looks like a ladder with two north-south, all-weather highways forming the legs—US 99 in the Central Valley just west of the foothills, and in the high desert to the east of the Sierra escarpment, US 395, one of the West's most beautiful scenic drives. The rungs are a series of east-west roads—highways in the north and increasingly narrow and twisting (though gorgeous) lanes as you progress south: **HIGHWAY 70**, from Oroville to Quincy; **HIGHWAY 49**, from Grass Valley to Sierraville; **INTERSTATE 80**, from Sacramento to

Truckee and Reno; **US 50**, from Sacramento to South Lake Tahoe and Carson City; **HIGHWAY 88**, from Jackson to Kirkwood and the Hope Valley; **HIGHWAY 4**, from Stockton to Angels Camp to Markleeville; **HIGHWAY 108**, from Modesto to Sonora to just north of Bridgeport; and **HIGHWAY 120**, from Manteca to Groveland. Some are closed in winter.

FRESNO–YOSEMITE INTERNATIONAL AIRPORT (559/251-7554; www.fresno.com/flyfresno) is approximately 65 miles from Yosemite and the southern Sierra. It is served by Allegiant, America West, American, American Eagle, Horizon, United, United Express, and Skywest. **MERCED AIR TERMINAL**, approximately 65 miles from Yosemite, is served by United Express. **MAMMOTH AIRPORT** is served by Mountain Air Express from Long Beach (800/788-4247 or 310/595-1011).

RENO/TAHOE INTERNATIONAL AIRPORT, approximately 45 miles from Lake Tahoe and 175 miles from Mammoth and the eastern Sierra, is served by Alaska, America West, American, Continental, Delta, Northwest, Southwest, TWA, United, and Shuttle by United. **SACRAMENTO INTERNATIONAL AIRPORT** is approximately 100 miles from Lake Tahoe and the northern and central Sierra. It is served by Alaska, American, America West, Continental, Delta, Horizon, Northwest, Southwest, United, and United Express Airlines.

AMTRAK's (800/USA-RAIL; www.amtrak.com) **CALIFORNIA ZEPHYR** from San Francisco to Chicago stops at Truckee, with Amtrak bus service to South Lake Tahoe; the **SAN JOAQUIN** from Oakland to Bakersfield stops at Merced, with Amtrak bus service to Yosemite.

GREYHOUND (800/229-9424; www.greyhound.com) has daily service from Los Angeles to Mammoth, from Sacramento to Lake Tahoe and Reno, and from Sacramento to Truckee and Reno. **VIA ADVENTURES** (Grey Line; 800/369-PARK; www.via-adventures.com) has four buses each day from Merced to Yosemite. The South Shore Chamber of Commerce's **TAHOE-CASINO EXPRESS** (775/588-2412) makes 14 to 18 round trips each day between Reno and South Lake Tahoe. **MAMMOTH SHUTTLE** (760/924-8249) offers deluxe van service between Reno, June Lake, and Mammoth Lakes.

YARTS (877/98-YARTS; www.yarts.com), the Yosemite Area Regional Transportation System, began running regional transit buses on May 19, 2000. YARTS offers an affordable, dependable alternative to travelers in the region who would rather ride on a bus from outlying communities into Yosemite Valley than drive their vehicles into Yosemite and park. It provides service to and from Mariposa, Merced, and Mono Counties.

Visitor information is available from a variety of locations: **JUNE LAKE CHAMBER OF COMMERCE** (760/648-7584; www.junelake.com), **LAKE TAHOE CENTRAL RESERVATIONS** (800/824-6348 or 530/583-3494; www.tahoefun.org), **LAKE TAHOE VISITORS AUTHORITY**

(800/AT-TAHOE; www.virtualtahoe.com), **LEE VINING CHAMBER OF COMMERCE AND MONO LAKE VISITOR CENTER** (Hwy 395 and 3rd St, Lee Vining; 760/647-6629), **MARIPOSA COUNTY VISITORS BUREAU** (888/554-9012; maripose.yosemite.net/visitor), **TUOLUMNE COUNTY VISITORS BUREAU** (209/533-4420 or 800/446-1333; www.thegreatun fenced.com), **YOSEMITE-SIERRA VISITORS BUREAU** (559/683-4636; www.yosemite-sierra.org), and **YOSEMITE AREA TRAVEL INFORMATION** (www.yosemite.com).

Lake Tahoe Area

Frontiersman Kit Carson was guiding General John Frémont's expedition across the Sierra Nevada in 1844 when he stumbled on an immense, deep-blue body of water, a lake so vast the native Washoe Indians were calling it *tahoe* ("big lake"). Carson was the first white man to see Tahoe, North America's largest alpine lake and the eighth-deepest in the world (its deepest point is at 1,645 feet). If completely drained, Tahoe would cover the entire state of California with 14 inches of water.

Despite all its great skiing, Tahoe is actually most crowded in the summer, when thousands flock here to cool off at the lake (although what constitutes public shoreline versus private waterfront is still a matter of heated debate between home owners and county supervisors). Warm-weather activities abound: boating, waterskiing, bicycling, hiking, rock climbing, hot-air ballooning, horseback riding . . . you name it. Unfortunately, the area pays dearly for its myriad attractions, in the form of tremendous traffic jams, water and air pollution, and a plethora of fast-food joints and condos erected before tough building restrictions were imposed. Despite these glaring scars, Lake Tahoe remains one of the premier outdoor playgrounds of the West, dazzling visitors with its soaring Sierra peaks and twinkling azure waters.

For a grand introduction to the area, take a leisurely 72-mile drive around the lake itself. **HIGHWAYS 50, 89, AND 28** hug the shore, providing gorgeous views from the car. Several stellar sights merit pulling over for a closer look, so be prepared to stop and haul out your camera (or camcorder) along the way. Topping the not-to-be-missed list are **EMERALD BAY** (off Hwy 89), one of the most photographed sights in the world; **CAVE ROCK TUNNEL**, the 200-foot-long, drive-through granite tunnel along Highway 50 on the East Shore; and **SAND HARBOR STATE PARK** (off Hwy 28, on the East Shore), one of the lake's prettiest—and least visited—beaches. Allow about three hours to loop around the lake, or longer if you're traveling on a summer weekend, holiday, or when the road is covered with snow.

SIERRA NEVADA THREE-DAY TOUR

Note: This itinerary is only possible from early summer to fall, when the High Sierra mountain passes are snow-free and open to traffic. It begins in **Oakhurst** in the foothills just south of Yosemite.

DAY ONE: Into the woods. Arrive the night before and check in at **Château du Sureau**, one of the most elegant inns in the West. Have dinner and breakfast at the château's four-star restaurant to fuel up for the mountaineering ahead. On the way to **Yosemite** take a short detour to see the **Mariposa Grove** of sequoias, including one of the world's largest trees, the **Grizzly Giant**. Entering the park by the southern entrance, you'll see **Tunnel View**, one of the best scenic views of the park and the site of a famous Ansel Adams photograph. Once you're in the valley, stop at the visitor center and take the two-hour open-air tram tour, or grab a map, rent bikes, and conduct your own tour. And don't worry if you don't get to see everything, because once you've been here you're hooked; you'll return again and again. Finish your tour early enough to check into your room at the majestic **Ahwahnee Hotel** and have a drink in the granite-and-timbered great lounge before dinner in the hotel's legendary dining room.

DAY TWO: Summits and spooks. Breakfast at the Ahwahnee, then cross the High Sierra on Highway 120. The road is barely two lanes, but the scenery is as breathtaking as the altitude, so take your time and enjoy the ride. Before you make your assault on 9,600 foot **Tioga Summit**, stop and stretch your legs at beautiful **Tuolumne Meadows**, with the **Tuolumne River** on one side and soaring granite peaks on the other. Then drop down some 3,000 feet to Highway 395, and just north of the town of Lee Vining, stop at the **Mono Basin Scenic Visitors Center** to get the scoop on

Dutch Flat

RESTAURANTS

Monte Vista Inn / ★

OFF I-80, DUTCH FLAT; 530/389-2333
For about 60 years, the Monte Vista has been a roadhouse catering to locals—and to travelers lucky enough to find it. The comfortable inn is built of logs and indigenous stone, with a wood-burning stove in the bar and large sofas near the petrified-wood fireplace in the lounge. Kerosene lamps light the wooden dining tables, and old farm implements hang on the walls. The kitchen prepares generous portions of California cuisine, ranging from mesquite-grilled steaks to scampi sautéed with fresh mushrooms and garlic; they're famous for their prime rib. They also smoke their own ribs and chicken using local fruit wood. You can admire the dozen or so freshly baked pies sitting neatly on the counter along the dining-room

the eerie lake and its otherworldly tufa towers of calcium. Don't tarry, because you need to take the lonely 12-mile detour to the magical mining town of **Bodie**. Eat lunch at the **Mono Inn**, but don't tarry, because you'll swear this road doesn't go anywhere, but then you go over a rise, and you're transported back in time to 1920. From here it's north on Highway 395 to Highway 89, over the **Monitor Pass**, and on to **Markleeville** for dinner at the small Italian restaurant **Villa Gigli**. After dinner it's a short trip to Hope Valley and a night in one of the rustic cabins at **Sorensen's Resort**. Quite a change from the luxury of the Ahwanee and du Surreau, it's just right for this side of the Sierra.

DAY THREE: By the big blue water. Enjoy your country breakfast at Sorensen's, because you're about to leave the simple, timeless charm of the remote High Sierra and head 15 miles north over the **Luther Pass** for the glitz, glamour, and gambling of Tahoe. To best see the lake, take the two-hour cruise aboard the **M.S. Dixie II** (775/588-3508), a paddle wheeler out of **Zephyr Cove**, just over the state line in Nevada. The cruise takes you from the east shore to the west shore at **Emerald Bay** with a close-up glimpse of the storied **Vikingsholm Mansion & Visitors Center** (9999 Emerald Bay Rd, Tahoma; 530/535-7232), a mansion replicating a Viking castle. Pick up a picnic lunch at **Sprouts**. Back at Zephyr Cove some beach time is in order, and this is the place to do it, though you may be torn between that and the parasailing, waterskiing, Jet Skis, and paddle boats. As the sun sets in the west, check into the **Christiania Inn**. Enjoy dinner at **Evan's American Gourmet Cafe**, and after dinner head for the tables at Caesars Tahoe to try your luck. Save enough money to get home.

wall, which taste as good as they look (the blackberry pie is tangy with lemon). Live music livens up the bar on the weekend. *$$; MC, V; local checks only; breakfast, lunch Sun, dinner every day; full bar; reservations recommended; at the Dutch Flat exit, 9 miles E of Colfax.* &

Soda Springs

RESTAURANTS

Engadine Cafe / ★★★

RAINBOW RD (ROYAL GORGE'S RAINBOW LODGE), SODA SPRINGS; 530/426-3661

Within Royal Gorge's Rainbow Lodge (see review, below) is the charming and cozy Engadine Cafe, which boasts a large fireplace that's continuously ablaze on those freezing Sierra winter nights. Breakfasts are planned for folks with hearty let's-scale-a-mountain appetites and feature a wide range of choices, from a belly-packing stack of whole-wheat pancakes to three-egg omelets bursting with smoked ham, mushrooms, scallions, and Swiss cheese, accompanied by a pile of country fries. Lunches at the Engadine are simple and satisfying and might include pasta with fresh eggplant, tomato, and mushroom sauce; a juicy burger with all the fixin's; and a luscious (and messy) sandwich provençal with grilled vegetables, sun-dried tomatoes, artichoke hearts, and melted provolone on a toasted sourdough roll. In the evening the kitchen turns out an eclectic mix of terrific fare such as Swiss fondue for two, roast rack of lamb breaded with pistachio nuts and basted with Dijon mustard, and several daily seafood specials. The deck in back looks out over the garden into the pines and is great for summer dining. *$$; MC, V; no checks; breakfast, lunch, dinner every day; full bar; reservations recommended; www.royalgorge.com; take Rainbow Rd exit off I-80 S and drive W.* &

LODGINGS

Royal Gorge's Rainbow Lodge and Wilderness Lodge / ★★

RAINBOW RD, SODA SPRINGS; 530/426-3871, 530/426-3661, OR 800/500-3871 (OUTSIDE NORTHERN CALIFORNIA ONLY)

In 1922, the Rainbow Lodge was built of hand-hewn pine timbers and local granite at a bend in the Yuba River. The owner of the popular Royal Gorge cross-country ski resort, the largest cross-country center in the United States, bought this charming retreat several years ago. The lodge's 32 simple, pine-paneled rooms come with either a private bath, shower, and sink or just a sink (with a bath down the hall). Rooms 12, 14, 23, and 24 overlook the river. Within the lodge is the very pleasant Engadine Cafe (see review, above), which serves some of the best food in the region and is open to nonguests, too. Breakfast is included with a night's stay. Royal Gorge also offers cross-country skiers accommodations in its Wilderness Lodge, a handsome wood lodge with a huge stone fireplace that's tucked away in a remote part of the cross-country course. Guests arrive at the lodge by jumping aboard an open sleigh pulled by a Sno-Cat. The private knotty-pine guest rooms are equipped with bunks or double beds covered with floral-print comforters. *$$–$$$; MC, V; no checks; main lodge open year-round, Wilderness Lodge open during ski season only; take Rainbow Rd exit off I-80 S and drive W.* &

Norden

LODGINGS

Clair Tappaan Lodge / ★

19940 DONNER PASS RD, NORDEN; 530/426-3632

This is no place for wimps, but those hardy souls who want to meet new people and limit expenses and don't mind a few housekeeping tasks should pack their bags and hike on in. Built by Sierra Club volunteers in 1934, Clair Tappaan Lodge is a massive, rustic three-story structure near Donner Summit. Guests carry their own bedding and luggage 100 yards uphill from the road to a building that accommodates up to 140 people. Dorm-style rooms vary from two-person cubicles with thin walls to family bunk rooms and a men's and a women's dorm (psst . . . the romantically inclined should note that all beds are single bunk beds). The pine-paneled living room is warmed by a rock fireplace in the winter, and a library, hot tub, and resident masseuse help keep you relaxed. Breakfast, lunch, and dinner are included in the room rate, and you're expected to help with basic caretaking chores such as dishwashing or mopping the floors. Guests get a hot breakfast and sack lunches to take skiing or hiking (tracks, slopes, and trails are close by). The dinners here are casual, healthy, and filling affairs served family style. They might include chips and salsa, a tossed green salad, warm corn bread, chili con carne (there's a vegetarian version), and, for dessert, big melt-in-your-mouth brownies. *$; MC, V; checks OK; from I-80, take the Soda Springs/ Norden exit; it's 2.4 miles E of the highway.*

Donner Summit

A whirl of white in the winter, the Donner region was named after the 89 members of the ill-fated Donner party who journeyed by wagon train to the area in October 1846. They had come from the Midwest and were bound for the West Coast but were trapped here by an early winter storm. The **EMIGRANT TRAIL MUSEUM** in **DONNER MEMORIAL STATE PARK** (12593 Donner Pass Rd, S of I-80; 530/582-7894 or 530/582-7892 for general park information, 800/444-7275 for camping reservations) tells their grim story of starvation, cannibalism, and (for some members) survival. Nowadays the snow-blanketed Donner region is a major downhill and cross-country ski destination in the winter, and in the summer the long fingers of its sparkling azure lake are dotted with sailboats, dwarfed by the imposing forested slopes and granite palisades. **DONNER LAKE** is a great fishing and boating retreat (a public boat ramp is on the west side), and a public beach rims the east end of the lake. The 350-acre state park, adjacent to the lake, also offers campsites, picnic tables, and hiking trails.

LODGINGS

Donner Country Inn / ★★

10070 GREGORY PL, DONNER LAKE; 530/587-5574 OR 925/938-6866
A B&B that wasn't restored from another lifetime, Donner Country Inn was built in 1986, a rarity for this part of the state, where 19th-century architecture is de rigueur. The attractive and comfortable inn, decorated with country pine furnishings and Laura Ashley prints, sits in a grove of pine trees just across the road from Donner Lake. Its five guest rooms have private entrances and baths, queen-size beds with down comforters, and wood-burning stoves. The cooked-to-order breakfast, served in the

main house's spacious second-floor living/dining area or on the sunny deck, includes an entree such as sour-cream waffles, plus fresh fruit, muffins, and croissants. There's also an evening happy hour with appetizers and refreshments. Advance reservations are required. *$$; no credit cards; checks OK; on the lake.*

Loch Leven Lodge / ★

13855 DONNER PASS RD, DONNER LAKE; 530/587-3773 OR 877/436-6637
If you want to get away from the crowds in Tahoe but would like easy access to the area's restaurants and shops, this quiet, simple lodge might be for you. Each of its eight small units faces beautiful Donner Lake and all but one have a kitchen. You can bask in the sun on the 5,000-square-foot redwood deck or put on your lime-green pants and head over to the Astroturf putting green (clubs and balls are provided). The lodge also has picnic tables, lawn chairs, a barbecue, a spa, and a rowboat. The rooms on the lower level offer the best lake views, but they don't offer the most privacy (passersby occasionally walk past the exposed windows). If you're traveling with the gang, reserve the two-level town house that sleeps eight and has a fireplace, a fully equipped kitchen, a living room with a queen-size hideaway bed, an upstairs bedroom, and an adjoining bunk room with four single beds. *$$; MC, V; checks OK; 1½ miles from I-80 (take the Donner Lake exit and turn left on Donner Pass Rd).*

Truckee

This popular little city packed with quaint shops, restaurants, and some terrific bed-and-breakfast inns started out in the mid-1800s as a railroad-lumber town with the construction of the first transcontinental railroad over Donner Summit. Its transformation from a dirty, run-down, one-horse town to a bustling city began in the 1970s. Today visitors arrive by car, bus, or the eastbound or westbound Amtrak passenger trains that stop at the yellow depot. If you need hiking, rock-climbing, and back-country skiing guidebooks or topographical maps and hiking supplies, stop by **SIERRA MOUNTAINEER** (Bridge St at Jibboom St; 530/587-2025), housed in the stone building that was once a livery and garage. Another notable shop is the **BOOKSHELF AT HOOLIGAN ROCKS** (11310 Donner Pass Rd, at the W end of the Safeway shopping center; 530/582-0515 or 800/959-5083), one of the Sierra Nevada's best bookstores (it's named after a nearby outcropping of rocks where miscreants were once tarred and feathered). The Bookshelf also has branches in Quincy (353 W Main St; 530/583-2665) and Tahoe City (in the Boatworks Mall; 530/581-1900). In the summer, popular Truckee attractions include the **CANNIBAL CAR CRUISE** in June, the **FOURTH OF JULY PARADE,** and the **TRUCKEE CHAMPIONSHIP RODEO** in August. The **TRUCKEE RIVER REGIONAL**

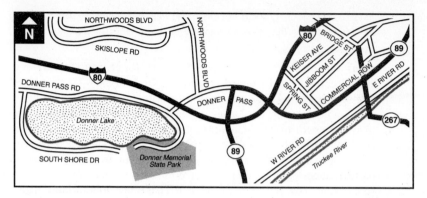

PARK (½ mile S of town on Hwy 267) has softball diamonds, picnic tables, tennis courts, and an outdoor amphitheater offering music programs (many are free) throughout the summer.

In December, when snow blankets the town and bright little white lights twinkle in the windows of the century-old facades along **COMMERCIAL ROW**, Truckee truly looks like a picture from a fairy tale. All winter long the town swarms with skiers who take advantage of its proximity to many first-rate alpine and cross-country ski areas. Others brave the freezing temperatures to engage in the 10-day winter carnival called **SNOWFEST IN MARCH**, or take a ride over the river and through the woods in a sleigh drawn by Clydesdales or Percherons. For more information call the **TRUCKEE CHAMBER OF COMMERCE** (530/587-2757).

RESTAURANTS

Andy's Truckee Diner

10144 W RIVER ST, TRUCKEE; 530/582-6925

Andy's classic diner is a fairly recent addition to the Truckee scene, but it feels like it's been around forever. Perhaps that's because the 1940s diner had an earlier life in West Chester, Pennsylvania, where it lived on the rails until it was restored and relocated here by the Carey family in 1995. Breakfast features fairly standard diner fare: omelets, pancakes, waffles, French toast, and, if you're not planning to eat again for a day or two, a hefty platter of chicken-fried steak smothered with country gravy. Burgers, dogs, and diner classics like a hot turkey sandwich with mashed potatoes, your basic BLT, and a Philly cheese steak on a roll are offered for lunch. The homey dinner entrees range from the roast turkey plate with all the fattening trimmings to Mabel's killer meat loaf and seafood jambalaya. Andy's kitchen crew proudly mash their potatoes by hand, make their own soups, and have a full fountain churning out shakes, malts, banana splits, and a variety of other diet-busting desserts.

$; AE, DIS, MC, V; local checks only; breakfast, lunch, dinner every day; beer and wine; no reservations; junction of Hwy 267. &

Coburn's Station / ★

10007 BRIDGE ST (THE TRUCKEE HOTEL), TRUCKEE; 530/550-8455
The recently opened Coburn's Station in the landmark Truckee Hotel (see review, below) is already a local favorite. Some say it's even better than its predecessor, the Passages. The attractive, spacious bar has its own menu with all the old favorite finger foods—chicken wings, breaded zucchini, teriyaki chicken skewers, and prosciutto-wrapped prawns. There's also a nice variety of soups, salads, and sandwiches, plus several pastas and desserts. The dinner menu is more elaborate, with choices like veal saltimbocca, pork tenderloins in a Thai sauce, loin of lamb with a rosemary dijonnaise finished with blue cheese, and grilled Pacific salmon. Located in the heart of downtown Truckee, Coburn's is a convenient and happy place to pile on the calories you've surely earned in the glorious surrounding mountains. In nice weather ask to eat under the stars on the patio out back. *$$; MC, V; checks OK; lunch Wed–Sun, dinner every day, brunch Sat–Sun; full bar; reservations recommended; downtown.*

Cottonwood / ★

10142 RUE HILLTOP, TRUCKEE; 530/587-5711
Cottonwood stands high on a hill on the south side of Truckee at the base of what was once California's first ski jump. The ski jump is long gone, but the restaurant affords a great view of the bright lights of Truckee from its spacious dining room. The eclectic seasonal menu ranges from Southwestern to Creole to Mediterranean fare. Begin the evening by sharing the Cottonwood's famous garlic-slathered whole-leaf Caesar salad meant to be eaten with your fingers—it's one of the best dishes on the menu. Entrees might include a braised free-range rabbit cassoulet with andouille sausage and white beans; a seafood stew of shellfish, prawns, scallops, and boudin sausage in a saffron-tomato broth served over linguine; or Denver leg of venison with a port wine and green peppercorn demi-glace. If available, the fresh berry-apple crisp à la mode makes a sweet finale. *$$; DIS, MC, V; checks OK; dinner every day; full bar; reservations recommended; above town, right off Hwy 267 at Hilltop Lodge, just beyond the railroad tracks.*

Truckee Trattoria / ★

11310-1 DONNER PASS RD, TRUCKEE; 530/582-1266
Conveniently located right off Interstate 80, this good, casual Italian cafe focuses primarily on pastas and roasted meats. Appetizers include garlic soup, portobello mushrooms stuffed with marinated goat cheese, and grilled artichokes. For a main course, try the fettuccine with tender strips of chicken and broccoli in a garlic cream sauce or the capellini with plump shrimp, arti-

choke hearts, tomatoes, and spinach in a white wine and garlic sauce. Desserts often include gelato, tiramisu, biscotti, and strawberry napoleon. Savor an espresso and hit the road again, well fed and raring to go. *$–$$; DIS, MC, V; checks OK; dinner Wed–Mon; beer and wine; reservations recommended; at the W end of the Safeway shopping center.* ⅄

LODGINGS

Hania's Bed & Breakfast Inn / ★★

10098 HIGH ST, TRUCKEE; 530/582-5775 OR 888/600-3735
Built in 1884, this pretty Victorian bed-and-breakfast has guest rooms decorated in Southwestern style with lodgepole pine furniture, colorful bedspreads, and original artwork. All the rooms have queen-size beds with down comforters and private baths. Located on a hillside within walking distance of downtown Truckee, the inn opened in 1997 and has rapidly gained a loyal clientele. There's a year-round hot tub with a mountain view, and a hearty breakfast is provided in the dining room, on the deck, or in your room. In the afternoon, wine is served in front of the wood-burning stove. Innkeeper Hania Davieson acquired her considerable innkeeping skills in Europe and can chat with you in English, Polish, German, or Russian. If you're coming to the area by train, plane, or bus, she'll even pick you up. *$$; AE, MC, V; checks OK; downtown.* ⅄

Richardson House / ★★★★

10154 HIGH ST, TRUCKEE; 530/587-5388 OR 888/229-0365
Perched on a hill overlooking downtown Truckee and the Sierra Nevada, the lavishly restored Richardson House (built in 1886) sets the standard that other B&Bs in the area will have to strive for. Its eight beautiful guest rooms are elegantly appointed with plush carpeting, color-coordinated drapes and wallpaper, vintage fixtures, featherbeds and comforters, and claw-footed tubs. Six rooms have private bathrooms and two adjoining suites share a bath. Some units have fireplaces, and Aunt Klara's Room offers every convenience for wheelchair-bound patrons. The vittles are first-rate, too. Soufflés, quiche, French toast, pancakes, hot cereal, and freshly baked scones are just some of the treats typically offered at the buffet breakfast. And if you ever manage to get hungry again, there's a 24-hour snack bar. Guests are welcome to lounge in the parlor, which has a player piano, a stereo with a CD player, and cable TV with a VCR; or spend your time outdoors among the fountains, sundials, and native aspens on vintage wicker furniture. Discount plans for skiers include lift tickets and bus transportation to nearby ski resorts. *$$–$$$; AE, DIS, MC, V; checks OK; at Spring St.* ⅄

The Truckee Hotel / ★★

10007 BRIDGE ST, TRUCKEE; 530/587-4444 OR 800/659-6921
Built in 1873, this handsome hotel is one of the oldest operating hotels in the Sierra Nevada. The original building was destroyed by a fire in

1909, and it was rebuilt with a steam heating system—the first hotel in the region to boast such a convenience. In 1992 and 1993, owners Karen and Jeff Winter renovated the place, and their hard work was acknowledged by the California Heritage Council with an award for historic restoration. The hotel's showpiece is the new Victorian-style parlor, a grand room with oak wainscoting, etched-glass doors, brass ceiling fans and light fixtures, and a marble fireplace. Upstairs there are 37 guest rooms with antique dressers, glass chandeliers, and full-, queen-, or king-size beds, many with elaborately carved wooden headboards; 8 rooms have private baths and the other 29 have basins and share bathrooms. The multiple configurations of rooms and suites can accommodate one to five people, and the units at the back of the hotel facing north—away from the railroad tracks and the bustling main street—are the quietest. Included in the rate is an expanded continental breakfast of hot and cold cereals, warm breads, and fresh fruit, served in the parlor. Late-afternoon tea is served in the parlor on weekends. Skiers will appreciate the ski racks and lockers. The hotel also houses Coburn's Station restaurant (see review, above), which serves brunch, lunch, and dinner. $–$$; AE, MC, V; no checks; at Donner Pass Rd.

North Shore Lake Tahoe

Although the California-Nevada border basically bisects Lake Tahoe down the middle, leaving its west side in California and its east side in Nevada, the lake is more commonly referred to in terms of its north and south shores. The **SOUTH SHORE** area (see below) is the most populous and urban, where you'll hear all those slot machines ringing. If you'd rather steer clear of the one-armed bandits, head for the **NORTH SHORE**. There you'll find fewer casinos (and tourists) and more of everything else, including Tahoe's best alpine and cross-country ski resorts, first-rate restaurants, and luxurious lodgings.

Make a quick stop in Tahoe City at the **LAKE TAHOE CENTRAL RESERVATION SERVICE AND VISITOR INFORMATION CENTER** (245 N Lake Blvd, just E of Hwys 89 and 28; 530/581-6900 or 800/824-6348; www.tahoefun.org), where you can sort through a mountain of brochures on local attractions ranging from indoor wall climbing to ice skating and horseback riding. If you plan to hike or ride bikes here, load up on the free trail maps, too. This is also the place to visit or call if you're having trouble finding a North Shore hotel room or campsite (a common problem during peak seasons) or need information on ski packages.

The hot summer weather brings a phenomenal array of lakeside activities, many of which don't cost a dime. Day hikers should head for the trail next to the **FOREST SERVICE VISITORS CENTER** (south shore of the lake, 5 miles S of Emerald Bay; 530/573-2674). It's the starting point for several well-marked trails, ranging from an easy half-mile stroll to a 10-mile leg-burning trek. Serious mountain bikers shouldn't miss huffing up and down the famous 24-mile **FLUME TRAIL**, which provides fantastic views of the lake; the trailhead begins at **NEVADA STATE PARK AT SPOONER LAKE** on the lake's eastern shore. Casual and asphalt-only pedalers can vie with in-line skaters, joggers, and strollers for room on North Tahoe's 15-mile-long paved trail, beginning at **SUGAR PINE POINT STATE PARK** on the West Shore and stretching north along the lake to Dollar Point on the North Shore. There's also a 3½-mile paved trail that parallels the Truckee River and passes through Tahoe City; the trail starts at the turnoff to **ALPINE MEADOWS** ski resort on Highway 89. For the truly lazy (or crazy) rider, Northstar-at-Tahoe, Ski Kirkwood, and Squaw Valley USA ski resorts offer miles of pedal-free trails accessible by chairlift or cable car—simply let the lifts tote you and your bike up the mountains, then spend the day cruising (or careening like a deranged daredevil) down the slopes.

If you weren't able to pack all your recreational toys, **PORTER'S SKI & SPORT** (501 N Lake Blvd, Tahoe City; 530/583-2314) in Tahoe City has the best prices in town for outdoor rental equipment—everything from bikes to skates to rackets, as well as a full line of snow skis, water skis, and snowboards.

To try your luck at blackjack or spinning the big wheel, make the short drive to Nevada, where the folks in the casinos will be delighted to see you. Although the North Shore's casinos are more subdued and less glitzy than the South Shore's high-rolling high-rises, the dealers are still adept at taking your money. If you're a greenhorn, this is a good place to learn the ABCs of the games, especially during off-hours. North Shore casinos include the **TAHOE BILTMORE LODGE AND CASINO** (775/831-0660); **CAL-NEVA RESORT, SPA, AND CASINO** (775/832-4000); **HYATT REGENCY LAKE TAHOE** (775/831-1111); and **CRYSTAL BAY CLUB CASINO** (775/831-0512).

North Lake Tahoe also offers a few nocturnal alternatives to the dice and the slots. You can dance any night of the week at **PIERCE STREET ANNEX** (850 N Lake Blvd, behind Safeway, Tahoe City; 530/583-5800), which caters primarily to a thirtysomething crowd but attracts swingers of all ages. **HUMPTY'S** (877 N Lake Blvd, across from Safeway, Tahoe City; 530/583-4867), on the other hand, resembles a college-town hangout, though this is where you'll find some of the area's top dance bands and the cheapest drinks. During the ski season, the lounge of the **RIVER RANCH LODGE** (see review under Alpine Meadows) has a raging après-ski scene, with ski bums from all over kicking back and chowing down on cheap hors d'oeuvres.

Tahoe Vista

RESTAURANTS

The Boulevard Cafe & Trattoria / ★★

6731 N LAKE BLVD, TAHOE VISTA; 530/546-7213

The breads, pastas, and just about everything else on the Boulevard's menu are made here, in the North Shore's most popular Italian restaurant. It's a small, casual roadside establishment run by talented chef Daniel Paolillo. Start with a bottle of wine from the extensive Italian list and the crab cake or potato–white truffle ravioli appetizer. Then sink your fork into one of the delicious entrees, such as the osso buco (braised veal shank), rack of lamb with Gorgonzola and kalamata olives, or one of the several seafood specials. Top it all off with a dish of the delectable house-made ice cream. In the summer, dine on the small patio among the pines. *$$; MC, V; no checks; dinner every day (Thurs–Tues only Apr, May, Nov, and Dec); beer and wine; reservations recommended; on Hwy 28, 1½ miles W of Hwy 267.*

Le Petit Pier / ★★★

7238 N LAKE BLVD, TAHOE VISTA; 530/546-4464

One of Tahoe's more exclusive French restaurants is elevated just above the shore with a dazzling view of the lake. The menu features such mouthwatering appetizers as escargots in Roquefort butter, warm foie gras with truffle sauce, and oysters on the half shell. The exquisite entrees range from seafood (swordfish with ginger raspberry sauce) and fowl (grilled breast of duck in a zinfandel sauce) to beef (grilled filet mignon with a sauce of port, figs, and fresh crepes) and a superb rack of lamb. Also deservedly popular is the order-ahead pheasant Souvaroff for two with foie gras and a rich demi-glace encrusted in puff pastry. Le Petit Pier's wine list recently won *Wine Spectator* magazine's Award of Excellence. When making a reservation, request a table by the window and be sure to arrive before sunset—you don't want to miss this view, which extends clear across Lake Tahoe. *$$$; AE, DC, DIS, MC, V; local checks only; dinner Wed–Mon; full bar; reservations recommended; on Hwy 28 at the W end of town.* &

Sunsets on the Lake / ★★★

7320 LAKE BLVD, TAHOE VISTA; 530/546-3640

Rare in Tahoe is a lakeside restaurant serving food that's equal to the spectacular view. Yet here even the Kodak moment beyond the windowpanes shares star billing with chef Lew Orlady's fantastic braised lamb shank, a hefty hunk of tender meat with shiitake mushrooms, caramelized vegetables, and garlic mashed potatoes—one of the best lamb dishes in Tahoe. If the duck is among the daily specials, you're in luck: each tender slice of this expertly prepared fowl explodes with flavor. Another superb entree is the linguine with fresh red Manila clams, garlic, shallots, chile flakes, Roma tomatoes, white wine, and olive oil. Just about every dish on the large Northern Italian/California menu is a winner, which explains the carloads and boatloads of patrons (Sunsets' "boat valet" will even clean your boat and top off its tank while you dine). *$$$; AE, DC, DIS, MC, V; no checks; lunch every day mid-July–late Aug, dinner every day (closed Nov–Dec 15); full bar; reservations recommended; on Hwy 28 at the E end of town.* &

LODGINGS

Franciscan Lakeside Lodge / ★

6944 N LAKE BLVD, TAHOE VISTA; 530/546-6300 OR 800/564-6754

The best of the area's motel scene, the Franciscan offers access to a private beach and pier, mooring buoys, a heated swimming pool, volleyball nets, a croquet set, horseshoe pits, a children's play area, and nearby tennis courts, ski areas, and a golf course. Its 54 plain but adequate units include studios, one- or two-bedrooms (and a four-bedroom house), full kitchens, private bathrooms, TVs, phones, and daily housekeeping service. The lakefront cottages have large porches overlooking the water (of course, they're the first to get booked, so make your reservations early). *$$; AE, MC, V; checks OK; on Hwy 28, 1 mile W of Hwy 267.*

Kings Beach

RESTAURANTS

Log Cabin Caffe / ★

8692 N LAKE BLVD, KINGS BEACH; 530/546-7109

Originally a summer home, the funky Log Cabin Caffe is now *the* place to have breakfast in Lake Tahoe. The owner's penchant for freshness is what makes the Log Cabin such a hit: croissants and muffins are baked every morning, the orange juice is fresh-squeezed, and the fluffy Belgian waffles are topped with fresh fruit and nuts. The large lunch menu features everything from fresh vegetable soup and tofu burgers to pizza, pasta, and sliced turkey-breast sandwiches filled with cranberries and cream cheese. Behind the restaurant near the lakeshore is a picnic area where you can cool off with ice cream sundaes and sodas, served from 11am to 11pm throughout the summer. *$; MC, V; checks OK; breakfast, lunch every day; beer and wine; reservations required; on Hwy 28, ⅓ mile E of Hwy 267.* &

Squaw Valley

LODGINGS

PlumpJack Squaw Valley Inn / ★★★

1920 SQUAW VALLEY RD, SQUAW VALLEY; 530/583-1576 OR 800/323-7666

Restaurateurs Bill Getty (yes, those Gettys) and Gavin Newsom, the brains—and money—behind the highly regarded PlumpJack Cafe in San

Francisco, have teamed together to create Tahoe's most stylish and sophisticated hotel and restaurant. Though it lacks the big-dollar toys offered by its competitor across the valley (the Resort at Squaw Creek), the PlumpJack Squaw Valley Inn is undeniably more stylish. The entire hotel bears a strong resemblance to the San Francisco restaurant, draped in muted tones of taupe and soft greens and highlighted with custom metalwork that imparts a handsome industrial-deco theme. Guest rooms are loaded with comforts, from plush hooded robes and terry-cloth slippers to thick down comforters atop expensive mattresses. The hotel boasts mountain views from each of its 60 rooms, as well as a swimming pool, two spas, a retail sports shop, ski rentals and storage, complimentary parking, and room service from the terrific cafe from 7am to 10pm. The adjoining PlumpJack Cafe is the latest showcase for award-winning chef Keith Luce, who oversees the kitchen both here and at the sister restaurant in San Francisco. Expect impeccable service regardless of your attire (this is, after all, a ski resort) and tempting menu choices that might include risotto with shiitake mushrooms and fava beans (with chianti, of course), roasted rabbit atop a golden potato purée, and a fabulous dish of braised oxtails paired with horseradish mashed potatoes and carrots. Those already familiar with PlumpJack in San Francisco know that the reasonably priced wine list is among the nation's best. *$$$; AE, DC, DIS, MC, V; checks OK; off Hwy 89.* &

Resort at Squaw Creek / ★★★

400 SQUAW CREEK RD, SQUAW VALLEY; 530/583-6300 OR 800/327-3353
The $130 million Resort at Squaw Creek—Tahoe's only superluxury resort hotel—is a paradise for skiers, golfers, and tennis players. Tucked away in an inconspicuous corner of Squaw Valley, the nine-story resort opened in 1990, offering a plethora of amenities—from parking valets, a concierge, and room service to children's activity programs, a shopping promenade, three swimming pools, a fitness center and spa, cross-country ski trails, an equestrian center with stables, and even an ice-skating rink. Furthermore, it's only a stone's throw from the Squaw Creek chairlift, which accesses the entire Squaw Valley USA ski area. In the summer, golfers may tee off at the resort's 18-hole championship golf course designed by Robert Trent Jones Jr. while tennis buffs may rally at the resort's eight tennis courts. The 405 rooms, suites, and bilevel penthouses feature custom furnishings, original artwork, minibars, closed-circuit televisions, Nintendo, Starbucks in-room coffee and tea service, and telephones with speakerphones. Unfortunately, with the hotel rooms in one building and the front desk, restaurants, and other facilities in another, guests are sometimes forced to walk outdoors—even in the middle of a wicked winter storm—but the journey takes less than 30 seconds and brollies are available for wimps. Ask about the midweek

package deals, which can knock a hefty amount off the normally exorbitant rates. In addition to a deli, pub, game lounge, and outdoor cafe, the Resort at Squaw Creek offers three restaurants: the elegant Glissandi, which serves French-American cuisine, the continental restaurant Cascades, and the Ristorante Montagna, where you can dine alfresco on wood-oven-baked pizzas, rotisserie-grilled meats, and house specials such as the *agnello alla griglia*—an oakwood-roasted rack of lamb with grilled vegetables. A new $3 million refurbishment of the 10,000-square-foot spa was recently completed with such state-of-the-art bliss inducers as full-service salon, body wraps, and mud baths. *$$$$; AE, DC, DIS, MC, V; checks OK; off Hwy 89.*

Alpine Meadows

LODGINGS

River Ranch Lodge / ★★

HWY 89, ALPINE MEADOWS; 530/583-4264 OR 800/535-9900
Established in 1888 as the Deer Park Inn, this historic lodge was a popular watering hole for passengers traveling by narrow-gauge railway. In 1950 the old building was replaced with the rustic, wood-shingled lodge that now stands on the banks of the picturesque Truckee River. The River Ranch's best rooms feature private balconies that overlook the river as it winds its way from Lake Tahoe to the town of Truckee, then east to Pyramid Lake in Nevada. All of the 19 recently refurbished rooms have private baths, antique or lodgepole pine furnishings, down comforters, TVs, and phones with data ports. Rooms 9 and 10, the farthest from the road, are the top choices because they're quiet and have the best river views from their private decks. In the winter, the lodge is a skier's paradise, a mere five-minute drive from both Squaw Valley USA and Alpine Meadows ski resorts (the Alpine Meadows stay-and-ski packages are outstanding); in the summer, guests relax under umbrellas on the huge patio overlooking the river, watching rafters float by while they munch on barbecued chicken and sip iced tea. A continental breakfast is included in the surprisingly reasonable rates. The River Ranch's spectacular circular cocktail lounge, which cantilevers over the river, has been a locals' haven for years and is an immensely popular après-ski spot for those who have been schussing the slopes of Alpine Meadows and Squaw Valley. Also a big hit is the handsome River Ranch Lodge Restaurant, which serves fresh fish, such as mountain rainbow trout sautéed with lemon butter, steaks, a full New Zealand rack of lamb, and something you probably don't cook at home: wood-oven-roasted Montana elk loin with a dried-bing-cherry–port sauce. *$–$$$; AE, MC, V; no checks; at Alpine Meadows Rd, 3½ miles from Lake Tahoe and Tahoe City.* &

Tahoe City

RESTAURANTS

Bridgetender Tavern and Grill / ★

30 W LAKE BLVD, TAHOE CITY; 530/583-3342

Any bar that has Jaegermeister on tap is worth a visit. The fact that the Bridgetender has 20 other beers on tap and great burgers is icing on the cake. Tahoe's foremost tavern, a rough-hewn log-and-stone structure built around a trio of healthy ponderosa pines, is frequented by folks who know each other on a first-name basis. The menu is basic—burgers, salads, sandwiches, and various appetizers like pork ribs, fish and chips, and deep-fried chicken strips—but the food is filling and cheap. Cholesterol-phobes will appreciate the healthy, low-fat chicken salad sandwich. In the summer the outside patio is always packed with giddy tourists unfamiliar with the effects of alcohol at high altitudes. *$; DIS, MC, V; no checks; lunch, dinner every day; full bar; no reservations; on Hwy 89 at Fanny Bridge, downtown.* &

Christy Hill / ★★★

115 GROVE ST, TAHOE CITY; 530/583-8551

Perched high above the lake in one of the most romantic fireside settings in Tahoe, the venerable Christy Hill restaurant has weathered droughts and recessions, yet still retains its title as one of the finest—and most expensive—restaurants in Tahoe City. The menu, presided over by chef Claudio Mejio, changes seasonally but always offers a wide selection of fresh seafood—Fanny Bay oysters, broiled salmon, and Alaskan halibut oven-baked with garlic bread crumbs and served over endive with a shallot, garlic, and white wine butter sauce, plus choice-cut meats such as Australian lamb marinated in wine, honey, and herbs, broiled and served with a fresh peach, ginger, and garlic chutney. Christy Hill's experienced servers (most have been here at least 10 years) know the menu and extensive wine list well, so don't hesitate to seek their advice. Dessert is a wonderful excuse to extend your evening here; try the warm summer fruit cobbler with house-made vanilla ice cream or the chocolate pot de crème with crème Chantilly. Arrive before sunset to admire the spectacular view. *$$$; AE, MC, V; checks OK; dinner Tues–Sun; beer and wine; reservations recommended; off Hwy 28/N Lake Blvd, behind the Village Store.*

Fire Sign Cafe / ★★

1785 W LAKE BLVD, TAHOE CITY; 530/583-0871

This converted old Tahoe home has been a favorite breakfast stop for locals since the late 1970s. Just about everything here is made from scratch, including the coffee cake and muffins that accompany generous

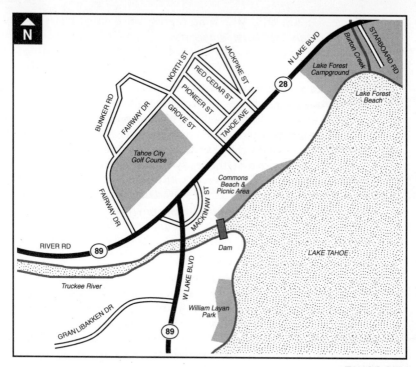

TAHOE CITY

servings of bacon and eggs. Even the savory, thinly sliced salmon used in the cafe's legendary eggs Benedict is smoked on the premises. Popular lunch items include the garden burger, the chicken burrito, the grilled turkey sandwich with green chiles and cheese, and a scrumptious raspberry cobbler. In the summer, dine on the deck under the pines. Expect a long wait on weekends. *$; AE, MC, V; local checks only; breakfast, lunch every day; beer and wine; no reservations; on Hwy 89, 2 miles S of town.* &

Jake's on the Lake / ★★

780 LAKE BLVD, TAHOE CITY; 530/583-0188

If you're in the mood for steak and seafood, Jake's serves some of the best in Tahoe. One link in a wildly popular California and Hawaii chain, this handsome lakefront restaurant offers consistently good food and service, provided in part by a candidate for California's most affable bartender, who's known simply as Montana. Specialties include rack of New Zealand lamb and fresh fish, such as the favored flame-broiled seven-spice ahi tuna with a saffron mustard sauce. And the terrific Hula Pie dessert (an Oreo cookie crust topped with mounds of macadamia-nut ice cream and smothered with fudge sauce and whipped cream) is worth the splurge. *$$; AE, DIS, MC, V; no checks; lunch every day June–Sept (lunch Sat only Oct–May), dinner every day; full bar; reservations recommended; on Hwy 28, downtown.* &

Rosie's Cafe / ★★

571 N LAKE BLVD, TAHOE CITY; 530/583-8504

Most folks who spend a few days or more in North Lake Tahoe eventually wind up at Rosie's for breakfast, lunch, dinner, drinks, or all of the above. This humble Tahoe institution serves large portions of traditional American fare—sandwiches, steaks, burgers, salads—but the dish that tourists always return for is the hearty Yankee pot roast (the perfect dish for those cold winter nights), served with mashed potatoes and gravy and a side of sautéed vegetables. *$$; AE, DC, DIS, MC, V; no checks; breakfast, lunch, dinner every day; full bar; no reservations for breakfast and lunch, reservations recommended for dinner; downtown.*

Wolfdale's / ★★★

640 N LAKE BLVD, TAHOE CITY; 530/583-5700

Chef/owner Douglas Dale is well known for his innovative California cuisine that's often accented with Japanese touches. His short, frequently changing menu offers an intriguing mix of truly one-of-a-kind, light, and beautifully arranged dishes that vary from very good to sublime. Everything served in this casually elegant restaurant—from the herb-kissed focaccia to the savory sausages, smoked fish, and divine desserts—is prepared on the premises. You might begin your meal with a cured salmon salad or a vegetable spring roll with a Thai curry-ginger sauce, followed by grilled Columbia River sturgeon with mushroom duxelles and tomato coulis or roasted quail stuffed with fennel sausage and onions served on a bed of kale. Many of Wolfdale's regular patrons dine at the small bar, and in the summertime you can sit outdoors and enjoy the view of Lake Tahoe through the trees. *$$$; MC, V; no checks; dinner Wed–Mon (dinner every day in July and Aug); full bar; reservations recommended; on Hwy 28, downtown.* &

Za's / ★★

395 LAKE BLVD, TAHOE CITY; 530/583-1812

When the front half of the "PIZZAS" sign fell off this restaurant long ago, the owner decided it was an auspicious omen and renamed the place Za's. Sure enough, Za's turned out to be a hit. In fact, it's one of the most popular restaurants in Tahoe, serving very good Italian food at bargain prices. Start with the Caesar salad or the baked polenta with wild mushrooms and marsala sauce, and follow that with the golden-brown calzone stuffed with fresh vegetables and mozzarella or the smoked-chicken fettuccine with fresh artichoke hearts and a garlic-cream sauce. Wash it all down with a tumbler of Chianti but skip the lackluster desserts. There are only a dozen tables, so during peak hours you'll have to join the line of salivating patrons snaking out the door. *$; MC, V; local checks only; dinner every day; beer and wine; no reservations; on Hwy 28, across from the fire station.*

LODGINGS

The Cottage Inn / ★★

1690 W LAKE BLVD, TAHOE CITY; 530/581-4073 OR 800/581-4073
This is one of the more appealing places to stay in Tahoe City. Each of the inn's 17 cabins has Swedish-pine furniture, a stone fireplace, a private bath with a ceramic-tile shower, a thick, colorful quilt on the bed, and a TV with a VCR. A full country breakfast, included in the price, may be delivered to your doorstep or served at the family-style tables in the dining room or on the outside deck. After breakfast, kick back in the comfortable sitting room in front of the large stone fireplace, in the Scandinavian sauna, or at the nearby beach and dock. *$$; MC, V; checks OK; on Hwy 89, 2 miles S of town.*

Sunnyside Restaurant & Lodge / ★★

1850 W LAKE BLVD, TAHOE CITY; 530/583-7200 OR 800/822-2754
Restored about 15 years ago, this attractive mountain lodge has 23 rooms, each with a deck. All but four have an unobstructed view of Lake Tahoe, and the best of the bunch are the bright and airy lakefront units (suites 30 and 31 and rooms 32 to 39). A complimentary continental breakfast buffet is served every morning, and in the afternoon locals and visitors assemble for lunch, dinner, or a drink on the huge redwood deck overlooking the lake. The Chris Craft Dining Room serves well-prepared California cuisine and specializes in fresh seafood, such as Hawaiian ahi and baked salmon with Roma tomatoes, fresh basil, and Gorgonzola. In the winter the lodge attracts a sizable après-ski crowd, which watches Sunnyside's ski flicks while munching on the inexpensive food at the bar. *$$$; AE, MC, V; no checks; on Hwy 89, 2 miles S of town.*

Homewood

RESTAURANTS

Swiss Lakewood Restaurant / ★★

5055 W LAKE BLVD, HOMEWOOD; 530/525-5211
This handsome Swiss-style edifice, first opened in 1920, is the home of the oldest operating restaurant in Lake Tahoe. Its current owners, Helga and Albert Marty, continue the tradition of offering fine French-Continental cuisine in a traditional Swiss setting (think knotty-pine walls covered with clocks, old photographs, and Swiss cowbells). Though the menu changes frequently, among the secrets of the Martys' unwavering success are their

perfectly executed sauces, such as the tangy caper-lemon-mustard sauce drizzled over their delicate crab cake appetizer or the tasty Madagascar green-pepper sauce poured over the hearty Black Angus pepper steak flambé, which is prepared at your table with fiery aplomb. And, but of course, there's the cheese fondue for two, served on weeknights and throughout the week in the winter. For dessert, consider the Grand Marnier soufflé or the cherries jubilee flambé for two. *$$$; AE, MC, V; no checks; dinner Tues–Sun; full bar; reservations recommended; on Hwy 89, 6 miles S of Tahoe City, next to Ski Homewood.* &

LODGINGS

Chaney House / ★★★

4725 W LAKE BLVD, HOMEWOOD; 530/525-7333

Built in the 1920s, the European-style Chaney House features 18-inch-thick stone walls, Gothic arches, and a massive stone fireplace that extends to a cathedral ceiling. Each of the four individually decorated rooms has a private bath and a queen- or king-size bed. The attractive Honeymoon Hideaway is a detached, very private unit with a fireplace and a granite Jacuzzi for two. Gary and Lori Chaney—two of Tahoe's more vivacious and friendly innkeepers—serve an elaborate breakfast on the patio (weather permitting) overlooking their private beach and pier. Lori likes to get creative in the kitchen—she often whips up such treats as French toast stuffed with cream cheese and topped with hot homemade blackberry sauce and crème fraîche, or a scrumptious concoction of scrambled eggs mixed with artichokes, vermouth, and cheese. The Chaney House books up quickly, so make your reservations at least a month in advance. *$$; DIS, MC, V; checks OK; on Hwy 89, 1 mile N of Ski Homewood.*

Rockwood Lodge / ★★★

5295 W LAKE BLVD, HOMEWOOD; 530/525-5273 OR 800/LE-TAHOE

Innkeepers Louis Reinkens and Constance Stevens bought this native stone and timber house in 1984 and, after a meticulous refurbishing, opened it as a bed-and-breakfast a year later. Although you may be disconcerted by their requirement that you remove your shoes before entering, all is forgiven when your feet sink into the plush, cream-colored carpet. The lodge, located just across the street from the lake, has five rooms, each furnished with antiques, featherbeds, and down comforters covered in Laura Ashley fabrics. Terry-cloth robes hang in the bedroom closets, and the extravagant private bathrooms feature brass fixtures, hand-painted tiles, and double showers or a tub for two. In the evening guests often play backgammon and sip cordials by the fireplace in the sitting room. A generous breakfast is served at 9am in the dining room or on the outdoor patio (early-rising skiers and golfers are also provided for). *$$–$$$$; no credit cards; checks OK; on Hwy 89, next to Ski Homewood.*

Tahoma

LODGINGS

Tahoma Meadows Bed & Breakfast / ★★

6821 W LAKE BLVD, TAHOMA; 530/525-1553 OR 800/355-1596

Ulli and Dick White, the new owners of Tahoma Meadows Bed & Breakfast, are just the couple to run the finest moderately priced B&B in Lake Tahoe. Both are veterans of the hospitality industry—Ulli here and in her native Germany, and Dick here in Lake Tahoe. This popular B&B consists of 11 cabins perched on a gentle forest slope among sugar pines and flowers. The units are individually decorated; in each cozy cabin you'll find framed paintings of bucolic settings. All have a private bath, a discreetly placed TV, and comfy king- or queen-size beds; four have gas-log fireplaces. The largest cabin, the Treehouse, sleeps six and is ideal for families seeking privacy and plenty of elbow room. A full breakfast is served at the main lodge upstairs, from the independently owned Stoneyridge Cafe. Nearby activities include skiing at Ski Homewood, fly-fishing at a private trout-stocked lake (Dick, an avid fly-fisherman, can give you some tips), and sunbathing on the lakeshore just across the street. Tahoma Meadows is popular with the hiking and biking crowds, who like not only the value but the superb hiking and biking trails nearby. *$$; AE, DIS, MC, V; checks OK; on Hwy 89, 8½ miles from Tahoe City.*

South Shore Lake Tahoe

Three premier attractions separate sassy South Lake Tahoe from its sportier northern counterpart: glitzy casinos with celebrity entertainers, several sandy beaches, and the massive **HEAVENLY SKI RESORT**, the only North American ski area that straddles two states. If 24-hour gambling parties or schussing down the slopes of Heavenly is your idea of paradise, then you're in for a treat.

Most of the weekend warriors who flock here on Friday afternoons book their favorite lodgings weeks—if not months—in advance. Follow their lead and plan early. For long-term stays, consider renting a condo with a group of friends. As soon as you roll into town, stop at the **SOUTH LAKE TAHOE CHAMBER OF COMMERCE** (3066 Lake Tahoe Blvd, 530/541-5255; www.tahoeinfo.com), where you'll find an entire room filled with free maps, brochures, and guidebooks to the South Lake region. And if you risked traveling to Tahoe without a hotel reservation, call **LAKE TAHOE RESERVATIONS** (800/AT-TAHOE) for help finding a room.

In the summer, droves of tourists and locals arrive by bike, car, or boat at the **BEACON** (see review, below) to scope out the beach, babe, and bar scene—easily the best on the lake. In addition to **JAMISON BEACH**, the other popular public beaches are **NEVADA BEACH** (on Elk Point Rd, 1 mile E of Stateline, Nevada), which has spectacular views of Lake Tahoe and the Sierra Nevada, and **EL DORADO BEACH** (off Lakeview Ave, across from Pizza Hut, in downtown S Lake Tahoe)—not as pretty but much closer to town.

Tahoe's brilliant-blue lake is so deep it never freezes, so it's navigable even in the dead of winter. Capitalizing on that fact, the **TAHOE QUEEN** (530/541-3364 or 800/23TAHOE; reservations required), an authentic Mississippi stern-wheeler regularly used for scenic lunch and dinner cruises, doubles as a ferry for South Shore skiers who want to explore the North Shore's resorts. Skiers hop aboard at the base of Ski Run Boulevard in South Lake. The 25-mile ride takes about two hours, disembarking at the West Shore's tiny town of Homewood, where a waiting shuttle transports riders to Squaw Valley USA ski resort. Passengers return to South Lake the same way they came; however, on the trip back the bar is open, the band is playing, and the boat is rockin'. The round-trip fare is reasonable, and for an extra fee skiers can fill up on a big breakfast on the morning ferry.

The South Lake's number one nighttime entertainment is—you guessed it—the casino. The top guns on this side of the lake are **HARRAH'S, CAESARS TAHOE, HARVEYS**, and the **HORIZON**, which are squeezed next to each other on Highway 50 in Nevada and burn enough bulbs to light a small city. Even if you can't afford to gamble away your money, stroll through the ruckus to watch the high rollers or gawk at those "just-one-more-try" players mesmerized by the flashy money machines. If you want to try your luck, a mere $10 can keep you entertained for quite a while on the nickel slots. Or spend the night kicking up your heels on the dance floor at **NERO'S 2000 NIGHTCLUB** (55 Hwy 50, Stateline, Nevada; 702/588-3515) in Caesars. Or visit **TURTLE'S SPORTS BAR AND DANCE EMPORIUM** (4130 Lake Tahoe Blvd, S Lake Tahoe; 530/544-5400) in the Embassy Suites.

For more than a century, **WALLEY'S HOT SPRINGS RESORT** (2001 Foothill Blvd, 2 miles N of the E end of Kingsbury Grade, near Genoa, Nevada; 702/782-8155) has been the place for South Lake residents to unwind after a hard day of skiing or mountain biking, even though it's about an hour-long drive from town. For less than the price of a pair of movie tickets, you can jump into the six open-air pools (each is set at a different temperature) and watch ducks and geese at the nearby wildlife area. If a good soak doesn't get all the kinks out, indulge in a rubdown at the resort's massage center. No children under 12 are allowed in the resort.

South Lake Tahoe

RESTAURANTS

The Beacon / ★★

1900 JAMISON BEACH RD, S LAKE TAHOE; 530/541-0630

On a warm summer afternoon there is no better place on the lake to sit outside, sip on a frosty Rum Runner (a blend of light and dark rums and seven juices), and say to yourself, "*This* is the life." Located right on Jamison Beach, the Beacon is where locals arrive by car, bike, or boat to bask in the sun, chow down on a bucket of steamed clams, and gawk at the tourist scene. The motto here is: "A Sunny Place for Shady People." The lunch fare is mostly salads, hamburgers, sandwiches, and the like, whereas dinner specialties include fresh seafood, such as blackened salmon with Cajun spices or a New York steak sautéed and glazed in a bourbon sauce. In the summer the Beacon shakes with live jazz, reggae, country, and rock 'n' roll. *$$; AE, DIS, MC, V; no checks; lunch, dinner every day, brunch Sat–Sun; full bar; reservations recommended; off Hwy 89, 2½ miles N of the Hwy 50 junction, at Camp Richardson.* &

Evan's American Gourmet Café / ★★★

536 EMERALD BAY RD, S LAKE TAHOE; 530/542-1990

The food at this family-run establishment is its raison d'être. Entering the small, softly lit dining room of this 1930s vintage house nestled in the woods, you will be greeted by one of the owners, Candice or Evan Williams. The ever-changing menu features an eclectic and impressive mix of Italian, Caribbean, Oriental, and Southwestern cuisines. These folks were doing the chic fusion cuisine thing before it had a name. The wine list, with nearly 300 labels, is as engaging as the food. A recent repast featured sautéed Dungeness crab cakes on roasted red pepper purée with crème fraîche, house-smoked duck breast salad with micro greens and papaya vinaigrette, and roast venison with balsamic roast cherries and "lacquered" root vegetables. After dinner be sure to try one of Candice's lavish desserts. *$$$; DIS, MC, V; no checks; dinner every day; beer and wine; reservations required; on Hwy 89, 1 mile N of the Hwy 50 junction, at 15th St.*

The Red Hut / ★

2749 HWY 50, S LAKE TAHOE; 530/541-9024

This all-American coffee shop, complete with an L-shaped Formica counter, booths, and a bubble-gum machine, has become so popular the owners have added a waiting room. The Red Hut's success is based primarily on its good coffee, hefty omelets with a variety of fillings, friendly waitresses, and, best of all, low prices. Lunch follows the same big-and-cheap all-American formula with a menu of mostly burgers and sandwiches. While the food isn't anything to swoon over, it beats the buns off the fast-food chains down the street. *$; cash only; breakfast, lunch every day; no alcohol; no reservations; ½ block S of Al Tahoe Blvd, 4 miles E of Stateline, Nevada.*

Samurai / ★★

2588 HWY 50, S LAKE TAHOE; 530/542-0300
Despite Tahoe's far-from-the-sea location, there is decent seafood in the area, and you'll certainly find some of the freshest sea creatures at Samurai, one of the best Japanese restaurants in South Lake Tahoe. Settle down at the sushi bar for some hamachi or tekka maki, or take a table in the dining room, where you may order such traditional Japanese dishes as tempura, teriyaki, seafood yosenabe (fresh vegetables, tofu, noodles, mushrooms, bamboo shoots, and various seafood stewing in a soy-sauce and lemon broth), and *tonkatsu* (deep-fried breaded pork cutlets). You may also dine at the Japanese *robata* (a table around a volcanic-rock fireplace), or, if you're with a large party, request a private tatami room. *$$; AE, MC, V; no checks; dinner every day; beer and wine; reservations recommended for parties of 6 or more; 1½ miles E of Hwy 89 junction.* &

Scusa! on Ski Run / ★★

1142 SKI RUN BLVD, S LAKE TAHOE; 530/542-0100
Don't let the restaurant's "Pasta Power" sign scare you away. And though the decor is an untraditional art deco with nary a wax-crusted chianti bottle or checkered tablecloth, this is the place where South Lake Tahoe foodies come for Italian fare. As soon as you're seated, order the terrific rosemary-and-garlic bread, served with extra-virgin olive oil. Then peruse the varied menu for a favorite Italian dish, which might include the seafood fettuccine tossed with shrimp, mussels, clams, scallops, and calamari in a spicy Alfredo sauce or the tricolored eggplant Parmesan, breaded with focaccia and oven-roasted with Alfredo, pesto, and marinara sauces. Desserts are simple but satisfying, and the wines are fairly priced. *$$; AE, DIS, MC, V; no checks; dinner every day; beer and wine; reservations recommended; off Hwy 50.*

Sprouts Natural Foods Cafe / ★★

3123 HARRISON AVE, S LAKE TAHOE; 530/541-6969
You don't have to be a granola-loving long-haired type to figure out that Sprouts is among the best places to eat in town. If the line out the door isn't a big enough hint, then perhaps a bite of the marvelous mayo-free tuna sandwich (made with yogurt and lots of fresh veggies) will make you a convert to feel-good food. Owner Tyler Cannon has filled a huge culinary hole in this area with the South Lake's premier vegetarian hangout. Almost everything is made on the premises, including the soups,

tempeh burgers, sandwiches (try the Real Tahoe Turkey), huge burritos, muffins, fruit smoothies (a meal in themselves), coffee drinks, and fresh-squeezed juices. Order at the counter, then scramble for a vacant seat (outdoor tables are coveted) and listen for one of the buffed and beautiful servers to call out your name and deliver your tray of earthy delights. This is also an excellent place to pack a picnic lunch for a skiing, hiking, or mountain biking expedition. *$; no credit cards; local checks only; breakfast, lunch, dinner every day; beer and wine; no reservations; on the corner of Hwy 50 and Alameda St.*

LODGINGS

Christiania Inn / ★★

3819 SADDLE RD, S LAKE TAHOE; 530/544-7337 ★

Located only 50 yards from Heavenly Ski Resort's main chairlift, this European-style bed-and-breakfast inn, built in 1965 as a Scandinavian-style après-ski lodge, has four suites that are frequently occupied by honeymooners. Each suite has a wood-burning fireplace and a king-size bed. One has a dry sauna, one a whirlpool, and one a mirror over the bed. A continental breakfast and an afternoon cognac are included in the rates. The elegant and expensive Christiania Inn Restaurant offers continental cuisine, such as pan-seared spring venison with red currant cabernet sauce, boneless breast of Long Island duck with black currant sauce, and Chilean sea bass with fresh fruit salsa. Guests with lighter appetites may order from the appetizer menu in the lounge. *$$; MC, V; local checks only; closed 3 weeks in May; off Ski Run Blvd, at the base of Heavenly Ski Resort.* &

Historic Camp Richardson Resort & Marina / ★

JAMISON BEACH RD AND HWY 89, S LAKE TAHOE; 530/541-1801 OR 800/544-1801

Richardson's, a popular family retreat, seems worlds away from the high-rise casinos and bustle of South Lake Tahoe, yet it's actually just a few miles outside town. Since the resort was taken over from the Forest Service in 1985, the owners have restored the 65-year-old lodge, upgraded the inn and cabins, and added a large courtyard spa. The lodge, graced with a stately stone fireplace in the lobby, offers 29 sparsely furnished rooms with private baths and is only a five-minute walk from the lake. Even closer to the water are 39 homey cabins named after classic American cars and the small, seven-room Beach Inn (the rooms are slightly larger than the main lodge's and they have lake views, TVs, and telephones). The best cabins are near Jamison Beach and are usually reserved far in advance (only some of them are available to rent in the winter). In the summer the resort provides guests with an ice cream parlor, a general store (which includes beer and wine in its inventory), camping facilities, hiking and biking trails, volleyballs and nets, horseshoes and pits, and

KEEP TAHOE BLUE

By the time explorers Kit Carson and John Frémont ventured upon the brilliant blue waters of "Da-ow-wa-ga" (edge of the lake), it had been a gathering place and spiritual site of the Washoe Indians for centuries. Fortune seekers soon followed the explorers, first for gold and silver, later for timber. Then wealthy San Franciscans in a quest for vacation sites fell in love with the lake, and hotels and gambling halls sprang up to shelter and entertain them. Tourism boomed. The 1960 Olympics at Squaw Valley revealed a first-class skiing area to the whole world. Today the lake is the focus of more than 20 million annual visitors—as many as 200,000 on fine summer weekends.

Love has taken its toll. One of the clearest lakes in the world, Tahoe has seen its famous transparency drop from 105 feet to around 70 feet. Algae coats the shoreline rocks in the spring. Wood-burning fireplaces, automobile exhaust, outboard motors, golf course fertilizers—all these by-products of human activity have an impact on the lake. If current levels of pollution continue, scientists say, by the end of the next 30 years the lake will have lost half its transparency, changing color from blue to green. Local wildlife and forests are also suffering from urbanization. That's the bad news.

The good news is that the pitched warfare between environmentalists and businesses/developers/property owners has abated, and a cooperative public-private partnership to preserve the lake and its environs seems to be genuinely under way. Federal

equipment rentals for almost anything that floats or rolls. Another perk: one of South Lake's best restaurants and bars, The Beacon Bar and Grill (see review, above) is just a short walk away. Staying at Richardson Resort is sort of like being at camp again, and it's a great place to take the kids. *$$; AE, MC, V; no checks; 2½ miles W of the Hwy 50 junction.*

Lakeland Village Beach & Ski Resort / ★★

3535 LAKE TAHOE BLVD, S LAKE TAHOE; 530/544-1685 OR 800/822-5969
Although a few of Lakeland Village's light-brown, two-story wood buildings are located on busy Highway 50, the 19-acre resort has more than 1,000 feet of beachfront property, two tennis courts, and two swimming pools—all beyond the sight and sound of the traffic. The Village's 260 units, ranging from studios to five-bedroom town houses, are individually owned. Interior decor varies, but owners are required to meet or exceed AAA three-diamond standards. The most desirable town houses front the lake, and they get booked quickly during peak season—some also command hefty $600-per-night rates. The studio rooms in the main lodge and the one-bedroom suites are the least expensive, starting at about $100. All units come with fireplaces, fully equipped kitchens, private balconies, and daily housekeeping service. *$$–$$$; AE, MC, V; checks OK; between Ski Run Blvd and Fairway Ave.* &

and state funds for restoration and conservation efforts are in the pipeline. In addition to the nature front, cooperative efforts are manifesting themselves in a clean-up of the tackier sections of urban areas. Low-rent motels, T-shirt stores, and souvenir shops in the commercial strip at the north end of South Lake Tahoe, for instance, will be bull-dozed out of existence, if all goes according to plan. They will be replaced by upscale hotels and restaurants, a major shopping mall, an outdoor ice rink, and a convention center. While this may not seem like the stuff of a nature lover's dreams, it is, sort of. In the name of arresting urban sprawl, the tentative agreement is to have new develop-ment take place in already urbanized areas, preserving the surrounding forests. Cur-rently, 95 percent of the ground in the commercial areas is covered in concrete, allowing polluted snowmelt and rainwater to go straight into the lake. Redeveloped areas will have holding and treatment ponds to clean up the runoff. Plans include a city transit center with a ski gondola and a high-tech bus system to lure people out of their cars.

Perhaps the most visible sign of changing attitudes is the prevalence of *Keep Tahoe Blue* bumper stickers. At one time considered a symbol of the environmental perspec-tive, like gang colors, the sign could get your car defaced. Now they are everywhere. Faced with the desecration of one of the world's natural wonders, admirers are at last united in efforts to save the lake. —*Mary Anne Moore*

Hope Valley

LODGINGS

Sorensen's Resort / ★★

14255 HWY 88, HOPE VALLEY; 530/694-2203 OR 800/423-9949

This resort's cluster of 30 cabins, nestled among the meadows and aspen groves of alpine Hope Valley, offers first-rate cross-country skiing in the winter, prime hiking and llama treks in late spring and summer, and a ter-rific display of colors in the fall, when the aspens turn vibrant shades of yellow, gold, and red. There's good trout fishing here, too. Accommoda-tions range from inexpensive, rustic-but-comfy cabins to grand, modern chalets. Norway House, a 13th-century Norwegian-style home with a hand-carved wooden facade and a sod roof, was actually built in Norway and transported here. It features a large open-loft bedroom, a kitchen, and a living/sleeping room, and is ideal for groups of up to eight people. The country decor, with quilts and vintage furniture, is attractive and unfussy. The cozy, creekside Waterfir Cabin with its brass bed, kitchen, wood-burning stove, and natural-stone hearth is the best choice for couples. If you rent one of the three smaller, less-expensive cabins (Piñon, Lupine, and Larkspur), which, unlike the others, don't have kitchens, breakfast is included in the cost of your stay. There are also fully furnished homes for rent, which are ideal for families—kids can explore the log playhouse nearby and dip a fishing pole in the stocked fish pond. Sorensen's Country Cafe is open only to guests for breakfast, lunch, and dinner. The food is a cut above most mountain-resort fare, with good breakfasts of quiche, waffles, and fresh fruit, and your basic steak, pork chops, grilled salmon, and pasta for dinner. In snow season the resort rents cross-country skis and snowshoes. Sorensen's also runs the nearby Hope Valley Store and Cafe, which offers a modest menu of hot dogs, hamburgers, fries, and similar fare from Memorial Day through Labor Day—a good place for a quick, inexpensive meal. *$$; AE, MC, V; checks OK; 5 miles NW of Woodfords.* &

Markleeville

This tiny mountain town's claim to fame is the annual **DEATH RIDE TOUR OF THE CALIFORNIA ALPS**, a grueling 128-mile bike trek over five mountain passes (16,000 feet of climbing) that's renowned among bicyclists as one of the top-10 cycling challenges in the United States. The tour, limited to the first 2,500 prepaid applicants, is held the first Saturday after July 4; contact the **ALPINE CHAMBER OF COMMERCE** (530/694-2475; deathride@alpinecounty.com) for more information.

The only place worth visiting in Markleeville besides the exceptional Villa Gigli restaurant (see review, below) is the **CUTTHROAT BAR**, located in the Alpine Hotel and Restaurant downtown. Belly up to the bar, order a whiskey or two, and contemplate why the owners decided to hang a collection of brassieres from the bar's ceiling. (By the way, women are encouraged to add their bras to the display; payment is a free Cutthroat Bar T-shirt. Whoopee!) Just outside of town is the popular **GROVER HOT SPRINGS STATE PARK** (4 miles W of Markleeville at the end of Hot Springs Rd; 530/694-2248; open 9am–9pm every day in summer, 2pm–9pm weekdays and 9am–9pm weekends in winter), where you may soak in the plain but soothing cement mineral pools year-round (bathing suits are required).

RESTAURANTS

Villa Gigli / ★★★

145 HOT SPRINGS RD, MARKLEEVILLE; 530/694-2253

Located on a remote hillside in this tiny Sierra town is Gina and Ruggero Gigli's Villa Gigli, a quintessential mom-and-pop cafe—it's situated alongside their modest home of 25 years. Every Friday, Saturday, and Sunday morning, Ruggero, who was raised in a small town in the hills of Tuscany, rolls pasta dough, bakes breads, and stuffs cannelloni in preparation for his two dozen or so nightly guests, most of whom have traveled hours to get here and made reservations weeks in advance—it's that special. The menu usually consists of four pasta dishes, two vegetarian and two with meat (such as lasagne al forno, tagliatelle with tomato sauce, or cannelloni), salad in the summer and soup in the winter, a dessert, and fresh-brewed coffee. Sparse, yes, but when you consider that Ruggero makes all the breads, pastas, sauces, and desserts by hand, without assistance and in his tiny kitchen, it's amazing there are any choices. Prices are surprisingly low: an entree with a bottle of the house red costs about half as much as you'd pay in other three-star establishments in the Sierra Nevada. In the summer, Ruggero often cooks on his wood-burning barbecue on the deck, where guests dining alfresco can watch him prepare their main course. The Giglis also rent out a small house on Markleeville's main street: Grandma's House is a modest three-bedroom, two-bath abode that sleeps up to eight people. It's simply decorated but exceptionally clean and comes with a fully stocked kitchen, a laundry room, cozy down comforters, a small yard, and views of Markleeville Creek from most of the rooms. *$$; no credit cards; checks OK; dinner Fri–Sun; beer and wine; reservations recommended; 2 blocks W of downtown.* &

The Lakes Basin Area

The scenic **GOLD LAKE ROAD**, which starts at Highway 49 just east of Sierra City and ends several miles south of Graeagle, is a spectacular 14-mile stretch of tarmac that zigzags through verdant valleys dotted with farms, historic buildings, deer, cows, and horses, and passes nearly a dozen sky-blue lakes—there are 30 lakes within the Lakes Basin area—most of them either visible from the highway or within easy walking distance. The **LAKES BASIN CAMPGROUND**, located right off the road, offers 24 sites on a first-come, first-served basis; call the Mohawk ranger station (530/836-2575) for details. Most of the lodges in the basin are quite rustic, and folks in the area like it that way. Whether you fancy horseback riding through meadows rife with wildflowers, fishing in roaring rivers, hiking through magnificent red-fir forests, or mountain-biking on rugged, hilly trails, you'll find it here. The lakeside lodges book up quickly, so make reservations well ahead of time or try your luck at catching a last-minute cancellation. Bear in mind that the seasonal resorts tend to have a high turnover of chefs, so menus and the quality of the fare may change considerably from one season to the next. In the winter, the basin closes and the unplowed road becomes a haven for snowmobilers.

RESTAURANTS

Sardine Lake Resort / ★★★

END OF SARDINE LAKE RD AT LOWER SARDINE LAKE, LAKES BASIN AREA; 530/862-1196 (SUMMER); 530/862-6363 (WINTER)
When the stress of daily life begins to take its toll, and you long for an escape to some peaceful, far-from-it-all retreat, some places quickly spring to mind. Sardine Lake is one of those places. The towering, craggy peaks

of the Sierra Buttes are mirrored in this lake, where the tranquil forest is restorative for even the most frazzled city folk. The resort's proprietors, Dorothy and Chandler Hunt, take full advantage of the splendid setting, serving cocktails before dinner on a small gazebo that juts over the lake. The food is good—perhaps the best in the Plumas-Eureka area—with a small but nicely rendered selection of meat, seafood, and poultry dishes. Restaurant reservations are a must—make them several weeks in advance. Unfortunately, the resort's nine cabins are often filled by a long list of returning clients, so the chance of getting a cabin reservation is, as one frustrated lad put it, "downright impossible." *$$; no credit cards; checks OK; dinner Fri–Wed (open mid-May–mid-Oct); full bar; reservations required; off Gold Lake Rd, 2 miles N of Hwy 49.*

LODGINGS

Gold Lake Lodge / ★

GOLD LAKE RD, LAKES BASIN AREA; 530/836-2350 (JULY 1–SEPT 30), 530/836-2751 (OCT 1–JUNE 30)
Gold Lake Lodge sits in the heart of the Lakes Basin Area (at an elevation of 6,620 feet) and within hiking distance of stunning High Sierra scenery, wildflower-filled meadows, and numerous lakes ideal for water play. Bear Lake is the closest (a third of a mile hike), and Gold Lake is a five-minute drive by car. Eleven tidy little cabins line the edge of a pretty meadow and a stand of old-growth red fir trees. Most of the cabins sleep three to four people; each of the seven standard cabins has a private bathroom, and the other four more rustic units share a detached bathing facility just a skip across the lawn. Every cabin has electricity, a small front patio with a table and chairs, and housekeeping service. Breakfast and dinner are included in the rates, and meals are served in the lodge's dining room (open to nonguests, too), which is furnished with a nickel-plated Franklin stove, picnic tables, and wagon wheel chandeliers. Dinner specials range from lasagne and pot roast to lobster and fried chicken, and the lodge's sun tea is the perfect antidote to a hot summer day. *$$$; MC, V; checks OK; open Father's Day–Sept 30; 7 miles S of Hwy 89.*

Gray Eagle Lodge / ★★★

GOLD LAKE RD, LAKES BASIN AREA; 530/836-2511 OR 800/635-8778
Gray Eagle Lodge is set in the heart of spectacular scenery at the northern edge of the Lakes Basin Area. Ironically, there isn't a lake nearby, but you will see a lovely stream, a waterfall, and Sierra trails trimmed with wild-flowers. The resort's 18 refurbished cabins have small decks, private baths, wall-to-wall carpeting, mini-refrigerators, and queen- or king-size beds with electric blankets and comforters. Breakfast and dinner, included in the room rates, are served in the impressive lodge's dining room. Constructed of enormous sugar-pine beams, the light-filled, high-ceilinged inn, with its tall windows and rock fireplace, is all that a grand

mountain hideaway ought to be. Dinner might include a carrot-curry soup with fresh ginger, a mixed baby greens salad with roasted walnuts and crumbled Roquefort cheese, and an entree of grilled swordfish with papaya-and-bell-pepper chutney accompanied by potato pancakes and French green beans. The extensive wine list features primarily California labels and is the best in the Lakes Basin Area. If you're not staying at the lodge, dinner reservations are required. *$$–$$$; MC, V; checks OK; open May–Oct; W of Gold Lake Rd.* ⅄

Packer Lake Lodge / ★★

PACKER LAKE RD, LAKES BASIN AREA; 530/862-1221 (LATE MAY–OCT), 415/921-5943 (OCT–LATE MAY)

What separates the 1926 Packer Lake Lodge from its neighbors in the Lakes Basin Area is its combination of good food and—at a 6,218-foot elevation—great scenery. The tall pines, gently rippling waters, and profusion of wildflowers provide an atmosphere of serene seclusion. Accommodations are in 14 simply furnished cabins, ranging from rustic, lakeside log cabins with shared bathrooms to three-room buildings with kitchens and private baths. Each cabin has its own rowboat, too. The single-room main lodge features a large stone fireplace, a tiny store that primarily sells candy bars and fishing supplies, a full bar, a reading and games nook, and a small dining room. Dinner fare includes fillet steaks, lamb, baby back ribs, pasta, and the "you-catch-it-and-clean-it-and-we'll-cook-it" trout special. Non-guests are welcome for dinner. *$–$$$; MC, V; checks OK; open mid-May–Oct; off Sardine Lake Rd, 4½ miles N of Hwy 49.*

Salmon Lake Lodge / ★

SALMON LAKE RD, LAKES BASIN AREA; 530/757-1825

You can't drive to this 1920s resort; instead, you have to drive to the north shore of Salmon Lake, telephone the lodge to send over a ferry, then hop aboard the boat to cross the lake (or you can hike a little less than a mile around the lake's splendid western rim). The 10 tent cabins offer canvas roofs, rough-wood walls, built-in double beds and single bunks, mini-refrigerators, and electric stoves; you need to bring a sleeping bag, towels, dishes, cooking gear, an ice chest, and groceries (showers and a washing machine—but no dryer—are available in a separate building). The three ridge-top cabins with their beautiful high-mountain views are the favorites, and each has a fully equipped kitchen (bring towels, bedding, and food). Also highly sought after is the lakeshore cabin, which has its own dock. Salmon Lake is great for swimming and boating, and rowboats, sailboats, canoes, and kayaks are provided to guests at no extra cost. You can also paddle a boat or take a barge to a lake island for a biweekly barbecue. *$$; no credit cards; checks OK; open June–mid-Oct, weather permitting; 1 mile W of Gold Lake Hwy.* ⅄

Clio

LODGINGS

White Sulphur Springs Resort Bed and Breakfast / ★

HWY 89, CLIO; 530/836-2387 OR 800/854-1797

Owned by descendants of the McKenzie family since 1867, the White Sulphur Springs Resort was once a main stop on the Truckee-Quincy stagecoach route. It's located in Clio, formerly known as Boozetown, thanks to the 13 saloons and 14 bordellos that once dominated its streets. The ranch's large restored wood-frame house with a two-story porch offers six guest rooms decorated with period antiques. All the rooms share bathrooms except the Fern Room, which has its own bath, a queen-size bed, and easy access to the swimming pool and patio. Guests wake up to a hearty ranch breakfast of eggs, potatoes, fruit, and freshly ground coffee. During the day, you can dive into the inn's huge 78°F mineral water pool or head across the road to the beautiful Whitehawk Ranch for a round of golf. In the evening, unwind on the front porch and watch the sun set over the Mohawk Valley. *$$; AE, DIS, MC, V; checks OK; 2 miles S of town.*

Mohawk, Blairsden, and Graeagle

The tiny towns of Mohawk, Blairsden, and Graeagle sit cheek by jowl, so to speak—each is located less than a mile from the other. In Mohawk, an old lumber town at a crossroads on the middle fork of the Feather River, there's not much left except an old, well-maintained little cemetery; a deteriorating but interesting log cabin that was once the town's stage stop; a pleasant little deli-restaurant; and the funky little **MOHAWK TAVERN** (530/836-2610), a friendly watering hole adorned with signs labeling it the Mohawk Convention Center and City Hall. Blairsden boasts two nurseries, as well as a car-repair garage, a hardware store, several restaurants, and a great bakery (and coffee shop), the **VILLAGE BAKER** (340 Bonta Rd, Blairsden; 530/836-4064).

About a quarter mile south of Blairsden is the picturesque little city of Graeagle, a former company town of the California Fruit Growers Exchange. Fruit Growers once had a lumber mill here that made wooden boxes for storing its produce, but the old mill is gone and the millpond has been converted into a family swimming area with grassy banks, gravel beaches, brown trout, and paddleboat rentals; in the winter, the pond is often a resting ground for gaggles of Canada geese. Graeagle modestly bills itself the "Home of the World's Finest Golf Clubs" (there's a custom golf-club store here), and there are six golf courses in the area; for **GOLFING INFORMATION**, call or stop by Williamson Realty (Hwy 89; 530/836-0112) in the Graeagle Village Center. Other outdoor activities include tennis, hiking, and horseback riding. The rest of the town consists of a little grocery store, a tearoom, an antique shop, and a handful of other small businesses—most are located in former company houses painted barn-red with white trim. For more information and a brochure on the area, contact the **PLUMAS COUNTY VISITORS BUREAU** (800/326-2247; www.plumas.ca.us/visitors_bureau/). If you're looking for a place to stay, numerous condos that double as vacation homes are available for rent; call 530/836-0313 or 530/836-2525 for information.

RESTAURANTS

Grizzly Grill Restaurant and Bar / ★★★

250 BONTA ST, BLAIRSDEN; 530/836-1300

Owner Lynn Hagen is a true pioneer in this neck of the woods: she's introduced baby greens, Muscovy duck, and Asiago cheese into the meat and potato belt. Can you believe that? Next thing you know she'll be hosting martini and cigar nights. Her light, woodsy, and relaxed restaurant is a fine spot to have dinner or just a drink at the long bar staffed by a congenial crew. The Grizzly's menu will warm a yuppie heart: a baby greens salad with walnuts, blue cheese, and a vinaigrette dressing; New England crab cakes with a red bell-pepper cream garnish; and a tasty Caesar salad. And that's just for starters. Among a number of very good pasta selections is a terrific linguine with wild mushrooms, sun-dried tomatoes, scallions, fresh basil, olive oil, and balsamic vinegar. Main courses range from a perfectly grilled Norwegian salmon with a sweet onion confit to a zesty cassoulet brimming with French lentils, vegetables, chicken, pork, and sausage in a white wine sauce. The small, daily dessert menu often holds some gems, and there is an extensive wine list. *$–$$; MC, V; checks OK; dinner every day (closed Jan 2–20); full bar; reservations recommended; near the junction of Hwys 70 and 89.*

LODGINGS

Feather River Inn / ★★

65899 HWY 70, BLAIRSDEN; 530/836-2623

Back in the '20s and '30s, when train-trip vacations were all the rage, the Feather River Inn was one of the prime destinations in the High Sierra. The palatial, rustic 1914 lodge is located off Highway 70 in a quiet woodland area, and it now functions primarily as a conference center operated by the University of the Pacific in Stockton. The inn is reserved for conference groups (ranging from 15 to 150 people), but other guests are accommodated on a space-available basis (nonconference reservations are taken no more than 60 days in advance). A half-dozen attractive chalets, which hold six to eight rooms each, and seven cabins are rented to guests. All accommodations are quite rustic, and some share bathrooms; the plain-Jane units are equipped with two twin beds and a double bed or just one twin and perhaps a small dresser or desk. Upstairs in the lodge, 24 rooms and 2 suites have been recently redecorated. Some of the rooms look out at the inn's nine-hole golf course and the surrounding mountains. The inn's broad veranda—its roof supported by enormous tree-trunk columns and rafters—faces the ninth green and lovely pine trees. The inn also has a swimming pool and volleyball, basketball, and tennis courts. Conference attendees are offered a buffet-style breakfast, lunch, and dinner. *$–$$; AE, DIS, MC, V; checks OK; open mid-Apr–Jan; ½ mile NW of town.*

River Pines Resort / ★★

8296 HWY 89, GRAEAGLE; 530/836-0313 OR 800/696-2551

Set alongside the Feather River, a National Wild and Scenic River, this resort is a popular family retreat that folks return to year after year. It's fun and affordable, and it offers enough activities to keep any hyperactive vacationer entertained. River Pines has a large pool and Jacuzzi with a poolside bar and snack bar, trout fishing, table tennis, shuffleboard, and horseshoes. It's also only a quarter mile from a stable with horseback riding excursions; nearby are several tennis courts and six golf courses. The resort has 63 units, including 18 one- and two-bedroom cabins constructed of stacked cedar. Each cabin has a fully stocked kitchen and a private bathroom; the one-room cabins have either a queen-size bed or two twins, while the two-room cabins have a queen, two twins, and a futon that folds out into a double bed. The resort's other rooms are reminiscent of a standard motel, with knotty-pine walls and comfortable, albeit plain, furnishings; some rooms have kitchens and sitting areas, too. Lunches of hamburgers, hot dogs, and pizza are served poolside at the umbrella-topped tables or at the pool bar. Sharing the grounds is the popular Coyote Bar & Grill (530/836-2002), serving very good Southwestern food, including a variety of steaks, blackened salmon, tequila-lime chicken and seafood enchiladas. And they make a margarita that'll knock your huaraches off. *$$; DIS, MC, V; checks OK; at the N end of town, on the S side of the Feather River.* &

Johnsville

This tiny, charming town, established by the Sierra Buttes Mining Company in the 1870s, is a California treasure. It was built for the gold miners and their families who didn't want to live next to the brothels and gambling centers in the nearby mining camps. Surrounded by the densely forested **PLUMAS-EUREKA STATE PARK**, Johnsville is a mix of old abandoned miner's shacks and restored ones that serve as private residences. In between the historical buildings are some new homes, most built to meet the Johnsville Historical Society's strict design guidelines. As you drive down Main Street, note the striking old barn-red **JOHNSVILLE**

HOTEL, now a private home, and the toylike firehouse across the street with a bell in its steeple and a horse-drawn fire wagon inside. Among the many wonderful artifacts at the **PLUMAS-EUREKA STATE PARK MUSEUM** are a working blacksmith shop and a five-story 60-stamp mill where gold was processed. A nearby campground area straddles pretty Jamison Creek, and across the street from the museum is the diminutive **MORI-ARITY HOUSE,** a completely restored miner's home with furnishings and equipment used by the 10-member Moriarity family in 1901. For museum and campground information, call 530/836-2380.

A mile up Johnsville's main road is **SKI GOLD MOUNTAIN** (530/836-2317), a quaint, no-frills downhill ski resort for beginner to expert skiers. There are two poma lifts, and hidden behind the one-room lodge is a lift for snow-tubers. The resort was recently taken over by the classy Gold Mountain development (on the east side of the Mohawk Valley), and the management is making many positive changes, including a new chairlift and expansion of winter hours (weather permitting) to seven days a week.

RESTAURANTS

The Iron Door / ★★

5417 MAIN ST, JOHNSVILLE; 530/836-2376
Johnsville supports one business, and this is it. The Iron Door restaurant has occupied the century-old general store and post office building since 1961, and it hasn't changed much since then. The bar and dining room are decorated with antique farm equipment, lanterns, floral wreaths, and Gibson Girl–style hangings, and behind the bar is a drawing of the last miner in Johnsville, who worked his claim on Jamison Creek until the 1950s. The Iron Door's soups are thick and hearty, and the main bill of fare is heavy with beef, lobster, and fowl. And since the restaurant's owner is from Bavaria, you can also bite into several excellent and authentic schnitzels. A good selection of beer and wine rounds out the offerings. *$$; MC, V; local checks only; dinner Wed–Mon (open Apr–Nov); full bar; reservations required; in Plumas-Eureka State Park, 5 miles W of Graeagle.*

Cromberg

RESTAURANTS

Mount Tomba Inn / ★★

HWY 70, CROMBERG; 530/836-2359

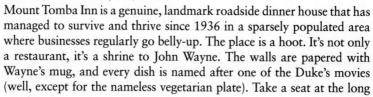

Mount Tomba Inn is a genuine, landmark roadside dinner house that has managed to survive and thrive since 1936 in a sparsely populated area where businesses regularly go belly-up. The place is a hoot. It's not only a restaurant, it's a shrine to John Wayne. The walls are papered with Wayne's mug, and every dish is named after one of the Duke's movies (well, except for the nameless vegetarian plate). Take a seat at the long bar, pardner, and order a tall one, or sit in front of the stone fireplace as you wait for a table. Mount Tomba's specialty is prawns—big, meaty, tender prawns, the way Duke would have liked 'em. You can get them deep fried, boiled with drawn butter, or sautéed in garlic butter, olive oil, lemon, and white wine. And of course, no John Wayne shrine would be complete without every cut of beef, from filet mignon (named after *The Quiet Man* flick because the slabs of meat are "known for their tenderness") to prime rib (a.k.a. True Grit, a reference only the author of the menu understands). For those who like innards, there's calf liver and onions. Diners also can choose from several chicken and fish dishes. Included in the price of every cowboy-size dinner is an excellent made-from-scratch soup (served in a large tureen), a nothing-special tossed green salad, a basket of warm bread, rice or a baked potato with all the trimmings, coffee, and a choice of sherbet, vanilla ice cream, or a chocolate sundae. *$–$$; DIS, MC, V; checks OK; dinner Tues–Sun Apr–Oct (Fri–Sun Nov–Mar); full bar; reservations recommended; ½ mile E of town; 17 miles from both Quincy and Portola.* ♿

LODGINGS

Twenty Mile House / ★★★

OLD CROMBERG RD, CROMBERG; 530/836-0375

Take the Old Cromberg Road back in time to Twenty Mile House. Set on the middle fork of the Feather River, this inn has been a tranquil haven for travelers since 1854, when it served as a stagecoach stop. The two-story brick building is set amid 250 acres of wildflowers, evergreens, and wildlife, and only an occasional train rumbling by on the Feather River route disturbs the silence. The house has been carefully restored with New England pine paneling, decorative fretwork, and carved Victorian furnishings. It offers three guest bedrooms with private bathrooms, including the Old Parlor Room, which has a private porch entrance, a double brass Victorian bed, and a wood-burning fireplace, and the Old Trading Post Room, which also has its own entrance, and boasts a queen and a single bed. Tucked into the nearby forest next to Jackson Creek are two cabins, each with a kitchen, bedroom, and beds for four. Anglers are particularly partial to Twenty Mile House, since 2 miles of the Feather River—designated a National Wild and Scenic River—run through the inn's private property. Some years ago proprietor Barbara Gage stocked the river with wild and native trout, and their population is maintained by limiting the number of fly fishers to four per day and restricting them to catch-and-release fishing. Breakfast is served in the country kitchen or on the front porch of the Old General Store next door, which has been restored and is now used as a local meeting and activities hall. *$$$; no credit cards; checks OK; 1 mile S of Hwy 70, 7 miles NW of Graeagle, and 18 miles SE of Quincy.*

Quincy

RESTAURANTS

Moon's / ★

497 LAWRENCE ST, QUINCY; 530/283-0765

A popular local hangout since the mid-'70s, Moon's is a roomy, ramshackle, rustic wooden building with four separate dining areas, including a formal dining room and an open-air patio covered with lush plants. The strong scent of garlic and yeast is a dead giveaway to the house specialties: pizza and pasta. The thick lasagne, heavily laden with sausage, and some of the beef entrees are among the kitchen's best efforts. Another favorite is the Mushrooms St. Thomas—a spinach, mushroom, and Italian-sausage casserole. Moon's is ideal for families, offering something to suit just about all tastes. *$; MC, V; checks OK; dinner Tues–Sun; beer and wine; reservations recommended; at Plymouth St.* &

Morning Thunder Cafe / ★

557 LAWRENCE ST, QUINCY; 530/283-1310

With its stained-glass window, vine-laced trellis, and macramé plant holder, the Morning Thunder Cafe may look a bit like a hippie haven, but those details are just leftovers from its impetuous youth. Breakfast has always been the draw here, with dishes like biscuits and gravy, huevos rancheros, and three-egg spinach, cheese, and mushroom omelets. The portions are huge, and the biscuits are as large as a prizefighter's fist. The restaurant also serves lunches of enormous hamburgers and freshly made soups (the delicious Boston clam chowder has become such a hit that the cafe's regulars insist on having it every Friday). *$; MC, V; checks OK; breakfast, lunch every day; beer and wine; reservations recommended; downtown.*

Ragged Jack Cafe and Bakery / ★★

189 W MAIN ST, QUINCY; 530/283-1974

The newest restaurant in Quincy, the charming Ragged Jack Cafe and Bakery (named after a particularly pretty variety of kale) is committed to good, healthy fare that incorporates fresh ingredients and predominantly organic foods, many grown in the garden in the backyard. The restaurant was created within owner Jen Terhune's home (she still lives in the back), an Arts and Crafts bungalow in the pretty downtown section of Quincy. Everything is cooked from scratch; these folks even grind their own whole wheat flour. The menu is casual but extensive, with items like fish tacos, chicken burgers, stuffed potatoes, all kinds of vegetarian sandwiches, salads, and stir-fries. There's also a fresh juice bar, smoothies, and beer and wine. The bakery and dessert selections change daily, there's a very reasonably priced kids' menu, and there are tables on the front porch for alfresco dining. *$; DIS, MC, V; local checks only; lunch, dinner Mon–Fri (open at 9 for coffee); beer and wine; no reservations; downtown.* &

LODGINGS

The Feather Bed / ★

542 JACKSON ST, QUINCY; 530/283-0102 OR 800/696-8624

This 1893 Victorian inn, proudly punctuated with colonnades on its teal-and-peach front porch, features five cozy, turn-of-the-century country-style guest rooms with private baths. There are also two quaint little cottages set behind the house. Floral-print wallpaper and beautiful patchwork quilts give the rooms a homey, old-fashioned feel. Some rooms have terrific deep claw-footed soaking tubs; others have gas fireplaces. After refueling on the full breakfast served in the dining room, borrow a bike from proprietors Bob and Jan Janowski and take a spin around Quincy. You can also easily walk from the Feather Bed to the heart of the quaint town. *$$–$$$; AE, DC, DIS, MC, V; checks OK; at Court St, 1 block from Hwy 70.*

Meadow Valley

RESTAURANTS

Ten-Two / ★

8270 BUCKS LAKE RD, MEADOW VALLEY; 530/283-1366

The road to this restaurant is 10.2 miles away from the town of Quincy, hence the name. Ten-Two is built right over a rushing flume, and although it's off the beaten track, many Quincy residents make the trek here for dinner. The menu offers sturdy standbys such as fish and chips, as well as fancier fare like salmon braised in sesame oil and topped with a delicate, secret sauce culled from an old Chinese cookbook, or filet mignon topped with sautéed portobello mushrooms in a walnut-merlot sauce. Service is casual, friendly, and attentive. When the weather is warm, consider dining on the deck. *$$; MC, V; checks OK; dinner every day; full bar; reservations recommended; 10.2 miles W of Quincy.*

Bear Valley Area

Tucked away in the central Sierra Nevada some 7,000 feet above sea level is the small town of Bear Valley, home of the popular **BEAR VALLEY MOUNTAIN RESORT COMPANY** and the **BEAR VALLEY CROSS-COUNTRY AREA**. (See the Skiing the Sierra Nevada section at the end of this chapter for contact information.) In the summer, more than 100 miles of the cross-country ski trails become prime mountain biking territory.

Bear Valley

LODGINGS

Bear Valley Lodge and Restaurant / ★★

BEAR VALLEY RD, BEAR VALLEY; 209/753-2327

Bear Valley Lodge, the center of this small mountain community, is a full-service year-round resort catering to families and sports enthusiasts. There are cross-country and downhill ski facilities nearby (ask about the great skiing/lodging package deals here) and plenty of mountains, trails, lakes, and streams to explore. Another bonus is the resort's high 7,000-foot elevation, which helps keep the scorching summer heat at bay. There are 51 guest rooms (including three suites), a restaurant and bar, and a heated swimming pool (open in summer only). Bear Valley Lodge Restaurant, catering to a mostly captive audience, offers California cuisine—steak, fish, chicken, pasta, vegetarian entrees, salads—and a children's menu. White tablecloths and candles set the mood in the dining room, although the dress code is casual. *$$; AE, MC, V; checks OK; from Hwy 4E go left on Bear Valley Rd.* &

Lake Alpine Lodge / ★

4000 HWY 4, BEAR VALLEY; 209/753-6358

This quaint Sierra resort situated on Lake Alpine was built in the '20s and remodeled in the '30s and again in '95. It features lodgepole-pine pillars, a fireplace so large you can walk into it, and a game room equipped with a pool table and video games. Eight of the nine rustic, fully equipped cabins have kitchens and outdoor barbecues, and all come with a shower, a deck, and a view of the lake. The lodge also offers "upscale camping" via three tent cabins, each furnished with four twin beds, a barbecue ring, and access to public bathrooms (available mid-June–Labor Day only). The Lake Alpine Lodge Cafe serves breakfast, lunch, and dinner in the summer (pancakes, burgers, sandwiches, etc.), and there's a small saloon as well as a convenience market that sells bait, tackle, and camping equipment. A laundromat and public showers are also available, as are boats and mountain bike rentals. *$$; MC, V; local checks only; open Memorial Day weekend–Oct; at Ebbets Pass/Lake Alpine.* &

Dorrington

LODGINGS

The Dorrington Hotel and Restaurant / ★★

3431 HWY 4, DORRINGTON; 209/795-5800

A few miles from magnificent Calaveras Big Trees State Park sits the Dorrington Hotel, built in 1852 and used as a stagecoach stop, a depot for stockmen, and—because of its 5,000-foot elevation—a summer resort where people could beat the heat. The country hotel, surrounded by some of the largest pines and sequoias in California, has been dressed up with lace curtains, period wallpaper, and decorative pillows. The five antique-filled rooms, which share bathrooms, have brass beds with homemade quilts. There is also a newly restored 1-room cabin next door with a kitchenette and spa-tub. Complimentary sherry and fruit are left in the room, and a continental breakfast is served there in the morning. The hotel's casual dining room offers Northern Italian–style dinners. *$$; DIS, MC, V; checks OK; near Board's Crossing.*

Arnold

RESTAURANTS

Tallahan's Café / ★★★

1225 OAK CIRCLE, ARNOLD; 209/795-4005

A happy surprise in this rustic setting, partners Kathleen Minahan and Bruce Tallakson have been serving up hearty yet sophisticated fare in their comfortable country cafe for years. Appetizers include grilled polenta and roasted veggie "potstickers" with balsamic chile sauce. For dinner, try the red chard and onion ravioli with mushrooms, dried cherries, white wine, and feta cheese or the risotto with tiger prawns and New Mexico sausage. Even sandwiches are imaginative creations here, such as the thinly sliced tri tip with red onion, spinach, avocado, cheddar cheese, and red-chile aioli in a chipotle chile tortilla. Best spot to dine is on the deck, if weather permits. Desserts include yummy bread pudding and pumpkin cheesecake that you can walk off on a stroll through the Harbinger Gallery across the street. *$$; AE, DIS, MC, V; local checks OK; lunch, dinner Fri–Tues (closed 2 weeks in early Dec, 1 week in May); beer and wine; reservations recommended; off Hwy 4 at Cedar Center.* &

Pinecrest

RESTAURANTS

Steam Donkey Restaurant / ★

421 PINECREST LAKE RD, PINECREST; 209/965-3117

Named after a steam-powered logging machine used to drag timber from the woods to the railroad, this popular barbecue house is usually packed with Sonorans, who make the 32-mile trek up to Dodge Ridge every weekend for the Steam Donkey's highly rated ribs, steaks, and chicken. Many of the regular patrons are ex-loggers, who likely feel right at home amid all the logging memorabilia scattered throughout the restaurant. *$–$$; MC, V; checks OK; lunch Sat–Sun (every day in summer), dinner every day; full bar; reservations recommended; off Pinecrest Ave and Hwy 108.* &

Yosemite National Park and Beyond

What was once the beloved home of the Ahwahneechee, Miwok, and Paiute Indians is now a spectacular international playground for 4 million annual visitors. Designated a national park in 1890, thanks in part to Sierra Club founder John Muir, 1,170-square-mile Yosemite is only slightly smaller than the state of Rhode Island. During the peak season, however, Yosemite seems more like a 1,200-square-*foot* park. Crowds more typical of Disney World clog the 7-square-mile valley for a glimpse of some of nature's most incredible creations, including 4,500-foot-high **EL CAPITAN**, the largest piece of exposed granite on earth, and 2,425-foot-high **YOSEMITE FALLS**, the highest waterfall in North America and fifth highest in the world.

The Yosemite area also offers access to the bird-watching shores of **MONO LAKE** and the outdoors haven of the **MAMMOTH LAKES** region.

Yosemite National Park

To avoid most of the crowds, visit Yosemite in the spring or early fall, when the wildflowers are plentiful and the weather is usually mild. You can virtually escape civilization by setting up a tent in Tuolumne Meadows (closed in winter), where numerous trails wind through the densely forested and sparsely populated high country. This grande dame of national parks is actually most dazzling, and least crowded, in the winter, the time of year Ansel Adams shot those world-renowned photographs of the snow-laced valley. Unfortunately, most of the hiking trails (and Tuolumne Meadows) will be inaccessible then and the drive may be treacherous. Snow and ice limit access to the park, and many of the eastern passes are closed; call for **HIGHWAY CONDITIONS** (800/427-ROAD). Those who do brave the elements, however, will be rewarded with a truly unforgettable winter vista.

No matter what the time of year, visitors to Yosemite National Park must pay its friendly rangers a $20-per-car entrance fee ($10 for seniors or persons arriving by bus). In return, you receive a seven-day pass, a detailed park map, and the **YOSEMITE GUIDE**, a handy tabloid featuring the park's rules, rates, attractions, and current exhibits. One of the best ways to sightsee on the valley floor is by bike. **CURRY VILLAGE** (209/372-8319) and **YOSEMITE LODGE** (209/372-1208) have bike stands that rent one-speed cruisers (and helmets) daily. More than 8 miles of paved bicycle paths wind through the eastern end of the valley, but bicycles (including mountain bikes) are not allowed on the hiking trails.

Day hikers in the valley have a wide variety of trails to choose from—some boring, some mind-blowing—and all are well-charted on the visitors' map. The best easy hike is the **MIRROR LAKE/MEADOW TRAIL**, a

2-mile round-trip walk (5 miles if you circle the lake) that provides a magnificent view of Half Dome. More strenuous is the popular hike to **UPPER YOSEMITE FALLS**, a 7.2-mile round-trip trek with a spectacular overview of the 2,425-foot drop. (Don't wander off the trail or you may join the unlucky souls who have tumbled off the cliffs to their deaths.) The granddaddy of Yosemite hikes is the very steep ascent to the top of 8,840-foot-tall **HALF DOME**, a 17-mile, round-trip, 10- to 12-hour-long thigh-burner that requires Schwarzenegger-like gusto and the nerve to hang onto climbing cables anchored in granite—clearly not a jaunt for everyone. When the snowstorm season hits, many people haul out their snowshoes or cross-county skis for valley excursions or snap on their alpine skis and schuss down the groomed beginner/intermediate hills of **BADGER PASS SKI** (Glacier Point Rd; 209/372-8430).

If you'd rather keep your feet firmly planted on lower ground, tour the **YOSEMITE VALLEY VISITORS CENTER** (Village Mall, Yosemite Valley; 209/372-0200), which houses some mildly interesting galleries and museums. The center's Indian Cultural Museum hosts live demonstrations of the native Miwok and Paiute methods of basket weaving, jewelry making, and other crafts. Nearby are a reconstructed Miwok-Paiute village, a self-guided nature trail, and an art gallery showcasing the master photographer whose name is almost synonymous with this place: Ansel Adams.

Unless bumper-to-bumper traffic is your idea of a vacation in the woods, skip Yosemite Valley during summer weekends and join the rebel minority who know there's more than one way to view the area. **GLACIER POINT** (at the end of Glacier Point Rd), a rocky ledge 3,215 feet above the valley floor, has what many consider one of the best vistas on the continent: a bird's-eye view of the entire valley and a panoramic expanse of the High Sierra. The view is particularly striking at sunset and under a full moon. The point is open only in the summer.

At the southern entrance to the park, 35 miles south of the valley, lies **MARIPOSA GROVE**, home to some of the planet's largest and most ancient living things. The most popular attraction is the 2,700-year-old **GRIZZLY GIANT**, the world's oldest sequoia. Pick up a self-guided trail map in the box at the grove trailhead or attend one of the free ranger-led walks, offered regularly; check the *Yosemite Guide* for current schedules.

Due north of Yosemite Valley is the famous **TIOGA PASS** (Hwy 120), the highest automobile pass in California, which crests at 9,945 feet (and is closed in the winter). The ideal time to tour the 60-mile east-west stretch is in early summer, when the meadows are dotted with wildflowers and you can occasionally spot some wildlife lingering near the lakes and exposed granite slopes. Numerous turnouts offer prime photo opportunities, and roadside picnic areas are located at **LEMBERT DOME**

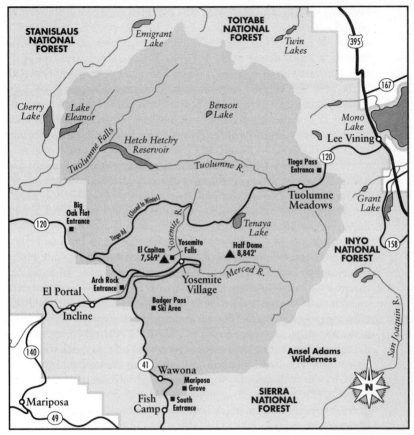

STANISLAUS NATIONAL FOREST

Emigrant Lake

TOIYABE NATIONAL FOREST

Twin Lakes

395

167

Cherry Lake

Lake Eleanor

Benson Lake

Mono Lake

Lee Vining

Tuolumne Falls

Hetch Hetchy Reservoir

Tuolumne R.

Tioga Pass Entrance

120

Tuolumne Meadows

Grant Lake

Big Oak Flat Entrance

120

Tioga Rd (Closed in Winter)

Yosemite R.

Tenaya Lake

INYO NATIONAL FOREST

158

El Capitan 7,569'

Yosemite Falls

Half Dome 8,842'

Arch Rock Entrance

Merced R.

El Portal

Yosemite Village

Incline

Badger Pass Ski Area

140

San Joaquin R.

Ansel Adams Wilderness

41

Wawona

Mariposa Grove

Mariposa

Fish Camp

South Entrance

SIERRA NATIONAL FOREST

N

49

YOSEMITE NATIONAL PARK

and **TENAYA LAKE**. This is also the route to **TUOLUMNE MEADOWS**, the gorgeous subalpine meadows along the Tuolumne River. The meadows are a popular camping area (half the campsites are available on a first-come, first-served basis and half require reservations) and the base for backpackers heading into Yosemite's beautiful high country.

Backpackers are required to obtain a **WILDERNESS PERMIT** in person (call 209/372-0740 for more information). The permits are free but only a limited number are distributed. The 3½-mile hike to **MAY LAKE** is a favorite route for backpackers, and the 6-mile hike to the **GLEN AULIN HIGH SIERRA BACKPACKER'S CAMP** offers a spectacular spot for pitching a tent. Five clusters of canvas cabins (call 559/454-2002 for details), for four to six occupants, are available to backpackers in the High Sierra region; prices average $150 for two per night and include breakfast, dinner, and a shower. These cabins are booked through an annual lottery each fall.

If you're partial to viewing Yosemite by car, pick up a copy of the **YOSEMITE ROAD GUIDE** or the *Yosemite Valley Tour* cassette tape at the Yosemite Valley Visitors Center. It's almost as good as having Ranger Rick in the back seat of your car. City slickers might also want to consider seeing the park on **HORSEBACK**; the thrill (and ease) of riding a horse into Yosemite's beautiful backcountry just might be worth the splurge. Select a stable in either Yosemite Valley, Wawona, or Tuolumne Meadows, then call 209/372-8348 or 209/372-8427 to make a reservation.

While the sightseeing in Yosemite is unparalleled, the dining is not. Bring as much of your own food as possible, because most of the park's restaurants offer mediocre (or worse) cafeteria-style food; the only exception is the lofty Ahwahnee Restaurant, but you'll have to fork over a bundle to eat there.

Park accommodations range from less than $15 per night for a campsite to more than $200 nightly for a room at the Ahwahnee Hotel. Reservations (accepted no more than eight weeks in advance) are required for most Yosemite **CAMPSITES**—only a few are available on a first-come, first-served basis. The valley campsites near the Merced River offer easy access to the park's most sought-after attractions but not much in the way of privacy. Moderately priced **MOTEL ROOMS** are available at the valley's bare-bones but adequate Yosemite Lodge (a quick walk from Lower Yosemite Falls). Spartan **CABINS** (some are nothing more than wood frames with canvas covers, others are heated in the winter) offer inexpensive alternatives to camping, and they're popular with families. There are also 69 tent cabins at Tuolumne Meadows Lodge. For camping **RESERVATIONS** call 800/365-CAMP; for reservations at all other Yosemite National Park accommodations call 559/252-4848. Vacation-home rentals (with full kitchens) can also be reserved, but they cost a pretty penny; for more information call **YOSEMITE WEST COTTAGES AND VACATION HOME RENTALS** (559/642-2211). Additional information on Yosemite National Park is available on the park's Web page at www.yosemitepark.com.

LODGINGS

Ahwahnee Hotel / ★★★

YOSEMITE VALLEY, YOSEMITE NATIONAL PARK; 209/372-1407 (HOTEL), 559/252-4848 (HOTEL RESERVATIONS)

 The majestic Ahwahnee Hotel stands regally against the soaring cliffs of Yosemite. It is among the most idyllic hotels in California, with a VIP guest list that ranges from Winston Churchill and John F. Kennedy to Greta Garbo and Queen Elizabeth. Built in 1927 with native granite boulders and redwood-hued concrete at a cost of $1.5 million, the multitiered six-story building blends comfortably into its surroundings. The lobby, dressed in a Native American motif, is oversized in all dimensions: thick-beamed high ceilings, walk-in fireplaces worthy of a medieval castle, and opulent chandeliers suitable for an opera house. For some folks, the contrast between the hotel's rustic mountain venue and its upscale image—overeager bellhops and a dress code that requires men to wear a jacket or sweater (though recently relaxed to exclude a tie) at dinner—might be a bit much. The 123 rooms are spacious, with double or king-size beds and large bathrooms; a few even boast a view of Half Dome. If money's no object, request one of the hotel's luxury suites or private cottages. The Ahwahnee Restaurant—an immense and impressive chamber highlighted by 50-foot-tall, floor-to-cathedral-ceiling leaded windows—is more noteworthy for its ambience than for its food (arrive well before nightfall to admire the view). Starched white tablecloths, tall candles, and a pianist tickling the ivories manage to give the colossal room a warm, almost intimate feel. The food is certainly the best in the region, but don't expect a gourmet affair; while the prices are equal to those of San Francisco's finer restaurants, the quality of the fare is not, though it has improved of late. Those in the know apply far in advance to get in the lottery for tickets to the Bracebridge Dinner, a three-hour feast held every Christmas that 60,000 people try to sign up for—though, alas, only 1,750 gain admission. *$$$–$$$$; DC, DIS, MC, V; checks OK; take 120 E into Yosemite Valley and follow signs to hotel.* &

Wawona Hotel / ★

HWY 41, YOSEMITE NATIONAL PARK; 209/375-6556
Four miles from the park's entrance, the Wawona—the Ahwahnee Hotel's more rustic cousin—is the oldest resort hotel in the state. A pair of century-old white buildings, adorned by pillars and a veranda, face an expansive manicured lawn, giving the Wawona the look of an antebellum mansion (you almost expect to see Scarlett O'Hara gracing the entryway). The majority of its 104 rooms are small, and about half of them have private bathrooms. This National Historic Landmark's biggest drawback is its lengthy distance from the park's most popular attractions. The giant sequoias in the nearby Mariposa Grove are inviting, but they don't compare to the cliffs and vistas elsewhere in Yosemite. Amenities include a nine-hole golf course, a tennis court, a riding stable, and a 1917 "swimming tank." For all its pretensions, the Wawona Hotel dining room has usually offered little more than upscale institutional food, though lately the quality has improved considerably. However, the Wawona's year-round Sunday brunch and the Saturday-evening summer lawn barbecues are a treat. *$$; AE, DC, DIS, MC, V; checks OK; closed Mon–Thurs Jan 12–Mar; SW corner of the park, 27 miles from Yosemite Valley.* &

MADAME MOUSTACHE AND THE ITALIAN GHOST

"Good-bye God, I'm going to Bodie," wrote a little girl whose family was moving to the most infamous gold rush boomtown in California.

Located in high desert country along the western slopes of the Sierra Nevada mountain range, Bodie had a population of about 8,000 brave souls in 1879 and a lurid history of stagecoach holdups, robberies, killings, saloons and dance halls, and loose women (Madame Moustache was a favorite). During one brief lull in the action, the local newspaper, tongue in cheek, commented, "Bodie is becoming a summer resort—no one killed here last week."

The town bustled with white-topped prairie schooners, horses and wagons filled with ore, wood, hay, and lumber, and daily stages carrying bars of gold bullion guarded by men with sawed-off shotguns. Some $32 million in gold was mined in the Bodie hills in the area's intense but short-lived heyday. After the mines played out, the town went into decline, and by 1882 most of the townsfolk had moved on. Fires finished off a large number of the remaining buildings. Today Bodie is a ghost town, designated a National Historic Site and State Historic Park. It is maintained in a state of "arrested decay," which means the remaining buildings are preserved but not rebuilt or changed in any way.

What you see is so eerily authentic and strange—pants still hanging next to a steamer

Fish Camp

RESTAURANTS

Narrow Gauge Inn / ★★

48571 HWY 41, FISH CAMP; 559/683-7720

An attractive old inn and restaurant nestled in the thick of the Sierra National Forest at a 4,800-foot elevation, the Narrow Gauge is one of the Mariposa Grove area's best restaurants. You'll find down-home service here, as well as views of Mount Raymond and a cozy country ambience enhanced by candlelight and a crackling fire. The inn's specialties include pork tenderloin with a fruit-and-nut stuffing and topped with an apricot-brandy glaze, and scallops sautéed in a champagne cream sauce with mushrooms. All dinners include a house-made soup or salad, fresh vegetables, and rice or potatoes (baked or garlic mashed). There's a well-edited wine list, too. The inn offers 26 rooms with balconies; ask for one of the four creekside rooms, which have particularly splendid views. Narrow Gauge also offers a heated swimming pool and a spa. *$$; DIS, MC, V; no checks; dinner every day (open Mar 30–Dec 31); full bar; reservations recommended; 4 miles S of Yosemite National Park's S gate.*

trunk, dusty schoolbooks tossed on desks, desert winds howling through a town jail known for vigilante justice—that ghost stories naturally abound. A little girl, buried in the cemetery and known as "the Angel of Bodie," has been heard calling for her daddy and plays with the occasional unsuspecting visitor's child. Park aides tossing rocks down a mine shaft claim to have heard a calm voice saying "Hey, you," coming from within the blocked-up, caved-in mine. Another employee opened a house that had been locked up for the winter and smelled fresh-cooked Italian food.

In addition to its ghostly inhabitants, Bodie is open to visitors all year, but winters can be fierce. At 9,000 feet, even summer months can get chilly. Mark Twain once said that the breaking up of one winter and the beginning of the next were the only two seasons he could distinguish in Bodie. The *Carson Tribune* observed, "The weather is so cold in Bodie that four pairs of blankets and three in a bed is not sufficient to promote warmth." There's no food, drink, or tourist accommodations in the park either—just the pure remains of the wild, wild West.

To get to Bodie, take US 395; 7 miles south of Bridgeport, take State Route 270. Go 10 miles to the end of the paved road and continue 3 more miles on the unfinished road to Bodie. Call ahead (760/647-6445) for road and weather conditions. Admission is $2 a person and $1 for children under 6. —*Mary Anne Moore*

LODGINGS

Tenaya Lodge at Yosemite / ★★★

1122 HWY 41, FISH CAMP; 559/683-6555 OR 800/635-5807

Tenaya Lodge is a full-service resort that offers just about everything, and its location is just 2 miles from the entrance to Yosemite National Park. Built in 1990 and rebuilt in 1999, the lodge has 244 rooms, all with mountain and forest views, private baths, and tasteful Southwestern decor. The lodge's showpiece is the immense front lobby, with its stone floors, high ceiling, huge fireplace, and Native American motif. Amenities include outdoor and indoor pools and a small fitness center with a steam room, sauna, and whirlpool. Sierra Restaurant offers breakfast and such Cal-Ital entrees as grilled sterling salmon, New York pepper steak, and lobster with orecchiette pasta for dinner. The Parkside Deli specializes in picnic lunches to go, and Jackalope's Bar and Grill offers more casual fare like pizza, pasta, and burgers. You can sign up for mountain bike rentals, tours of Yosemite, the children's Camp Tenaya, and other outdoor activities at the lodge's events desk. *$$$; AE, DC, DIS, MC, V; checks OK; 2 miles S of Yosemite National Park's SW gate.* &

Bridgeport

LODGINGS

The Cain House: A Country Inn / ★★

340 MAIN ST, BRIDGEPORT; 760/932-7040 OR 800/433-2246

James Stuart Cain made his fortune as the principal landowner in the rough-and-tumble boomtown of Bodie (known in its day as the wickedest town in the West). However, later generations of Cains (perhaps weary of Bodie's sanitation problems and the proliferation of whorehouses) moved over the hill to the comparatively genteel cowtown of Bridgeport. Set in one of the most picturesque valleys in the eastern Sierra, Bridgeport is backed by granite peaks in the west and by round sage- and piñon-covered desert hills in the east. This modest turn-of-the-century inn, owned by the obliging Marachal Gohlich, is a tribute to Cain. It combines European elegance with a Western atmosphere, and each of the seven individually decorated guest rooms has a private bath, a king- or queen-size bed with a quilt and down comforter, and a TV tucked inside an armoire. In the morning expect good, dark coffee (a rare treat on this side of the Sierra) and a full breakfast, including house-made muffins. $$; AE, DIS, MC, V; checks OK; at the N end of town.

Mono Lake

Set at the eastern foot of the craggy Sierra Nevada and ringed with fragile limestone tufa spires, this hauntingly beautiful 60-square-mile desert salt lake is a stopover for millions of migratory birds that arrive each year to feed on the lake's trillions of brine shrimp and alkali flies (mono means "flies" in the language of the Yokuts, the Native Americans who live just south of this region). While numerous streams empty into Mono (pronounced "MOE-no") Lake, there is no outlet. Instead, the lake water evaporates, leaving behind minerals washed down from the surrounding mountains. The result is an alkaline and saline content that is too high for fish but ideal for shrimp, flies, and swimmers (the brackish water is three times saltier than the sea). Right off Highway 395 is the **MONO BASIN SCENIC AREA VISITORS CENTER** (760/647-3044; www.mono-lake.org; open every day in summer and Thurs–Mon in winter), a modern, high-tech edifice that would make any taxpayer proud. The center offers scheduled walks and talks, and it has an outstanding environmental and historical display with hands-on exhibits that will even entertain the kids. After touring the visitors center, head for the **SOUTH TUFA AREA** at the southern end of the lake and get a closer look at the tufa formations and briny water.

RESTAURANTS

The Mono Inn / ★★★

HWY 395, MONO LAKE; 760/647-6581

After years of neglect, the historic Mono Inn, a popular respite for travelers to the Mono Lake region since 1922, was purchased several years ago by the Adams family (relatives of legendary photographer Ansel Adams). They hired architect Peter Bolin to revamp the aging structure to include a restaurant, an arts and crafts gallery, and a lounge, yet still retain the rustic charm and stellar views of Mono Lake. Proprietor Sarah Adams (Ansel's granddaughter) oversees the upper-level gallery/lounge and lower-level dining room, while chef Linda Dore—formerly of the highly reputable Anything Goes Cafe in Mammoth Lakes—runs the kitchen. Dore prepares hearty California-style cuisine ranging from pan-seared Black Angus top sirloin with brandied green peppercorn mustard sauce to prime rib (on Friday and Saturday nights only), grilled salmon fillets, sautéed prawns, and the Vegetarian's Delight, fresh seasonal vegetables roasted and served over creamy polenta. There's also a good wine list. Be sure to arrive early to admire the gallery (featuring original Ansel Adams photographs) and the panoramic view from the cocktail lounge—and beg for a dinner table near the window, particularly on moonlit nights when Mono Lake is most dazzling. *$$; AE, CB, DIS, MC, V; checks OK; dinner Wed–Mon mid-Apr–Oct (Thurs–Sun Dec–mid-Mar); full bar; reservations recommended; 4 miles N of Lee Vining.*

June Lake

RESTAURANTS

Carson Peak Inn / ★★

JUNE LAKE LOOP, JUNE LAKE; 760/648-7575

This barn-red building, located a few miles past the town of June Lake, has led several former lives, most recently as an American Legion headquarters, dance hall, and pizza parlor. Now it's one of the better restaurants in the area, serving hearty dinners such as steak-and-lobster brochette and a melt-in-your-mouth filet mignon smothered with sautéed mushrooms. Many regulars come for the Australian lobster tail (a rarity in these parts). Fish, chicken, and pork are served broiled, deep-fried, pan-fried, or barbecued. Dessert is an ice-cream sundae or sherbet. *$–$$$; AE, DIS, MC, V; checks OK; dinner every day; beer and wine; reservations recommended; off Hwy 395.* &

Mammoth Lakes

At the base of 11,053-foot Mammoth Mountain are nearly a dozen alpine lakes and the sprawling town of Mammoth Lakes—a mishmash of inns, motels, and restaurants primarily built to serve patrons of the popular Mammoth Mountain Ski Area. Ever since founder Dave McCoy mortgaged his motorcycle for $85 in 1938 to buy his first ski lift, folks have been coming here in droves (particularly from Southern California) to carve turns and navigate the moguls at one of the best downhill ski areas in the United States. In addition to skiing, this section of the eastern Sierra Nevada has been famous for decades for its fantastic fishing holes. In fact, the trout is king here, and several fishing derbies celebrate its royal status. This natural kingdom is no longer the exclusive domain of anglers and skiers, however. Word has gotten out about Mammoth's charms, attracting every kind of outdoor enthusiast and adventurer to this spectacular region in the heart of the High Sierra.

Whether you've migrated to the Mammoth area to ski, fish, golf, play, or simply rest your weary bones, stop by the **MAMMOTH LAKES VISITORS CENTER/RANGER STATION** (Hwy 203, just before the town of Mammoth Lakes; 760/924-5500), or contact the **MAMMOTH LAKES VISITORS BUREAU** (760/934-2712 or 888-GO-MAMMOTH; www.visit mammoth.com). You'll find wall-to-wall maps, brochures, and day planners, as well as copies of the Forest Service's excellent (and free) "Winter Recreation Map" and "Summer Recreation Map," which show the area's best routes for hiking, biking, sledding, snowmobiling, and cross-country skiing. If you need to rent ski gear or practically any other athletic or outdoor equipment, visit the bustling **KITTREDGE SPORTS** shop (Main S, next to the Chevron gas station, Mammoth Lakes; 760/934-7566).

Once you've unpacked your bags, it's time to lace up your hiking boots and explore. A top attraction is **DEVIL'S POSTPILE NATIONAL MONUMENT** (760/934-2289 in summer, 760/872-4881 in winter), one of the world's premier examples of basalt columns. The 60-foot-tall, slender rock columns rise 7,560 feet above sea level and were formed nearly 100,000 years ago when molten lava from the erupting Mammoth Mountain cooled and fractured into multisided forms; they've become such a popular attraction that between June 15 and September 15, rangers close the access road to daytime traffic and require visitors without a special permit to travel by shuttle. Shuttles pick up riders every 15 minutes at the Mammoth Mountain Ski Area parking lot on Minaret Road, off Highway 203 West, and drop them off at a riverside trail for the less-than-half-mile walk to the monument. (To reach the access road, take Hwy 203 W from US 395, go through the town of Mammoth and continue 17 miles W.)

After you've seen the Postpile, follow the trail for another 2 miles to the beautiful **RAINBOW FALLS**, where the **SAN JOAQUIN RIVER** plunges 101 feet over an ancient lava flow into a deep pool, often creating rainbows in the mist. If you follow the trail another 3 miles to **RED'S**

MEADOW, you'll be at one of the entrance points to the 228,500-acre **ANSEL ADAMS WILDERNESS**, a popular backpacking destination highlighted by the jagged **MINARETS**, a series of steep, narrow volcanic ridges just south of massive Mount Ritter.

True to its name, the Mammoth Lakes area boasts 10 lakes (none of which, oddly enough, are named Mammoth). The largest and one of the most striking is **LAKE MARY** (head W on Main St, which turns into Lake Mary Rd, drive past Twin Lakes, and continue on until you see it), and even though it's set high in the mountains, it's easy to get to. Numerous hiking trails at Lake Mary lead to nearby smaller, less crowded lakes, including **HORSESHOE LAKE**, a great place for swimming (the water is slightly warmer than in neighboring lakes). Trout fishers frequently try their luck at Lake Mary, although most anglers prefer to cast their lines in **CONVICT LAKE**, where you can rent a boat and stock up at the Convict Lake Resort's tackle shop (from Hwy 395 a few miles S of town, take the Convict Lake Rd exit, just S of Mammoth Lakes Airport; 760/934-3800). Another hot spot for snagging some meaty trout is **HOT CREEK** (on Hot Creek Hatchery Rd, just off Hwy 395 at the N end of Mammoth Lakes Airport), the most popular catch-and-release fishery in California (on average, each trout is caught and released five to six times a month). Only a few miles of the creek are accessible to the public—the rest is private property.

MOUNTAIN BIKING is another hugely popular sport here in the summer, when the entire Mammoth Mountain Ski Area is transformed into one of the top bike parks in the country. The national Norba mountain bike championship race (on Minaret Rd, off Hwy 203 W) takes place here, too; call the Mammoth Lakes Visitors Bureau for details. You can buy an all-day pass to 60 miles of single-track trails and a gondola that will zip you and your bike up to the top of the mountain. From there it's downhill all the way (be sure to wear a helmet), with trails ranging in difficulty from the mellow "Paper Route" ride to the infamous "Kamikaze" wheel-spinner. If you don't want to pay to ride a bike, there are dozens of great trails in the area where mountain bikes are permitted.

With winter comes an onslaught of downhill skiers, who journey here to schuss the slopes of **MAMMOTH MOUNTAIN SKI AREA** (see Skiing the Sierra Nevada section, below). Unfortunately, it can be one of the country's most crowded ski areas, particularly on weekends, when more than 10,000 Los Angelenos make the lengthy commute. (Tip: About 90 percent of the skiers arrive on Friday night and leave Sunday afternoon, so come on a weekday.) If you've ever seen the several-mile-long traffic jams converging on the ski area's parking lot, then you know why veteran Mammoth skiers always park their wheels in town and take the shuttle to the resort. These shuttles are not only convenient, they're free.

And no matter where you're staying in Mammoth Lakes, a **MAMMOTH AREA SHUTTLE** (MAS) stop (760/934-2571) is most likely nearby. The ubiquitous buses run from 7am to 5:30pm every day during the ski season, and they swing by their stops every 15 minutes to shuttle skiers to one of the resort's three entrances.

Mammoth Lakes also has mile upon mile of perfectly groomed cross-country ski trails, winding through gorgeous stretches of national forest and immense meadows. Nordic skiers of all levels favor the **TAMARACK CROSS-COUNTRY SKI CENTER** (Lake Mary Rd, 2½ miles SW of town; 760/934-2442) at Tamarack Lodge in Twin Lakes, which offers 25 miles of groomed trails, extensive backcountry trails, lessons, rentals, and tours.

Dozens of natural hot springs dot the Mammoth area, although most of the remote ones are kept secret by tourist-weary locals who probably wouldn't make you feel very welcome even if you discovered one. Visitors are definitely welcome, however, at the more accessible springs, including the free **HOT CREEK GEOLOGIC SITE** (take the Hot Creek Hatchery Rd exit off Hwy 395, at the N end of Mammoth Lakes Airport, and follow the signs), where the narrow creek feeds into a series of artificial pools—some only big enough for two, others family size. These pools are equipped with cold-water pipes that usually keep the water temperature toasty yet not unbearably hot. The Forest Service discourages soaking in the pools because of sporadic spurts of scalding water— yes, there *is* a small risk of getting your buns poached—but most people are more concerned about whether or not to show off their birthday suit (swimsuits are optional). Call the Mammoth Lakes Visitors Bureau for more details.

Granted, life is often one big outdoor party in Mammoth Lakes, but when the annual **MAMMOTH LAKES JAZZ JUBILEE** swings into gear in July, hold on to your Tevas—nearly everyone in this toe-tapping town starts kicking up their heels when a dozen world-class bands start tootin' their horns. This three-day jazz extravaganza usually happens the first weekend after the Fourth of July, and opening day is free (after that it's about $25 or more per day). A much more sedate but definitely worthwhile musical event is the annual **SIERRA SUMMER FESTIVAL**, a tribute to everything from chamber to classical music that begins in late July and winds down in early August.

RESTAURANTS

The Mogul / ★

1528 TAVERN RD, MAMMOTH LAKES; 760/934-3039
Your server skillfully charbroils fresh fish, shrimp, and steak under your watchful eye here at the Mogul, the steak house voted Mammoth's best by *Mammoth Times* readers several years in a row. Although it's not

cooked at the table, prime rib is a local favorite. The restaurant's success is based in part on the use of old family recipes for such favorites as baked beans and sweet Cinnamon Charlotte, a cupcake topped with ice cream and cinnamon sauce. *$$; AE, DIS, MC, V; no checks; dinner every day; full bar; reservations recommended; 1 block S of Main St, off Old Mammoth Rd.*

Nevados / ★★★

ON MAIN ST, MAMMOTH LAKES; 760/934-4466
Mammoth's finest restaurant is packed almost every night with an equal split of locals and Los Angelenos on their annual ski or summer holiday. Ebullient owner/host Tim Dawson darts about the small dining room and adjacent bar, seating guests, opening wine, and making sure everyone's enjoying themselves. The entrees are so utterly satisfying—and reasonably priced—that nary a complaint is heard about the food or service (that is, if you keep in mind that your server is a skier first, waitperson second). A cheerful trompe l'oeil of a European village is painted on the dining room walls and melds well with the often crowded and boisterous dinner scene. Though all menu items are available à la carte, for only a few dollars more you can enjoy a prix-fixe three-course meal with any dish on the three-part menu. A recommended trio is the strudel appetizer of wild mushrooms and rabbit with roasted shallots and grilled scallions, followed by an entree of braised Provimi veal shank with roasted tomatoes and garlic mashed potatoes and, for dessert, a fantastic warm pear and almond tart sweetened with caramel sauce and vanilla bean ice cream. Other commendable choices include the tuna tartare and tuna sashimi layered with wonton skins and wasabi aioli, the duck confit and grilled duck breast with plum wine sauce and duck fried rice, or the chocolate tiramisu in a chocolate cup with espresso ladyfingers. *$$–$$$; AE, MC, V; checks OK; dinner every day; full bar; reservations recommended; at Minaret Rd.*

Skadi / ★★★

587 OLD MAMMOTH ROAD, MAMMOTH LAKES; 760/934-3902
Ian Algerøen, chef/owner of Skadi, was formerly chef at the popular Nevados (see review, above), then moved on to realize his own unique culinary vision. The food here is a mix of Scandinavian and Italian Alpine, with a bit of San Francisco thrown in. *Bon Appétit* magazine has called Skadi (named for the Viking goddess of hunting and skiing) "the most inventive restaurant in Mammoth," and so it is. The appetizers range from a Caprese salad of fresh mozzarella, tomatoes, and basil to a smorgasbord plate of Norwegian style gravlax, smoked red trout with horseradish, dilled shrimp steamed in Carlsberg beer, and ahi tuna tartare. Entrees include lamb shanks braised in zinfandel, garlic, and rosemary with rosemary-garlic mashed potatoes and a side of garlic

confit; roast maple leaf duck with juniper, aquavit, and lingonberries; and pan-roasted, crispy-skin salmon with horseradish and chives, served with mashed potatoes and roasted beets. The desserts are noteworthy, particularly the special tasting of four of the house-made chocolate delights and the wild honey roasted strawberries with passion fruit sorbet. *$$$; AE, MC, V; checks OK; dinner every day; beer and wine; reservations recommended; corner of Chateau and Old Mammoth Rds.*

LODGINGS

Mammoth Mountain Inn / ★

MINARET RD, MAMMOTH LAKES; 760/934-2581 OR 800/228-4947

This inn is a popular haven for downhill skiers—it's just steps away from the chairlifts at Mammoth Mountain Ski Area—and in the summer the guests are primarily mountain bikers, fly fishers, hikers, and horseback riders. The 214 rooms have thin walls and a predictably humdrum decor but come with all the usual amenities such as telephones, TVs, and queen-size or double beds. Your best bet is to rent a junior suite in the refurbished section that has a view of the ski area. Other perks include a whirlpool spa, child-care facilities, and shuttle-bus service. The only downside is the 10-minute drive into town, but if your goal is to ski-till-you-drop, you can't get any closer to the slopes. The hotel's Mountainside Grill—a semiformal restaurant serving pasta, seafood, lamb, chicken, and prime rib—and Dry Creek Lounge are open year-round. *$$–$$$; AE, MC, V; checks OK; at Mammoth Mountain Ski Area, 4 miles from downtown.*

Sierra Lodge / ★★

3540 MAIN ST, MAMMOTH LAKES; 760/934-8881 OR 800/356-5711

Unlike most lodges in the area, Sierra Lodge, built in 1991, has no rustic elements in any of its 35 spacious rooms. The decor here is quite contemporary: soothing earth tones, framed modern prints, track lighting, blond wood furnishings, and big comfy beds. Amenities include cable TV, telephones, kitchenettes, and partial mountain views from your private balcony. After a hard day of skiing, relax your bones in the lodge's

 outdoor Jacuzzi, then kick back by the fireplace for a game of backgammon in the cozy Fireside Room. Skiers are pampered with their own ski locker; all guests enjoy free covered parking and a continental breakfast. But wait, there's more: free shuttle service right outside the front door, and Mammoth's best restaurant, Nevados (see review, above), is within easy walking distance. The lodge is the area's only non-smoking hotel. You'll like the Sierra Lodge's friendly staff, too—a team that definitely has its act together. *$–$$; AE, DIS, MC, V; checks OK; at Sierra St.*

Tamarack Lodge Resort / ★★

TWIN LAKE RD, MAMMOTH LAKES; 760/934-2442 OR 800/237-6879

Built in 1924 by the movie-star Foy family of Los Angeles, the 6-acre Tamarack Lodge sits at an elevation of 8,600 feet on the edge of Twin Lake. Come summer or winter, it's an extremely romantic retreat, nestled deep within the pines and overlooking a serene alpine lake. The resort's 11 rooms and 25 cabins, which were upgraded and redecorated in 1986 with pine furnishings and soft-hued fabrics, are currently undergoing another major, multiyear redo. Rooms 1, 2, and 7 have a view of the lake. Six of the rooms have private baths, and five share two baths. The cabins range from studios to three-bedroom suites that sleep up to nine people, and a few have wood-burning fireplaces (the best units are the lakefront cabins—Fisherman's, Lakeside, and numbers 8, 36, and 37). The rustic Lakefront Restaurant, with its antique furnishings and fringed lamps, offers the most romantic dinner setting in Mammoth Lakes. Its seasonally changing menu may feature such well-prepared fare as grilled medallions of elk fillet with a blueberry–juniper berry sauce, veal tenderloin, and fresh sea scallops in a caper-chardonnay-tarragon beurre blanc, and the restaurant gets an air-shipment of fresh Hawaiian fish daily. In the winter, the lodge opens the Tamarack Cross-Country Ski Center, with 25 miles of groomed trails, lessons, rentals, and tours. *$$–$$$; AE, MC, V; checks OK; off Lake Mary Rd, 2½ miles above town.*

Convict Lake

RESTAURANTS

The Restaurant at Convict Lake / ★★★

AT CONVICT LAKE, CONVICT LAKE; 760/934-3803

The anglers who toss their lines into Convict Lake to catch rainbow and German brown trout have kept this restaurant a secret for many years. Their secret, however, is slowly slipping out, as others have begun to journey here for a meal at this glorious lakeside spot. The lounge's open-beam ceiling and bare wood floors are warmed by a wood-burning stove and overstuffed chairs and sofas. Some patrons make a meal out of the appetizers at the bar, while others settle into the cozy booths in the elegant dining area, where a freestanding fireplace with a glistening copper chimney glows in the center of the room. The chef's specials might include Chilean sea bass with mango-pineapple-cilantro relish or lamb loin in a hazelnut-and-rosemary sauce. Popular entrees from the seasonal menu include beef Wellington, local Alpers trout, and duck confit flavored with sun-dried cherry sauce and garnished with candied orange zest. For dessert try the tasty meringue topped with kiwi fruit and whipped cream or the bananas Foster flambé. *$$$; AE, DIS, MC, V; checks OK; dinner* *every day; full bar; reservations recommended; from Hwy 395 take the Convict Lake exit; 3½ miles S of Mammoth Lakes.* &

Skiing the Sierra Nevada

When the Golden State's denizens gear up for the ski season, they all usually have one destination in mind: **LAKE TAHOE**, the premier winter playground for deranged daredevils and cautious snowplowers alike. Whether you're a 6-year-old hotshot schussing down chutes and cornices, a 60-year-old granddaddy trekking through cross-country tracks in a serene Sierra valley, or someone in between, the Tahoe region will surely please you. A smorgasbord of downhill slopes encircles the famous twinkling alpine lake, while the cross-country ski trails are some of the most scenic and challenging in the country.

Top on the list of **CROSS-COUNTRY FAVORITES** is the North Shore's **ROYAL GORGE** (Soda Springs exit off I-80; 530/426-3871), the largest cross-country ski resort in North America, with 200 miles of trails for skiers of all levels, 9,172 acres of skiable terrain, an average annual snowfall of more than 650 inches, 10 warming huts (for defrosting those frozen fingers and toes), and two lodges. More experienced Nordic skiers should head over to **EAGLE MOUNTAIN** (from I-80, exit at Yuba Gap, turn right, and follow the signs; 530/389-2254 or 800/391-2254), one of the area's best-kept secrets, which offers 47 miles of challenging trails with fantastic Sierra vistas. The South Shore's choicest cross-country tracks are at Sorensen's Resort in **HOPE VALLEY**, and they're open to the public at no charge. You'll find more than 60 miles of trails winding through the **TOIYABE NATIONAL FOREST**—plenty of room for mastering that telemark turn and escaping the Tahoe crowds. Rentals, lessons, tours, and trail maps are available at the **HOPE VALLEY CROSS-COUNTRY SKI CENTER** (from Hwy 50 in Myers, take Hwy 89 S over the Luther Pass to the Hwy 88/89 intersection, turn left, and continue for ½ mile to Sorensen's; 530/694-2266), located 300 yards east of Sorensen's Resort. Farther south is the **BEAR VALLEY CROSS-COUNTRY** area (209/753-2834; off Hwy 4), with 43 miles of groomed Nordic track—one of the largest track systems in the United States. **YOSEMITE CROSS-COUNTRY SKI SCHOOL** (209/372-8444), at **BADGER PASS SKI AREA** (off SR 41), offers rentals, lessons, and excursions on 90 miles of groomed trails (there's a total of 350 miles of cross-country trails in the park). There are also two major cross-country ski centers at **MAMMOTH MOUNTAIN SKI AREA** (off Hwy 395), where L.A. folk flock on winter weekends; for more information, call the Mammoth Lakes Visitors Bureau (760/934-2712 or 800/367-6572).

For **DOWNHILL** thrill-seekers, Lake Tahoe offers a plethora of first-rate resorts that cater to every age, ability, and whim. Families fare best at **NORTHSTAR**, while serious skiers find the most challenging terrain at **SQUAW VALLEY USA, KIRKWOOD, HEAVENLY SKI RESORT**, and **ALPINE MEADOWS**. If you plan to stay overnight, call the **TAHOE VISITORS BUREAU** (800/TAHOE-4-U) for the lowdown on ski-package deals. Although most Northern Californians rarely tote their skis beyond Tahoe's sunny slopes, a host of top-notch ski resorts dot the landscape south of the lake, including one of the state's best: **MAMMOTH MOUNTAIN SKI AREA**. Aside from Mammoth, these south-of-Tahoe ski spots are often less crowded and less expensive than their lakeside counterparts. Here's a roundup of the Sierra's major downhill ski areas, from the outer reaches of North Lake Tahoe to as far south as Badger Pass, just outside Yosemite National Park.

Lake Tahoe Ski Resorts

ALPINE MEADOWS (off Hwy 89; 530/583-4232 or 800/441-4423). A favorite among locals, Alpine has runs on a par with Squaw Valley's best but without the holier-than-thou attitude of the Squaw staff. Alpine also has the West's first six-passenger high-speed chairlift, and, bowing to the popularity of snowboarding, the resort has lifted its ban on snowboarders. The ski/lodging combo packages offered by **RIVER RANCH LODGE** in Alpine Meadows are often outstanding.

BOREAL (off I-80; 530/426-3666). Small and easy, Boreal is a good beginner's resort. It's also one of the few places in the Lake Tahoe area that offers night skiing (open until 9pm), and, thanks to its extensive snowmaking equipment, is usually one of the first ski areas to open.

DIAMOND PEAK (from Hwy 28, exit on Country Club Dr, turn right on Sky Wy, and drive to Incline Village; 775/832-1177). Located in Incline Village on the Nevada side of Tahoe's North Shore, this small, family ski resort guarantees good skiing—if you don't like the conditions, you may turn in your ticket within the first hour for a voucher that's good for another day.

DONNER SKI RANCH (Soda Springs exit off I-80; 530/426-3635). Just up the road from Sugar Bowl is Donner, whose best attribute is its price—a ski pass is about half the cost of its neighbors! And despite its small size, this unpretentious ski area has a lot to offer skiers of all levels: tree skiing, groomed trails, and a few steeps and jumps, not to mention convenient parking and a cozy, down-home lodge.

GRANLIBAKKEN (off Hwy 89 at the junction of Hwy 28; 530/583-4242 or 800/543-322). Tiny and mainly for tots, this is a great place to teach kids the fundamentals. Later, when you'll surely need a libation, you won't have far to go to find the Tahoe City nightspots.

HEAVENLY SKI RESORT (off Hwy 50; 702/586-7000 or 800/2-HEAVEN). South Lake Tahoe's pride and joy has something for skiers of all levels. Heavenly is so immense it straddles two states (California and Nevada); those in the know park on the Nevada side to avoid the crowds.

KIRKWOOD (off Hwy 88; 209/258-6000). When skiing conditions just don't get any better, Tahoe locals make the pilgrimage over the passes to where the snow is the deepest and the skiing is the sweetest. Kirkwood also offers some very tempting ski/lodging packages.

NORTHSTAR-AT-TAHOE (off Hwy 267; 530/562-1010 or 800/GO-NORTH). Northstar is consistently rated one of the best family ski resorts in the nation, due to its numerous amenities. It also has the dubious honor of being called "Flatstar" by the locals because of its penchant for grooming. It's a completely self-contained ski resort (you'll find everything from lodgings to stores to a gas station here), so you can park your car and leave it in the same spot for the duration of your stay.

SIERRA-AT-TAHOE (off Hwy 50; 530/659-7453). Formerly named Sierra Ski Ranch, Tahoe's third-largest ski area is a good all-around resort, offering a slightly better price than most comparable places in the area. It's not worth the drive from the North Shore, but it's a good alternative to Heavenly Ski Resort if you want a change of venue near the South Shore.

HOMEWOOD MOUNTAIN RESORT (off Hwy 89; 530/525-2992). This underrated midsize resort has a little of everything for skiers of all levels, as well as one of the best views of Lake Tahoe. Midweek specials often knock down the price of a ticket by as much as 50 percent (call ahead for quotes), easily the best deal around.

SQUAW VALLEY USA (off Hwy 89; 530/583-6985 or 800/545-4350). Site of the 1960 Winter Olympic Games, Squaw is a resort that people either love (because it has everything a skier could hope for) or hate (because the staff here knows it has everything). Squaw offers some of the country's most challenging terrain, intensive ski-school programs, top-of-the-line chairlifts, night skiing from 4pm to 9pm, and a snowboard park, plus a variety of nonskiing activities including ice skating, swimming, and even bungee jumping. Unfortunately, the resort tends to attract the most obnoxious snowboarders and the most egotistical skiers in North America.

SUGAR BOWL (Soda Springs exit off I-80; 530/426-9000). Here's another good all-around midsize ski resort, with about 50 runs. Sugar Bowl's top feature is its accessibility—it's the closest resort from the valley off Interstate 80, about 30 minutes closer than Squaw Valley USA (and several bucks less a pass, thank you). Whether it's worth the drive from the North Shore, however, is questionable.

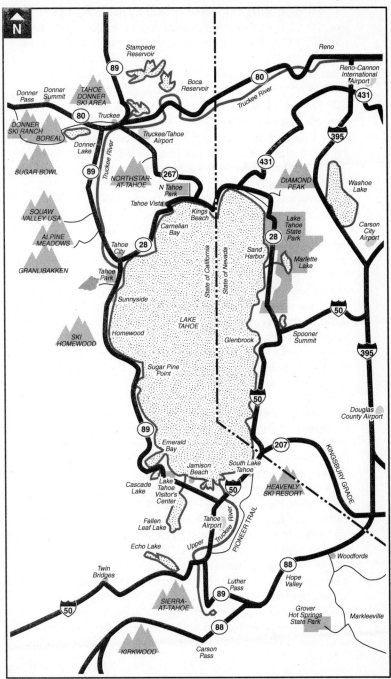

TAHOE DONNER SKI AREA (from I-80, take the Donner State Park exit, turn left on Donner Pass Rd, and go left on Northwoods Blvd; 530/587-9444). If you're a beginner or a beginner/intermediate skier and are staying on the North Shore, Tahoe Donner is a viable option, offering short lift lines, no car traffic, and relatively low prices.

South-of-Tahoe Ski Resorts

BADGER PASS SKI AREA (off SR 41; 209/372-1000). Badger Pass, 23 miles from Yosemite Valley, keeps its predominantly intermediate ski runs well manicured and offers some unique family activities, such as daily snowshoe walks led by a ranger/naturalist and ice skating in the shadow of Half Dome.

BEAR VALLEY MOUNTAIN RESORT COMPANY (off Hwy 4; 209/753-2301). Nestled in the small town of Bear Valley, this is one of the undiscovered gems of downhill skiing in Northern California. The eighth-largest ski area in the state, it has a network of 60 trails for skiers of all levels, serviced by 11 lifts that can accommodate 12,000 skiers per hour. Considering the relatively inexpensive lift tickets and the diversity of the terrain, Bear Valley offers one of the best deals in the state.

DODGE RIDGE SKI AREA (off SR 108; 209/965-3474). This small ski resort in the tiny town of Pinecrest has a decades-long reputation as a friendly, low-key ski area that's short on frills but high on family conveniences such as a top-ranked children's ski school. Its lift lines are often short, and Dodge Ridge is the closest ski resort to the Bay Area (it's just above Sonora and Columbia). More advanced skiers, however, would be happier driving the few extra miles to Bear Valley for more challenging terrain.

JUNE MOUNTAIN (on June Lake Loop off Hwy 395; 760/648-7733). Purchased by Mammoth Mountain Ski Area owner Dave McCoy in 1986, June Mountain offers skiers a calmer and less-crowded ski experience than its colossal cousin across the valley. It may be about one-fifth the size of Mammoth, but June also offers great skiing—wide bowls, steep chutes, forested trails—with the added attraction of a spectacular Sierra view from its two peaks: 10,050-foot Rainbow Summit and 10,135-foot June Mountain Summit.

MAMMOTH MOUNTAIN SKI AREA (off Hwy 395; for ski-resort information, call the Mammoth Lakes Visitors Bureau at 760/934-8006 or 800/367-6572). Mammoth vies with Heavenly for the title of largest ski resort in the state, and it's L.A.'s prime weekend ski destination. What makes it so great? The numbers speak for themselves: 8 to 12 feet of consistently deep snowpack, 31 chairlifts, a 70 percent chance of sunny skies, 150 runs, 1,800 employees, 3,100 vertical feet, 3,500 acres of skiable terrain, up to 15,000 skiers a weekend, and more than 30,000 hotel beds.

GOLD COUNTRY

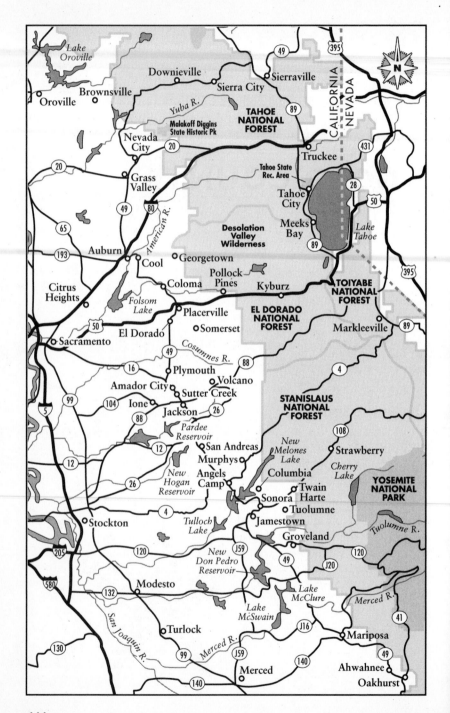

GOLD COUNTRY

By 1849, word had spread throughout the United States, Europe, and other corners of the globe that gold miners in California were becoming millionaires overnight. In just one year, more than 80,000 eager souls stampeded across water and land to reach the hilly terrain now known as the Gold Country and the Mother Lode. By 1852, more than 200,000 men were working the mines. Many of the "forty-niners" had to fight for their claims to the land, claims that left the average miner with little more than dirt and grime in his pocket. Crime and starvation were rampant, and when the exhausted miners put away their picks and pans for the night, most sought comfort in drinking, gambling, and prostitutes. It was a wild and heady time that brought riches to relatively few but changed the Golden State forever.

You can follow in the miners' footsteps (geographically, at least) by cruising along the aptly numbered Highway 49, the zigzagging, 321-mile Gold Rush road that links many of the mining towns. Yep, there are precious nuggets in those hills and mountain streams, and you can hire a prospector to show you how and where to try your luck. But spend any time in the Sierra foothills and you'll soon discover the real gold lies in the history of the tiny towns that characterize this region, and in the grassy foothills that turn golden beneath the summer sun.

ACCESS AND INFORMATION

The Gold Country is truly a region for all seasons, with wineries, antique shops, historic parks, caverns, and museums open throughout the year. Late spring and early summer bring explosions of wildflowers and rafting down the American, Merced, Tuolumne, and Yuba Rivers. The crisp air of autumn ushers in apple and grape harvests, and the vibrant turning of leaves on the Chinese pistache, dogwood, and maple trees. During the winter, when the Sacramento and San Joaquin Valleys are shrouded in fog, the sun is often shining in the Gold Country, and the region is only a short drive away from most ski resorts. On the other hand, you'll want an air-conditioned room on the hottest summer days and tire chains in the winter if you're heading up to Kyburz or Sierra City.

If, like most visitors to the area, you decide to drive, there are several ways to enter the region. With **INTERSTATE 5** or **HIGHWAY 99** as your motoring-off point, you will find a slew of highways and county roads (marked with a "J") running east toward **HIGHWAY 49**. A California map or Gold Country region map are your best bets for finding the quickest route as well as for deciphering all those tempting side roads that pop up along the way.

Though the easiest way to explore the towns on and off Highway 49 is by automobile or motorcycle, there are a few other ways to reach the area.

AMTRAK trains (800/872-7245; www.amtrak.com) run daily along the valley floor, with Frontier Tours buses departing from the Sacramento station (401 I St at 5th; 916/444-7094) to Placerville, Auburn, Grass Valley, and Nevada City several times a day, and from the Merced station (324 W 24th St; 209/722-6862) to Mariposa four times a day. The train also arrives at 6:40pm in Auburn from the San Francisco Bay Area every day. (Check the train schedule for any time changes.)

Nine noncommercial small passenger and private plane airports dot the Gold Country from Nevada City to Mariposa. Check your **AOPA DIRECTORY** or **WESTERN FLIGHT GUIDE** (or even a California road map) for their locations. **COLUMBIA AIRPORT** (10767 Airport Rd, Columbia; 209/533-5685) is an easy half-mile walk away from Columbia State Historic Park, and you can borrow a car at **CALAVERAS AIRPORT** (3600 Carol Kennedy, San Andreas; 209/736-2526) for a few hours on weekdays if you let them know ahead of time. Staff at most of the other airports can help you arrange for taxi or a rental car (best to call ahead) if you don't want to walk the 2 to 5 miles into town.

Northern Gold Country

You'll find some of the most authentically preserved towns in the northern Gold Country, including Grass Valley, where more than a billion dollars in gold was extracted, and Nevada City, former home of one of the region's more famous miners, President Herbert Hoover. The farther east you travel in the Gold Country, the closer you move toward the Sierra Nevada mountains. In towns like Downieville, Sierra City, Kyburz, and Twain Harte, the Gold Country foothills begin to lose their gentle climb; slopes get steeper, oak trees fade into forests of fir and pine.

Sierra City

The first thing all visitors do upon entering Sierra City is tilt their heads back to take in the magnificent view of the **SIERRA BUTTES** towering above them. Don't worry if you forgot your binoculars: just about every restaurant and lodging in town has a telescope pointing straight up at these majestic mountains. Black bear lumber through this little town on a daily basis, so unless you are willing to sacrifice a back window, be careful not to leave any food in your automobile. Dozens of nearby hiking and cross-country-ski trails wind through Tahoe National Forest to more than 30 mountain lakes, which offer great trout fishing. Local activities include mountain biking, horseback riding, kayaking, snowmobiling, and enjoying the pristine scenery.

RESTAURANTS

Buckhorn Lodge Restaurant and Tavern / ★★

225 MAIN ST, SIERRA CITY; 530/862-1170 OR 800/991-1170

What's left of a winsome-looking deer greets the customers at the tavern door of this 1889 building, where those desiring a hearty dinner during the warm months are treated to the sight and sound of a babbling Sierra creek cascading down the center of a terraced garden patio. Wander up to the top of the garden and check out the totem pole with the history of the town carved into its sides. Once you've settled into this garden oasis, prepare to more than satisfy your appetite. The menu includes New York strip steak, charbroiled salmon or Chilean sea bass, international specials such as the (1-pound!) Bavarian roast pork, and, on Saturday nights, a barbecue. *$$; MC, V; checks OK; dinner Tues–Sat (Fri–Sat, Dec–May); full bar; reservations recommended; downtown.*

Herrington's Sierra Pines Resort / ★★

104 MAIN ST, SIERRA CITY; 530/862-1151 OR 800/682-9848

In a log- and wood-paneled dining room on the gorgeous north fork of the Yuba River, the Herrington family serves house-baked bread and their specialty: fresh trout reeled right out of their trout pond. The evening menu also offers New York steak and such specials as filet mignon wrapped in bacon, stuffed shrimp, and clam and shrimp fettuc-cine. For dessert, don't pass up the fresh berry cobbler or the Harvey Wallbanger cake. The Herringtons serve breakfast, too, which might include strawberry pancakes, eggs Benedict, or biscuits and gravy. The resort also offers 21 motel-style units with covered decks, and most have views of the Yuba River. If you have a group of three or more, inquire about the two apartments—each has a bedroom with two double beds, a fully equipped kitchen, and a living room with a Franklin fireplace. *$$; DIS, MC, V; checks OK; breakfast, dinner every day; closed Nov (or when the pipes freeze)–Apr; full bar; reservations recommended; S side of Hwy 49 at the W end of town.*

LODGINGS

High Country Inn / ★★★

100 GREENE RD, SIERRA CITY; 530/862-1530 OR 800/862-1530

Aspen flutter in the breeze along the north fork of the Yuba River, the backdrop to this welcoming five-room inn. Mother Nature's handiwork is reason enough to stay here, but the high point of the High Country Inn is the spectacular view of the Sierra Buttes from its deck. And while there is a view from every room, the Sierra Buttes Suite takes full advantage of the gorgeous mountain scenery. The room encompasses the entire second floor, with a cathedral ceiling, a king-size bed, and a fireplace. The bath-room is almost a suite of its own, with a 6½-foot-long 1846 bathtub and

GOLD COUNTRY THREE-DAY TOUR

DAY ONE: Vineyards and vistas. After a gourmet breakfast at **The Shafsky House** in Placerville, ask your hosts to make your reservations for dinner at **Cafe Luna** before driving down to nearby **Gold Bug Park**. Take the self-guided tour of the 52-degree **Gold Bug Mine**, then check out the giant ore stamps at Joshua Hendy Stamp Mill. Head back toward town for a visit to the **El Dorado County Historical Museum** to see what a Studebaker looked like before it became a car. Pick up a picnic lunch at **A Main Street Cafe** (325 Main St; 530/642-1700) and a map of the wineries across the street at the **WineSmith** (346 Main St; 530/622-0516). A short drive into the country down Schnell School Road to Carson Road brings you to the historic **Boeger Winery** for a sip of its 1998 barbera. Relax and enjoy your picnic on the tables in the surrounding pear orchards or by the pond beneath the redwoods. Continue on through the countryside for more wine tasting and a gorgeous view of the valley at **Lava Cap** (2221 Fruitridge Rd, Placerville; 530/621-0175). Finish your tour by sampling the intense reds at **Madroña Vineyards** (High Hill Rd, Camino; 530/644-5948), then swing back into town from Highway 50 and explore the eclectic shops along Main Street. Enjoy dinner at Cafe Luna, then settle in for the night at The Shafsky House.

DAY TWO: Laughter to the rafters. Arrange for an early breakfast at The Shafsky House, then drive 8 miles north on Highway 49 to **the Marshall Gold Discovery State Historic Park** in **Coloma**. Peek into the American River Conservancy Nature Center to learn about the wildlife in the area, then walk over to the park's visitor center to pick up a walking tour map. Spend about an hour wandering through the buildings and the site where gold was first discovered. Grab a sandwich and slice of fresh fruit pie

a dressing room complete with terry-cloth robes. Families often opt for the spacious Howard Creek Room because it has both a king-size and a double bed as well as room for a roll-away. The High Country Inn offers gourmet breakfasts in addition to the tray of coffee and tea that's set outside each room by 7am for those who want to get an early start. *$$$; AE, DIS, MC, V; checks OK; blatta@sccn.net; www.hicountryinn.com; 5 miles E of town, on the S side of Hwy 49 and Gold Lake Rd.*

Holly House / ★★★

119 MAIN ST, SIERRA CITY; 530/862-1123

Tucked beneath the breathtaking Sierra Buttes, this carefully restored Italianate Victorian, owned and run by Mary and Rich Nourse, is sure to bring a "wow" to the lips of the road-weary traveler. High medallioned ceilings, classic antiques, and a wraparound porch add to the charm and elegance of the six-bedroom air-conditioned B&B. The

for an early lunch at the Argonaut, located in the park. The extra calories will help get you through the half-day river rafting trip with **American River Recreation** (530/622-6802 or 800/333-7238) down the South Fork of the American River. You'll be tired but hungry after shooting the rapids, so join the other river rafters for gourmet pizza on the outdoor patio at **Marco's Cafe** (7221 Hwy 49; 530/642-2025) in nearby Lotus. If you have any energy left after you arrive back at your room, wander over to **Placerville Coffee Co.** (594 Main St; 530/642-8481) for a glass of wine or beer and a little live music at The Shafsky House.

DAY THREE: South to Sutter Creek. Treat yourself to an early breakfast in town at **Sweetie Pies**, then take a leisurely drive south on Highway 49 for a day of antiquing in Amador City and Sutter Creek. Drop off your luggage at the **Eureka Street Inn** in Sutter Creek, then walk one block to **Susan's Place** (15 Eureka St; 209/267-0945) for lunch. Design your own sandwich or create your own pasta, polenta, or rice entree by choosing from a variety of sauces and toppings. If you have the time, take the 12-mile scenic Sutter Creek/Volcano Road into **Volcano**. Make a reservation for dinner at the **St. George Hotel Restaurant**. While you're waiting, sip a beverage in the **Whiskey Flat Saloon** at the historic hotel and try your hand at tacking a dollar bill to the 14-foot-high ceiling in a single toss. After dinner, head back to your B&B in Sutter Creek via Pine Grove/Volcano Road for a last night in the Gold Country. If it's still light out, make a short stop along the way at **Indian Grinding Rock State Historic Park**, and take a moment to stretch your legs on the half-mile nature trail where the Miwok once walked, hundreds of years before anyone in the region even cared about that shiny stuff shimmering in the creeks.

grandest room in the house is The Engel, decorated in pale blues and white, with a large mirrored armoire, a love seat/hide-a-bed in the bay window, and a luxurious private bath with a claw-footed tub and shower. The red plaid wallpaper bordered by wide white molding in the downstairs H. Watt Hughes Room (also known as the Fire Room) is more charming than alarming, and the double-size spa in the private bath is a perfect place to relax those muscles after a day of exploring the great outdoors. Guests are welcome to enjoy their evening wine and hors d'oeuvres in the parlor and to eat their breakfast in the formal dining room, but most eventually end up at the large table in the spacious country kitchen or out on the shaded patio. *$$$; MC, V, checks OK; open weekends only Memorial Day weekend–first 2 weeks of June, and all of Sept; www.hollyhouse.com; W of downtown, on the N side of Hwy 49.*

Downieville

This scenic little mountain town at the junction of the Yuba and Downie Rivers hasn't changed much since the 1850s: venerable buildings still line the boardwalks along crooked Main Street, and trim homes are cut into the canyon walls above. Downieville's population hovers around 350 now (closer to 500 in the summer), though during its heyday 5,000 prospectors panned the streams and worked the mines here. The lusty gold camp even had the dubious distinction of being the only place in California where a woman was lynched.

A former Gold Rush–era Chinese store houses the **DOWNIEVILLE MUSEUM** (330 Main St; no phone; open daily in summer, weekends in spring and fall). The **SIERRA COUNTY COURTHOUSE** (100 Courthouse Sq; 530/289-3698) displays gold dug out of the rich Ruby Mine, and next door stands the only original gallows in the Gold Country. For more Gold Rush history and lore, check out the **SIERRA COUNTY HISTORICAL PARK** (530/862-1310) on Highway 99, 1 mile north of Sierra City, where the restored Kentucky Mine and a stamp mill still stand. It's open Wednesday through Sunday, Memorial Day through September, and on weekends in October, weather permitting.

For local news and current Downieville events, pick up a copy of the **MOUNTAIN MESSENGER** (100 Main St; 530/289-3262), a weekly newspaper published since 1853. To tour this scenic area by bicycle, visit the folks at **OUTFITTERS** (310 Main St; 530/289-0155; dvoutfit@sirius.com; www.downivilleoutfitters.com) or **YUBA EXPEDITIONS** (corner of Main and Commercial Sts; 530/265-8779; www.yubaexpeditions.com). Both shops will plan a mountain bike tour for you. Bike rentals are available at Outfitters only.

RESTAURANTS

The Downieville Bakery and Cafe / ★★

109 COMMERCIAL ST, DOWNIEVILLE; 530/289-0108

Housed in the historic Craycroft Building (which, by the way, is where Juanita, the aforementioned hangee, unsuccessfully fled to avoid the lynching mob), this bakery and cafe is engulfed daily by the heavenly aroma of breads and pastries. Take a seat in the small, six-table restaurant for a cup of joe and a pastry, or choose from a tasty lunchtime array of wraps, sandwiches made with fresh-baked breads, homemade soups, and salads. The dinner menu changes weekly but will usually include a beef, a chicken, and a fish dish. The appetizing jumbo tiger prawns sautéed in garlic and rosemary served with a rice pilaf or baby red potatoes will almost always be found on the menu, along with fresh fruit pies for dessert. *$$; no credit cards; checks OK; breakfast, lunch Wed–Mon, dinner Fri–Mon (hours vary after Labor Day); beer and wine; reservations recommended; Hwy 49 at the Jersey Bridge.* &

Brownsville

If you're driving anywhere near this remote region of the Gold Country, consider making a reservation for a tour of the **RENAISSANCE VINEYARD & WINERY** (12585 Rice's Crossing Rd, Oregon House; 530/692-3104 or 800/655-3277; sales@rvw.com; www.renaissancewinery.com; 7 miles S of Brownsville, call for directions), a spectacular 365-acre winery with rose gardens fit for a queen's palace. Located in the nearby village of Oregon House, Renaissance is at an elevation of 2,300 feet and is one of the largest mountain vineyards in North America. It is owned and operated by a wealthy religious group known as the Fellowship of Friends. The visitors' schedule is subject to change, but tours and tastings are usually available on Friday and Saturday, and appointments are essential, even if you just want to smell the roses. The **APOLLO BISTRO** (12587 Rice's Crossing Rd, Oregon House; 530/692-9243) next to the winery, however, is not under the same restrictions—it's open for lunch and dinner Wednesday through Sunday almost year-round.

For a glimpse of life from the 1800s, visit the **YUBA FEATHER MUSEUM** (19096 New York Flat Rd, Forbestown, 95941; 530/675-1025; www.YFHmuseum.org), just 15 minutes outside of Brownsville. The museum features more than 3,000 photographs and life-size exhibits, including a schoolhouse, barbershop, jail, Native American Maidu village, and a Chinese laundry. This miniature town of yesteryear is only open on the weekends from noon to 4pm, Memorial Day through Labor day.

Nevada City

Established in 1849 when miners found gold in Deer Creek, Nevada City occupies one of the most picturesque sites in the Sierra foothills. When the sugar maples blaze in autumn, the town resembles a small New England village, making it hard to believe this was once the third-largest city in California. This is also B&B heaven, and with so many beautifully restored houses to choose from, you'll have a tough time selecting a favorite. To understand the lay of the land, put on your walking shoes and pick up a **FREE WALKING-TOUR MAP** at the Chamber of Commerce (132 Main St at Coyote St; 530/265-2692). Town highlights include the **NATIONAL HOTEL**, where the cozy Gold Rush–era bar is ideal for a cocktail or two, and the white, cupola-topped **FIREHOUSE NUMBER I MUSEUM** (214 Main St at Commercial St; 530/265-5468), featuring Gold Rush memorabilia, rare Indian baskets, a fine Chinese altar from a local 1860s joss house, and relics from the infamous and ill-fated Donner Party. The museum is open daily, 11am to 4pm, April through November, and weekends December through March.

North of Nevada City is the 3,000-acre **MALAKOFF DIGGINS STATE HISTORIC PARK** (530/265-2740), home of the world's largest hydraulic gold mine and a monument to mining's devastating results. During the Gold Rush days, nearly half a mountain was washed away with powerful jets of pressurized water, leaving behind a 600-foot-deep canyon of minaret-shaped, rust-colored rocks—eerily beautiful to some but an eyesore to most. Inside the park is the semirestored mining town of North Bloomfield, where you can hike along a 3-mile loop trail that shows hydraulic-mining memorabilia. The easiest way to reach the park is to drive 5 miles past the Yuba River on Highway 49 north, turn right on Tyler-Foote Crossing, then continue up 14 miles to the park.

If you've ever visited downtown Nevada City or Grass Valley on a weekend, you know how hard it is to find a parking spot (and to think you came here to get away from it all!). This time, why not leave the car at the inn and let **GOLD COUNTRY STAGE**'s drivers (530/477-0103 or 888/660-7433; www.co.nevada.ca.us/gcstage/) do all the navigating? A couple bucks buys you an all-day shuttle pass good for both towns as well as rides to major attractions in outlying areas. Call for a free map and riders' guide.

RESTAURANTS

Citronée / ★★★

320 BROAD ST, NEVADA CITY; 530/265 5697

Whether you are seated in the bistro-like room upstairs or in the more intimate back room downstairs, you will soon understand why this Nevada City restaurant was recommended by the *New York Times*. Begin your meal with an appetizer like the black and white sesame-seed-coated ahi seared rare, with a chile soy dip and wasabi crème fraîche, or

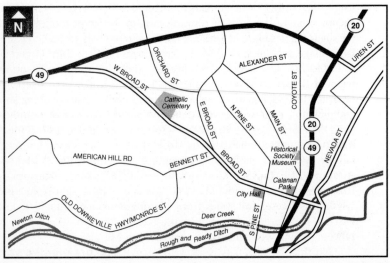

NEVADA CITY

the hazelnut-breaded goat cheese, served warm with homemade mango chutney and Tuscan white beans. Entrees include sautéed sea bass served with wasabi mashed potatoes (you'll wish you had a second helping) and the domestic lamb shanks, braised with lambrusco and served with porcini risotto. Choose from one of the 140 international and California wines to complement your meal. *$$$; AE, MC, V; local checks; lunch Mon–Fri, dinner Mon–Sat; beer and wine; reservations recommended; across from City Hall.*

Country Rose Cafe / ★★

300 COMMERCIAL ST, NEVADA CITY; 530/265-6248

Within this tall, stately brick building you'll find chef/owner Michael Johns cooking some mighty fine French country fare. The afternoon offerings often include a savory salmon-cucumber sandwich served on a baguette with an herb spread, ratatouille, beef stroganoff, and a delicate salmon quiche. For dinner, expect plenty of fresh fish, rack of lamb, beef tournedos, and a range of well-prepared poultry entrees. Fortunately, sunny days are in abundance here, enabling diners to sit on the cafe's pretty walled-in garden patio. The wine and beer lists are terrific, and more than a dozen wines are poured by the glass. *$$$; AE, DC, MC, V; local checks only; lunch, dinner every day, brunch Sun; beer and wine; reservations recommended; near the center of town at Commercial and Pine Sts.* &

Kirby's Creekside Restaurant & Bar / ★★★

101 BROAD ST, NEVADA CITY; 530/265-3445

This attractive two-story restaurant is perched precariously over Deer Creek. You can choose from the lunch menu's large selection of salads and sandwiches, or indulge in a healthy serving of meat loaf with garlic mashed potatoes or the seafood or chicken special of the day. Dinner is a more elaborate affair, kicked off with appetizers such as the marinated portobello served with roasted tomato aioli, or the steamed mussels in a chardonnay-tomato coulis. For your next course, select from one of a half-dozen pasta dishes and entrees such as braised beef in a red wine sauce, stuffed pork loin in crème de cassis sauce, or roasted leg of lamb. Prix-fixe multicourse dinners are also available, and children can choose from the kids' menu. Kirby's takes its wine list as seriously as its food and maintains a very good selection. The wine and beer bar, located on the main floor, offers live music Tuesday through Saturday. The main restaurant is downstairs, but dinner can also be served at the bar. *$$$–$$$$; AE, DIS, MC, V; checks OK; lunch Mon–Sat, dinner every day; beer and wine; reservations recommended; W side of Hwy 49 at Broad and Sacramento Sts.* &

New Moon Cafe / ★★★

203 YORK ST, NEVADA CITY; 530/265-6399

Set inside a cedar cabin lined with glass windows and decorated with Mediterranean touches and large paintings from local artists, this restaurant is popular with locals and tourists alike. But it isn't just the pleasant ambience that keeps folks coming back. Everything, down to the restaurant's organic-grain bread, is made from scratch. Whenever possible, the food is purchased locally, and the rib-eye steak, or any other meat dish you may order, comes from an "all naturally raised" beast. Five to seven fresh vegetables are served with every entree, including the sumptuous Navarro Scampi and the vegetarian wild mushroom lasagne, made with New Moon's own fresh pasta, three different Italian cheeses, and a smoked tomato sauce. *$$$; AE, DC, MC, V; checks OK; lunch Tues–Fri, dinner Tues–Sun; beer and wine; reservations recommended; 1 block from Broad St.* &

LODGINGS

Deer Creek Inn / ★★★

116 NEVADA ST, NEVADA CITY; 530/265-0363 OR 800/655-0363

Set on the banks of pretty Deer Creek, which was famous in the Gold Rush days as a "pound-a-day" source for gold panners, this Queen Anne Victorian house has been completely restored and attractively decorated as a bed-and-breakfast. The five guest rooms have either king- or queen-size four-poster or canopy beds with down comforters, private baths with marble or claw-footed tubs, and private verandas. If you're contemplating getting engaged, you might be interested to know that Winifred's Room has been the site of at least a half-dozen marriage proposals (perhaps it's the romantic veranda overlooking the creek that inspires couples to commit?). In the morning, guests are treated to a gourmet breakfast served on the deck overlooking the creek and rose garden or in the formal dining room. Wine and hors d'oeuvres are served each evening. There's a two-night minimum stay on weekends. *$$$; AE, MC, V; checks OK; deercreek@gv.net; www.deercreekinn.com; at Nevada and Broad Sts.*

Emma Nevada House / ★★★★

528 E BROAD ST, NEVADA CITY; 530/265-4415 OR 800/916-3662

Although it was built in 1856, the immaculately restored Emma Nevada House (the childhood home and namesake of 19th-century opera star Emma Nevada) is one of the newer stars in Nevada City's fine array of bed-and-breakfast inns. Many of the home's antique fixtures, such as the gas-lit chandeliers, claw-footed bathtubs, transoms, and doors, have been refurbished and modernized, and the six guest rooms have private baths and recently added queen-size beds. One of the preferred units is

Nightingale's Bower, a room on the main floor with bay windows, an antique stove, elegant Italian bedding, and a Jacuzzi. Another popular choice is the romantic Empress's Chamber. A full breakfast of fresh fruit, juices, muffins or scones, and an entree such as onion-caraway quiche or pumpkin waffles, plus Emma's special cobbler, is served in the dining room and sunroom overlooking the garden. There's a minimum stay of two nights on weekends from May through December and on holidays. *$$$; AE, DC, MC, V; checks OK; emmanev@nevadacityinns.com; www.nevadacityinns.com; right fork of the "Y" at the top of Broad St.*

Grandmere's Inn / ★★★★

449 BROAD ST, NEVADA CITY; 530/265-4660

Generally considered the grande dame of Nevada City's hostelries, Grandmere's Inn is indeed a showplace, with quite a history to boot. This three-story colonial revival mansion was once owned by Aaron and Ellen Clark Sargent, and Susan B. Anthony was a regular guest. A suffragette, Ellen helped champion women's rights, while Aaron authored the legislation that ultimately allowed women to vote; he was also a major catalyst in the founding of the Transcontinental Railroad. The mansion is set amid old terraced gardens and offers six guest rooms. The downstairs suite is the finest, with blond hardwood floors, a sitting area, an antique gas fireplace, and a private porch. If you want a bit more privacy, ask for Ellen's Garden Room, which has a private garden entrance and a bathroom with a deep soaking-tub and shower. The wonderful breakfast spread consists of hot dishes, baked goods, and fresh fruits. *$$$–$$$$; AE, MC, V; checks OK; grandmere@nevadacityinns.com; www.nevadacityinns.com; left side of Broad St at Bennett St.*

Kendall House / ★★★

534 SPRING ST, NEVADA CITY; 530/265-0405 OR 888/647-0405

This sunny bed-and-breakfast, set amid a 2-acre garden with apple trees, is a quiet, serene, and comfortable escape for city dwellers—and it's only 2 blocks from downtown Nevada City. The Garden Room downstairs is a private retreat that's near the large heated swimming pool and garden. If you like to wake up in the morning sun, try the French Country Room. Some folks prefer staying in the cottage (a converted barn), which has a tiled kitchen, a breakfast nook, a wood-burning stove, and a private deck with built-in seating and a view of the pool and fruit trees. All rooms have queen-size beds and private baths. Ask proprietor Ted Kendall, an avid jogger, for the lowdown on the best local running trails. Jan Kendall's scrumptious three-course breakfast makes for a fine morning send-off. *$$$; DIS, MC, V; checks OK; kenhouse@jps.net; www.cabbi.com; just S of W Broad St.*

National Hotel

211 BROAD ST, NEVADA CITY; 530/265-4551

The 42-room National Hotel is truly a California institution. It opened in the mid-1850s and is the oldest continuously operating hotel west of the Rockies. President Herbert Hoover slept here, as did entertainers Lotta Crabtree and Lola Montez. Heck, even former governor Jerry Brown spent the night, presumably in a four-poster bed and not on the floor. Sure, the place shows its age, and the decor (particularly the carpets) is a mishmash from every era from the 1850s to the 1950s. But, hey, such color keeps the fastidious and faint of heart away, and a few of the rooms have been updated as the hotel slowly undergoes a renovation. The 42 guest rooms are furnished with antiques, and all but eight units have private bathrooms. Families are welcome at the National, and children 12 and under stay for free if they sleep in the same room as their parents. The hotel also has a swimming pool and a dining room serving perfunctory American fare. The hotel's bar features live music on Friday and Saturday. *$$; AE, MC, V; local checks only; located at the center of town.* &

Parsonage Bed and Breakfast Inn / ★★

427 BROAD ST, NEVADA CITY; 530/265-9478

Once home to the ministers of the Nevada City Methodist Church, the Parsonage is quiet, unassuming, and an essential stop for California history buffs. Owned and operated by a great-granddaughter of California pioneer Ezra Dane, the place is something of a living museum. Deborah Dane lovingly maintains the home, which is decorated with collections from three generations of Californians—everything from a Sheraton dining room set to Chinese rice-paper-and-silk peacock screens. All six guest rooms have private baths and are furnished with the family's museum-quality heritage antiques. The Moue House, a cute cottage that was originally an old woodshed, is set apart from the inn, making it ideal for honeymooners seeking privacy or for couples with a particularly rambunctious young child. *$$; MC, V; checks OK; www.innsofthegoldcountry.com/pars.htm or www.christianbandb.com; in historic downtown.*

Piety Hill Cottages / ★★★

523 SACRAMENTO ST, NEVADA CITY; 530/265-2245 OR 800/443-2245

Originally built in 1933 as an auto court, Piety Hill Cottages has been imaginatively and charmingly restored and redecorated by owners Joan and Steve Oas. The inn consists of nine cottages clustered around a grassy, tree-shaded courtyard and garden. Each of the one-, two-, and three-room cottages has a kitchenette stocked with complimentary hot and cold beverages, at least one king- or queen-size bed, a private bath, cable TV, and air conditioning. One unit also has a wood-burning stove. Between 8:30am and 10am (you pick the exact time), the innkeeper delivers a breakfast basket filled with juice, fresh fruit, and lemon poppy seed bread or orange sourdough French toast. Guests are free to linger in the lodge-style living room, soak in the gazebo-sheltered spa nestled among cedars, and barbecue on the outdoor grills. The larger cottages may be rented by the week in the summer. *$$$; AE, MC, V; checks OK; www.pietyhillcottages.com; 2 blocks SE of Hwy 49.*

The Red Castle Historic Lodging / ★★★★
109 PROSPECT ST, NEVADA CITY; 530/265-5135 OR 800/761-4766
A towering, four-story red brick manse detailed with lacy white icicle trim, the Red Castle is a Gothic revival gem. The seven guest rooms (three are suites) have either a private porch or a garden terrace, and all of the bathrooms have recently been restyled in 1860 fashion. The oft-photographed Garden Room on the mansion's entry level is furnished with a canopy bed, French doors, and two mannequin arms that reach out for your towels in the bathroom. Smaller quarters are upstairs on the former nursery floor, but climb a bit higher and you'll find the three-room Garret Suite, where the private veranda provides a superb view of Nevada City. The Red Castle's ever-changing breakfast (prepared by an in-house chef) is a feast. Spirits were once rumored to visit the inn, which may explain a mix-up in reservations one reader experienced a few years ago. Call early for reservations if you are planning to visit in December. *$$$; MC, V; checks OK; www.historic-lodgings.com; call for directions.*

Grass Valley

Once known for rich quartz mines, Cornish pasties, and Gold Rush entertainers like dancers Lola Montez and Lotta Crabtree, Grass Valley

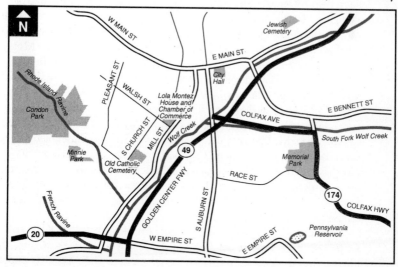

GRASS VALLEY

THE FAMOUS AND INFAMOUS

Gold! From Sutter's Mill the word spread like wildfire, bringing hordes of fortune seekers and adventurers from around the world to the Sierra foothills. But who would write their stories? Who would entertain them? And who would rob them of their gold?

It was *The Jumping Frog of Calaveras County* that first brought international fame to **Mark Twain**—and he heard the story while drinking in a saloon in Angels Camp. Between writing for newspapers in San Francisco and Carson City, Nevada, Twain hung out with his mining buddies on Mokelumne Hill near Jackson. This author and humorist has since become the George Washington of the Sierra foothills, with seemingly every third lodging claiming that "Mark Twain slept here."

Once mistress to Czar Nicholas I and the lunatic King Ludwig I of Bavaria, the beautiful and voluptuous **Lola Montez** arrived in Grass Valley on the arm of her second husband. But after she threw him out, she returned to doing what she thought she knew best—the Spider Dance. Wearing a scandalous knee-length skirt covered with cork tarantulas, Lola could always pack a theater—for one night. Despite her lack of talent, Lola took her act on the road, where the miners she entertained in the camps loved her—and Lola, in turn, loved them back.

Whatever Lola Montez lacked in talent, her Grass Valley neighbor **Lotta Crabtree** had in spades. Pushed by her mother, the gifted little girl performed in mining camps throughout the Sierras before moving to Boston, where she became a famous actress

has a historic and slightly scruffy downtown that's a pleasure to explore, as well as elegant bed-and-breakfasts and good restaurants. Stop at the **CHAMBER OF COMMERCE** (248 Mill St; 530/273-4667 or 800/655-4667; info@gvncchamber.org; www.gvncchamber.org), site of the Lola Montez home, for a free walking-tour map of the town and two terrific brochures listing more than two dozen scenic walking, hiking, and mountain biking trails. As you tour the town, be sure to stop at the 10-ton Pelton Waterwheel (at 30 feet in diameter, it's the world's largest) on display at the exemplary **NORTH STAR MUSEUM AND PELTON WHEEL EXHIBIT** (S end of Mill St at McCourtney Rd; 530/273-4255). The museum building, open daily from May through October, was once the powerhouse for the North Star Mine. Part of the park is wheelchair accessible. Make getting around town easy with an all-day pass on a **GOLD COUNTRY STAGE** (530/477-0103 or 888/660-7433; www.co.nevada.ca.us/gcstage/) shuttle; see Nevada City, above, for details.

Just outside of town is the 785-acre **EMPIRE MINE STATE HISTORIC PARK** (10791 E Empire St; 530/273-8522; www.cal-parks.ca.gov), the oldest, largest, deepest, and richest gold mine in California; its underground passages once extended 367 miles and descended 11,007 feet into

and the first female millionaire in the country.

Famous for saying "please" when he pointed his (empty) double-barrelled shotgun at Wells Fargo Stage drivers and demanded their strongbox full of gold, **Black Bart**—the "gentleman bandit"—never stole from the passengers riding the stage. Much of his success as a thief can be attributed to his skill as a backwoodsman and to his double life as a distinguished gentleman living in San Francisco, where he was known only as Charles E. Bolton.

The murderous activities attributed to outlaw **Joaquin Murieta** may have been the work of as many as five different Joaquins. More myth than man, and much romanticized in an 1854 biography, "Murieta" was a name soon whispered in fear by miners and printed in newspapers throughout California whenever gold was missing and bodies were found. Eventually killed by the California Rangers, Murieta's head was lopped off and placed in a jar, where it toured the state for one year. But was it Murieta's head, or that of another Joaquin?

The foothills are filled with stories of Gold Rush heroes whose fame may not have crossed the Sierra Nevada—like one-eyed **Charley Parker**, the woman who handled the reins of Wells Fargo stagecoaches in the guise of a man, and **Snowshoe Thompson**, who carried the miners' mail to Nevada and back over the snow-covered Sierra. Theirs are the stories that make up the lore of this region, and they can be heard in every town along the forty-niner trail. —*Susan Lyn McCombs*

the ground. A museum occupies a former stable, and the impressive granite and red brick **EMPIRE COTTAGE**, designed by San Francisco architect Willis Polk in 1897 for the mine's owner, is a prime example of what all that gold dust could buy. For the most part, the park is wheelchair accessible, and dogs on a leash are okay.

After touring Grass Valley, head about 5 miles west on Highway 20 for a pleasant side trip to the tiny town of **ROUGH AND READY**, which once chose to secede from the Union rather than pay a mining tax. Then continue on Highway 20 for another couple of miles and turn north on Pleasant Valley Road; 15 miles up the road is **BRIDGEPORT**, home of California's longest covered bridge. Built in 1862, the bridge provides a good spot for dangling your fishing line.

RESTAURANTS

Arletta's / ★★

212 W MAIN ST (THE HOLBROOKE HOTEL), GRASS VALLEY;
530/273-1353 OR 800/933-7077

The scrumptious meals at Arletta's make this restaurant more than just a convenient place to eat if you are staying at the Holbrooke Hotel.

Lunch offerings range from a club sandwich to a Chinese chicken salad, and dinner entrees include mesquite-smoked prime rib, oven-roasted breast of chicken stuffed with boursin cheese, pine nuts, and roasted red peppers; and seared salmon fillet in a three-peppercorn crust with lemon caper butter. Save room for one of the terrific desserts of the day. If you're a Mark Twain fan, you'll want to attend a Sunday brunch at the hotel, where local Chris Legate entertains diners as the notable 19th-century author and humorist. *$$$; AE, DC, DIS, MC, V; checks OK; lunch Mon–Sat, dinner every day, brunch Sun; full bar; reservations recommended; holbrooke@holbrooke.com; www.holbrooke.com; between S Church and Mill Sts, inside the Holbrooke Hotel.* &

Tofanelli's / ★★

302 W MAIN ST, GRASS VALLEY; 530/272-1468

Tofanelli's is one of Grass Valley's cultural and culinary meeting places. And when people convene here for lunch, they often order the restaurant's famous veggie burger. The tostadas also make a very good lunch, including the version topped with marinated chicken breast (or marinated tofu), brown rice, the house pinto beans, greens, carrots, and tomatoes. Tofanelli's whips up several vegetarian dishes, but the kitchen can also turn out a mean hamburger and Reuben sandwich. Each week the chefs prepare a new dinner menu, which might feature Brie chicken breast with pesto, red peppers, and garlic (also served as a sandwich for lunch), as well as the favored vegetarian lasagne with three cheeses, fresh spinach, and house-made marinara. Be sure to save room for Katherine's Chocolate Cake, complemented perfectly by one of Tofanelli's dozen coffee or espresso drinks. *$; AE, MC, V; checks OK; breakfast, lunch, dinner every day; beer and wine; reservations required for parties of 6 or more; next to the Holbrooke Hotel.* &

LODGINGS

The Holbrooke Hotel / ★★★

212 W MAIN ST, GRASS VALLEY; 530/273-1353 OR 800/933-7077

Mark Twain slept here. And so did entertainers Lola Montez and Lotta Crabtree, as well as the notorious gentleman-bandit Black Bart. Other heavyweight visitors to this historic Gold Rush hostelry include champion boxers Gentleman Jim Corbett and Bob Fitzsimmons and political prizefighters Ulysses S. Grant, Benjamin Harrison, Herbert Hoover, and Grover Cleveland. But don't be intimidated; despite its rugged Gold Rush grandeur, the 140-year-old brick Holbrooke Hotel is a relaxed and accommodating establishment. Many of the 27 guest rooms have private balconies, and all contain antiques, cable TVs tucked away in armoires, and contemporary bathrooms with those delightful (though not so contemporary) claw-footed bathtubs. A continental breakfast is served in the library. The hotel restaurant, Arletta's, is excellent (see review, above), and the Holbrooke's Golden Gate Saloon is the best bar on Main Street, so light sleepers should request a suite far from the libations. *$$; AE, DC, DIS, MC, V; checks OK; holbrooke@holbrooke.com; www.holbrooke.com; between S Church and Mill Sts.* &

Murphy's Inn / ★★★

318 NEAL ST, GRASS VALLEY; 530/273-6873 OR 800/895-2488

Once the personal estate of North Star and Idaho Mines owner Edward Coleman, Murphy's Inn has become one of Grass Valley's premier B&Bs. Marc and Rose Murphy established this well-known, highly regarded inn more than a decade ago, and now proprietors Ted and Nancy Daus are running the show. The main house has remained true to its 19th-century origins with its downstairs parlors and a bold brass-fronted fireplace, though the kitchen has taken a more contemporary turn. Families with young children are welcome to stay in one of the two suites in the Annex across the street from the building. The first-floor suite comes with a full kitchen, but guests are welcome to the full breakfast in the main house. In true Victorian style, all eight guest rooms are tastefully gussied up in an understated floral motif. Breakfast is a feast. *$$$; AE, MC, V; checks OK; www.murphysinn.com; at School St, 1 block from Main St.*

Auburn

The Gold Country's largest town, Auburn is sprawled on a bluff overlooking the American River and has been the seat of Placer County since 1850. Nowadays, Auburn serves mainly as a pit stop for vacationers headed for Lake Tahoe. Its few noteworthy sights, including **OLD TOWN** and the impressively domed **PLACER COUNTY COURTHOUSE** (101 Maple St; 530/889-6550), are best seen out the car window as you head toward the far more congenial towns of Grass Valley and Nevada City to the north. But if you're here to stretch your legs or get a bite to eat (there are some very good restaurants), stroll by the numerous bustling shops and restaurants that grace Old Town's streets. Many of these enterprises are housed in historic Gold Rush buildings, including the **SHANGHAI RESTAURANT** (289 Washington St; 530/823-2613), a Chinese establishment that has been open continuously since 1906 and displays a wonderful collection of memorabilia in its bar (where part of the movie *Phenomenon* was filmed starring John Travolta). A gigantic stone statue of Claude Chana, who discovered gold in the Auburn Ravine in 1848, marks the historic section. Other Old Town highlights include the whimsical **FIREHOUSE** (Lincoln Wy at Commercial St), the former 1852 **WELLS FARGO BANK** (Lincoln Wy, 1 block S of the firehouse), and the **POST OFFICE** (Lincoln Wy at Sacramento St), which first opened its doors in 1849. For more information, contact the Chamber of Commerce (601

Lincoln Wy; 530/885-5616). The north and middle forks of the American River in the **AUBURN STATE RECREATION AREA** (Hwy 49, 1 mile S of Auburn; 530/885-4527) are popular destinations for gold panners, swimmers, picnickers, and rafters. The recreation area also has great camping sites, hiking trails, equestrian trails, and mountain biking routes.

RESTAURANTS

Bootlegger's Old Town Tavern & Grill / ★★★

210 WASHINGTON ST, AUBURN; 530/889-2229

Located in a handsome old brick building in the heart of Auburn's historic center, Bootlegger's offers a large, eclectic seasonal menu that's so chock-full of interesting choices you'll want to come back several times to sample them all. One lunchtime winner is the *tacos de pescado*—marinated white fish on white corn tortillas with jack cheese, Napa cabbage, and a jalepeño cilantro aioli, topped with pico de gallo. For dinner, choose from an extensive list of pastas, grilled steak, ribs, lamb, or chicken, including Southern fried chicken, Mom's Meat Loaf, Maryland-style crab cakes, and sautéed pork loin with fresh pineapple and crimini mushrooms in a rosemary demi-glace. If that isn't enough to stimulate your appetite, Bootlegger's features special-occasion theme menus such as the Oktoberfest selection of sauerbraten and schnitzel. *$$$; AE, DIS, MC, V; checks OK; lunch Tues–Sat, dinner Tues–Sun; beer and wine; reservations recommended; bootlegg@foothill.net; www.bootleggers.com; in Old Town.* &

Latitudes / ★★★

130 MAPLE ST #200, AUBURN; 530/885-9535

Latitudes, which chef/owners Pat and Pete Enochs call their "world kitchen," is located in a lovely Victorian building just above Auburn's Old Town. Most of their cuisine is truly adventurous and wide-ranging (for example, you might find an African dish sharing the menu with a Cajun specialty), reflecting their desire to encourage people to try foods from other cultures. The lunch menu includes a terrific tofu Florentine (grilled with cashews, green onions, and spinach), a tenderloin fajita (pepper-coated tenderloin strips grilled with vegetables and red wine, served in a sun-dried tomato tortilla with lettuce and Caesar dressing), and a first-rate burger served with the best fries in town. Dinner is equally rewarding, with a juicy fillet of fresh Atlantic salmon, gingered prawns, East Indian curried tofu, and a fork-tender filet mignon. (If you brought the kiddies, ask for the children's menu.) The extensive wine and beer lists feature brands from around the world. And as if the great food weren't enough, Latitudes often has live music in its downstairs bar on Fridays and Saturdays. *$$; AE, DIS, MC, V; local checks only; lunch Mon–Fri (closed on Tues after Memorial Day), dinner Wed–Sun,* *brunch Sun; full bar; reservations recommended; latitudes@neworld.net; www.Latitudes@eatingsacramento.com; across from the courthouse.* &

Le Bilig / ★★★★

11750 ATWOOD RD, AUBURN; 530/888-1491

The sign in front of the modest building says "Bail Bonds," but open the correct door and you will discover what looks like a slice of the French countryside. This small jewel-box restaurant is the creation of husband-and-wife team Marc and Monica Deconinck. Marc is an accomplished and dedicated chef from Lille in northern France, and his specialty is hearty, rustic French comfort food—not unctuous, sauced French fare or prissy nouvelle cuisine. In winter, Deconinck might be dishing out a definitive French onion soup or ham hocks with lentils; in early spring, look for his lamb shanks roasted with fennel and thyme-scented tomatoes. There are also a few house specialties served nearly year-round—steak with Belgian fries, and Brittany-style whole-wheat or buckwheat crepes (*le bilig* means cast-iron crepe pan) with savory fillings like poached fresh salmon. The wine list has some rarities and bargains, including reasonably priced French bottles from the '70s and '80s as well as some local wines from El Dorado and Amador Counties. A few divine desserts are offered, such as the classic crème caramel and crepes suzette. For a great culinary treat, visit Le Bilig on the second Sunday of each month, when the Deconincks serve a prix-fixe French country feast. *$$$; MC, V; checks OK; dinner Wed–Sat (closed Suns June 21–Sep 21); beer and wine; reservations recommended; off Hwy 49, 1 block W of the Bel Air Shopping Center, at the N end of town.* &

Georgetown

When the tent city located here burned in 1852, this mountain town was rebuilt with much wider streets, which are now graced by a few noteworthy old buildings: **I.O.O.F. HALL** (at Main St and Hwy 193), **GEORGETOWN HOTEL** (6260 Main St), and the **AMERICAN RIVER INN** (see review, below), which had an earlier life as a boardinghouse. In the spring, spectacular displays of wild Scotch broom cover the Georgetown hillsides. At first glance there isn't much to do in this town, and after you've examined the **SIGNPOST FOREST** pointing the way to at least a dozen destinations out of town (feel free to put up your own) and sipped on a beverage at the karaoke bar in the Georgetown Hotel, you'll realize there isn't much to do at second glance either. But that's what your car is for, and if you want to experience small-town life in the foothills or, like Garbo, you just want to be alone, Georgetown is the place to be.

LODGINGS

American River Inn / ★★

**CORNER OF MAIN AND ORLEANS STS, GEORGETOWN; 530/333-4499
OR 800/245-6566**

This is the hotel that gold built. In the nearby community of Growlers-
burg, the gold nuggets were so big they growled as they rolled around the
miners' pans. One nugget taken from the Woodside Gold Mine (which
has tunnels running underneath the inn) weighed 126 ounces—the equiv-
alent of winning the Super Lotto today. Innkeepers Will and Maria Collin
and manager Betty Reed have done an exemplary job of maintaining the
inn's 25 guest rooms, which are spread out between two well-appointed
buildings dating back to the 1850s. Once you make your way past the
ceramic masks, teddy bears, and Elvis jigsaw puzzles spilling out into the
hallway from the gift shop, you will soon notice that most of the inn is
filled with interesting and beautiful antiques. The most luxurious room
is number 18, which takes up a generous portion of the second floor of
the handsome Queen Anne house. The hotel has a pool and spa, as well
as bicycles, a putting green, horseshoes, table tennis, badminton, a
driving range, and a croquet ground. If you arrive in Georgetown by
plane, take advantage of the inn's free airport limo. *$$; AE, MC, V;
checks OK; corner of Main and Orleans Sts.* ♿

Coloma

As every California schoolchild knows, the Gold Rush began here when
carpenter James Marshall found traces of the precious metal on January
24, 1848, at the sawmill he and John Sutter owned. A full-scale working
replica of the famous sawmill and other gold-related exhibits are dis-
played at **MARSHALL GOLD DISCOVERY STATE HISTORIC PARK** (Hwy
49; 530/622-3470; www.windjammer.net/coloma), a 280-acre expanse
of shaded lawns and picnic tables that extends through three-quarters of
the town. Most of the park is wheelchair accessible. Stop at the park's
small **GOLD DISCOVERY MUSEUM** (530/622-1166) for a look at Native
American artifacts and James Marshall memorabilia and pick up the self-
guided tour pamphlet outlining the park's highlights.

Coloma is silly with tourists and river rafters on summer weekends,
so try to plan your visit during the week, when you can picnic in peace
and float down the **AMERICAN RIVER** without fear of colliding into
others. To plan your **RIVER RAFTING TRIP**, contact www.caloutdoors.org
for a list of outfitters in the Sierra foothills or try the **EL DORADO
COUNTY CHAMBER OF COMMERCE** (542 Main St; 530/621-5885). Or
get completely away from the crowds and up into the clouds with **RIVER
CANYONS BY BALLOON** (530/622-4942). Alan Erghott offers hot-air
balloon rides for a one-of-a-kind, bird's-eye view of the Gold Country.

Visitors who have nerves of steel may find the whitewater-ballooning trips more enticing: Erghott will take your breath away as he swings the balloon's carriage within inches of the river, then soars 2,000 feet back into the sky. For a more mellow but certainly no less dramatic experience, attend an audience participation melodrama at the **OLDE COLOMA THEATER** (380 Monument Blvd; 530/626-5282). Performances are held Friday and Saturday nights from Memorial Day through late December. Popcorn throwing and booing are required.

RESTAURANTS

Adam's Red Brick Restaurant / ★★

1006 LOTUS RD, COLOMA; 530/621 4562

The decor on the beautiful brick walls of this former 1855 general store is definitely eclectic, and the bathrooms are a bit rustic, but the food, served up by husband-and-wife team Bruce and Jill Smith, makes up for whatever idiosyncrasies you may encounter here. The specialty of the house is the beef vindaloo—a spicy curry dish served with homemade mango chutney, rice, and in-season vegetables. Other standards include pork Madeira—a boneless pork cutlet sautéed in a Madeira wine gravy, a stuffed portobello (order ahead), and beef bourguignon. For dessert, Jill bakes fresh fruit cobblers, lemon or Key lime tart, chocolate fudge cake, and triple chocolate pie. The restaurant is only open on weekends, but special arrangements can be made for larger groups. Tucked behind the restaurant is the Smith's Golden Lotus B&B. A bit intimidating at first glance, it has six delightful rooms inside, each decorated floor to ceiling in themes ranging from Western to Tranquility. All have private baths. *$$$; MC, V; local checks only; dinner Fri–Sun; beer and wine; reservations required; 1 mile off Hwy 49, just past Henningsen Lotus Park.*

LODGINGS

Coloma Country Inn / ★★★

345 HIGH ST, COLOMA; 530/622-6919

Candi and Kerry Bliss are the new owners of this five-room B&B set in the heart of the Marshall Gold Discovery State Historic Park. (Adventure seekers, do not fear: former owner Alan Ehrgott is still offering hot-air balloon rides—see introduction.) The intimate 1852 inn provides a tranquil retreat from the summer crowds. The Rose room has both a private bath and its own patio. The lavender East Lake room comes with a private balcony and a view of the pond, as well as a private bath. Families might prefer the Cottage Suite, with a queen-size bed, and a daybed fitted with a trundle bed that can be used in combination to make a king-size bed. The suite also has a kitchenette, a sitting area, and private courtyard. Every day ends in a most civilized manner with iced tea and homemade cookies in the garden gazebo. *$$; MC, V; checks OK; www.colomacountry inn.com; in Marshall Gold Discovery State Historic Park.*

El Dorado

Three miles south of Placerville on Highway 49 sits the small town of El Dorado, whose denizens tolerate but in no way cultivate tourism. In fact, most travelers pass right on through—except for those who know about Poor Red's (see review, below), a bar and restaurant that may not look like much from the outside (or the inside, for that matter) but is known throughout the land for its famous cocktail.

RESTAURANTS

Poor Red's / ★

6221 PLEASANT VALLEY RD, EL DORADO; 530/622-2901

It's not often that small-town bars garner an international reputation, but this Cheers of the Gold Country has had its name translated into more tongues than a Robert Ludlum novel. It all started one night when the proud new owners of a gold-colored Cadillac asked the bartender to whip up a commemorative drink to celebrate their purchase. Grabbing the only thing behind the bar that was gold-colored (Galliano liqueur), the bartender dusted off the bottle, added a shot of this and a jigger of that, and eureka!—the frothy Golden Cadillac was born. By alchemic accident, this tiny Golden State saloon soon became the largest user of Galliano in North America (as the gilded plaque, sent from Italy and proudly displayed behind a glass showcase, attests). Legend has it that during Poor Red's, er, golden era, dozens of bottles were emptied per day as celebrities, dignitaries, and plain folks all queued up at the door for a chance to squeeze inside. Nowadays a line of motorcycles might be parked outside the bar on a weekend night, but inside the bar will be packed with friendly tourists and locals. The days are a bit more placid, with lawyers, doctors, and ranchers in baseball caps and boots politely ordering from a memorized menu of barbecued steak, ham, chicken, and pork (in fact, Dorothy, the lunchtime waitress, has been scribbling the same orders in her notepads for nearly two decades). *$; AE, DC, DIS, MC, V; checks OK; lunch Mon–Fri, dinner every day; full bar; no reservations; downtown.*

Placerville

One of the first camps settled by miners who branched out from Coloma, Placerville was dubbed Dry Diggins because of a lack of water. Its name was changed to Hangtown in 1849 after a series of grisly lynchings; it became Placerville in 1854 to satisfy local pride. Among the town's historical highlights is the brick-and-stone CITY HALL (487 Main St; 530/642-5200), which was built in 1860 and originally served as the town's firehouse, and PLACERVILLE COFFEE CO. (594 Main St; 530/642-8481), located in the Historic Soda Works building, home of the 150-foot gold mine. Another noteworthy edifice is the **HISTORIC CARY HOUSE HOTEL** (see review, below), where Mark Twain once lodged. Across the street, note the dangling dummy that marks the location of the town's infamous hanging tree. If you get a sudden longing for the *Wall Street Journal* or the *New York Times,* step into **PLACERVILLE NEWS** (409 Main St; 530/622-4510). The store has been run by the same family since 1912. Just a few doors down is **PLACERVILLE HARDWARE** (441 Main St; 530/622-1151), established in 1852. A single brass tack marks each foot along a section of the 100-foot-long store (two tacks mark every 5 feet), which is handy for measuring lumber or lengths of rope, and may just explain the origins of the expression "getting down to brass tacks."

A mile north of downtown Placerville is **GOLD BUG PARK**, home of the city-owned **GOLD BUG MINE** (Bedford Ave; 530/642-5238). Tours of the mine lead you deep into the cool, lighted shafts. **EL DORADO COUNTY HISTORICAL MUSEUM** (104 Placerville Dr; 530/621-5865), adjacent to the county fairgrounds, is open Wednesday through Sunday and showcases Pony Express paraphernalia, an original Studebaker wheelbarrow, a replica of a 19th-century general store, and a restored Concord stagecoach, plus other mining-era relics.

Every autumn, droves of people—about half a million each year—come to a small ridge just east of Placerville called **APPLE HILL ORCHARDS** (from Hwy 50, take the Carson Rd exit and follow the signs). What's the attraction? Why, apples, of course. Baked, fried, buttered, canned, candied, and caramelized apples, to name just a few variations. Dozens of vendors sell their special apple concoctions, and in September and October (peak apple-harvest season), if you don't mind the crowds, it's definitely worth a stop.

RESTAURANTS

Cafe Luna / ★★

451 MAIN ST #8, PLACERVILLE; 530/642-8669

Be sure to come with an appetite when you sit down at Cafe Luna. Not only is the food delicious and the portions generous, but the restaurant charges a table setting fee for just sitting down and sipping an iced tea while your dining partner gorges him- or herself with an entree. Sharing a meal will cost you as well. Since most lunches cost around $7, you might as well eat. And the eating is good here. The menu changes frequently, but a recent lunch included a fresh roasted turkey breast sandwich with avocado, artichoke hearts, and provolone cheese, and a penne pasta with eggplant, roasted red bell peppers, zucchini, and mushrooms. Dinner might include thinly sliced pork loin marinated in Southwestern spices, charbroiled on an open flame and topped with a sweet and spicy jalepeño and orange marinade, or the Pasta Raphael—a rich blend of salmon, fresh tomatoes, artichoke hearts, sweet onion, fresh basil, and white wine. *$$;*

MC, V; checks OK; lunch Mon–Sat, dinner Wed–Sat; beer and wine; reservations recommended; 2 doors from the courthouse. ♿

Sweetie Pies / ★★

577 MAIN ST, PLACERVILLE; 530/642-0128

Stop for lunch at this cute little house on Main Street and order one of the freshly made soups served with house-baked sourdough bread. Or you might fancy a slice of the vegetable quiche and a freshly tossed garden salad. Whatever you choose, save room for the pie. Better yet, eat dessert first—it's that good. Don't miss the knockout thick, rich olallieberry pie or the rhubarb pie filled with tart chunks of the real thing. Other sweet-tooth delights include cream pies and cinnamon and pecan rolls. Should you need more than a sugar rush to get you pumped, various coffee drinks ought to do the trick. Breakfasts at Sweetie Pies can be rich and filling: waffles, pancakes, egg dishes, and biscuits topped with a spicy sausage gravy; or sweet and simple: coffee, tea, pastries, muffins, and, of course, pies. *$; MC, V; checks OK; breakfast every day, lunch Mon–Sat; beer and wine; reservations recommended; across from the Historic Soda Works building.* ♿

Zachary Jacques / ★★★★

1821 PLEASANT VALLEY RD, PLACERVILLE; 530/626-8045

The decor at Zachary Jacques may be French country with touches of California Western, but the cuisine is definitely all French country, and it's superb. Chef/owners Christian and Jennifer Masse offer a seasonal menu that recently featured a sweetbread appetizer sautéed in port wine and mushrooms; roast pork tenderloin served in garlic, honey, and rosemary; and lamb tenderloin in a Côtes du Rhone sauce, served with ratatouille and potato pancake. On Wednesday nights the house specialty is cassoulet, the classic French stew of white beans, duck, sausage, and lamb that takes days to prepare and is rarely served in American restaurants. Finding the perfect bottle of wine to accompany your order is never a problem: the wine list, which received an award of excellence from the highly respected *Wine Spectator* magazine, features more than 300 French and American labels. In June, July, and August the restaurant hosts popular wine tastings featuring French and local foothill wines as well as French hors d'oeuvres. *$$$; AE, MC, V; no checks; dinner Wed–Sun; beer and wine; reservations recommended; www.eldoradomall.com; 3 miles E of Diamond Springs.* ♿

LODGINGS

Chichester-McKee House / ★★

800 SPRING ST, PLACERVILLE; 530/626-1882 OR 800/831-4008

This gracious Victorian home, built in 1892 by lumber baron D.W. Chichester, was the finest house in Placerville at the time and the first to have the luxury of indoor plumbing. Today the refurbished home still has the look and feel of the late 1800s—except, of course, for its updated plumbing. All four guest rooms have queen-size, Victorian-era bedsteads, stained glass, fireplaces trimmed with carved wood and marble, and private baths. You won't find televisions in the guest rooms of this B&B, but the grand old house offers something even better—a library. And despite the location on occasionally busy Spring Street, all is peaceful inside Chichester-McKee. Guests can munch on homemade caramel brownies in the evening and feast in the morning on a full breakfast served in the dining room. *$$; AE, DIS, MC, V; checks OK; info@innlover.com; www.innlover.com; on Hwy 49, 1½ blocks N of Hwy 50.*

Combellack Blair House / ★★

3059 CEDAR RAVINE RD, PLACERVILLE; 530/622-3764

A spectacular sight, the recently renovated Combellack Blair House is trimmed with gingerbread and guarded by a white picket fence. White wicker furniture graces the large front veranda and a love swing hangs on the back porch. (Sounds like the setting for a Hallmark commercial, right? But wait—there's more.) Just off the porch you'll see a gazebo, a rose garden, and a little waterfall. Of course, proprietors Marlene and Loren DeLaurenti have made sure the Queen Anne Victorian theme continues inside—from the sweeping spiral staircase to the rich wood moldings and the floral carpets. The three guest rooms have private baths and queen-size beds and are tastefully appointed. Unfortunately, the house fronts a relatively busy street. *$$; MC, V; checks OK; comblair@c-zone. net; www.c-zone.net/comblair; E end of Main St, turn right on Cedar Ravine Rd.*

Historic Cary House Hotel / ★★

300 MAIN ST, PLACERVILLE; 530/622-4271

Originally built in 1857, refurbished in the late 1980s, and redecorated between 1997 and 2000, the Cary House is a historically significant Victorian inn centrally located on Main Street. The four-story brick building was the headquarters of the Wells Fargo stage lines during the Gold Rush, and according to local lore, $90 million worth of bullion was dumped over time on the hotel's porch before it was transported to the U.S. Mint in San Francisco. Years later, newspaper editor Horace Greeley used the balcony above the porch to make his "Go West, young man" presidential campaign speech to miners. All 36 of the simple, comfortable guest rooms are decorated with antiques and have received a fresh coat of paint, new beds, carpets, and drapes; each has a private bath, a remote-control TV, and a phone. A continental breakfast is served in the pantry, but many units have kitchenettes. Six rooms overlook the street, though old Hangtown ain't as noisy and rambunctious as it was in its wild youth.

*Who is? $$$; AE, DIS, MC, V; no checks; hchh@caryhouse.com; www.
caryhouse.com; between Bedford and Spring Sts.*

The Shafsky House / ★★

2942 COLOMA ST, PLACERVILLE; 530/642-2776

Guests slip off their shoes and step into the early 1900s when they enter
this absolutely charming Queen Anne–style house. A soothing refresh-
ment and a pair of slippers awaits new arrivals. Lining the walls of the
stairway to the second floor are photographs of the Shafsky family,
including Albert Shafsky, who came to the United States from Moldavia
in the late 1800s, and his daughter Alberta Shafsky (who celebrated her
101st birthday in 2000). Decorated with antiques, the three guest rooms
come with private baths and king- or queen-size beds (with featherbeds
and goose-down comforters in the winter months). Breakfast is served on
china and silver in the elegant dining room between 8am and 10am;
guests can dine in private or in the company of the other guests. Of
course, if you are staying in the Sapphire Suite, your breakfast can also
be delivered to your room. *$$; DIS, MC, V; local checks only;
shafsky@directcon.net; www.shafsky.com; 1 block N of Hwy 50, at the
corner of Spring and Coloma Sts.*

Kyburz

LODGINGS

Strawberry Lodge / ★★

17510 HWY 50, KYBURZ; 530/659-7200

Wedged between the giant conifers and granite headwalls of Lake Tahoe's
southwestern rim, Strawberry Lodge has been the headquarters for a cor-
nucopia of year-round outdoor activities for more than a century. Named
for the wild strawberry patches that once covered the area, the lodge has
45 rooms (most with private baths) that often get booked up during the
peak months of summer and winter (the place does a fierce wedding business). The rooms overlooking the river are the quietest. In the new section
(built in 1997), the rooms feature cabin-style log furniture, and all come

with private baths. The rooms in Annex Lodge (across the highway) vary
in size, also come with private baths, and are among the least expensive.
Families or small groups might prefer the Hawks Nest, with two queen-
size beds and a single, in the new wing of the lodge, or the River House—
a cabin at the edge of the American River's south fork. The Strawberry
Lodge's dining room serves breakfast, lunch, and dinner and offers fresh-
baked bread, steaks, chicken, seafood, and a daily pasta special. *AE, MC,
V; no checks; open every day Memorial Day–Labor Day (Fri–Sat and
holidays only Labor Day–Memorial Day); www.strawberry-lodge.com;
43 miles E of Placerville, 9 miles E of Kyburz.*

Somerset

LODGINGS

Fitzpatrick Winery and Lodge / ★★

7740 FAIRPLAY RD, SOMERSET; 530/620-3248 OR 800/245-9166

If you've never experienced true Irish hospitality, reserve a night at Brian and Diana Fitzpatrick's country-style winery and lodge. Sitting atop a hill with a commanding 360-degree view of the countryside, their lodge has five guest rooms: French Basque, Irish, Old Fairplay, the Wine Maker's Suite, and the Log Suite. Guests may also dive into the new 25-meter lap pool and bask in the sun at tables on the expanded deck, where meats and breads are often cooked on the outdoor wood-fired oven. A full breakfast and complimentary glasses of the Fitzpatricks' wine are included in the room rate. On Friday nights during the extended evenings of daylight saving time, the Fitzpatricks serve wood-fired oven pizza, salad, cheesecake, and, of course, wine. Reservations are required. *$$$; AE, DC, DIS, MC, V; checks OK; www.fitzpatrickwinery.com; off Mount Aukum Rd, 6 miles SE of town.* ⅃

Southern Gold Country

The rolling hills of the southern Gold Country are honeycombed with mysterious caverns and abandoned mines, including the deepest gold mines on the continent. The mining boom went bust by 1860, and most of the Gold Rush towns were abandoned by the 1870s. Some have survived by mining for tourist dollars instead, and as a result it's not always easy to steer clear of tourist trappings. Most people journey to this area for the fishing, camping, hiking, rafting, and mountain biking, though some still come to pan for gold.

Plymouth

Plymouth may be best known as the starting point of the **AMADOR COUNTRY WINERIES** (209/267-2297), located along the Shenandoah Valley Road. The town's **POKERVILLE MARKET** (18170 Hwy 49; 209/245-6986) carries almost all of the wines produced in the area and sells them at a low price. If you are planning to visit the wineries, the market is also a great place to pick up a picnic lunch to take with you.

LODGINGS

Indian Creek Bed and Breakfast / ★★★

21950 HWY 49, PLYMOUTH; 209/245-4648

 Part of Indian Creek's popularity is simply a matter of location—it's right off Highway 49 and conveniently close to Amador County's Shenandoah

Valley wineries. But it's not just the location that keeps folks coming back. Steve Noffsinger and Lena Stiward run this beautiful B&B on 10 wooded acres outside Plymouth, where you can relax by the artesian-fed pond, peer into a secret gold mine, sunbathe on your private deck, or drink whiskey in the way-cool Cowboy Bar (bring your own booze, though, 'cause they don't have a liquor license). Indian Creek B&B was originally built in 1923 by Hollywood producer Arthur Hamburger, who entertained such celebrity guests as John Wayne. Hence the playful (but tastefully done) cowboy/Indian theme running throughout the lodge. Indian Creek offers four guest rooms (all with private baths, queen-size beds, air conditioning, and ceiling fans), and the top gun is the decidedly feminine Margaret Breen room, which has French doors that open onto a private deck. Cowboy wannabes may prefer the Way Out West room, festooned with real cowboy toys. After a bounteous gourmet breakfast, rest yer tired dogs by the pool or in one of the shaded two-person hammocks—it's a fantastic place to unwind from the hustle and bustle of daily life. *$$$; DIS, MC, V; checks OK; info@indiancreek.com; www.indiancreek.com; 3 miles N of Plymouth.*

Amador City

RESTAURANTS

Imperial Hotel Restaurant / ★★★

14202 HWY 49, AMADOR CITY; 209/267-9172 OR 800/242-5594

This elegant restaurant is under the domain of talented chef Bill Waldear, who prepares first-rate California-French cuisine. The menu changes seasonally, but a summer menu might include a smoked pork chop with fig and onion confit or the pan-broiled rib eye with a provençal herb crust. Fresh seafood is offered nightly; the restaurant flies in fresh fish several times a week. Pastry chef Ingrid Fraser is in charge of a dessert menu that features such delights as crème brûlée, custom-made ice cream, and a selection of cakes and tortes. On warm summer evenings request a table on the back patio. *$$$; AE, DC, DIS, MC, V; checks OK; dinner Tues–Sun, brunch Mother's Day and Easter; full bar; reservations recommended; host@imperialamador.com; www.imperialamador.com; downtown.* &

LODGINGS

Imperial Hotel / ★★★

14202 HWY 49, AMADOR CITY; 209/267-9172 OR 800/242-5594

Proprietors Bruce Sherrill and Dale Martin restored this century-old brick hotel in 1988, striking a marvelous balance between elegance and whimsy. One of the best examples of their playful talent is on display in the Oasis Bar: a fresco fantasy of a Saharan oasis complete with palm trees, belly dancers, and camels. The six upstairs guest rooms house numerous antiques as well as hand-painted furnishings by local artist John Johannsen. Room 6 is one of the quietest, but room 1 is everyone's favorite, with its high ceiling, queen-size canopy bed, giant windows, and French doors that open onto a private balcony overlooking Main Street (granted, you have to put up with some traffic noise, but the old brick hotel is located on a slow curve, so no one's going terribly fast). Breakfast is served downstairs, in your room, or on the patio or balcony. *$$; AE, DC, DIS, MC, V; checks OK; host@imperialamador; www.imperial amador.com; downtown.*

Sutter Creek

"Big Four" railroad baron Leland Stanford made his millions at Sutter Creek's Lincoln Mine, then used his wad to invest in the Transcontinental Railroad and fund his successful campaign to become governor of California. Sutter Creek is the self-proclaimed "nicest little town in the Mother Lode" and was named after sawmill owner John Sutter. It boasts some beautiful 19th-century buildings that you can admire from the street, including the recently reopened landmark **KNIGHT'S FOUNDRY HISTORIC WATER-POWERED IRON WORKS** (81 Eureka St; 209/267-0201), the last water-powered foundry and machine shop in the nation, and the **DOWNS MANSION** (Spanish St, across from the Immaculate Conception Church), the former home of the foreman at Leland Stanford's mine. Also worth exploring: the Asian furnishings and Native American and Mexican folk art at the **COBWEB COLLECTION** (83 Main St; 209/267-0690) and the gallery/home accessories store at **PASSAGES** (73 Main St; 209/267-5225). For the pooch you left at home, fetch a doggie treat or two from the **THREE DOG BAKERY** (16 Eureka St; 209/267-1500).

RESTAURANTS

Zinfandels / ★★★

51 HANFORD ST, SUTTER CREEK; 209/267-5008
Chef Greg West, a six-year veteran of Greens (San Francisco's most famous vegetarian restaurant), has teamed up with pastry chef/baker/wife Kelley West to provide their version of light (but not meatless) California cuisine to the southern Gold Country. The Wests' menu changes monthly, incorporating the best local farm produce and seasonal ingredients. A meal might begin with two popular appetizers: crisp polenta topped with mushrooms, garlic, shallots, and fresh herbs and cream, and Medicated Goo—a small round of homemade bread hollowed out and filled with blue Castello cheese, toasted walnuts, pan-fried garlic, and fresh herbs. For the main course, standouts include a butternut squash risotto with pancetta, leeks, crimini mushrooms, and spinach; and the Copper River salmon topped with Morello cherry beurre rouge (red

THERE'S WINE IN THEM THAR HILLS

Those forty-niners had more than gold to keep them company—they had wine! During the Gold Rush, dozens of wineries existed in the Sierra foothills. Sadly, the end of the mining boom and Prohibition brought a severe wine-making drought to the region. Today, however, there are more than 60 wineries in the area from Mariposa to Nevada Counties, producing, naturally enough, gold-medal-winning wines. Most of the wineries are only 20 or 30 years old, but you can still find 100-year-old mission grapevines growing in some of the vineyards.

Thirty-two varietals flourish within the microclimates of the foothills, resulting in wines from barberas to gewürztraminers to zinfandels. Fortunately, wine enthusiasts do not have to travel all over the counties and down isolated roads to taste them. Most of the **Amador County Wineries** (209/267-2297; www.amadorwine.com) are situated along the Shenandoah Valley Road out of Plymouth. The nine wineries in **Calaveras County** (800/225-3764, ext. 25; www.calaveraswines.org) are within a 3-mile radius of the town of Murphys, and five tasting rooms are right in town. The majority of wineries in **El Dorado County** (800/306-3956; www.eldoradowines.org) are centered around the Apple Hill area and between the towns of Fairplay and Mount Akum. A map to all the wineries can be found throughout the region in the *Vine Times*, a complimentary wine newspaper, and county winery maps can be picked up in visitors centers and in most lodgings. Many of the wineries are open daily and most offer free wine tasting, with a friendly staff ready to answer all your questions.

While the "quaint" factor of the tasting rooms has little to do with how a wine tastes, the atmosphere surrounding the wine adds to the wine taster's experience. Listed below are just a few among the more interesting to see.

Boeger (1709 Carson Rd, Placerville; 530/622-8094; www.boegerwinery.com).

butter) and served with orange pumpkin seed, wild rice, and basmati rice pilaf. Zinfandels also offers a well-edited list of locally produced wines, and the chef thoughtfully highlights the perfect wine to accompany each dish on the menu. There are even a couple of very reasonably priced "Just for Kids" plates available. *$$$; AE, DIS, MC, V; checks OK; dinner Thurs–Sun; beer and wine; reservations recommended; Wild4Zin@aol.com; N end of downtown.*

LODGINGS

Eureka Street Inn Bed and Breakfast / ★★
55 EUREKA ST, SUTTER CREEK; 209/267-5500

 Owners Chuck and Sandy Anderson took over this quaint Craftsman-style inn, formerly known as the Picturerock Inn, in 1999. Step into the

Started by the Lamardo Fossati Family in 1850, this winery is surrounded by both vineyards and pear orchards—a perfect picnic spot. Try the Gold Medal barbera served in the 1857 Swiss Italian stone wine cellar and tasting room.

Sierra Vista (4560 Cabernet Wy, end of Leisure Ln; 530/622-7221; www.sierravista winery.com). Taste the flagship Rhône-style wines of this family-operated winery while gazing at the magnificent view of the snowcapped Sierra Nevada Mountains. Picnic tables rest on the shaded lawn, circled by a flower garden. Tours of the winery are available by appointment.

Stevenot (2690 San Domingo Rd, Murphys; 209/728-0638; www.stevenotwinery. com). Guests can sip the winery's signature chardonnay in the 1887 Shaw ranch house. Across the dirt driveway, a sod roof and the surrounding vineyards camouflage the winery's 1906 Alaska house, soon to become a museum. Grapevines grow so close to the building, you'll be tempted to pick the grapes yourself. During the summer, Shakespearean plays are performed on the pretty lawn.

Story Winery (10525 Bell Rd, Plymouth; 209/245-6208). Hundred-year-old mission grapevines grow in the vineyards of this family-operated winery that produces mission, zinfandel, and chenin blanc wines. The cabinlike tasting room and picnic area are dramatically perched above the Consumnes River, offering visitors an exciting view of the canyon.

Villa Toscano (106000 Shenandoah School House Rd; 209/245-3800; www.villa toscano.com). The faux-red-clay tasting room rises above the formal grounds of this Tuscan-style villa with two koi ponds, roses, and round mosaic cafe tables. This is one of the newest wineries in the region, and it produces barbera and sangiovese, among other wines. —*Susan Lyn McCombs*

living room with its overstuffed leather sofa and stained glass windows, and you'll feel instantly feel at home. The downstairs common areas are comfortable and cozy, and the four guest rooms on the second floor are bright, cheerful, and tastefully decorated with antiques. Chuck is in charge of the gourmet breakfasts (eggs Benedict on artichoke hearts, cheese blintzes, French toast, poached pears), served in the formal dining room. *$$; DIS, MC, V; checks OK; may be closed last 2 weeks of Dec and all of Jan; innkeeper@eurekastreettinn.com: www.eurekastreet inn.com; 1½ blocks off Main St, near the Foundry.*

The Foxes in Sutter Creek Bed and Breakfast Inn / ★★★

77 MAIN ST, SUTTER CREEK; 209/267-5882 OR 800/987-3344

 For nearly two decades Pete and Min Fox have run the finest B&B in Sutter Creek. An immaculate garden fronts the Gold Rush–era foundation, and from there it only gets better. Each of the seven guest rooms is furnished with antiques, including massive, elaborate Victorian head-boards and armoires that seem too priceless to actually use. All of the rooms have private baths, and five have fireplaces. What helps account for this B&B's popularity is the breakfast experience: you get to choose your meal from the Foxes' menu (special dietary requests are accommodated, too), and the hearty spread is delivered with the morning paper on a silver platter to your room or at the garden gazebo. Located on Main Street, the inn is only steps away from Sutter Creek's shops and restaurants. Reserve ahead to avoid a two-month wait for weekend stays during peak seasons. *$$$; DIS, MC, V; checks OK; foxes@cdepot.net; www.foxesinn.com; downtown.*

Grey Gables Inn / ★★

161 HANFORD ST, SUTTER CREEK; 209/267-1039 OR 800/473-9422
This adorable Victorian retreat is run by Roger and Sue Garlick, two ever-friendly British expatriates. Surrounded by terraces of colorful, meticulously manicured gardens, their three-story inn has eight plushly carpeted guest rooms named after British poets and writers. Sue's favorite, the Byron Room, is bedecked in hues of deep green and Normandy rose, which pairs well with the dark wood furnishings and Renaissance revival bed. Aside from the king-size bed in the Brontë Room, all of the boudoirs have queen-size beds, gas-log fireplaces, large armoires, air conditioning, and private baths (a few with claw-footed tubs). A bounteous breakfast, delivered on fine English bone china, is served either in the formal dining room or in your room. And in true English fashion there is an informal tea every afternoon from 3pm to 4pm; wine and cheese is served daily from 6pm to 7pm. The only drawback to this English Eden is that the house abuts heavily traveled Highway 49, though the rooms are soundproofed. On the plus side, Sutter Creek's shops and restaurants are only a short walk away. *$$$; AE, DIS, MC, V; checks OK; greygables@aol.com; www.greygables.com; on Hwy 49, at the N end of town.* &

Ione

When you pull out your map and search for Ione, your suspicions will immediately be confirmed: the town exists smack dab in the middle of nowhere. But within this little town's borders lie the 18-hole **CASTLE OAKS CHAMPIONSHIP GOLF COURSE** (1000 Castle Oaks Dr; 209/274-0167) and the pretty **GREENSTONE WINERY** (Hwy 88 at Jackson Valley Rd; 209/274-2238), open for wine tasting Friday through Sunday year-round (Wed–Sun July–Aug). True, there isn't much else in the way of entertainment 'round these parts, but Sutter Creek, Jackson, and the wineries along Shenandoah Valley Road are only 11 miles away.

LODGINGS

The Heirloom Bed and Breakfast Inn / ★★★

214 SHAKELEY LN, IONE; 209/274-4468 OR 888/628-7896

One of the most charming B&Bs in the Gold Country has recently been purchased by innkeepers Sherry and Richard Scagliola. Well-loved gardens grace this Southern antebellum mansion, a favored sight for weddings and receptions. Each of the inn's six guest rooms (all with private baths) is cleverly named to correspond to its seasonal advantages. The Summer Room is shaded by a 150-year-old walnut tree; the Springtime Room's private balcony overlooks the garden; and the Winter Room has a fireplace, an extra-long tub, and a hand-carved four-poster bed. The Room for All Seasons is in a detached cottage built of handcrafted 16-inch-thick rammed-earth walls (which maintain pleasant temperatures year-round), framed by California cedars, redwoods, and pines. A family might prefer the small (even cramped) two-room Carriage House with its TV and extra trundle bed. A full breakfast, whipped up by Sherry (a former caterer and baker), can be served in the garden or in the dining room. Golf buffs will be happy to know an 18-hole golf course is only five blocks away. *$$; AE, MC, V; checks OK; www.heirloominn.com; first left off Preston from Main St.*

Jackson

Just beyond an enormous Georgia Pacific lumber mill lies Jackson, the seat of Amador County. Jackson hides most of its rowdy past behind modern facades, but old-timers know the town (once called "little Reno") as the last place in California to outlaw prostitution. For a trip back in time, take a gander at the **NATIONAL HOTEL** (2 Water St; 209/223-0500), which has been in continuous operation since 1862 and has built up quite a guest list: Will Rogers, John Wayne, Leland Stanford, and almost every other California governor in the 19th century stayed here. Ragtime tunes and classic oldie sing-alongs are played on the grand piano, and guests register for the spartan rooms with the bartender through a wooden cage at the back of the saloon.

A sight Gold Rush buffs shouldn't miss is the **AMADOR COUNTY MUSEUM** (225 Church St; 209/223-6386), which has scale models of the local hard-rock mines. It's open Wednesday through Sunday. There's also **KENNEDY TAILING WHEELS PARK** (take Main St to Jackson Gate Rd, just N of Jackson; no phone), site of the Kennedy and Argonaut Mines, the Mother Lode's deepest. Though these mines have been closed for decades, their head frames and huge tailing wheels (some are 58 feet in diameter) remain to help show how waste from the mines was conveyed over the hills to a settling pond. If you're a wannabe gold panner, hire a guide to take you to **ROARING CAMP MINING COMPANY** (209/296-4100) on the Mokelumne River, where you can try your luck and enjoy a cookout.

RESTAURANTS

Upstairs Restaurant & Streetside Bistro / ★★

164 MAIN ST, JACKSON; 209/223-3342

Chef Layne McCollum, who learned his trade at the California Culinary Academy, presides over this two-story restaurant housed in a handsome Gold Rush–era building made of exposed brick and petrified wood. The bright, cheery Streetside Bistro—tastefully furnished with wrought-iron furniture, tile flooring, and colorful oil paintings—offers quiche, soups, salads, and gourmet sandwiches such as smoked pork loin with red chile pesto for lunch. For dinner, take the stairway to the Upstairs Restaurant, a long, narrow room of exposed brick and glass furnished with white-linen-topped tables graced with fresh flowers and oil lamps. McCollum's small, contemporary American menu changes weekly, though you might encounter pasta puttanesca prepared with tomato-basil fettuccine, smoked vegetables grilled with pesto, or grilled boneless breast of duck topped with blackberry-ginger sauce. A prix-fixe five-course special is offered on every menu. *$$$; AE, DIS, MC, V; checks OK; lunch, dinner Wed–Sun; beer and wine; reservations recommended; downtown.*

Volcano

This tiny town with fewer than 100 residents is so wonderfully authentic that it borders on decrepit (it doesn't get more Gold Rush–genuine than this, folks). During the heady mining days, this unusually sophisticated town built the state's first library and its first astronomical observatory. Nowadays you can see some preserved buildings and artifacts, including a Civil War cannon. An outdoor amphitheater, hidden behind stone facades along Main Street, is the site of popular summer theatricals performed by the **VOLCANO THEATRE COMPANY** (on Main St, 1 block N of the St. George Hotel; 209/296-2525). And at nearby **INDIAN GRINDING ROCK STATE HISTORIC PARK** (located 1 mile S of Volcano off Pine Grove/Volcano Rd; 209/296-7488) you'll find 3,000-year-old petroglyphs and an enormous limestone outcropping—the largest of its kind in America—dotted with thousands of holes created by generations of native Miwoks who ground their acorn meal on the rock here. The park also has a fine Indian artifacts museum and a replica of a Miwok ceremonial roundhouse. After touring the town, take the side trip up winding Ram's Horn Grade to cool off in the funky, friendly bar at the **ST. GEORGE HOTEL**. Or, in early spring, picnic amid the nearly half-million daffodils (and more than 100 varieties) in bloom on **DAFFODIL HILL,** a 4-acre ranch 3 miles north of Volcano (follow the signs on Ram's Horn Grade; no phone).

RESTAURANTS

The St. George Hotel Restaurant / ★★★

16104 MAIN ST, VOLCANO; 209/296-4458

There's a super chef in town and he works at the St. George Hotel restaurant. After 40 years of a menu that was basically pancakes for breakfast and a slab of prime rib for dinner, chef/owner Mark Berkner has introduced a seasonal menu based on his own version of California cuisine. Appetizers during the summer might include a smoked salmon and cheese tart or a Mediterranean bruschetta. Locals drive in from Jackson for lamb and fish entrees like the South of the Border Grilled Salmon topped with mango salsa. For those who long for that traditional slab of meat, Berkner may grill up a thick-cut pork chop served in a caramelized onion and red wine sauce, or a New York steak topped with wild mushrooms. Choosing from the dessert menu isn't easy, but the Frozen Chocolate Nut Mousse with macadamia nut filling and Oreo cookie crust is definitely something to sigh over. *$$$; AE, MC, V; checks OK; dinner Thurs–Sun, brunch Sun (closed 3 weeks in Jan or Feb); full bar; reservations recommended; stgeorge @volcano.net; www.stgeorgehotel.com; downtown.*

LODGINGS

The St. George Hotel / ★★

16104 MAIN ST, VOLCANO; 209/296-4458

In its heyday in the 1860s, the burgeoning village of Volcano offered a tired miner his choice of 17 hotels. Those whose pockets held the largest nuggets chose the St. George. The three-story hotel wrapped with balconies and entwined with Virginia creeper is still a gold mine for anyone spending an evening in this little town. Owners Tracey and Mark Berkner have spent the past few years recapturing some the hotel's original charm: the restaurant (see review, above) is delightful, the parlor and grounds exquisite (think weddings), and the rooms in the modernized Annex bright and comfortable. The 14 guest rooms in the main building are by far the most interesting. Each room is decorated with antiques and the personal effects donated by admired friends and relatives. The rooms in back have great views of the garden and are perfect for morning people who like to rise with the sun. Otherwise, your best bet is to ask for a balcony room in front. On the downside, all 14 rooms share a total of five bathrooms. A continental breakfast, served in the large downstairs parlor, can also be enjoyed in the garden. *$$; AE, MC, V; checks OK; open Wed–Sun, closed 3 weeks in Jan or Feb; stgeorge@volcano.net; www.stgeorgehotel.com; downtown.* &

Angels Camp

Cruise right through the overcommercialized and truly uninspiring town of San Andreas and you'll eventually pull into Angels Camp, made famous by Mark Twain's short story "The Celebrated Jumping Frog of Calaveras County." Every year on the third weekend in May, thousands of frog fans flock to the **CALAVERAS COUNTY FAIR** (at the county fairgrounds; 209/736-2561; 2 miles S of town) to witness the **JUMPING FROG JUBILEE**, one of the premier frog-jumping contests in the world. The festival also features a rodeo, carnival rides, live music, and—for those of you who forgot to bring one—frogs for rent. *Ribbit.*

RESTAURANTS

Camps / ★★★

676 MCCAULEY RANCH RD, ANGELS CAMP; 209/736-8181

A bit hard to find, Camps is ensconced within sprawling Greenhorn Creek golf resort on the western fringes of Angels Camp. Head chef Renee Gianettoni (who worked under the former executive chef Jean Paul Lucy) continues to provide a cuisine that pairs local produce with European, Asian, and Caribbean cooking techniques. The menu changes frequently, but you can count on a variety of cuts of certified Angus beef, fresh fish, and organically grown vegetables. The crisp roasted duck with kumquat and sun-dried cherries is a popular dish and an example of some of the unusual flavors Gianettoni uses to enhance her entrees. With a thoughtful eye toward the families that have private homes at the resort, Camps offers a kids' menu for around $5. Come see for yourself; request a table on the veranda, or relax amid the natural earth tones and antique wood furniture. Oh, and PGA wannabes should bring their golf clubs. *$$$; AE, MC, V; checks OK; breakfast, lunch, dinner every day, brunch Sun; full bar; reservations recommended; www.greenhorncreek.com; ½ mile W on Hwy 4, from N junction of Hwys 4 and 49.* &

LODGINGS

The Cottages at Greenhorn Creek / ★★★

626 MCCAULEY RANCH RD, ANGELS CAMP; 209/736-8120 OR 888-736-5900

More than 30 individual, newly built houses are available for rent on a daily basis at the quiet Greenhorn Creek Resort. Each cottage is roughly 1,300 square feet, with two master suites, two bathrooms, and a fully equipped kitchen in a "great room" that includes a dining area and a comfortable living room, complete with TV and VCR. If an entire house is more than you need, each cottage can be separated into a one-bedroom suite and a one-bedroom hotel room with the turn of a key. It's not exactly the traditional Sierra foothills experience, but if you've ever wanted to live at a golf resort, these cottages are ideal. Not only is the restaurant Camps (see review, above) within walking distance, but guests have access to the swimming pool and fitness center. *$$$$; AE, MC, V; checks OK; request@greenhorncreek.com; www.greenhorncreek.com; ½ mile W on Hwy 4, from N junction of Hwys 4 and 49.*

Murphys

Gingerbread Victorian homes behind white picket fences and tall locust trees border the streets in Murphys, a former trading post set up by brothers Dan and John Murphy in cooperation with local Native Americans (John married the chief's daughter). It's worth taking the detour off Highway 49 just to stroll down Murphys' tree-lined Main Street or, better yet, to sample the regions' brews at the **MURPHYS HISTORIC HOTEL AND LODGE** (see review, below). Most of the **CALAVERAS WINERIES** (209/736-6722 or 800/225-3764, ext. 25; www.calaveraswines.org) have tasting rooms right in the heart of town. Peer below the foundations of **MURPHYS CREEK ANTIQUES** next the hotel to find the cave-like interior of the tasting room at **ZUCCA** (209/728-1623). Just a few steps farther and you'll find **MALVADINO**'s (209/728-9030). Pick up a map in town to visit the wineries located just outside of town. A word of warning to those who are not motorcycle fans: With Angels Camp only a few miles away, Murphys becomes a roaring two-wheeled town on the third weekend in May—the date of the famed frog-jumping contests.

Eighteen miles northeast of Murphys on Highway 4 is **CALAVERAS BIG TREES STATE PARK** (209/795-2334), a popular summer retreat that offers camping, swimming, hiking, and fishing along the Stanislaus River. Many of the numerous caverns in the area were discovered in the mid-1800s by gold prospectors and can now be toured, including **MERCER CAVERNS** (209/728-2101), which has crystalline stalactites and stalagmites in a series of descending chambers; **MOANING CAVERN** (209/736-2708), where a 100-foot stairway spirals down into a limestone chamber so huge it could house the Statue of Liberty, and is a great place to try out your rappelling skills; and **CALIFORNIA CAVERNS** (209/736-2708; www.caverntours.com; reservations required; closed Dec–Apr/May, when the cavern fills with water) is the West's first commercially developed cave and the largest single cave system in Northern California. It has yet to be fully explored.

RESTAURANTS

Grounds / ★★

402 MAIN ST, MURPHYS; 209/728-8663

River Klass, a handsome young transplant from the East Coast, opened this fantastic coffeehouse and cafe in 1993. Many locals have become addicted to the Grounds' potato pancakes (served with every made-to-order omelet), and lunch favorites include the grilled eggplant sandwich stuffed with smoked mozzarella and fresh basil and the sausage sandwich on house-baked bread. The dinner menu changes frequently, but recent winners were pork tenderloin stuffed with white fig and encrusted with English walnuts; angel hair pasta with spinach, crimini mushrooms, garlic, shallots, and white wine; the fettuccine topped with sautéed shrimp, halibut, and mussels in a garlic cream sauce; a juicy pot roast with steamed red potatoes; oven-roasted sweetheart ham with glazed yams; and a good ol' New York steak with caramelized onions and horse-radish mashed potatoes. The long, narrow dining rooms are bright and airy, with pine furnishings, wood floors, and an open kitchen. *$$; AE, DIS, MC, V; checks OK; breakfast, lunch every day, dinner Wed–Sun; beer and wine; reservations recommended; E side of street, center of town.* &

LODGINGS

Dunbar House, 1880 / ★★★

271 JONES ST, MURPHYS; 209/728-2897 OR 800/692-6006

Without question, Dunbar House is among the finest B&Bs in the Gold Country. Century-old gardens adorn this lovely Italianate home built in 1880 by Willis Dunbar, a superintendent for the Utica Water Company, for his bride. The lush grounds are complemented by a two-person ham-mock, a gazebo, a rose garden with benches, and a swing. All five guest rooms are furnished with gas-burning stoves, heirloom antiques, down pillows and comforters, and vases of fresh flowers for dashes of vibrant color. The Cedar Room offers a private sun porch and a two-person whirlpool bath, while the two-room Sugar Pine suite comes with English towel warmers, a CD/stereo system, and a balcony perched among the elm trees. For breakfast, fresh juices, coffee, house-made pastries, and a main dish such as the fabulous concoction of crab and cheese atop an English muffin are served in your room, at the dining room table, or in the gorgeous garden. *$$$; AE, MC, V; checks OK; innkeep@dunbar house.com; www.dunbarhouse.com; just off Main St at S end of town.*

Murphys Historic Hotel and Lodge / ★

457 MAIN ST, MURPHYS; 209/728-3444 OR 800/532-7684

When this hotel opened in 1856, who could have known what kind of characters would pass through its doors? The illustrious guest register includes Ulysses S. Grant, Mark Twain, Horatio Alger, Susan B. Anthony, and Black Bart, to name just a few. Although its days of housing digni-taries are long past, this national- and state-registered landmark still maintains its hold as Murphys' social center. Any time of day or night you'll find a few locals here hunched over stools, voicing their opinions, and politely ignoring the tourists who stop in for a bed or a drink or both. The main building has nine historic guest rooms that reflect turn-of-the-century lifestyles (that is, thin walls, no phones, televisions, or private baths), while the newer building offers 20 modern rooms with private bathrooms and hair dryers. In the dining area, open for breakfast, lunch, and dinner, you'll find huge platters of chicken, beef, seafood, and pasta, but the lackluster service and mediocre cuisine usually discourages most visitors from coming back (especially now that the estimable Grounds and Murphy's Grille restaurants are just down the street). *$$; AE, DC, DIS, MC, V; checks OK; downtown.* ♿

The Redbud Inn / ★★

402 MAIN ST, MURPHYS; 209/728-8533 OR 800/827-8533

A town in great need of luxury accommodations, Murphys hadn't celebrated the opening of a new inn in more than a century until October 1993, when the Redbud opened its doors. Proprietors Pam and Steve Hatch have been busy ever since, and their painstaking attention to detail is evident in each of the 13 individually decorated guest rooms. All are exquisitely furnished with brass or antique beds, family heirlooms and mementos, antique baths and sinks, fireplaces, wood-burning stoves, and original artwork. The immaculate Anniversary Suite features a private balcony, a wet bar, a double-sided fireplace, a peach-and-white king-size bed, and an enormous, inviting spa tub. Guests are treated to a full breakfast and, in the evening, hors d'oeuvres and locally produced wine. You can also pamper yourself with a massage or an herbal bath at the Redbud by appointment. *$$$; DIS, MC, V; checks OK; innkeeper@redbudinn.com; www.red budinn.com; in the Miner's Exchange Complex.* ♿

Columbia

Some mighty fortunate forty-niners unearthed a staggering $87 million in gold in this former boisterous mining town, once the state's second-largest city (it was only two votes shy of becoming the state capital over Sacramento). But when the gold no longer panned out in the late 1850s, Columbia's population of 15,000 nearly vanished. In 1945 the entire town was turned into **COLUMBIA STATE HISTORIC PARK** (209/532-4301 or 209/532-0150), a true Gold Country treasure. This is the Mother Lode's best-preserved park, filled with historic facades and mining artifacts. Now only three blocks long (okay, maybe four), it has no addresses to mark the buildings, but nothing is difficult to locate—except, perhaps, a vein of gold. Follow the free, short, self-guided park tour, and don't miss the **WELLS FARGO EXPRESS OFFICE**, a former stagecoach center, and the restored **COLUMBIA SCHOOLHOUSE**, which was in use until 1937. Big-time Gold Rush buffs who want more area history should pick up the inexpensive walking-tour booklet at the visitors center or sign up for a guided mine tour. For a more leisurely view of the park, hop aboard one of the horse-drawn stagecoaches. And to learn how to pan for gold, stop by **HIDDEN TREASURE GOLD MINE TOURS** (209/532-9693) at the corner of Main and Stage Streets.

RESTAURANTS

The City Hotel Restaurant / ★★★

MAIN ST, COLUMBIA; 209/532-1479 OR 800/532-1479

The City Hotel Restaurant is a rarity—a culinary palace in the heart of a state park. Inside, it's decked out with red velvet drapes, oil paintings, and antique furniture topped with crisp linens and flowers. The restaurant and hotel are a hotel-hospitality training center for the nearby Columbia College, and the students assist the staff here. If this is Hotel Hospitality Class 101, these are 4.0 students—the serving staff even dresses in period costumes. You may order from the small prix-fixe or à la carte menus featuring dishes like grilled tournedos of beef tenderloin with potato and blue cheese twice-baked soufflé or pan-seared fillet of salmon over stir-fried vegetables with shiitake mushroom compote. For dessert, diners who can wait 30 minutes will be justly rewarded with a lemon soufflé crowned with Grand Marnier sauce. California vintages feature prominently on the wine list. While you wait for your dinner table, spend some time in What Cheer, the hotel's saloon. *$$$; AE, DIS, MC, V; checks OK; dinner Tues–Sun, brunch Sun; full bar; reservations required on weekends, recommended on weekdays; info@cityhotel. com; www.cityhotel.com; between Jackson and State Sts.*

LODGINGS

City Hotel / ★★★

MAIN ST, COLUMBIA; 209/532-1479 OR 800/532-1479

City folk who frequented this opulent hotel in 1856 called it the Gem of the Southern Mines. Predictably, the building has gone through several incarnations since then, including stints as a gold-assay shop and a dance hall. When the town was turned into a state historic park in 1945, visitors once again returned to this venerable landmark. In the '70s, nearby Columbia College obtained grant money to renovate the structure and turn it into a hotel-hospitality training center, and now students assist the staff here. The lobby is fitted with period settees and marble-topped tables, and six of the ten high-ceilinged rooms face a central parlor where you can relax and read the newspaper or chat with your fellow travelers. Rooms 1 and 2 have balconies overlooking Main Street. All of the rooms have half-baths, with showers down the hall, and the hotel provides comfy robes, slippers, and wicker baskets full of toiletries to ease the trip. *$$; AE, DIS, MC, V; checks OK; info@cityhotel.com; www.cityhotel. com; between Jackson and State Sts.*

Twain Harte

RESTAURANTS

Cottage Cafe / ★★

22975 JOAQUIN GULLY RD, TWAIN HARTE; 209/586-6448

This restaurant is slow on service but scores high marks on food. Part of the delay may be that this cafe truly is a cottage—a tiny cottage, which is also why reservations are required on weekends. Once you squeeze in at a table on the small front porch or inside in the mini-dining room, take a moment to savor the choices before you: salmon baked in parchment dressed with lemon butter; osso buco—a veal shank sautéed with carrots, wine, celery, and herbs and served with a rich wine gravy; or sautéed chicken, mushrooms, and artichokes in a light wine sauce. For lunch almost all sandwiches start with *biga* (an old-world bread). Choose the grilled chicken rosemary sandwich with melted jack cheese, or the vegetarian with roasted red peppers, portobello, caramelized onion, and melted cheese. Delicious! *$$; AE, MC, V; checks OK; breakfast, lunch every day, dinner Thurs–Sat (Fri–Sat Labor Day–Memorial Day); beer and wine; reservations required; next to the Twain Harte arch.*

LODGINGS

McCaffrey House Bed & Breakfast Inn / ★★★

23251 HWY 108, TWAIN HARTE; 209/586-0757 OR 888/586-0757

Located in the Stanislaus National Forest, Michael and Stephanie McCaffrey's gorgeous, sprawling three-story country home was built specifically as a B&B, and it's one of the top 10 in the Gold Country. Each of the seven immaculate guest rooms has its own bath with a shower and tub, blow dryers, an individually controlled thermostat, access to a video library of 400 movies, and a private phone and modem jacks. All but two units have private decks. But it's the details that make the difference: a nearby creek to lull you to sleep; a view of the forest from your deck; queen-size quilts handmade by the Amish of Pennsylvania; a black iron stove in every room; exceptional gallery-quality art adorning the walls; TVs with VCRs stored in pine wood armoires; a library of paperbacks that are yours to keep; an outdoor hot tub perfectly situated to watch the full moon passing overhead—and more. In the summer, breakfast and hors d'oeuvres, wine, and sparkling cider are served on the huge redwood deck, which surrounds the house and overlooks the verdant hollow. Winter attracts families of skiers, who opt for McCaffrey House's ski packages to make use of nearby resorts (also ask about its theater and fishing packages). Every room in this B&B is a winner, but top honors go to the Evergreen and Burgundy boudoirs, which have unobstructed views of the forest. And the McCaffreys and their gaggle of pets are all incredibly friendly—reason enough to return again and again. *$$$; AE, MC, V; checks OK; innkeeper@mccaffrey.com; 11 miles E of Sonora.*

Sonora

When the traffic starts to crawl along Highway 49, you're probably closing in on Sonora. In forty-niner days, Sonora competed with Columbia for the title of wealthiest city in the southern Mother Lode. Today, it is the Gold Country's largest and most crowded town and the Tuolumne County seat. If you have time to spare, search for a parking space along Washington Street (no easy feat on weekends) or park in one of the lots a block east of Washington on Stewart Street, and take a look at the well-preserved 19th-century **ST. JAMES EPISCOPAL CHURCH**, at the top of Washington Street, and the **TUOLUMNE COUNTY MUSEUM** (158 W Bradford St; 209/532-1317), located in the century-old jail. In the charming old lumber town of Standard, now part of East Sonora, is the **SNOWSHOE BREWING COMPANY** (19040 Standard Rd; 209/536-1445; www.snowshoebrewing.com), housed in the spacious former office of the now-defunct Standard Lumber Company and serving up its own Grizzly Brown and ESB (Extra Special Blizzard) brews along with several specialty beers. If you really have time to kill, take a leisurely drive along the picturesque **DETOUR ROUTE 108**, which heads west into the Sierra Nevada over **SONORA PASS** and through several scenic alpine communities.

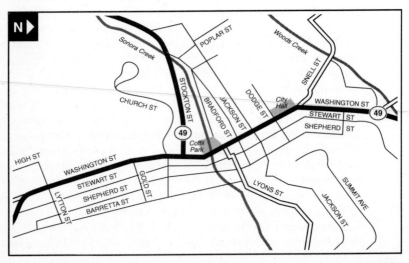

SONORA

RESTAURANTS
Banny's / ★★

83 S STEWART ST, SONORA; 209/533-4709
French innkeeper Bruno Trial at Barretta Gardens Inn (see review, below) not only sends his guests here; he and his wife Sherri often eat here themselves. The decor is not elaborate, but chef/owner Rob Bannworth is a passionate spice man who takes his sauces seriously, and you certainly can't complain about the reasonable prices he charges for pan-roasted duckling with apricot port wine sauce; spicy Moroccan lamb chops; chicken breast alfredo; and grilled prawn salad with mango lime dressing. Expect to pay almost half of what you'd pay in the San Francisco Bay Area for fare of equal quality. *$$; DIS, MC, V; checks OK; lunch Mon–Sat, dinner every day; beer and wine; reservations recommended; in Old Town.*

LODGINGS
Barretta Gardens Inn / ★★

700 S BARRETTA ST, SONORA; 209/532-6039 OR 800/206-3333
There is always something blooming in the expansive gardens of native flowering shrubs surrounding this small country inn on a hillside southeast of downtown Sonora. The wraparound porch is perfect for curling up with a good book (or your honey) in spring or autumn. Winter conversation takes place on soft sofas around the fireplace in the comfortable living room. Barretta Gardens has five guest rooms, and the most impressive is the pretty Odette Room, fashioned after a late-18th-century Italian suite. Innkeepers Sally and Bruno Trial greet guests in the afternoon with a beverage and treat them the following morning to a generous breakfast of apple puff pancakes, freshly baked French pastries made by Bruno (he has a real French accent!), and fresh-squeezed juices served in the dining room or, when it's warm, on the screened-in breakfast porch. *$$$; AE, MC, V; checks OK; barrettagardens@hotmail.com; www.barrettagardens. com; a few blocks E of Washington St.*

Ryan House, 1855 / ★★

153 S SHEPHERD ST, SONORA; 209/533-3445 OR 800/831-4897 (CALIFORNIA ONLY)
When Dennis and Susan Ryan came to the United States in 1855 from Cork, Ireland, to escape the potato famine, they settled in booming Sonora and built their dream house, which stayed in the family until the early 1980s. It is now a picture-perfect B&B, owned by Guy and Nancy Hoffman, that retains its authentic 19th-century architectural details— everything from the square nails to the handmade windows (with original glass, no less!). The only drawback is its small size, but the three guest rooms have unexpectedly high ceilings, cheerful wallpaper, antique furnishings, queen-size beds with handmade quilts, and private baths. In

1992, the Hoffmans converted the attic into a spacious three-room suite with a parlor, a gas-log cast-iron stove, a two-person soaking tub, a queen-size brass-and-iron bed, and a pleasant view of downtown Sonora. In the morning, if the weather's nice, breakfast is served in the rose garden; otherwise, the repast is enjoyed in the formal dining room. Be sure to sample Nancy's special scones—so good they were featured in *Country Inns* magazine. *$$; AE, MC, V; checks OK; www.ryan house.com; 2 blocks E of N Washington St.*

Jamestown

Jamestown has been preoccupied with gold since the first fleck was taken out of Woods Creek in 1848; a marker even commemorates the discovery of a 75-pound nugget. For a fee, you can pan for gold at troughs on Main Street or go prospecting with a guide. But gold isn't Jamestown's only claim to fame. For decades, this two-block town lined with picturesque buildings has been Hollywood's favorite Western movie set: Scenes from famous flicks like *Butch Cassidy and the Sundance Kid* were shot here, and vintage railway cars and steam locomotives used in such TV classics as *Little House on the Prairie*, *Bonanza*, and *High Noon* are on display at the **RAILTOWN 1897 STATE HISTORIC PARK** (5th Ave at Reservoir Rd, near the center of town; 209/984-3953). You can view the vehicles at the roundhouse daily or ride the rails on weekends from April through October and during holiday events, such as the Santa Train ride in December.

RESTAURANTS

Michelangelo's / ★★

18228 MAIN ST, JAMESTOWN; 209/984-4830
For three years the town watched the large round Michelangelo's sign hang in front of its abandoned restaurant, a cruel reminder of the Italian dinners they had to go without. Then in 1999, Neal Parrish rode into town and reopened their beloved Michelangelo's, saving the town from their painful marinara withdrawal. Diners from all over come to sit beneath the white tin ceiling of this old Gold Rush–era building and just breathe in the aromas of the marsala wine sauces, the prosciutto-wrapped veal and chicken, and the sizzling pasta dishes. Focaccia herb bread is served with all the entrees, and wines from the Gold Country are available from the bar at the side of the restaurant. *$$; AE, DIS, MC, V; checks OK; lunch Fri–Sun, dinner Wed–Mon; full bar; reservations recommended; www.jamestownca.com/michelangelo; downtown.*

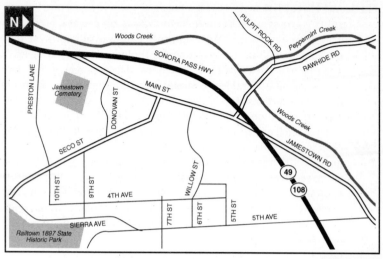

LODGINGS

Jamestown Hotel / ★★

18153 MAIN ST, JAMESTOWN; 209/984-3902 OR 800/205-4901

Built at the turn of the last century and converted into a hospital in the 1920s, this two-story brick charmer with its Western facade and wood veranda was transformed into a country inn more than a decade ago. Upstairs, each of the eight engaging guest rooms—named after female Gold Rush personalities—are furnished with antiques and private Victorian baths with brass showers. The romantic one-room Lotta Crabtree Suite is furnished with lots of wicker, floral fabrics, and a claw-footed tub. A black iron bed and claw-footed tub are part of the Lola Montez suite, a site rumored to be haunted by the fiery countess herself (more likely a ghostly impersonator, as no one can confirm that the lady ever stayed at the hotel). Downstairs is the handsome saloon, with a fabulous bar that's worth a gander even if you're just passing through. The dining room serves traditional favorites like bacon-wrapped filet mignon, salmon steak poached in white wine, prime rib, and pepper steak. *$$; AE, DC, DIS, MC, V; checks OK; jthotel@sonnet.com; www.james townhotel.com; downtown.* &

National Hotel / ★★

18183 MAIN ST, JAMESTOWN; 209/984-3446 OR 800/894-3446

The restoration of the 1859 National Hotel was so impressive that both the Tuolumne Visitors Bureau and the Tuolumne County Lodging Association bestowed awards for its new look. The restorers of the nine guest rooms did an admirable job of blending 19th-century details (handmade quilts, lace curtains, brass beds) with 20th-century comforts (private bathrooms). The saloon, with its handsome redwood bar, is the best place in town to catch up on local gossip. A generous continental breakfast includes cereals, house-made muffins, hard-boiled eggs, fresh fruit, fresh-squeezed juices, coffee and tea, and the morning paper. Brunch, lunch, and dinner are served to the public in the handsome old-fashioned dining room, replete with antiques, old photos, and Gold Rush memorabilia. You'll find an extensive array of hearty steak, prime rib, chicken, seafood, and pasta dishes, as well as numerous fine wines and house-made desserts. On sunny days or warm summer nights, ask for a table in the Garden Courtyard, draped by a century-old grape arbor. *$$; AE, DC, DIS, MC, V; checks OK; info@national-hotel.com; www.national-hotel.com; downtown.*

Groveland

LODGINGS

Berkshire Inn / ★★

19950 HWY 120, GROVELAND; 209/962-6744

By the time you reach this modern Tudor-style B&B, you will have driven over the foothills and into the mountains. Most guests come for a weekend of white-water rafting on the Tuolumne River, for boating, golfing, or hiking at nearby Pine Mountain Lake Recreation Area, or stop for a night on their way to Yosemite. Perched on 20 wooded acres, the Berkshire Inn has six large bedrooms and four suites with private entrances (some also have decks), as well as two large common areas with comfy couches, TVs, and VCRs. Guests share access to the large gazebo overlooking the countryside. Other perks include complimentary wine and a large continental breakfast. This is a great place for families or groups of rafters. *$$; AE, DIS, MC, V; checks OK; www.berkshire bandb.com; 2 miles E of town, look for the international flags.*

Groveland Hotel / ★★

18767 MAIN ST, GROVELAND; 209/962-4000 OR 800/273-3314

Constructed in 1849, the adobe Groveland Hotel is one of the Gold Country's oldest buildings; an addition was erected some 65 years later to serve as a rooming house. Several years ago, the hotel underwent a million-dollar renovation, adding a modern conference center and a saloon. Despite the costly upgrades, the place still manages to retain some of the charm of yesteryear. Its 17 guest rooms aren't large, but down comforters and private baths make them quite comfortable, and they're furnished with attractive European antiques. The best rooms are the two-room suites equipped with spa tubs and fireplaces. The old-fashioned hotel restaurant serves American classics such as rack of lamb, baby back ribs, fresh fish, and pasta, and the wine list won the *Wine Spectator* Award of Excellence. Another plus: This hotel is pet-friendly. *$$$; AE, DC, DIS, MC, V; checks OK; peggy@groveland.com; www.groveland.com; downtown, E side of Main St.* &

Coulterville

There's gold in Maxwell Creek running alongside the town of Coulter-ville, but before you even think of searching for it, check with the locals about which sections of the creek are more likely to earn you a tres-passer's derriere full of buckshot than a vial flecked with gold. Named in 1853 by a draw of straws, this historic little town once hosted 25 saloons, 10 hotels, and a large Chinese population. Pick up a walking-tour map from the **COULTERVILLE VISITORS CENTER** (5007 Main St; 209/878-3074) to learn the history of the other buildings in this small historic town, most of which are currently inhabited by businesses and funky antique shops. If you're looking for a place to hang your hat for the night, you might try the **HOTEL JEFFERY** (1 Main St; 209/878-3471 or 800/464-3471; www.hoteljeffery.com). It's clean, it's family run since 1851, it's got a heck-of-a-lotta character, and it's home to the **MAGNOLIA SALOON AND GRILL**, where you can get some not-too-fancy grub. 'Course you might not want to chow down too much if you're planning to head south on Highway 49 anytime soon—there are 161 curves in 13 miles between Coulterville and Mariposa.

Mariposa

The town clock in the two-story **MARIPOSA COUNTY COURTHOUSE** (Bul-lion St between 9th and 10th Sts; 209/966-3222) has been marking time since 1866. Another town landmark is **ST. JOSEPH'S CATHOLIC CHURCH** (4985 Bullion St) built in 1863, and behind it lies the entrance to the **MARI-POSA MINE**, discovered by Kit Carson in 1849 and later purchased by John C. Frémont, who owned most of the land around these parts.

Two miles south of Mariposa in the Mariposa Country Fairgrounds is the **CALIFORNIA STATE MINING AND MINERAL MUSEUM** (5007 Fair-grounds Rd; 209/742-7625), a state geology center with one of the finest collections of gems and minerals in the country. One wing showcases 20,000 glittering gems and minerals; another holds artifacts and photos that tell California's mining story.

A side trip off Highway 49 leads to **HORNITOS** (Spanish for "little ovens"), a name that refers to the shape of the tombs on Boot Hill. This formerly lawless burg is nearly a ghost town, though it was once a favorite haunt of Gold Country bandido Joaquin Murieta, whose pickled head was turned over to state authorities in a glass jar for a $1,000 reward in 1853. Weathered old buildings (saloons, fandango halls, and gambling dens) stand around the plaza, some flaunting bullet holes from bygone battles.

RESTAURANTS

Charles Street Dinner House / ★★

5043 CHARLES ST, MARIPOSA; 209/966-2366
This 18-year-old landmark isn't as formal as its name might suggest. Rather, it's a place where the Old West reigns over decor, food, and service. The wait staff are dressed in period costume and look as though they just stepped out of the historic photos on the wall. Although the culinary offerings—steaks, chops, chicken, fresh seafood—are fairly common fare, they are skillfully prepared and well presented. Dinner specials might include broiled chicken breast, rack of lamb, duck, lobster, scampi, or prime rib, and all dinners are served with soup and salad. Charles Street Dinner House's latest addition is a 2,000-bottle wine cellar offering an impressive array of vintages. *$$; AE, DIS, MC, V; local checks only; dinner Wed–Sun (closed Jan); beer and wine; reservations recommended; www. yosemite.net/mariposa/restaurants/csdh; Hwy 140 and 7th St.*

Ocean Sierra / ★★★

3292 E WESTFALL RD, MARIPOSA; 209/7742-7050
This little cabin in the woods is home to some of the best cuisine in the county. Chef/owner Pam Toney does all the cooking, preparing everything fresh right as it's ordered. Dinner begins with a soup (the spicy gazpacho is fantastic) and a green salad served with a chilled fork. Entrees include lemon grilled prawns, New York pepper steak, a savory vegetarian stir-fry, and Australian lobster. Complete your meal with homemade ice cream, the oh-so-tasty So Slim Key Lime Cheesecake, or other desserts of the day. The restaurant, with its high pine ceiling, chipped-wood walls, brick fireplace, and white linen tablecloths, has the feel of a French inn in the mountains. Even the deer come by at dusk to graze on the lawn. *$$$; DIS, MC, V; checks OK; dinner Fri–Sun; beer and wine; reservations recommended; www.yosemite.net/oceansierra/; at Triangle and E Westfall Rds.*

LODGINGS

Meadow Creek Ranch / ★★

2669 TRIANGLE RD, MARIPOSA; 209/966-3843 OR 800/853-2057
 A stage stop in the 1850s, this refurbished ranch house is one of the most secluded bed-and-breakfasts in the Gold Country—a good choice for those looking for romantic solitude. There are only two guest rooms, each

decorated in an Early American style. The Garden Gate Room, located in an annex to the main house with a private entrance, offers a queen-size bed, a twin bed in the alcove, sitting area, private bath, and a patio that overlooks the meadow. The cozy Country Cottage, a converted chicken coop that has been beautifully decorated in mahogany, has a queen-size bed imported from Austria, a private bath with a claw-footed tub, and a sitting area. As you enjoy that early-morning cup of coffee, wander around the waterwheel and arbor or take a seat on the patio and soak in the scenic surroundings. A hearty breakfast is served family style in the ranch house's spacious dining room. *$$; AE, DIS, MC, V; checks OK; meadowcreekranch@sierratel.com; www.mariposa.yosemite.net/csdh/; about 11½ miles S of town on Hwy 49.*&

Oakhurst

RESTAURANTS

Erna's Elderberry House / ★★★★

48688 VICTORIA LN, OAKHURST; 559/683-6800
Vienna-born Erna Kubin-Clanin selected this Oakhurst hillside more than a decade ago as the site for her now-famous restaurant and inn. The location is reminiscent of a corner of Provence, and, indeed, after indulging in one of her meals you'll think you've been transported to some European gastronomical paradise. Ever since the *New York Times* praised Erna's Elderberry House as "one of the most elegant and stylish restaurants in the nation," epicureans from around the world have made the pilgrimage to the elaborate Mediterranean-style dining room ensconced among pine trees and elderberry bushes. The prix-fixe dinner is a six-course affair that changes daily. A meal might begin with a grilled vegetable and goat cheese terrine, followed by chilled Yukon potato soup. Dungeness crab sandwich served with yucca root cake, avocado, and saffron aioli; foie gras–apricot spaetzle; or curry-roasted pork tenderloin rounds out the meal. The sweet finale might be a caramelized banana-chocolate tart. Order a bottle of wine from sommelier Renée-Nicole Cubin's award-winning list to match the vintage to the course. Erna also runs the spectacular Château du Sureau (see review, below). *$$$$; AE, DIS, MC, V; no checks; dinner every day, brunch Sun (closed Jan 3–23); full bar; reservations recommended; chateaux@chateaux sureau; www.elderberryhouse.com; off Hwy 41, just W of town.* &

LODGINGS

Château du Sureau / ★★★★

48688 VICTORIA LN, OAKHURST; 559/683-6860
 In 1991, when the opulent Château du Sureau was completed (*sureau* is French for elderberry), Erna Kubin-Clanin was able to offer her guests a

magnificent place to stay after indulging in the exquisite cuisine at her Elderberry House (see review, above). Erna's desire for perfection doesn't stop in the kitchen, as you'll instantly notice once you see the château's massive chandeliers and 19th-century paintings, the cathedral windows framing grand Sierra views, and the imported tiles that complement the limestone in the baths. The 10 guest rooms come replete with goose-down comforters, canopy beds, antiques, provençal fabrics, tapestries, fresh flowers, and even a CD sound system. The elegant Thyme Room is designed to easily accommodate wheelchairs; the Mint Room has a private entrance for those seeking seclusion; and the Saffron Room has a breathtaking Napoleon III–era bedroom set made of ebony and inlaid ivory. A European-style breakfast is served to all château guests in the cozy breakfast room or alfresco on the patio. Elsewhere on the grounds lie a fountain, a swimming pool, and a giant outdoor chess court with 3-foot-tall pieces. There's even a tiny chapel where wedding bells occasionally ring. If you find the exquisite decor is still too mundane for your tastes, you might be interested in the château's pièce de résistance—the Villa Sureau, a private two-bedroom, two-bath guest residence, featuring a salon, a library, and a fully insured Jeep Cherokee LTD to use during your stay. Outside the villa is a private Roman spa, where you can soak under the stars or receive a massage to relax all those muscles you used picking up the phone to call your butler. (Oh yes, the villa comes with a 24-hour butler.) If you feel you can do without the use of Jeeves and the Jeep, you are welcome to rent only half the villa. All this luxury comes at a price, of course. But the Elderberry House and Château du Sureau are one-of-a-kind Gold Country finds—and just about as precious and rare as those golden nuggets in the surrounding countryside. *$$$$; AE, MC, V; no checks; closed Jan 3–23; chateaux@chateaux.com; www.integra. fr/relaischateaux/sureau; off Hwy 41, just W of town.* &

SACRAMENTO AND THE CENTRAL VALLEY

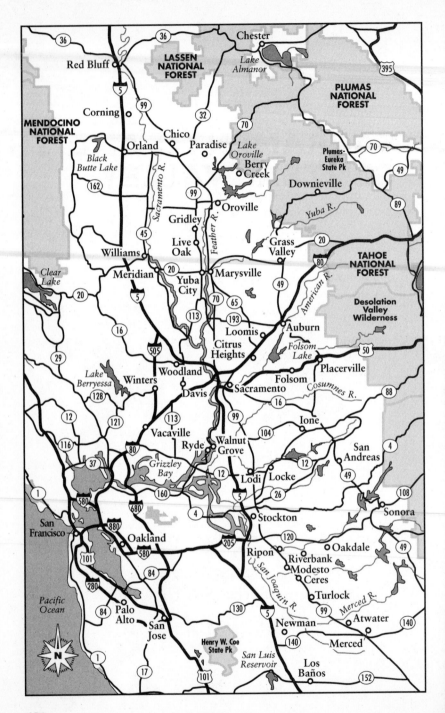

SACRAMENTO AND THE CENTRAL VALLEY

California's Central Valley is nearly 300 miles long and 50 miles wide—the largest expanse of flatland west of the Continental Divide. Stretching from Los Banos in the south to Red Bluff in the north, this great plain is bordered by the Sierra Nevada Mountains on the eastern flank and the Coast Ranges to the west. At the heart lies the capital city, Sacramento, the legislative pulse of the state. For the most part, the Central Valley is slightly above sea level, with the exception of the Sutter Buttes (the world's smallest mountain range), located just north of Sacramento, and the Sacramento River Delta, which is largely below sea level. Like a huge patchwork quilt, the Central Valley encompasses miles of farmland, orchards, and vineyards, stitched with irrigation canals, lakes, and rivers.

ACCESS AND INFORMATION

INTERSTATE 5 AND HIGHWAY 99 are the primary north-south routes through the Central Valley. Among the many east-west arteries are Highway 152 between Los Banos and Merced, and Highway 132 between the Altamont Pass and Modesto in the south, while to the north, Highway 20 serves as an artery from the foothills near Grass Valley to Clear Lake. Interstate 5 provides easy access to **SACRAMENTO INTERNATIONAL AIRPORT**, while Interstate 80 will take you east to the Reno/Lake Tahoe region or west to San Francisco. Visiting the Delta, Highway 12 is the major thoroughfare from 99 or Interstate 5, and from Sacramento, Highway 160 winds along the Sacramento River, across drawbridges and swing bridges, and is by far the most scenic. There is no public transportation system for the region (only within the cities), so it is best to explore this area by car. However, take notice that the Central Valley is often blanketed with thick fog during the winter months (Dec–Feb is the worst). Driving can be hazardous, and often flights are delayed at Sacramento's International Airport due to poor visibility. Always call the airline to confirm schedules, and for news on current road conditions throughout the Central Valley and the state, visit www.dot.ca.gov or call 800/427-ROAD.

Stockton and the South Central Valley

The communities between Los Banos and Stockton—some tiny, some rapidly developing (like Modesto)—are worth exploring. This region of the Central Valley can be defined as the east-west midway point between Yosemite National Park and the San Francisco Bay Area. Closer inspection, however, finds this agriculturally abundant area rich in history, cultural diversity, and small-town flavor.

Merced

Merced has claimed the title "Gateway to Yosemite" for more than a century, and the majority of its visitors are San Francisco Bay Area residents just passing through. Those who stop long enough to look around usually end up at **APPLEGATE PARK** (between M and R Sts), a 23-acre greenbelt with more than 60 varieties of trees, an immaculate rose garden, a small, free zoo, and, in the summer, amusement rides to whirl and twirl you and the kids. On Thursday evenings, local farmers sell their fresh produce from 6pm to 9pm on Main Street (between N and K Sts), a good place to buy picnic basket ingredients. One of the more interesting sights in the area is the **MERCED COUNTY COURTHOUSE MUSEUM** (2222 N St; 209/723-2401), the pride and joy of Merced and a monument to the early settlers of the great Central Valley.

RESTAURANTS

Branding Iron Restaurant / ★☆

640 W 16TH ST, MERCED; 209/722-1822

This paean to the American Beef Council has delighted Mercedites for nearly half a century, thanks in part to chef Bob Freitas, who has presided over the kitchen for almost three decades. Owners Kara and Greg Parle have added to the Branding Iron's Old West ambience by decorating its rough-hewn redwood walls with registered livestock brands from all over California. Dinner begins with soup and salad, followed by such carnivorous delights as a thick cut of choice prime rib seasoned with coarse-ground pepper, garlic, rosemary, and thyme, and a large baked potato with all the fixins. If your stomach (or waistline) will allow it, finish the evening with a sweet treat from the well-stocked dessert tray. *$$; AE, MC, V; local checks only; lunch Mon–Fri, dinner every day; full bar; reservations recommended; next to the Santa Fe Railway Depot.* &

Atwater

RESTAURANTS

Out to Lunch / ★★

1301 WINTON WY, ATWATER; 209/357-1170

Word got out a long time ago about the delicious thick sandwiches that emerge from this little veranda-wrapped cottage. Almost anything piled between the warm, sweetly spiced slices of house-made zucchini bread is a good bet, including the crunchy veggie sandwich with cream cheese, cucumbers, bell peppers, shredded carrots, avocado, and sprouts. Other great choices are the English muffin topped with sautéed mushrooms, Jack cheese, and crumbled bacon or any of the house-made quiches. No alcohol is served here, but you're welcome to bring your own bottle of wine. If you're en route by car from Los Angeles to the Sacramento area (or vice versa), this is one of the best places for a lunch break—and it's just a minute away from the highway. *$; MC, V; checks OK; lunch Mon–Fri, dinner Fri only Memorial Day–Labor Day; no alcohol; no reservations; out2lunch@cell2000.net; at Drakely St: from Hwy 99, take the Applegate exit.* &

Turlock

RESTAURANTS

El Jardín / ★★

409 E OLIVE ST, TURLOCK; 209/632-0932

True to its name, El Jardín has a fragrant, colorful flower garden surrounded by several outdoor tables—*the* place to sit when the weather is mild. The authentic south-of-the-border fare—all offered at south-of-the-border prices—includes such house specials as the Milanesa breaded

beef fillet with fresh green salsa and the tender and tasty *pollo a la parilla* (grilled chicken breast). For *los niños* there are kid-size enchiladas, quesadillas, taquitos, burritos, and tostadas served with rice and beans. If you're in the mood for a late breakfast (the kitchen doesn't open until 11am), stop by for huevos rancheros, steak, scrambled eggs with chorizo, and other Mexican standards. *$; V; no checks; late breakfast, lunch, dinner every day; beer and wine; reservations recommended; 1 block W of Golden State Blvd, 1 block N of Main St.*

Modesto

RESTAURANTS

Appetèz / ★★

825 W ROSEBURG AVE, MODESTO; 209/577-5099

Hidden in a small shopping center within a shady residential district, Appetèz is a jewel. Soft lighting, beige colors, and classical music create a relaxed, comfortable atmosphere. For lunch try one of the many creative wraps (a variation on traditional sandwiches) served with a side salad. The dinner menu features a nice selection of pastas like the Creole chicken farfalle with kielbasa, chicken, sun-dried tomatoes, red onion, and roasted red peppers in a Creole cream sauce. The champagne-port scallops are poached in champagne and cream, then drizzled with a delicious port sauce. Speaking of port, on Friday and Saturday nights, Appetèz hosts a late-night port and dessert alternative to the caffeine ritual. Full vertical tastings or single servings of fine ports are comple-

SACRAMENTO AREA THREE-DAY-TOUR

DAY ONE: Just like old times. After breakfast at the **Fox and Goose**, start your first day in Old Sacramento with a stop at the visitor center on Second Street; pick up a map of attractions. Spend some time exploring the **California State Railway Museum**, for an understanding of how the railroads shaped California history. Browse the rest of **Old Sacramento** by foot, or consider a **paddle wheel sightseeing cruise** (916/552-2933 or 800/433-0263) aboard the historic *Matthew McKinley*. Wander over to the **Rio City Cafe** for a tasty lunch with a view of the river. If you're ready for more history, don't miss the **Crocker Art Museum**, or if you'd rather, visit the **Sacramento Zoo**. When you're ready to kick back, board the *Delta King* and head for the fourth-floor lounge for an early evening aperitif and view of the sunset. Lodging at the centrally located **Sterling Hotel** is highly recommended. Enjoy tonight's dinner at **Paragary's Bar and Oven**.

DAY TWO: State of the Arts. Begin today with breakfast and people-watching at the **Tower Cafe** (1518 Broadway; 916/441-0222), birthplace of Tower Records. Then head over to **Sutter's Fort** and the **California State Indian Museum**. Arrive at the Pavilions Shopping Mall before the lunch crowd, for a remarkable deli experience at **David Berkley**. Dine there and browse Sacramento's most exquisite shopping center, or pack a picnic and head for **Capitol Park** for lunch under the huge trees. From here, take the **state capitol** tour (free), then walk to the **California Vietnam Veterans Memorial**.

mented by the pastry chef's light, seasonal creations, designed to enhance the flavor of the wine, without burdening the stomach. Examples include chocolate-covered strawberries and heavenly house-made truffles. *$$; AE, DIS, MC, V; local checks only; lunch Mon–Fri, dinner Mon–Sat; beer and wine; reservations recommended; www.appetez.com; in the Roseburg Square shopping center.* &

Hazel's / ★★

431 12TH ST, MODESTO; 209/578-3463

This old pink house, converted 30 years ago into a restaurant, is a favorite romantic weekend retreat for many Modesto residents. It may pale next to the hoity-toity culinary castles in San Francisco, but in this part of the valley Hazel's is the place to be for a candlelit dinner. Owner Jeff Morey, a graduate of the California Culinary Academy, maintains original owner Hazel Saylor's time-honored menu, featuring dishes as simple as liver and onions topped with sautéed mushrooms and as deluxe as the rich lobster Macedonia. Hazel's version of cannelloni, stuffed with seasoned veal, chicken, and mushrooms, is still a lunchtime favorite. The wine list is well edited and reasonably priced, with several selections available by the glass.

For dinner with music (Spanish classical and flamenco guitar), try **Tapa the World**, or for a wonderfully elegant and exotic meal, try Sacramento's famous **Lemon Grass**.

DAY THREE: Cruisin' country roads. After breakfast at **33rd Street Bistro**, leave the city for a tour of the rural levee roads of the **Sacramento River Delta** and the century-old vineyards of Lodi. From Sacramento, take scenic Highway 160 South through Freeport and Hood. Explore the tiny town of **Locke**, built by Chinese immigrants in 1915. Have lunch at the popular **Orilla del Rio** in Walnut Grove. Cross the Sacramento River just past town and head south. If it's the weekend, visit the **Levee Gallery**, displaying peaceful Delta landscapes captured on canvas by local artist Marty Stanley, and don't miss the Ryde Hotel, a former boardinghouse/speakeasy. Turn west between the gallery and the Ryde Hotel and head toward the **Grand Island Mansion**, a 1917 Italian Renaissance–style inn with lush gardens. Just south of the mansion, hop on the **J-Mack ferry** (free) and cross Steamboat Slough. Turn left and follow the water to the next ferry crossing—the *Real McCoy*. This ferry (also free) takes you across Cache Slough, where you disembark just a few miles from **Rio Vista**. On Highway 12, head east toward Lodi, driving over drawbridges and through patchworks of sunflowers, vineyards, and corn. Between Interstate 5 and Lodi, stop in at Phillips Farm and again at the **Van Ruiten–Taylor Winery** (340 W Hwy 12; 209/334-5722) to sample or purchase some of Lodi's respected and popular varietals. Finish the long day with a relaxing dinner and pampered lodging at Lodi's **Wine and Roses Country Inn**.

$$–$$$; AE, DC, DIS, MC, V; local checks only; lunch Tues–Fri, dinner Tues–Sat; full bar; reserations recommended; jeffhazel@softcom.net; www.hazelsmodesto.com; between E and F Sts. &

Tresetti's World Caffe / ★★

927 11TH ST, MODESTO; 209/572-2990

Located a few blocks from City Hall, this popular hangout attracts a steady gaggle of lawyers, lobbyists, politicians, and other professionals, who congregate at the stylish galvanized steel and polished-wood wine bar. The adjacent high-ceilinged dining room is equally chic, with its burgundy drapes, matching cement floor, pale yellow walls, a glass facade overlooking downtown Modesto, and only a dozen tables. The chef strives for a global culinary theme, focusing on classic dishes from around the world. Recent offerings included baked Moroccan chicken, with currant couscous and a curry-lime yogurt, and potato-encrusted Australian lamb loin with Shiraz balsamic demi-glace and a cilantro-lime-Dijon aioli on roasted garlic mashed potatoes. Tresetti's also has a large assortment of single-malt whiskeys and ports. *$$; AE, DIS, MC,*

V; checks OK; lunch, dinner Mon–Sat; full bar; reservations recommended; www.tresetti.com; at J St, adjacent to Tresetti's Wine Shop. ♿

LODGINGS

Doubletree Hotel Modesto / ★

1150 9TH ST, MODESTO; 209/526-6000 OR 800/222-TREE
Towering 14 stories above the Modesto landscape, the Doubletree is the Central Valley's premier business/luxury accommodation. Guests are pampered with such amenities as a spa, sauna, sundeck, heated outdoor pool, weight room, two restaurants, two bars, and extensive conference facilities. Each of the 258 rather plain but comfortable guest rooms (including six suites) are equipped with a TV, three telephones with a fax/PC data port, a king- or queen-size bed, a separate desk and table, a coffeemaker, an iron and ironing board, and a hair dryer. A free shuttle will whisk you to the Modesto airport; if you have your own wheels, take advantage of the free parking in the sheltered lot. *$$$; AE, DC, DIS, MC, V; checks OK; www.doubletreehotels.com; at K St.* ♿

Oakdale

Sitting on Highway 120, en route to Yosemite, this "Cowboy Capital of the World" is the home of the monolithic **HERSHEY CHOCOLATE FACTORY**. Believe it or not, 150,000 annual visitors line up for the free 30-minute tours of the chocolate-making plant offered Monday through Friday, 8:30am to 3pm. Tours depart from the **HERSHEY VISITORS CENTER** (120 S Sierra Ave; 209/848-8126; at Yosemite Ave and East F St), which has a few low-tech displays from the history of Milton Hershey's chocolate empire. The **OAKDALE COWBOY MUSEUM** (355 East F St; 209/847-7049) houses items from world-renowned rodeo champions, and succulent lovers, don't miss **POOT'S HOUSE OF CACTUS** (on the way to Oakdale, 5 miles E of Hwy 99; 17229 E Hwy 120; 209/599-7241)—an incredible collection of cactus and unusual plants from around the world. Another town highlight is the **SATURDAY OAKDALE LIVESTOCK AUCTION** (6001 Albers Rd; 209/847-1033). Just be careful not to scratch your nose—you could become the dumbstruck new owner of a 600-pound Black Angus.

RESTAURANTS

H-B Saloon and Bachi's Restaurant / ★

401 EAST F ST, OAKDALE; 209/847-2985

For a real Central Valley experience, don your shit-kickers and cowboy hat and head for the H-B saloon, a decidedly funky old bar and restaurant festooned with faded photos of ranches and rodeos, mounted game, old-fashioned tack, branded wainscoting, and other mementos of ranching life. During any time of the day or night you'll find aging cattlemen in baseball caps and cowboy hats playing shuffleboard or poker in the saloon, drinking $1 beers, listening to Johnny Cash on the jukebox, and doing their best to ignore the occasional wayward tourist. Dinner, served family style in the adjacent Bachi's Restaurant, will satisfy even the hungriest cowboy: choose from rib-eye steak, pork chops, lamb chops, chicken, baby back ribs, halibut, or, on Friday and Saturday only, prime rib. Each inexpensive meal includes red wine, soup, salad, french fries, bread, beans, potato salad, and ice cream. *$; DIS, MC, V; local checks only; lunch Mon–Fri, dinner Wed–Sat; full bar; no reservations; next to the Hershey Visitors Center.* よ

Ripon

RESTAURANTS

Christopaolo's / ★★

125 E MAIN ST, RIPON; 209/599-2030
If there were ever a reason to roll your wheels into Ripon, this is it. Owner Christopaolo Bonora has kept many of the original fixtures in this handsome, high-ceilinged 1886 edifice, including the marvelous exposed brick walls, intricate mahogany woodwork, and an authentic dumbwaiter. The menu offers a large array of Italian dishes such as *nocetta di maiale ai porcini* (pork loin sautéed with porcini mushrooms and wine), spaghetti Bolognese, and *zuppa di pesce*, an Adriatic fisherman's stew laden with a variety of shellfish and chunks of fresh fish. Grilled items, such as center-cut rib steak, salmon, and a half-chicken, are also available. The small wine bar offers a smart selection of California wines—a good reason to arrive a little early. *$$; DIS, MC, V; checks OK; lunch Wed–Fri, dinner Wed–Sun, brunch Sun; beer and wine; reservations recommended; at Stockton Ave.* よ

Stockton

The birthplace of Caterpillar tractor inventor Benjamin Holt, heartthrob rock star Chris Isaak, and Summer Home of the San Francisco 49ers, Stockton used to be a simple, blue-collar town. In 1999 it was chosen as an All-American City by the National Civic League. A multicultural blend of European, Mexican, and Asian immigrants who own businesses and provide services and labor in this agriculturally abundant region make diversity a watchword here. Some 75 languages are spoken within the city limits.

For a taste of regional history and fine art, a visit to the **HAGGIN MUSEUM** (1201 N Pershing Ave; 209/940-6300) is a must. Maestro Peter Jaffe conducts the innovative **STOCKTON SYMPHONY** (209/951-0196; www.stocktonsymphony.org) along with high-caliber guest artists. The

STOCKTON CIVIC THEATRE (2312 Rose Marie Ln; 209/473-2424) puts on affordable quality productions, and the historic **FOX THEATRE** (242 E Main; 209/462-2694) is the place to see big-name performers.

On those scorching summer days, what better way to cool off than a trip to the **OAK PARK ICE ARENA** (3545 Alvarado St; 209/937-7433)? The **STOCKTON CHILDREN'S MUSEUM** (402 W ßer Ave; 209/465-4386) is a hands-on discovery and learning center for kids as well as parents. **MICKE GROVE PARK & ZOO** (11793 N Micke Grove Rd; 209/331-7270; take the Eight-Mile Rd Exit from Hwy 99) is shaded by huge oak trees—a great place to picnic. It also features a zoo known for its endangered species breeding program, a golf course, driving range, Japanese gardens, and a small amusement park for the younger ones. For a rundown on the agricultural history of the San Joaquin Valley, check out the **SAN JOAQUIN COUNTY HISTORICAL MUSEUM** (located inside Micke Grove Park; 209/331-2055).

From May through October the **STOCKTON CERTIFIED FARMERS MARKETS** (209/943-1830) offer superb local produce and are held Thursday through Sunday mornings at various locations around town. And speaking of produce, the **STOCKTON ASPARAGUS FESTIVAL** (Oak Grove Regional Park, Eight-Mile Rd Exit off I-5), held every fourth weekend in April, has grown into one of the most popular food and entertainment events in Northern California. This three-day event features more than 50 entertainers, gourmet asparagus dishes, a wine and beer pavilion, a classic car show, a 5K run, and more, all celebrating—you guessed it—asparagus. For more information on this event or any other activities in the Stockton area, call the **SAN JOAQUIN CONVENTION AND VISITORS BUREAU** (46 W Fremont St; 209/943-1987).

RESTAURANTS

Bella Fresca / ★★★

678 GRIDER WY, STOCKTON; 209/478-0856

It's nowhere near the water, but Bella Fresca still delivers fine seafood dinners. Owner Cal Bowser is a seafood wholesaler who has put together the right combination of cuisine, ambience, and service to make this establishment one of Stockton's finest. Located in an industrial-type metal building, it has a decor that's sophisticated but with a twist of the salty fisherman: there's a large sailfish mounted on the wall and aging fishing gear and an old skiff stashed in the corner. Patio dining is available, with a fireplace to warm those cool delta breezes. Salads are on the light side, portionwise, but the dressings and flavor combinations are zesty and creative. Recent entree offerings included a grilled rare fillet of ahi tuna with sake-braised Asian mushrooms, cellophane noodles, and wasabi-ginger *nage*, and house-made smoked Pacific salmon ravioli with light tomato cream and fresh basil chiffonade. The wine list is lacking in local vintages, but is otherwise extensive. For dessert try the frozen Valencia orange soufflé with blood orange coulis. *$$$; MC, V; checks OK; dinner Thurs–Sat; beer and wine; reservations recommended; just off Lower Sacramento Rd, S of Eight-Mile Rd.* &

Ernie's on the Brick Walk / ★★

296 LINCOLN CENTER N, STOCKTON; 209/951-3311

In 1998, chef/owner Warren K. Ito moved his Ernie's Pasta Barn from the country northeast of Stockton to this brick walk location, tucked among the coffeehouses and gift shops of Lincoln Center North. Ernie's concise menu still reflects quality as opposed to quantity (that applies to portions as well). For starters try the polenta Castello, topped with melted blue cheese, sautéed mushrooms, and marsala sauce. The mixed mushroom fusilli is tossed with a light roasted garlic–cream sauce with shiitake, oyster, portobello, and porcini mushrooms; or if you're craving something more filling, try the New Zealand lamb chops with kalamata olive and rosemary soubise. The restaurant also offers nightly specials and an impressive wine list with the largest selection of ports in the area. *$$; AE, DC, DIS, MC, V; no checks; lunch Mon–Fri, dinner every day; full bar; reservations recommended; center of Lincoln Center N at Benjamin Holt Dr.* &

Sho Mi Japanese Cuisine / ★★

419 LINCOLN CENTER, STOCKTON; 209/951/3525

When you go to Sho Mi, whether for lunch or dinner, be prepared to stand in line. After expanding the place once in 1999, Shoji Akai and his team of talented sushi chefs and prep cooks continue to pack 'em in at this unassuming Japanese restaurant. Akai, the proprietor, a 1994 transplant from Shiba City, Japan, has been creating artistic delicacies for more than two decades. Order first and wait for a table, or seat yourself at the L-shaped sushi bar and observe the efficiency of this extremely popular and profitable eatery. Try the spicy shrimp eel roll or one of the daily specials. If sushi is not your thing, the ginger pork or chicken combines tender pieces of browned meat with zucchini and mushrooms in a potent ginger-teriyaki sauce. The combination plates are guaranteed to satisfy even the biggest appetites. Everything at Sho Mi is consistently fresh and flavorful, the portions are generous, and drinks (nonalcoholic) are included with all meals over $4.75. *$; cash only; lunch, dinner Mon–Sat; beer and wine; no reservations; SW corner of Lincoln Center at Benjamin Holt Dr.* &

Lodi

For more than a century, vineyards have thrived in Lodi. Situated just east of the fertile Sacramento River Delta and west of the Sierra Nevada

THE LODI ON WINES

Delicato Winery (12001 Hwy 99, Manteca; 800/924-2024; www.delicato.com). Established in 1924 by Gaspare Indelicato, this large vineyard and winery is presently run by Gaspare's three sons. Delicato has a busy gift shop/tasting room filled with cutesy merchandise and medal-draped bottles displaying awards from various wine competitions. Tasting 9am–5:30pm; tours at 11am every day.

The Lucas Winery (18196 N Davis Rd, Lodi; 209/368-2006). This charming winery was built specifically for the gentle handling of classic, old-vine zinfandel wine grapes from the surrounding fields. The trendy tasting room (a former tractor barn) sits next to a climate-controlled, gravel-floored aging room known as the "Grand Chai" (French for barrel room). Tasting Sat–Sun 12–5pm; tours by appointment only.

Oak Ridge Vineyards (6100 E Highway 12, Lodi; 209/369-4758). This 66-year-old winery was founded just after the repeal of Prohibition. Step inside the 50,000-gallon, redwood-barrel tasting room and sample the petite syrah and chardonnay. Picnic tables are available, surrounded by colorful gardens. Tasting Mon–Sat 9am–5pm; Sun 12–5pm; tours by appointment only.

Peirano Estate (21831 N Highway 99, Acampo; 209/369-9463; www.peirano.com). Conveniently located on the Highway 99 frontage road, Peirano owns the largest single block of head-trained, natural-rooted zinfandel remaining in the country. The cheerful tasting room is actually the remodeled Peirano Estate farmhouse, built in 1904.

foothills, with alluvial soil, abundant water, warm days, and cool nights (thanks to the Delta breezes), Lodi is geographically ideal for growing wine grapes. Check out the **LODI GRAPE FESTIVAL AND HARVEST FAIR** (209/369-3771), held each third weekend in September. The **DISCOVER LODI! WINE AND VISITOR'S CENTER** (2505 Turner Rd; 209/367-4727; www.lodiwine.com) is a great place pick up a map and learn more about the Lodi area wines and wineries.

RESTAURANTS

Wine and Roses Country Inn / ★★★

2505 TURNER RD, LODI; 209/334-6988

Talented chef and proprietor Sherri Smith, a graduate of the California Culinary Academy in San Francisco, consistently presents delectable creations with attention to detail at this 1902 homestead estate (listed with the San Joaquin County Historical Society). For lunch, try the classic Caesar salad or the chicken *vol-au-vent* (dressed in a cheese sauce and served in a puff-pastry shell). The dinner menu will tempt you with marinated sirloin of lamb, accompanied by brandied cherry and mint chutney, or prosciutto-stuffed chicken breast on a creamy herbed polenta

Enjoy a picnic among the 90-year-old vines or browse the gift shop while you sample the popular wines. Tasting Thurs–Sun 10am–5pm.

Phillips Vineyard (4580 W Hwy 12, Lodi; 209/368-7384; www.phillipsvineyards. com). These award-winning wines are available to sample at the Phillips Farm Produce Market, packed full of fresh asparagus, sweet corn, cherries, and whatever else is in season. Phillips specializes in Rhône varietals and blends. The small cafe serves burgers made with Phillips's own range-fed beef, along with killer fresh-fruit milk shakes and pies. Tasting daily 10am–5pm; tours by appointment only.

The Van Ruiten-Taylor Winery (340 W Hwy 12, Lodi; 209/334-5722). In 1998, vineyard manager Randy Taylor teamed up with generations-old Lodi area grape growers Jim and John Van Ruiten to create this state-of-the-art winery. Surrounded by vineyards and featuring a glass-fronted, two-story tasting room, Van Ruiten-Taylor will offer one of the first cab-shiraz wines produced in this country.

Woodbridge by Robert Mondavi (5950 Woodbridge Rd, Acampo; 209/365-2839; www.robertmondavi.com). Robert Mondavi was raised among the vineyards of Lodi. In 1979, he established Woodbridge, just northeast of town. Here Mondavi produces cabernet sauvignon, chardonnay, merlot, muscat, sauvignon blanc, white zinfandel, and a specialty dessert wine called Portacinco. Tasting and retail sales Wed–Sun 9:30am–4:30pm; tours Wed–Sun 9:30am (or by appointment).

with molten mozzarella and sun-dried tomato vinaigrette. Order a bottle of one of the increasingly popular Lodi wines to round out the meal. The inn hosts special events including musical and theatrical productions in the garden between June and September. During these affairs a grand buffet is served in place of the regular menu and reservations are required. $$; AE, DC, DIS, MC, V; checks OK; lunch Tues–Fri, dinner Wed–Sat, brunch Sun; full bar; reservations required; www.winerose.com; 5 miles E of I-5, 2 miles W of Hwy 99, at Turner and Lower Sacramento Rds. &

LODGINGS

Wine and Roses Country Inn / ★★★

2505 W TURNER RD, LODI; 209/334-6988

Martha Stewart and former British Prime Minister Lady Margaret Thatcher are among the guests who've signed the register at this tasteful country inn situated on five acres of towering 100-year-old deodar cedars, cherry trees, and beautifully landscaped gardens. The 1902 estate, owned and operated by Del and Sherri Smith and their partners Russ and Kathryn Munson, has recently expanded. Included in this $5 million project are the Discover Lodi! Wine & Visitor's Center (see above), 40 new rooms, each with private courtyard entries, spa tubs, fire-places, large televisions, garden verandas, and room service; two 5,000-square-foot banquet facilities; a spa and therapy center; flower shop; pool; Jacuzzi; a large catering kitchen; and a small cafe. The 10 original rooms (named after songs) have queen-size beds, turn-of-the-century decor, and handmade comforters. In the rose-toned sitting room, camel-back couches and wing chairs are clustered around a wide fireplace that's always ablaze in the winter. Guests are treated to evening wine and a gourmet breakfast served in the popular restaurant, located on the ground floor. *$$–$$$; AE, DC, DIS, MC, V; checks OK; www.winerose. com; 5 miles E of I-5, 2 miles W of Hwy 99; at Turner and Lower Sacramento Rds.* &

Sacramento and the Delta Region

Five rivers, 57 islands, and 1,000 miles of navigable waterways make up the Sacramento River Delta, which is easily mistaken, at high tide, for a vast inland lake. It is the largest estuary on the West Coast, touching six counties, and containing half the freshwater runoff in California. After the completion of the Transcontinental Railroad in 1869, a workforce of some 10,000 Chinese laborers began work on the levee system, reclaiming the fertile farmland. Today's Delta is dotted with old-fashioned island towns, from Rio Vista to the tiny hamlets just south of Sacramento, connected by drawbridges, ferries, and winding levee roads. For a true Delta experience, **RENT A HOUSEBOAT** and cruise this labyrinth of waterways for a few days. **HOUSEBOAT, SKI-BOAT, AND WAVE-RUNNER RENTALS** are available several miles north of Stockton at **HERMAN AND HELEN'S MARINA** (off I-5, at the W end of Eight-Mile Rd; 209/951-4634; www.houseboats.com) and **PARADISE POINT MARINA** (8095 Rio Blanco; 209/952-1000 and 800/752-9669). If you'd rather explore by car, keep in mind that many folks miss the beauty of the Delta as they speed by, navigating the rivers of highway that bisect this unique and delicate ecosystem. Slow down; relax a bit, and get on "Delta time."

Rio Vista

This slow-paced Delta town, located at the junction of Highways 12 and 160, is considered by many to be the heart of the Delta. With a population of under 5,000, its residents include speed-demon Craig Breedlove—former land speed record holder—and Dennis Hope of Lunar Embassy–Celestial Property Sales, who can sell you a piece of property anywhere in the universe. There's not much to do in town—the river is the main attraction here—although you might check out the

RIO VISTA MUSEUM (16 N Front St; 707/374-5169; weekends only) for a rundown on the history of farming and dredging in the area. Even if you don't have the nerve to eat at **FOSTER'S BIGHORN** (143 Main St; 707/374-2511), it's worth a peek. This stuffy bar and restaurant displays some 300 wild game trophies from Bill Foster's private collection, including a full-grown bull elephant—complete with ivory tusks—and a giraffe! (Who could shoot a giraffe?). Humphrey the wayward humpback whale cruised this part of the river back in 1985 (good thing Foster was already dead); and there's a stone monument to Humphrey on the waterfront, adjacent to city hall.

Isleton

Once the asparagus capital of the world, and an original stop for the *Delta King,* Isleton today is known as **CRAWDAD TOWN USA**—home of the Crawdad Festival each Father's Day weekend. This sleepy little town on Highway 160 has a sense of humor (the local bait shop is the "Master-Baiter") and a Chinatown, where decrepit buildings stand beside refurbished ones.

RESTAURANTS

Riverboat II / ★★

106 W BRANNAN ISLAND RD, ISLETON; 916/777-4884

High ceilings and a nautical theme set the mood for this casual-yet-stylish floating restaurant. Formerly Moore's Riverboat (which burned in 1993), Riverboat II, located on the scenic "Delta loop," offers fine dining, excellent service, and an impressive wine list. Executive chef Micheal Cummesky is consistent and somewhat conservative—and his loyal clientele like it that way. If your party consists of four or five diners, call and reserve the Catfish McGuire room—a somewhat intimate, windowed chamber overlooking the Mokelumne River. Share the 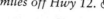 prawns and Rio Vista endive salad with walnuts, blue cheese, and a sassy basalmic vinagrette. Have your fillet of salmon blackened or broiled, or try the herb-crusted prime rib, served with Yukon gold mashed potatoes and fresh seasonal veggies. All entrees come with warm sourdough bread and your choice of thick clam chowder or salad. For dessert, if there's still room, the Delta mud cake is a specialty—a decadent chocolate cake and Jamoca almond fudge ice-cream roll, drizzled with piping-hot fudge sauce. Loosen that belt! *$$; AE, MC, V; local checks only; lunch Mon–Sat, dinner every day, brunch Sun; full bar; reservations recommended; www.riverboat2.com; 3.5 miles off Hwy 12.* &

Ryde

RESTAURANTS

The Ryde Hotel / ★★

14340 HWY 160, RYDE; 916/776-1318 OR 888/717-RYDE

Walk past the lively fountain, under the black awning, and into another era. This art deco–themed restaurant with its grand piano and black-laquered bar will transport you to a day when liquor was illegal and steamships regularly cruised this part of the Sacramento River. Look out over the golf course through expansive windows, or watch the sunset paint magenta hues along the river as you dine alfresco. The menu showcases fresh local ingredients, and dinner entrees are elegant in both taste and presentation. Try the pan-seared salmon with sage and mustard butter sauce, served with steamed asparagus. Complement your dinner with a glass of 1997 Bogle Chardonnay (Gold Medal); the vineyards are just upriver in Clarksburg. There's live jazz on Saturday nights, and if you plan to partake of the extremely popular Sunday brunch, bring your appetite and make sure you have reservations. *$$–$$$; MC, V; checks OK; dinner Fri–Sat (Apr–Nov), brunch Sun (Apr–Jan); full bar; reservations required; rydehotel@hotmail.com; www.rydehotel.com; 3-miles S of Walnut Grove on the W bank of the Sacramento River.* &

LODGINGS

The Ryde Hotel / ★★

14340 HWY 160, RYDE; 916/776-1318 OR 888/717-RYDE

Originally built as a boardinghouse, this four-story peach stucco inn on the banks of the Sacramento River became famous as a speakeasy during Prohibition, when steamers and paddleboats brought crowds of city folk in search of jazz and illicit liquor. The Ryde attracted movie stars, politicians, and presidents: Herbert Hoover announced his candidacy here in 1940. In 1997, the hotel changed hands and underwent major renovations. The new owners, Jan LeRoy and Cathy Hartrich, have managed to maintain the original historical design, while integrating modern amenities. The hotel now has 32 guest rooms decorated in a 1920s art deco style with a mauve, gray, and black color scheme. The two master suites offer sweeping views and are furnished with antique armoires, floor lamps (with beaded shades), and large Jacuzzi tubs that overlook the river. Three golf suites face the executive nine-hole golf course, which winds through a stately pear orchard. Four of the rooms exemplify the original European-style accommodations, with shared bathroom facilities. Continental breakfast is included, served in the salon or outside on one of the patios. (The Ryde's trendy restaurant, located inside the main entrance facing the river, is open on weekends.) Hotel and restaurant guests may arrive by car or tie their vessels at the private boat dock. *$$–$$$; MC, V; checks OK; rydehotel@hotmail.com; www.ryde hotel.com; 3 miles S of Walnut Grove.*

Walnut Grove

RESTAURANTS

Orilla del Rio / ★★

14133 MARKET ST, WALNUT GROVE; 916/776-2007

This family-owned restaurant pumps out the best Mexican food in the Delta. Meals seem to be health-conscious, so if you order wisely, your cholesterol count won't skyrocket too seriously. Try the chile-lime chicken wings for starters and the alligator tacos for something totally different. The chile verde, made with lean pork, is very good. A variety of house-made salsas are always available at the salsa bar, and if you're really not watching that cholesterol, finish off your meal with an order of the delightfully rich flan. *$; no credit cards; checks OK; breakfast Sun, lunch, dinner Tues–Sun; beer and wine; no reservations; 1 block E of Hwy 160.* &

Locke

The town of Locke was established in 1915, soon after a devastating fire destroyed the neighboring Chinese community of Walnut Grove. Since Asian Americans at that time could not legally own property, a committee of Chinese merchants, led by (Charlie) Lee Bing, approached landowner George Locke and persuaded him to allow a new community to be built on his land. Chinese architects designed Lockeport, which became Locke as it exists today. At one time this hamlet claimed more than 600 permanent residents. Businesses flourished; illicit activities also thrived in the form of gambling houses, brothels, speakeasies, and opium dens.

Locke was the educational center for the region. The Joe Shoong Chinese School was built in 1926, with funding from Joe Shoong, the millionaire who founded National Dollar Stores. Shoong endorsed Chinese language, art, and culture in schools built specifically for Chinese youth. Located at the north end of town, the school is still in use today and is open for public viewing. Next door, **YUEN CHONG MARKET**, established in 1916 by a Chinese cooperative, stocks a nice selection of cold drinks. Today, you can wander Locke's Main Street and easily imagine what it must have been like in the days of Prohibition. Notice the worn wooden sidewalks; like the town, they seem warped in time. Visit the **DAI LOY GAMBLING HOUSE MUSEUM**, and step into **AL THE WOP'S**, Lee Bing's original restaurant. For information regarding a guided tour of Locke, given by a resident historian, stop in at **LOCKE ART CENTER** (916/776-1661).

THE BOK-BOK MAN

Bok . . . bok . . . bok . . . the hollow sound of bamboo-mallet on wooden-box echoed through the darkness. Residents, knowing he was there, rested peacefully. Every hour on the hour, year after year, through heavy rain, winter fog, and summer winds, he walked up and down Main Street. Today, no one remembers his name—he is simply the bok-bok man. Because of the fire hazard associated with numerous households living in tightly packed wooden-framed buildings, the town of Locke hired this man to walk Main Street every night and serve as a night fire-watchman. He could very well be the reason that Locke, the only town built by the Chinese for the Chinese, still stands today. Other Chinese communities in the Delta were destroyed by major fires, some of them twice.

The small, rectangular, bok-bok box was hand carried and struck on the hour (the number of hits reflected the hour) beginning at 1am and continuing through the early morning until 5am. The sound could be heard for surprisingly long distances and served as the signal that all was well. For many residents, especially the farmworkers, the bok-bok man was an alarm clock. His salary was collected from the community: 25 cents per month, per household. The bok-bok man patrolled Locke until his death in 1955. His original bok-bok box and mallet are on display at the Dai Loy Gambling House Museum on Main Street (13951 Main St, Locke; 916/776-1661).   —*Lori Makabe*

RESTAURANTS

Al the Wop's / ★

13943 MAIN ST, LOCKE; 916/776-1800

Al Adami bought this former Chinese restaurant in 1934. When Al died in 1961, his bartender Ralph Santos Sr. took over this venerable and legendary delta institution. Ralph, in turn, was succeeded by his son in 1981, who changed the name of this restaurant to Al's Place—a more politically correct moniker. Alas, the name change didn't go over too well, in part because people drove the phone company crazy asking for "Al the Wop's" and got very surly when the name didn't come up in the database. In June 1995, Ralph's nephews, Lorenzo and Steve Giannetti, took over the place and, by popular demand, reinstated the old name. Everything else here remains pretty much the same. The low-ceilinged dining room in the back of the building is furnished with long tables and benches—just as it was in the '30s. The food is simple but adequate and the assorted tourists, boaters, and local characters who hang out here like it that way. For lunch, try Al's traditional steak or chicken dishes or one of the newer menu items: hamburgers and cheeseburgers. Tuesday's are steak and lobster nights; otherwise, Al's dinners are limited to chicken and New York steaks (12 or 18 ounces) served with a side of spaghetti or french fries and maybe a bowl of homemade minestrone. *$; no credit cards; checks OK; lunch, dinner every day; full bar; no reservations; middle of Main St.*

Sacramento

Heart and center of the Central Valley and capital city of the state, Sacramento has long been regarded as the second-class stepsister of San Francisco. But with its increasing number of skyscrapers, upscale restaurants, and swanky hotels (as well as the NBA's Sacramento Kings, the women's NBA Sacramento Monarchs, and Class AAA baseball's Rivercats), California's capital city is no longer the sleepy little valley town folks whiz through on their way to Lake Tahoe. Located 90 miles northeast of the Bay Area, the city is best known for its dual status as the seat of state government and the epicenter of California's biggest industry—agriculture. But disregard any disparaging words you may have heard about this fertile hot spot: there are no cows (or even cowboy hats) within city limits, and most of the city slickers do not pick tomatoes for a living.

A former Gold Rush boomtown, Sacramento sprang up where the American and Sacramento Rivers meet—a tourist area now known as Old Sacramento. In 1839 Swiss immigrant John Sutter traversed both waterways, built his famous fort, and established his colony called New Helvetia (New Switzerland). But his hopes that the thriving colony would evolve into his own vast empire were dashed when gold was discovered up near his sawmill in 1848. Sutter's colonists deserted New Helvetia to search for the precious nuggets, and as word of the discovery spread, thousands more wound their way to the hills above Sacramento to seek their fortune. Ironically, Sutter himself never prospered from the Gold Rush and he died a bitter, penniless man.

Today Sacramento is home to more than a million people, many of whom play politics with the capital crowd or practice law. They dote on their spectacular Victorian homes and fine Craftsman-style bungalows, and are justly proud of the tree-lined streets and thick carpets of grass that surround their houses and parks.

In the scorching summer months, when thermometers often soar above three digits for days, many folks beat the heat by diving into swimming pools, chugging around the Delta on a houseboat, or floating down the American River in a raft or an inner tube. Once the sun sets, however, things usually cool off dramatically. Winters are punctuated by the famous tule fog—so thick it can block the sun for weeks at a time. But as all ski buffs know, Sacramentans get the jump on their Bay Area neighbors racing to the snowy slopes of Tahoe, thanks to the city's proximity to the Sierra Nevada.

ACCESS AND INFORMATION

Conveniently located just 15 minutes from downtown, the **SACRA-MENTO INTERNATIONAL AIRPORT** (916/874-0700) is easily accessible from Interstate 5. **SUPERSHUTTLE** Sacramento (www.supershuttle.com; 800/BLUE-VAN) provides door-to-door service, while taxi and van service is available 24 hours a day from **SACRAMENTO INDEPENDENT TAXI** (916/457-4862) and Yellow Cab (800/464-0777). **AMTRAK**'s Capitol Routes (5th and I Sts; 800/872-7245) connect Sacramento and the Bay Area several times a day. City **BUS** and **LIGHT RAIL** service is operated by **SACRAMENTO REGIONAL TRANSIT DISTRICT** (916/321-BUSS) and the **GREYHOUND** terminal (7th and L Sts; 800/231-2222) is open 24 hours and can connect you to just about anywhere. By car, Interstate 5 and US Highway 99 reach Sacramento on the north-south route; Interstate 80 is a direct route from the Bay Area, and US Highway 50 will get you there from Lake Tahoe/Reno. Once downtown, it's nice to know that the "lettered" city streets (C–Z) run from north to south, with M Street also being known as Capitol, and the "numbered" streets (2nd–29th) run west to east, with 1st Street referred to as Front Street due to its location on the waterfront. **PARKING** can be a challenge along the streets, so look for the large public lots, which usually have spaces available. For more information, contact the **SACRAMENTO CONVENTION AND VISITORS BUREAU** (1303 J St, Ste 600; 916/264-7777; www.sacramentocvb.org) or drop in at the **VISITOR INFORMATION CENTER** (1101 2nd St; 916/442-7644), located in Old Sacramento.

MAJOR ATTRACTIONS

To best appreciate this thriving city, visit **OLD SACRAMENTO** (a.k.a. Old Sac), the historic district. Perched along the Sacramento River, this four-block-long stretch is filled with dozens of restaurants, gift shops, and saloons. An Old Sac highlight is the **CALIFORNIA STATE RAILROAD MUSEUM** (125 I St at 2nd St; 916/323-9280), a grand monument to the glory days of locomotion and the Big Four; it's the largest museum of its kind in the nation. The granddaddy of Old Sac attractions is the Sacramento Dixieland Jubilee, the world's largest Dixieland jazz festival, which attracts thousands of toe-tappers and bands from around the world each Memorial Day weekend (916/372-5277). One mile south of this historic district is the **TOWE FORD MUSEUM OF AUTOMOTIVE HISTORY** (2200 Front St; 916/442-6802), which boasts the largest antique Ford collection in the world. Nearby is the **CROCKER ART MUSEUM** (216 O St at 3rd St; 916/264-5423), home of the region's largest art collection, including a stunning collection of European master drawings and a fine selection of contemporary California art by local talents who made the big time, such as Wayne Thiebaud and Robert Arneson. **LA RAZA GALLERIA POSADA** (704 O St at 7th St; 916/446-5133) is a Chicano, Latino, and Native

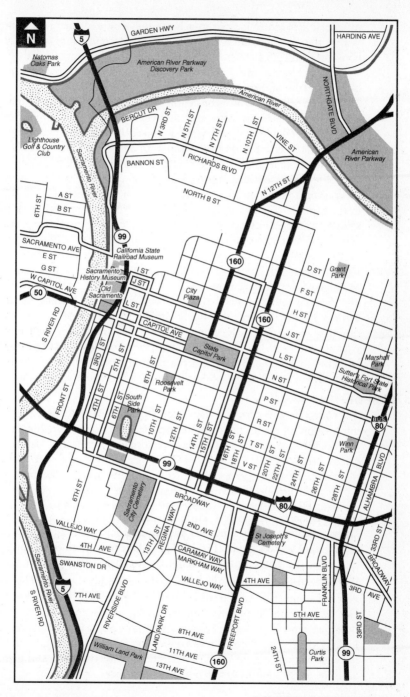

DOWNTOWN SACRAMENTO

American arts center located in a beautifully restored Victorian house. Within this complex are a cultural center, a contemporary art gallery, bookstore, and gift shop stocked with wonderful Mexican folk art.

A few blocks northeast of the gallery is the awe-inspiring **STATE CAPITOL** (10th St, between L and N Sts; 916/324-0333), restored in the 1970s to its original turn-of-the-century magnificence with $67.8 million in taxpayers' dollars (so come see what you paid for). You may wander around the building on your own, but you really shouldn't miss the free tours given daily every hour between 9am and 4pm. Tours include an overview of the legislative process and, if you're lucky, a chance to see the political hotshots in action. Tickets are handed out a half hour before the tour on a first-come, first-served basis in the basement of room B-27 in the capitol. While you're getting your tickets, pick up a copy of the **STATE CAPITOL TREE TOUR** brochure so you can saunter through marvelous **CAPITOL PARK** and admire more than 340 varieties of trees from around the world. Also worth a visit, the **SACRAMENTO ZOO** (Sutterville Rd and Land Park Dr; 916/264-5888) houses 400 animals, including 32 endangered or threatened species.

If you're a big history buff, step back in time by strolling through **SUTTER'S FORT** (between K and L Sts, at 27th; 916/445-4422), where you can view the restored self-contained community that Sutter built in the wilderness in 1839. On the same grounds is the **CALIFORNIA STATE INDIAN MUSEUM** (916/324-0539), with artifacts from more than 100 California Indian tribes, including one of the finest basket collections in the nation.

PERFORMING ARTS

The **SACRAMENTO CONVENTION CENTER** (1400 J St; 916/264-5291) has information on the Sacramento Philharmonic (box office 916/264-5181) and other big-name jazz and classical performers. Just up the road is the **CREST THEATER** (1013 K St; 916/442-7378), a refurbished art deco palace that hosts rock, folk, reggae, and world beat concerts and runs classic movies.

Sacramento has a thriving live theater scene, and two top venues are the **SACRAMENTO THEATER COMPANY** (1419 H St; 916/446-7501) and the **B STREET THEATER** (2711 B St; 916/443-5300), cofounded by TV and film star Timothy Busfield and his brother Buck. The **SACRAMENTO LIGHT OPERA ASSOCIATION** (1419 H St; 916/557-1999) hosts one of the city's most popular summer pastimes, the **MUSIC CIRCUS**, an annual festival of Broadway musicals presented under a big-top tent. This 50-year-old summer musical tradition revives the music of Cole Porter, the Gershwins, and Stephen Sondheim using professional casts from Broadway and Hollywood. Equally if not more popular, the Sacramento Light Opera Association's **BROADWAY SERIES** runs from September through May, featuring as many as nine Broadway shows and giving Sacramento 11 months of top-notch performances.

RECREATION

Sacramento's two most notable natural attractions are its two rivers: the boat-filled, bustling, brown Sacramento River and the raft-filled, sparkling blue American River. For cyclists and joggers, nothing beats the **AMERICAN RIVER PARKWAY**, a 5,000-acre nature preserve with a 22-mile-long, pothole-free bike trail, which starts in Old Sac and follows the water all the way to the town of Folsom. You can rent a bike for about $15 a day at **CITY BICYCLE WORKS** (2419 K St; 916/447-2453). In the sweltering Sacramento summers many locals and visitors alike abandon their bikes for a leisurely raft trip down the American River with **AMERICAN RIVER RAFT RENTALS** (11257 S Bridge St, Rancho Cordova; 916/635-6400) or head for **SIX FLAGS–WATERWORLD USA** (1600 Exposition Blvd; 916/924-0556). **SHADOW GLEN RIDING STABLES** (4854 Main Ave, Orangevale; 916/989-1826) offers hourly horseback riding and guided trail rides around Folsom Lake and the Iceland ice skating rink (1430 Del Paso Blvd; 916/925-3121) provides a cool indoor alternative. If you're cruising through town during the last two weeks of August, set aside a day or night to visit the **CALIFORNIA STATE FAIR** (916/263-3000; www.bigfun.org), Sacramento's grandest party. The carnival rides are not for the faint of stomach, but the livestock exhibits and wine tasting are worth the admission price. Located at Cal Expo (at Expo Boulevard, off the I-80/Capital City Fwy).

RESTAURANTS

Biba / ★★★★

2801 CAPITOL AVE, SACRAMENTO; 916/455-2422

Biba is a study in understated neo-deco design—the sort of place where you'd expect precious, trendy foods to dominate the menu. Fortunately, they don't. Bologna-born chef/owner Biba Caggiano is a traditionalist to the core, and what comes out of her kitchen is exactly what she learned at her mother's elbow: classical Italian cooking based on the finest ingredients available and a painstaking attention to detail. The menu changes seasonally, but expect to find such entrees as grilled shrimp wrapped in basil and Parma ham, melt-in-your-mouth nutmeg-and-ricotta tortellini, angel hair pasta tossed with sun-dried tomatoes, a phenomenal shrimp-studded linguine, duck cooked with port and Italian cherries, and rosemary-infused lamb chops. As if all that weren't enough, the service is superb and the long list of domestic and Italian wines should please even the snootiest connoisseur. Top off your marvelous meal with Biba's divine double-chocolate trifle. In addition to running one of the region's finest restaurants, Biba has written more than half a dozen books on Italian cooking—her latest is *Italy Al Dente*. $$$; AE, DC, MC, V; no checks; lunch Mon–Fri, dinner Mon–Sat; full bar; reservations recommended; biba@infovillage.com; www.infovillage.com/biba; at 28th St. &

David Berkley / ★★★

515 PAVILIONS LN, SACRAMENTO; 916/929-4422

Located in the Pavilions, Sacramento's most upscale shopping mall, David Berkley is essentially a delicatessen—but, wow, what a deli! Just about everything served here is perfect. There's even a superior selection of wine and beer, and the deli section offers nearly two-dozen different salads every day, including several low-fat options. Try sinking your teeth into the savory smoked-chicken salad, the wild rice and pear salad, or the luscious shrimp, avocado, cucumber, and fresh dill combination. David Berkley (named after the owner) also offers a takeout dinner menu, which changes weekly and features four entrees and a selection of side dishes. A takeout meal might include a salad of jicama and orange slices tossed with a citrus vinaigrette; a thick, grilled New York steak crusted with Dijon mustard and horseradish; herbed mashed potatoes; and sautéed baby vegetables. Finish your feast with a decadent cheesecake or tart. Arrive early if you're planning to eat here, since seating is limited (most tables are outdoors) and this place packs 'em in. *$$; AE, MC, V; checks OK; lunch every day; beer and wine; no reservations; dberkley@spyderwebb.com; in the Pavilions shopping center, on the N side of Fair Oaks Blvd, between Howe and Fulton Aves.* &

Dos Coyotes Border Cafe / ★★

1735 ARDEN WY, SACRAMENTO; 916/927-0377

With its leaping lizards and chile pepper decor, this Arden Fair branch of the popular eatery in Davis is always hopping—serving up consistently fresh and creative fare like mango-charbroiled chicken quesadillas or paella burritos. For a full review, see the Restaurants section of Davis. *$; AE, MC, V; no checks; lunch, dinner every day; beer and wine; no reservations; at Market Square in the Arden Fair shopping mall.* &

The Fox and Goose / ★★★

1001 R ST, SACRAMENTO; 916/443-8825

You'll see chaps chugging down pints of bitter and having a jolly good time over a game of darts at this bustling British pub, almost as genuine as any neighborhood spot you're likely to find in the United Kingdom. Owned by Allyson Dalton, the Fox and Goose is a River City institution, offering a wee bit of everything—beer, breakfast, lunch, and live music—and doing it all wonderfully. There are 13 beers on tap, including brews from England, Ireland, and Scotland. For breakfast, choose from a variety of omelets, as well as kippers (Atlantic herring), grilled tomatoes, crumpets, and such authentic English treats as bangers and mash; or you can take the California-cuisine route and order the vegetarian pub grill (scrambled tofu mixed with pesto and red onions or curry and green onions). The Fox and Goose is famous for its burnt cream (a rich, velvety custard topped with caramelized brown sugar), but the other desserts are equally delectable. Be forewarned: This is a popular pub and reservations are not accepted, so arrive a little early, particularly for lunch. At night the place swings to folk, jazz, and bluegrass tunes. *$; AE, MC, V; local checks only; breakfast, lunch every day, dinner Sat–Sun; beer and wine; no reservations; www. infovillage.com/fox&goose; at 12th St, just S of the capitol.* &

Lemon Grass / ★★★★

601 MONROE ST, SACRAMENTO; 916/486-4891

This elegant restaurant, offering a unique blend of Vietnamese and Thai cooking, keeps getting better and better and is approaching nirvana. Husband-and-wife owners Mai Pham and Trong Nguyen use local organically grown produce, fresh seafood, Petaluma free-range chicken, and little or no oil in many of their culinary masterpieces. The Siamese Seafood Feast, a Thai bouillabaisse, comes bubbling with fresh clams, sea scallops, mussels, and prawns in a spicy, hot-and-sour broth infused with lemongrass, galangal (Thai ginger), kaffir lime leaves, and chiles. Other standout dishes include the fillet of farm-raised catfish cooked in a caramelized garlic sauce and the Thai green curry, made with slices of chicken breast, bamboo shoots, and peas simmered in a curry-based coconut milk. The wide-ranging dessert menu features such delicacies as Saigon by Night, a blend of Vietnamese espresso, hazelnut syrup, whipped cream, and vanilla ice cream; a silky house-made caramelized Australian ginger ice cream with Grand Marnier sauce; and a banana cheesecake drizzled with warm coconut sauce. Mai, a best-selling author, has been featured in *Martha Stewart Living* and on National Public Radio's program *Fresh Air*. Her latest cookbook is entitled *Life, Love, and a Bowl of Pho*. *$$; AE, DC, MC, V; no checks; lunch Mon–Fri, dinner Mon–Sat; full bar; reservations recommended; maipham@ibm.net; just N of Fair Oaks Blvd, near Loehmann's Plaza shopping center.* &

Paragary's Bar and Oven / ★★★

1401 28TH ST, SACRAMENTO; 916/485-7100
2220 GOLD SPRINGS COURT, SACRAMENTO; 916/852-0214

Paragary's Bar and Oven restaurants (there are two in Sacramento alone) were voted Best Overall Restaurants by the readers of the *Sacramento Bee* and *Sacramento Magazine*. The 28th Street branch is the small chain's flagship. Both locations are well known for zesty pizzas cooked in wood-burning ovens, mesquite-grilled entrees that typically have a strong Italian accent, and freshly made pastas and desserts. Part of the Randy Paragary empire, each Sacramento branch has different and wonderfully imaginative menus that change frequently and feature produce from the restaurant's own garden. Recent offerings included grilled asparagus with shallots, marinated beets, and capers; prosciutto-wrapped pears with warm goat cheese, hazelnuts, and arugula; a pizza with Italian sausage, cilantro pesto, sautéed red onions, and sweet peppers with mozzarella; and a grilled lamb sirloin with garlic mashed potatoes, fava beans, and black olive relish. The 28th Street location has a courtyard and a well-stocked bar. *$$$; AE, DC, MC, V; no checks; lunch Mon–Fri, dinner every day; full bar; reservations recommended; www.paragarys.com; at N St.* &

Rio City Cafe / ★★

1110 FRONT ST, SACRAMENTO; 916/442-8226

Located on the Sacramento River smack dab in the middle of "Old Sac," the city's premier tourist attraction, the Rio City Cafe has a commanding view up and down this Old Man River. The pleasantly light, airy, attractive dining room also offers a view of the glassed-in kitchen so you can watch the cooks as they sauté and grill the evening's entrees—a scene reminiscent of drones in a busy beehive. The fare here is primarily Southwestern with a dash of California and a soupçon of New Orleans. For lunch, expect a large variety of soups, salads, and sandwiches; the dinner entrees change as regularly as the delta tides. Rio's extensive wine list features a thoughtful collection of California vintages. *$$; AE, DC, DIS, MC, V; no checks; lunch, dinner every day; full bar; reservations recommended; between J and K Sts.* &

Tapa the World / ★★

2115 J ST, SACRAMENTO; 916/442-4353

Choose from a wide selection of flavorful tapas (Spanish appetizers) and other specialties in this extremely popular dinner house, one of the few in Sacramento that serves until midnight. Tapa your feet to the live Spanish and flamenco guitar performances every night of the week. The wine list offers numerous varietals from both Spain and California to complement your meal. Try one of the paellas; the deep-dish, saffron-simmered rice feasts, available in *mariscos* (seafood), *mixta* (combination of chicken, seafood, and chorizo), or vegetarian versions; or try the *Lomo de Cordero*, marinated grilled lamb loin served with wild mushroom rice and three specialty sauces—Rioja wine, avocado, and balsamic. The menu also features a braised tri-tip dinner and a grilled venison, served with an apricot-sangría glaze and grilled zucchini, garnished with a pâté of duck. And don't miss the most popular dessert specialty, chocolate addiction—a double-layered chocolate mousse cake topped with a warm simmered and reduced sangría and fresh strawberries. *$$; AE, DIS, MC, V; no checks; lunch, dinner every day; beer and wine; no reservations; on J St between 21st and 22nd Sts.* &

33rd Street Bistro / ★★★

3301 FOLSOM BLVD, SACRAMENTO; 916/455-2282

The 33rd Street Bistro was a huge success right from the start, and it just keeps getting better. Chef/owner Fred Haines has combined a casual, trendy ambience—a handsome red brick wall, high ceilings, polished wood floors, and vibrant oversize paintings of vegetables—with terrific food at reasonable prices. You can order the excellent salads in a large or "lite" size, including a knockout Mediterranean salad tossed with wood-roasted chicken, sweet red peppers, red onions, white beans, and feta. The entrees, called "large plates," usually include your choice of salmon, chicken, or pork and are served with grilled or sautéed seasonal vegetables. The daily soups are always outstanding, and so are the seasonal desserts. Expect a crowd during peak dining hours—and this is probably not the place for a marriage proposal (or even a proposition), unless you don't mind yelling a bit. *$$; AE, MC, V; checks OK; breakfast, lunch, dinner every day; full bar; no reservations; at 33rd St.* &

Twenty Eight / ★★★★

2730 N ST, SACRAMENTO; 916/456-2800
Twenty Eight, transformed from the Capitol Grill, is a romantic, upscale restaurant with plump, cozy chairs, mirrored walls, chandeliers, and large tables. The food is delectable, both in taste and presentation, and the service is excellent. Recent culinary creations included lobster pot stickers with curry sauce and a pea sprout salad, as well as a sesame-crusted ahi tuna steak with crispy noodles, shiitake mushrooms, bok choy, and a Chinese black bean sauce. The extensive wine list includes more than 200 of the best labels from California and France. This is a dining experience that's definitely on a par with what you'll find at fine restaurants in San Francisco. *$$$; AE, DC, MC, V; local checks only; lunch Mon–Fri, dinner Mon–Sat; full bar; reservations recommended; www.paragarys.com/twentyeight; at 28th and N Sts.*

The Waterboy / ★★★

2000 CAPITOL AVE, SACRAMENTO; 916/498-9891
Chef/owner Rick Mahan insists on fresh, high quality ingredients like naturally raised beef and lamb from Niman Ranch, organic produce from Winter Creek Gardens and Fiddlers Green Farm, and outstanding breads from the Grace Baking Company. Named after the Celtic rock band the Waterboys, this midtown restaurant is a bright and cheery gem, serving bold and imaginative dishes inspired by recipes from southern France and northern Italy. The menu changes monthly to stay in sync with the seasons. A recent dinner menu included handmade potato gnocchi with pesto and vine ripe cherry tomatoes; carnaroli risotto with veal cheeks, porcini mushrooms, tomatoes, Reggiano, and sage; and a sweet corn soup. If there's room for dessert, don't miss the heavenly creations of Edie Stewart, like the warm fruit crostada with vanilla bean ice cream and caramel. The wine list promotes fine California varietals and ports with choices available by bottle, glass, or half-glass. *$$–$$$; AE, DC, DIS, MC, V; no checks; lunch Tues–Fri, dinner Tues–Sun; beer and wine; reservations recommended; info@waterboyrestaurant.com;www. waterboyrestaurant.com; at 20th St and Capitol Ave.* &

Zinfandel Grille / ★★★

2384 FAIR OAKS BLVD, SACRAMENTO; 916/485-7100

The two Zinfandel Grilles (there is one in Folsom, see review) were formerly known as Paragary's Bar and Oven, owned by John Hankard and once affiliated with Randy Paragary's fine dining establishments. The name changed in September 2000, but the menu (which changes every two months) still shines with the creative talents of executive chef Doug Eby. Readers of the *Sacramento Bee* have voted this establishment "Best American," and Eby and his staff continue to please the population with entrees like four-mushroom lasagne (porcini, oyster, crimini, and shiitake), with beautifully blended flavors and béchamel sauce, or grilled, spice-crusted pork tenderloin with Anaheim chiles and zucchini, with cilantro pesto and fried polenta. And don't miss the opportunity to try one (or more) of the award-winning desserts from pastry chef Pat Conroy—seasonal crème brûlée, tiramisu, Boston cream pie—any of which will leave you speechless. *$$$; AE, MC, V; no checks; lunch, dinner every day; full bar; reservations recommended; between Howe and Fulton Aves.* ঌ

LODGINGS

Amber House / ★★★★

1315 22ND ST, SACRAMENTO; 916/444-8085 OR 800/755-6526

Amber House is actually three restored historic homes—two set side by side (a 1905 Craftsman and a 1913 Mediterranean) and one across the street (an 1895 colonial revival). The 14 guest rooms, named after artists, poets, and musicians, have private, Italian-marble-tiled baths stocked with plush robes (11 also have Jacuzzi tubs for two), private phones with voice mail, cable TVs with VCRs, and CD players. The Van Gogh Room offers a spectacular bathroom with a heart-shaped Jacuzzi for two that perhaps even Vincent would have liked. Guests may enjoy their gourmet breakfast at whatever time they wish, served in their room, the dining room, or in one of the inn's several delightful gardens. Amber House is located on a quiet, shady street eight blocks from the capitol and is within easy walking distance of half a dozen of Sacramento's finest restaurants. *$$; AE, DC, DIS, MC, V; checks OK; innkeeper@amberhouse.com; www.amberhouse.com; between Capitol Ave and N St.*

Hyatt Regency Sacramento / ★★★★

1209 L ST, SACRAMENTO; 916/443-1234 OR 800/233-1234

This is the only lodging in Sacramento that truly feels like a big-city hotel. It boasts a vaulted marble entryway; a sumptuous, light-filled atrium lounge; 500 beautifully appointed rooms with pretty views of palm-tree-lined Capitol Park; and excellent service. There are two fine restaurants on the hotel's main floor: Dawson's, a chophouse that caters mostly to meat eaters with its prime rib, pepper steak, and filet mignon; and the cross-cultural Ciao-Yama, an Italian/Japanese restaurant offering a variety of creative salads, entrees, and desserts. The outstanding artwork displayed throughout the hotel—murals, paintings, and wrought-iron railings and banisters—is by local artists. *$$$; AE, DC, DIS, MC, V; checks OK; www.hyatt.com; at 12th St, across from the capitol.* &

Sterling Hotel / ★★★★

1300 H ST, SACRAMENTO; 916/448-1300 OR 800/365-7660

From the outside, this striking, turn-of-the-century Victorian inn with its beautiful garden and manicured lawn immediately draws the attention of all who pass by. Inside, it's a sleek luxury hotel aimed at the upper echelon of corporate travelers. The Sterling's interior is awash in Asian-influenced, neo-deco flourishes, and the artwork has a decidedly Zen twist. The 16 guest rooms are large, airy, and spotless; each has a marble bathroom equipped with a Jacuzzi, replicas of antique furniture, big, CEO-style desks, voice mail and data ports, and numerous brass fixtures. Chanterelle, the hotel's small but highly regarded restaurant, is located on the ground floor with a charming patio for fair-weather dining. *$$$; AE, DC, MC, V; checks OK when mailed in advance; www.sterlinghotel.com; at 13th St.* &

Northern Central Valley

Leaving the urban, political sprawl of Sacramento, the Northern Central Valley opens into a patchwork of farmland and orchards, stitched together by country roads and small towns. From historic Sutter Street in Folsom to the charming college town of Chico, with its abundance of outdoor activity options, this region of the Golden State has something for everyone.

Folsom

RESTAURANTS

Alexander's Meritage / ★★★★

6608 FOLSOM-AUBURN RD, STE 9, FOLSOM; 916/988-7000

Chef/owner Vincent Paul Alexander consistently delivers excellence. From the appetizers to the French roast, your dining experience here will be memorable. Try, for example, the butter-poached lobster served on a bed of risotto tossed with sweet pumpkin and sprinkled with asiago cheese, or the roasted corn blini stuffed with Atlantic king salmon and topped with a dollop of caviar. On one visit, choices of tempting entrees included smoked boneless quail stuffed with a brandy cherry dressing served with a port wine demi-glace, and seared ahi tuna with a cumin seed crust served over baby greens tossed with a jalapeño cilantro vinaigrette. The wines were equally engaging, especially Meritage's rare cabernets, such as the Beringer Reserve 1992. Desserts included a chocolate coconut cheesecake and a poached pear in a buttery flaky pastry, smothered with a rich caramel sauce. *$$$; AE, DIS, MC, V; no checks; dinner Tues–Sun; full bar; reservations recommended; in the Folsom Pavilions Center.* &

Christophe's French Restaurant / ★★★★

2304 E BIDWELL ST, FOLSOM; 916/983-4883

Voted Best French Restaurant by *Sacramento Magazine* 2000, Christophe's, and new owners Ali Mazkani and Lisa Watts, are off to a very good start. The talented new chef, Kenneth Llewellyn, a graduate of the Culinary Institute of America in Hyde Park, New York, is formerly from the Sacramento area. On a recent visit, his creations included a sautéed wild mushroom medley in a creamy vegetable au jus, stuffed in a fresh puff pastry shell for a starter, and the soup du jour was a gently spiced fresh tomato blend, sprinkled with chives. Entrees on this menu, which changes seasonally, included a sautéed mapleleaf duck breast with blackberry coulis and olive oil potato purée, and a tender "Mountain Meadows" brand loin of lamb served with ratatouille and au gratin potatoes. The atmosphere is open, light, and airy, with a courtyard, gardens, and a dramatic fountain. The wine list is extensive, covering both French and California recommendations. And don't skip over the dessert selections carefully prepared by dessert chef Jasmine Jackson. Notables include her elegant chocolate crème brûlée, the fresh fruit tarts, and the fresh berry compote. *$$$; AE, DIS, MC, V; no checks; dinner Tues–Sat; full bar; reservations recommended; lisa@christophes.com; www. christophes.com; between Creekside Dr and Oak Ave.* &

Zinfandel Grille / ★★★

705 GOLD LAKE DR, FOLSOM; 916/985-3321

Located near Lake Natoma, this branch of the well-liked eatery in Sacramento is very popular, even at lunchtime, so reservations are strongly advised. On par with the other fine dining establishments in Folsom, the Zinfandel serves such culinary delights as grilled portobello mushrooms and sweet onion risotto-fontina cake with a balsamic vinegar sauce for starters and spinach linguine with smoked salmon and mussels with leeks, fresh dill, shallots, and a touch of vermouth. For a full review, see the main branch in the Sacramento section. *$$$; AE, MC, V; no checks; lunch, dinner every day; full bar; reservations recommended; in The Lakes shopping center.* &

Loomis

LODGINGS

Emma's Bed and Breakfast / ★★★

3137 TAYLOR RD, LOOMIS; 916/652-1392

 Perched on a hill overlooking apple, walnut, and mandarin orange orchards, this stately manor situated on 45 acres is impressively furnished and decorated. It has five guest suites with opulent private baths, down-filled duvets, TVs with VCRs, and fax/PC hookups. Three of the suites are in the immaculately renovated 1912 farmhouse, and two are in a new, matching building next door. The Orchard Suite features mahogany antiques, including a beautiful Louis XV queen-size bed. Lovebirds may opt for the luxurious Honeymoon Suite. The full breakfasts are different every day and include juice, an entree such as German pancakes, and coffee or tea. *$$; DIS, MC, V; checks OK; info@emmasbnb.com; www.emmasbnb.com; between King and Penryn Rds.* &

The Old Flower Farm Bed and Breakfast Inn / ★★★

4150 AUBURN-FOLSOM RD, LOOMIS; 916/652-4200
Set in a bucolic countryside and oozing charm from every 100-year-old board, the Old Flower Farm looks out over (what else?) a flower farm. With its century-old architecture lovingly painted and restored, it looks like a cover shot for *Sunset* magazine. And inside it's even more impressive. Owner Jenny Leonard, a longtime professional decorator, has turned this into a special place indeed. The living room's focal point is a red Vermont stove set on a rock hearth, which, with the two antique wing-back chairs, a large upright wicker chair, and an overstuffed celadon green sofa, cry out for a good book and a willing reader. Upstairs are three guest bedrooms, each with a queen-size bed topped with overstuffed down pillows and a private bath with a claw-footed tub and shower. The largest unit, the Country Checker Room, is filled with antiques, a white wicker chaise longue, a high poster bed with a Victorian dresser, and red- and white-checked curtains. Adjacent to the main house is the Honeymoon Cottage, decorated in neutral tones with a net-draped queen-size bed. The swimming pool beckons on hot summer days, and Folsom Lake, a mecca for boaters and anglers, is only a five-minute drive away. Breakfasts are healthy and hearty, served with fresh fruit, home-made jams, and juices made from the farm's own produce. *$$–$$$; AE, MC, V; checks OK; flowerbnb@jps.net; members/aol.com/rosiesmile/offi.html; halfway between the towns of Auburn and Folsom, at Horseshoe Bar.*

Davis

The **UNIVERSITY OF CALIFORNIA AT DAVIS** (UCD) is this little city's claim to fame, particularly the college's respected veterinary science and enology schools. A former farming town, Davis is also famous for its city officials who pride themselves on finding more ecological ways of living on the planet. For example, to encourage people to cut down on fuel consumption, the city has built 67 miles of bike lanes and trails. The urban-village atmosphere of downtown Davis draws shoppers, diners, and browsers to its charming streets. Great minds of Davis get their world-shaking ideas while sipping espresso at **MISHKA'S CAFE** (514 2nd St; 530/759-0811); they spend hours studying the works of other great

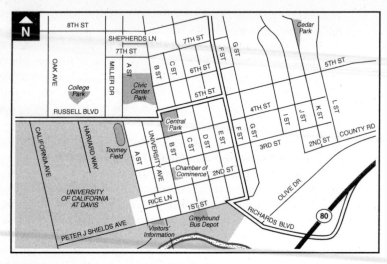

DAVIS

minds at the **AVID READER** (617 2nd St; 530/758-4040); and they take out their aggressions by climbing the walls (literally) at **ROCKNASIUM** (720 Olive Dr; 530 757-2902). The **PALMS PLAYHOUSE** (726 Drummand Ave; 530/756-9901) features nationally known blues, country, jazz, and folk acts, and the **DAVIS MUSICAL THEATRE COMPANY** (530/756-3682) stages 10 musical productions each year. Or, if you've always wanted to jump out of an airplane, try **SKYDANCE SKYDIVING** (Yolo County Airport; 800/759-3483; www.1800skydive.com). For more information on what to see and do in Davis, call the **DAVIS CHAMBER OF COMMERCE** (530/756-0191).

RESTAURANTS

Dos Coyotes Border Cafe / ★★

1411 W COVELL BLVD #108, DAVIS; 530/753-0922

This distant outpost of Southwestern cuisine is one of the hottest places in Davis. The crowds come for the fresh, consistently good food, such as the house-made salsas (help yourself to the salsa bar), shrimp tacos, and ranchero burritos with marinated steak, chicken, or vegetarian fillings.

Equally good are the more unconventional offerings, such as the mahimahi taco or the Yucatán salad with marinated charbroiled chicken breast, black beans, red onion, carrots, cabbage, sweet peppers, and corn served on a flour tortilla. If you have room for dessert, sample the light-as-a-feather Santa Fe wedding cookies dusted with powdered sugar. Owner Bobby Coyote has turned his cafe into a howling success—even the branch in Sacramento (1735 Arden Wy; 916/927-0377) attracts crowds. *$; AE, MC, V; local checks only; lunch, dinner every day; beer and wine; reservations recommended; in the Marketplace shopping center, just E of Hwy 113.* &

Soga's Restaurant / ★★★

217 E ST, DAVIS; 530/757-1733
If you didn't know about this exquisite slip of a restaurant, you might pass right by it. Word of mouth has transformed the classy spot into a bustling establishment where reservations are highly recommended. Chef/owner Matt Soga prepares innovative appetizers such as smoked salmon served alongside cornmeal pancakes smeared with cream cheese, onions, and chives, and medallions of lamb with fresh artichoke hearts, tomatoes, and mushrooms. He also makes a superb double-thick pork chop that's marinated for 48 hours, roasted to perfection, and served with garlic mashed potatoes and gravy. Desserts are simple but heartwarming: strawberry shortcake, warm apple crisp, and lemon-mint sorbet scooped onto a cookie shell and topped with a raspberry purée. *$$; AE, DC, DIS, MC, V; local checks only; lunch Mon–Fri, dinner every day; beer and wine; reservations recommended; between 2nd and 3rd Sts.* &

LODGINGS

Palm Court Hotel / ★★★

234 D ST, DAVIS; 530/753-7100 OR 800/528-1234
This chic, unobtrusive jewel is reminiscent of a fine little boutique hotel. The lobby is small and intimate with a kind of Raffles Hotel look—English with a dash of East Indian. The 28 suites (all for nonsmokers) have lots of goodies for the serious traveler, including irons and ironing boards, hair dryers, TVs and telephones in every room, and sofa beds (in addition to the beds in the adjoining rooms). The two Palm Suites are the ritziest, with fireplaces, marble bathrooms with whirlpool baths, and full-length balconies. The decor in the rooms has an East Indian/English flair, too, with dark wooden blinds, Regency furnishings in hues of rust, maroon, and gold, and handsome armoires that conceal TVs, honor bars, and refrigerators. *$$; AE, DC, DIS, MC, V; no checks; www.stayanight.com/palmcourt; at 3rd St.* &

Woodland

RESTAURANTS

Morrison's Upstairs / ★★

428½ 1ST ST, WOODLAND; 530/666-6176
Tucked into the attic of one of Woodland's most striking buildings, an 1891 Queen Anne Victorian that was originally a luxury apartment house, Morrison's Upstairs combines old-fashioned elegance with a

predinner aerobic workout; guests must climb three flights of stairs. (The elevator is an option for those who are easily winded.) Favorite entrees include an abundance of creatively prepared fresh fish dishes, plump beer-batter prawns, fettuccine with prawns in a Parmesan cream sauce, perfectly cooked prime rib, and steak Morrison, a 12-ounce prime-cut New York strip smothered with mushrooms and shallots. Early birds dining between 5pm and 6pm Monday through Thursday get the same fare at bargain prices. Morrison's wine list is the best in town. *$$; AE, DC, DIS, MC, V; local checks only; lunch Mon–Fri, dinner every day; full bar; reservations recommended; at Bush St.* &

Yuba City

RESTAURANTS

City Cafe / ★★☆

667 PLUMAS ST, YUBA CITY; 530/671-1501

By golly, Yuba City's gone trendy with this chic, little cafe smack-dab in the middle of the town's historic section. Take a seat inside the bistro-like dining room (a bit cramped) or sit outside in the courtyard in front of the restaurant, where you have more room. The lunch menu focuses on an assortment of panini prepared with focaccia and herb mayo, including the popular grilled eggplant, sautéed spinach, mild banana pepper, and feta sandwich. Dinner is a more ambitious affair, with such items as sautéed duck breast served medium rare with a port wine sauce, and grilled rack of pork with a roasted red pepper and shallot demi-glace served with mashed potatoes. City Cafe has a good selection of beer and wine, with many wines available by the glass. *$$; DIS, MC, V; checks OK; lunch Mon–Fri, dinner Mon–Sat; beer and wine; reservations recommended; at Colusa Hwy.* &

Ruthy's Bar and Oven / ★★

229 CLARK AVE, YUBA CITY; 530/674-2611 OR 800/455-LAKE

If you're a big breakfast eater, make a beeline to Ruthy's. You'll find such belly-packing fare as French toast made with Ruthy's own cinnamon-raisin bread, terrific whole-wheat and buttermilk pancakes, and creative egg dishes such as the omelet stuffed with Monterey Jack cheese and prawns sautéed in garlic-herb butter. For lunch, head straight for the salad bar or order a sandwich served on house-made bread. Dinner is more elaborate, with interesting appetizers like little chicken quesadillas, tiny New Zealand clams steamed in a garlic and white wine sauce, and spicy Cajun prawns in a garlic red pepper sauce. Entrees vary from house-made fettuccine tossed with house-smoked salmon to a spicy chicken stir-fry. *$$; AE, DC, DIS, MC, V; checks OK; breakfast, lunch,* *dinner Tues–Sat, brunch Sun; full bar; no reservations; ruthys@syix. com; in the Hillcrest Plaza mini-mall, S of Franklin Rd.* &

LODGINGS

Harkey House / ★★

212 C ST, YUBA CITY; 530/674-1942

This cream-colored 1874 Victorian Gothic B&B trimmed in gold offers four guest rooms with private baths, as well as such diversions as a spa, a chess table, and an antique Chickering piano. The spacious Harkey Suite is swathed in a paisley pattern and has a small sitting room that doubles as a library; a gas-burning stove keeps the room toasty on chilly winter nights. The soft green Empress Room features a gas fireplace, and a water fountain graces the room. In the solarium-style dining area guests are treated to a full breakfast: Belgian waffles, zucchini croquettes, Canadian bacon, fresh fruit, scones, juice, and coffee. *$$; AE, DIS, MC, V; checks OK; www.harkeyhouse.com; in old downtown, across from the courthouse.*

Marysville

RESTAURANTS

Silver Dollar Saloon / ★

330 IST ST, MARYSVILLE; 530/743-0507

As you amble up to the Silver Dollar Saloon, be sure to pay your respects to the massive wooden cowboy standing guard at the entrance. This restaurant and saloon is a lively relic of Marysville's frontier past, with Western memorabilia scattered throughout the building. Place your order, grab a table, and watch 'em cook your order on the open-pit grill. The Silver Dollar's menu features terrific grilled steaks and steak sandwiches, grilled chicken, hot pastrami sandwiches, and delectable barbecued ribs. For those craving a lighter meal, they also serve up some tasty grilled vegetables, a Cajun broiled catfish, and tempting pasta dishes. Friday and Saturday nights the place is packed with cowpokes tappin' their boots to the beat of country music mixed by a DJ. *$; MC, V; checks OK; lunch, dinner Mon–Sat; full bar; no reservations; in Old Town, between C and D Sts.* &

Williams

LODGINGS

Wilbur Hot Springs / ★★

3375 WILBUR SPRINGS RD, WILBUR SPRINGS; 530/473-2306

This sanctuary was named after Ezekial Wilbur, who, with a partner in the 1860s, purchased 640 acres along Sulfur Creek to mine copper. When the mining venture failed, Wilbur bought out his partner, built a small wooden hotel, and opened Wilbur Hot Springs. The current owner purchased the retreat in the 1970s, restored the hotel, added a third floor, and managed to keep its original charm and simplicity. Today Wilbur sits 22 miles west of Williams, on private property within a 15,000-acre nature preserve. You'll find no electricity here—the hotel is softly lit with solar power and warmed by centrally located gas fireplaces. There are 17 private guest rooms (toilets are located, European style, throughout the hotel), a spacious suite with private bath and kitchen, and a comfortable 11-bed bunk room. Since there is no restaurant at Wilbur, guests bring their own groceries and use the well-equipped commercial kitchen, where dry spices, cookware, utensils, dishes, and refrigeration/freezer storage are supplied. The hot springs area (the highlight of your stay) is dimly lit with Japanese lanterns and sheltered by a cedar A-framed bathhouse where clothing is optional and noise is a no-no. Registered guests have 24-hour access to the hot springs. A spacious redwood deck surrounds the bathhouse and leads to an 80°F outdoor pool, a dry sauna, and private outdoor showers. $$–$$$; MC, V; checks OK; www.wilburhotsprings.com; from I-5, take Hwy 20 W, N on Wilbur Rd (go 4 miles), turn left onto the Wilbur Silver Bridge, drive 1 mile, and enter gate.

Oroville

Oroville has been largely, and undeservedly, overlooked by tourists. This historic **GOLD RUSH** town is the site of the second major gold discovery after Coloma and the center of a rich agricultural industry (specializing in cattle, citrus, nuts, and olives). The **OROVILLE CHINESE TEMPLE AND GARDEN** (1500 Broderick St; 530/538-2496) was built in 1863 to serve the 10,000 Chinese who worked the mines here. It has an extensive collection of tapestries, costumes, and puppets used in Chinese opera, and its lovely gardens, planted exclusively with plants from China, offer a great place for meditation. The 770-foot-tall **OROVILLE DAM** (from Hwy 70, head E on Oroville Dam Blvd) is the tallest earthen dam in the country, and **LAKE OROVILLE** (530/538-2219) is regularly rated as one of the best bass fishing spots in the United States. It is also a houseboaters' paradise, with 24 square miles of surface area and 167 miles of shoreline. Just south of the dam you can rent a houseboat, ski boat, or wave-runner and find out where to reel in the big ones by visiting the folks at **BIDWELL CANYON MARINA** (801 Bidwell Canyon Rd; 530/589-3165). The 640-foot-high **FEATHER FALLS**, the sixth tallest waterfall in the country, is a worthy side trip if you're up for a moderately strenuous hike. Your reward: spectacular views of the falls, the Sacramento Valley, and the Coast Range; for directions and details, call the **OROVILLE AREA CHAMBER OF COMMERCE** (530/538-2542).

Berry Creek

LODGINGS

Lake Oroville Bed and Breakfast / ★★★

240 SUNDAY DR, BERRY CREEK; 530/589-0700 OR 800/455-LAKE

"Silent, upon a peak in Darien. . . ." With apologies to Mr. Keats, make that "upon the outskirts of Oroville" and you have a pretty fair description of the Lake Oroville Bed and Breakfast, sitting in lonely yellow splendor on 40 acres high above the lake, with views in every direction. Built in 1992 specifically to be an inn (as opposed to a reconfigured residence), the B&B has six guest bedrooms with private entrances and baths, and five of them have whirlpool tubs. The Rose Petal Room is appropriately covered with rose print wallpaper, and a white Battenberg bedspread is draped over the king-size bed, from which you have a view of the lake. The Monet Room, Max's Room, the Arbor Room, and the Vine Room all have queen-size beds and views of the surrounding woods. Breakfast is a hearty affair, with a main course of either quiche, eggs Benedict, crepes, waffles, or French toast. Proprietors Ron and Cheryl Damberger welcome children and maintain a small playroom for them, and they like to host family reunions and other group events, too. A gas grill is available for guests who get so downright relaxed they'd rather barbecue than drive into town for dinner. Pets are welcome. *$$; AE, DIS, MC, V; checks OK; lakeinn@cncnet.com; www.lakeoroville.com/lake oroville; from Hwy 70 take Oroville Dam Blvd/Hwy 162 E for 1.7 miles, turn right at Olive Hwy, continue for 13½ miles, then turn left at Bell Ranch Rd, bear right, and go ½ mile to Sunday Dr.* &

Chico

This charming little city was founded in 1860 by John Bidwell, a member of the first wagon-train expedition to reach California. After he struck gold near Oroville and purchased land along Chico Creek, he built a three-story Italian-villa-style mansion. After Bidwell's death, the mansion and its surrounding grounds were donated for the establishment of a Christian school and later became California State University–Chico (Chico State). Today, **BIDWELL MANSION STATE HISTORIC PARK** stands adjacent to the beautifully landscaped campus grounds surrounded by hundreds of varieties of trees Bidwell introduced to the area. Across town, Bidwell Park is a 3,600-acre playground for outdoor enthusiasts, with swimming holes, hiking, biking and equestrian trails, picnic areas, and facilities for organized sports. These days, Chico, once known as the nation's number-one party school, has a new designation as the nation's number-one bike town, with user-friendly bike paths leading both in and out of town. **UPPER BIDWELL PARK** has become somewhat of a mecca for mountain bikers.

To find out what's currently going on around town, settle in at one of the espresso bars and thumb through the *Chico News and Review* (642 W 5th St; 530/343-0704), the city's fine alternative-press newspaper. Or simply relax à la Chico by observing the brewing-to-bottling process and sampling the award-winning ales and lagers at **SIERRA NEVADA BREWING COMPANY** (1075 E 20th St; 530/893-3520; www.sierra-nevada.com); free tours are offered at 2:30 on Tuesdays through Fridays and noon to 3pm on Saturdays.

RESTAURANTS

The Albatross / ★★

3312 THE ESPLANADE, CHICO; 530/345-6037
Set in a neighborhood of old mansions, the Albatross was a private home before it was converted into a dinner house with several small, casual dining rooms and a wonderfully landscaped garden patio. The service is excellent, and despite the wait staff's aloha attire and the restaurant's tropical decor, you won't find any pounded taro root or papaya salsa on the menu. What you will find is well-prepared mahimahi, fresh salmon topped with champagne butter, and broiled swordfish with tarragon, as well as steak and prime rib. All the entrees come with steaming hot sourdough and squaw bread and choice of potato and include unlimited trips to the first-rate salad bar. Top off your meal with the ultrarich Island Pie: macadamia-nut ice cream piled onto a cookie-crumb crust and smothered with fudge, whipped cream, and a sprinkling of almonds. *$$; AE, MC, V; checks OK; dinner Tues–Sun; full bar; reservations recommended; N of downtown.* &

The Black Crow Grill and Taproom / ★★★

209 SALEM ST, CHICO; 530/892-1392
Voted Best Dinner Place two years in a row by the *Chico News and Review*, this popular downtown restaurant has reasonably priced meals, good service, and a lively atmosphere. Check the daily specials menu, which features a choice of wines, starters, entrees, and desserts. Try the Fuji apple salad with organic baby greens, blue cheese, currants, and caramelized walnuts with aged balsamic vinaigrette for a start. Entrees range from house-made linguine with bay scallops, corn, roasted tomato, and white wine/artichoke basil pesto to a lemon roasted half chicken served with garlic mashed potatoes and herbed pan gravy to pan-roasted Atlantic salmon, seared and smothered with an orange stone-ground mustard butter sauce. And if it's on the menu, don't miss their creamy lemon brûlée, a perfect end to a perfect meal. *$$; AE, MC, V; checks OK;*

lunch Mon–Sat, dinner every day; full bar; reservations recommended; www.theblackcrow.com; corner of 2nd and Salem Sts. ♿

Kramore Inn / ★★

1903 PARK AVE, CHICO; 530/343-3701

Owner Bill Theller started at the Kramore as a dishwasher, worked his way up to become cook and manager, then bought the place and clearly figured out how to keep his customers happy . . . the inn's food has kept people coming back for more than 20 years. The Kramore specialty is crepes. You'll find 30 different kinds—everything from a shrimp-and-broccoli combo to the old favorite ham-and-cheese. There are plenty of vegetarian varieties as well (to keep the conscience as pure as the body), and the Kramore serves organic and pesticide-free vegetables whenever possible. Other good dishes on the lengthy menu are the Italian roast chicken, the Hungarian mushroom soup, and the daily stir-fries. The excellent breads, pasta, and ice creams are made locally. For a sweet finale, top off your meal with the decadent chocolate mousse crepe. *$; AE, DIS, MC, V; local checks only; lunch Tues–Fri, dinner Tues–Sun, brunch Sat–Sun; beer and wine; reservations recommended; jpw@cmc.net; at W 19th St.* ♿

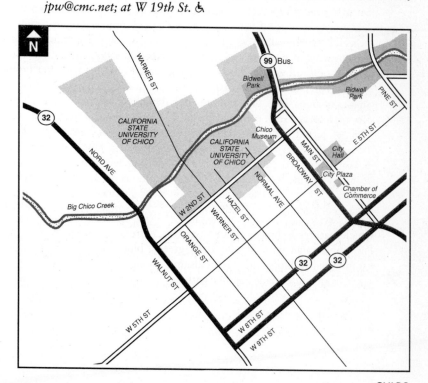

LODGINGS

The Esplanade Bed and Breakfast / ★

620 THE ESPLANADE, CHICO; 530/345-8084

This B&B is located on one of Chico's most beautiful boulevards, The Esplanade, which is lined on both sides with lush lawns, tall trees, and stately Victorian mansions. The charming turn-of-the-century house sits across the street from the famous Bidwell Mansion and is close to downtown and the university. Five guest rooms are offered here, each with a cable TV and a private bath. Susan's Room is a favorite, with its luxurious queen-size poster bed and a great view of the Bidwell Mansion. Natalie's Room is downstairs and has lavender decor and a bay window. The attached bathroom features a Jacuzzi tub situated under a stained-glass window. Proprietor Lois Kloss pampers her guests with a hearty breakfast in the formal dining room, and she pours everyone a glass of wine each evening in the parlor or on the garden patio. *$; DIS, MC, V; checks OK; www.now2000.com/esplanade; near Memorial Wy.*

Johnson's Country Inn / ★★★★

3935 MOOREHEAD AVE, CHICO; 530/345-7829

Set in the heart of a picture-perfect almond orchard, this Victorian-style farmhouse is an ideal place for a wedding, an anniversary, or simply a peaceful retreat—and you'd never guess that it's only five minutes from downtown Chico. Built specifically as a B&B in 1992, the inn has four guest rooms, all with private baths. The Icart Room, named after Louis Icart, a Parisian art deco artist, is furnished in a French country style in shades of green, blue, and rose (and it's wheelchair accessible). The Jarrett Room, adorned with paintings by the 1930s San Francisco artist Charles "Dixie" Jarrett, is decorated in soft greens and blues and has a view of the orchard from an upstairs window. Named after a family member, the Sexton Room is decked out in floral hues of rose, beige, and blue with furnishings designed by William Morris, the famous pre-Raphaelite English artist and poet. The romantic Harrison Room, named after the owners' great-great-great-great grandfather, the 23rd president, has an 1860s Victorian double bed, a fireplace, and a private Jacuzzi. Owners David and Joan Johnson provide a coffee and juice tray for each room early in the morning, then later bring out an ample breakfast of locally made apple sausages, peach French toast, frittata, and almond coffee cakes (guess where the almonds come from). Wine is provided each afternoon to allow guests to decompress from a hard day on the croquet court. *$$; MC, V; checks OK; j.c.inn@pobox.com; www.chico.com/johnsonsinn; travel W on W 5th for 1 mile, past Walnut to Moorhead Ave.* ⅚

Orland

LODGINGS

The Inn at Shallow Creek Farm / ★★

4712 COUNTY RD DD, ORLAND; 530/865-4093 OR 800/865-4093

Who would have thought there'd be an elegant and absolutely peaceful refuge so close to Interstate 5? Mary and Kurt Glaeseman are the proprietors of this gray-and-white, ivy-covered farmhouse surrounded by citrus trees and set at the end of a long drive lined with fruit and nut trees. The inn offers four guest rooms, including the Heritage Room upstairs, a favorite with its striking morning-glory wallpaper and wonderful antiques. The Brookdale Room has twin beds and a wide window overlooking the wild verdant tangle along the creek. If total privacy is what you're after, stay in the four-room Cottage, with a fully equipped kitchen, a sunporch, and a wood-burning stove. Mary serves a breakfast of home-baked breads and muffins, fresh fruit from the farm's orchards, juice, and coffee. When the day turns cold and wintry, sink into one of the overstuffed sofas in front of the roaring fire with a good book and nibble on some mandarin oranges—a local delicacy. *$; MC, V; checks OK; innfarm@orland.net; take the Chico/Orland exit off I-5, drive 2½ miles W, then turn right on County Rd DD and drive ½ mile.*

Red Bluff

LODGINGS

The Faulkner House / ★★

1029 JEFFERSON ST, RED BLUFF; 530/529-0520 OR 800/549-6171

No use looking for the *Absalom, Absalom* room or the *As I Lay Dying* suite in this 1890 Queen Anne Victorian, for it was named after a local doctor who practiced here in the '30s—not the writer. The Faulkner House features a red-velvet parlor, a casual living room, and a spacious blue dining room. Its four guest rooms are upstairs, and each has a private bath. The two smallest rooms are often preferred: the octagonal Tower Room is a light-filled corner room decorated in tan florals, and the Wicker Room is wallpapered in dark green with mauve roses and has an iron bed draped with an antique bedspread, plus wicker accessories and views of the shade trees. In the evening, owners Mary and Harvey Klingler leave a full decanter of sherry for you in the upstairs hall. *$$; AE, MC, V; checks OK; faulkner BB@snowcrest.net; www.snowcrest.net/faulknerbb; off Union St.*

San Francisco Bay Area Restaurant Index

SAN FRANCISCO

THE CASTRO
2223 Restaurant and Bar

CHINATOWN
Great Eastern

COLE VALLEY
EOS Restaurant & Wine Bar

FINANCIAL DISTRICT
Boulevard
Oritalia
Pastis
Restaurant Elisabeth Daniel
Rubicon
Mandarin Oriental
Palace Hotel

THE HAIGHT
Cha Cha Cha
Thep Phanom

HAYES VALLEY
Absinthe Brasserie and Bar
Jardinière
Zuni Cafe

MARINA/COW HOLLOW
Betelnut
Cafe Marimba
Greens
Pane e Vino

THE MISSION
Blowfish Sushi to Die For
Foreign Cinema
La Taqueria
The Slanted Door
Universal Cafe

NOB HILL
The Dining Room at the Ritz-Carlton
Fleur de Lys
Swan Oyster Depot

NOE VALLEY
Firefly

NORTH BEACH
Helmand
MC2
Moose's
Peña PachaMama
Rose Pistola

PACIFIC HEIGHTS
Cafe Kati
The Meetinghouse

POTRERO HILL
42 Degrees

THE RICHMOND
Hong Kong Flower Lounge

RUSSIAN HILL
Antica Trattoria
La Folie
Zarzuela

SOMA (South of Market Street)
Azie
Bizou
Fringale
Hawthorne Lane

UNION SQUARE
Campton Place
Farallon
Le Colonial
Postrio

MARIN COUNTY

KENTFIELD
Half Day Cafe

LARKSPUR
Chai of Larkspur
Emporio Rulli
Lark Creek Inn
Left Bank

MILL VALLEY
Buckeye Roadhouse
Piazza D'Angelo

SAN ANSELMO
Bubba's Diner
Insalata's

SAN RAFAEL
The Rice Table

SAUSALITO
Alta Mira Restaurant
Mikayla
Ondine
Sushi Ran

TIBURON
Guaymas
Sam's Anchor Café

EAST BAY

ALBANY
Britt-Marie's

BENECIA
Camellia Tea Room

BERKELEY
Ajanta
Bette's Oceanview Diner
Café Fanny
Café Rouge
Cambodiana's
Chez Panisse
Kirala
Lalime's
O Chamé
Rivoli
Spenger's Fresh Fish Grotto
Xanadu

DANVILLE
Blackhawk Grille
Bridges

EMERYVILLE
Bucci's
Hong Kong East Ocean Seafood Restaurant

FREMONT
Pearl's Cafe

LAFAYETTE
Miraku

LIVERMORE
Wente Vineyards
　Restaurant

OAKLAND
Asmara Restaurant and
　Bar
Bay Wolf Restaurant
Caffe 817
Citron
Jade Villa
Jojo
Le Cheval
Mama's Royal Cafe
Nan Yang Rockridge
Oliveto Cafe and
　Restaurant
Pho Anh Dao
Pizza Rustica
Soizic Bistro-Cafe
Spettro
Tsing Tao
Yoshi's
Zatis

SAN RAMON
Bighorn Grill
Mudd's Restaurant

WALNUT CREEK
Lark Creek Cafe
Le Virage
Prima

THE PENINSULA

BURLINGAME
Kuleto's
Tavern Grill

MENLO PARK
Bistro La Luna
Carpaccio
Dal Baffo

MILLBRAE
Hong Kong Flower
　Lounge

PALO ALTO
Beppo
Bistro Elan
Evvia
Higashi West
L'Amie Donia
Maddalena's Continental
　Restaurant
Spago Palo Alto

REDWOOD CITY
The Redwood Cafe &
　Spice Company
2030

SAN CARLOS
Creo La.
Kabul Afghan Cuisine

SAN MATEO
Buffalo Grill
Gibson
Lark Creek Cafe
Ristorante Capellini
Spiedo Ristorante
231 Ellsworth
Viognier

WOODSIDE
Buck's
John Bentley's
　Restaurant
The Village Pub

SOUTH BAY

CAMPBELL
Chez Sovan Restaurant

LOS ALTOS
Beauséjour
Chef Chu's

LOS GATOS
Café Marcella
Cafe Trio
I Gatti
Los Gatos Brewing
　Company
Pigalle

MOUNTAIN VIEW
Amber India Restaurant
Hangen

SAN JOSE
Agenda
Chez Sovan Restaurant
Eight Forty North First
Emile's
Gombei Restaurant
La Forêt French
　Restaurant
Orlo's
Paolo's
71 Saint Peter

SANTA CLARA
Birk's

SARATOGA
Le Mouton Noir
Sent Soví

SUNNYVALE
Kabul Afghan Cuisine
Il Postale

Index

We Stand By Our Reviews

Sasquatch Books is proud of *Best Places Northern California*. Our editors and contributors go to great lengths and expense to see that all of the restaurant and lodging reviews are as accurate, up-to-date, and honest as possible. If we have disappointed you, please accept our apologies; however, if a recommendation in this 4th edition of *Best Places Northern California* has seriously misled you, Sasquatch Books would like to refund your purchase price. To receive your refund:

1. Tell us where and when you purchased your book and return the book and the book-purchase receipt to the address below.
2. Enclose the original restaurant or lodging receipt from the establishment in question, including date of visit.
3. Write a full explanation of your stay or meal and how *Best Places Northern California* misled you.
4. Include your name, address, and phone number.

Refund is valid only while this 4th edition of *Best Places Northern California* is in print. If the ownership, management, or chef has changed since publication, Sasquatch Books cannot be held responsible. Tax and postage on the returned book is your responsibility. Please allow six to eight weeks for processing.

Please address to Satisfaction Guaranteed, *Best Places Northern California*, and send to:

Sasquatch Books
615 Second Avenue, Suite 260
Seattle, WA 98104

Best Places Northern California Report Form

Based on my personal experience, I wish to nominate the following restaurant, place of lodging, shop, nightclub, sight, or other as a "Best Place"; or confirm/correct/disagree with the current review.

_____

_____

_____

(Please include address and telephone number of establishment, if convenient.)

REPORT

Please describe food, service, style, comfort, value, date of visit, and other aspects of your experience; continue on another piece of paper if necessary.

_____

_____

_____

_____

_____

_____

I am not concerned, directly or indirectly, with the management or ownership of this establishment.

_____

SIGNED

_____

ADDRESS

_____

_____

PHONE   **DATE**

Please address to Best Places Northern California and send to:
SASQUATCH BOOKS
615 SECOND AVENUE, SUITE 260
SEATTLE, WA 98104
Feel free to email feedback as well: **BOOKS@SASQUATCHBOOKS.COM**

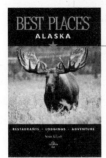

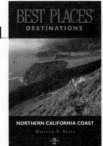